CCCC
CCCC**ONVIVIUM**PRESS
CCCC

José Antonio Pagola

Jesus: An Historical Approximation

Translated by Margaret Wilde

CONVIVIUMPRESS

SERIES KYRIOS

REVISED EDITION
FOURTH PRINTING

2013

Jesus: An Historical Approximation

Original Title: *Jesús. Aproximación histórica*

© JOSÉ ANTONIO PAGOLA 2007

© PPC, EDITORIAL Y DISTRIBUIDORA, SA. 2007

Translation: *Jesus: An Historical Approximation*

© CONVIVIUM PRESS, 2009 *(Original edition)*

© CONVIVIUM PRESS, 2011 *(Second printing)*

© CONVIVIUM PRESS, 2012 *(Third printing)*

© CONVIVIUM PRESS, 2013 *(Fourth printing)*

All rights reserved
For the English Edition
Under license by PPC, EDITORIAL
Y DISTRIBUIDORA, SA

http://www.conviviumpress.com
sales@conviviumpress.com
ventas@conviviumpress.com
convivium@conviviumpress.com

7661 NW 68th St, Suite 108,
Miami, Florida 33166. USA.
Phone: +1 (786) 8669718
Fax: +1 (305) 8875463

Edited by Rafael Luciani
Translated by Margaret Wilde
Designed by Eduardo Chumaceiro d'E
Series: *Kyrios*

ISBN: 978-1-934996-09-6

Printed in Colombia
Impreso en Colombia
Panamericana Formas e Impresos, S.A.

Convivium Press
Miami, 2013

Jesus: An Historical Approximation

Contents

Preface

Who was Jesus? What secret lies within this fascinating Galilean, born two thousand years ago in an unimportant village of the Roman Empire, executed as a criminal near an old quarry on the outskirts of Jerusalem when he was about thirty years old? Who was this man who has so decisively shaped Western religion, culture and art, that even the calendar changed for him? Probably no one has had such power over human hearts; no one has expressed human concerns and questions as he did; no one has awakened so many hopes. Why has his name not been forgotten? Why is the faith of so many millions of men and women still being nourished by his person and message — even today, in the midst of a crisis of ideologies and religions?

1

Why have I written this book?

This is not a new idea for me[1]. I have always felt the need to spread the word of his person and his message. I am convinced that Jesus is the best we have in the Church and the best we can offer today to modern society. Even more: I believe, as many other thinkers do, that Jesus is the best that humanity has ever produced. He is the most admirable power of light and hope available to us as human beings. The horizon of history would be impoverished if Jesus were to be forgotten.

So it hurts me to hear him described in vague terms, or in ways that are inconsistent with the sources we have about him. Jesus is slowly being extinguished in our hearts, while we listen to «clichés» that impoverish and distort his person: such a Jesus cannot attract, seduce, or enamor us. It also hurts to hear him described in routine, worn-out language. It does not ignite our hearts or set fire to the world; it does not start a conversation.

I grieve to see how thoughtlessly we blur the proclamation of Jesus' real purpose, how easily we condense his message and mutilate his good news: for example, how can we speak and write so much about him without mentioning his proclamation of the reign of God? It is even more painful to pick up works of «science fiction», delirious fantasies that promise to reveal at last the real Jesus and his «secret teachings», which are only a fraud cooked up by impostors as a money-making scheme.

---

1   In 1981 I published *Jesús de Nazaret. El hombre y su mensaje,* Idatz, San Sebastián.

My fundamental purpose is to «approximate» Jesus with historical rigor and in simple language, to bring his person and message closer to today's men and women. I hope to put in their hands a book that can guide them away from the attractive but false paths of so many science fiction novels, which ignore and contradict modern scholarship. But more than that, I hope to awaken in modern society a «desire for Jesus», and suggest some «first steps» toward grasping that mystery.

From the beginning my book on Jesus was received much more widely and positively than I could have hoped. I have received testimony from both Christians and non-Christians, expressing appreciation for what it meant in these moments of their life. But my work has also received negative criticism, and has awakened questions and doubts that can lead to misunderstanding. This has led me to prepare a new edition, revising the text and, above all, offering a more detailed presentation of my study and expanding the final chapter. My only purpose is that Jesus may continue doing good in those who approach him through these pages.

2

What do I offer in this book?

As a Christian I have tried to follow Jesus, not always as faithfully as I would like, in the heart of the Catholic Church. That is where I nourish and celebrate my faith in Jesus Christ, and try to serve the reign of God that he proclaimed. But I did not write this book in order to study and expound the content of my faith in Jesus Christ, the Son of God incarnate for our salvation.

As the subtitle says, this is an «historical approximation» to the figure of Jesus, using the methodology and the means employed in modern scholarship. Readers will find in these pages an historical study of Jesus which tries to answer questions like these: What was he like? How did he understand his life? What were the basic characteristics of his activity, the thrust and essential content of his message? Why did they kill him? How did the adventure of his life end?

For some years scholars have talked about the «historical Jesus» and the «Christ of faith» as if they were two different ways or paths to reach Jesus. By «historical Jesus» we mean the knowledge of Jesus that historians can obtain through the scientific methods of modern historical research. In contrast, when we say

«Christ of faith», we mean the knowledge to which the Church comes by responding in faith to the revealing acts of God incarnate in Jesus. My study of the «historical Jesus» should not be confused with a study on the «Christ of faith» in whom we Christians believe.

But why do Christians need historical research, if by faith we can understand the mystery of Jesus? Is this a legitimate study? Is it necessary? It is not only legitimate; it is an ineluctable task of the Church. The reason is simple. If we believe in Jesus as the Son of God incarnate in our own history, how can we not use all the methods available to us to understand better his historical dimension and his concrete human life? Our faith itself demands it[2].

Nevertheless we must be modest and realistic in this approach to Jesus. It is not possible through historical research to gain access to «the total reality of Jesus»; we can only begin by gathering an incomplete and flawed portrait of his activity in Galilee in the decade of the thirties in the first century. Historical research on the life of Jesus clearly cannot by itself awaken faith in Jesus Christ, the Son of God incarnate for our salvation. The Church's faith in Jesus Christ is not dependent on the work of the scholars. If we Christians believe in Jesus Christ, it is not because of the studies published by J.P. Meier, J. Gnilka, R.E. Brown, J. Schlosser and others[3].

But that said, we must affirm that historical research, rigorously applied, can awaken in many people an attraction, interest and admiration for Jesus. For many men and women today, overwhelmed by religious crisis and upheaval, knowing him vividly and concretely can be the first step toward a more vivid, real and profound relationship with him. It can help renew the faith of believers in Jesus Christ. For those with little or no belief, it is an invitation to seek him more sincerely.

What makes the historical figure of Jesus so attractive? Simply that it brings us a «flesh and blood» Jesus, makes his humanity concrete and alive. We Christians confess Jesus as «true God and true man». Both together. But we often

---

2   In his recent book *Jesus of Nazaret* the Pope reaffirms the legitimacy and need for this historical research in clear, precise terms: «The historical method is and continues to be an ineluctable dimension of the exegetical task (...). If factual history forms an essential part of Christian faith, it must confront historical methods. Faith itself demands it». *Jesús de Nazaret*, La Esfera de los Libros, Madrid 2007, 11. (English: *Jesus of Nazareth*, Doubleday, New York 2007).

3   On the other hand, the study and analysis of christology has also been unable, by itself, to generate faith in Jesus Christ. This faith is the fruit of God's action in us and our faithful response in different and complementary ways: among them are personal searching, hearing the Word of God, participating in the Christian community, faithfully following Jesus, and listening to his Gospel in the heart of the Church.

emphasize much more forcefully that he is God. We have to do so, because otherwise our faith would be destroyed. But if by emphasizing his divine nature we forget that Jesus is a man, if we ignore his concrete human life, that can also dissolve our faith[4]. It is significant that the pope has expressed his «highest appreciation» to modern exegesis «for all that it has given and continues to give us». Concretely, J. Ratzinger is grateful that «it has given us a great quantity of material and knowledge through which the figure of Jesus can become present to us with a vitality and depth that we could not even imagine a few decades ago»[5].

3

How have I developed this approach to Jesus?

18

To put it briefly, my book is a study of historical research on Jesus, written by a believer who not only seeks to recover scientifically the history of Jesus in the Galilee of the thirties, but does so in hopes of bringing his person closer to today's men and women, for I am convinced that in him is the «best news» that they could hear in these days. Is that too much to hope? Is it possible to open such a path? I shall explain what I have attempted and how I have done it.

For my research on Jesus I have followed the methods of historical-critical analysis. Like the other sciences, history has its own autonomy and its own laws. The fact that I am a believer does not give me a special advantage as a researcher. «Catholic exegesis does not have its own, exclusive method of interpretation; rather, starting from a basis of historical criticism, without philosophical presuppositions or any others contrary to the truth of our faith, it uses all the methods now available, seeking in each one the seed of the Word»[6]. On this basic principle, I have tried at each step to follow the scientific criteria accepted today by the large majority of Jesus scholars, and I have tried to do so with the greatest

---

4 To be faithful to the very heart of Christian dogma (the Council of Chalcedon), we must defend with equal firmness the divine and human natures of Jesus.
5 *Jesús de Nazaret*, La Esfera de los Libros, Madrid 2007, 19-20. (English: *Jesus of Nazareth*, Doubleday, New York 2007).
6 Speech given by John Paul II on April 23, 1993, in presenting the document *La interpretación de la Biblia en la Iglesia*, PPC, Madrid 2007, 16. (English: *The interpretation of the Bible in the Church*, Pontifical Biblical Commission, 1993).

possible objectivity[7]. As I shall explain, my faith has had great importance in other ways, but I have not used it as an instrument of historical interpretation.

In principle I have tried to base my research on all the available *literary sources*[8]. On this there is general consensus among both Christian and non-Christian scholars. That does not at all mean an equal acceptance of their value or credibility. Indeed the four gospels are, beyond all doubt, the most important and decisive source. Not because they are the writings officially accepted by Christian churches, but because they come from the group closest to Jesus' followers, and provide the framework in which his memory has been most completely and authentically preserved. Attentive readers will observe that my study is totally based and centered on an analysis of the gospel sources.

Indeed the other sources, so highly esteemed today in the Anglo-Saxon world, do not in practice contribute reliable information from which to approach Jesus. Along with more prestigious scholars, I subscribe to the conclusion expressed by the eminent scholar J.P. Meier: «I do not believe that the rabbinical material, the *agrapha*, the apocryphal gospels and the codices of Nag Hammadi (especially the Gospel of Thomas) offer new and reliable information or authentic sayings independent of the New Testament»[9]. Readers who stop to examine the footnotes will observe that I pay attention to the apocryphal gospel of Thomas and similar writings, not as a basis for my positions but in order to analyze them critically, or in some cases to reaffirm some aspect of the canonical gospels[10].

Obviously, in order not to judge arbitrarily or lightly, it is necessary to keep in mind throughout the research clear *criteria* which allow us to evaluate the content of the sources. Indeed, although the gospels have a privileged place in Jesus research, they do not automatically guarantee the historicity of his words and actions as they are narrated in a specific text. The gospel writers have not composed a «biography» of Jesus in the modern sense of that word. The writings are infused with their faith in the risen Christ, they are highly selective, they have

---

7 PONTIFICAL BIBLICAL COMMMISSION, *La interpretación de la Biblia en la Iglesia*, 36. (English: *The interpretation of the Bible in the Church*, Pontifical Biblical Commission, 1993).

8 For my view of the literary sources and their overall value in the study of Jesus, see Appendix 3, pp. 471-477.

9 MEIER, J.P., *Un judío marginal. Nueva vision del Jesús historico. 1. Las raíces del problema y de la persona*, Verbo Divino, Estella 2001, 159. (English: *A marginal Jew. 1. The root of the problem and the person*, Doubleday, New York 1991, 139ff). Cf. Appendix 3, pp. 486-487.

10 This attention to apocryphal literature may seem superfluous. Perhaps it is. But I do it to show that the apocryphal writings, which have recently generated such interest among readers of the novelistic literature about Jesus, need to be studied critically.

been related in terms of the problems and needs of the early Christian communities, and they are arranged and oriented toward concrete theological objectives. Thus they require careful critical study before we can draw reliable information from them for our research.

Naturally I have followed the *criteria of historicity* most widely accepted among scholars: the criterion of *difficulty* (if a report presents difficulty, it probably comes from Jesus and not from a later development in the Christian tradition); of *discontinuity*, as a measure of plausibility (if a report cannot be explained in the context of Judaism or the early Church, it very possibly should be attributed to Jesus); of *multiple testimony* (if a report appears in multiple and independent sources, its historical reliability is increased); and of *coherence* (we can rely more on what fits the historical circumstances or well established facts)[11].

20

We must remember that history is not an exact science. The reader will note that on many occasions, I have nuanced my claims with varied expressions («probably», «perhaps», «surely», «everything suggests that», or «it is hard to tell»). This is the modest language of the historian. The important thing is to try to grasp the essential: the basic profile of Jesus; the most common characteristics of his activity, the content and thrust of his message[12].

Following the general approach of modern scholarship, which is not limited to the critical study of the literary sources we have on Jesus but uses the most relevant contributions of all kinds of *methods* and *sciences*, I also draw on such fields as archaeology, cultural anthropology, the sociology of agrarian societies in the Mediterranean Basin, and economics[13]. This interdisciplinary way of addressing the study of Jesus has helped to contextualize Jesus in the Galilee of the decade of the thirties in the first century, shedding new light on his activity and message (his healing, eating with «tax collectors and sinners», the way he lived among them, the concrete demands of the reign of God, and his concrete call to conversion). I have paid special attention to this research, because by patiently gathering often-neglected nuances and details, we can bring into our vision of the Jesus of the gospels the «vivacity» and «profundity» of which J. Ratzinger speaks. Believers who are used to seeing Jesus only in the context of liturgical

11 See Appendix 4, pp. 479-483.
12 The titles of each chapter are carefully chosen in order to bring together basic aspects of the profile of Jesus, his message, and his activity.
13 I have been especially attentive to the criteria and guidance of the Pontifical Biblical Commission on the need for a sociological approach, the importance of an approach from cultural anthropology, and the contribution of the liberationist and feminist approaches. See Appendix 2, pp. 463-467.

celebration and homiletical preaching, so often routinized, can perhaps contemplate that same Jesus in a new light by seeing him in the context of his concrete Galilean life.

Finally I want to say that I have tried to understand as completely as possible the most important works of those who are devoted to the study of Jesus. Within my own limitations I have studied, evaluated and synthesized the work of the authors most recognized for their historical rigor and the solidity of their positions[14].

I have not done this in an uncritical way. I have distanced my work from a sector of scholarship whose methodology, use of apocryphal sources, or radical positions particularly separates them from the most balanced and recognized research[15]. I try to avoid the tendency of some authors to understand scholarship as a drastic effort to remove from the tradition all that has subsequently been added or revised by the Christian tradition, in search of a «pure Jesus» who in practical terms would replace the «Christ of faith». Rather I have followed the lead of James D.G. Dunn and others who focus on the impact of Jesus on his nearest followers. We can best approximate Jesus by studying especially the memory he left among his people[16].

I have also tried not to be tied to the personal «reconstruction» of even a highly respected author. Scholars in recent years have designed different models of Jesus, such as the «social reformer», the «itinerant cynic», the «eschatological prophet», the «wisdom teacher», the «pious charismatic». The great scholars run the risk of focusing their research on what best fits their «model» of Jesus, neglecting other important aspects that are also solidly established in the tradition. I have tried to be attentive to the most solid contributions of these diverse «models», bringing in the ones that work together reasonably well[17].

---

14 My 1981 study *Jesús de Nazaret. El hombre y su mensaje* was based on the great scholars of that time (such as Jeremias, Käsemann, Bornkamm, Fuchs, Schürmann, Schnackenburg, Schlier, Léon-Dufour, Grelot, Taylor, Perrin, and Dodd). This book retains what has been confirmed in their work, and directly uses some of their studies on concrete issues (Schürmann, Jeremias, Perrin, Léon-Dufour), but my work is based especially on research published from the 1980's to the present.

15 I am thinking particularly of J.D. Crossan, the members of the Jesus Seminar, and those around them. This critical distance does not prevent me from occasionally using details or interpretations that confirm and enrich more solid and balanced scholarly positions.

16 DUNN, J.D.G., *Redescubrir a Jesús de Nazaret. Lo que la investigación sobre el Jesús histórico ha olvidado*, Sígueme, Salamanca 2006. (English: *A New Perspective on Jesus*, Baker Academic, Grand Rapids/Michigan 2005); also DUNN J.D.G., *Jesus Remembered*, Eerdmanns, Grand Rapids/Cambridge 2003, 96-136.

17 This entails problems, but my study seeks to synthesize and build on current research in a balanced way.

What is the role of my faith?

I must say that I have not found my work of historical research at all incompatible with my faith in Jesus Christ. As I said, I have not used my faith as an instrument of research. But setting aside the faith to study Jesus historically does not mean a negation of faith.

On the contrary, faith has been the main stimulus for my work from the beginning. This book was born of my faith and my love for Jesus Christ. I shall never research the history of the emperor Tiberius or the life of Aristotle. We Christians are much more interested in learning all we can about the person and life of Jesus, precisely because we believe that in that person and that concrete life God is revealed to us in a unique, exceptional and unrepeatable way. If in Jesus I encounter the mystery of God incarnate, how could I not be interested in learning as concretely as possible what sort of person he is, what he defends, whom he approaches, his attitude toward those who suffer, how he seeks justice, how he relates to women, how he understands and lives his religion?[18]

During the writing of this book I did something I had never done before. After examining a concrete issue, critically evaluating the information provided by scholars, I have spent many hours in silence, trying to become attuned to the protagonist himself. Sometimes I did so as an historian (in the third person): «Who is this Jesus who has left us with so many questions and debates?» «What can we say today about his activity and his message?» At other times I did so as a believer (in the second person): «Who are you?» «What was your first reaction when you saw people suffering?» «How can I tell your story truly to men and women today?» Please understand. I have not done this to alter the critically established information, but to enter more fully into the meaning of the information and to be more vitally attuned to the person and message of Jesus.

I also want to say that stimulated by the faith, I have tried to nourish two «existential» attitudes, which go beyond any confessional or agnostic position. The first is *affinity*. If the scholar has a living affinity with the subject of research, that

18 In the above-mentioned discourse of John Paul II at the presentation of the Document *The interpretation of the Bible in the Church*, he solemnly affirms that "the Catholic Church takes seriously the realism of the incarnation, and therefore attributes great importance to the historical-critical study of the Bible». *La interpretación de la Biblia en la Iglesia*, 1.

clearly helps in grasping and expressing its meaning[19]. Certainly being attuned to the message of Jesus, having an open and positive attitude to his summons, and being in sympathy with his fundamental attitudes, can increase the exegete's ability to grasp his truth. I have tried to be attuned to Jesus, but I surely have missed many things by not being a more faithful follower.

In the second place, the faith challenges me to narrate the history of Jesus in a way that is meaningful to modern society. This concern for what Jesus can mean to human life today is legitimate in any scholar and serves to spur the historical search[20]. I have tried to bring today's men and women in together with Jesus. Thus in editing my work, I have moved away from the literary discourse usually employed by scholars. I have not sought to expound conclusions coldly, by establishing the most reliable data. I do not dwell on academic technicalities or on scholastic interests. I have spent a long time looking for clear, simple, good words to tell a living story. I have tried to tell today's men and women about Jesus in a simple way, but without distorting or disfiguring the results of the research[21].

My choice of this *narrative genre* comes from my wish to bring today's readers — believers or not — into the experience lived by those who encountered Jesus, and help them to be attuned to the Good News they have found in that experience. If Jesus was understood and remembered as something «new» and «good» by those who met him, can it not also give us something renewing, liberating, hope-giving? Is it not also «Good News» for believers and non-believers, to recover the human dimension of Jesus rigorously and vividly?[22]

19 According to the Pontifical Biblical Commission, it is good to remember that «the true knowledge of the biblical text is only accessible to those who have a living affinity with what the text is speaking about» (*La interpretación de la Biblia en la Iglesia*, 74). Cf. Appendix 2, pp. 463-467.

20 Some years ago, Albert Nolan wrote a book with a very evocative title: *Jesús antes del cristianismo: ¿Quién es este hombre?* Sal Terrae, Santander 1981. He described his purpose this way: «We will seek the historical truth about Jesus, but that is not even our principal objective. The method is historical, but the goal is not… We are not moved by history's academic obsession with history. This book has an urgent and practical goal. I am extraordinarily concerned with people, the suffering of so many millions of people, and the prospect of much greater suffering in the near future. What I'm looking for is what we can do about that» (9-10). Original in English: *Jesus before Christianity: The Gospel of Liberation*, Darton, Longman and Todd, London 1976.

21 For this reason the book can be read, we might say, on two levels. One can simply read the explanations in the main text, or also read the footnotes for a better understanding of the state of the research on each specific point and the reasons that justify the explanations in the main text.

22 According to experts in narrative theory (P. Ricoeur, G. Genette, D. Rhoads, J.D. Kingsbury), «narration is the most elemental way to communicate the foundational experiences of humanity». Concretely, «to tell the experience that gave birth to the Christian faith is one way to reactivate the presence of Jesus today, helping non-Christians to come closer to him, and enriching Christians in their believing access to the Christ of Faith». MARGUERAT, D., *Le Dieu des premières chrétiens*, Labor et Fides, Genève 1997, 147-163.

It is hard to come near him and not be attracted by his person. Jesus brings a new horizon to life, a deeper dimension, a more essential truth. His life becomes a summons to live our existence from its ultimate root, a God who only wants a better and happier life for his sons and daughters. Contact with him invites us to set aside routines and posturing: it frees us from the deceptions, fears and selfishness that paralyze our lives; it introduces in us something as decisive as joy in living, compassion for the least of these, or tireless effort toward a more just world. Jesus teaches us to live with simplicity and dignity, with meaning and hope.

There is more. Jesus leads us to believe in God without making God's mystery an idol or a threat, but a friendly and nearby presence, an inexhaustible source of life and compassion for all. Unfortunately we sometimes live with sick images of God, and transmit them from generation to generation without weighing their disastrous effects. Jesus invites us to live his experience of a Father God more human and greater than all our theories: God as savior and friend.

5

How should you read this book?

The chapters of this book are not stages in an historical biography of Jesus. They should not be read as such, because as we know, it is not possible to write a «biography» of Jesus in the modern sense of that word. The first thirteen chapters bring him nearer by tracing his principal features step by step: (1) Galilean Jew, (2) resident of Nazareth, (3) seeker of God, (4) prophet of the reign of God, (5) poet of compassion, (6) healer of life, (7) defender of the least of these, (8) friend of women, (9) teacher of life, (10) creator of a renewal movement, (11) faithful believer, (12) troublemaker and endangerer, (13) martyr of the reign of God.

Non-Christians can read these chapters for a better understanding of a man who put his mark on human history. Perhaps some will begin to understand why passing time has not been able to undo his seductive power or mute the echo of his words. Some may feel that his person and message are still there, calling humanity to a more worthy, human and hope-filled life. A few may feel a personal invitation to bring more truth, more meaning and more hope into their own lives, coming closer to his mystery.

Christians, from their faith in Jesus Christ, can read the same chapters with a different feeling: the joy of knowing more concretely the human life of the one in whom God is revealed to us in a unique and unrepeatable way. They will give thanks to God that his incarnation was not an abstraction, but an event so human that it makes him our «neighbor» in that village of Nazareth. They will praise God as they become more aware that the incarnation has not revealed to us the powerful figure of a Roman emperor or a high priest in Jerusalem, nor yet the law as taught by an ascetic «monk» of Qumran; rather it has revealed the distinctive features of a «prophet» passionately proclaiming God's reign of life and justice for all, and of a «poet» telling of his compassion toward all humanity. They will be moved to see how the incarnate God lived among human beings doing good: «healing lives», «defending the least of these», «loving women» and seeking their true dignity. Perhaps their commitment to Jesus will grow as they become attuned to him as «teacher of life» and «faithful believer», and they will reaffirm their desire to follow him faithfully as they see how he entrusted his mission to a «renewal group» of which they themselves are a part. And again, they can all silently worship the unfathomable Love of God revealed in the Son who was crucified for the salvation of the world.

Strictly speaking, an historical study of Jesus has to end where his story ends, with his execution at Calvary around 30 A.D. The resurrection of the Crucified One is outside the earthly history of Jesus, since according to his followers, it was not a return to the life we live in the world, but a step to the Life of God. That is why most scholars end their study with the crucifixion. But I have chosen not to end my book at the cross. I have added two chapters that overflow the history of Jesus: chapter 14, on Jesus «raised by God», and chapter 15, titled «Going deeper into the identity of Jesus». Why?

I did not want to leave readers standing in confusion before a Jesus cruelly executed on a scaffold. It did not end there. If the crucifixion were the last memory Jesus left us, the gospels would not have been written and the Church would not have been born. It is hard to imagine who would have kept his memory, and how the echo of his life and message would have reached us. «Something» happened, something hard to explain. His closest followers, who had fled to Galilee leaving Jesus to his fate, returned to Jerusalem, met together in his name, and began to proclaim that the convict crucified a few days earlier was alive: He had been raised by God!

Chapter 14 does not cover everything we Christians confess about Jesus Christ, raised by the Father from among the dead. I will simply outline the historical sources to see what we can say about what happened. I hope to bring readers, who have followed my study up to the execution of Jesus on the cross, nearer to the experience lived by those who first dared to confess that Jesus is still full of life after his death. I will address three questions that belong to an historical study. One is, what did those first witnesses mean when they began talking about Jesus' «resurrection»: How did they understand it? What were they thinking about? Next we will examine what can be said historically about the process that led them to such a shocking belief: What could have provoked such a radical change in these disciples who had so recently given Jesus up as lost? What happened to them after his execution? What can we say about the experience that sparked their excitement over the risen Christ? Finally, we can focus on the early conclusions they drew from their faith in the resurrection: God has vindicated Jesus and has done him justice.

Of course not everyone will read that chapter, so decisive for faith in Jesus Christ, in the same way. Non-believers will respond with radical doubts. Some will look on with great detachment, thinking it is too beautiful to be true; others will respect the Christian faith or even try to understand it; some may feel invited to keep searching, without closing any doors. Christians, on the other hand, will be joyfully attuned to the experience of the first witnesses to the Risen One. It is the «foundational experience» from which the Church was born. Perhaps these pages will inspire more than one reader to renew that faith in the risen Christ which we Christians celebrate every Sunday.

Chapter 15 briefly evokes the work that Christians must still begin, starting with their experience of the risen Christ, in order to deepen their understanding of Jesus' identity. The first disciples, in the early development of their faith in Jesus Christ, felt called to answer this question: Who is this Jesus whose life was so attractive and surprising — and whose death was even more so, ending as it did in resurrection? With whom did he meet in Galilee? Who is this Prophet whose life had awakened so much hope in their hearts, and whose rising from the dead now inspired them to hope in God's eternal life? What is the true identity of this crucified man whom God raised up, infusing God's own life in him? What should they call him? How should they proclaim him?

It is not the purpose of this book to unravel the complex paths of the early development of christological faith. I only hope to help readers discern some of the first steps taken in the Christian communities to deepen the mystery that lies within Jesus. Toward that end I will point out two things. First, the gospel writers were re-reading the story of Jesus in the light of the risen Christ, in order to deepen their understanding of his person, activity and message. I will now present those gospel writers — who have been my source in historically approximating Jesus through critical analysis — as witnesses to the faith in Jesus Christ, Son of God, which emerged from the Jesus they knew in Galilee, interpreted in the light of their encounter with the Risen One. In the second place, I will briefly summarize the efforts of the early Christians to find «names» and «titles» for Jesus, capable of expressing his true identity.

6

Of whom am I thinking as I write?

∽

First of all I have in mind Christians whom I know closely. I know how their faith can be enlivened, how much they will enjoy being believers, if they come to know Jesus better. Many of them, good women and men, live on the «epidermis of faith», nourished by a conventional Christianity. They find religious security in the beliefs and practices that are within their reach, but they do not live in joyful relationship with Jesus Christ. They have heard about him since they were children, but they are not seduced or enamored by what they know of him. Meeting Jesus could transform their lives. I know how tempting it is to live correctly within the Church, without worrying about the one thing Jesus sought: the kingdom of God and its justice. We have to return to the roots, to the experience that set off the long chain reaction. It does no good to confess Jesus as God incarnate, if we never try to find out what this man who revealed God to us was like, how he lived and acted. Nothing can be more important to the Church than knowing, loving, and following Jesus Christ more faithfully.

But Jesus does not only belong to Christians. His life and message are the legacy of all humanity. The French writer Jean Onimus was right to protest: «Why should you be the private property of preachers, doctors, and a few scholars, you who spoke so simply and directly, in words that are still words of life for everyone?» As I wrote these pages I was thinking of people who know almost nothing of Jesus. Men and women for whom his name has no serious meaning, or his memory was long ago erased from their consciousness. I thought of young people who don't know much about the faith, but who feel a secret attraction to Jesus. I grieve to hear them say they have left religion for a better life. Better than with Jesus? I would rejoice if any of them found in these pages a way back to him.

I think a lot about those who have moved away from the Church out of discouragement with the Christianity they see there, and who are now looking in other directions for light and warmth for their lives. I know some of them well. They do not find a source of life and liberation in their religion. Unfortunately the Christianity they know has come in decadent forms, not very faithful to the gospel. With or without the Church, so many people have «lost their way», not knowing which door to knock at. I know that Jesus can really be good news for them.

But nothing would make me happier than knowing that the Good News is reaching the least of these, through means that I might never expect. They were and still are Jesus' favorites: the sick who suffer without hope, the starving, those who walk through life without love, home or friendship; women abused by their husbands or partners; those condemned to a lifetime in prison; those who feel overwhelmed by guilt; prostitutes enslaved by so many evil interests; children who have never known their parents' love; people forgotten or excluded by the Church; those who die alone and are buried without a cross or a prayer; those whom only God loves.

I know that Jesus doesn't need me or anyone else to open his way into people's hearts and stories. I also know that others can write of him from much deeper historical knowledge, from more vivid experience, and above all, from a more radical following of his person. I feel far from having grasped the whole mystery of Jesus. I only hope I have not too seriously betrayed it. In any case, an encounter with Jesus is not the fruit of historical research or of doctrinal reflection. It only happens through personal commitment and faithful following. We begin to encounter Jesus when we begin to trust God as he did, when we believe in love as he did, when we come to suffering people as he did, when we defend life as he did, when we look at people as he did, when we confront life and death with hope as he did, when we pass on the contagion of the Good News as he did.

A Galilean Jew

They called him *Yeshua*, and he probably liked that. Etymologically, the name means «Yahweh saves»[1]. His father had given it to him at his circumcision. The name was so common in those days, that something more was needed to identify him[2]. In his village he was called *Yeshua bar Yosef*, «Jesus, son of Joseph». Elsewhere they would say *Yeshua ha-notsri*, «Jesus of Nazareth»[3]. In first-century Galilee that was what people needed to know about a person: Where is he from? What family does he belong to? Knowing where he comes from, and his extended family, tells us a lot about his person[4].

To the people who met him, Jesus was a Galilean. He was not from Judea; neither was he born in the diaspora, in one of the Jewish colonies established by the Roman Empire. He came from Nazareth, not from Tiberias; from a backwater town, not the holy city of Jerusalem. Everyone knew he was the son of a «craftsman», not a tax collector or a scribe. Can we find out what it meant to be a Galilean Jew in the decade of the thirties A.D.?[5]

1

Under the Roman Empire

Jesus had no reason to know Augustus Caesar or Tiberius. They never set foot in his small country, a province of the Roman Empire ever since General Pompey entered Jerusalem in the spring of 63 B.C. But he heard about them, and saw their images engraved on some coins. Jesus knew very well that they ruled the world and were the owners of Galilee. That was even more obvious when he was about 24 years old. Antipas, the tetrarch of Galilee, vassal of Rome, built a new city on the shore of his beloved Lake Gennesaret and made it the new capital of Galilee. The city's name said everything. Antipas called it Tiberias in honor of Tiberius, the new emperor who had just succeeded Octavian Augustus. He wanted the Galileans to know who was their supreme lord.

---

1   *Yeshua* is the abbreviated form of *Yehoshua*, meaning «Yahweh saves». Philo of Alexandria, a Jewish philosopher of Jesus' time, says in one of his works that Jesus means «the Lord's salvation».
2   The Jewish historian Flavius Josephus mentions at least ten people in Jesus' time who had the same name. Before the Babylonian Exile, the common form of the name was Joshua.
3   In European languages the name comes from the Greek form, *Iesous*.
4   In his culture, one's identity comes from one's group. People are less interested in a «psychological description» than in knowing what group one belongs to (Malina/Rohrbaugh).
5   The purpose of this study is to situate Jesus in the context of Galilee in the decade of the thirties, not in the broader context of first-century Judaism.

For more than sixty years no one could oppose the Roman Empire. Octavian and Tiberius dominated the political scene with ease. Around thirty legions of 5,000 men each, and other auxiliary troops assured them absolute control of an immense territory that extended from Spain and Gaul to Mesopotamia; from the banks of the Rhine, the Danube and the Dead Sea to Egypt and North Africa. In Nazareth with no geographic knowledge, no maps, and hardly any news about what was happening outside Galilee, Jesus had no inkling of the power of the Empire into which his small country had fallen.

This immense territory was sparsely populated. In the early first century it might have contained 50 million people. Jesus was one of them. The population was mostly concentrated in large cities, mostly along the shore of the Mediterranean, large rivers, or the protected areas of the most fertile plains. Two of these cities were especially important. They were certainly the ones most talked about by the Jews of Palestine: Rome, the great capital with a million inhabitants, where people went to resolve big conflicts in front of Caesar; and Alexandria with more than half a million residents, including an important colony of Jews who made periodic pilgrimages to Jerusalem. In this enormous empire Jesus was only an insignificant Galilean, without Roman citizenship, a member of a subject people.

The cities can be described as the nerve center of the Empire. Political and military power, culture and government were concentrated there. In general the ruling classes, the large property owners and those who held Roman citizenship lived there. These cities formed a sort of archipelago surrounded by sparsely populated regions, inhabited by the uncouth members of subject peoples. That explains the importance of the Roman highways which provided transportation and communication among the cities, and rapid deployment for the military legions. Galilee was a key point in the Near Eastern network of roads and commercial highways, linking the towns of the desert with those of the sea. In Nazareth, Jesus lived far from these important routes. Only when he went to Capernaum, a major city northeast of Lake Galilee, did he see the *via maris* or «sea highway», a great commercial route that began at the Euphrates River, crossed Syria, passed through Damascus, cut diagonally across Galilee and went on to Egypt. Jesus never ventured out on the highways of the Empire. His feet trod only the paths of Galilee and the roads that led to the holy city of Jerusalem.

To facilitate the administration and control of such a large territory, Rome had divided the Empire into provinces ruled by a governor who was charged with maintaining order, overseeing the collection of taxes, and imparting justice. So when

Pompey intervened in Palestine, taking advantage of internal struggles among the Jewish leaders, the first thing he did was to reorganize the region and place it under the control of the Empire. Thus Rome put an end to the independence that the Jews had enjoyed for eighty years as a result of the Maccabean Revolt. Like Judea, Galilee became part of the Roman province of Syria. The year was 63 B.C.

The Palestinian Jews swelled the rolls of «subjugated peoples» inscribed by Rome on the monuments of the Empire's cities. When a people was conquered after a violent military campaign, the «victory» was celebrated with special solemnity. The victorious general would lead a civic-religious procession through the streets of Rome: people could contemplate not only the rich spoils of war, but also the defeated kings and generals who filed past in chains toward their ritual execution. The military power of the conquerors and the humiliating defeat of the conquered were clear to everyone. The glory of these conquests was then inscribed in perpetuity on buildings, coins, literary works, monuments, and above all, on the triumphal arches raised throughout the Empire[6].

The subjugated peoples were not allowed to forget that they lived under the Roman Empire. The statue of the emperor, erected beside those of the traditional gods, was there to remind them. His presence in the temples and public spaces of the cities invited the peoples to worship him as their true «lord»[7]. But by far the most effective way to keep them in submission was by punishment and terror. Rome could not afford to show any weakness in the face of rebellion. The legions might take a while, but they always got there. The practice of crucifixion, massive beheadings, the capture of slaves, the burning of villages and urban massacres had no other purpose than to terrorize the population. It was the best way to secure the *fides* or loyalty of the peoples[8].

6 More than three hundred of these are known. The most famous, and the most significant for us, is the Arch of Titus in the center of Rome, celebrating the victory of the general who destroyed Jerusalem in the year 70 A.D.

7 The *apotheosis* of Octavian, his title *Augustus* «Sublime», and his acclamation as «Savior» of the world, bringer of «peace» and «prosperity» to all humanity, decisively established the cult of the emperor which was developed especially in the Orient.

8 The most serious episodes in Palestine, recorded by Flavius Josephus, will serve as examples: Around 53 or 52 B.C., some fifty years before Mary Magdalene was born, the general Cassius enslaved some 30,000 (!) Jews around Tarichea (Magdala), on the shore of Lake Galilee. In 4 A.D., when Jesus was two or three years old, general Varus burned Sepphoris and the surrounding villages, then completely destroyed Emmaus and finally took Jerusalem, enslaving innumerable Jews and crucifying some 2,000. All the earlier actions paled in comparison with the destruction of Jerusalem by Titus in August of 70 A.D., described in horrifying detail by Flavius Josephus. According to that Jewish historian, the Roman troops sought only to «destroy» the city and «lay waste the earth» in order to punish and terrify the Jewish people forever.

The grandiose and sinister memory of Herod

Palestine was never occupied by the Roman soldiers. That wasn't the way they did things. Once a territory was under control the legions marched back to Syria, where they were stationed in strategic locations. Palestine held a vital place between Syria, the gateway to the wealth of Asia Minor, and Egypt, one of the most important «bread baskets» supplying Rome. The legions were needed there to defend the zone from invasion by the Parthians on the other side of the Euphrates, who represented the only military threat to the Empire. Apart from that, Rome followed its custom of not occupying the subjected territories but ruling them through sovereigns, preferably from the area, who exercised their authority as vassals or «clients» of the emperor. It was these rulers who directly, sometimes brutally, controlled their peoples in his name.

Herod the Great was surely the cruelest of them. Jesus never met him, for he was born just before Herod's death, when at around age 70 he was obsessed by fear of a conspiracy. A few years earlier he had consolidated his power by ordering the death of family members who might put his sovereignty at risk. They were wiped out one after another: first his brother in-law Aristobulus, drowned in a pool at Jericho; then his wife Mariamme, accused of adultery; his mother in-law Alexandra, and others. He was the same in his last years. Three years before his death he had his sons Alexander and Aristobulus, the legitimate heirs to his throne, strangled. Later, crazy with terror but still backed by Augustus, he ordered the execution of his son Herod Antipatris. Five days later Herod died in his palace at Jericho. Jesus was then two or three years old, taking his first steps around the house in Nazareth[9].

A man like Herod was the right type to control Palestine, and Rome knew it. Thus in the fall of the year 40 B.C., the Roman Senate bypassed other candidates and named him «allied king and friend of the Roman people». It took Herod three years to bring his kingdom under control, but in 37 B.C. he succeeded in taking Jerusalem with the help of Roman troops. He was never a beloved king

---

9 The memory of Herod's sinister behavior toward anyone who might threaten his power is certainly behind the legend of the «slaughter of the innocents» in Bethlehem at the hands of his soldiers (Matt 2:1-18). It is said that Augustus once joked that he would rather be Herod's pig (*hus*) than his son (*huios*).

to the Jews. The son of a rich Idumaean family, he was always seen as a foreign meddler in the service of Roman interests. But for the Empire he was the ideal vassal for their two main purposes: to maintain a stable region between Syria and Egypt, and to squeeze the maximum profit out of those lands through a rigid system of tribute. Rome's conditions were clear and concrete: Herod was to defend the eastern borders, especially against the Arabs and Parthians; he must not allow any revolt or insurrection in his territory; and finally, as an allied king, he must contribute his troops to any action taken by Rome in the surrounding countries.

Herod was always a realist. He knew his first duty was to control the territory, avoiding any uprising or subversion. Therefore he built a network of fortresses and palaces and placed his own troops in them. In Galilee he occupied Sepphoris and turned it into a stronghold, the main administrative center of the region. Concerned with the defense of the borders, he built the fortress of Herodium near Bethlehem, Machaerus to the east of the Dead Sea, and Masada to the south. In Jerusalem he raised the Antonia Tower to control the temple area, especially during the Passover festivals. In this way he gradually built a monumental and grandiose kingdom. He had an admirable way of combining security, luxury, and a pompous life style. His palace on the terraces of Masada, the almost impregnable complex at Herodium, and the royal residence in the walled oasis of Jericho were envied throughout the Empire. But it was the construction of Caesarea by the Sea and the Jerusalem temple that confirmed Herod as one of the great builders of antiquity.

Herod never forgot who owned him. He regularly made exquisite gifts to the emperor and other members of the imperial family. In Caesarea every five years he organized athletic games in honor of Caesar. But above all he developed the cult of the emperor. He erected temples and dedicated whole cities to him. In Samaria he restored the old capital and named it *Sebaste*, the Greek translation of Augustus. In Jerusalem he built a theatre and an amphitheatre, decorated with inscriptions celebrating Caesar and trophies recalling his own military victories. But his boldest and most grandiose project was the construction of Caesarea by the Sea. Its port facilitated the arrival of the Roman legions by sea, and at the same time, the transport of wheat, wine and olive oil to Rome. The new city graphically portrayed the grandeur, power and wealth of Herod, but also his unbreakable submission to Rome. The palace facades, the mosaic pavements, the painted frescos, the abundant use of marble and the column-lined walks suggested a miniature Rome. Travelers arriving by sea or by land could see from a distance the enormous temple, where gigantic statues of the emperor Augustus and the goddess Roma dominated the city. The polished white stone that covered the building shone in the sunlight, illuminating the whole city. The people must be «educated» to the veneration of their lord, the Roman emperor, who was called *Augustus*, «the Sublime», a name usually reserved for gods.

Herod always harshly repressed any act of rebellion or resistance to his policy as a vassal king of Rome. One of the more dramatic episodes occurred at the end of his life and had great repercussions because of the symbolic weight of the events. The temple works were well underway. A grandiose edifice in Greco-Roman style was rising before the surprised eyes of the inhabitants of Jerusalem. They could already see the impressive royal portico, adorned with Corinthian columns of white marble. Herod had it all figured out. As well as endearing himself to the Jewish people by raising a temple to their God, he was proving his own grandeur to the whole world. But Herod also wanted to make clear where the supreme power lay. For that reason he ordered a golden eagle, symbolizing the power of Rome, placed over the great entrance. Almost nothing could have so humiliated the Jews, as to have to pass beneath the «imperial eagle» on their way in to the house of their God. Judas and Matthias, two prestigious teachers of the law, probably Pharisees, pressed their disciples to tear them down and destroy them. Herod acted swiftly. He arrested forty young men who had committed the act, along with their teachers, and had them burned alive. The crime was still remembered after Herod's death, and the 42 martyrs were mourned by the temple gate[10]. Jesus probably heard about them when he went to the temple in Jerusalem.

Herod's death unleashed a long-suppressed rage, and there was agitation and rebellion in several parts of Palestine. In Jericho one of his slaves, named Simon, took advantage of the confusion and with a few other men, sacked and burned the royal palace. Near Emmaus, probably around the same time, the shepherd Athronges confronted Herodian troops who were transporting grain and weapons. The most serious episode occurred in Sepphoris where one Judas (also Theudas), son of a longtime bandit chieftain named Ezekias, and his group of desperados took the city, sacked the royal palace, and made off with the weapons and merchandise stored there.

---

10 FLAVIUS JOSEPHUS, *La Guerra Judía* 1, 648-655. (English: *The Jewish War*).

The reaction from Rome was not long in coming. Quintilius Varus, the governor of Syria, took two legions, added four cavalry regiments, recruited auxiliary troops from regional vassals — at least 20,000 men in all — and set off to regain control of Palestine. He marched directly to the Jerusalem area, to take over the capital and block any effort to shore up its perimeter. It was a brutal action: he enslaved a large number of Jews and mercilessly crucified the most rebellious of them. Flavius Josephus says there were «some two thousand in all». Meanwhile he sent Gaius to Galilee to repress the main hub of the rebellion. This was done brutally and with almost no resistance. He seized the city of Sepphoris and burned it. Then he terrorized the peasants by burning some of the surrounding villages, and carried off many inhabitants of the zone as slaves[11].

Jesus was three or four years old at the time and lived in the village of Nazareth, only five kilometers away from Sepphoris. We don't know how it affected his family. We can be sure that the brutal Roman intervention was remembered for a long time. Peasants in the small villages do not easily forget such things. The stories must have terrified Jesus as a child. Later when he described the Romans as «rulers of the nations» who «lord it over them» and «are tyrants over them», he knew what he was talking about[12].

The situation did not change much with Herod's death in 4 B.C. His sons contested their father's will, and Augustus settled the succession issue in his own way: Archelaus would get Idumea, Judea and Samaria; Antipas would rule in Galilea and in Perea, a region east of the Jordan; Herod Philip II was given Gaulanitis, Trachonitis and Auranitis, sparsely populated Gentile areas north and east of Galilee. None of them was named king. Antipas received the title of «tetrarch», that is, sovereign of one-fourth of the reign of Herod the Great.

Antipas ruled Galilee from 4 B.C. to 39 A.D.; then he was deposed by the emperor and ended his life as an exile in the Gauls. Jesus lived his whole life as his subject. Antipas was educated in Rome and acted as a tetrarch, vassal of the emperor[13]. We can see some of his father's traits in him. Like Herod he reigned for

11 FLAVIUS JOSEPHUS, *La Guerra Judía* II, 55-79. (English: *The Jewish War*).
12 Those words are attributed to Jesus in Mark's gospel: "You know that among the Gentiles those whom they recognize as their rulers lord it over them, and their great ones are tyrants over them. But it is not so among you; but whoever wishes to become great among you must be your servant, and whoever wishes to be first among you must be slave of all» (Mark 10:42-44). Scholars believe that this text reflects the thinking of Jesus, although his words were adapted as a criticism of the rivalries that were emerging among the Christians.
13 We have surprisingly little information on Antipas from Flavius Josephus or the rabbinic literature, considering the length of his reign.

many years; he too tried to build his «little kingdom», and constructed a sort of miniature of the Caesarea that Herod had raised on the Mediterranean shore. Also following his father's example, he did not hesitate to eliminate the criticism that a prophet named John the Baptist had directed at him from the desert, but mercilessly ordered his execution. Jesus probably never felt safe in the dominions of Antipas[14].

3

Galilee in the time of Antipas

Galilee was green and fertile, different from the austere but serene hills of Samaria, and even more different from the harsh, rugged terrain of Judea. First-century writers speak of three clearly defined regions. *Upper Galilee* in the north was the border region, sparsely inhabited, with elevations up to 1,200 meters; not always easy to reach, it was a refuge of fugitive bandits and criminals; from it came the torrential headwaters of the Jordan. *Lower Galilee,* further south, was a land of low hills overlooking the great plain of Jezreel, one of the richest areas in the whole country, which was punctuated by two solitary mountains, Tabor and Hermon. Numerous villages are scattered across the area.[15] Nazareth is in the hills; a little to the north, in an enchanting valley, lies Sepphoris, the capital of Galilee during Jesus' childhood. The *lake region* was a rich and densely populated area, around a freshwater lake with an abundant fishery. Three important cities lay around it: Capernaum, Magdala, and Tiberias. The territory of Galilee covered some 20,000 square kilometers. Although it was one of the region's more densely populated areas, in the time of Antipas it almost certainly had no more than 150,000 inhabitants[16].

---

14 The situation was different in Judea. Archelaus, who had been named «ethnarch» with the promise of later receiving the title of king, was dismissed after a few years because of his subjects' complaints. Augustus did not name another vassal. He chose instead to subject Judea to direct Roman rule through prefects who lived in Caesarea by the Sea. After Archelaus was deposed in 6 A.D., Coponius became the first of these prefects.

15 Flavius Josephus speaks of 204 towns in Galilee. Recent excavations in different areas indicate that this is not exaggerated.

16 Exact population figures are hard to confirm. New methods of calculation have significantly reduced the estimates accepted a few years ago, which closely followed Flavius Josephus (Reed, Freyne, Horsley).

Nothing gets us closer to the country than the description by the Jewish historian Flavius Josephus, who knew it well; he was the general in charge of defending the Galilean territory against the invasion of Rome in 66 A.D. Here is what he said about the «lake region» so often traveled by Jesus:

> Extended along the Lake of Gennesaret is a land of the same name, admirable for its natural beauty. The fertility of the terrain supports all kinds of vegetation. Its inhabitants cultivate the whole area. Moreover its climate is good for all kinds of plants. Walnuts, which need a cooler climate than other trees, flower in abundance here. There are also palm trees, which need higher temperatures. Not far away we find figs and olives, which require a more temperate climate. One might say that nature has worked to bring the most incompatible species together here, in one place, or that the seasons of the year compete with one another in a noble struggle to claim the rights of each one to this land. Not only does the soil produce the most diverse fruits, but it strives to keep them ripe as long as possible. The noblest of them, the grapes and figs, are gathered without interruption over a period of ten months. Because along with the gentle climate, the fertility of this land is nourished by the waters of an artesian well, to which the people have given the name of Capernaum[17].

Even without the flowery exaggerations of Flavius Josephus, we can easily see how beautiful was Jesus' homeland[18]. Its gentle climate, the moist sea breezes which easily penetrated inland, and the fertile soil made Galilee an exuberant country. By the evidence we have, the valleys of Jezreel and Beth Netopha produced excellent wheat and also barley, which was bitter and hard to digest, and so comprised the daily bread of the poorest people. Vineyards were to be seen everywhere, even on the gentle hillsides. Apparently Galilee produced an excellent, Aegean-type wine[19]. Olive trees were highly valued and abundant. Fig trees, pomegranates, and fruit trees grew around the villages or in the middle of the vineyards. Greens and vegetables were cultivated in the more humid, shady areas.

Galilee was an agrarian society. Jesus' contemporaries lived by farming, like most people in the Roman Empire of the first century. According to Josephus, «the whole region of Galilee is devoted to farming, and there are no idle lands»[20].

---

17 FLAVIUS JOSEPHUS, *La Guerra Judía* III, 516-519. (English: *The Jewish War*).
18 The Galilee of Jesus' time was probably greener than it is now.
19 As we know, vineyards were a symbol of the «promised land» and a traditional Israelite image.
20 FLAVIUS JOSEPHUS, *La Guerra Judía* III, 516-519. (English: *The Jewish War*).

Practically everyone worked the land, except for the urban elite who held positions of government, administration, tax collection or military control[21]. Farming was hard work, assisted only by a few oxen, donkeys or camels. The villagers wore themselves out plowing, harvesting, or hoeing the grain fields[22]. In the lake region where Jesus was so much at home, fishing was also important. The families of Capernaum, Magdala and Bethsaida made their living from the lake. Fishing was a rudimentary art: people fished with different types of nets, traps, and spears. Many used boats; the poorest of them fished from the lakeside. In general, the fishing life was no easier than that of the peasants. Their work was watched by Antipas' tax collectors, who charged for fishing rights and access to the docks[23].

Despite what was thought until recently, apparently neither foreign trade nor local commerce was important in the Galilee of Jesus' time. Land transport was difficult and costly: one could only «do business» with small luxury items. Oil and other products were exported from Upper Galilee to Tyre and the Phoenician coast, but this was never an intensive activity. The clay pottery from Kefr Hananiah and vessels from Shechem which are found throughout Galilee, were not commercially produced and traded except in response to local village demand.

In an agrarian society, land ownership is vitally important. Who controlled the land in Galilee? In principle the Romans thought of the conquered territories as goods belonging to Rome, so they demanded tribute from the people who worked the land. In the case of Galilee, ruled directly by a vassal tetrarch, land distribution was complex and inequitable.

Antipas probably inherited the large holdings of fertile land that his father, Herod the Great, owned in the valley of Jezreel south of the Nazareth hills. He also had properties around Tiberias; that enabled him to build the new capital and settle it with people from the surrounding area. According to Flavius Josephus, Antipas received 200 talents as rent from his land in Perea and Galilee[24]. Besides controlling their own properties, the sovereigns could assign lands to

---

21 Comparative studies suggest that in Jesus' time farmers made up 80-90% of the population, while 5-7% belonged to the ruling elite (Lenski, Malina/Rohrbaugh, Hanson and Oakman).

22 Jesus lived among these Galilean peasants. Many of his parables seem to have as a backdrop the valley of Beth Netophah, north of Nazareth and Sepphoris, near the Lake of Galilee (Hanson/Oakman).

23 Jesus fit well into the fishing life, though it was not his. He ate fish and told parables of «fish», «nets», and «fishing» (From the Q source = Luke 11:11, Matt 7:10, Matt 13:47-50; also the apocryphal *Gospel of Thomas* 8:1-2. For the Q source, cf. Appendix 3, pp. xxx).

24 FLAVIUS JOSEPHUS, *La Guerra Judía* I, 95. (English: *The Jewish War*).

their family members, court officials, or military veterans. These large landowners usually lived in the cities, rented out their lands to peasants in the area, and supervised them through administrators acting in their name. The leases were almost always very burdensome for the peasants. The owner demanded half or a significant portion of their production, which varied according to the results of the harvest; sometimes they made advances of grain or agricultural inputs, charging high prices for everything. There were often conflicts with the administrators or owners, especially when the harvest was poor. There are signs that in Jesus' time, these large landowners were expanding their holdings with new lands from debt-ridden families, and coming to control a good part of Lower Galilee.

Clearly many peasants worked their own land, with the help of their families; these were usually modest parcels situated near their villages. There were also quite a few day laborers, who for one reason or another had lost their land. They went through the villages looking for work, especially at harvest time; they were usually paid at the end of the day. They made up a substantial part of the population, and many of them lived between day labor and begging. Jesus knew this world well. One of his parables is about a landlord who leased his vineyard to tenants, and the conflict that ensued when they refused to hand over his share of the produce[25]. In another he tells of «laborers» in a village square at harvest time, waiting to be hired by some landowner. He had probably seen them as he went about the villages of Lower Galilee[26].

One of the most characteristic features of the agricultural societies of the Roman Empire was the enormous inequality of resources between the great majority of the peasant population and the small elite who lived in the cities. That was the case in Galilee. The village peasants sustained the country's economy; they worked the land and produced enough to support the ruling minority. The cities didn't produce; the elites needed the labor of the peasants. So they used different mechanisms to control the production of the rural areas and obtain the maximum possible benefit from the peasants. That was done with tributes, fees, taxes and tithes. From the viewpoint of power, this policy of extraction and tribute was the peasants' legitimate obligation to the elite who defended the country, protected their lands, and performed diverse administrative services. In reality

25 Mark 12:1-9.
26 Matt 20:1-16.

this economic organization did not promote the common good of the country, but favored the growing well-being of the elites[27].

The first tribute payment was required by Rome: the *tributum soli*, corresponding to cultivated land, and the *tributum capitis* or per capita tax paid by every adult member of the household[28]. It was paid in kind or in coin: the administrators liked to receive their tribute in grain so as to avoid the food shortages that often occurred in Rome[29]. The tributes provided food for the legions that controlled each province, and funded the construction of highways, bridges or public buildings, and above all, the support of the ruling classes. Refusal to pay was considered an act of rebellion against the Empire by Rome, and the vassal kings were responsible for organizing the collections. We do not know the amount involved. It is estimated that in Antipas' time, it might have come to 12% or 13% of total production. We do know that according to the Roman historian Tacitus, it was a very heavy burden on the peasants[30].

Like his father, Antipas had his own tax system. He usually contracted with collectors who, after paying the sovereign a certain amount, set out to extract the maximum benefit from everyone else[31]. The fees must have been steep. That is the only way Herod the Great could have carried out his ambitious construction program. Something like that was happening in Jesus' time when Antipas, in only twenty years, rebuilt the city of Sepphoris which had been burned by the Romans, and then built the new capital at Tiberias. The Galilean peasants must have felt all this in the taxes they paid.

27 Studies by Lenski, Freyne, Hanson, Oakman, Horsley and others are contributing to a more precise awareness of the Galilean economic organization. In practice there was not a reciprocal economic exchange between the peasants and the elites, but an imposed policy that can be summed up in three words: «extraction», «tribute», and «redistribution» by the powerful (Oakman).

28 Apparently the *tributum soli* consisted of one fourth of the product every other year. For the *tributum capitis*, each person paid one denarius every year, men from age 14 and women from age 12.

29 Flavius Josephus mentions «Caesar's wheat which was stored in the villages of Upper Galilee». *Autobiografía*, 71. (English: *Autobiography*).

30 According to Tacitus, around 17 A.D. when Jesus was 24 or 25 years old, Judea, drained by the tributes, begged Tiberius to reduce the taxes; we don't know his answer. But Sanders is probably right in observing that the situation of the peasants in Egypt and North Africa, the two great «breadbaskets» of Rome, was even worse.

31 «Publicans» (*telonai*) and «tax collectors» often appear in the gospels. There were apparently three levels: the great families entrusted by Rome with the collection of tributes; these families, who served their own interests, had servants who did the «dirty work» of collecting from the rural villages or the fishing boats on the lake; the «chief tax collectors» (*architelonai*), like Zaccheus, hired by the ruling classes to collect in a specific zone; finally, the «publicans» (*telonai*) were servants or even slaves who directly carried out the unpleasant task of collection in the service of the great collectors and the chief tax collectors. It was probably these who talked with Jesus.

We don't know if that was all, or if religious taxes were also imposed from the temple in Jerusalem. In the Hasmonean period, before the Roman Empire came to power, the rulers of Jerusalem extended to Galilee the complex, traditional Jewish system of tithes and first fruits. It was considered a sacred obligation to God, who was present in the temple, and whose representatives and mediators were the priests. Apparently it came to 20% of the annual harvest. What was collected in the rural areas, plus the half-shekel per capita tax that every Jewish adult had to pay each year, provided assistance to the priests and Levites who, according to the legal prescription, had no lands of their own to cultivate; it also paid for the high costs of running the temple and to maintain the priestly aristocracy in Jerusalem. The collection took place in the villages themselves, and the produce was stored in the temple for distribution. Rome did not suppress this administrative apparatus, and the tithes were still collected under Herod. We don't know what happened in Galilee when it became a jurisdiction separate from Judea, ruled by Herod's son Antipas. We also don't know by what means the priests in Jerusalem brought pressure on the peasants in Galilee[32].

The total charge was probably overwhelming. Tributes and taxes probably amounted to a third or a half of many families' production[33]. It was hard to get away from the collectors. They came in person to carry off the produce for storage in Sepphoris, the main administrative center, or in Tiberias. The peasants' problem was how to keep enough seed for the next planting, and how to live from harvest to harvest without falling into a spiral of debt. Jesus knew well the suffering of these peasants who, struggling to eke out as much as possible from their modest land, sowed in rocky soil, among thistles, and even in areas that were used as footpaths[34].

The spectre of debt was feared by all. Extended family members helped one another defend against the tax collectors' pressure tactics, but many fell into debt sooner or later. The Galilee Jesus knew was trapped in debt. For the great majority the biggest threat was losing their land and resources for survival. When families lost their land to debt, alienation and degradation set in. Some became day workers and spent painful lives looking for work on other people's land.

---

32 There is debate over whether the Galileans of Jesus' time paid tithes and tributes to the temple. Many authors (Sanders, Oakman, Freyne, Horsley, etc.) believe they did. Others, like Fiensy, disagree.

33 Sanders, Safrai, Oakman, Horsley, Reed, and others support this theory.

34 Parable of the sower (Mark 4:3-8).

Some sold themselves into slavery. Some became beggars, or prostitutes. A few joined gangs of bandits or highwaymen in the more inhospitable regions of the country[35].

4
Urbanization in Galilee

This difficult situation grew worse for the peasants when Antipas rebuilt Sepphoris and built the new capital of Tiberias, in a period of only twenty years. Jesus was not yet 25 years old. Galileans who had lived for centuries in villages and hamlets, working their own small parcels of land, became aware for the first time of two cities in their own area which would rapidly change the Galilean panorama, leading to grave social disintegration[36].

The Hasmoneans had earlier established an armed base in Sepphoris, from which to control the area and ensure the payment of taxes. Herod continued using it as the principal administrative center of Galilee until his death, when it was destroyed by the uprising of Judas and the subsequent intervention of the Roman soldiers. Antipas wasted no time in rebuilding it when he came to power. Built on a small rise overlooking fertile lands, at the time it was the best place for the Galilean capital. Antipas called it the «Imperial» (*Autocratoris*)[37]. That lasted until 18/19 A.D. when Antipas built Tiberias, the splendid new capital, on top of an old cemetery on the shores of Lake Galilee.

In the Roman Empire, the cities were built as residences for the ruling classes: the government and military leaders, tax collectors, managers and administrators, judges and notaries, large landowners, and those responsible for the storage depots. The countryside was administered, and its taxes extracted, from the cities. There was an obvious difference between the standard of living in the cities and in the villages. In the peasant towns of Galilee, people lived in very

35 According to E.W. Stegemann and W. Stegemann, the indebtedness and expropriation of small farmers were marks of the Roman era.
36 The construction of Sepphoris and Tiberias has drawn considerable attention from modern scholars, who believe that the social, economic and cultural situation behind it is the best context in which to understand Jesus' teachings and activity.
37 Josephus calls it «the charm of Galilee». It was described as «standing at the top of a hill like a little bird (*zippori* is the Hebrew word for «bird».) It had an impressive view of the valley of Beth Netophah and the highway that linked the Sea of Galilee with Tolemaida and the Mediterranean coast.

modest houses of adobe or unfinished stone, with roofs made of branches; the streets were of unpaved dirt; marble and decorative trim were totally absent. In Sepphoris on the other hand one saw sturdy buildings with red tile roofs, mosaic floors, and painted frescos; also paved streets, and even an avenue some thirteen meters wide, lined on both sides by showy columns[38]. Tiberias was even more monumental with the palace of Antipas, a variety of administrative buildings, and the city gate with two rounded towers, purely ornamental and symbolic, to mark the separation between the people of the city and of the countryside.

Between 8,000 and 12,000 people lived in Sepphoris, and about 8,000 in Tiberias. These cities were not nearly as powerful and wealthy as Caesarea by the Sea, where the Roman prefect lived, or Aeschitopolis or the coastal cities of Tyre and Sidon[39]. They were small urban centers, but their presence introduced an important new element into Galilee. Their people did not work the land, but had to be supplied from the countryside. Peasant families, already struggling to produce what they needed to live, now had to increase production to support the ruling classes[40].

Sepphoris and Tiberias were the taxation and administration centers for all Galilee. Now for the first time the peasants felt close up the pressure and control of the Herodian rulers. They could not avoid paying rents and fees. The administration of fees and storage of produce became more and more efficient. Newly developing administrative centers required more and more supplies. While the standard of living and the availability of luxury goods increased in Sepphoris and Tiberias, insecurity and the struggle for survival increased in the villages. Sepphoris and Tiberias had introduced unprecedented relations of control, administrative power, and taxation.

Galilean family farming was traditionally very diversified. The peasants grew different crops on their land, in view of their varied needs and the marketplace of exchange and reciprocity that existed among the village families and neighbors. The new situation led to increasing reliance on monoculture. The large landowners wanted to increase production, run the tax system more efficiently, and make

38 Archaeologists have recently concluded that the beautiful theatre dates to the end of the first century; the sumptuous villa, with decorative motifs reflecting the worship of Dionysius and other Syrian divinities, is believed to be from the third century.

39 Both Caesarea and Aeschitopolis were twice the size of Sepphoris or Tiberias, with populations between 20,000 and 40,000.

40 On the other hand some rural inhabitants, such as craftsmen, found work in the construction of the two new cities and in some urban services (Freyne, Sanders).

money on crop storage. That left the small landholders and day workers more and more vulnerable. The urban elites were not concerned with the needs of poor families who ate barley, kidney beans, millet, onions and figs, but rather with crops like wheat, olive oil and wine, which were easier to store and more profitable.

Around then, silver coins minted by Antipas in Tiberias began to circulate in Galilee. Monetization facilitated the purchase of produce and the payment of tribute to Rome[41]. It also allowed the rich to accumulate their wealth and protect against future times of scarcity. The circulation of coins was controlled by the urban elites and favored the wealthy. Gold and silver coins in particular were used to accumulate «treasure» or *mammona*, which in turn brought honor, public reputation and power; only in the cities could one «build up treasure»[42]. Silver coins were used to pay the per capita tribute and other taxes. Bronze coins were used as small change, to «balance» the exchange of products; that was what the peasants normally used.

Throughout his life, Jesus apparently saw the growth of an inequality that favored the privileged minority in Sepphoris and Tiberias at the cost of insecurity, poverty and disintegration for many peasant families. Indebtedness and loss of land increased among the weakest families. The courts in the cities seldom upheld the peasants' claims. The number of indigents, day workers and prostitutes increased steadily. So did the number of poor and hungry people, who could not enjoy God's gift of land to his people[43].

Jesus' activity in the Galilean villages and his message of the «reign of God» amounted to a strong critique of this state of affairs. His firm defense of the indigent and hungry, his preferential embrace of the least in that society, and his condemnation of the sumptuous life of the urban rich, were a public challenge to the socio-political program of Antipas, which favored the interests of the most powerful and plunged the weakest into indigence. The parable of the beggar Lazarus and the rich man who lived fatuously, ignoring the starving man at

41 Soldiers were usually paid in coins throughout the Empire.
42 The Aramaic word *mammon* (from the root '*mn*) meant «what is certain» or «what gives security». According to Jesus, the accumulation of *mammon* is incompatible with the service of God: «You cannot serve God and wealth (*mammon*)» (Q source = Luke 6:13; Matt 6:24; [apocryphal] *Gospel of Thomas* 47:1-2).
43 In the Galilee Jesus knew, most people were «poor» (*penetes*), but they had their small homes and parcels of land, and could survive because of their hard working life. The gospels do not speak of those poor, but of the «indigent» (*ptochoi*) who had no land, were often homeless, and lived under the threat of hunger and malnutrition.

the gate of his palace;[44] the story of the thoughtless landowner who only cared about building storage barns for his grain[45]; his severe reprimand to those who build up treasures without a thought for people in need[46]; his proclamation of blessedness for the indigent, the hungry, and those who weep over their lost lands[47]; his exhortations to his followers to share the living conditions of the poorest people in the villages and walk as they did without gold, silver, copper, a change of tunic or sandals[48]; his calls to have compassion on those who suffer and forgive their debts[49]; and many other sayings can help us understand even today how Jesus shared the suffering of his people and how passionately he sought a new, more just and loving, world in which God would reign as Father of all[50].

5

A different kind of Jews

Who were these Galileans who inhabited Jesus' country? From the Judean capital of Jerusalem, the prophet Isaiah had talked about the «Galilee of the gentiles». That was never entirely true. We don't know exactly what happened to the northern tribes after the Assyrians conquered the territory and turned Galilee into an Assyrian province. Until recently it was thought that the Assyrians had only deported the ruling classes, leaving the peasants farming the land. However, more recent excavations show a great depopulation during this period[51]. Probably only a few peasants remained.

44 Luke 16:19-31.
45 Luke 12:16-21.
46 Q Source (Luke 16:13 // Matt 6:24; Luke 12:33-34 // Matt 6:19-21).
47 Luke 6:20-21.
48 Matt 10:9-10.
49 Luke 6:36-38.
50 The gospels never mention any visit by Jesus to Sepphoris or Tiberias. That is surprising, and probably not an accidental oversight, in view of his itinerant ways. Scholars debate the reason for this. Recent studies tend to dismiss religious-cultural explanations, since neither Sepphoris nor Tiberias was a paganized, Hellenic city. Many believe that Jesus avoided them so that his message would not be mediated by the elites (Horsley, Theissen, Reed, and to some extent Crossan); by acting in the villages, he probably sought to present as clearly as possible the social implications of the reign of God (Freyne). Also, Jesus may have been trying to avoid coming near Antipas; the border region of Capernaum, with its easy access across the lake, facilitated Antipas' movement outside his dominions (Hochner, Reed, Sanders).
51 The most recent excavations show a period of depopulation after the Assyrian conquest in the eighth century B.C. On the other hand there was a substantial demographic increase during the Hasmonean period (167-63 B.C.) (Reed).

We know almost nothing of these «Galileans» who lived far from Jerusalem, in a territory that was invaded over six centuries by Assyrians, Babylonians, Persians, Ptolemids, and Seleucids. They probably remained faithful to Yahweh, the God of Israel, and conserved the great traditions of the Exodus, the Covenant, the law of Moses or the Sabbath celebration, but not without difficulty. On the one hand, they had no worship center like the one in Jerusalem. On the other, they did not have a native priestly aristocracy or a ruling class to guard and cultivate the Israelite traditions, as did Judea. Thus it is not surprising that local traditions, customs and practices developed differently in Galilee than in Judea.

Something important happened after the Maccabean revolt. The Hasmonean sovereigns of Judea subjected Galilee to the State-Temple at Jerusalem and obligated its inhabitants to live «according to the Jewish laws»[52]. The integration must not have been hard for them, for they considered themselves members of the Jewish Covenant people. But after so many centuries away from Jerusalem, they were not used to living in subjection to the high priests. The temple was clearly God's home, but now it also represented a power center that subjected them directly to the collection of tithes and other sacred fees.

The colonization carried out by the Hasmonean rulers contributed decisively to the integration and assimilation of Galilee into the Jewish State. Apparently many Jewish families went from Judea to farm Galilean lands[53]. In any case, the inhabitants of Galilee in Jesus' time can properly be called «Jews». Their religious roots were in Judea. Indeed Rome, Herod and Antipas treated them as Jews, respecting their traditions and their religion. Archaeological excavations also confirm with certainty the Jewish character of the Galilee Jesus knew. *Miqwaot* or purification pools have been found everywhere: the Galileans practiced the same rites of purification as the Judeans did[54]. The absence of pork in their diet, the presence of stone vessels, and the type of burials clearly show that they belonged to the Jewish religion[55].

---

52 FLAVIUS JOSEPHUS, *Antigüedades de los judíos* 13, 318. (English: *Antiquities of the Jews*).

53 Probably most of the inhabitants of Galilee in the first century were descendents of these settlers from Judea (Reed, Dunn) rather than ancestral Israelites integrated by the Hasmoneans in their conquest of Galilee (Horsley).

54 These pools are less often seen in Capernaum. The people of that region probably practiced their ritual cleansing in the lake (Reed).

55 Information collected by Reed from different excavations.

Geographically, Galilee was a sort of island surrounded by important Hellenist cities. To the south, in the hostile region of Samaria, the new and markedly Hellenistic capital called Sebaste was being built. To the west, on the Mediterranean coast, three important urban centers stood out: Ptolemais, which strongly influenced the Jezreel plain; and Tyre and Sidon, whose presence was felt in the northern border regions. To the east lay the Decapolis, an important confederation of cities which comprised the center of Hellenistic development in the area. When Pompey laid out the region, he gave these ten cities their own statutes and integrated them directly into the new Roman province of Syria. But in the midst of these strongly Hellenistic surroundings, Galilee in the time of Jesus stood out as a perfectly defined region, with a different population, linked to Judea with its own personality. Even in Sepphoris and Tiberias there are no signs of a significant number of Roman, Greek, or Syrophoenician gentiles. Both cities were somewhat more Hellenized than the rest of Galilee, but they were still Jewish cities[56].

It is hard to know exactly how the religious connection to Jerusalem affected Galilee. There was certainly a geographic and spiritual distance. The Galileans never felt the religious influence as intensely as did the people of Jerusalem or the peasants of the Judahite villages around it. There apparently was not a very active presence of scribes or teachers of the law. When Jesus and his disciples went up to Jerusalem they faced some sort of «barrier», coming to the center from the geographical margins of Galilean Judaism. Nevertheless, Jerusalem played a unique symbolic role and for the Galileans, held an attraction that neither Sepphoris nor Tiberias could match. We know from Flavius Josephus that the Galileans made pilgrimages to Jerusalem. Probably many of them had grandparents or parents born in Judea, and had stayed in touch with them. Also, pilgrimages were not only a religious phenomenon but a very important social event. The pilgrims participated in religious festivals, but they also went to eat, drink, sing, and make small purchases. The religious festivals were a very attractive sort of holy vacation.

---

56 The signs of Jewish ethnicity in Sepphoris and Tiberias (ritual pools, burials with ossuaries, no pork in the diet, stone vessels) are practically identical to the rest of Galilee (Reed). Recent scholarship is moving away from the view of a strongly Hellenized Galilee in Jesus' time. This reduces the plausibility of the hypothesis that Jesus was a «cynic» in the Greek mold (Downing, Mack, and to a large extent Crossan).

On the other hand we can understand the special appreciation of the Galileans for the Israelite traditions of the north, where Galilee was located. The gospel sources speak of the northern «prophets», such as Elijah, Elisha or Jonah, but they barely mention the «kings» and «priests» who were typical of Jerusalem and Judea. They speak of the Israelites as «children of Abraham», and avoid the theology of Zion and the holy city. The Galileans were probably accustomed to a more relaxed interpretation of the law, and were less strict about certain purity laws than were the Judeans.

The Galileans spoke Aramaic, a language that since the Assyrian expansion had become increasingly separate from Hebrew. It was Jesus' maternal language. Aramaic was spoken in his home, and his first names for his parents were *abba* and *imma*. It was surely the language in which he proclaimed his message, for it was the everyday language of the Jewish people, in both Galilee and Judea. There are still clear vestiges of Aramaic in the gospel texts[57]. The Galileans spoke an Aramaic slightly different from that of the Judean Jews. They did not pronounce guttural sounds well, which made them the object of jokes and mockery in the capital. Jesus' accent, like Peter's, identified him as a Galilean[58].

Hebrew, the language of Israel in the time of the great prophets, had declined greatly after the Babylonian exile but was not completely lost. In Jesus' time it was still spoken in some parts of Judea, but it was mostly conserved as the sacred language in which the books of the law were written, and used in temple worship and in certain prayers. The scribes spoke it fluently and even used it in their debates. But the people no longer understood it well; when the holy Scriptures were read in Hebrew in the synagogues, the text was translated and explained in Aramaic[59]. Jesus probably had some knowledge of biblical Hebrew, but he apparently did not speak it regularly in ordinary conversation.

With the Hellenizing influence of Alexander the Great, the Greek language increasingly took root in the conquered territories and became the official language of culture, administration, and commercial exchange. Something like this also occurred in Galilee and Judea. It did not displace Aramaic, but largely be-

---

57 Scholars have identified up to 26 Aramaic words attributed to Jesus. Certainly the most familiar of these is *abba*, which he used to address God, his Father.

58 In Matthew 26:73 a bystander tells Peter: «Certainly you are also one of them, for your accent betrays you».

59 We know of many *targumim* or commentaries written in Aramaic and intended to make the Hebrew text of the holy Scriptures understandable. Jesus may have been familiar with the so-called «Isaiah Targum» (Chilton).

came the common language of members of Herod's court, the ruling classes and the top administrators. Greek may have been spoken more in Sepphoris than in Tiberias, but Aramaic remained alive in both cities. The priestly aristocracy and ruling groups in Jerusalem also knew Greek[60]. There are signs of bilingual people in Jesus' time who spoke both Aramaic and a rudimentary Greek[61]. Jesus certainly spoke and thought in Aramaic, but he may have had more intense contact with the Greek language than is commonly assumed, especially if he ever looked for work in Sepphoris. Some of his followers spoke Greek. A tax collector named Levi must have known it to exercise his profession. Andrew and Philip, who had Greek names and came from Bethsaida (Caesarea Philippi), surely spoke Greek and may have helped Jesus communicate with pagans, like the Syrophoenician woman.

Latin never prevailed, even with the arrival of the Romans. It was apparently used only by Roman government and military officials. Certainly there were impressive Latin inscriptions on buildings, aqueducts and public monuments, but the people did not understand their content; they only got the message of power and domination. There is no reason to believe that Jesus spoke Latin. In this linguistically complex region, Jesus was a rural Galilean who taught the people in his mother tongue, Aramaic; he probably knew enough biblical Hebrew to understand and quote the Scriptures; he may have been able to get along in Greek, but did not know Latin[62].

60 Jerusalem may have had a population of about 100,000, of whom 10,000 or 15,000 could also speak Greek.
61 Inscriptions in Aramaic (= Hebrew) and Greek, found in Lower Galilee and the shores of Lake Gennesaret, suggest a bilingual population. They were very likely a small minority.
62 The inscription over the cross, which according to John 19:20 could be read in Hebrew (= Aramaic), Latin, and Greek, is a clear reflection of the linguistic situation.

Life in Nazareth

According to the Christian sources, Jesus turned up suddenly as an itinerant prophet on the roads of Galilee after distancing himself from John the Baptist. It was as if he hadn't been around before[1]. But he was not a newcomer. People knew he had grown up in Nazareth. They knew his parents and brothers. He was the son of a craftsman. They called him Jesus, the one from Nazareth. What can we find out about his life in that small town?[2]

1

Jesus' home town

Nazareth was a small town in the mountains of Lower Galilee[3]. There were significant variations in the size, layout, and placement of Galilean villages. Some were in protected areas, others on the hilltops. None of them shows evidence of prior design, as the Hellenic cities do.

We know that Nazareth was about 340 meters above sea level, on a hillside, far from the big highways, in the region of the tribe of Zebulun. A gully cascaded down to Lake Gennesaret. Apparently there were no real roads between the villages. Perhaps the one most traveled went to Sepphoris, the capital of Jesus' home district of Galilee. Otherwise the town was isolated in the midst of a beautiful landscape surrounded by hills. Houses were scattered on the sunniest slopes, to the south; nearby there were artificial terraces for vineyards of black grapes; olive

1   The first two chapters in the gospels of Matthew and Luke give a set of stories about the conception, birth and infancy of Jesus. They are traditionally called the «infancy gospels». There are notable differences between them with respect to content, general structure, literary style and points of emphasis. An analysis of their literary style shows that rather than biographical narratives they are Christian compositions, written in the light of faith in the risen Christ. They resemble a literary genre called *haggadic midrash*, describing the birth of Jesus in the light of events, characters or texts of the Old Testament. They were not collected to give information on the actual events (about which probably little was known), but to proclaim the Good News that Jesus is the Davidic Messiah that Israel was waiting for, and the Son of God born to save humanity. This is the opinion of specialists like Holzmann, Benoit, Vögtle, Trilling, Rigaux, Laurentin, Muñoz Iglesias and Brown. For this reason most Jesus scholars begin their studies with Jesus' baptism in the Jordan.

2   Jesus was probably born in Nazareth. Only the infancy gospels of Matthew and Luke speak of his birth in Bethlehem, surely for theological reasons, as the fulfillment of the words of the prophet Micah in the eighth century B.C.: «But you, O Bethlehem of Ephrathah, who are one of the little clans of Judah, from you shall come forth for me one who is to rule in Israel» (Micah 5:2 [5:1 in the Hebrew]). All the other sources say he came from Nazareth (Mark 1:9; Matt 21:11; John 1:45-46; Acts 10:38) and was called «Jesus, the Nazarene (*nazarenós*)» or «of Nazareth» (Mark 1:24; 10:47; 14:67; 16:6; Luke 4:34; 24:19).

3   Different excavations have located 19 towns in the hill country around Nazareth.

trees grew in the rocky areas. On the broad hillsides were fields of wheat, barley and millet. In the shadiest areas greens and vegetables were grown in alluvial soil; a large spring flowed at the western edge. These were the surroundings of Jesus' first years: uphill, downhill, an occasional stroll through the olive trees or over to the spring[4].

Nazareth was a small, unknown town of barely 200 or 400 inhabitants. It is not mentioned in the sacred texts of the Jewish people, not even on the list of towns of the tribe of Zebulun[5]. Some of its inhabitants lived in caves built into the hillside; the majority had small, primitive houses, with dark walls of adobe or stone, roofs thatched of dry branches and clay, and floors of tamped-down dirt. Many had subterranean cavities for water or grain storage. In general they had only one room where the whole family lived and slept, including animals. The houses usually opened onto a patio shared by three or four families of the same group, where most domestic life took place. They shared a grindstone where the women ground the grain, and an oven for cooking bread. Work tools were also kept there. This patio was the favorite place for children to play, and for adults to rest and chat in the evening.

Jesus lived in one of these humble homes, and knew the smallest details of everyday life. He knew where was the best place to place a candle, to light the whole room despite its dark, unwhitewashed walls. He had seen women sweeping the stony ground with a palm frond, in search of a coin lost in some corner. He knew how easy it was to dig an opening in the wall and steal the few valuables inside[6]. He had spent many hours in the patio of his house, and knew family life well. There were no secrets to keep. He had seen how his mother and the neighbors went out to the patio at dawn to knead a little yeast into the bread dough. He had seen them mending clothes, and noticed that one could not sew a patch of new cloth on an old dress. He had heard children ask their parents for bread or an egg, knowing they would always be given good things. He also knew how neighbors help one another. He had probably heard someone get up at night after the house was closed, to answer a friend's plea for help[7].

---

4   This is how Reed envisions the area around Nazareth, on the basis of recent excavations which showed terraces built for vineyards on a hillside, a round stone tower associated with a vineyard, a space dug out of the rock for treading grapes, a millstone for extracting oil from olives, etc.
5   Flavius Josephus lists 45 towns in Galilee, but not Nazareth. It is also not among the 65 towns mentioned in the Talmud.
6   Matt 5:15; Luke 15:8-9; Matt 24:45.
7   Matt 13:33; Matt 9:16; Luke 11:5-8, 9-13.

Later as he walked around Galilee inviting people to a new experience of God, Jesus would not make great theological speeches, or quote from the sacred texts that people read on the Sabbath in a language they did not know well. No special understanding, no book learning, was needed to understand Jesus. He talked to them from life. Everyone could understand his message: the women who put yeast in the bread dough, the men who went out to sow seeds. They needed only to have lived everyday life with intensity, and to hear with simple hearts the lessons Jesus drew from it, in order to understand a Father God.

As a child Jesus ventured out into the village and its surroundings. Like all children he soon noticed the animals that wandered about: the hens that hide their chicks under their wings, or the dogs barking when beggars approached. He saw how the doves came right up to him, and was sometimes startled to come upon a snake resting in the sun by the walls of his house[8].

Life in Nazareth was a rural life. Jesus grew up surrounded by nature, with eyes open to the world around him. You knew that by the way he talked. His abundant images and observations from nature revealed a man who understood the creation and how to enjoy it. Jesus had often watched the birds circling around his village; they neither sowed nor reaped nor gathered into barns, but they were filled with life on the wing, fed by God, their Father. He had been dazzled by the red lilies that blanket the Nazareth hills in April; not even Solomon in all his glory was dressed as they were. He watched the branches of the fig trees: when they put out tender new leaves, you knew summer was coming. People saw him enjoying the sun and the rain, and giving thanks to God who «makes his sun rise on the evil and the good, and sends rain on the righteous and on the unrighteous». He watched the grey clouds that announced a coming storm, and felt on his skin the damp south winds that announced a coming heat wave[9].

Jesus was not only open to nature. Later he would encourage people to see what was behind it. He saw with eyes of faith. He admired the flowers of the field and the birds of the air, but behind them he saw God's loving care for all God's creatures. He rejoiced at the sun and the rain, but even more at God's goodness to all his children, whether they were good or evil. He knew that the wind «blows where it chooses... you do not know where it comes from or where it goes», but in the wind he saw a deeper, more mysterious reality: the Holy Spirit of God[10].

8 Matt 23:37; Luke 16:21; Matt 10:16.
9 Matt 6:26; 6:28; 24:32; 5:45; Luke 12:55.
10 Matt 6:25-30; Matt 5:45; John 3:8.

Jesus could only speak from the experience of life. To be attuned to him and share his experience of God, one had to love life and plunge into it, open up to the world, and listen to the creation.

2

In the heart of a Jewish family

In Nazareth, family was everything: one's birthplace, life school and job security. Outside the family an individual was unprotected, unsafe. One's true identity came from the family. Such a family was more than the small circle formed by parents and children. It included the whole family clan, presided over by a patriarchal authority and formed by all who were linked to it by blood or by marriage. Close social and religious ties were established in this «extended family». They owned their tools and olive oil mills in common; they shared the various farm tasks, especially harvesting the grain and grapes; they came together to protect their land or defend the family honor; they arranged marriages for their sons and daughters, thus protecting the family's goods and reputation. Groups united by family relationship often established a new village.

Jesus belonged to such a family; he did not live, as we might imagine, in a small family circle with his parents. The gospels tell us he had four brothers named James, Joses, Judas and Simon, and some sisters whose names are unknown because women were not considered important. These brothers and sisters were probably married and had small families of their own. An «extended family» like Jesus' might represent a large part of the population of a village like Nazareth[11]. To leave one's family was a serious matter. It meant losing the tie to one's protective group and to one's town. The individual must find another «family» or group. Thus, leaving one's family of origin was a bizarre and risky decision. But at some

11 In Mark 6:3, the people of Nazareth said: «Is not this the carpenter, the son of Mary and brother of James and Joses and Judas and Simon, and are not his sisters here with us?» The early church was quick to comment on this and other texts that mention Jesus' «brothers and sisters» (Mark 3:31-32; 1 Cor 9:5; Gal 1:19). The most widely accepted interpretation came from Jerome, who considered them «cousins or near relatives». Meier and other recent scholars discount this interpretation, mostly for philological reasons; they believe the texts are speaking of real «brothers» of Jesus. This makes sense in the context of a patriarchal culture based on *agnatio* (family lines traced through the sons); in that culture to say that two persons are «brothers» simply means that they have the same father. The Catholic Church has always assumed that the texts are not referring to other sons of the Virgin Mary.

point Jesus did just that. His family, even his extended family, must have seemed too small. He was looking for a «family» big enough for everyone who was willing to do God's will[12]. The break with his family initiated his life as an itinerant prophet.

There were at least two aspects of the families that Jesus would come to criticize. One was patriarchal authority which dominated everything; the father had absolute authority; everyone owed him obedience and loyalty. The father arranged marriages and decided the fate of his daughters. He organized the work of the household and defined everyone's rights and duties. Everyone was subject to him. Jesus would later talk about more fraternal relations, in which dominion over others would be replaced by mutual service. Matthew attributes these words to Jesus: «And call no one your father on earth, for you have one Father — the one in heaven»[13].

The other aspect Jesus challenged was the situation of women. Women were mostly appreciated for their fecundity and their work in the house. They bore the burden of raising and clothing children, preparing meals, and other domestic tasks. Apart from that they participated very little in village social life. Their place was in the home. They had no contact with men, except for their relatives. They did not sit at the table with invited guests. Women had their own world of friendship and mutual support. Indeed, every woman belonged to someone. Ownership was passed on from her father to her husband. Her father could sell her as a slave to pay a debt, but not his son who would become responsible for the continuity of the family. Her husband could repudiate her, abandoning her to her fate. Especially tragic was the situation of repudiated women and widows, who were left without honor, goods or protection, unless they could find another man to take charge of them. Later Jesus would defend women against discrimination, count them among his disciples, and firmly oppose the right of repudiation exercised by men: «Whoever divorces his wife and marries another commits adultery against her»[14].

Like all the children of Nazareth, Jesus lived his first seven or eight years in the care of his mother and the women of his extended family. In these Galilean villages, children were the weakest and most vulnerable members, the first to

---

12 Mark 3:34-35.
13 Matt 23:9. Although these words were written in the Christian community to warn against a growing danger of hierarchizatioin, they reflect the authentic thinking of Jesus.
14 Mark 10:11.

suffer the effects of hunger, malnutrition and disease. Infant mortality was very high[15]. Moreover, very few reached adolescence without having lost a father or mother. Of course children, even orphans were appreciated and loved, but their life was especially harsh and difficult. At around age eight, boys were introduced with very little preparation into the authoritarian world of men, where they were taught to affirm their masculinity by cultivating courage, sexual aggressivity and wisdom. Years later, Jesus would adopt an attitude toward children that was unusual in that kind of society. It was not normal for an honorable man to show children the attentiveness and affection that Christian sources attribute to Jesus, contrasting them with other, more typical reactions. His attitude is faithfully reflected in these words: «Let the little children come to me; do not stop them; for it is to such as these that the kingdom of God belongs»[16].

60

3

Among the people of the countryside

In the cities, the rural villagers were called *'am ha-'arets*, which literally means «people of the countryside», but it was also used pejoratively to describe rude and ignorant people[17]. «Can anything good come out of Nazareth?»[18]. This was how people thought of Jesus' village and its inhabitants. Life was hard in Nazareth. Hunger was a real threat in times of severe drought, or after a bad harvest[19]. Families did everything possible to live from the fruit of their land, rather than depending on others. The peasant diet was limited. It consisted mainly of bread, olives and wine; they ate kidney beans or lentils, sometimes with greens; figs, cheese or yoghurt were a welcome addition. Occasionally they ate saltfish; meat

---

15 Infant mortality is estimated to have been around 30%. Certainly 60% died before age 16. Malaria and tuberculosis were common in Galilee.

16 Mark 10:14. Jesus showed the same affectionate, protective attitude toward children as toward the weakest and most defenseless members of society. In turning the children away, the disciples reflected the normal attitude in that society.

17 The expression *am-ha-'arets* originally referred to the Canaanites who inhabited these lands before the arrival of the Hebrews.

18 John 1:46.

19 Jesus was not there during the two famines that occurred in Palestine, one at the time of Herod the Great and the other after Jesus' death. The itinerant life of Jesus and his group was especially difficult. The sources tell of one time when the disciples, under the pressure of hunger, started plucking sprigs of wheat to eat the grains (Mark 2:23-27).

was reserved for big celebrations and the pilgrimage to Jerusalem. The average life expectancy was around thirty years. Few lived to be 50 or 60 years old[20].

These peasants had two main concerns: survival and honor. The first meant subsisting after paying all the taxes and fees, without falling into a spiral of debt and blackmail. The real problem was having enough to feed the family and animals, and at the same time, keep seed back for the next planting[21]. There was very little circulation of money in Nazareth. Goods were bartered, or traded for short-term work in the fields, lending out work animals, and other services. Except for some construction workers, potters or tailors, all the people in these Galilean villages worked in the fields, following the rhythm of the seasons. According to the Mishna[22], everyday Jewish work was distributed as follows: women worked in the house, preparing meals and washing clothes; men worked outside the house, in the various farming tasks. It was probably different in the small villages. At harvest time, for example, everyone including women and children did the gathering. Women also went out to get water or wood, and it was not unusual to see men weaving or repairing shoes.

Jesus knew this peasant world well. He knew the importance of plowing a straight line without looking back. He knew the sometimes unrewarded labor of the sowers. He saw that seeds could only germinate deep in the ground, and that the farmer never knew how the seedlings grow. He knew how hard it is to separate the wheat from the weeds that come up in its midst, and how patiently one must wait for the fig tree to bear fruit[23]. All this would later help him proclaim his message in clear and simple words.

Along with survival, families cared about their honor. Reputation was everything. The ideal was to uphold the honor and position of the family group, without usurping that of others and without letting others harm theirs. The whole clan was vigilant against attempts to stain the family honor. They kept especially close watch on their women, who could endanger the good name of the family. That could happen in several ways: by not bringing sons into the fam-

20 Most of the skeletons discovered from that period show a great deficiency of iron and protein. Many also showed signs of severe arthritis.
21 Jesus was speaking very realistically when he invited his disciples to pray to the Father, «Give us this day our daily bread». This formulation of the prayer, in Matt 6:11, is earlier and more authentic than the one in Luke 11:3.
22 The Mishna is a collection of rabbinic commentaries on the law of Moses. It was essentially codified around the end of the second or beginning of the third century. The Mishna and the later commentaries of the Gemara make up the Talmud, one of the most important works of Judaism.
23 Luke 9:62; Mark 4:3-9; John 12:24; Mark 4:26-29; Matt 13:24-30.36-43; Luke 21:29-30.

ily; by establishing sexual relations without the consent of the group; by telling family secrets, or by acting in a way that shamed everyone. Women were taught chastity, silence, and obedience. These were probably the most important virtues for a woman in Nazareth.

Jesus put the honor of his family at risk when he left. His vagabond's life, far from home, without fixed employment, performing exorcisms and strange healings, and proclaiming a disturbing message without authorization, brought shame to the whole family. Their reaction was understandable: «When his family heard it, they went out to restrain him, for people were saying, "He has gone out of his mind"»[24]. Jesus for his part, a child of the same culture, protested to his neighbors in Nazareth that they had not given him the appreciation and respect due a prophet: «Prophets are not without honor, except in their hometown, and among their own kin, and in their own house»[25].

4

The religious environment

Galilee was not like Judea. The holy city of Jerusalem was a long way away. In the far away, hill country village of Nazareth, religious life did not revolve around the temple and its sacrifices. The great teachers of the law did not come to Nazareth. The villagers themselves took charge of nourishing their faith in the home and in the Sabbath meetings. It was a rather conservative and elemental faith, probably unconstrained by the more sophisticated traditions, but deeply rooted in the people's hearts. What could comfort them in their life of hardship, if not their faith in God?[26]

Jesus in Nazareth could not have been very aware of the pluralism then prevailing among the Jews. He might have heard only occasionally and vaguely about the Sadducees in Jerusalem, the various groups of Pharisees, the monks

24 Mark 3:21. Most scholars believe that his parents really thought Jesus had gone crazy, and were trying to take him home.
25 Mark 6:4. This complaint by Jesus is considered very authentic. It also appears in Luke 4:24, John 4:44, and in the [apocryphal] *Gospel of Thomas* 31.
26 Apparently the faith and piety of the Galilean villages was conservative in nature (Freyne, Riesner). However, there seems to have been no significant presence by the scribes and teachers of the law (Sanders).

of Qumran, or the Therapeutae of Alexandria[27]. Their faith was nourished by the religious experience of the Galilean villages. It is not hard to describe the basic features of this religion.

Like all the Jews of their time, twice a day the Nazarene villagers confessed their faith in one God, creator of the world and savior of Israel. In a Jewish home that was the first thing people did in the morning, and the last at night. They were not exactly reciting a creed, but an emotion-laden prayer that invited Jewish believers to live in love with God as their only Lord: «Hear, O Israel: The Lord is our God, the Lord alone. You shall love the Lord your God with all your heart, and with all your soul, and with all your might»[28]. These words, repeated every day on rising and going to bed, were deeply engraved in Jesus' heart. Later he would tell the people: This prayer which we recite every day reminds us what is most important in our religion: to live life totally in love with God[29].

Even in that poor village, the people of Nazareth knew they belonged to a people loved by God. All the nations made alliances and treaties among themselves to defend against their enemies, but the Jewish people had a very different, unusual kind of covenant. There was a special relationship between that unique God and Israel. God had chosen that small, defenseless people as his very own, and had established a covenant with them: the Lord was their God and protector, and Israel was the «people of God». To be an Israelite meant belonging to that chosen people. Jewish boys were circumcised in order to carry in their own flesh the sign that identified them as members of the chosen people. Jesus knew that. He too had been circumcised according to the law, by his father Joseph, eight days after his birth. The rite was probably performed one morning in the patio of the family house. That was how it was done in the small villages. The rite of circum-

27 Researchers today tend to distinguish between normative or «common Judaism» (Sanders) and the «diverse Judaisms» or faces of Jewish religion as it was lived by different groups: Sadducees, Pharisaic groups with different tendencies, the «monks» of Qumran or «Essenes» of the *Damascus Document*, Alexandrian Therapeutae. Dunn speaks of a «common Judaism», comprised of «the practices and beliefs of the large majority of people», and of «Jewish factionalism» including the diverse factions or groups within Judaism which competed for recognition as the true heirs of Israel.

28 The prayer known as *Shema Israel* («Hear, Israel») began with these words from Deut 6:4-5. Apparently this prayer was recited before the year 70 (Schürer).

29 In Mark 12:29-30 a scribe asks Jesus, «Which commandment is the greatest of all?» Jesus replies with the first words of the *Shema Israel*. The famous teacher Hillel, a contemporary of Jesus, taught the same.

cision meant that Jesus was accepted as a son by his father, but it also meant he belonged to the community of the Covenant[30].

The Jews were proud of the Torah. Yahweh himself had given his people the law that revealed what they must do to live in faithful response to their God. No one doubted that. No one considered it a heavy burden, but rather a gift that helped them to live a life worthy of their Covenant with God. In Nazareth as in any Jewish village, all of life took place within the sacred framework of this law. Jesus had learned day by day to live according to the great commandments of Sinai. His parents had also taught him the rituals and social and family customs prescribed by the law. The Torah was woven into everything. It was Israel's mark of identity, the one thing that distinguished the Jews from the other peoples[31]. Jesus never belittled the law, but he did come to teach a different way of living it, of heartfelt listening to a Father God who seeks to reign among his sons and daughters and to offer them all a life of dignity and happiness.

There was no temple in Nazareth. Foreigners were surprised that the Jews did not build temples or worship divine images. There was only one place in their land where God could be worshipped: the holy temple in Jerusalem. That was where the God of the Covenant lived among his people, invisible and mysterious. The villagers of Nazareth went there on pilgrimage to praise God, as did Jews all over the world. There they solemnly celebrated the Jewish festivals. There they offered sacrifices for the sins of the whole people in the «feast of the atonement»[32]. For Jews, the temple was the heart of the world. They knew that in Nazareth. That was why they looked toward Jerusalem when they prayed. Jesus probably learned to pray that way. But later, people would see him pray «looking up toward heaven»[33], according to an ancient custom known also from the Psalms. For Jesus, God was the «Father in heaven». He was not tied down to one sacred place. He did not belong to a specific people or race. He was not the property of any religion. God belonged to everyone.

---

30 The rite of circumcision came to be called *berit*, that is, «covenant», because it signified the child's entry into the people of the Covenant (Chilton).

31 Flavius Josephus proudly underlines this distinctiveness of his people, ruled by God's law, and says the Jewish people can be called a *theocracy*.

32 Only at this festival, *Yom Kippur*, did the high priest enter the most hidden and sacred part of the temple to perform atonement for the sins of the people.

33 Mark 6:45; 7:34; Luke 9:16.

Nazareth was transformed on every sabbath day. Nobody rose with the dawn. The men did not go out into the fields. The women did not bake bread. All work stopped. The Sabbath was a day of rest for the whole family. Everyone waited for it joyfully. For these people it was truly a festival in the family circle; its most joyful moment was the family meal, always better and more abundant than on other days of the week. The sabbath was another essential feature of Jewish identity. The pagan peoples, who did not practice a weekly rest, were surprised by this festival which the Jews observed as a sign of their chosenness. To profane the sabbath was to dishonor their election and their covenant.

The day of absolute rest for all, the peaceful time with family members and neighbors, and the synagogue meeting, enabled the whole people to live an experience of renewal[34]. It was like a «refreshment» ordained by God, who «rested, and was refreshed» on the seventh day after creating heaven and earth[35]. Relieved of the burdensome rhythm of their daily labor, that day they were free to remember that God had led them out of slavery and into the enjoyment of their own land[36]. In Nazareth they probably had not kept up with the scribes' debates over just which tasks were prohibited on the sabbath. They couldn't have known how rigorously the Essenes observed the weekly rest. For the country people, the sabbath was a «blessing from God». Jesus knew that very well. Later when he was criticized for so freely healing the sick on the sabbath, his words went to the heart of the matter: «The sabbath was made for humankind, and not humankind for the sabbath»[37]. Could there be a better time to free people from their suffering and sickness?

On sabbath mornings, all the neighbors met at the village synagogue for prayer. It was the most important event of the day. The synagogue at Nazareth was surely a humble place. Perhaps a simple house served both as a place of prayer, and for taking up matters of common interest to everyone, the work to be done together, the people who needed help[38]. Nearly everyone went to the sabbath

---

34 The sabbath was a day of total rest. Not only work, but every physical effort was to be avoided. No one could carry a load. They could only walk a little more than a kilometer.

35 Exodus 31:17.

36 Deut 5:12-15.

37 Mark 2:27.

38 Scholars debate whether there were synagogues in Galilee during Jesus' time. Some say there is neither literary nor archeological evidence to identify a particular building as a synagogue (Gutmann, Horsley). Others, based particularly on the most recent archaeological information from Magdala-Tarichea, Gamala or Capernaum, are certain that there were synagogues, probably with diverse functions (Ben Witherington III, González Etchegaray, Barbaglio). Certainly in the

meeting, although women were not required to attend. It began with a prayer, like the *Shema Israel,* or a blessing. Then there was a reading from the Pentateuch, sometimes followed by a prophetic text. Everyone could hear the Word of God: men, women, children. This religious custom, surprising to foreigners, helped the Jews nourish their faith directly from its most authentic source. But most could not understand the Hebrew text of the Scriptures. So the text was translated and paraphrased in Aramaic. Then came preaching; any adult male could take a turn[39]. The «Bible» that the villagers knew by heart was not the Hebrew text we know today, but this Aramaic translation that they heard every sabbath in the synagogue. It was apparently what Jesus had in his mind when he taught the people.

After the sabbath, people went back to work. Their hard, monotonous daily life was broken only by religious festivals and weddings, which were clearly the country people's favorite celebrations. A wedding was a spirited family and community festival. The very best. Friends and family members accompanied the young couple for several days, eating and drinking with them, performing wedding dances and singing love songs. Jesus must have taken part in more than one, since he came from a large family. He apparently loved being with the couples during these festive days, eating, singing and dancing with them. Later when they accused his disciples of not living austerely as John's disciples did, Jesus surprised them with his defense. He simply explained that while they were with him, life should be a party like the days of a wedding. One would hardly celebrate a wedding without eating and drinking: «The wedding guests cannot fast while the bridegroom is with them, can they?»[40]

Everyone loved the religious festivals, but we don't know how they were celebrated in the small towns by people who could not make pilgrimage to Jerusalem. The fall was an especially festive season. The «festival of the new year» (*Rosh hashana*) was celebrated in September. Ten days later came the «day of atonement» (*Yom kippur*), celebrated mainly inside the temple where special sacrifices were

Galilean villages of Jesus' time there were assemblies (*synagogai*), both of a religious nature and for community purposes. In the small villages these were probably held in the plaza, in a patio or in a space prepared for such activities; the larger towns would gradually have built more adequate structures. We don't know anything about Nazareth in particular (Reed, Dunn). This seems to me the most likely conclusion for now. The scene described in Luke 4:16-22 is probably the gospel writer's own re-creation.

39 This re-creation of the service is based on rabbinic literature from after 70 A.D. Scholars believe it also describes the practice in Jesus' time.

40 Mark 2:19. Scholars are certain that this saying came from Jesus in some form.

offered for the sins of the people. A much more joyful, popular festival began six days after that, and lasted for seven days. It was called «the feast of booths» (*Sukkoth*). It had probably begun as a «harvest festival» celebrated in the countryside, in small booths set up in the vineyards. At this festival, eagerly awaited by the children, the families camped outdoors in these booths, recalling the tents that had sheltered their ancestors in the desert when God led them out of Egypt.

In the spring came the great «Paschal feast» (*Pesaj*), which brought thousands of Jewish pilgrims from all over the world. The paschal lamb was ritually slaughtered on the eve of the first day; in the evening each family gathered for an emotion-filled dinner to commemorate the liberation of the Jewish people from slavery in Egypt. The festival continued for seven days, filled with the joy and pride of belonging to the chosen people, and also with anxious waiting for the restoration of the freedom they had lost under the yoke of the Roman emperor. Fifty days later, as summer approached, they celebrated the «feast of Pentecost» or «harvest festival». In Jesus' time this was associated with the memory of the Covenant and the gift of the law at Sinai.

Jesus' faith grew in this religious environment in his village, at sabbath meetings and the great Jewish festivals, but especially in his family where he was nourished by the faith of his parents, learned the deep meaning of the traditions, and learned to pray to God. The names of his parents and siblings, all drawn from Israelite history, suggest that Jesus grew up in a deeply religious Jewish family[41]. In his first years his mother and the women of his extended family had the closest relationship with him and were best able to initiate him in the faith of his people. Later it was surely Joseph who not only taught him a trade, but also brought him into the life of an adult faithful to God's Covenant[42].

Jesus learned to pray as a child. Devout Jews did not only pray in the synagogue liturgy or with the prayers prescribed for rising and going to bed. At any time of the day they might lift their hearts to praise God in a typically Jewish prayer called a «blessing» (*beraka*). These prayers began with a shout of admiration: *Baruk atá Adonai*, «Blessed art Thou, O Lord», followed by mention of whatever had inspired the moment of thanks. To an Israelite, anything can inspire

---

41 His father's name, Joseph, belonged to one of the sons of Jacob. His mother's, Miryam, came from the sister of Moses. His brothers Simon (=Simeon), Joses (=Joseph) and Judas (=Judah) were named after three of Jacob's sons; James (=Jacob) was the name of the great patriarch himself.

42 Joseph's influence on his son may have been more important than we have recognized. Jesus was accustomed to call God *Abba*, using the same name he used for his «father» Joseph.

a «blessing»: a beautiful morning or evening, the bounteous heat of the sun and the spring rains, the birth of a child or the gathering of grain, the gift of life and enjoyment of the promised land. From childhood Jesus breathed in this faith filled with thanksgiving and praise to God. An ancient Christian source has conserved a «blessing» that sprang spontaneously from his heart on seeing that the little ones had understood his message: «I thank you, Father, Lord of heaven and earth, because you have hidden these things from the wise and the intelligent and have revealed them to infants»[43].

5

A worker's life

ℭ∿

68   We don't know for sure whether Jesus received any education outside the home. In that remote village we don't know whether there was a school linked to the synagogue, as there were later on in many Palestinian towns[44]. Among the humble classes in the Roman Empire, apparently few people knew how to read and write[45]. The same was probably true in Galilee[46]. People in towns as small as Nazareth had neither books nor ways to learn in their homes. Only the ruling classes, the Jerusalem aristocracy, the professional scribes or the «monks» of Qumran had access to a certain level of written culture. People in the small villages of Galilee didn't feel a need for it. So we don't know if Jesus learned to read and write. If he did, he had little chance to practice; there were no books to read in his house, nor ink and parchment for writing. But the ease with which Jesus discussed scriptural texts and religious traditions suggests that he had a natural intelligence, which compensated for his low level of formal education. In the oral culture of these towns, people had a well-developed memory for the songs, prayers, and popular traditions that were transmitted from parents to children. One could be wise without reading or writing in this kind of society. That was probably true of Jesus.

---

43 Q Source (Luke 10:21; Matt 11:25).

44 Later rabbinical descriptions of schools (*bet ha-sefer*) in the Palestinian towns, are probably not applicable to the Galilee of Jesus' time (Schürer).

45 Literacy is estimated at only about 10% of the population of the Empire (Harris, Horsley, Kloppenborg).

Certainly he never attended a school for scribes, nor was he a disciple of any teacher of the law. He was simply a wise and intelligent villager, who listened attentively and remembered the holy words, prayers and psalms that he loved most. He didn't need to look them up in a book, in order to meditate on them in his heart. Later as he taught the people, he would not cite the authority of any rabbi or quote the holy texts of Scripture word for word. He spoke about what flowed from his heart[47]. And the people were amazed. They had never heard a teacher speak with such authority[48].

What Jesus certainly learned in Nazareth was a trade by which to support himself. He was not a peasant farmer, although more than once he would help those who were, especially at harvest time. The sources say very clearly that he was a «craftsman», as his father was[49]. His work was different from a modern carpenter's. He worked in wood, but also stone. A village carpenter's activity involved different tasks. It is not hard to guess what Jesus was asked to do: repair the roofs of thatch and clay eroded by the winter wind, tighten the beams of the house, build wooden doors and windows, simple chests, rough-hewn benches, lampstands, and other simple objects. But maybe also to build a house for a newly married couple, repair a vineyard terrace, or dig a hole in the rock for treading grapes.

In Nazareth itself there was not enough work to support a craftsman. For one thing the humble homes were modestly furnished with ceramic and stone vessels, baskets, straw mats, the basic necessities of everyday life. For another, the poorest families built their own houses, and in the winter the peasants repaired their own work tools. To find work, both Joseph and his son had to leave Nazareth and go from town to town. Did Jesus ever work in Sepphoris? When he began to earn his livelihood as a craftsman, Sepphoris was the capital of Galilee, only five kilometers from Nazareth. Razed to the ground by the Romans when Jesus was about six years old, Sepphoris was now being completely rebuilt. Workers were in great demand. Stonecutters and construction workers were especially needed. Many young men from the nearby villages probably found work there. In a little over an hour Jesus could walk from his town to Sepphoris, and return home

---

46 Some researchers believe literacy in Palestine did not exceed 3% of the population (Horsley, Kloppenborg, Reed). Others suggest that the Jewish religion, centered on the holy Scriptures, may have led to literacy rates higher than those in the rest of the Empire (Riesner, Dunn).

47 Jesus said, «For out of the abundance of the heart the mouth speaks» (Matt 12:34).

48 Mark 1:27.

49 Mark 6:3; Matt 13:55. The Greek term *tekton* should not be translated as «carpenter», but rather «builder». The word describes a craftsman who works with different materials, such as stone, wood, or even iron.

in the evening. He may even have stayed to work for a period in the city, although that is just a guess[50].

Even with modest employment, Jesus was as poor as most Galileans in his time. He was not at the bottom of the social and economic ladder. His life was not as hard as that of a slave, nor did he experience the misery of the beggars who wandered through the villages asking for help. But he also didn't have the security of the peasants who farmed their own land. His life was more like that of the day laborers who were constantly looking for work. Like them, Jesus had to keep moving in order to find someone who would hire him.

6

Unmarried, without children

70

Jesus lived a quiet life, with no big events worth noting. The silence of the sources can probably be explained very simply: nothing special happened in Nazareth[51]. The one important exception was something strange and unusual in those Galilean towns, which probably was frowned on by his neighbors: Jesus did not get married. He did not seek out a wife to ensure his family's posterity[52]. Jesus' behavior must have been disconcerting to his family and neighbors. The Jewish people had a more positive and joyful view of sex and marriage than is seen in other cultures. In the synagogue Jesus had heard the words of Genesis more than once: «It is not good that the man should be alone»[53]. What pleases God is a man with a fertile wife at his side, surrounded by children. It is not surprising that we read sayings like this in the later rabbinical literature: «Seven things are condemned by heaven, and the first of these is a man without a woman». What could have moved Jesus to adopt a behavior so absolutely strange to the Galilean towns,

---

50 Some scholars believe Jesus did work in the reconstruction of Sepphoris (Batey, González Etchegaray). If so, he would have had much more contact with the urban culture than we usually think. It is a very interesting subject of speculation, but for now we have no real evidence (Reed).

51 The fantastic stories of the *Protoevangel of James*, the *Gospel of Pseudo-Matthew*, *The History of Joseph, the Carpenter*, and other apocryphal gospels written to satisfy popular curiosity with details of Jesus' childhood or youth, do not provide any reliable information.

52 The Christian sources speak of many women in Jesus' circle of friends. They also mention his mother and sisters. But nothing is said about a wife and children. The theory that the sources might have taken for granted that he was married (Phipps) is not very convincing.

53 Genesis 2:18.

known only in a few marginal groups like the Essenes of Qumran or the Therapeutae of Egypt?

Jesus' renunciation of sexual love does not seem to have been motivated by an ascetic ideal like that of the «monks» of Qumran, who sought extreme ritual purity, or the Alexandrian Therapeutae, who practiced «dominion over the passions». His life style was not that of a desert ascetic. Jesus ate and drank with sinners, talked with prostitutes, and did not live in fear of ritual impurity. Nor can we see in him a rejection of women. His renunciation of marriage is not like that of the Essenes of Qumran, who did not take wives because they might cause discord in the community. Jesus accepted women in his group without hesitation, did not shy away from their friendship, and responded tenderly to the special affection of Mary Magdalene.

We also have no reason to suspect that Jesus heard a call from God to live without a wife like Jeremiah, who according to the tradition had been asked by God to live alone, not enjoying the company of a wife or feasting with his friends, but staying away from his wayward people who went on with their merrymaking, heedless of the punishment that awaited them[54]. Jesus' life, attending weddings, sitting at table with sinners, and celebrating meals as a foretaste of the final banquet with God, was nothing like the wild-eyed loneliness that the prophet adopted as a critique of his impenitent people.

The celibate life of Jesus was also unlike that of John the Baptist, who abandoned his father Zechariah despite his obligation to provide him with descendants to continue the priestly line. John's decision to live without a wife made some sense. It would have been hard to take a wife with him to the desert, to live on locusts and wild honey while he proclaimed the imminent judgment of God and called everyone to repentance. But Jesus was not a man of the desert. He traveled around Galilee, not proclaiming the terrible judgment of God but the nearness of a forgiving Father. In contrast with the austerity of John, who came «eating no bread and drinking no wine», Jesus shocked people with his festive life style: he ate and drank without regard to what people thought[55]. There were men among the disciples who traveled with him, but also women he loved dearly. Why wasn't a wife beside him?

---

54 Jeremiah was a tender-hearted prophet, born to love, but he felt obligated to proclaim punishment and misfortune to his people. He was obsessed by his mission and gave prophetic meaning to his solitary life: «I did not sit in the company of merrymakers, nor did I rejoice; under the weight of your hand I sat alone».

55 Thus the ancient Q Source (Luke 7:33-34; Matt 11:11-19).

The Pharisees didn't practice celibacy. There was one rabbi after Jesus, named Simon ben Azzai, who recommended marriage and procreation to others but had no wife of his own. When he was accused of not practicing what he preached, he used to reply: «My soul is in love with the Torah. Others can keep the world going». Totally devoted to studying and observing the law, he did not feel called to spend time with a wife and children. That wasn't Jesus' reason either, for his life was not devoted to studying the Torah.

But he was totally dedicated to something that was increasingly seizing control of his heart. He called it the «reign of God». It was his life's passion, the cause to which he gave himself, body and soul. The laborer from Nazareth ended up living only to help his people take hold of the «reign of God». He abandoned his family, left his work, walked into the desert and joined the movement of John; later he left that, sought out collaborators, and began to go around the towns of Galilee. His one obsession was to proclaim the «Good News of God»[56]. Caught up in the reign of God, he lived out his life without ever having time to create his own family. His behavior was strange and disconcerting. According to the sources he was called a «glutton», «tippler», «friend of sinners», «Samaritan», «crazy man». Probably they also mocked him as a «eunuch». That was a devastating insult which not only challenged his manhood, but linked him with a marginal group of men who were seen as impure because they were not physically whole. Jesus reacted by explaining his behavior: there are eunuchs who were born without testicles; others were castrated in order to serve the families of the high administration of the Empire. But «there are eunuchs who have made themselves eunuchs for the sake of the kingdom of heaven». This graphic language could only have come from someone as unique and scandalous as Jesus[57].

If Jesus did not live with a woman, it was not because he disapproved of sex or belittled the family. It was because he could not marry anything or anyone that might distract him from his mission of service to the reign of God. He did not embrace a wife, but let himself be embraced by prostitutes who were entering into the dynamic of that reign, after recovering their dignity in his presence.

---

56 This expression originated in the first generation of Christians, but it reflects the content of Jesus' activity very well (Mark 1:14).

57 This metaphor of «castrating oneself» for the reign of God has no parallels in Judaism. It comes from a saying which circulated independently in the Christian communities, and which surely came from Jesus. Matthew 19:12 gives it as follows: «For there are eunuchs who have been so from birth, and there are eunuchs who have been made eunuchs by others, and there are eunuchs who have made themselves eunuchs for the sake of the kingdom of heaven».

He had no children to kiss, but he hugged and blessed the children who came to him, seeing them as a «living parable» of how to embrace God. He did not create his own family, but he worked to raise up a more universal family, made up of men and women doing God's will. Of all Jesus' features, this is the one that most forcefully reveals his passion for the reign of God and his total dedication to the struggle of the powerless and humiliated. Jesus knew tenderness, experienced affection and friendship, loved children and defended women. He only turned away from what could interfere with his love, his universality, and his unconditional commitment to those who were deprived of love and dignity. Jesus would not have understood any other celibacy besides the one that flowed out of his passion for God, and for the poorest of God's sons and daughters.

A Seeker of God

We don't know when or why, but at some point Jesus left his craftsman's trade, left his family, and left Nazareth. He wasn't looking for a new occupation. He didn't seek out a recognized teacher to study Torah, or to learn more about the Jewish traditions. He didn't go to the shores of the Dead Sea, seeking admission to the Qumran community. Neither did he go to Jerusalem, to see up close the sacred place where sacrifices were offered to the God of Israel. He just walked away from the inhabited world and into the desert[1].

For Jesus as for all Jews, the wilderness recalled the birthplace of the people: the place they must return to at times of crisis, in order to begin again the history cut short by their unfaithfulness to God. Orders from Rome and the bustle of the temple did not reach the desert; no one heard the discourse of the teachers of the law. What they could hear was God's voice in the silence and loneliness. According to the prophet Isaiah, the desert was the best place to «make straight a highway for our God» and let God enter the heart of the people[2]. The dissident «monks» of Qumran had withdrawn into the desert around 150 B.C.; the popular prophets led their followers there; that was where the Baptist roared out his message. Jesus also went into the desert. He wanted to listen to the God who «speaks tenderly» to his people in the wilderness[3].

But there is no evidence that he was looking for a more intense experience of God to satisfy his internal thirst, or to bring peace to his heart. Jesus was not a mystic in search of personal harmony. What we know suggests that he was seeking God as the «power of salvation» for his people. It was the people's suffering that made him suffer: the brutality of the Romans, the oppression suffocating the peasants, the religious crisis of his people, the debasement of the Covenant. Where was God? Wasn't he the «friend of life»? Wasn't he going to intervene?[4]

Jesus had not yet worked out a plan of action when he met John the Baptist. He was immediately seduced by this desert prophet. He'd never seen anyone like that. He was also fascinated by the idea of creating a «renewed people» in

---

1 The depth and maturity of his religious inclination lead some people to believe that Jesus was engaged in this search before he found John the Baptist. Flavius Josephus mentions his own search, which began when he was about sixteen; he too went into the desert, and lived for three years with a «man of the desert» named Banus. (*Autobiography* 2:10-12).

2 Isa 40:3.

3 Hos 2:14.

4 Jesus' later preaching wasn't about a mystical experience of God, but about his total trust in the nearness of God, who would bring justice and salvation (the reign of God among human beings). So I don't think it's enough to think of him as a charismatic «filled with the Spirit of God» (Borg) or as a «pious Jew» (*hasid*) along the lines of Honi the «circle-drawer», or of Haninah ben Dosa (Vermes).

order to start history over again, grasping for the saving intervention of God. Jesus had never admired anyone as he did John the Baptist. He never talked about anyone else in the same way. For Jesus, John was not just a prophet. He was «more than a prophet»[5]. He was the greatest «among those born of women»[6]. What was it that so seduced Jesus? What did he see in John's person and in his message?

1
John's radical diagnosis

A new and different kind of prophet had appeared on the religious horizon of Palestine between the fall of 27 and the spring of 28 A.D., provoking a strong impact on everyone. His name was John, but people called him the «Baptizer», because he practiced a startling and usual ritual in the waters of the Jordan. More than anyone else, he influenced the trajectory of Jesus[7].

John came from a rural priestly family. His crude language and the images he used came from a village peasant environment[8]. At some point John parted company with the temple and its whole system of ritual purification and forgiveness. We don't know what motivated him to abandon his priestly role. His behavior suggests a man shaken up by the Spirit. He didn't follow the lead of any teacher. He didn't explicitly quote the holy Scriptures. He didn't invoke any authority to legitimate his action. He just left the sacred land of Israel and went out in the desert to roar out his message.

John understood more than the deep crisis the people were suffering. Unlike other movements of the time, which looked at different aspects of the crisis, he focused all the power of his prophetic gaze on the root of it all: Israel's sin and rebelliousness. His diagnosis was brief and to the point: the history of the chosen people had ended in total failure. God's plan had been frustrated. This was not just another crisis. It was the last link in a long chain of sins. The people were now facing God's definitive reaction. Like a woodcutter tapping the base of a

---

5 Q Source (Luke 7:26; Matthew 11:9).

6 Q Source (Luke 7:28; Matt 11:11); [apocryphal] *Gospel of Thomas* 46.

7 The principal sources on the activity, preaching and death of the Baptist are Mark 1:2-11; 6:17-29; the Q Source (Luke 3:7-9; 3:16-17; 7:24-28; 16:16 - Matt 3:7-10; 3:11-12; 11:7-11; 11:12-13); Flavius Josephus in *The Antiquities of the Jews* 18, 5, 2.

8 According to many authors (Meier, Theissen-Merz, Ernst, Webb), this is the only part of the information in Luke's narrative of the «infancy of John» (Luke 1) that we can accept as historical.

tree before striking the last powerful blows, God had placed his ax at their roots[9]. It was too late for them to «flee from the wrath to come», like snakes from an approaching grass fire[10]. They could no longer rely on the old ways to renew the history of salvation. Sacrifices of atonement would no longer work. The people were quickly coming to their end.

Evil was corrupting everything, according to the Baptist. The whole people was contaminated, not only its individual members; all Israel must confess its sin and be radically converted to God, or it would be irremediably lost. The temple itself was corrupt; it was no longer a holy place; it could no longer eradicate the evil from the people; the atonement sacrifices celebrated there were useless; they needed a new rite of radical purification, not linked to the temple cult. Evil had infected even the land where Israel lived; it too must be purified and inhabited by a renewed people; they must go out to the desert, away from the promised land, in order to come back as a people converted and forgiven by God.

No one should be under any illusions. The Covenant was broken. It had been annulled by the sin of Israel. It wouldn't help to say they were God's chosen people. Being «children of Abraham» would do them no good at all[11]; God could make children of Abraham even out of the rocks scattered around the desert. Nothing would take the place of a radical conversion. Israel was no better off than the Gentiles. They couldn't go back to their past history with God. They needed a total purification to re-establish the Covenant. The «baptism» John offered was precisely the new rite of conversion and radical forgiveness that Israel needed: the beginning of a new election and a new covenant for that failed people.

Jesus was seduced and impacted by this grandiose vision. This man was putting God at the center and on the horizon of any search for salvation. The temple, sacrifices, interpretations of the law, even belonging to the chosen people: all that was relative. Only one thing was decisive and urgent: to be converted to God and embrace God's forgiveness.

---

9 Q Source (Luke 3:9; Matt 3:10). «Even now the ax is lying at the root of the trees; every tree therefore that does not bear good fruit will be cut down and thrown into the fire».

10 Q Source (Luke 3:7; Matt 3:7). «You brood of vipers! Who warned you to flee from the wrath to come?»

11 Q Source (Luke 3:8; Matt 3:9). «Do not begin to say to yourselves, 'We have Abraham as our ancestor'; for I tell you, God is able from these stones to raise up children for Abraham».

The new beginning

John wasn't trying to plunge his people into despair. On the contrary, he felt called to invite them into the desert to engage in a radical conversion, to be purified in the waters of the Jordan, and once they were forgiven, to return to the promised land and welcome the imminent arrival of God.

John himself led the way into the desert. He left his small village and turned toward an uninhabited region to the east of the Jordan River. The region was called Perea, at the edge of the promised land but just outside it[12].

He had apparently chosen the location with care. It was beside the Jordan River, with plenty of water for the rite of «baptism». An important commercial route also ran through the area, from Jerusalem to the regions east of the Jordan; there John could cry out his message to the many passers-by. But there was another, more important reason. The Baptist could have found more water on the shores of Lake Gennesaret. He could have reached more people in the city of Jericho, or even Jerusalem, which also had small public and private tanks called *miqwaot* where he could easily have performed the baptismal rite. But the «desert» he chose was opposite Jericho, in the very place where according to the tradition, Joshua had led his people across the Jordan River and into the promised land[13]. It was an intentional choice.

There John began living as a «man of the desert». His clothing was a garment of camel's hair with a leather belt; his food was locusts and wild honey[14]. This crude way of dressing and eating expressed more than a desire to live an ascetic, penitential life. It was the life style of a man who is at home in the desert and feeds on the natural products of an uncultivated land. John wanted to remind people of Israel's life in the desert, before they entered the land that God was giving them as an inheritance[15].

---

12 The most recent studies on John the Baptist (Stegemann, Meier, Webb, Vidal) place his baptizing activity *east of the Jordan* in the territory of Perea, which was under the jurisdiction of Antipas. That explains how Antipas could imprison and execute him in the fortress of Machaerus, south of Perea. Pontius Pilate ruled Judea at the time.

13 Josh 4:13-19.

14 Mark 1:6.

15 Despite what is usually believed, it appears that John's residence in the desert was intended to symbolize «life outside the promised land», rather than the asceticism of a penitent (Stegemann, Gnilka, Meier, Vidal).

John was bringing his people back into the wilderness At the gates of the promised land, but outside it. The new liberation of Israel must begin again, where it began before. The Baptist called the people to return symbolically to their point of departure, before they crossed the river. Like the «first generation of the desert», now too the people must listen to God, purify themselves in Jordan's waters, and thus renewed, come back to the land of peace and salvation.

On this symbolic stage John appeared as the prophet calling for conversion, offering baptism for the forgiveness of sins. The gospel writers showed this with two texts from the biblical tradition[16]. John was «the voice of one crying out in the wilderness: "Prepare the way of the Lord, make his paths straight"»[17]. That was his task: helping the people to prepare the way for God's arrival. In other words, he was «the messenger» who once more guides Israel through the wilderness and leads them into the promised land.

3

The baptism of John

When John arrived in the Jordan desert, sacred baths and rites of purification with water were commonly practiced throughout the Orient. Many cultures have attributed a sacred, symbolic meaning to water: it cleanses, purifies, refreshes, and gives life. The Jewish people also used baths and ablutions to obtain purification in God's eyes. It was one of the most expressive means of religious renewal. The deeper they sank into their sin and misfortune, the more they yearned for a purification that would cleanse them of all evil. They still remembered the moving promise of Ezekiel, around 587 B.C.: «I will take you from the nations, and gather you from all the countries, and bring you into your own land. I will sprinkle clean water upon you, and you shall be clean from all your uncleannesses, and from all your idols I will cleanse you. A new heart I will give you, and a new spirit I will put within you»[18].

---

16 We don't know if John used these texts to present himself to the people, as did other prophetic leaders in his time. Many authors generally say he did not.

17 All the gospel writers used this familiar text from Isaiah 40:3 in speaking of John: Mark 1:3; the Q Source (Luke 3:4; Matt 3:3); and John 1:23.

18 Ezek 36:24-26.

This desire for cleansing led to a surprising diffusion of rites of purification among the Jews of the first century[19], and the emergence of a variety of baptizing movements. Their awareness of living far from God, their need for conversion, and their hope for salvation at the «last day», led many people to seek purification in the desert. Less than twenty kilometers from where John baptized was the «monastery» of Qumran, where a large community of white-robed «monks», obsessed with ritual purity, practiced daily baths and rites of purification in small pools specially built for that purpose. The desert must have held a very intense attraction as a place of conversion and purification. Flavius Josephus tells about «a certain Banus who lived in the desert, wore a garment made of leaves, ate wild food, and washed himself several times every day and night with cold water to purify himself»[20].

Yet John's baptism, and the meaning he gave it, were absolutely new and unique. It was not to be practiced any old way. First it was not done in tanks or pools, as was customary in the Qumran «monastery» or in the temple area, but in the strong current of the Jordan River. That was not by chance. John's purpose was to purify the people from the radical impurity caused by their evil; he knew that for very grave and contagious impurities, the Jewish tradition required water that was «not still or "dead"», but «living water», water that rushed and flowed.

Those who accepted his baptism were plunged by John into the waters of the Jordan. His baptism was a full-body bath, not the sprinkling or partial washing of the hands or feet that marked other purification rites in that period. His new baptism aimed for a total purification. For that reason it could only be done once, like starting life over again, not like the immersions that the Qumran «monks» practiced several times daily to restore the ritual purity they had lost during the day.

There was something even more unusual. Before John the Jews were not accustomed to baptizing others. They had many rites of purification and immersion, but the people seeking purification always washed themselves. John was the first to assume the authority to baptize others. That is why they called him the «baptizer» or «submerger». This gave his baptism a singular character. On the one hand it created a strong bond between the baptized ones and John. The ablutions practiced by the Jews were individual, private rites, to be done when-

19 Archaeologists have discovered «tanks» and small «pools» (*miqwaot*) from Jesus' time, which were used in purifications. They could be used privately or publicly. Some were dug out of rock and had channeling systems to collect water from the rain or from a nearby spring.

20 *Autobiography* 2, 11-12.

ever they thought it necessary. Baptism in the Jordan was different. People talked about «the baptism of John». To be plunged by him into the living waters of the Jordan meant accepting his call and incorporating themselves into the renewal of Israel. On the other hand, because it was done by John and not by themselves, it felt like a gift of God. God himself was offering purification to Israel. John was only the mediator[21].

Thus John's baptism became a sign and commitment to a radical conversion to God. The act solemnly expressed renunciation of the sin into which the people had fallen, and their return to God's Covenant. This conversion had to occur at the deepest personal level, but it must also be translated into behavior worthy of a people faithful to God: the Baptist demanded «fruits worthy of repentance»[22]. This «conversion» was absolutely necessary and could not be replaced by any religious rite, not even by baptism[23].

Yet the rite did create the proper atmosphere to awaken the desire for radical conversion. Men and women, whether or not they belonged to the category of «sinners», whether they were considered pure or impure, were baptized by John in the Jordan River while they confessed their sins in a loud voice[24]. It was an individual baptism, not collective: each person assumed personal responsibility. But the confession of sins was not only for individual behavior; it included the sins of all Israel. It may have been similar to the public confession of sins that the whole people made when they gathered for the festival of Atonement.

«John's baptism» was much more than a sign of conversion. It also included God's forgiveness. Repentance alone would not erase the sins accumulated by Israel, and create the renewed people that John had in mind. He proclaimed a baptism of «repentance for the forgiveness of sins»[25]. This forgiveness, given by God at the last moment to an utterly lost people, is probably what moved people most deeply. But the priests in Jerusalem were scandalized: the Baptist was acting outside the temple, in contempt of the one place where people could re-

---

21 Some see memories of John's priestly role in this activity, since the priests acted as God's mediators in the purification rites at the temple.

22 Q Source (Luke 3:8; Matt 3:8).

23 Jews often used the word *teshuva* (conversion); literally it means «turn» or «return», and it describes the proper response to the call so often made by the prophets to their people: «Return to Yahweh».

24 The rite is thus described in Mark 1:5: they «were baptized by him in the river Jordan, confessing their sins».

25 Mark 1:4.

ceive God's forgiveness. John's arrogance was unheard-of: offering God's forgiveness to the people, so far away from the corrupt temple in Jerusalem!

As he came near the Jordan, Jesus saw a moving spectacle: people from many places were being baptized by John, confessing their sins and begging for God's forgiveness. In the whole crowd there were no temple priests, no scribes from Jerusalem. Most of the people were from the villages; among them were prostitutes, tax collectors, and suspicious-looking characters. An attitude of «conversion» infused the whole group. Purification in the living waters of the Jordan symbolized movement from the desert to the land that God was once again offering them, to be enjoyed in the way it should be[26]. The new people of the Covenant were being formed there.

John did not have in mind a «closed community» like Qumran; his baptism was not a rite of initiation into a select group. He offered it to everyone. In John's view, the «restoration» of Israel was beginning at the Jordan. The newly baptized returned home to live in a new way, as members of a renewed people, prepared to welcome the imminent arrival of God[27].

4

What the Baptist expected

⁓

John never thought of himself as the Messiah of the end times. He was only beginning the preparation. His vision was fascinating. John was thinking of a dynamic process with two distinct stages. The first was the moment of preparation. Its protagonist was the Baptist, and the wilderness was its setting. This preparation revolved around baptism in the Jordan: that was the great sign expressing conversion to God and acceptance of his forgiveness. A second stage would fol-

---

26 Some authors suggest that the people being baptized may have entered the water from the east side, the «desert», and come out on the other, into the «promised land». This is an interesting hypothesis, but cannot be confirmed.

27 There is debate over whether the Baptist had some relationship, or even belonged for a time, to the Qumran community. His activity in the desert (justified by reference to Isaiah 40:3 like that of Qumran), his radical call to conversion, his critique of the temple, his rite of purification, and his eschatological framework, are similar to Qumran (Hollenbach, Paul, Barbaglio). But the uniqueness of John's rite, the bond of the newly baptized with his person and message, his universal offer of salvation, the coming of the «more powerful one», and other aspects distinguish him from the «monks» of the Dead Sea (Stegemann). Many authors place John in the middle of a much broader religious phenomenon of baptismal movements and practices (Meier, Perrot, Scobie).

low immediately, inside the promised land. It would not be led by the Baptist, but by a mysterious figure whom John called «the more powerful one». The baptism by water would be followed by a «baptism by fire», which would definitively transform the people and lead them into fullness of life[28].

Who exactly would come after the Baptist? John did not say exactly. It would clearly be the central character of the last days, but John did not call him the Messiah or give him any other title. He only said it was «the one who was to come», the one «more powerful than I»[29]. Was he thinking of God? It was very common in the biblical tradition to call God «the powerful one»; God was also the Judge of Israel, the only one who could judge his people or infuse them with his Spirit. But it seems odd to think of John speaking of God as «more powerful» than he, or saying that he was not worthy «to untie the thong of his sandals»[30]. He was probably thinking of someone else who would come, through whom God would carry out his ultimate plan. He didn't have a clear idea who that would be, but he expected him to be the definitive mediator. This person would not come to «prepare» the way for God, as John had. He would come to make God's judgment and salvation a reality. He would carry forward the process initiated by the Baptist, leading everyone to the destiny chosen by each one through their response to John's baptism: either judgment or restoration.

It is hard to know exactly how the Baptist imagined what would happen then. Certainly the first event in this definitive stage would be a great, purifying judgment, the time of a «baptism by fire» which would completely purify the people, eliminate evil, and implant justice. The Baptist saw two large groups forming: those like Antipas and his courtesans who did not hear the call to repentance, and those who had come from all over to receive baptism and begin a new life. The «fire» of God would definitively judge his people.

John used the agricultural images one would expect from a man of rural origin. They were violent images, and surely had a great impact on the peasants who heard him. He saw Israel as God's plantation, which needed a radical cleansing. The time was coming to clear out all the useless brush, cutting and burning

28 Against what is commonly believed, the Baptist did not consider this second stage as «the end of this world», but as the radical renewal of Israel in a transformed land (Webb, Stegemann, Vidal).

29 This language of the «one more powerful» (Mark 1:7) or «the one who is to come» (Matt 11:3) was never used to speak of Christ in the Christian communities. It almost certainly reflects the original preaching of John.

30 Mark 1:7: «The one who is more powerful than I is coming after me; I am not worthy to stoop down and untie the thong of his sandals».

the trees that did not bear good fruit[31]. Only the fruitful trees would remain alive and standing: the authentic plantation of God, the true Israel. And John made use of another image. Israel was like a people whose threshing floor is full of everything: grain, chaff, and straw. It needed to be completely cleared out, separating the grain for storage in the granary, and gathering the straw for burning. With his judgment, God would eliminate all the waste and bring the harvest in clean[32].

The great purifying judgment would lead to a new situation of peace and fullness of life. The «baptism of fire» alone would not accomplish that. John also expected a «baptism of the Holy Spirit»[33]. Israel would feel the transforming power of God, the life-giving outpouring of his Spirit. At last the people would know the fullness and justice of life in a transformed land. They would live in a new Covenant with their God.

5

The «conversion» of Jesus

℘

At some point Jesus came to the Baptist, heard his call to conversion, and was baptized by him in the waters of the Jordan River. It happened around 28 A.D.; that we know for certain. No one in the early Christian communities would have invented such an embarrassing episode, for it could only create problems for Jesus' followers.

Jesus' baptism created two problems in particular. If he accepted baptism from John, didn't that mean he was inferior to the Baptist? Worse yet, if he had gone down to the Jordan as everyone else did, confessing his sins, didn't that mean he too was a sinner? These were not just hypothetical questions, since some Christians were probably in touch with baptist groups that followed John and not Jesus.

The Christians could not deny the event, but they presented it in a way that would not undermine Jesus' worthiness. Mark, the first of the gospel writers, affirms that Jesus «was baptized by John in the Jordan», but immediately he adds that Jesus had a strange experience. He saw the Holy Spirit descending on him

---

31 Q Source (Luke 3:9; Matt 3:10).
32 Matt 3:12.
33 Mark 1:8; Q Source (Luke 3:16; Matt 3:11).

«like a dove», and heard a voice from heaven saying: «You are my Son, the Beloved». This way everyone would understand that although he had allowed John to baptize him, Jesus was really the «one more powerful» of whom the Baptist spoke, the one who would come after and would «baptize with the Holy Spirit»[34].

Matthew goes a step further. When Jesus comes to be baptized, the Baptist tries to prevent him, saying: «I need to be baptized by you, and do you come to me?» Jesus replies, «it is proper for us in this way to fulfill all righteousness». This makes it clear that Jesus did not need to be baptized; he did it for some unknown, compelling reason[35]. Luke doesn't need to explain it, for although he mentions Jesus' baptism, he leaves out the intervention of the Baptist (who was already imprisoned by Antipas). Here Jesus has the stage to himself: he was praying when he had the religious experience described by Mark[36]. The fourth evangelist doesn't even mention the baptism: John no longer appears as the baptizer of Jesus, but as the witness who declares him the «Lamb of God who takes away the sin of the world» and «the one who baptizes with the Holy Spirit»[37].

Let us set aside these later Christian interpretations for the moment. We know for sure that Jesus was baptized by John. It was a decisive moment for Jesus, a complete about-face in his life. That young craftsman from a small Galilean village would never again be seen in Nazareth. From then on he would devote body and soul to a prophetic task that would amaze his family and friends: they had never imagined anything like this when he was among them. What can we know about the time Jesus spent with the Baptist, which would so decisively change his life?[38]

Apparently Jesus did not yet have a well-defined mission of his own. Still, his decision to be baptized by John gives us a clue to his search. Accepting «John's baptism» meant that he shared John's vision of the hopelessness of Israel's situation: the people must go through a radical conversion in order to receive God's

34 Mark 1:9-11.
35 Matt 3:14-15.
36 Luke 3:21-22.
37 John 1:29-30, 33-34. The apocryphal writings continued evolving in the same direction. In one fragment of the *Gospel of the Ebionites*, John kneels before Jesus saying, «I beg you, Lord, baptize me». And in a passage of the *Gospel of the Nazarenes*, when Jesus' mother and brothers invite him to go with them to the Baptist, Jesus answers: «How have I sinned, that I should go and be baptized?»
38 Surprisingly few scholars have considered the importance of the Baptist, which Jesus himself affirmed so vigorously, in looking for the sources of Jesus' early inspiration. Nevertheless, Jesus' baptism is the only historically verifiable event that can bring us close to the starting point of his mission.

forgiveness[39]. But more importantly, he shared the hope of the Baptist. He was drawn to the idea of preparing the people for the encounter with their God. Soon they would all see the saving irruption of God in history. Israel would be restored, the Covenant would be renewed, and the people would enjoy a fuller life. Jesus would never forget this hope, which he first caught from the Baptist. Later, moving within a different horizon, Jesus' main purpose would be to make that hope a reality, especially among the most unfortunate. He would call the people to hold on to God, awaken hope in their hearts, work for the restoration of Israel, seek a more just and faithful participation in the Covenant. There in the Jordan desert, Jesus was probably already beginning to see the broad outlines of his mission.

Jesus accepted baptism as a sign and commitment to a radical change. That was what the Baptist demanded of everyone who came to be immersed in the Jordan river. Jesus also wanted to make his «conversion» real; his first step was to decide that from now on, he would collaborate with John the Baptist in his service to the people. Was this not the best way to welcome the God who was already coming to purify and save Israel? He separated from his family and committed himself to his people. He also forgot about his work. His only goal was to collaborate in that wonderful conversion movement that John had begun. At night in the silent desert, when the roars of John the Baptist subsided and he could no longer hear the people confessing their sins as they plunged into the Jordan, Jesus heard the voice of God calling him to a new mission[40].

He did not return immediately to Galilee, but stayed some time with the Baptist in the wilderness. We don't know what life was like for those who made up John's circle. It is plausible to think he had two types of followers. Most of them returned home after baptism, but kept alive their awareness of belonging to the renewed people that was forming around the Baptist. But some stayed with him in the desert, deepening their understanding of his message and helping him with his task. They probably practiced a life style of austerity and prayer, inspired by the Baptist[41]. Jesus not only took up John's mission, but joined this

---

39 Although some authors believe Jesus sought forgiveness for his own personal sins in baptism (Hollenbach), his acceptance of baptism gives us no concrete information on which to base an understanding of his state of mind.

40 The Christian sources mention Jesus' habit of withdrawing at night to a solitary place, to communicate with God. This seems to be an historical fact, attested by all the authors. Jesus probably kept in his heart the nostalgic memory of his nights at prayer in the Jordan desert.

41 Q Source (Luke 5:33; Matt 9:14); Luke 11:1-2.

group of disciples and collaborators[42]. The sources do not allow us to say much more than that. He was probably an enthusiastic assistant in John's baptisms. There he met two brothers named Andrew and Simon, and a friend of theirs named Philip, all from the same town of Bethsaida. Those three belonged to the Baptist's circle, although later they would give their allegiance to Jesus[43].

6
The new mission of Jesus

The movement launched by the Baptist was beginning to be felt everywhere in Israel. Even people who were written off as reprobates and sinners, like tax collectors and prostitutes, embraced his message. Only the religious elites and the Herodians around Antipas opposed it[44].

People's enthusiasm for a new way of doing things is always disturbing to their rulers. To make it worse, the Baptist was boldly condemning the sins of all, including the immoral behavior of the king. He was becoming a dangerous prophet, especially after Herod repudiated his wife and married Herodias, the wife of his stepbrother Philip, whom he had known as a young man in Rome. It is not hard to imagine the distress this had caused. Antipas was married to the daughter of Aretas IV, the king of Nabatea. The marriage had been well received, since it sealed a peace agreement between Perea and the perennially hostile border area of Nabatea. Now that stability was threatened by the divorce. The Nabateans took it as an insult to their people, and were preparing to fight against Herod Antipas.

The situation became explosive when the Baptist, preaching within twenty kilometers of the Nabatean border, publicly condemned the king's action as a violation of the Torah. According to Flavius Josephus, «Herod feared that John's great influence on the people would lead to a kind of revolt... and he considered it much better to eliminate him than to face a difficult situation of revolt

---

42 This information is widely accepted in recent scholarship (Jeremias, Hollenbach, Becker, Meier, Webb, Murphy-O'Connor, Stuhlmacher, Vidal).

43 Many authors have tried to re-create Jesus' time with the Baptist on the basis of material from the fourth gospel (John 1:35-51; 3:22-36; 4:1-2), but that seems too risky. Meanwhile Meier's theory, that Jesus probably went on baptizing throughout his life, has not been widely accepted.

44 Q Source (Luke 7:33; Matt 11:18; Luke 7:29-30; Matt21:21-32); Luke 3:10-14.

later on, when he might regret his indecision»[45]. Rather than let the situation deteriorate, Antipas ordered the Baptist imprisoned at the fortress of Machaerus, and later had him executed[46].

The death of the Baptist must have caused great consternation. He was the prophet who was preparing Israel for the definitive arrival of God. John's whole mission had been interrupted. Not even the first stage could be carried out. The conversion of Israel remained incomplete. What would become of the people now? What would God do? A great unrest and anxiety took hold of John's disciples and collaborators.

Jesus' reaction was surprising[47]. He did not give up the hope that inspired the Baptist, but radicalized it to an unimaginable degree. He did not go on baptizing like John's other disciples, who carried on his mission after his death. He accepted the end of the preparation that the Baptist had been carrying out, and transformed his mission into something new. He never questioned John's mission and authority, but set out on a new plan of action for the renewal of Israel. A different conviction was awakening in Jesus: God was going to act in this hopeless situation, in an unexpected way. The death of the Baptist did not mean the failure of God's plans, but the beginning of his saving action. God was not abandoning his people. On the contrary, God was about to reveal his mercy even more clearly.

Jesus was beginning to see things in a new perspective. The time of preparation in the desert had come to an end. Now the definitive irruption of God in history was beginning. To receive it, one had to stand in a different place. John's hope for the future was beginning to be realized. The time now beginning was not the old time of preparation, but a new age. God's salvation was coming now.

Jesus was thinking of more than a change in time frame. His insight of faith and his total confidence in God's mercy were leading him to transform John's hope at its very roots. In John's logic, the preparation in the desert would be followed by God's great purifying judgment on the people, a «baptism by fire»; his transforming and saving irruption through the «baptism of the Spirit» would

---

45 *Antiquities of the Jews* 18, 5, 2.

46 Mark's gospel (6:17-29) repeats a popular legend that was circulating about the execution of the Baptist. The gist of the story fits the information provided by Flavius Josephus.

47 As we shall see later on (pp. 309-312), Jesus' prophetic activity began with his intense and powerful experience of God beside the Jordan river. That experience, soon to be followed by the Baptist's disappearance from the stage of history, impelled Jesus to move forward and carry out his new trajectory beyond the desert environment.

only come after that. Jesus was beginning to see it all in the context of God's mercy. What was beginning now for this people, who had not been able to complete their conversion, was not God's judgment but the great gift of salvation. In this hopeless situation the people would see the incredible compassion of God, not his devastating wrath.

Soon Jesus began using a new kind of language: the «reign of God» was coming. They did not need to wait any longer, but to embrace it. What seemed so far away to John was now breaking in on them; soon they would see its saving power. It was time to proclaim the «Good News» to all. The people needed conversion; that conversion did not consist of preparation for judgment, as John thought, but of «entering» the «reign of God» and accepting his saving forgiveness.

Jesus offered it to everyone. Not only to those whom John had baptized in the Jordan, but also to the unbaptized. Jesus did not cancel out the idea of judgment, but put it in a totally new perspective. God comes to everyone as a savior, not as a judge. But God does not force anyone; he only invites them. His invitation can be accepted or rejected. Everyone had a choice of destiny. Some would hear the invitation, embrace the reign of God, enter into its dynamic and let it transform them; others would not hear the good news, would reject God's reign, would not enter into God's dynamic, and would close themselves off to salvation.

Jesus left the desert stage on which the preparation was being enacted, and moved out into the land of Israel to proclaim and «act out» the salvation which was already being offered with the arrival of God. The people no longer needed to go into the desert, as they had in John's time. Jesus himself, in the company of his closest disciples and collaborators, would walk through the promised land. His itinerant life in and around the Galilean towns would be the best symbol of the arrival of God, who was coming as a Father to establish a fuller, more just life for all his children.

Jesus also moved away from John's prophetic manner and strategy. He replaced the austere life of the desert with a festive life style. He set aside the Baptist's way of dressing. It also made no sense to go on fasting. The time had come to offer meals open to everyone, to welcome and celebrate the new life that God was instilling in his people. Jesus offered a banquet to be shared by all, and made it an expressive symbol of a people embracing the fullness of life that God willed for them[48].

---

48 John was called the «baptizer», because his activity revolved around baptism in the Jordan river. Jesus was called a «glutton» and «friend of sinners», because he celebrated the acceptance of God by eating with undesirables.

Even baptism was no longer meaningful as a rite of re-entry into the promised land. Jesus replaced it with other signs of forgiveness and healing, to express and make real the liberation that God willed for his people. To receive forgiveness one need not go up to the Jerusalem temple and offer a sacrifice of atonement; nor was it necessary to plunge into the waters of Jordan. Jesus offered it free of charge to whoever would accept the reign of God. To proclaim God's mercy in a concrete, understandable way, he began doing something that John never did. He healed people that no one else could heal; he soothed the pain of the forsaken; he touched lepers that no one else would touch; he blessed and embraced children and the little ones. They would all feel the saving nearness of God, even the most forgotten and despised of them: the tax collectors, the prostitutes, the demon-possessed, the Samaritans.

Jesus also left behind the language of the desert. Now the people must hear Good News. His words turned into poetry. He invited people to look at life in a new way. He began to tell parables that the Baptist could never have imagined. The people were enchanted. Suddenly everything spoke to them of the nearness of God: the seeds they sowed and the bread they baked, the birds in the sky and the grain in the field, their family weddings and their meals shared with Jesus.

With Jesus everything was different. Their fear of judgment gave way to the joy of clinging to God, the friend of life. No one talked any more of his coming «wrath». Jesus invited everyone into total trust in a Father God. And the change was not only in the people's religious experience. The very figure of Jesus was changing. People no longer saw him as a disciple or collaborator of the Baptist, but as the prophet who passionately proclaimed the reign of God. Could this be the person John had called the «one more powerful»?

A Prophet of the Reign of God

Jesus left the desert, crossed the Jordan River, and walked back into the land that God had given his people. It was around the year 28; Jesus was about 32 years old. He did not go to Jerusalem or stay in Judea. He went straight to Galilee. There was fire in his heart. He needed to proclaim to those poor people the news that was burning inside him: God was coming now to liberate his people from so much suffering and oppression. He knew what he wanted to do: he would «bring fire to the earth» by proclaiming the irruption of the reign of God[1].

1

An itinerant prophet

Jesus did not move back into his house in Nazareth, but went on to the region of Lake Galilee and took up residence in Capernaum, in the home of Simon and Andrew, the two brothers he had met in the company of the Baptist[2]. Capernaum was a town of between 600 and 1,500 inhabitants, built along the lakeshore in the far north of Galilee, at the edge of the territory ruled by Herod's brother Philip. Jesus may have chosen this as a strategic setting for his activity as an itinerant prophet. It made sense, because Capernaum had good communication with the rest of Galilee and its neighbor territories: the tetrarchy of Philip, the Phoenician coastal cities, and the region of the Decapolis.

Capernaum was an important village in comparison with Nazareth, Nain, and many others in Lower Galilee, but very modest in comparison with Sepphoris or Tiberias. It didn't have paved streets on an urban grid but well-worn dirt paths, dusty in the summer, muddy in the rainy season, and malodorous all year round. There were no marble buildings, no mosaic adornments. The homes were modestly built of black basalt stone, with roofs of mud-covered thatch and branches. Usually three or four houses were clustered around a common patio, the setting for much of the family's life and work[3].

---

1 Luke 12:49: «I came to bring fire to the earth». Many scholars believe these words are an echo of Jesus' feelings. In the [apocryphal] *Gospel of Thomas* we can also read this saying of Jesus: «Whoever is near to me, is near the fire. Whoever is far from me, is far from God's reign» (82).

2 The Christian sources say only that Jesus «withdrew to Galilee. He left Nazareth and made his home in Capernaum by the sea» (Matt 4:12-13).

3 Archaeologists have found fishhooks, work tools, grindstones, and wine presses scattered around such patios.

The people of Capernaum were Jewish, except perhaps for the tax collectors, a few government officials, and probably a small detachment of Antipas' soldiers. Outside Capernaum were customs booths to monitor the flow of merchandise along the highway, which brought caravans from the Orient with valuable goods like perfumes from India or silk from China. The customs agents, who charged taxes, tolls and border entry fees, were not viewed favorably and probably kept their distance from the local people[4]; the same was true of the officials who collected fees for fishing rights at the lakeside docks. And there was always a military presence in a border town like Capernaum. Antipas had his own army, equipped and trained in the Roman style, but mainly comprised of foreign mercenaries. There was probably also a small detachment of Herodian soldiers to monitor the border and keep order in that part of the lake, where fishing and port activities were fairly intensive[5].

The people of Capernaum lived modestly. Many were peasants who lived from their farm produce and nearby vineyards, but the majority were engaged in fishing. Some of the peasants lived comfortably; some of the fishers owned their own boats. But there were also landless peasants who worked as day laborers for the large landowners, or hired themselves out for a day or a season around the major ports[6].

Capernaum was above all a fishing village, whose people moved back and forth between their modest homes and the jetties and wharves by the lake. That was probably also Jesus' habitual environment. The north part of the lake, which had the richest fishing banks, was fished mostly by people from Capernaum and Bethsaida. They went out on the water at night. If the catch was large they would go south to the port of Magdala, to sell to the curers of saltfish[7]. Jesus apparently hit it off right away with the fishing families. They let him use their boats

---

4 According to one gospel story, Jesus annoyed some of the leading sectors in Capernaum when he went to the house of Levi and ate with his circle of tax collectors (Mark 2:14-17).

5 Although the Q Source (Luke 7:1-10; Matt 8:5-13) tells about Jesus healing the slave of a centurion living in Capernaum, the presence of a 100-man division in Capernaum is historically improbable. At that time the Roman legion that guarded the whole region was based in Syria. Jesus did not meet Roman soldiers in Galilee.

6 Archaeologists have not found luxury objects, imported porcelain, jewels, or fine dishes in the area. There are no signs of affluent homes.

7 The lake traffic was apparently intensive. Magdala, famous for its saltfish, was the best place to unload the fishing boats. The remains of a boat from Jesus' time were found, sunk in the lake, at Magdala in 1986. It was made of cedar, 8.12 meters long and 2.35 meters at its widest point. It must have had a central mast for a square sail, but there were also oars. It probably sank in a storm around the beginning of the first century.

to go across the lake, and to preach to the crowds gathered on the shore. His best friends were fishermen: Simon and Andrew, who came from Bethsaida but had a house in Capernaum; James and John, the sons of Zebedee and Salome, one of the women who stayed with him to the end; Mary, from the port town of Magdala, whom Jesus had healed and who gave him undying love.

But he did not put down roots in Capernaum. He wanted to spread the news of God's reign everywhere. We cannot reconstruct his itinerary, but we know he went from town to town along the lakeshore: Capernaum, Magdala, Chorazin or Bethsaida. He visited the towns of Lower Galilee: Nazareth, Cana, Nain. He went to other places around Galilee: Tyre and Sidon, Caesarea Philippi, and the Decapolis. But according to the sources he stayed away from the large Galilean cities: Tiberias, the splendid new capital built by Antipas beside the lake only sixteen kilometers from Capernaum, and Sepphoris, the lovely city in Lower Galilee, only six kilometers from Nazareth. Even when he went near Tyre and Sidon, or visited the area of Caesarea Philippi or the Decapolis, he did not go into the urban centers; he stopped in the surrounding villages or on the outskirts of the city. There he met the most marginalized people, the travelers and vagabonds who slept outside the walls. His mission was to visit the villages of Galilee, in the company of a small group of followers. When they visited nearby towns like Chorazin, only three miles from Capernaum, they probably went back to their homes at sundown. When they went from village to village, they looked for people willing to give them food and a simple place to sleep, probably in the patio of the house. We don't know how they withstood the rain and chill of the winters.

When he came to a town, Jesus went looking for the residents. He walked the streets, just as he had when he was a craftsman looking for work. He would stop at a house, wishing peace to the mothers and children in the patio. His favorite place was surely the synagogue or wherever the people met, especially on the sabbath. There they prayed, sang psalms, debated the town's problems, or shared information about recent local events. On the sabbath they read and commented on the Scriptures, and prayed to God for their long-awaited liberation. This was the best place to spread the good news of God's reign.

This apparently was not a casual approach, but a well thought-out strategy. The people no longer needed to go out to the desert to prepare for God's imminent judgment. Jesus himself was walking through the villages, inviting everyone to «enter» the reign of God that was already irrupting in their lives. Their own land had become the place to accept salvation. The parables and images that Jesus drew from village life became the «story of God». Healing the sick and liberating the demon-possessed were his way of pointing to a society of healthy men and women, called to enjoy fullness of life as sons and daughters of God. Meals open to all the people were the symbols of an invitation to share the great table of God, the Father of all.

Jesus saw in these villagers the best starting point for the renewal of the whole people. The peasants spoke Aramaic as he did, and they had most authentically kept the religious tradition of Israel. The cities were different. There along with Aramaic the people spoke some Greek, a language Jesus did not know well; the Hellenist culture was also stronger there.

But another reason was probably closer to his heart. In these Galilean villages lived the poorest and most marginalized people, dispossessed of their right to enjoy the land God had given them; here more than anywhere else, Jesus found the sick and suffering Israel, abused by the powerful; here is where Israel felt the harshest effects of oppression. The powerful lived in the cities, along with their diverse collaborators: managers, large landowners, tax collectors. They did not represent the people of God but the oppressors, the cause of the misery and hunger of these families. The coming of the reign of God must begin among the most humiliated people. These poor, hungry, afflicted people were the «lost sheep» who represented all the dispirited people of Israel. Jesus was very clear about this. The reign of God could only be proclaimed out of a close, direct contact with the people who most needed breathing space and liberation. The good news of God could not come from the splendid palace of Antipas in Tiberias, or from the sumptuous villas in Sepphoris, or from the wealthy neighborhood where the priestly elites lived in Jerusalem. The seeds of God's reign would only find fertile soil among the poor of Galilee[8].

Jesus' itinerant life among them was a living symbol of his freedom and his faith in the reign of God. He had no paid employment, no house or land; he owed nothing to the tax collectors; he carried no coins with the image of Caesar. He had given up the security of the system to «enter» trustingly into God's reign[9].

---

8 We cannot discount the theory of some scholars that Jesus' itinerant life in the Galilean villages, avoiding Tiberias and Sepphoris and staying near the lake, which would permit him to flee Galilee quickly if needed, was partly due to his fear of being imprisoned by Antipas (Hoehner, Reed).

9 The [apocryphal] *Gospel of Thomas* attributes these words to Jesus: «Be wanderers». According to some experts, this brief saying authentically reflects Jesus' choice of an itinerant, countercultural life style.

His itinerant life in the service of the poor also made clear that the reign of God has no center of power and control[10]. It is not like the Empire, governed by Tiberius from Rome, nor like the tetrarchy of Galilee, ruled by Antipas from Tiberias, nor like the Jewish religion, overseen by the priestly elites from the temple in Jerusalem. The reign of God was coming wherever good things happen to the poor.

2
Passion for the reign of God

There is no doubt about this information from the sources: Jesus «went on through cities and villages, proclaiming and bringing the good news of the kingdom of God»[11]. We can say without hesitation that from then on Jesus devoted his time, his energy, and his whole life to what he called the «reign of God». That was certainly the core of his preaching, his deepest conviction, the passion that inspired all his activity. Everything he said and did was in the service of God's reign. That reality gave everything its coherence, true meaning, and passionate force. The reign of God is the key to the meaning that Jesus gave to his life, and to the mission he wanted to carry out in Galilee, in the people of Israel, and ultimately in all the peoples[12].

All the sources agree on this: Jesus in Galilee was not teaching a religious doctrine for his listeners to learn and follow. He was proclaiming an event, so they could accept it joyfully and faithfully. No one saw him as a teacher devoted to explaining the religious traditions of Israel. They knew a prophet with a passion for a fuller life for everyone, who only wanted people to embrace God, so that God's reign of justice and mercy would become ever wider and more joyful. His goal was not to perfect the Jewish religion, but to hasten the coming of the long-awaited reign of God, which meant life, justice, and peace.

Neither was Jesus teaching the peasants new moral norms and laws. He was telling them the news: «God is already here, seeking a happier life for everyone. We must change our outlook and our hearts». He was not giving the villagers a

10 This is suggested by Theissen, Crossan and other authors, who emphasize the itinerant aspect of Jesus' mission.

11 Luke 8:1.

12 Although it will surprise some readers, Jesus only spoke of the «reign of God», not of the «church». The reign of God appears 120 times in the synoptic gospels; the church only appears twice (Matt 16:18 and 18:17), and it clearly is not a term Jesus used.

more perfect moral code, but offering insight into God's way of being and acting, and what the world and their lives would be like if everyone followed his example. That is what he was communicating with his teaching and with his whole life.

Jesus always talked about the «reign of God», but he never said exactly what that was. Somehow the people guessed what he was talking about, because they knew his coming was the hope that sustained them. But Jesus would surprise them with his explanations of how this reign was coming, for whom it would turn out to be good news, and how they could receive its saving power. There was something new and fascinating in his message for those people. It was what they wanted to hear. What was it in his talk about the «reign of God» that got them so excited? What did they see in that metaphor? How did they come to think of God as good news?

3
An ancient hope

The reign of God was not a new idea with Jesus, but a well known metaphor that drew on Israel's deepest aspirations and hopes. He found that hope already in the people's hearts, and he was able to recreate it in a surprising new perspective out of his own experience of God. It was not Israel's only symbol, or even the most central to their thinking, but it was increasingly widespread before Jesus began to use it. The actual words «reign of God» were relatively new, however, and not yet so widely used[13]. It was Jesus who decided to use it regularly. There was no better way to express what he believed in.

As a child he had learned to believe in God as creator of the heavens and the earth, the absolute sovereign over all the gods and lord of all the peoples. Israel felt secure in that belief. Everything was in God's hands. His reign was absolute, universal, and everlasting. The people expressed their faith by singing joyfully:

---

13 The expression «reign of God» seldom appears in the Old Testament. Its writers said that God was «king» (*melek*), or that God «reigns» (*malak*). The gospels indicate that Jesus used the expression «reign of God» (*basileia tou theou*). That is the Greek translation of the Aramaic form that Jesus used: «*malkutá di ʿelahá*».

«Say among the nations, "The Lord is king! The world is firmly established; it shall never be moved. He will judge the peoples with equity"»[14].

That great God, lord of all the nations, was Israel's God in a very special way. He had brought them out of slavery in Egypt, and led them through the desert to the promised land. The people knew him as their «liberator», their «shepherd», and their «father», for they had felt his protective love and care. At the beginning they did not call him «king». But after the monarchy was established, when Israel had its own king like other nations, they felt a need to remember that God was the only king of Israel. A king could only rule his people in God's name, and in obedience to God's will.

Their earthly kings had been a big disappointment. God had liberated Israel from slavery in Egypt, in order to create a people free of all oppression and slavery. He had given them that land to share as brothers and sisters. Israel would be different from other nations; there would be no slaves among them; widows and orphans would not be abused; they would have compassion on foreigners. Despite the warnings of the prophets, Israel had become a disaster because of the kings' favoritism toward the powerful, the exploitation of the poor by the wealthy, and every other kind of abuse. The consequence of all this was their exile in Babylonia.

That was a tragic experience, hard for Israel to understand. Once more the people were being oppressed by a foreign king, dispossessed of their land, with no king, temple or institutions of their own, and subjected to humiliating slavery. Where was God, the king of Israel? The prophets never gave up hope: God would restore that humiliated people, and liberate them again from slavery. This was the message of one prophet in the sixth century B.C.: God still loved his people and was again offering them forgiveness. God would bring Israel out of captivity, the people would experience a new «exodus», the dispersed tribes would come back together, and they would all enjoy the promised land in peace. Jesus knew, and was perhaps reminding them on his travels through the Galilean hills, of the forceful and beautiful message that the prophet had given them near the end of their exile: «How beautiful upon the mountains are the feet of the messenger who announces peace, who brings good news, who announces salvation, who says to Zion, "Your God reigns"»[15].

14 Ps 96:10. At the time of the new year's festival, a liturgy of enthronement of Yahweh as king was celebrated at the temple in Jerusalem. We can still read some of the psalms (93-99) that were sung especially for this occasion. Jesus probably knew them and sang them from time to time.

15 Isa 52:7. Near the end of the exile (around 550 B.C.) this great, anonymous prophet wrote what we now call the «Book of Consolation», which later became chapters 40-55 of the Book of Isaiah.

Some groups of exiles did return to their land, and the temple was rebuilt, but those marvelous promises remained unfulfilled. The tribes remained in dispersion. The old lies and injustices came back. True peace seemed out of reach, for the threatening shadow of Alexander the Great was looming on the horizon. But later prophets kept on encouraging the people. Malachi had the audacity to put this good news in the mouth of Yahweh: «See, I am sending my messenger to prepare the way before me»[16]. Jesus lived by this faith, as did many of his contemporaries. When they heard about the coming of God, it awakened a double hope in their hearts: God would soon liberate Israel from the oppression of the foreign powers, and would establish justice, peace, and fullness of life among them.

4

A burning hope in the heart of the people

Israel's situation became even more desperate, first with the invasion of Alexander the Great, and then with the Roman legions. The prophets no longer dared raise their voices. Israel seemed doomed to disappear. Soon the anguished cry of this oppressed people could be heard again, in unexpected apocalyptic writings that kept Israel's ardent hope alive[17]. The situation was so chaotic that everyone saw it as an unsolvable puzzle. Where was God? They needed God himself to reveal his secret plans and assure his people that he was still in control of history. Only these writers, who had seen the deepest plans of God in dreams and visions, could shed some kind of light on the situation the people were experiencing.

The message of these visionaries was fearsome, and at the same time hopeful. The world had been corrupted by evil. The whole creation was contaminated. A final, violent combat would be unleashed between the forces of good and the forces of evil, between the powers of light and darkness. God would have to destroy this world through a cosmic catastrophe, in order to create «new heavens

---

16 Mal 3:1. Malachi is considered the last of the prophets.

17 The writers are called apocalyptic because they communicated to the people the «revelation» (*apokalypsis*) they said they had received from God. This literature emerged forcefully at the beginning of the second century B.C., and did not fade until after the first century A.D. One of the most famous writings is the book of Daniel, which was accepted into the Bible. The others are called «apocryphal» books (*apokrifoi*), that is, books left out of the biblical canon. Among them are the books of *Enoch*, the book of *Jubilees*, the *Psalms of Solomon*, the *Ascent of Moses*, the *Testaments of the Twelve Patriarchs*, the *Oracles of the Sybil*, and others. These books were well known in the Qumran community, and some of them were probably written in that «monastery».

and a new earth». The present, dark period of chaos would give way to a new era of peace and blessing[18].

Jesus certainly knew the book of Daniel, the most popular of the apocalyptic writings, which appeared during a brutal persecution by Antioch IV Epiphanes (168-164 B.C.) The level of oppression was unimaginable. The power of evil was greater than any human force. Daniel depicted the oppressor kingdoms as savage beasts destroying the people of God. But after so much oppression would come a human kingdom. God would take power from the oppressor kingdoms and deliver it to Israel[19].

Jesus and the Galilean peasants probably did not know these apocalyptic writings in detail, since they only circulated in cultured environments like that of the Qumran «monastery». But they might have known two prayers that were recited in Jesus' time. The *Kaddish*, written in Aramaic, was prayed in public at the synagogues during the sabbath and feast day liturgies. That prayer said in part:

> May the great Name of God be exalted and sanctified, throughout the world, which he has created according to his will. May his Kingship be established in your lifetime and in your days, and in the lifetime of the entire household of Israel, swiftly and in the near future... May there be abundant peace from Heaven, and life, upon us and upon all Israel... He who makes peace in his high holy places, may he bring peace upon us, and upon all Israel[20].

The prayer of the *Eighteen Blessings* was also well known; the men recited it every morning and evening. In one of them the people cried out to God: «Take all suffering and affliction from us, and be Thou our only King»[21].

---

18 Most scholars believe that the apocalyptic writings were proclaiming a final intervention by God to destroy the present, tangible world and replace it with «another world» beyond history. But a growing number of authors think that the apocalyptic language and imagery were really focused on a transformation of this tangible world, which would begin with the historical transformation of Israel (Wright, Horsley, Vidal).

19 Daniel 7.

20 The double request that «the great Name of God be exalted and sanctified», and that his Kingship be established, lead many authors to believe that Jesus drew on this popular prayer in the first part of the «Lord's Prayer».

21 *Shemoné esré*. According to the Babylonian Talmud, this prayer dates back to the first generation after the exile.

Jesus might also have known the *Psalms of Solomon*, written by a group of Pharisees from the depth of their crisis, when general Pompey entered Jerusalem in 63 B.C. and profaned the temple. These devout Jews expressed their trust that God, the true king of Israel, would soon intervene to establish his eternal kingdom through the Messiah, of the family of David. Although the Roman legions had occupied the promised land, one of these psalms begins and ends with a moving affirmation of faith: «Lord, only you are our king forever and ever»[22].

5
God is already here!

Jesus surprised everyone with this declaration: «The reign of God has come». His certainty must have caused quite an impact. His attitude was awfully bold: wasn't Israel still under Roman domination? Weren't the peasants still oppressed by the powerful classes? Wasn't the world full of corruption and injustice? But Jesus was speaking and acting out of a surprising conviction: God is already here, acting in a new way. His reign has begun to prevail in these Galilean villages. God's saving power is on the march. Jesus had already experienced it and wanted to communicate it to everyone. The decisive, divine intervention that everyone was waiting for was not at all a distant dream; it was something real that could be grasped here and now. God had begun to make his saving presence felt. They could perceive it even in this dark time of their life.

The gospel of Mark accurately pinpoints this original, surprising message of Jesus. Mark says that Jesus proclaimed «the good news of God» in the villages of Galilee: «The time is fulfilled, and the kingdom of God has come near; repent, and believe in the good news»[23]. This language was new. Jesus was not talking, as his contemporaries did, about a future manifestation of God; he wasn't saying that the reign of God is more or less close. It has arrived. It is here. Jesus has experienced it. And in spite of all the evidence to the contrary, he was inviting people to believe this good news.

22 *Psalms of Solomon*, 17. We don't know if Jesus was familiar with the Pharisaic environments where this spirituality was practiced.

23 Mark 1:14-15. This summary of Jesus' message probably comes from the early Christian teachers, but according to many scholars its central affirmation, «the kingdom of God has drawn near», is certainly from Jesus (Beasley-Murray, Schlosser, Meier).

It is not hard to understand the skepticism of some, and the confusion of almost everyone: How could he say the reign of God was already here? Where could they see it or experience it? How could Jesus be so sure that God had already arrived? Where could they see him getting rid of the pagans and establishing justice in Israel? Where were the final cataclysm and the terrible signs that would accompany God's powerful intervention? They must have asked Jesus that many times. His reply was disconcerting: God would not come in a spectacular way, «nor will they say, "Look, here it is!" or "There it is!" For in fact, the kingdom of God is among you»[24].

These words have not always been well understood. They are sometimes wrongly translated: «The reign of God is *within* you»[25]. This has unfortunately led to a distortion of Jesus' thinking, reducing the reign of God to something private and spiritual that people feel inside them when they open up to God's action. Jesus wasn't thinking that way when he talked to the Galilean peasants. Rather he was trying to convince them that the coming of God to establish justice was not a terrible, spectacular intervention but a liberating force, humble yet effective, and that it was there in the midst of life, within reach of anyone who accepted it with faith.

To Jesus this was not a perverse world, hopelessly subjected to the power of evil while it waited for God's final intervention, as the apocalyptic writings said. Along with the terrible destructive power of evil, people could already see the saving power of God, who was now bringing their life to its definitive liberation. The [apocryphal] *Gospel of Thomas* attributes these words to Jesus: «The kingdom of God is within you and outside you»[26]. That is true. Acceptance of the reign of God begins within a person in the form of faith in Jesus, but it is realized in the life of the people wherever evil is being overcome by God's saving justice.

Jesus' certainty was puzzling. It was a privileged moment: those Galilean peasants were experiencing the salvation that their ancestors had dreamed of. In the *Psalms of Solomon*, so popular in Pharisaic groups during Jesus' time, they could

---

24 There is a scholarly consensus that these words (Luke 17:21) express the authentic thinking of Jesus. The [apocryphal] *Gospel of Thomas* picks up the same idea: «The Father's kingdom has spread over all the earth, and the people do not see it» (113).

25 Although the Greek expression *entos hymin* can also mean «within you», modern researchers now generally translate it as «The kingdom of God is *among you*»; for Jesus it was not an intimate spiritual reality, but a transformation that involved the whole of life and of people.

26 *[Apocryphal] Gospel of Thomas* 3. This saying was written down in a context with noticeable Gnostic influences. But according to some authors, it reflects the style and the thinking of Jesus.

read lines like this: «Blessed are they who will live in those days, and see the good things that the Lord is preparing for the coming generation»[27]. Jesus called his followers blessed because with him they were experiencing what so many of the great personalities of Israel had waited for: «Blessed are the eyes that see what you see! For I tell you that many prophets and kings desired to see what you see, but did not see it, and to hear what you hear, but did not hear it»[28].

6

The best news

∞

The arrival of God is a good thing. That is how Jesus thought of it: God is coming near because God is good, and it is good for us that he comes near. God is not coming to «defend» his rights and settle accounts with those who do not fulfill his commandments. He is not coming to impose his «religious dominion». In fact, Jesus didn't ask the peasants to fulfill their obligation of paying the tithes and first fruits, he didn't tell the priests to observe the purity laws more carefully when they conduct atonement sacrifices in the temple, and he didn't encourage the scribes to enforce the sabbath and other laws more faithfully. The reign of God was different. What God cared about was liberating the people from whatever dehumanized them and caused them suffering.

Jesus' message had an impact from the beginning. His way of talking about God provoked enthusiasm in the simplest, least educated sectors of Galilee. This is what they needed to hear: God cared about them[29]. The reign of God that Jesus proclaimed was the answer to their deepest hope: to live in dignity. All the sources point to one thing beyond any doubt: Jesus saw himself as the bearer of good news. Indeed his message would inspire great joy among those poor, humiliated peasants, people without prestige or material security, for whom not even the temple held out any hope.

27 *Psalm of Solomon* 18:6. The *Oracles of the Sybil*, an apocalyptic writing from the diaspora around 150-120 B.C., said something similar: «Blessed is the man or the woman who lives in that time» (3:371).
28 From the Q Source (Luke 10:23-24; Matt 13:16-17). According to many authors, they reflect the essence of Jesus' thinking. In another saying, Jesus affirms that the new reality of the reign of God had arrived after John: «The law and the prophets were in effect until John came; since then the good news of the kingdom of God is proclaimed» (Luke 16:16; Matt 11:12-13). It is however difficult to recreate the original form of the saying and confirm its authenticity.
29 The Christian sources always, and in many ways, present the message and activity of Jesus as *euaggelion*, that is, «good news».

The apocalyptic writers gave a dark description of Israel's situation. Evil had invaded everything. Everything was under Satan's power. He was the personification of all the evils, sufferings and misfortunes that afflicted them. This mythical vision was not naïve. Those visionaries knew very well that evil grows in the heart of every individual, but they also saw how it shaped the society, laws and customs, and finally corrupted everything. It wasn't just the depraved Herod, or the corrupt priestly family of Annas. The large landowners were not the only oppressors, nor were the tax collectors the only wicked ones. There was «something more». The Roman Empire that enslaved the peoples, the vested interests that ran the temple, the exploitation of the peasants with all kinds of tributes and taxes, the self-serving interpretation of the law by some scribes: everything seemed to be driven and ruled by the mysterious power of evil. Evil was more than individual activity; people absorbed it from the social and religious environment as a satanic force that conditioned, subjected, and dehumanized them.

In this apocalyptic environment, Jesus announced that God had already begun to invade the reign of Satan and destroy his power. The decisive combat had begun. God was coming to destroy, not the people, but the evil that lay at the root of everything and poisoned all of life. Jesus was convinced: «I watched Satan fall from heaven like a flash of lightning». These words may be an echo of an experience that had marked his life forever[30]. Jesus had seen the beginning of the defeat of evil. What some groups had been hoping for was now becoming a reality: «Then the kingdom of God will come upon his creatures, the final hour of the devil will sound, and sadness will disappear with him»[31]. Satan was the enemy they had to combat, and no one else. God was not coming to destroy the Romans or to obliterate sinners. He was coming to liberate them all from the power of evil. This battle for control of the world between God and the forces of evil was not a «mythical combat», but a real and concrete confrontation that was constantly taking place in human history. Wherever the sick are rescued from suffering, wherever demoniacs are freed from their torment, wherever the poor recover their dignity, the way is being opened for the reign of God. God is the «anti-evil»: he seeks to «destroy» everything that damages human beings[32].

---

30 This saying, quoted in Luke 10:18, is believed to be directly from Jesus. Many authors believe he was talking about a personal experience (Stegemann, Hollenbach, Otto, Theissen/Merz, Merklein).

31 *Ascent of Moses* 10:1.

32 In Mark 1:24 the evil spirits that were tormenting a man challenged Jesus: «Have you come to destroy us?»

For that reason Jesus, unlike the Baptist, did not speak of God's «wrath» but of his «compassion». God was not coming as a pompous judge, but as a father overflowing with love. The people listened with amazement, for they were all prepared to receive him as a terrible judge. That was what the temple writings said: «He will rise up from his throne with indignation and anger», «he will have vengeance on all his enemies», «he will erase from the earth those who have set fire to his wrath», «none of the wicked will be saved on the day of the judgment of his wrath»[33]. Jesus sought the destruction of Satan, the symbol of evil, but not of the pagans and sinners. He never identified with the Jews in opposition to the pagan peoples: the reign of God would not be an Israelite victory, forever destroying the gentiles. Nor did he identify with the righteous against sinners: the reign of God would not be a victory of the saints, punishing the wicked for their sins. He identified with all those who suffer, against evil; the reign of God was about liberation for everyone deprived of a full, happy life.

God was coming to «reign», but not to exhibit his power over everyone; rather, to show his goodness and put it to work. It is interesting that Jesus, who talked constantly about the «kingdom of God», never called God a «king» but a «father»[34]. His reign would not be imposed by force, but to bring his mercy to all life and fill the whole creation with his compassion. That mercy, responsibly embraced by all, is what would destroy Satan, the personification of that hostile world that works against God and against human beings[35].

Where did Jesus get this way of understanding the «reign of God»? He certainly did not learn it on the sabbath in the synagogue, or absorb it from the temple liturgy. Apparently Jesus was communicating his own experience of God, not the experience that people routinely talked about. Of course the face of a compassionate God was present in the best tradition of Israelite prayer. It was reflected in a familiar psalm: «But you, O Lord, are a God merciful and gracious, slow to anger and abounding in steadfast love and faithfulness»[36]. However,

---

33 This is the message of writings like the *First Book of Enoch*, the *Ascent of Moses*, and the *Psalms of Solomon*.

34 The few passages that speak of God as a «king» are secondary, or are found only in the special material originating with Matthew (5:35; 18:23; 22:2; 25:34).

35 Jesus' parables emphasize «compassion» as the main characteristic of God (Luke 15:11-31; Matt 18:18-35; 20:1-16). In the gospels it also characterizes his own attitude toward those who suffer (Mark 1:41; 6:34; Matt 9:36; 14:14; 15:32; 20:34; Luke 7:13). The writers use a very expressive Greek word, *splanjnizomai*, which literally means that Jesus' (and God's) «bowels shook» when they saw people suffering.

36 Ps 86:15. The words Jesus used to speak of God suggest the meaning of three Hebrew words that appear in this psalm. «Merciful» (*rahum*) describes a compassion that comes from the bowels

Jesus was not quoting Scripture to convince people of God's compassion. He found it instinctively by contemplating nature, and invited the peasants to discover that the whole creation is full of God's goodness. God «makes his sun rise on the evil and the good, and sends rain on the righteous and on the unrighteous»[37]. God doesn't reserve his love for the Jews alone, or bless only those who live in obedience to the law. He also has compassion on gentiles and sinners. This activity of God, which so scandalized the most fanatical sectors of society, was what moved Jesus. It's not that God is unjust, or indifferent to evil. Rather, he does not want to see anyone suffer. Therefore his love has no boundaries, not even to keep out the wicked. That is the God who was coming.

7
God, the friend of life

Everyone agrees on this: Jesus brought excitement to the Galilean peasants[38]. As he described the reign of God, it was something simple and accessible to the people. Something very good and tangible, that even the least educated could understand: what mattered most to Jesus was their life, not their religion. When they heard him speak, and especially when they saw him healing the sick and liberating the demon-possessed from their torment, they could believe that God truly cared more about their lives than about the «religious» issues that lay beyond their understanding. The reign of God was the answer to their deepest aspirations.

The Galilean peasants saw something new and unique in him: Jesus proclaimed God's salvation by healing people. He announced God's reign by initiating a process of healing, both individual and social. His underlying goals were clear: to heal, to dispel suffering, to restore life[39]. There was nothing random or sensationalistic about his healings. Neither was he trying to prove his message or reaffirm his authority. He healed because he was «moved by compassion,» so

and involves the whole person; «gracious» (*hannún*) expresses a gratuitous, unconditional, overflowing love; «steadfast love» (*hesed*) speaks of God's faithfulness to his love for the people.

37 Matt 5:45. Luke's gospel also shows Jesus' thinking about God: «for he is kind to the ungrateful and the wicked» (6:35). It is generally believed that this saying, from the Q Source, expresses Jesus' own conviction.

38 Despite the depth of the «Galilean crisis» (Dodd, Mussner, Schillebeeckx), apparently the excitement Jesus sparked among the Galilean peasants never waned.

39 John's gospel quotes a saying that sums up the people's memory of Jesus: «I came that they may have life, and have it abundantly» (John 10:10).

that the sick, downtrodden and tormented could experience the life of health that God wanted for everyone. That was how he saw his own healing activity: «But if it is by the finger of God that I cast out demons, then the kingdom of God has come to you»[40].

According to an old Christian story, when the disciples of John the Baptist ask him, «are you the one who is to come?» Jesus simply tells them what is happening: «Go and tell John what you hear and see: the blind receive their sight, the lame walk, the lepers are cleansed, the deaf hear, the dead are raised, and the poor have good news brought to them. And blessed is anyone who takes no offense at me»[41]. Jesus understood that God was acting in power and mercy, healing the sick and defending the life of the wretched. That is what was happening, even if it went against the expectations of the Baptist and many others. What was being fulfilled, instead of the dark prophecies of the apocalyptic writers, was the promise of the prophet Isaiah: the coming of God to liberate and heal his people[42].

According to the gospel writers, Jesus dismissed the sick and sinners with the words, «Go in peace», enjoy life[43]. Jesus wished them all the best: integral health, complete well-being, a happy life in their families and villages, a life full of God's blessings. The Hebrew word *shalom,* or «peace», describes the most complete kind of happiness: the opposite of a life of indignity, misfortune, the torments of illness or poverty. Following the tradition of the great prophets, Jesus understood the reign of God as a reign of life and peace. His God was a «friend of life»[44].

Jesus only performed a few healings. In the Galilean villages many blind people, lepers and demoniacs went on suffering their afflictions without a cure. Only a handful experienced his healing power. Jesus never thought of «miracles» as a

---

40 These words from the Q Source (Luke 11:20; Matt 12:28) express Jesus' conviction. Luke says that Jesus cast out demons «by the finger of God»; Matthew, «by the Spirit of God». Luke's word is closer to the concrete, vivid language that Jesus used.

41 Matthew 11:4-6 and Luke 7:22-23 give Jesus' words exactly as they were in the Q Source. Many researchers believe it is a formulation from the Christian community to show that the prophecies of Isaiah were fulfilled in Jesus. But Meier, Scolie, Wink, and others have offered convincing evidence that this material authentically records Jesus' conviction that the time of salvation prophesied by Isaiah was already here.

42 Isaiah 35:5-6; 61:1.

43 Mark 5:34; Luke 7:50; 8:58. We do not know whether this was Jesus' custom, or if it was added by the early Christian community. In any case, that is how they remembered Jesus (Dunn).

44 Jesus may not have been familiar with that beautiful description of God from the Book of Wisdom (11:26), which was written in Alexandria around 100 or 50 B.C.

magic formula to eradicate suffering from the world, but as a sign to indicate the type of action that was needed to welcome and spread God's reign in human life[45]. For this reason he wasn't thinking only of curing sick people. All his activity was aimed at establishing a healthier society: his rebellion against pathological religious attitudes such as legalism, rigorism, or the meaningless cult of righteousness; his efforts toward justice and solidarity; his offer of forgiveness to people overwhelmed by guilt; his embrace of people abused by life or society; his determination to liberate them all from fear and security for a life of absolute trust in God[46]. Healing, liberating from evil, lifting out of depression, reprimanding the religious leaders, building a more friendly society, were all paths toward the reign of God. These are the paths that Jesus followed.

8

The fortunate poor

Jesus left no one out. He announced the good news to everyone, but not everyone would hear it in the same way. Everyone could enter God's reign, but not in the same way; God's mercy meant doing justice first of all for the poorest and most humiliated. For that reason God's coming meant good luck for those who suffered exploitation, but it was threatening to their exploiters.

Jesus declared emphatically that the reign of God is for the poor. He was looking at people who lived in humiliation in their villages, defenseless against the powerful landowners; he knew the hunger of those children; he had seen peasants crying in helpless rage, as the tax collectors carried off the best of their crops to Sepphoris or Tiberias. They more than anyone else needed to hear the news of God's reign: «Blessed are you who are poor, for yours is the kingdom of God. Blessed are you who are hungry now, for you will be filled. Blessed are you who weep now, for you will laugh»[47]. Jesus called them blessed, even in the midst of their unjust suffering, not because they would soon be rich like the large

---

45 When Jesus entrusted the mission to his followers, he always charged them with two tasks: to proclaim the nearness of God's reign, and to heal the sick.

46 In Mark's gospel, Jesus explained his embrace of sinners with this popular saying: «Those who are well have no need of a physician, but those who are sick».

47 There is widespread consensus that these three beatitudes, addressed specifically to the poor, the hungry, and those who weep, were formulated by Jesus. It also appears that Luke's version (6:20-21) is more authentic than Matthew's (5:3-11), which spiritualizes these blessings and adds others.

landowners, but because God was already coming to take away their misery, put an end to their hunger, and bring a smile to their lips. He was already rejoicing with them. He invited them, not to resignation but to hope. He wasn't holding out false illusions, but a chance to recover their dignity. They must all know that God is the defender of the poor. They are God's favorites. If they accepted God's reign, everything would change, for the benefit of the least of these. That was Jesus' faith, his passion, and his struggle.

Jesus was not talking abstractly about «poverty», but about the poor whom he met on his travels through the villages. Families that were barely surviving, people who struggled against losing their land and their honor, children threatened by hunger and malnutrition, prostitutes and beggars despised by all, the sick and demon-possessed who were denied even a minimum of dignity, lepers marginalized by the society and the religion. Whole villages living under the oppression of the urban elites, suffering their scorn and humiliation. Men and women with no chance for a better future. Why would the reign of God be good news for these poor people? Why should they be the privileged ones? Could it be that God isn't neutral? Could it be that he doesn't love everyone the same? If Jesus had said that God was coming to make the righteous happy, that would have made sense and everyone would have understood; but a God who favors the poor, without taking their moral behavior into account, that was scandalous. Were the poor better than everyone else, more deserving of preferential treatment in the reign of God?

Jesus never praised the poor for their virtues or qualities. The peasants were probably no better than their powerful oppressors; they too took advantage of people who were weaker than they, and mercilessly demanded payment from those who had borrowed from them. In blessing them, Jesus never said they were good or virtuous, only that they were suffering unjustly. God takes their side, not because they deserve it but because they need it. God, the merciful Father of all, could not reign if he did not do justice first of all for those who had never received justice. This is what made Jesus so joyful. God defends those whom nobody else defends!

This faith was rooted in a long tradition. The people of Israel had always hoped that their kings would defend the poor and marginalized. A good king would protect them, not because they were better citizens than the others, but simply because they needed protection. The king's justice did not depend on being «impartial» to everyone, but on doing justice for those who are unjustly oppressed. A psalm about the ideal of a good king makes that point clearly: «May he defend the cause of the poor of the people, give deliverance to the needy, and crush the oppressor»[48]. The message Jesus drew from this was clear. If any king knew how to do justice for the poor it was God, the «lover of justice»[49]. He is not deceived by the worship offered him in the temple. Sacrifices, fasts, and pilgrimages to Jerusalem mean nothing to him. For God, the first thing is to do justice for the poor. Jesus had probably often recited the psalm that describes a God «who executes justice for the oppressed; who gives food to the hungry... The Lord watches over the strangers; he upholds the orphan and the widow»[50]. If Jesus had known this beautiful prayer from the Book of Judith, he would have loved it: «But you are the God of the lowly, helper of the oppressed, upholder of the weak, protector of the forsaken, savior of those without hope»[51]. That was the God that Jesus knew.

9
Things have to change

What exactly was Jesus hoping for? How did he expect God's reign to be established? What needed to happen so that the reign of God would truly develop into something good for the poor? Was he thinking only of the conversion of his hearers, so that God could transform their hearts and reign in a growing number of followers? Was he simply trying to purify the Jewish religion? Was he thinking of deep-rooted social and political transformation in Israel, in the Roman Empire, and ultimately in the whole world? Certainly the reign of God was not something vague or ethereal for him. The irruption of God in history required a profound change. He was proclaiming God's reign in order to awaken hope and call people to change their way of thinking and acting[52]. The people must «enter» the reign of God, let themselves be changed by its dynamic, and begin to build their lives in accordance with God's will.

48 Ps 72:4 and 12-14. This psalm, dedicated to Solomon, describes Israel's vision of an ideal king.
49 Ps 99:4.
50 Ps 146:7 and 9. This is one of a group of psalms that begin with the acclamation, *alleluia!* (Praise the Lord!), which the Jews recited in the morning.
51 Judith 9:11. This work, by an unknown author around 150 B.C., is attributed to Judith («the Jewish woman»), a legendary heroine devoted to the liberation of her people.
52 In speaking of the «conversion» Jesus required, the gospels use the word *metanoein*, which means a change of both «thinking» and «acting».

How would the reign of God take shape? Apparently Jesus wanted to see his people restored and transformed according to the ideal of the Covenant: a nation where God reigns. For the Jews, returning to the Covenant meant belonging to God alone: a people free of foreign slavery, where everyone could enjoy their land in justice and peace, without being exploited by anyone. The prophets dreamed of a «people of God» where children would not die of hunger, old people would live a full life, peasants would not suffer exploitation. One of them said: «No more shall there be in it an infant that lives but a few days, or an old person who does not live out a lifetime… They shall build houses and inhabit them; they shall plant vineyards and eat their fruit. They shall not build and another inhabit; they shall not plant and another eat»[53]. In Jesus' time, some people thought that the only way to live as the «people of the Covenant» was to expel the impure and idolatrous Roman occupiers; to make no alliances with Caesar; to disobey him and refuse to pay the tributes. The Essenes of Qumran had a different view. For them it was impossible to be the «holy people of God» in that corrupt society; the restoration of Israel had to begin with the establishment of a «separated community» in the desert, made up of pure and holy men. The Pharisees took yet another position. It would be suicidal to rebel against Rome and refuse to pay its taxes, and it was a mistake to withdraw into the desert. All they could do was survive as God's people, by insisting on the ritual purity that distinguished them from the pagans.

From what we know, Jesus never had in mind a concrete political and religious strategy for building the reign of God[54]. The important thing, he said, was for everyone to recognize God and «enter» into the dynamic of his reign. It was not a merely religious matter, but a commitment with profound political and social consequences. The very words «reign of God», chosen by Jesus as the central symbol of his message and activity, were political words that would naturally arouse political expectations; they also provoked the jealousy of the Roman governor and the Herodian circles in Tiberias. The only empire recognized in the Mediterranean world and beyond, was the «empire of Caesar». What was Jesus implying, when he proclaimed that the «empire of God» was arriving?[55]

---

[53] Isa 65:20-22. These are the words of an anonymous prophet, written after the exile.

[54] Although Christians today speak of «building» or «building up» the reign of God, Jesus never used that language.

[55] The gospels translated Jesus' word for «reign» with the Greek word *basileia*, which in the decade of the thirties was only used with reference to the Roman «empire» (Crossan, Patterson, Kaylor, Horsley).

It was the Roman emperor and his legions who established peace and imposed justice on the whole world, subjecting the peoples to their empire. The emperor gave them well-being and security, and at the same time implacably demanded the payment of tribute. What was Jesus' goal in trying to convince everyone that instead of the rule of Tiberius, who only sought prestige, wealth and power, they must enter into «God's empire», which sought to do justice especially for the poorest and most oppressed inhabitants of the Empire?

The people saw Jesus challenging the emperor's absolute and exclusive sovereignty. It is not surprising that at one point «Pharisees» and «Herodians» from Antipas' circle raised one of the most delicate and controversial issues with him: «Is it lawful to pay taxes to the emperor, or not?» Jesus borrowed a denarius from someone, and asked whose image and title were stamped on it. Naturally it was Tiberius' image; the inscription read *Tiberius, Caesar, Divi Augusti Filius, Augustus.* That coin was the most universal symbol of the emperor's «divine» power[56]. Jesus then spoke the words that would be forever engraved in his followers' memory: «Give to the emperor the things that are the emperor's, and to God the things that are God's»[57]. No one, not even Tiberius, is above God. Return to Caesar this sign of his power, but never give any emperor that which only belongs to God: the dignity of the poor and the happiness of those who suffer. They belong to God; God's kingdom belongs to them[58].

Jesus made his position clearer on the subject of rich landowners. Their wealth was «unjust»; the only way to get rich in that society was to exploit the peasants, the only social group that produced wealth. God's reign required an end to that iniquitous exploitation: «You cannot serve God and wealth»[59]. One cannot enter God's reign by recognizing God as lord, defender of the poor, and go on accumulating wealth at the cost of those same poor. That must change. «Entering» the reign of God meant building a life not according to the will of Tiberius, the Herodian families or the rich Galilean landowners, but according to God's will. Thus, «entering» God's reign meant «leaving» the empire imposed by the «chiefs of the nations» and the powerful rich.

56 In the ancient world, the right to mint one's own coins was one of the most important symbols of sovereignty.
57 The episode is narrated in Mark, in the Q Source and in the [apocryphal] *Gospel of Thomas.* A general consensus affirms that these words authentically reflect Jesus' reply (Mark 12:17; Matt 22:21; Luke 20:25; [apocryphal] *Gospel of Thomas*).
58 There is no scholarly consensus on Jesus' own specific position with regard to the payment of tribute to Rome.
59 From the Q Source (Matt 6:24; Luke 16:13).

Jesus did more than denounce whatever is opposed to God's reign. He also recommended a way of living more in accordance with the Father's will. He sought more than individual, personal conversion. He was trying to introduce in the towns and villages a new model of social behavior. He saw their anguish over the most basic necessities: bread to put on the table and clothing to cover their bodies. Jesus understood that the dynamic of God's reign could change that situation: «do not worry about your life, what you will eat, or about your body, what you will wear... Instead, strive for his kingdom, and these things will be given to you as well» [60]. He's not talking about a miraculous intervention of God, but a change of behavior that can lead to a fuller and more secure life for all. What was happening in those villages could not be pleasing to God: quarrels among families, insults and aggression, abuse by the most powerful, neglect toward the most defenseless. That is not living in the reign of God. Jesus was proposing a different style of life, and demonstrating it with examples that everyone could understand: they must put an end to hatred among neighbors, and adopt a friendlier attitude toward enemies and those who slander them. They must go beyond the ancient *lex talionis*: God cannot reign in a village where the neighbors insist on returning evil for evil, «an eye for an eye and a tooth for a tooth». They must restrain their aggressive reaction against physical insults: «If anyone strikes you on the cheek, offer the other also». They must give generously to the beggars in the village: «Give to everyone who begs from you; and if anyone takes away your goods, do not ask for them again». When someone in need «takes your coat, do not withhold even your shirt». They must have a big heart for the poorest people. They must be like God: «Be merciful, just as your Father is merciful». If the village peasants lived like this, no one would go without bread or clothing [61].

One source of painful conflicts and disputes was the spectre of indebtedness. Everyone tried by any means possible to avoid falling into a spiral of debt, losing their lands and being left at the mercy of the large landowners. Everyone pressed their neighbors to repay the small loans they had made them, in order to meet the demands of the tax collectors. Jesus was trying to create a different climate, proposing even mutual forgiveness and the cancellation of debts. God

---

60 Q Source (Luke 12:22; Matt 6:25 and 33). The nucleus of this teaching comes from Jesus.

61 This collection of sayings from the Q Source (Luke 6:27-35; Matt 6:25-34) conveys the substance of Jesus' teachings. It was probably his message to the peasants in the Galilean villages (Horsley, Kaylor), although it may also have been part of his teachings to his closest followers (Theissen, Ben Witherington III).

was coming to offer everyone forgiveness. How could they accept that forgiveness in a climate of mutual pressure and implacable demands for the payment of debts? God's forgiveness should lead to a more fraternal and solidary behavior. That is why Jesus wanted his followers to pray from the heart: «And forgive us our debts, as we also have forgiven our debtors»[62].

It is worth noting that when Luke describes Jesus' activity, he suggests that Jesus was proclaiming the great «Jubilee of God». By ancient tradition, every 49 years «the Year of Jubilee» was to be declared in Israel, to restore social equality and stability among the people of the Covenant. In that year all who had sold themselves as slaves to pay their debts would be set free, all land would be restored to its original owners, and all debts were to be forgiven[63]. In Luke's narrative, Jesus begins his ministry with these words: «The Spirit of the Lord is upon me, because he has anointed me to bring good news to the poor. He has sent me to proclaim release to the captives and recovery of sight to the blind, to let the oppressed go free, to proclaim the year of the Lord's favor»[64]. Whether or not he understood his mission in the context of the Jubilee, is certain that Jesus was proclaiming the reign of God as a reality that requires the restoration of social justice[65].

10

The best is yet to come

The reign of God had come and its power was already in action, but not much could be seen of it in Galilee. The people of Israel and Jesus himself were hoping for much more at the end of time. The reign of God was already breaking in, but its saving power could be felt only in partial and fragmentary ways, not in their ultimate totality and fullness. So while Jesus invited his followers to «enter» the reign of God now, he also taught them to pray continually: «Your kingdom come».

---

62 This petition is from the Q Source (Matt 6:12; Luke 11:4). Matthew's version is apparently closer to the original.

63 The Jubilee laws are in chapter 25 of Leviticus, a compendium of laws, rites and prescriptions collected by the priests of Israel.

64 Luke 4:18-19. Jesus was reading from the book of Isaiah 61:1-2. According to some experts, this was one of the texts prescribed for reading in the synagogues at the beginning of the Year of Jubilee (Ringe, Fuellenbach).

65 In general, the authors believe that this was Luke's own theological vision.

Jesus spoke quite naturally of the reign of God as something that was already present, and at the same time as something still to come. He didn't see it as a contradiction. God's reign is not a timed intervention, but an ongoing action of the Father which calls for responsible acceptance; however no amount of resistance can stop it from coming, until it is fully realized. A new world is already «germinating», but it will only be fully realized in the future[66].

Jesus ardently hoped for that fulfillment. The Christian tradition preserves two cries that certainly came from his passion for the reign of God. They are direct, concise petitions that reflect his yearning and his faith: «Father, hallowed be your name. Your kingdom come»[67]. Jesus could see that the «name of God» was not honored or blessed. People would not let him be the Father of all. The tears and hunger of those Galileans were the clearest proof that God's name of Father was ignored and held in contempt. That explains Jesus' cry: «Father, hallowed be your name»; make them respect you, show your saving power soon! He also prayed directly: «Your kingdom come». This was a new expression, revealing his most heartfelt desire: Father, come to reign. Injustice and suffering are still present everywhere. No one can eradicate them completely from the earth. Reveal the fullness of your saving power. Only you can change things once and for all, by revealing yourself as Father of all and transforming life forever.

The reign of God is already here, but it is still only a «seed» sown in the world; one day it will be time for the final «harvest». The reign of God is irrupting in human life like a measure of «yeast»; one day God will cause the yeast to transform everything. God's saving power is secretly acting in the world, but it is still a «hidden treasure» that many people have not been able to find; one day everyone will enjoy it. Jesus had no doubts about that good and liberating end. Despite all the resistance and failure it produces, God will bring to fruition that utopia, as old as the human heart: the disappearance of evil, injustice and death[68].

---

66 In the *War Scroll* found at Qumran, the ultimate confrontation between «the sons of light» and the «sons of darkness» would last for «forty years», during which good would gradually triumph over evil.

67 Q Source (Luke 11:2; Matt 6:9-10a). No one doubts that these two petitions came from Jesus.

68 In the Book of Revelation, which was probably written around 95 A.D. during the persecution by the emperor Domitian, the author comforts the persecuted Christians with this faith that Jesus taught: on that day, God «will wipe every tear from their eyes. Death will be no more; mourning and crying and pain will be no more, for the first things have passed away» (21:4).

When would that end come? Jesus was not concerned with dates or calendars; he did not make calculations as the apocalyptists did; he did not specify time frames or speculate about the sequence of periods or ages[69]. Probably like most of his contemporaries, Jesus felt it as something near and imminent. One must remain alert, because God's reign could come at any time. But Jesus did not know when it might come, and he humbly made that clear: «But about that day or hour no one knows, neither the angels in heaven, nor the Son, but only the Father»[70].

Jesus maintained his trust in the definitive reign of God, and emphatically reaffirmed it at the dinner where he bid farewell to his disciples, a few hours before he was crucified. This was the last of those festive meals that he had so joyfully celebrated in the villages and towns, symbolizing the ultimate banquet in the reign of God. How joyfully he had «anticipated» the final party in which God would share his table with the poor and hungry, with sinners and the impure, even with pagans from outside Israel! This was his last festive meal in the world. Jesus sat at the table, knowing that Israel had not listened to his message. His death was near, but hope still burned in his grieving heart. The reign of God would come. God would triumph at the end, and Jesus with him, in spite of his failure and his death. God would fulfill his reign, and invite Jesus to sit at the table to drink a «new wine» at the final banquet. This was his indestructible hope: «Truly I tell you, I will never again drink of the fruit of the vine until that day when I drink it new in the kingdom of God»[71].

69 Most investigators believe that the reign of God as predicted by Jesus included two great moments: its historical gestation and its final consummation (Meier, Sanders, Theissen-Merz, Meyer, Allison, Beasley-Murray, Perrin and others). Recently some authors have advanced different hypotheses, affirming that in proclaiming God's reign, Jesus was thinking of a «renewal of this life» here and now, with no other horizon of eschatological consummation. This «historical reign of God» is variously understood as a «sapiential reign» (Mack), a «reign of social revolution» (Horsley), a «reign of the experience of the Spirit» (Borg), a «brokerless kingdom» without intermediaries (Crossan), a «reign of acceptance of the Torah» (Vermes). The main argument against these new hypotheses on the reign of God is that Jesus began with the apocalyptic vision of John the Baptist, and was followed by Christian communities which lived in the expectation of «new heavens and a new earth». It is hard to explain how, in between these two realities, Jesus could have preached a reign of God only for this life, without eschatological expectations.

70 Mark 13:32. These words give the substance of Jesus' affirmation. The early Christians would not have dared invent a saying in which Jesus appears not to know the most important of all dates. It appears that Jesus was expecting the imminent arrival of the ultimate reign of God, but he never situated it within a specific time frame (Meier, Theissen-Merz, Jeremias, Bultmann, and others).

71 Mark 14:25. The great majority of researchers affirm the authenticity of this saying (Schlosser, Meier, Theissen-Merz, Pesch, Merklein, Léon-Dufour, and others).

A Poet of Compassion

Jesus did not directly explain his experience of the reign of God. Apparently it was hard for him to describe conceptually what he felt within him. He didn't use the language of the scribes in his dialogue with the Galilean peasants. He didn't use the solemn style of the priests in Jerusalem. He used the language of the poets. With infinite creativity he invented images, constructed beautiful metaphors, and suggested comparisons; above all he was a master storyteller whose parables captivated his listeners. The best way we have to «get inside» Jesus' experience of the reign of God is to take a walk through the fascinating world of these stories.

1

The seduction of the parables

Jesus' language is unique. There is nothing artificial or forced in his words; every-
thing is clear and simple. He didn't need to resort to abstract ideas or complicated sentences; he talked about life. His words were transfigured when he talked about God to these country people. He was teaching them a different view of life: God is good, his goodness fills everything; his mercy is already irrupting in human life. All Galilee is present in his language: its work days and its feast days, its sky and the seasons, its flocks and vineyards, its planting and harvesting, its beautiful lake, and its population of fishers and farmers. Sometimes he helped them see the world around them in a new light; other times he led them more deeply into their own experience. They could meet God there, in the depths of their life.

> Consider the ravens: they neither sow nor reap, they have neither storehouse nor barn, and yet God feeds them. Of how much more value are you than the birds!... Consider the lilies, how they grow: they neither toil nor spin; yet I tell you, even Solomon in all his glory was not clothed like one of these. But if God so clothes the grass of the field, which is alive today and tomorrow is thrown into the oven, how much more will he clothe you — you of little faith![1]

If God takes care of birds as ugly as the ravens, and dresses the humble field lilies so elegantly, they knew he would take care of them!

[1] Q Source (Luke 12:24.27-28; Matt 6:26.28-30). Perhaps the image of the ravens was especially addressed to the men, who knew about planting, harvesting, and building granaries; the image of the lilies would appeal to the women, who knew about weaving, spinning, and making clothes.

Jesus also looked at the sparrows, the smallest birds in Galilee, and thought again about God. Sparrows are sold in the village markets, but God does not forget them: «Are not five sparrows sold for two pennies? Yet not one of them is forgotten in God's sight. But even the hairs of your head are all counted. Do not be afraid; you are of more value than many sparrows»[2]. He used the most fragile details to speak of God's tenderness: the smallest bird, a human hair.

God is good! Jesus didn't need to back that up with logical arguments. Of course God is better than we are! Once he invited a group of parents to recall their own experience: «Is there anyone among you who, if your child asks for bread, will give a stone? Or if the child asks for a fish, will give a snake? If you then, who are evil, know how to give good gifts to your children, how much more will your Father in heaven give good things to those who ask him!»[3].

This poetic language was not entirely unfamiliar to these peasants. Hosea, Isaiah, Jeremiah and other prophets had also spoken that way: poetry offered the most vigorous way to shake the conscience and awaken the heart to the mystery of the living God. What was unique and surprising, however, were the parables Jesus told as they walked through the grain fields of Galilee, or watched the nets full of fish that the fishers were pulling out of the lake. He couldn't have found stories as evocative as these in the sacred Scriptures[4].

The Christian sources have preserved around forty parables with more or less developed story lines, along with some twenty images and metaphors that appear as sketches or notes for a parable. These are only a small sample of the many stories Jesus told. Naturally the ones we have are the stories he told most often, or the ones that most forcefully impacted people's hearts and memories[5].

---

2 Q Source (Luke 12:6-7; Matt 10:29-31). These vivid, real-life images for God's tender care come directly from Jesus.

3 Q Source (Luke 11:11-13; Matt 7:9-11). Matthew's version is considered closer to Jesus' original words.

4 The Hebrew Bible does not have «parables» as a well-defined literary genre. The word *mashal* (plural *meshalim*) is generally used to describe analogies, proverbs, visions, fables, and allegories. Some *meshalim* resemble parables: the story of the «poor man's lamb» with which the prophet Nathan condemned David's criminal behavior (2 Sam 12:1-7); the «song of the vineyard» praising God's love for his people (Isa 5:1-7); or the «allegory of the eagle» (Ezek 17:3-10).

5 In the [apocryphal] *Gospel of Thomas* are twelve parables that also appear in the canonical gospels, plus two others: the «broken pitcher» (97) and the «murderer» (98). There are eight parables in the [apocryphal] *Gospel of James*, of which two seem to be new: the «grain» and the «spike».

Only Jesus told parables about the «reign of God». The teachers of the law used several kinds of *mashal* in their teaching, some of them similar in form and content to Jesus' parables, but for very different purposes[6]. In general the rabbis began with a biblical text that they wanted to explain to their disciples, and used a parable to expound the correct interpretation of the law. Therein lies the fundamental difference: the rabbis were seeing things from a legal perspective, Jesus from the perspective of the reign of God that was already irrupting in Israel[7].

The Christian communities were unable to imitate Jesus' parabolic language. Probably they did not create new parables[8]. The first generations of Christians were generally content to apply Jesus' parables to their own situation. Sometimes they reinterpreted the original content; sometimes they turned them into «moral fables»; and there was apparently a tendency to allegorize stories that Jesus first told as simple parables[9].

Jesus did not compose allegories: that language was too complicated for the Galilean peasants. He told stories that surprised everyone with their freshness and their simple, vivid, penetrating style[10]. It is not hard to tell the difference between a parable and an allegory. In a parable each detail means just what it says: a sower is a sower, seed is seed, a field is a field. In an allegory, each detail of the story has a figurative meaning. The sower is the Son of Man; the field is the world; the good seeds are the sons and daughters of God's reign; the weeds are the children of the devil, and so on. Thus an allegory always has a subtle, elabo-

---

6 About 1500 rabbinic parables have been collected, but there is no confirmation as yet that they come from a period before 70 A.D. (Stern). Neither have any parables been found in the writings of Qumran.

7 Flusser suggests, however, that the rabbinic parables and those of Jesus had a common origin.

8 However some scholars (Funk, Scott, Butts) hold that a few of the parables might have come from the Christian communities: «the net filled with fish» (Matt 13:47-48); «the man who wanted to build a tower» (Luke 14:28-30); «the king going to war» (Luke 14:31-38); or «the closed door» (Luke 13:25).

9 In John's gospel we see some allegorical stories that present Jesus as «the true vine», «the good shepherd», or «the gate of the sheepfold» (15:1-7; 10:11-18; 10:1-5). They are not the same as parables, and they are far from the style of the Galilean teacher.

10 This is the practically unanimous view of scholars since Jülicher published his definitive study in the early twentieth century. The original meaning of Jesus' parables is not to be found in the allegorical interpretations elaborated by the Christian community. For example, Mark 4:3-9 is an allegorical reading of the parable of the sower, specifying which people made up the different kinds of soil on which the seed of the Word falls. In Matt 13:37-43 there is an allegorical reading of the parable of the weeds. These interpretations do not come from Jesus. They were composed for the use of Christian evangelists and catechists.

rate twist: if one doesn't have the key to its meaning, it becomes an enigma. Apparently this way of talking didn't fit Jesus' style[11].

What was the purpose of his parables? Although he was a master storyteller, he clearly wasn't doing it to entertain the ears and hearts of the peasants[12]. Nor was he using them as illustrations, to help these simple people grasp sophisticated teachings that they would not otherwise understand. Indeed, his parables had no real didactic purpose. What Jesus wanted was not to transmit new ideas, but to put the people in touch with their own experience, things they had lived as peasants or fishers, which could help them open up to God's reign[13].

Unlike the Baptist, who never told parables in the desert, Jesus used them to bring the reign of God close to each village, each family, each person. Through these captivating stories he was removing obstacles and overcoming resistance so that the people could open up to the experience of a God who was coming into their lives. Each parable is an urgent invitation to go from an old, conventional, closed-in world to a «new country», full of life, that Jesus was already experiencing and which he called «the kingdom of God». Those fortunate peasants and fishers heard his stories as a call to understand and live life in a completely different way. Jesus' way[14].

---

11 However, in a very matter-of-fact way Jesus' parables did refer to personalities and realities that his listeners, familiar with the Jewish Scriptures, would clearly have understood in an allegorical way. When he speaks of a «father» or a «king», the people easily took it to mean God. They knew that the «vine» referred to Israel. When he described a «banquet» or a «harvest», they began to imagine the last days. It is wrong to eliminate all allegorical meaning from the parables. Semitic cultures do not distinguish so clearly between parables and allegories (Brown, Drury, Gowler). Some recent analyses (Funk, Wilder, Crossan, Scott) have brought in new perspectives from modern linguistics, but they are not always helpful in understanding the linguistic context in which Jesus taught.

12 It was not Jesus' original purpose to tell «stories of an aesthetic nature», as Via suggests.

13 Jesus makes his purpose clear: «With what can we compare the kingdom of God, or what parable will we use for it?» (Mark 4:30). Sometimes the parables begin with an explanatory introduction: «The kingdom of heaven is like a mustard seed...» (Matt 13:31).

14 Jesus' activity in Galilee leaves no doubt: he proclaimed God's reign to all without discrimination, and told his parables not to harden anyone's heart but to help people «enter» that reign. However we read disconcerting words in Mark 4:11-12. Jesus tells his followers: «You already have the secret of the kingdom of God. But for those outside everything is left to them in enigmatic parables; thus no matter how much they look, they will not see; no matter how much they listen, they will not understand, unless they become converted and are forgiven». These words did not come from Jesus. This was a later Christian composition, at a time when some parables had become hard to understand, either because they were no longer in their original context, or they had suffered an allegorical reinterpretation. According to Mark, the parables could only be understood by Jesus' followers, who «have entered» into God's reign. «Those outside» cannot understand anything, unless they are converted. The above text has been endlessly debated. I follow the translation of V. Taylor and a reasonable line of interpretation (Gnilka, Dodd, Meyer, Lightfoot).

When Jesus told parables, something «happened» in his listeners; it wasn't like the other teachers' detailed explanations of the law. Jesus «made God present», irrupting into the lives of his listeners. His parables were moving and thought-provoking; they touched people's hearts and invited them to open up to God; they shook up conventional lives and gave them a new perspective from which to accept and live God's presence in a completely different way[15]. The people heard the parables as «good news», the best news that a prophet could bring them.

Jesus apparently did not explain the meaning of his parables, either before or after he told them; he did not sum them up or clarify them in more prosaic language. The parable itself had to penetrate its hearers. He had a habit of saying: «Those who have ears to hear, let them hear»[16]. His message was out there, open to anyone who would listen. It was not something mysterious, esoteric or enigmatic. It was «good news» that must be heard. Those who listened as spectators wouldn't get the point; those who resisted would remain outside. But those who entered in to the story and let its power transform them, were already «entering» the reign of God[17].

2

Life is more than meets the eye

Jesus was warmly welcomed by the Galilean people, but they surely did not find it easy to believe that God's reign was already coming. They didn't see anything particularly great in what Jesus did. They were expecting something more spectacular. Where were the «strange signs» of which the apocalyptists had spoken? Where could they see God's terrible power? How could they be sure that the reign of God was already among them?

---

15 Fuchs, Linnemann and others have highlighted this dimension of Jesus' parables as «word-events». We should note that the events occurred at the linguistic level (Scott, Gowler). Hearing the parables should not be thought of as a kind of «sacrament».

16 Crossan translates this as «those who have ears should use them». He considers it an authentic expression of Jesus, reflecting the oral culture in which he lived.

17 The parables cannot be translated into conceptual language without losing their original, transforming power (P. Ricoeur). When we interpret a parable, the goal should not be to «explain it» in clearer language than Jesus used, but to re-awaken the experience it provoked when Jesus first told it. This however does not exclude the possibility of thinking in depth about the implications suggested by the parable (Perrin, Weder, Funk, Crossan, Wilder).

Jesus had to teach them to «grasp» the saving presence of God in a different way, and he began by suggesting that life is more than meets the eye. While we go on distractedly living the life we see in front of us, something mysterious is happening at the heart of existence. Jesus showed them the Galilean fields: while they were walking along the paths without seeing anything special, something was happening in the soil; the seeds were being transformed into a beautiful harvest. The same thing was happening at home. Daily life went on as usual, but something was secretly happening in the bread dough the women mixed every morning; soon the whole loaf would rise. That's the way the reign of God works. Its saving power was already at work in their lives, mysteriously transforming everything. Can life really be like that? Is God quietly acting in the inner core of our own lives? Is that the ultimate secret of life?

Perhaps Jesus' most puzzling parable was the one about the mustard seed:

It is like a mustard seed, which, when sown upon the ground, is the smallest of all the seeds on earth; yet when it is sown it grows up and becomes the greatest of all shrubs, and puts forth large branches, so that the birds of the air can make nests in its shade[18].

Jesus could have talked about a fig tree, a palm tree, or a grape vine, as the tradition did. But surprisingly, intentionally, he chose the mustard seed which is proverbially thought of as the smallest of all. A grain the size of a pin head becomes, in time, a bush three or four meters high in which, every April, little flocks of finches make their nests and eat their favorite seeds. The Galilean peasants could watch it happening every evening.

Jesus' language was perplexing and unprecedented. Everyone was expecting the arrival of God as a great and powerful event. They especially recalled the image of the prophet Ezekiel, who spoke of a «noble cedar» planted by God «on a high and lofty mountain», which would «produce boughs and bear fruit»; all kinds of birds and winged creatures would nest in the shade of its branches. For Jesus the true metaphor of God's reign was not the cedar, which people think of as grandiose and powerful, but the little, weak and insignificant mustard seed[19].

18 This is the version from Mark 4:31-32. The parable also appears in Matt 13:31b-32; Luke 13:19; and the [apocryphal] *Gospel of Thomas*, 20.

19 Ezek 17:22-23. The gospel writers emphasize the contrast between the small seed and the high bush, but Jesus was probably contrasting the humble mustard bush with the powerful cedar of Lebanon (Crossan, Scott).

The parable must have affected them deeply. How could Jesus compare God's saving power with a bush growing from a tiny seed? Was he asking them to give up the tradition of a great and powerful God? Were they supposed to forget God's mighty acts of the past, and watch for a God who is already acting in such small and insignificant ways? Could he be right? Each listener had to decide: to go on waiting for a powerful and terrible God, or take the risk of believing in his saving presence in Jesus' modest activity.

It was a hard choice. What could they hope for in something as insignificant as what was happening in those remote Galilean villages? Shouldn't they do something more to hurry things along? Jesus could see their impatience. To convey his total trust in God's action, he talked about the seeds farmers plant in their fields.

> The kingdom of God is as if someone would scatter seed on the ground, and would sleep and rise night and day, and the seed would sprout and grow, he does not know how. The earth produces of itself, first the stalk, then the head, then the full grain in the head. But when the grain is ripe, at once he goes in with his sickle, because the harvest has come[20].

Jesus was calling attention to a scene they were used to seeing every year in the fields of Galilee: first the planting, a few months later ripe grain all over the countryside. Every year they knew that the harvest would follow the planting. No one knew how it happened, but something mysterious was going on underground. The reign of God is like that. God is already acting, quietly and secretly. We only need to wait for the harvest.

All the farmers do is put the seeds in the ground. Once they've done that, their job is done. The growth of the plants is not up to them; they can go to bed every evening, knowing the seeds are developing; they can rise in the morning and see that the growth has continued. Something is happening in their land, that they cannot explain. They will not be disappointed. In time they will reap the grain.

The farmers didn't do the important work. The seeds germinated and grew, by a mysterious power that the farmers didn't understand. Jesus described this growth in such detail that his listeners could almost see it happening. At first only

---

20 This parable appears only in Mark 4:26-29. We don't know why it was left out of Matthew and Luke.

tiny green sprouts would emerge from the ground; then the stalks; later they would see the abundant grains of wheat. It all happened with no intervention by the farmer, nor even an understanding of how the miracle occurred.

Everything worked together to bring on the day of the harvest: the farmer, the soil, and the seeds. But Jesus invited them to see God's hidden and powerful action in that growth. The new life they could see in the grain fields year after year was always a surprise, a gift, a blessing from God[21]. The harvest was greater than what they could do by their own effort. That also is true of the reign of God. It doesn't correlate with the efforts people put into it. It is a gift of God, far beyond all the aspirations and labor human beings devote to it. We should not lose patience when the results don't come immediately; we should not act under time pressure. Jesus is planting the seed; God is already growing our life; the harvest is sure to come. Can it be so? Can we put more trust in Jesus and his message? What do we hope to reap in the end? The results of our efforts, or the fruit of God's action? A reign we have built, or our trusting, responsible acceptance of God's salvation?

That salvation is already coming. The reign of God is like the springtime, when everything begins to fill up with life. There are no fruits yet, we can't go out to harvest, but the branches of the fig tree are becoming tender and putting out leaves. Life, which seemed dead, is beginning to awaken. The reign of God is like that. Jesus could not contemplate the springtime without thinking of the life that God was raising up in the world. «From the fig tree learn its lesson: as soon as its branch becomes tender and puts forth leaves, you know that summer is near»[22]. For Jesus the coming of spring was a symbol of the great mystery of life, and a sign of God's arrival as a blessing and life for human beings[23].

He evoked the mysterious presence of God's reign through other experiences as well. One small parable especially touched the heart of the peasants. Every week before the sabbath, the women rose early and went out to the patio to make bread. Before dawn they were mixing the dough, adding fresh yeast to ferment

---

21 Crossan rightly points out that in biblical cultures, unlike the modern understanding, germination and growth are not seen as an organic or biological process; they are an awesome «miracle», a sign of blessing from the God who feeds his creatures.

22 Mark 13:28. According to many scholars (Dodd, Jeremias, Crossan, Scott), this saying circulated separately in the first communities and referred to the nearness of God's reign. It was only later incorporated in the apocalyptic discourse, which speaks of the final coming of the Son of man.

23 In Israel the fig tree was a proverbial symbol of blessing and happiness. Micah, a beloved prophet of peasant origin, puts it this way: «nation shall not lift up sword against nation, neither shall they learn war any more; but they shall all sit under their own vines and under their own fig trees, and no one shall make them afraid» (4:3-4).

it, covering it with a woolen cloth and waiting for the dough to rise, slowly and silently. Meanwhile they lit the fire and heated the rock on which they would bake the bread. From their beds the children inhaled the unmistakable aroma of the loaves, lovingly prepared by their mothers. Jesus never forgot that family scene. It suggested to him the maternal nearness of God, infusing the world with yeast. The reign of God «is like yeast that a woman took and mixed in with three measures of flour until all of it was leavened»[24].

Is that how God's power works, hidden in life? Like the power of the yeast that works secretly in the dough and completely transforms it? Is God arriving almost imperceptibly, but with the power to transform everything?

Jesus worked one of his characteristic «exaggerations» into this parable. No Galilean woman would put in three measures of flour; that would make about forty kilos of bread, enough to feed some 150 persons. People laughed, but Jesus wasn't talking about the family's weekly ration of bread. He was talking about the abundant, generous banquet of the final feast with God.

Something else surprised them in this parable; it may have scandalized some people. Yeast was commonly used as a symbol and metaphor for the power of evil to corrupt everything; unleavened, unfermented bread was a symbol of purity and holiness. Nothing fermented could be offered to God, and at Passover they ate only unleavened bread[25]. What was Jesus suggesting with this confusing and provocative metaphor? How could he compare the reign of God with a handful of yeast? Does God act by turning the traditional measures of holiness and purity upside down? Would they also have to discern his reign in that world of lepers, the demon-possessed, sinners and prostitutes that Jesus frequented?

Some people were attracted by his words. Others probably had more than a few doubts. Was it reasonable to believe him, or was it craziness? Jesus told two stories to win them over. Breaking with his custom, he drew these not from everyday life but from the fantastic folk tales of the Orient. He was not trying to encourage impossible dreams that would help them endure the hard life of the countryside, but to awaken in them joyfulness and decisiveness toward God's arrival.

---

24 The parable is conserved in the Q Source (Luke 13:20b-21; Matt 13:33b). We also find it in the [apocryphal] *Gospel of Thomas* 96, with some small differences that were typical of Gnostic circles.

25 In Mark 8:14 Jesus also uses the metaphor of yeast in a pejorative sense, warning his disciples to «beware of the yeast of the Pharisees and the yeast of Herod».

In the first of these, «the kingdom of God is like a treasure hidden in a field, which someone found and hid; then in his joy he goes and sells all that he has and buys that field»[26]. A poor worker is digging on land he does not own, when he discovers the buried chest of treasure. It's not hard to imagine his surprise and joy. He doesn't think twice. This is his moment and he's not about to waste it: he hides the chest again, sells everything he has, buys the field and takes the treasure. The Galilean peasants loved this kind of stories. Over the centuries their region had been invaded by all kinds of armies, and they all knew that the best way to protect their valuables from becoming spoils of war was to bury them in a safe place[27]. Some peasants dreamed of one day finding such a treasure hidden in some corner.

The second parable is similar: «Again, the kingdom of heaven is like a merchant in search of fine pearls; on finding one pearl of great value, he went and sold all that he had and bought it»[28]. This time the protagonist is not a poor farmer, but a rich pearl merchant. His business is to buy pearls in the far-off lands of the Orient, and sell them at a much higher price. Suddenly he finds a pearl of immeasurable value. His expert's intuition does not fail him. He decides quickly, sells all his goods and gets the pearl. Jesus' hearers «understand» the story. Near Capernaum is the *Via Maris*, a great commercial route where caravans from the Orient pass through on their way to Egypt and the Mediterranean ports. The people sometimes see merchants with their stock of pearls from the Persian Gulf or the seas of India[29].

Jesus' listeners felt obligated to react. Could it be true that the reign of God is a hidden treasure they cannot see? That it is not an imposition by God, but a «treasure», pure and simple? Everyone was convinced of its value: they had

---

26 This parable in Matthew 13:44 has the characteristic marks of Jesus' narrative technique. In the [apocryphal] *Gospel of Thomas* there is a more developed version, which is probably an adaptation of a well-known rabbinic parable of the *Midrás Rabbá* (Jeremias, Crossan, Funk, Scott).

27 According to Flavius Josephus, after the fall of Jerusalem in 70 A.D. the Romans «dug up gold, silver and other precious objects, whose owners had hidden them in the ground in view of the uncertain outcome of the war» (*La guerra judía* [English: the Jewish War] VII, 115).

28 This parable is in Matt 13:45-46; the [apocryphal] *Gospel of Thomas* 76 has a different version. The [apocryphal] *Gospel of Thomas* also conserves the parable of the great fish, about «an intelligent fisherman who threw his net into the sea, and when he pulled it in, it contained a large quantity of small fish. Among them he found a large and beautiful fish. The intelligent fisherman did not hesitate but picked it up and threw all the small fish back into the sea» (8). Scholars see Gnostic elements in this parable, but it may still reflect Jesus' original idea: on unexpectedly capturing a large and beautiful fish, the fisherman discards all the rest (Jeremias, Espinel).

29 According to Pliny the Elder, Cleopatra, famous for her liaison with Mark Antony, possessed a pearl worth at least a hundred thousand sestertia (something over eighteen million Euros).

waited and prayed for it as the supreme good. Now Jesus was saying, you can find it now! Should they open up to the surprise? Was the reign of God something unexpected that we intuit and long for, but whose goodness and beauty is beyond our wildest imagination? That would be the culmination of their happiness, a total joy that relativizes everything else. The farmer had never seen a treasure like that; the merchant had never held such a precious pearl in his hands. Was the reign of God like that? Finding the most essential thing, having the immense good luck of finding everything a human being could ask or wish?

According to Jesus, the reign of God is an opportunity that no one can afford to pass up. They must risk whatever is needed in order to grasp it. Everything else is secondary, subordinate. Was Jesus right? The decision must be immediate and radical, but what was he talking about? Where was it hidden, this «treasure» that he had found? Where was the «mustard seed» germinating? Where could they recognize the springtime? What was it made of, this saving power of God that was already secretly transforming their life?

3
God is merciful

Jesus tried to answer these questions with the most beautiful and moving parables he ever told. He had surely spent a long time working them out in his heart. They all invited people to discern the incredible mystery of God. The most captivating one is about a good father[30].

> There was a man who had two sons. The younger of them said to his father, «Father, give me the share of the property that will belong to me». So he divided his property between them. A few days later the younger son gathered all he had and traveled to a distant country, and there he squandered his property in dissolute living.
>
> When he had spent everything, a severe famine took place throughout that country, and he began to be in need. So he went and hired himself out to one of the citizens of that country, who sent him to his fields to feed the pigs. He would gladly have filled himself with the pods that the pigs were eating; and no one gave him anything. But

---

30 It is a mistake to call this the parable of the «prodigal» or «wasteful» son. The father is the central figure. A better title would be «the father's love» or «the merciful father».

when he came to himself he said, «How many of my father's hired hands have bread enough and to spare, but here I am dying of hunger! I will get up and go to my father, and I will say to him, "Father, I have sinned against heaven and before you; I am no longer worthy to be called your son; treat me like one of your hired hands"». So he set off and went to his father.

But while he was still far off, his father saw him and was filled with compassion; he ran and put his arms around him and kissed him. Then the son said to him, «Father, I have sinned against heaven and before you; I am no longer worthy to be called your son». But the father said to his slaves, «Quickly, bring out a robe — the best one — and put it on him; put a ring on his finger and sandals on his feet. And get the fatted calf and kill it, and let us eat and celebrate; for this son of mine was dead and is alive again; he was lost and is found!» And they began to celebrate.

Now his elder son was in the field; and when he came and approached the house, he heard music and dancing. He called one of the slaves and asked what was going on. He replied, «Your brother has come, and your father has killed the fatted calf, because he has got him back safe and sound». Then he became angry and refused to go in. His father came out and began to plead with him. But he answered his father, «Listen! For all these years I have been working like a slave for you, and I have never disobeyed your command; yet you have never given me even a young goat so that I might celebrate with my friends. But when this son of yours came back, who has devoured your property with prostitutes, you killed the fatted calf for him!»

Then the father said to him, «Son, you are always with me, and all that is mine is yours. But we had to celebrate and rejoice, because this brother of yours was dead and has come to life; he was lost and has been found»[31].

Jesus knew Galilean family conflicts well: arguments between parents and children, the desire for independence, sibling rivalries over inheritance rights that put family cohesion and stability at risk. They caused unspeakable suffering, because family was everything: home, place of work and survival, source of identity, the assurance of safety and protection. It was very hard to survive outside the family. And one family could not survive apart from others. The villages

---

31 Although this parable appears only in Luke 15:11-32, there is no reason to doubt that it comes from Jesus (*contra* Schotroff, and Carlston in part). Luke understood the parable as Jesus' response to the «scribes and Pharisees» who criticized him for eating with sinners. Recent authors think Jesus must have told it in a broader context than the one suggested by Luke (McBride, Scott, Rohrbaugh).

were formed by families bound together with close links of kinship, neighborhood and solidarity. Together they planned the marriages of their children, helped one another gather the crops or repair the roads, and worked together to protect the widows and orphans. Solidarity among the village families was as important as loyalty within the family. Family problems and conflicts had serious effects on all the neighbors.

When Jesus started talking about a father's problems in maintaining family unity, everyone paid attention. They knew about conflicts like that, but the son's request was unforgivable. In demanding his part of the inheritance he was treating his father as dead, dishonoring him and breaking family solidarity. How could they divide the inheritance while the father was still alive? How could they divide the property, endangering the family's future? The demand was insane, and shameful to the whole community[32]. The father says nothing. He respects his son's unreason and divides his inheritance[33]. Jesus' listeners must have been puzzled. What kind of father is that? Why doesn't he impose his authority? How can he accept his son's crazy request, thus losing his own dignity and endangering the whole family?

After the inheritance is divided the son rejects his father, abandons his brother, and goes «to a distant country». A dissolute life soon leads him to ruin. With no more money to stave off hunger, absolutely alone in a foreign country, with no family or protection, he ends up enslaved to a pagan and feeding pigs. There could be no greater degradation. Without freedom or dignity, leading an infrahuman life in the midst of «impure» animals, he wishes in vain for some of the pods the pigs eat, since no one gives him anything. In that desperate situation, the young man comes to his senses. He remembers his father's house, where bread was plentiful. That was his home; he can no longer live so far from his family. So he decides: «I will get up and go to my father». He will acknowledge his sin. He has lost all the rights of a son, but perhaps he will be hired as one more day laborer.

---

32 The Book of Ecclesiasticus or Sirach, written by Ben Sira around 190-180 B.C., offers this wise counsel: «To son or wife, brother or friend, do not give power over yourself, as long as you live... At the time when you end the days of your life, in the hour of death, distribute your inheritance» (33:20.24).

33 The text says literally that the father «divided his life [bios] between them», the source of his life and sustenance.

34 Literally, «his bowels were shaken».

The father's response is incredible. While the son is still far off, outside the town, the father sees him exhausted by hunger and humiliation, and is «filled with compassion»[34]. Losing control, he runs to meet his son, embraces him tenderly without letting him fall to his knees, and kisses him effusively without a thought for his impure state. This is not the behavior of a landowner and family patriarch. These are the gestures of a mother. Those heartfelt kisses and hugs in front of the whole town are a sign of welcome and forgiveness, but also of protection and defense in the eyes of the neighbors. He interrupts his son's confession, to save him from further humiliation, and hastens to restore his dignity within the family: he dresses him with «the best robe» in the house[35], puts on his finger the ring that confers the role of a son, and has him wear the sandals of a free man. But he still needs to rebuild his own honor and that of his family within the village. So the father organizes a great banquet for all the townspeople. He kills the fatted calf[36] and arranges music and dancing in the town square. All this is more than justified: «this son of mine was dead and is alive again; he was lost and is found!» At last the family will live in dignity and happiness.

Unfortunately the older son isn't there. He comes in from the field in the evening, after faithfully completing another day of work. He's puzzled to hear the «music and dancing». He doesn't understand at all. He doesn't rejoice as his father did, to see his brother back; he is angry. He stays outside, refusing to go in to the party. He has never left home, but now he feels like an outsider in the eyes of his family and the neighbors gathered to welcome his brother. He has never been lost in a distant country, but now he is lost in his own resentment.

The father goes out to invite him in, with the same tenderness he showed for his other son's arrival from far away. He doesn't shout at his son, or order him to come in. He doesn't act like the lord of the household. On the contrary, like a mother, he begs him again and again to come to the party. That is when the older son explodes and reveals all his anger. He has followed his father's orders like a slave all his life, but he has never enjoyed his father's love. His life of self-sacrifice has hardened his heart. He is not a part of the family; if his father had given him a goat he would have organized a party, not with his father but with his friends. Now he can only humiliate his father and insult his brother, condemning his

---

34

35 The «best robe» was probably the father's (Plummer, Scott, Rohrbaugh).

36 For a farm family in Galilee, killing a calf was very costly and uncommon. It was only done at great feasts to be shared with the neighbors.

dissolute life with prostitutes. He doesn't understand his father's love for that miserable soul. He does not embrace, does not forgive.

The father speaks to him with a special tenderness[37]. From his fatherly heart, he sees everything differently. The son who came home is not a reprobate, but a «dead son who is alive again». The son who refuses to come in to the party is not a slave, but a beloved son who can celebrate with his father, sharing everything with him. His only desire as a father is to see his sons once more at the same table, sharing a festive banquet as brothers.

Here the story ends without further explanation. What must the other parents have felt, who had closed their doors forever to their children who had left home to seek adventure? What would the neighbors feel, who were so scornful of people who left the town to go and live in Sepphoris or Tiberias? How would it affect those who had spent years far away from God, at the margin of the Covenant, not trying to fulfill the law or make pilgrimages to the temple? Or those who had lived by the Covenant and despised sinners, tax collectors and prostitutes. They had all been quick to judge the foolishness of that father, his lack of authority over his sons; but they must have been confused and deeply moved to see his incredible compassion, his forgiveness and motherly protection for his lost son, his humility as he talks to his older son, his passionate search for reconciliation at the party.

Is God like that? A father who doesn't hold on to his inheritance, who is respectful of his sons' behavior, who is not obsessed with their morality but seeks a full and happy life for them even against the conventional norms of justice and etiquette? Is this the best metaphor for God: a father opening his arms to those who are «lost», away from home, and pleading with others to embrace them with compassion? The parable implies a true «revolution». Is that what the reign of God means? A Father who regards his creatures with incredible love, and seeks to lead human history toward a final feast in celebration of life, forgiveness, and ultimate liberation from everything that enslaves and degrades the human being? Jesus was talking about a splendid banquet for everyone, about music and dancing, about lost sons who awaken tenderness in their fathers, about brothers who are called to forgive each other. Is this the good news of God?

---

37 He speaks to his son as *teknon*, an affectionate term that can be translated as «my beloved son, my little one».

Again and again Jesus emphasized the compassionate love of God. Once he told a surprising, provocative parable about a vineyard owner who wanted employment and bread for everyone[38]. He might have told it at the time of the grape harvest, when laborers were waiting in the town square for someone to hire them. He said:

For the kingdom of heaven is like a landowner who went out early in the morning to hire laborers for his vineyard. After agreeing with the laborers for the usual daily wage, he sent them into the vineyard. When he went out about nine o'clock, he saw others standing idle in the marketplace; and he said to them, «You also go into the vineyard, and I will pay you whatever is right». So they went. When he went out again about noon and about three o'clock, he did the same. And about five o'clock he went out and found others standing around; and he said to them, «Why are you standing here idle all day?» They said to him, «Because no one has hired us». He said to them, «You also go into the vineyard».

When evening came, the owner of the vineyard said to his manager, «Call the laborers and give them their pay, beginning with the last and then going to the first». When those hired about five o'clock came, each of them received the usual daily wage. Now when the first came, they thought they would receive more; but each of them also received the usual daily wage. And when they received it, they grumbled against the landowner, saying, «These last worked only one hour, and you have made them equal to us who have borne the burden of the day and the scorching heat». But he replied to one of them, «Friend, I am doing you no wrong; did you not agree with me for the usual daily wage?» Take what belongs to you and go; I choose to give to this last the same as I give to you. Am I not allowed to do what I choose with what belongs to me? Or are you envious because I am generous?»[39].

---

[38] This parable is called «the workers in the vineyard», but the owner is the real protagonist. We could title it «the generous owner» (Jeremias), «the good contractor» (Etchells), or «the boss who wanted to let everyone work».

[39] This parable appears only in Matt 20:1-15, but no one doubts its authenticity. The exaggerated comings and goings of the owner to hire laborers in the town square, and the surprising ending, are unmistakable traits of Jesus' stories. The ending — «So the last will be first, and the first will be last» (20:16) — is a saying that circulated independently in the Christian community, which was added as an unfortunate application of the parable.

The large landowners in the area, like this one, belonged to the powerful ruling class. In general they did not live in the villages but in some city, and managed their land through an administrator. They only came to the vineyard at harvest time, to oversee the work directly. The laborers belonged to the lowest levels of society. They were farmers who had lost their land, and lived from day to day with no security: sometimes begging, sometimes stealing, always looking for an owner to hire them, if only for a day.

The work day begins at dawn and ends at sunset. The rich vineyard owner comes in person to the town square, early in the morning. He goes up to a group of workers, settles with them on the wage of one denarius, and puts them to work in his vineyard. It's not much, but it's enough to supply the needs of a peasant family for at least one day. The owner returns to the square at 9 a.m., noon and 3 p.m.; he doesn't mention the denarius to them, but only promises «whatever is right». They are in no position to demand anything. They go to work with no security, dependent on what the owner decides to pay them: probably a fraction of a denarius. At 5 p.m. the owner comes back, with only an hour left in the work day. In spite of that he hires a group that no one else has hired, and sends them to lend a hand. He doesn't even talk to them about wages.

Jesus' listeners couldn't understand the landowner's comings and goings to hire the workers. Large owners didn't negotiate directly with their workers. And they didn't keep going back to the square. The hiring was done in the early morning, after a careful calculation of the number of workers needed. What kind of landowner is this? Why does he act this way? No one goes out to hire workers in the late afternoon. Is he so anxious to bring in the grapes? The story doesn't say anything about the harvest. Rather it suggests that he didn't want to see anyone left without work. So he says to the last group: «Why are you standing here idle all day?»[40]

Then the time comes to pay the workers. It has to be done on the same day, before sunset, or they will have nothing to eat that evening. God's law requires it: «You shall not withhold the wages of poor and needy laborers... You shall pay them their wages daily before sunset, because they are poor and their livelihood depends on them»[41]. The owner orders the payment, first to the workers

---

40 Several authors call attention to the importance of this detail (Linnemann, Scott, McBride, Shillington).

41 Deut 24:14-15. This is one of the ancient laws collected in Deuteronomy, redacted in Jerusalem around 700 B.C., and completed in later years.

who have just arrived. This raises the expectations of the others: if the late-comers are receiving a denarius for only an hour's work, what might they receive? To their great disappointment they see that everyone is getting one denarius, even those who worked all day. How is that fair? Why only one denarius, since the work was so unequal? Jesus' listeners surely sympathized secretly with the people who had worked the most. They agreed with giving the late-comers a denarius, but wasn't he devaluing the work of the others? They didn't want him to give them just a fraction of a denarius, but didn't the others deserve the same generosity? It's fine to be generous with those who have only worked for an hour, but shouldn't he be equally generous toward those who worked all day?

The owner gives a firm reply to the worker who spoke up: «Friend, I am doing you no wrong... Am I not allowed to do what I choose with what belongs to me? Or are you envious because I am generous?» Those who complained are still thinking in terms of strict justice, but the vineyard owner is thinking differently. He has violated that justice out of kindness, and kindness harms no one. It was not an arbitrary action. It was only mercy and loving generosity to all. He gave everyone what they needed to live: work and bread. He was not concerned with the relative merits of each, but that they should all eat dinner that evening with their families. Justice and mercy were intertwined in his action.

The listeners were all surprised. What was Jesus suggesting? That God doesn't measure the merits of each person? That God's reign doesn't work on the basis of the same calculations and criteria we use to mete out justice and equality for everyone? Doesn't this violate all the religious standards of Israel? Was Jesus deliberately ignoring the differences that the law establishes between the righteous and sinners?

Jesus' parable seems to contradict all that. Is it true that God doesn't look at each person's merits, but rather at their needs? It would be nice if God was like that: everyone could trust in him, even those who had few merits. But isn't it dangerous to open ourselves up to that incredible world of God's mercy, which doesn't fit our calculations? Isn't it safer and more comforting, especially for those who have faithfully kept the law, to stick to the temple religion where duties, merits and sins are clearly defined?

They were even more puzzled when he told a small parable about a Pharisee and a tax collector who went up to the temple to pray, according to the custom of the Jews in Jerusalem:

Two men went up to the temple to pray, one a Pharisee and the other a tax collector. The Pharisee, standing by himself, was praying thus, «God, I thank you that I am not like other people: thieves, rogues, adulterers, or even like this tax collector. I fast twice a week; I give a tenth of all my income». But the tax collector, standing far off, would not even look up to heaven, but was beating his breast and saying, «God, be merciful to me, a sinner!» I tell you, this man went down to his home justified rather than the other[42].

There are three characters in this story: a Pharisee, a tax collector, and the temple where God lives. The parable doesn't speak only of two men praying, but of the action of God, present in the temple. The listeners got the point right away. They had made pilgrimages to the temple more than once. It was the center of their people and their religion. Only there could they worship Yahweh. They called it «the house of God», for the holy God of Israel lived there. From there he protected and blessed his people. No one could approach the temple without first undergoing ritual purification: as the psalm says, only «those who have clean hands and pure hearts»[43]. Long ago the Ark of the Covenant was kept in the most sacred part of the temple, and in it were two stone tablets engraved with the commandments of the law. The temple represented the presence of God, who reigned over his people through that law. How joyfully they came into his presence, those who had faithfully kept those commandments!

Jesus' story immediately sparked interest and curiosity among his hearers. What would happen in the temple? How would those men feel there, in God's presence, men as different from one another as a Pharisee and a tax collector. They all knew what a Pharisee was like: a pious man who faithfully keeps the commandments, strictly observes the norms of ritual purity, and scrupulously pays his tithes. Pharisees were the pillars of the temple. They went up to the sanctuary, sinless: of course God would bless them. The people also knew what

42 This parable appears only in Luke 18:10-14a. Luke has added his own introduction which says that Jesus told the story «to some who trusted in themselves that they were righteous and regarded others with contempt» (18:9). That gives the parable a strongly anti-Pharisaic thrust that Jesus did not originally intend (Bultmann, Plummer, Linnemann, Scott, McBride, and others). He has also added a conclusion that does not belong in the original story, but was an unrelated saying of Jesus: «for all who exalt themselves will be humbled, but all who humble themselves will be exalted» (18:14b). The parable is not about how to pray, but rather about where one can best listen to God.

43 The Jews sang Psalm 24 as they went up to the temple on pilgrimages. It says: «Who shall ascend the hill of the Lord? And who shall stand in his holy place? Those who have clean hands and pure hearts… They will receive blessing from the Lord, and vindication from the God of their salvation» (24:3-5).

tax collectors were like: Jews who made their living by despicable acts. They didn't work to collect tithes and uphold the temple, but to collect taxes and seek their own prosperity[44]. They were unredeemable. They could never repair the harm they had done, or repay their victims for what they took. They could never feel good in the temple. It wasn't their place[45].

The Pharisee prays standing upright, secure and fearless. His conscience doesn't accuse him of any sins requiring atonement. What rises spontaneously from his heart is gratitude: «God, I thank you». It's not an act of hypocrisy. What he says is real. He keeps the commandments faithfully: he does not belong to the category of sinners, as the tax collector naturally does. He fasts every Monday and Thursday for the sins of the people, although fasts are required only once a year, on the Day of Atonement[46]. He not only pays the mandatory tithe on farm products (grain, oil, wine), but on everything he earns. His life is exemplary. He faithfully meets and even exceeds his obligations. He doesn't claim the credit for himself, but thanks God for sustaining his holy life[47]. If this isn't a righteous man, who is? He is a model of faithfulness and obedience to God. Wouldn't we all like to be like him! He can be sure of God's blessing, Jesus' listeners were thinking.

The tax collector keeps his distance. He feels uncomfortable; he doesn't deserve to be in that holy assembly. He knows what the other faithful are thinking: he is a dishonest and corrupt official who doesn't work for the temple, but for the Roman system. He doesn't even dare look up from the floor. He beats his breast in acknowledgment of his sin and shame. He doesn't promise God anything. He can't give back all that he has stolen from so many unknown persons. He can't quit his job as a tax collector. He can no longer change his life. His only hope is to throw himself on God's mercy: «God, be merciful to me, a sinner!»[48] His prayer recalls the moving plea of a psalmist who said: «The sacrifice acceptable to God is a broken spirit; a broken and contrite heart, O God, you will not

---

44 The word *telonés*, used in the parable, indicates that this man did not directly collect the land taxes required by the Empire. He would be a lower-ranked employee who worked at the gates of cities like Capernaum or Jericho, and in collection booths along the great commercial highways, charging tolls and taxes for the importation and exportation of merchandise.

45 Probably the two men had gone up to the temple for the sacrifices of atonement for sin. While the priests carried out the sacred rite, they withdrew for an examination of conscience.

46 Many Pharisees did the same, even though the law only required solemn fasting on the great Day of Atonement (Lev 16:29-31).

47 There are similar prayers in the writings of Qumran and in the Talmud.

48 The literal meaning of the words is: «Oh God, atone for my sins».

despise»[49]. The poor man is only acknowledging what everyone knows. No one would want to be in his place. God cannot approve of his sinful life.

Jesus ends the parable with a surprising affirmation: «I tell you, this man went down to his home justified rather than the other». The pious man, who has done even more than the law requires, has not found favor in God's eyes. But the tax collector, who threw himself on God's mercy, without even promising to change his life, receives forgiveness. Jesus has taken them by surprise. Suddenly he has opened up a new world that breaks all the molds. This is not just about the relative piety of two people. With this apparently simple, naïve parable, isn't he threatening the whole religious system of the temple? What unforgivable sin has the Pharisee committed? Where is his fault? And by what merits is the tax collector justified as he leaves the temple? The God of the temple must surely have affirmed the Pharisee and reproved the tax collector. What Jesus says is incredible. In the temple, God welcomes the righteous into his presence and excludes sinners and the impure from his holy place. How can Jesus talk about a God who does not recognize the righteous, but instead offers grace to the sinner?

If Jesus is right, then nobody can be sure of anything. They must all appeal to God's mercy. What good then is the temple, and the spirituality it nourishes? What good does it do to observe the law and the temple cult? How can the reign of God be based, not on the justice formulated by religion, but on the bottomless mercy of God? Isn't Jesus playing with fire? By what authority does he invite people to live on mercy, and not on religion and the law?

One thing is certain in this parable: a despised tax collector has thrown himself on God's mercy and has found grace. Is Jesus trying to bring everybody into a real experience that they have all felt deep in their being? When we feel good about ourselves and in the eyes of others, life is dependable; we don't seem to need anything more. But when our conscience declares us guilty and we lose that security, don't we feel the need to cling to God's mercy and nothing else? When we act as the Pharisee did, we come to God through a religion that has no place for the tax collector. When we trust God's mercy, as the tax collector did, we are in a religion that has room for everyone. Does last word belong, not to the law which judges our conduct, but to God's mercy which accepts our prayer? Is this the true religion, the religion of God's kingdom?

---

49 Psalm 51(50):19.

Accustomed as we are to the religion of the temple, it is hard for us to rely on the unpredictable mercy of God. Jesus was trying to break through his listeners' resistance. One day he offered a puzzling parable about a man who was attacked by bandits on his way from Jerusalem to Jericho[50]:

A man was going down from Jerusalem to Jericho, and fell into the hands of robbers, who stripped him, beat him, and went away, leaving him half dead. Now by chance a priest was going down that road; and when he saw him, he passed by on the other side. So likewise a Levite, when he came to the place and saw him, passed by on the other side. But a Samaritan while traveling came near him; and when he saw him, he was moved with pity. He went to him and bandaged his wounds, having poured oil and wine on them. Then he put him on his own animal, brought him to an inn, and took care of him. The next day he took out two denarii, gave them to the innkeeper, and said, «Take care of him, and when I come back, I will repay you whatever more you spend»[51].

This story immediately got everyone's attention. They had made pilgrimages to Jerusalem and knew very well the dangerous, desert area through which the road passes between the capital and Jericho. They knew how hard it was to avoid the bandits who hid out in those cliffs and ravines. But many travelers made the trip. Every week there were priests and Levites returning from their service in the temple to Jericho, an important priestly city. Groups of pilgrims also passed through, and merchants bringing their wares to Jerusalem. What would happen this time on that dangerous road? The thought of a man robbed and left for dead in the roadside ditch inspires sympathy and pity. He's an innocent victim, tossed aside on a lonely road, in urgent need of help. It could have been any one of them. Of course they feel compassion![52]

---

50 This one is called the parable of the «good Samaritan». Certainly he is the protagonist of the story, but to get Jesus' point we need to read the story from the viewpoint of the man fallen by the wayside.

51 Although it is only found in Luke 10:30-36, this parable is clearly from Jesus. His narrative technique and the content are unmistakable. Luke has inserted the parable as part of a dialogue between Jesus and a teacher of the law. This is Luke's artificial placement, since both Mark and Matthew report the same dialogue without even mentioning the parable of the Samaritan. To understand Jesus' original intention we must separate the parable from the context imagined by Luke (10:25-29 and 10:36-37). The story is not a «morality tale» in response to the question, «who is my neighbor?» but rather a «parable of God's reign». It might have begun this way: «The kingdom of God is like a man who fell into the hands of robbers» (Funk, Crossan, Scott, McDonald, Etchells).

52 The injured man is never named in the story, and he cannot be identified even by his clothing (which was stripped from him). Since the narrator doesn't say otherwise, we must assume that he is a Jew.

Fortunately two travelers appear up the road, first a priest and then a Levite. They are both coming from the temple. They have been serving there all week, and with their obligations fulfilled, they are returning home to Jericho. The injured man watches them approach, filled with hope. They are Jews like him; they represent the temple; surely they will have pity on him. But they don't. They both do the same thing: they see him and «step aside». They do not come near him, but pass by. Why? Are they afraid of the bandits? Are they afraid of incurring ritual impurity by touching a stranger, covered with blood and half dead?[53]. Jesus' listeners must have been scandalized by their lack of compassion. How could they not help a man abandoned to an almost certain death?

Then a third traveler appears on the horizon. He is not a priest or a Levite; he's not coming from the temple; he doesn't even belong to the chosen people of Israel. He is a hated Samaritan[54]; probably a merchant dedicated to his business dealings. The injured man watches fearfully as he approaches. Jesus' listeners are also worried. The enmity between Samaritans and Jews was well known. One could only expect the worst from this man. Would he finish off the injured man? But the Samaritan sees him, «feels compassion», and goes up to him. Right away he does what he can: disinfects his wounds with wine, softens them with oil, bandages him, places him on his own animal, takes him to the nearest inn, cares for him and pays for other needed attention. This man doesn't look like a merchant thinking about his wares. His action is more like a mother tenderly caring for her injured son.

Jesus' listeners couldn't be more surprised. How can he see the reign of God in the compassion of a hated Samaritan? The parable breaks all the molds and classifications of friends and enemies, chosen people and impure foreigners. Can it be that God's mercy comes to us, not from the temple or the official religious channels, but from a proverbial enemy? They are puzzled. Jesus is looking at life from the roadside ditch, with the eyes of a victim needing help. For Jesus, the best metaphor for God is compassion for an injured man.

53 It appears that the priest and the Levite had no legal grounds on which to justify their action (Jeremias, Linneman, Scott, and others).

54 The Samaritans were descendants of the Assyrian conquerors and the Israelite women who were not deported to Assyria after the destruction of the Northern Kingdom in 721 B.C. The Jews returning from the Babylonian exile in 537 B.C. excluded them from the «chosen people» and did not let them participate in the reconstruction of the temple, due to their impure origin and their lax observation of the Jewish religion. There was a proverbial antagonism between the Jewish temple in Jerusalem and the Samaritan center of worship at Gerizim. The hatred between the two groups grew between the years 6 and 9 A.D., when on the eve of Passover a group of Samaritans scattered human bones in the temple, rendering it impure for any celebration.

The parable turns everything upside down. The representatives of the temple pass by, neglecting the injured man. The hated man turns out to be the savior. The reign of God is present wherever people show mercy. Even a traditional enemy, despised by all, can be the instrument and incarnation of God's compassionate love. Jesus' message is a true «revolution» and a challenge to everyone: must we now extend God's mercy even to the enemies of Israel, forgetting our prejudices and secular enmities? Can we really go on practicing a religion like that of the temple, which conveys hatred and sectarianism? Must we reorder everything, giving absolute primacy to mercy?[55] Must we even be «disloyal» to our own group, so as to identify with the suffering of any victim we find along any roadside? Is that what the reign of God means?

4

Be merciful like your Father

It was not easy to accept Jesus' message, but the people were beginning to sense the demands of God's reign. If God is like the father welcoming and reaching out to his lost son, there will have to be changes in family and village attitudes toward rebellious youth who not only get lost themselves, but also endanger the solidarity and honor of everyone around them. If God is like the vineyard owner who wants bread for all, even those who are left without a job, there will have to be an end to exploitation by the large landowners and rivalries among the workers, so that together they can seek a fuller, more solidary life for all. If God in his own temple embraces and justifies a dishonest tax collector who trusts his mercy, there must be a review and reframing of the religion that blesses those who observe the law and condemns sinners, opening an almost unbridgeable gap between them. If God's mercy can reach an injured man by the roadside, not through the religious representatives of Israel but through the compassionate action of a Samaritan heretic, sectarianism and secular hatreds must be put aside so that

---

55 Luke is on the right track when he turns this parable into a morality tale, in which Jesus audaciously tells a lawyer to learn from a Samaritan heretic about practicing mercy. The question we must ask is not, «Who is my neighbor?» or «how far does my obligation to love extend?» Neither our own religion nor our own cultural group can tell us whom to love and whom to hate, whom to help and whom to ignore. The right question is: «Who needs me to come closer, make myself a neighbor and respond to their need?» The suffering of any human being fallen by the roadside can teach us how to act with compassionate love.

we can see each other with eyes of compassion and hearts attentive to the suffering of those fallen by the wayside. Without these changes, God will never reign in Israel.

Jesus says it explicitly: «Be merciful, just as your Father is merciful»[56]. To accept the reign of God we don't need to create a «holy community» in the Qumran wilderness; we don't need to insist on a scrupulous observance of the law as the Pharisaic groups did; we don't need to plan violent uprisings against Rome, as some impatient sectors did; we don't need to strengthen the temple religion, as the priests in Jerusalem insisted. What we need is to introduce compassion into all human life, a compassion like God's; we need to look with compassion on a lost son, a worker without access to employment or bread, a delinquent unable to rebuild his life, a victim fallen by the roadside. We must plant mercy in families and villages, on the landowners' large estates, in the religious system of the temple, in relations between Israel and its enemies.

Jesus told a variety of parables to help the people see mercy as the best way into the reign of God. Perhaps the most important thing was to understand and share God's joy when a lost person is saved and recovers the fullness of life. Jesus wanted to place in their hearts what he felt deeply in his own heart. The lost ones belong to God; God looks for them passionately, and when he finds them his joy overflows. He wants us all to share God's joy.

He had two very similar parables: about «a shepherd» who looks for a lost sheep until he finds it, and about «a woman» who sweeps the whole house until she finds the coin she has lost[57]. Many of his listeners didn't get the point of these stories. How could Jesus compare God with a shepherd, who belongs to a group most people disdained socially, or with a simple village woman? Does God have to keep surprising us this way? As Jesus tells it:

Which of you, having a hundred sheep and losing one of them, does not leave the ninety-nine in the wilderness and go after the one that is lost until he finds it? When he has found it, he lays it on his shoulders and rejoices. And when he comes home, he calls

---

56 Q Source (Luke 6:36; Matt 5:48). In Matthew we read: «Be perfect, therefore, as your heavenly Father is perfect». The two gospel writers convey Jesus' thinking with different nuances.

57 These are traditionally called the parable of the «lost sheep» and the «lost coin». They are really about the «shepherd» and the «woman» searching for the lost object.

together his friends and neighbors, saying to them, «Rejoice with me, for I have found my sheep that was lost»[58].

Shepherds apparently were not viewed favorably in those villages. They couldn't be trusted, for they were apt to take the sheep to graze in the farmers' fields; they were seen as undesirables. But the image of «shepherds» was much loved in popular tradition, from a time when the tribes of Israel were still semi-nomadic. Moses, Saul, David and other great leaders had been shepherds. Everyone liked to imagine God as a shepherd who cares for, feeds and defends his people[59]. What would Jesus say about them now?

This time he begins the parable with a question: imagine that you are a shepherd, you have a hundred sheep and one gets lost. Won't you leave the ninety-nine and search for the one until you find it? His listeners must have hesitated before answering; it's a strange scenario. But Jesus starts talking about a shepherd who does just that. He feels that the sheep, though lost, belongs to him. It is his. So he doesn't hesitate to go looking for it, leaving the other sheep «in the wilderness». Isn't it crazy to put the whole flock in danger that way? Is the lost sheep worth more than the ninety-nine? The shepherd doesn't waste time with that kind of reasoning. His heart leads him to search until he finds the sheep. His joy on finding it is indescribable. In a gesture of tenderness and loving care for the weary and maybe injured sheep, he puts it on his shoulders, around his neck, and returns to the sheepfold. Then he calls his friends and invites them to share his joy. They will understand: «I have found my sheep that was lost».

His listeners can't believe it. How can such a foolish shepherd be a metaphor for God? Of course men and women are God's creatures, they belong to God.

---

58 The parable is found in Luke 15:4-6, in Matt 18:12-13, and in the [apocryphal] *Gospel of Thomas* 107. Both Luke and Matthew are using an original parable of Jesus, although each one adapts it for his own purposes. Matthew uses it to insist that the small and vulnerable should not be looked down on in the Christian community; Luke is emphasizing God's concern for those who are lost. It is hard to know which is closer to Jesus' original intent. Luke's text is quoted here, but in order to focus on Jesus' original meaning, we have left out the gospel writer's artificial conclusion referring to the repentance of sinners: «Just so, I tell you, there will be more joy in heaven over one sinner who repents than over ninety-nine righteous persons who need no repentance» (15:7). The story itself says nothing about that; the sheep has nothing to repent for!

59 There was a well-known text in Ezekiel (592-570 B.C.), comparing the bad shepherds of Israel with Yahweh, who says: «I myself will search for my sheep, and will seek them out. As shepherds seek out their flocks when they are among their scattered sheep, I will rescue them from all the places to which they have been scattered... I will seek the lost, and I will bring back the strayed, and I will bind up the injured, and I will strengthen the weak» (34:11-12, 16a).

And people will go to great lengths in order not to lose what belongs to them. But does God really feel such ownership for the «lost»? Besides, isn't it too risky to leave the flock for the sake of the «lost sheep»? Isn't it more important to assure the restoration of all Israel, than to waste time with prostitutes and tax collectors, who after all are undesirables and sinners?

The parable makes us think: can it be that God doesn't reject the «lost», whom everyone despises, but passionately seeks them out because, like Jesus, God doesn't give anyone up for lost? Should we learn to share and celebrate God's joy, as Jesus does by eating with them? But the parable may be saying more than that. The sheep doesn't return to the flock on its own. It is the shepherd who looks for it and brings it back[60]. Would God bring back sinners just because he loves them, even before they show signs of repentance? They know that God always welcomes back repentant sinners. Not even the Pharisees would refuse to offer friendship to a sinner who showed repentance. But isn't Jesus going too far? Is he suggesting that the sinner's return is not dependent on conversion, but on the God's mercy poured over him?

Jesus came back to this point with another parable about God's concern for the lost, and his joy on bringing them back. The second story is about a woman. There may have been many women among his hearers. He wanted them to understand too.

> Or what woman having ten silver coins, if she loses one of them, does not light a lamp, sweep the house, and search carefully until she finds it? When she has found it, she calls together her friends and neighbors, saying, «Rejoice with me, for I have found the coin that I had lost»[61].

This realistic story must have gotten everyone's attention. A poor woman who has ten drachmas loses one of them. It wasn't much. Everyone knew that little silver coin, worth only a denario, which was a day's wage for a field worker.

---

60 Luke and Matthew see no value in the sheep. The shepherd looks for it because it is his. In contrast, in the [apocryphal] *Gospel of Thomas*, the shepherd searches for the sheep because it is the most beautiful and beloved of them all. Then he leaves the ninety-nine and cares only about seeking the one until he finds it. At the end he tells the sheep: «I love you more than the ninety-nine» (107). Such an idea is foreign to Jesus (Funk, Scott, Jeremias and others).

61 This parable is found only in Luke 15:8-9. The gospel writer has linked it to the parable of the lost sheep (15:4-7). He has also added his own conclusion about «the conversion of sinners». Jesus' original meaning is better understood without this Lukan explanation (Funk, Scott, Schotroff, and others).

But to her it's worth a lot. She only has ten drachmas. She may even have worn it in her hair, an extremely poor ornament compared with the ones worn by the rich landowners' wives[62]. The woman doesn't resign herself to the loss of her small coin. She «lights a lamp», because her simple house has no windows and very little light comes in through the one door, usually a low one. She «sweeps the house» with a palm frond, listening for the sound of the coin on the stone floor in the dark. When at last she finds it she cannot keep her joy to herself but calls her neighbors to share it: «Rejoice with me».

That's what God does! He is like that poor woman who searches for her coin and is overcome by joy when she finds it. What might have little value for us, is a treasure for her. Again the listeners are surprised. A few women are moved to tears. Is God like that? Are the tax collectors and prostitutes, the lost souls and sinners who mean so little to certain religious leaders, so much loved by God?

150

Jesus was having a hard time persuading people to rejoice and enjoy God's mercy. Some of them not only didn't rejoice in his embrace of prostitutes and sinners, but even condemned him for eating with such undesirables. The Baptist had preached a threatening message of God's judgment, inviting people to repent by sharing his austere fasts, and some of them said: «He has a demon». Now Jesus was inviting everyone to rejoice over God's mercy to sinners, by eating and drinking with them as he did, and the people said: «Look, a glutton and a drunkard, a friend of tax collectors and sinners»[63].

So he challenged them with a dramatic example: you are like children who won't join the other children's game. «To what then shall I compare the people of this generation, and what are they like? They are like children sitting in the marketplace and calling to each other, "We played the flute for you, and you did not dance; we wailed, and you did not weep"»[64].

He knew how children play; he had sometimes watched them in the town square, since he loved being near the little ones. The little girls liked to play «funerals»: one group sang laments while another group cried and wailed like professional mourners. The little boys played at «weddings»: some played an instrument and others danced. The game doesn't work if some people refuse to play[65]. Something

---

62 Some authors (Jeremias, Brouwer, Bishop and others) connect such decorations with a woman's bridal dowry, in which case it would be her most precious possession. Some women wouldn't have taken it off even to sleep at night.

63 Q Source (Luke 7:33-34; Matt 11:18-19).

64 Q Source (Luke 7:31-32; Matt 11:16-17).

65 Compared with other possible readings, this interpretation by Jeremias is still the most plausible.

like that is happening here. Jesus wants to get everyone «dancing for joy» over God's mercy toward lost sinners, but some people don't want to play the game.

So he tried again; they had to learn to look differently at those lost souls whom almost everyone scorns. One of his small parables, told in the house of a Pharisee, expresses his thinking well[66]. Jesus has been invited to a festive banquet. The guests are comfortably reclined around a low table[67]. There are many guests, all men, and apparently there is not room for them all inside. The banquet is held in front of the house, where curious bystanders can watch the diners and listen to their conversation.

Then a local prostitute approaches them[68]. Simon immediately recognizes her and is annoyed: the woman might besmirch the diners' purity and disrupt the banquet. The prostitute goes directly to Jesus, throws herself at his feet, and breaks into tears. She doesn't say anything. She is overcome by emotion. She doesn't know how to express her joy and appreciation. Her tears fall on Jesus' feet. Ignoring everyone else, she loosens her long hair and uses it to dry his feet. It is shameful for a woman to loosen her hair in the presence of men, but that doesn't deter her; she is used to being shamed. She kisses his feet over and over, and opening a small flask tied around her neck, she anoints them with a precious perfume[69].

Sensing Simon's discomfort over the prostitute's actions and his own serene response, Jesus challenges him with a little parable: «A certain creditor had two debtors; one owed five hundred denarii, and the other fifty. When they could not pay, he canceled the debts for both of them. Now which of them will love him more?»[70]

The example is clear and simple. We don't know why the creditor forgave the two debts. Surely he is a generous man who understands the suffering of those who cannot pay what they owe. One of the debts is large: 500 denarii, the equivalent

---

66 It's not clear whether the episode described in Luke 7:36-50 in the house of Simon the Pharisee is the same one that Mark 14:3-9 places in the house of Simon the leper. Luke probably adapted the incident to connect the story of the Pharisee and the sinful woman with that of the two debtors. Even if the scene is not as Luke describes it, the episode does reflect a typical situation in which Jesus is shown authentically communicating his message. This is how he was remembered (Dunn).

67 This way of dining, in the Greek or Roman style, was reserved for great occasions.

68 Although the term «sinful woman» (*amartolós*) can have other meanings, the story suggests that she is a prostitute (Michaelis, Jeremias, Wenham, and others). This woman should not be identified with either Mary Magdalene or Mary of Bethany.

69 Apparently prostitutes wore such flasks between their breasts to enhance their attractiveness.

70 This parable is in Luke 7:41-42. Some recent authors believe it was made up by Luke (Funk, Scott). In any case the content is consistent with Jesus' message about God «forgiving debts».

of a farm worker's wages for almost two years, an impossible burden for a peasant. The second comes only to fifty denarii, which would be much easier, only seven weeks of wages. Which of the two will be more grateful?[71] Simon gives the logical answer: «I suppose the one for whom he canceled the greater debt». The other diners agree.

That's how it happens with the coming of God. His forgiveness brings joy and thanksgiving to sinners because they feel accepted by God, not for their merits, but out of the great goodness of the heavenly Father. The «perfect» react differently: they don't consider themselves sinners, or forgiven. They don't need God's mercy. Jesus' message doesn't impress them. But that prostitute, moved to tears by God's forgiveness and the new possibilities he has brought to her life, does not know how to express her joy and gratefulness. Simon the Pharisee sees in her the suggestive gestures of her profession: loosening her hair, kissing, caressing, and seducing with perfumes. Jesus sees in the behavior of that impure, sinful woman the tangible sign of God's immense forgiveness: «Her sins, which were many, have been forgiven; hence she has shown great love»[72].

God comes to everyone offering forgiveness and mercy. Living in his reign means setting in motion a dynamic of reciprocal forgiveness and compassion. Jesus doesn't know any other way to live. To shake their conscience he tells a new parable about a servant who, although he has been forgiven by his king, cannot learn to live by forgiveness:

> For this reason the kingdom of heaven may be compared to a king who wished to settle accounts with his slaves. When he began the reckoning, one who owed him ten thousand talents was brought to him; and, as he could not pay, his lord ordered him to be sold, together with his wife and children and all his possessions, and payment to be made. So the slave fell on his knees before him, saying, «Have patience with me, and I will pay you everything». And out of pity for him, the lord of that slave released him and forgave him the debt.
>
> But that same slave, as he went out, came upon one of his fellow slaves who owed him a hundred denarii, and seizing him by the throat, he said, «Pay what you owe». Then his fellow slave fell down and pleaded with him, «Have patience with me, and I will pay you». But he refused, then he went and threw him into prison until he would

---

71 There is no Aramaic word for «give thanks». Other verbs are used, like «love» or «bless».

72 Luke 7:47. This is the right translation, although traditionally it has been interpreted to say «She has been forgiven much because she loved much».

pay the debt. When his fellow slaves saw what had happened, they were greatly distressed, and they went and reported to their lord all that had taken place. Then his lord summoned him and said to him, «You wicked slave! I forgave you all that debt because you pleaded with me. Should you not have had mercy on your fellow slave, as I had mercy on you?» And in anger his lord handed him over to be tortured until he would pay his entire debt[73].

Jesus' listeners immediately saw that the story was not from their everyday world. That powerful king, the fabulous quantities of money, his cruel and arbitrary treatment of his servants (selling them as slaves or delivering them to torturers), all reminded them of the great pagan Empires. But they had also heard stories like this about Herod the Great and his sons. What is Jesus talking about?

Checking over his financial records, a king discovers that one of his employees owes him 10,000 talents, the equivalent of 100,000,000 denarii. An unimaginable amount, especially for these people who never had more than ten or twenty denarii in the house[74]. No one could ever put together that amount of money. The king's decision is cruel: he orders the employee and all his family sold as slaves. He won't get his money back that way, but it will serve as a warning to others[75]. The employee falls at his feet in despair: «Have patience with me, and I will pay you everything». He knows that would be impossible. But surprisingly, on seeing the employee humiliated at his feet, the king feels «pity» and forgives the whole debt. Instead of being sold as a slave, he is restored to his position.

When he meets an employee of lower rank who owes him a hundred denarii, he grabs him by the throat and demands immediate payment. Falling to the ground, the other man cries out the same words the employee addressed to the

73 This parable of the «merciless servant» is only found in Matt 18:23-34, but no one doubts its authenticity. However Matthew has incorrectly inserted it into a dialogue between Jesus and Peter on the need to «forgive seventy-seven times» (18:21-22). That is clearly not the subject of the parable, since the king only forgives once and then withdraws his forgiveness. Moreover, the final conclusion (v. 35) does not belong to Jesus' original parable. Matthew has unfortunately applied it in a way that distracts our attention from the king's initial generosity and focuses on his final «vengeance». This turns Jesus' parable into a fearful allegory, in which God uses torturers to carry out his merciless punishment! For the true message of the parable we should overlook Matthew's redaction (Jeremias, Linnemann, Via, Scott, McBride).

74 Flavius Josephus reports that Herod the Great collected some 900 talents per year. In the year 4 B.C., the amount collected in Perea and Galilee amounted to 200 talents.

75 It was not an uncommon practice outside Israel, but Jewish law prohibited the sale of the wife and children to pay the husband's debts.

king: «Have patience with me, and I will pay you». This is a smaller amount, not so impossible. Jesus' listeners expect him to show pity. He has just been forgiven a debt of a hundred million denarii; how can he not forgive a hundred for his fellow employee? But he does not; instead he mercilessly throws him in jail. It is easy to imagine the reaction of Jesus' listeners: «Nobody would be so heartless, when he owes his own life to the king's forgiveness!»

That is exactly what the king's other employees were thinking. Amazed by what has happened, they appeal to the king to do something. The king's reaction is terrible: «You wicked slave!... Should you not have had mercy on your fellow slave, as I had mercy on you?» In his rage he withdraws his forgiveness, renews his demand for the full payment, and puts the servant in the hands of torturers until it is all paid. Thus his punishment is no longer to be sold as a slave, but to be tortured for the rest of his life[76].

The parable began hopefully with the generous forgiveness of the king, but the brutal ending can only upset Jesus' listeners. Everything goes wrong. The king's generous act has not succeeded in erasing centuries of oppression: his subordinates go on acting as cruelly as before. The king himself is a prisoner of his system. For a moment it looked like the beginning of a new era of forgiveness, a new order inspired by compassion. But at the end, mercy is wiped out once more. Neither the king, nor the servant, nor his fellow employees can hear the call to forgive.

His fellow servants have asked the king for justice toward the servant who would not forgive. But if the king withdraws his mercy, won't they all be in danger again? They have just done what the merciless servant did: they have not forgiven him, but asked the king to punish him. If mercy is once more set aside in favor of strict justice, doesn't this take us back into the shadows? Could Jesus be right? Is the God of mercy the best news that we can hear? Is there any other way to be free from wickedness and cruelty, except by being compassionate like the heavenly Father? Jesus' listeners are caught in a «trap». They probably all agree that the forgiven servant should have forgiven his fellow servant; that was normal, the least one could expect of him. But if all men and women live by God's mercy, will there have to be a new way of doing things, in which compassion is no longer an exceptional and admirable gesture but a normal expectation? Can this be the most practical way to accept God's reign, and extend it among his sons and daughters?

---

76 Although Jewish law condemned torture, Herod the Great and his sons used it without any scruples.

A Healer of Life

The poet of God's compassion spoke in parables, but also in deeds. The Galilean peasants could see that Jesus, full of the Spirit of God, went from village to village healing the sick, casting out demons, and liberating people from evil, indignity and exclusion. God's mercy was not just a beautiful idea that he taught in parables. It was a fascinating reality. In Jesus' presence the sick recovered their health; demoniacs were rescued from their dark and shadowy world. He brought them into a new, better, healthier and more fraternal society that was moving toward the fullness of God's reign.

Jesus kept surprising everyone: God is coming, not as the «God of the righteous», but as the «God of the suffering». The prophet of the reign of God had no doubt about this. What God cares about is the suffering of the most unfortunate; what moves him to action is his compassionate love; the God who seeks to reign among men and women is a «healing God»[1]. The Christian sources unanimously affirm it: «Jesus went through Galilee... proclaiming the good news of the kingdom and curing every disease and every sickness among the people»[2].

Unlike the Baptist, who never healed anyone, Jesus proclaimed the reign of God by bringing health and life to individuals and to the whole society. What Jesus sought among the Galilean people, more than anything else, was not to reform their religious life but to help them live a healthier life, free from the power of evil. This image of Jesus was engraved in the memory of the first Christians: «how God anointed Jesus of Nazareth with the Holy Spirit and with power; how he went about doing good and healing all who were oppressed by the devil, for God was with him»[3]. Jesus did not look first at sinners who needed to be called to conversion, but at those who suffered illness or handicaps and yearned for a fuller life and health[4].

---

1 An ancient Israelite tradition says: «I am the Lord who heals you» (Ex 15:26).
2 Matt 4:23. See also Mark 1:39; Matt 9:35; Luke 6:18, and other passages.
3 Acts 10:38
4 John's gospel interprets Jesus' activity as entirely directed toward empowering life: «I came that they may have life, and have it abundantly» (John 10:10). The «eternal life» he speaks of begins in this life and achieves its fullness in the ultimate encounter with God.

Sickness in Galilee

Every culture experiences sickness in a different way. It is not the same thing to be sick in the western society of our time, as in Lower Galilee in the decade of the 30's of the first century. Sickness is not only a biological condition. It is also an experience that one interprets, lives, and suffers within the cultural framework of one's own society. What was it like to be sick in the villages Jesus knew? How did it affect the people? How did their family members and neighbors respond? What did they do to recover their health?[5]

The sick people Jesus met suffered the afflictions one would expect in a poor and underdeveloped country: there were blind people, paralytics, deaf mutes, people with skin diseases, the mentally ill. Many were incurable, abandoned to their fate, and left without means of earning a living; they hobbled through life as beggars, constantly confronted with misery and hunger. Jesus saw them lying by the roadside, at the village entrance, or in the synagogues, pleading for pity from the passers-by.

For these peasants illness was not mainly an organic condition, but an inability to live as other children of God did[6]. The great misfortune of the blind was not being able to understand the life around them. Without eyes they lost touch with reality; they could not see faces or fields; it was harder to think perceptively, measure the value of things, love people. The misfortune of the deaf mute was an inability to communicate. They could not hear messages from other people or express

---

5 Anthropologists distinguish between disease (a pathology or organic dysfunction), which can be biologically *cured*, and illness (an experience lived socially within a culture), where the proper response is to *heal* its harmful effects on both the individual and the social group (Young, Kleinman, Pilch, Avalos, and others). I use both terms, «curing» and «healing», to describe what Jesus did. In the *spanish* text I refer to Jesus more often as a «curer» (from the Latin *cura*, «care» or «solicitude» for the needy one), since I believe it better describes, in Spanish, the perception the sick must have had of him. Editor's note: in the translation done here, the term «healer» is used more often, since «cure» is almost exclusively organic; and «heal» is more integral, as Pagola intends and uses the term. There is no English equivalent for "curador," and its root meaning (care) is largely forgotten. As a noun there is no alternative to use but «healer» for this edition, which respects what the author intends. We have used the verb «cure» and the adjective «curative» only where appropriate, to avoid misunderstandings in English.

6 According to the anthropologists (Geradon, Malina, Pilch), the cultures of the Mediterranean Basin saw human beings as made up of three «zones»: thinking and emotion (eyes-heart); communication (ears-mouth); and activity (hands-feet). Anything that damages one of the three zones is called sickness or illness.

their own; they could not speak, bless, or sing; enclosed in their isolation, they could hear only themselves. Paralytics, unable to use their hands or feet, could not work, move, or take action; they could not walk or make pilgrimages to Jerusalem; they could not embrace another person, or dance. What they all yearned for was not only a cure for their affliction, but to be able to enjoy life fully as other people did.

Lepers experienced their illness differently. Among them were not only people with «leprosy» as we know it today, but those afflicted by different skin ailments (psoriasis, ringworm, boils, tumors, eczema, etc.); when these spread over the body, they were repugnant to everyone[7]. The tragedy of these sufferers is not mainly the physical effects of the disease on their bodies, but the shame and humiliation of being regarded and shunned as dirty and repulsive. Condemned to total ostracism, they could not marry and have children, or participate in feasts and pilgrimages.

Sickness in Galilee, as everywhere and in all times, led to the spontaneous question that arises from any grave illness: Why? Why me? Why now? The Galilean peasants did not look on their illness from a medical viewpoint, but a religious one. They did not look for organic explanations, but were mainly concerned with its meaning. If God, the creator of life, had withdrawn his life-giving spirit from them, it meant he was abandoning them. Why?

In the Semitic way of thinking, health and sickness come from God. The lord of life and death has total power[8]. Therefore as the Israelites saw it, a strong and vigorous life is a life blessed by God; a sick, wounded or mutilated life is a curse. In the villages Jesus visited, people usually saw blindness, leprosy, or any other grave illness as God's punishment for some kind of sin or unfaithfulness[9]. Similarly, they saw healing as a blessing from God. Since God does not want a sinner to die but to be converted and live, the people of Israel expected God's final intervention to bring a life full of health for everyone: «And no inhabitant will say, "I am sick;" the people who live there will be forgiven their iniquity»[10].

---

7 The Hebrew word *sara'at*, usually translated as «leprosy», is not what modern medicine calls Hansen's disease (G.H.A. Hansen discovered *mycobacterium leprae* in 1861), but refers to a range of skin diseases which produce discoloration, eruptions, purulent wounds, etc., and therefore cause repugnance (Lev 13). There have been no discoveries of remains belonging to a person with leprosy in ancient Palestine (Van Hulse).

8 In the Book of Deuteronomy there is an ancient hymn, attributed to Moses, in which Yahweh says: «I kill and I make alive, I wound and I heal» (Deut 32:39).

9 In John's gospel the disciples ask Jesus about a man blind from birth: «Rabbi, who sinned, this man or his parents, that he was born blind?» (9:2).

10 Isa 33:24. This was probably a poem from the Persian period, incorporated in the Book of Isaiah.

Because they were seen as abandoned by God, these sick people aroused unease and discomfort among the «people of God». Why doesn't God bless them like everyone else? Why does he deny them the nourishment of life? Something about their life must have displeased him. Therefore their presence among God's «holy people» had to be carefully watched. It was safer to keep them more or less outside the religious and social circle. According to Israelite tradition, «the blind and the lame shall not come into the house»[11]. The writings found at Qumran emphasize this exclusion even more: the blind and deaf were not respected because «those who do not see and hear, do not know how to practice the law». The blind were excluded not only from the temple, but from the city of Jerusalem: «No blind person shall enter it as long as they live; they shall not profane the holy city at whose center I live»[12]. This exclusion from the temple, the holy place of God's habitation, implacably reminds the sick of what they have already sensed from the depths of their illness: God doesn't love them as he loves other people.

«Lepers» were separated from the community, not for fear of contagion, but because they were seen as «impure» and might contaminate the holy people of God. It was a cruel prescription: «The person who has the leprous disease… shall cover his upper lip and cry out, "Unclean, unclean!" He shall remain unclean as long as he has the disease; he is unclean. He shall live alone; his dwelling shall be outside the camp»[13]. In a society like that of Galilee, where individuals could only survive as an integral part of their family and village, this exclusion was tragic. The lepers' greatest anguish was that they might never be able to return to their community.

Abandoned by God and by humanity, stigmatized by their neighbors, largely excluded from community life, these sick people were probably the most marginalized sector of the society. But are they really abandoned by God, or does the Father have a privileged place for them in his heart? The historical fact is beyond doubt: Jesus was devoted to them above everyone else. He came near to those who were seen as Godforsaken, touched the lepers whom no one else would touch, gained the trust of those who could not enter the temple, and brought them into the people of God as he understood it. They had to be the first to feel

---

11 This was a popular saying, cited in 2 Sam 5:8.
12 The full text is in 4QMMT 56-57, and in the *Temple Scroll* (11Q Temple 45, 12-14).
13 Lev 13:45-46. Although the gospels sometimes tell of lepers near the people, with fairly easy access to Jesus, it is believed that the prescriptions of Leviticus remained in force during that time (Baumgarten, Avalos).

the Father's mercy and witness the arrival of his reign. His care for them is the best «parable» to show that God is, more than anything else, the God of those who suffer abandonment and exclusion.

2

No easy way to healing

All sick people yearn some day to be free of their illness, to enjoy a life of health once more. But what could the sick in those villages do to recover their health?

When they were sick, Israelites generally turned first to God. They examined their lives, confessed their sins before God, and prayed for a cure. They could recite one of the many psalms which had been composed by sick people and collected in the Scriptures: «O Lord, be gracious to me; heal me, for I have sinned against you»[14]. The family had the first responsibility to care for the sick. Parents, the nearest relatives, the owner of the house, or the neighbors helped them to acknowledge their sin and call on God. At the same time they looked around them for a healer[15].

Apparently there were no professional physicians. Greek medicine, pioneered by Hippocrates (450-350 B.C.), had spread across the Mediterranean Basin and may have reached some important cities like Tiberias, Sepphoris or the Decapolis region, but not the Galilean villages. Hippocratic medicine did not invoke the healing power of the gods; based on different theories of the human body it tried to identify the illness, diagnose its causes, and seek some remedy that would help to restore balance to the body[16]. The Israelites generally rejected this type of medicine, since they saw God as the only source of health. But things were already changing in Jesus' time. Some Jewish sages recommended going to doctors, for «there may come a time when recovery lies in the hands of the physicians»[17].

---

14 Ps 41(40):4.

15 The gospel writings show that relatives cared for their sick (Mark 1:30); parents sought help for their children (Mark 7:25; 9:17-18), employers for their servants (Luke 7:2-10), neighbors for the people in their villages (Mark 2:3-4).

16 The well known tract *De Medicina* by Aulus Cornelius Celsus, who was born about twenty years before Jesus and died three or four years after his crucifixion, provides a broad overview of medical theory and practice in his time. However the signal figure in Roman medicine was Claudius Galenus (130-200 A.D.)

17 So says Ben Sirah in the Book of Sirach (Ecclesiasticus) 38:1-15, written around 190-180 B.C.

Unfortunately for the sick in Galilee, physicians were not a viable option; they lived far from the villages, and their fees were excessively high.

The villagers also could not make pilgrimage to the famous temples of Asklepios, the god of medicine, or visit the sanctuaries of the healing deities Isis and Serapis, or bathe in the sacred fountains believed to have therapeutic powers. There were many prestigious temples to Asklepios. The most famous in Jesus' time was probably at Epidaurus, not far from Corinth, which attracted thousands of sick people. After bathing and making an offering to Asklepios, they spent the night on a dark portico of the temple in hopes of being visited by the healing god. In their dreams they might receive a message indicating the appropriate remedies (ointments, bandages, diets), or instructions that the temple servants could interpret to restore their health[18]. There were also temples to Isis and Serapis in the most important cities of the eastern Mediterranean, but nowhere near Galilee. Sick Galileans could not undertake the long voyage to these famous centers of healing, or pay for the costly offerings required there[19].

Closer home were the popular healers who did not practice professional medicine and were not associated with sanctuaries. These magicians, exorcists, and holy men (*hasidim*) were famous for their powers of prayer. Some, like Honi or Haninah ben Dosa[20], relied more on their close relationship with God than on therapeutic techniques[21]. In this context Jesus began traveling through Galilee, proclaiming the reign of God and healing the sick.

18 It is not easy to separate the «medical» from the «magical» elements of these places of healing. In general the god would indicate some procedure which, applied on awakening, would restore the patient's health. In sanctuaries like Pergamon or the Isle of Cos there were real physicians exercising their profession.

19 It is hard to tell whether there were places of healing in Jerusalem (the pool of Bethesda?), although around 135 B.C. there was a temple of Asklepios in Roman Jerusalem, then called the *Aelia Capitolina* (Duprez, Parrot).

20 Honi was apparently active in the early first century B.C. in Galilee (Vermes) or in Jerusalem (Meier); he was best known for his successful prayers to God for rain during periods of drought. Miracles of powerful prayer are also attributed to Haninah ben Dosa. He lived in Galilee during the first century, possibly only a few kilometers from Nazareth (Vermes, Parrot).

21 In this period it is hard to distinguish among *medicine*, which sought to restore the natural balance of the organism; *magic*, which invoked mysterious powers for beneficial effects on a person; and *healing*, which was attributed to powerful divine intervention (Kee, Avalos, Meier, Crossan).

An unusual healer

$\mathcal{C}\!\!\mathscr{D}$

One fact is historically undeniable: Jesus was renowned as a healer and exorcist among his contemporaries[22]. All the Christian sources speak of his healings and exorcisms[23]. The Jewish historian Flavius Josephus, writing around 90 A.D., also reports that during Pontius Pilate's rule as prefect of Judea «there appeared a wise man named Jesus, who performed amazing deeds»[24]. Jesus' fame as a miracle worker must have been extraordinary; for years afterward exorcists and magicians outside the Christian circle used his name to perform their magic[25].

Jesus' activity must have amazed the Galileans: Where did he get his curative power? He seemed like other healers they had seen in the region, but at the same time he was different. Certainly he wasn't a professional physician. He didn't examine the sick to diagnose their illness; he didn't use medical techniques or prescribe remedies. He did things very differently. He was concerned not only with their physical affliction, but also with the situation of helplessness and humiliation it caused them. He gave the sick something the doctors' remedies could not offer: a new relationship with God, which helped them live with new dignity before him.

Jesus' specific methods didn't surprise them; some were like the procedures used by magicians and popular healers. According to the Christian sources, he once took a deaf mute aside in private, «put his fingers into his ears, and spat and touched his tongue». Another time they brought a blind man to him; he «led

---

22 Almost all modern scholars agree on this: Crossan, Sanders, Meier, Theissen, Wenham, Parrot, Twelftree, Evans, Blackburn. The one exception is B. Mack. This general critical consensus does not mean that the historicity of each specific event, as narrated in the gospels, can be proven. On the contrary, these are usually stereotyped stories which do not so much describe specific events as show the kind of healing that Jesus did, according to people's memory of him as a «miracle worker». Some of the stories probably come from witnesses, but have been embellished and developed to distinguish Jesus from other famous miracle workers. We also cannot discount the possibility that some were created to illustrate a theological understanding of Jesus and his activity.

23 The healings are attested in all the sources: the Q Source, Mark, the independent material in Matthew, the independent material in Luke and John. They are also found in every literary form: narratives, sayings of Jesus, summaries of his activity, controversies with his adversaries, etc.

24 *Antigüedades de los judíos* 18, 3, 3 (English: *Antiquities of the Jews*). This text is considered authentic by most experts.

25 This is attested in the Greek Magical Papyri, which include materials from the first or second century B.C. to the fifth century A.D. One of the magicians' names mentioned is Jesus, «the god of the Hebrews».

the blind man out of the village», and «put saliva on his eyes and laid his hands on him» to cure him[26].

But Jesus was never seen trying to manipulate invisible forces, as the magicians did to force the divinity to intervene. He did not rely on techniques, but on the healing love of God who has compassion for those who suffer. Thus his activity was not like that of a magician in his time. He never intervened to do harm, cause sickness, produce insomnia, interfere with love relationships or get rid of enemies, but to cure suffering and infirmity. He did not conjure or pronounce secret formulas; he did not use amulets, witchcraft, or charms[27]. He never acted out of economic interests, but was moved by compassionate love and a determination to proclaim the reign of God[28].

The figure of Jesus is closer to that of two pious men, well known in the rabbinical tradition. Honi, the «Circle Drawer», is said to have successfully prayed to God for rain during a period of drought[29]. And it was said that when Haninah ben Dosa prayed for the sick, he could tell by the ease with which the prayer came from his mouth whether or not God would provide the healing. The action of these two holy men was not like magic, but was attributed to God's favor. The rabbinical tradition specifically emphasizes the effectiveness of their prayers. Honi and Haninah ben Dosa were not exactly miracle workers. They did not perform miracles by words or gestures; the power of their prayers was miraculous. Jesus, however, healed by giving orders or performing gestures.

26 These stories appear in Mark 7:31-37 and 8:22-26. Saliva was known to have healing properties: Jesus touched the deaf mute's tongue with saliva to «release» it, and caressed the blind man's eyes with saliva to «open» them. Matthew and Luke leave these stories out, probably because they sound like acts of magic.

27 He was not like the magicians who appear in the Greek Magical Papyri, or like his famous contemporary Apollonius of Tyana, the subject of a biography written by the philosopher Philostratus at the end of the second century. Apollonius was credited with miracles that recall the gospel stories, but his character was very different. He used his power to take vengeance on and harm his adversaries; he was «an expert on the occult forces» that moved in a strange world of satyrs, magic stones and miraculous plants, far from the world of suffering that Jesus knew.

28 Some years ago Morton Smith, based on the Greek Magical Papyri he had discovered, called Jesus a «magician» and described his healing activity as magic. His view has been adopted by some authors (Aune, Crossan). Crossan holds that that society did not fundamentally distinguish between magical and miraculous activity; he therefore prefers to call Jesus a «magician» in a sociological sense, without pejorative connotations. I prefer the view of those who emphasize the differences, and who say that calling Jesus a «magician» does not help to clarify his healing activity (Kee, Meier, Twelftree, Theissen, Blackburn).

29 Flavius Josephus speaks of him, as does the Mishna. He is called the «Circle Drawer» because, when the rain did not come as he wished, he drew a circle on the ground and vowed that he would not leave it until God sent the rain as he wanted it.

The people probably did not see Jesus as a *hasid*, like Honi or Haninah ben Dosa, but rather as a prophet who healed by the Spirit of God. His activity may have reminded them of Elijah and Elisha, who were very popular prophets in the Northern Kingdom because of their miraculous deeds. They did not perform mighty acts for the people, as Moses did, but the tradition remembered them as miracle-working prophets[30]. Elijah was said to have revived the son of a poor widow, whom he had earlier miraculously provided with food. Elisha was credited, among other things, with the resurrection of a widow's son, a miraculous multiplication of loaves of bread, and the healing of Naaman, a chief of the Aramean army who suffered from leprosy. But the tradition also attributes to Elisha things that Jesus would never have done. He fatally cursed a group of boys who were mocking him, punished Naaman's servant with leprosy, and struck blind the soldiers who had come out to capture him. No one would imagine the poet of God's mercy taking the life of children, for whom he showed such affection, or causing blindness, or condemning a person to the perpetual stigma of leprosy.

But what most distinguishes Jesus from other healers is that for him the healings were not isolated acts; they were part of his proclamation of the reign of God. This was his way of telling everyone the good news: God is arriving, and even the most unfortunate can experience his merciful love here and now. These amazing healings were simple but real signs of a new world: the world that God wants for everyone.

4

Jesus' curative power

∽

When did Jesus discover his power to heal? Did his faith in God's mercy compel him to alleviate the suffering of the sick, or was it the other way round: his discovery of his healing power led him to proclaim the nearness of God and his coming salvation? We can never answer this type of question. They belong to the secret world of Jesus[31].

---

30 Elijah and Elisha lived in the ninth century B.C. Elijah's activity is narrated in 1 Kings 17-20, that of Elisha in 2 Kings 2-8.
31 Some researchers suggest that Jesus' first healing was that of Simon's mother in-law (Mark 1:29-31), or the man with leprosy (Mark 1:40-45). We cannot say anything with certainty.

What we do know is that Jesus was contagious with health and life. The people of Galilee sensed in him someone who was enabled to heal by the Spirit and by God's healing power. Although from time to time he apparently used popular techniques, like saliva, what is important is not the specific procedures he used but who he was: the healing power that burned within him. People did not go to him for remedies or prescriptions, but to be with him. It was their encounter with the healer that made the difference. The therapy that Jesus applied was his own person: his passionate love of life, his wholehearted acceptance of every sick person, his power to renew a person from the bottom up, the contagion of his faith in human beings. His power to awaken unrecognized energies in people created the conditions that made the recovery of health possible.

Underlying this healing power, and inspiring all his activity, was his compassionate love. Jesus suffered to see the terrible distance between the suffering of these stricken men, women, and children, and the life God wants for all his sons and daughters[32]. What moved him was his love for those who suffer, and his will that they should experience now, in their own bodies, God's mercy which liberates them from evil. Healing was Jesus' way of loving. When he came to them to awaken their trust in God, liberate them from evil, and restore them to community life, above all Jesus was showing them that they deserved to be loved.

For that reason his healing was always a free gift. He never asked anything for himself, not even that the people he cured join his followers. The healing prompted by the reign of God is free, and his disciples must also give it away without charge[33]. This gratuitous dimension was surprising and appealing. Everyone could come to Jesus without worrying about the expense. The people he healed were not at all like the wealthy clients who sought out the gods of healing[34].

Jesus had his own way of healing. He did it by the power of his word and gestures. He talked to the sick person and showed his will that the person be healed. That was one of his most fundamental traits. He did not pronounce secret formulas or mumble, as the magicians did. His words were clear. Everyone could

---

32 The gospels, usually reluctant to speak of Jesus' own feelings, constantly used the verb *splanjnizomai* to say that he cured the sick because he was «moved with pity»: literally, «his bowels were shaken» (Mark 1:41; 9:22; Matt 9:36; 14:14; 15:32; 20:34; Luke 7:13).

33 Matthew makes this explicit in Jesus' instructions to the Twelve: «Cure the sick, raise the dead, cleanse the lepers, cast out demons. You received without payment; give without payment» (10:8).

34 In the temples and places of healing there were charges for service, and costly offerings were to be given to the healing god. Physicians also charged high fees for their services. According to Pliny the Elder, who was born in the year 23 and died in the 79 A.D. eruption of Vesuvius, in his time there was no «more lucrative» profession than medicine.

listen and understand. At the same time, he «touched» them. The Christian sources emphasize this, describing his gestures in different ways. Sometimes he «took them by the hand», to transmit his power to them and draw them out of the illness. Other times he «laid his hands on them» in a gesture of blessing, to wrap them in the loving kindness of God. Or he «stretched out his hand» to touch them, expressing his nearness, acceptance and compassion. He did this especially with lepers, who were usually excluded from community relationships[35]. Jesus' hands brought blessing to people who saw themselves as cursed, touched the lepers whom no one else would touch, conveyed power to people sinking in helplessness, inspired trust in people who felt abandoned by God, caressed people excluded from human contact. It was his way of healing.

Jesus was offering more than a physical improvement. His healing action went beyond the elimination of an organic problem. Curing the organism is part of a more integral healing of the person. He was rebuilding sick people from the bottom up: building their trust in God, drawing them out of isolation and despair, liberating them from sin, restoring them to the heart of the people of God, opening to them a fuller, healthier life. How did he do it?

Jesus began by renewing the people's faith. In different ways he led them to trust the saving goodness of God, who seemed to have withdrawn all blessing from them. The Christian sources emphasize this part of his healing action: «Do not fear, only believe»; «All things can be done for the one who believes»; «Son, your sins are forgiven»[36]. The narratives suggest that at some point, Jesus and the sick person were fused into a single faith. The sick people no longer felt alone and abandoned; accompanied and sustained by Jesus, they opened themselves trustingly to the God of the poor and lost. Without trust, Jesus' curative action would be frustrated. That apparently happened in his home village of Nazareth, where he could cure almost no one because of their lack of faith[37]. In contrast, when they trusted him and were cured, Jesus openly attributed it to their faith: «Daughter, your faith has made you well; go in peace, and be healed

35 Jesus «takes by the hand» (*krátein*) the mother in-law of Simon (Mark 1:30), the daughter of Jairus (Mark 5:41), or the young epileptic (Mark 9:27). He «lays hands on» (*epithenai*) the bent-over woman (Luke 13:13), the blind man at Bethsaida (Mark 8:23), and one of the many lepers brought to him at sunset in Capernaum (Luke 4:40). He «stretched out his hand» to touch the leper in Mark 1:41. Although these stories do not describe Jesus' healings exactly as they happened, by repeating such details they show us how they were remembered by the first Christians.

36 Mark 5:36; 9:23; 2:5.

37 Mark says this bluntly: «And he could do no deed of power there, except that he laid his hands on a few sick people and cured them. And he was amazed at their unbelief» (6:5-6).

of your disease»[38]. Thus faith was clearly part of the healing process itself. Jesus did not cure in order to produce faith; he called for faith in order to cure the affliction. This faith does not come easily. Sick people feel called to hope for something that goes beyond the limits of possibility. In believing, they cross a barrier and throw themselves on God's saving power. That is not easy to do. We can understand the paradoxical cry of one sick boy's father: «I believe; help my unbelief!»[39].

Jesus was not asking for faith in his mysterious power or occult wisdom, but in the goodness of God who comes to save people from evil, even by drawing on unknown possibilities that are not usually available to human beings. He did it, not by resorting to hypnosis or magic, but by helping the sick to accept God in the midst of their painful experience. Jesus worked in their «heart», helping them to trust God, liberating them from the dark feelings of guilt and abandonment by God that lead to sickness. He healed them by bringing God's forgiveness, peace, and blessing into their lives[40]. In this way he opened up to them the possibility of living with a new heart, reconciled with God.

At the same time he reconciled them to the society. Sickness and marginalization are closely linked; the healing is not complete until the sick are integrated into the society. Therefore Jesus eliminated the barriers that kept them excluded from the community. Society must not fear them, but welcome them. In different ways, the Christian sources describe Jesus' determination to re-incorporate them into the community: «Stand up, take your mat and go to your home». «Go, show yourself to the priest, and offer for your cleansing what Moses commanded, as a testimony to them». «Go home to your friends, and tell them how much the Lord has done for you»[41].

His behavior toward the lepers was especially meaningful, since they were excluded from the community as impure. They didn't exactly ask Jesus to heal them but to «cleanse» them, to show them the «mercy» they could not find in society[42]. Jesus responded with a gesture: he stretched out his hand and touched

---

38 Mark 5:34; see also Mark 10:52.

39 Mark 9:24.

40 In Mark 2:5, Jesus explicitly tells the paralyzed man: «Son, your sins are forgiven». Some authors believe this was a later addition to a story that was originally about a simple cure. Even so, the declaration of forgiveness is a good expression of his way of healing.

41 Mark 2:11; 1:44; 5:19. Perhaps Mary Magdalene had no family and Jesus, after drawing out «seven demons» from her, brought her into his group of disciples.

42 On his travels through Galilee a leper begged him, «If you choose, you can make me clean» (Mark 1:40). Another time as he was entering a village, ten lepers called out to him: «Jesus, Master, have mercy on us!» (Luke 17:14). This story appears to be a later addition.

them. Those men and women were members of the people of God, as Jesus understood it. By touching them, he was liberating them from their exclusion. It was a purposeful gesture. He was not only curing them, but calling out to the whole society. The reign of God is coming. We have to live life differently. The impure can be touched; the excluded must be welcomed. The sick must not be regarded with fear, but with compassion. This is how God looks at them.

5

Liberation from demons

Jesus did not only heal the sick. Filled with the Spirit of God, he also came to the demon-possessed and freed them from the evil spirits. There is no doubt about this. Jesus was an exorcist of great renown, even outside Christian circles; for years after his death, other exorcists continued using his name as a powerful way to expel demons. His actions toward demoniacs caused a much greater impact than did his healings. People were amazed, and asked what was the secret source of this great power. Some felt threatened by him; they accused him of being «possessed» by an evil spirit, acting as an agent of Beelzebul. For Jesus, however, this power confirmed a belief that had been growing in his heart: if evil was being overcome, if it was possible to experience the defeat of Satan, then the reign of God was coming now. Who were these sick people? How can we understand, from the viewpoint of our own culture, the different way they were experienced by the people around Jesus? How did he heal them?

Modern scholars generally think of «diabolic possession» as an illness. The people were suffering from epilepsy, hysteria, schizophrenia, or «altered states of consciousness», in which the patients dramatically project onto an evil person the repressions and conflicts that fragment their inner world[43]. Certainly that is a legitimate way to think of it today, but what the Galilean peasants experienced was nothing like this model of conflicts «projected» onto another person. On the contrary, from their viewpoint, it was they who were invaded and possessed by one of those evil beings that infest the world. That is precisely their

[43] Recent researchers (Pilch, Crossan) have studied Jesus' activity using the category of «altered states of consciousness», proposed by modern anthropology (Erika Bourguignon, Goodman) as a «neutral definition» of strange phenomena that occur in all times and societies, but which are interpreted differently in each culture. However, this category of «altered states of consciousness» is also a cultural interpretation, developed in the context of modern psychology.

tragedy. The evil they suffered was not just another illness. It was life controlled by an unknown, irrational power that tormented them, and against which they were defenseless[44].

It is probably more correct to see demon-possession as a complex strategy, used in a dysfunctional way by oppressed people to protect themselves from an unbearable situation. When they have no other way to rebel, individuals can develop a separate personality that permits them to say and do what they could not under normal circumstances, at least not without great risk. Was there some connection between the oppression of Palestine by the Roman Empire, and the simultaneous phenomenon of so many people possessed by the devil? Was this a dysfunctional way to rebel against their subjection to Rome and the dominion of the powerful? Although the healing of the Gerasene demoniac is not a strictly historical narrative, it may help us to establish a vague connection between demon-possession and Roman oppression. In this story there is only one demon, but it calls itself «legion» because it is many, like the Roman military legions that controlled Palestine; the demons enter into «swine», the most impure of animals and the ones best used to describe the Romans; later the swine rush into the «sea», which is where the Jewish resistance wanted to see them drowned forever[45]. It is hard to imagine today the terror and frustration that the Roman Empire inspired in people who were absolutely defenseless against its cruelty.

There was also plenty of conflict and oppression within the peasant families, with their rigid patriarchal structure. More than a few of the demon-possessed were probably women, adolescents and children: infertile wives, frustrated and shamed before everyone; widows left defenseless against mistreatment by men; abused children. For them too, possession was a defense mechanism that enabled them to get attention, defend themselves from the people around them, and exercise a kind of power[46].

---

44 In these primitive societies we should not confuse an «illness» caused by an evil spirit with «diabolic possession» (Thiessen, Strecker).

45 Mark 5:1-20. Many scholars view demon-possession in Galilee as a form of secret resistance against Rome, typical of desperate people (Hollenbach, Horsley, Sanders, Crossan, Guijarro). It is worth noting that «demon-possession», so common in Jesus' time, was practically unknown in previous centuries.

46 Some authors (Davies, Lewis) have noted the presence of demon-possession in victims of family abuse and conflict. Luke recalls «some women who had been cured of evil spirits and infirmities», specifically including Mary Magdalene, «from whom seven demons had gone out» (Luke 8:2).

The demon-possessed whom Jesus healed were not just mentally ill. They were starving people, victims of endemic violence, helpless against unbearable abuse. They did not see themselves as rebelling against evil, but as victims of a strange and unknown power that tormented them and destroyed their identity. Mark describes in horrifying detail the Gerasene demoniac who lived «among the tombs and on the mountains», in a state of total isolation, excluded from the land of the living; «restrained with shackles and chains» by a society terrified of his presence; «howling» in his inability to communicate with anyone, and «bruising himself with stones», a victim of his own violence. What evil power lay behind that behavior? It is hard to tell. We only know that Jesus came near to that sinister world, and liberated those who were tormented by evil.

Jesus seemed like other exorcists of his time, but he was different[47]. His combat with evil spirits was probably not altogether foreign to the Galilean villages, but there was something in his activity that almost certainly surprised people who saw him up close. Jesus' language and gestures were not unlike those of the exorcists of his time, but he apparently established a different relationship with the demoniacs. He did not use the tools of other exorcists: rings, hoops, amulets, incense, human milk, hair. His power came from within him. His presence and the power of his words imposed themselves. Moreover, unlike the other exorcists who conjured the demons in the name of some divinity or sacred personality, Jesus felt no need to reveal the source of his power. He did not say in whose name he was expelling the demons; he neither pronounced magic names nor invoked secret powers[48]. He also didn't use conjuring or secret formulas. He didn't even call on his Father. Jesus confronted the demons with the force of his word: «Come out of him!» «Come out of him, and never enter him again!»[49]. Everything points to the interpretation that when he fought the demons, Jesus was convinced he was acting by God's own power.

47 Several sources describe the practices of exorcism in Jesus' time: Flavius Josephus' personal report of a Jewish exorcist named Eliezer; the narrative of a first-century Roman writer named Lucian of Samosata about a Syrian exorcist from Palestine; a curious description of Abraham as an exorcist in the apocryphal *Genesis* found at Qumran; the Book of Tobias, written around 200 B.C. The Greco-Roman Magical Papyri, although of later date and further away from Palestine, also give us an idea of the cultural background in which Jesus was probably acting.

48 The name most commonly invoked by Jewish exorcists at the time was Solomon. Flavius Josephus mentions King Solomon's fame in Jewish legends, as a wise man knowledgeable in the occult sciences and an expert exorcist.

49 Mark 1:25; 5:8; 9:25.

The sources describe his activity as a violent confrontation between people who felt possessed by Satan, and the prophet who knew he was inhabited by the Spirit of God. Both combatants attacked, and both defended themselves. The demons howled at Jesus; he threatened them and gave fierce orders. He invaded the field dominated by the evil spirits, conquered and expelled the demons, who «fled» in defeat[50]. This «combat», which looks to us like a literary composition, probably conceals terrifying episodes to which the Galilean villagers were witness. Recent researchers suspect that Jesus himself suffered a dramatic transformation during his activity as an exorcist. In struggling to subdue the demons he talked directly to them, penetrated their world, asked their names in order to dominate them, shouted orders at them, gesticulated, angered them and drove them out. In this way he destroyed the «demoniacs'» identity and built them a new identity, conveying to them the healing power of his own person[51].

172

This would help to explain certain reactions to Jesus' exorcisms. In the earliest gospel we read that Jesus' family members came from Nazareth to take charge of him, because they believed he had «gone out of his mind». What behavior was more likely to have encouraged that idea, than his strange activity with the demoniacs?[52] His adversaries went further; they said «He has Beelzebul, and by the ruler of the demons he casts out demons»[53]. Those who accused him did not think about the good Jesus was doing for these sick people. Rather they saw his exorcisms as some kind of threat to the social order. By liberating the demon-possessed Jesus was building a new Israel, made up of freer, more autonomous people; he was seeking a new society. His adversaries could best neutralize this dangerous activity by discrediting him socially, accusing him of deviant behavior: his power over the demons was not from God, but came from the evil power of the prince of demons. This type of accusation was a commonly used strategy of the powerful to control the society.

Jesus could not remain silent; he had to defend himself and explain the true meaning of his exorcising activities. He pointed out the logical inconsistency of the accusation: Satan cannot act against himself. «If Satan casts out Satan, he is

---

50 Jesus never laid his hands on the demoniacs. He reserved that gesture of blessing for the sick.
51 Recent researchers believe that Jesus himself went into a kind of «trance» and imitated the demoniacs' behavior in order to cure them (Smith, Crossan, Sanders, Davies).
52 Mark 3:21. The expression «he has gone out of his mind» (*éjeste*) is an appropriate way to describe a demoniac.
53 Mark 3:22. The gospel of John puts the accusation more clearly: «You have a demon!» (7:20; 8:48, 49, 52; 10:20, 21).

divided against himself; how then will his kingdom stand?»[54] Obviously Jesus did not belong to the reign of Satan; it was absurd to see an alliance with the evil one in his exorcisms. To dispel any remaining ambiguity, Jesus clearly explained the meaning of his activity: «But if it is by the finger of God that I cast out demons, then the kingdom of God has come to you»[55]. For Jesus there was no other explanation. This was «the finger of God». His struggle to «liberate» these unhappy people was a victory over Satan and the best sign of the coming of the reign of God, who wants a healthier, more liberated life for his sons and daughters.

Jesus apparently gave great importance to his exorcising activity. He explained his action toward the demons with a colorful image: «But no one can enter a strong man's house and plunder his property without first tying up the strong man; then indeed the house can be plundered»[56]. No one can invade the arena dominated by Satan without first reducing him to powerlessness. Jesus saw his exorcisms as a way of «tying up» the evil one and controlling his destructive power[57].

6
Signs of a new world

Jesus did not limit himself to alleviating the suffering of the sick and demon-possessed, but gave his healing activity a transcendent interpretation: he saw in it the signs of a new world. Faced with the catastrophic pessimism that prevailed in apocalyptic circles, where everything was seen as infested with evil, Jesus proclaimed something new: God is here. Healing the sick and liberating the demon-possessed are his reaction against human suffering: they show the final victory of his mercy here and now, by liberating the world from a destiny fatally marked by suffering and misfortune.

54 Matt 12:26.
55 Q Source (Luke 11:20; Matt 12:28). According to Luke, Jesus cast out demons «by the finger of God». In Matthew, he did it «by the Spirit of God». Luke's expression is closer to Jesus vivid and specific language.
56 Mark 3:27. The image also appears in the Q Source (Luke 11:21-22; Matt 12:29) and in the [apocryphal] *Gospel of Thomas* 35:1-2. It clearly comes from Jesus.
57 This small parable of Jesus must be understood in the cultural context of his time, when it was thought that although God holds supreme power over the world, he allows the demons a certain influence over the earth, until the end when he will re-establish his authority and destroy them forever. In the meantime, books known in Jesus time affirmed the possibility of «binding them hand and foot» (Tob 8:3; 1 Enoch 10:4) or «shutting them up in a prison» (Isa 24:21-22).

Jesus did not perform cures to prove his divine authority or the truth of his message. In fact, when people asked for a spectacular proof that would save them the risk of making a decision, he refused[58]. He didn't put on a show. In Jesus' understanding, his healings were not a proof of God's power but a sign of his mercy. Indeed for the Galileans, «miracles» were not a final proof of anything, although they did encourage people to see the miracle worker in some close relationship with God. The teachers of the law in particular were skeptical toward prodigious acts. In their eyes a «miracle» proved nothing unless the miracle worker strictly observed the law. That is why Jesus' act of healing on the sabbath, challenging the orthodox traditions, provoked such a scandal. In reality Jesus did not win a generalized following. Some people followed him; others rejected him.

Probably they were most aware of the great difference between Jesus' activity and that of John the Baptist. The Baptist's mission was conceived and organized in terms of sin. His highest concern was to denounce people's sins, and to purify of their moral filth those who came to him at the Jordan River. That is what he offered everyone: a purifying baptism for «the forgiveness of sins». Jesus' highest concern, in contrast, was the suffering of the most unfortunate. The sources do not show Jesus walking through Galilee in search of sinners, to convert them away from their sins, but coming to the sick and demon-possessed, to liberate them from their suffering. His activity was not oriented toward reforming the Jewish religion, but toward alleviating the suffering of those who were burdened by evil and excluded from a healthy life. It was more about eliminating suffering than condemning various types of sin. This does not mean he wasn't concerned about sin, but that for Jesus the gravest sin, the kind that most effectively resists the reign of God, is the sin of causing suffering or remaining indifferent to it.

The Christian sources sum up Jesus' activity by affirming that he was devoted to two tasks: proclaiming the good news of the reign of God, and curing disease and sickness[59]. That was his fundamental calling: to awaken faith in the nearness of God by struggling against suffering. When he entrusted his mission to his disciples, he charged them with the same task: «he sent them out to proclaim the kingdom of God and to heal»[60].

---

58 Although Jesus performed cures, he never gave them the «sign from heaven» that some groups of scribes wanted (Mark 8:11-12; Q Source [Luke 11:29-30; Matt 12:38-39]).

59 «Jesus went throughout Galilee... proclaiming the good news of the kingdom and curing every disease and sickness among the people» (Matt 4:23).

60 Luke 9:2. Luke also quotes Jesus: «Whenever you enter a town... cure the sick who are there, and say to them, "The kingdom of God has come near to you"» (Luke 10:8-9; Matt 10:7-8).

Jesus only performed a handful of healings and exorcisms. Many blind people, lepers and demoniacs were left in the Galilean villages, still suffering their affliction. Only a few who met him experienced his curative power. Jesus never thought of «miracles» as an easy way to end suffering in the world, but as a sign showing how his followers must act in order to welcome the reign of God.

This reaffirms the message of his parables. God's saving action is already in motion. The reign is God's response to human suffering. The most unfortunate people can experience, in their own flesh, the signs of a new world in which God will overcome evil at last. That sometimes filled Jesus with emotion: «I watched Satan fall from heaven like a flash of lightning»[61]. This is the kingdom of God that he yearned for: the defeat of evil, the irruption of God's mercy, the elimination of suffering, the acceptance of those previously excluded from community life, the establishment of a society liberated from all affliction. That is far from being an accomplished reality. We must go on bringing signs of God's mercy into the world. That is the mission Jesus would now entrust to his followers.

---

61 Luke 10:18. Although this is not quoted anywhere else, scholars consider it an authentic saying of Jesus.

Defender of the Last

It gave Jesus great joy to experience the reign of God, already present in the healing of the sick and the liberation of the demon-possessed. They needed him most, but they were not the only ones. Soon the poorest people in Galilee began coming to him. Some of them were homeless. They wandered through the villages, from one place to another. Soon they came across Jesus, who also lived an itinerant life and had «nowhere to lay his head»[1]. They needed to hear that the reign of God is for them too. They knew all too well what a reign built on power and on the oppression of the weakest was like: they had had to support Herod's family for years. Now he must show them the kind of life God wants for them: a reign of justice and compassion, where the large landowners are the «last» and the village beggars the «first».

1

The last in Galilee

Herod Antipas wanted to build his own «reign» as his father had, although Rome had only given Antipas the title of «tetrarch». He began by rebuilding the city of Sepphoris in Lower Galilee; later, recalling the city of Caesarea that his father had built on the Mediterranean coast, he built a new capital on the shore of Lake Gennesaret. Naturally he called it Tiberias in honor of Tiberius, the new emperor. The construction of these two cities brought the phenomenon of urbanization to the Galilean territory for the first time. Within a brief period, the first twenty years of Jesus' life, the development of these two cities less than fifty kilometers apart produced a profound social change. Jesus experienced that change at first hand.

Sepphoris and Tiberias became the administrative centers for control of the whole region. The ruling classes were concentrated there: military officials, collectors of tribute, judges, administrators, large landowners, and officials in charge of storing merchandise. There were not many of them, but they made up the urban elite protected by Antipas. They were the «rich» in Galilee during Jesus' time: they had wealth, power, and honor.

The rural situation was very different. The large construction projects, undertaken first by Herod and then by his son Antipas, led to even higher taxes on the peasants. Some families could barely survive. One bad harvest, an illness, or

1 Luke 9:58.

the death of a man in the family could bring on misfortune. A family without sufficient reserves to last until the next harvest, had to go first to their relatives and neighbors for help. Often these could not help, because their whole villages were affected by the same poverty. Their only option then was to seek a loan from those who controlled the grain storage. Everyone knew what that could mean. Villagers who could not repay the debt were forced to give up their lands, which further increased the property of the large landowners.

Other factors made the peasants' situation even more vulnerable. The central powers imposed monoculture, production specialized on one crop, in order to increase the profit from their land. The landowners decided what to cultivate on their large holdings, based on their commercial interests in wheat, oil, or wine. Meanwhile the peasants, renters, and day workers could not get the barley, kidney beans, and other modest foods needed to feed their families.

The use of coins circulated by Antipas also did not benefit the peasants, at least initially. Only the urban elites had significant sums of money with which to operate their businesses, and only they could accumulate gold or silver coins[2]. The peasants could only put their hands on a few, almost worthless, bronze or copper coins. In the villages, nearly everyone lived by bartering goods and services in a subsistence regimen.

The result was the same, whether in the empire of Tiberius, the reign of Herod, or the tetrarchy of Antipas. Luxurious buildings in the cities, misery in the villages; wealth and ostentation among the urban elites, debt and hunger among the rural people; growing enrichment of the large landowners, loss of land among the peasants. Insecurity and malnutrition increased; the families deprived of their land disintegrated; the number of day workers, beggars, vagabonds, prostitutes, and debt collection fugitives increased. There was nothing to hope for under either Tiberius or Antipas[3].

These people were the «poor» in Jesus' time. The sources always speak of them in the plural. They are the most oppressed social stratum or sector: those who have lost their land and are forced to seek work as day laborers or to live by beg-

---

2 In Aramaic this money was called *mammon* (what is certain, what gives security). This money was called «unworthy *mammon*» or dishonest wealth (Luke 16:9.11).

3 According to many researchers, the development of the cities of Sepphoris and Tiberias was largely responsible for provoking crisis and disintegration among the poorest families in the Galilean villages during Jesus' time. They point especially to three facts: the loss of land due to debt, the development of currency, and the growing impact of monoculture (Freyne, Horsley, Stegemann, Schotroff, Crossan, Oakman, Patterson).

ging or prostitution. In Galilee the immense majority of the population were poor; they were families who struggled to survive day by day, but at least they had a small piece of land or some stable employment to live on. But when Jesus talks about the «poor» he is referring to those who have nothing: people living on the edge, dispossessed of everything, at the opposite extreme from the powerful elites. The poor live without wealth, without power, and without honor[4].

They are not an anonymous mass. They have faces, almost always dirty and emaciated by malnutrition and extreme misery. Many of them are women; there are also orphans who live in the shadow of some family. Most are homeless vagabonds. They do not know what it is to eat meat or bread made from wheat; they are glad for a crumb of black barley bread or a few stolen onions, figs, or grapes. They clothe themselves as best they can, and almost always go barefoot. They are easy to recognize. There are beggars who go from town to town, blind or crippled people who beg along the roads or at the entrance to the village. There are also slaves running away from cruel masters, and peasants escaping their creditors. Among the women there are widows who cannot remarry, childless wives repudiated by their husbands, and more than a few who are trying to feed their children by prostitution. In this world of misery, women are beyond doubt the most vulnerable and defenseless, because they are not only poor but also women[5].

There are common traits within this sector. They are all victims of abuse and mistreatment by those who have power, wealth, and land. Dispossessed of everything, they live in a situation of misery from which there is no escape. They have no defense against the powerful. They have no patron to protect them, because they have nothing to offer in the prevailing patron-client relations. In short, nobody cares about them. They are the dregs of the Empire. Lives without a future[6].

---

4 Already in the fourth century B.C., the Greek language of the Empire distinguished between *penés* (the poor who live by hard work) and *ptojos* (those dispossessed of everything, who have nothing to live by). Jesus was always referring to the latter (Stegemann, Schotroff, Hanson, Oakman).

5 The situation of these people was particularly tragic in times of drought and epidemic. Flavius Josephus tells about two periods of extreme hunger: the year 25 B.C. under Herod, and in 46 A.D. in Jerusalem (*Antigüedades de los judíos*, 15:9,1; 20:1,5. [English: *Jewish Antiquities*]).

6 The prestigious anthropologist Gerhard Lenski describes this sector as «the expendables».

God belongs to those who have no one

Jesus' life as an itinerant brought him very close to this world of indigents. He lived practically as one of them, homeless and without stable employment. He carried no coins with Caesar's image: he had no problems with tax collectors. He had left the domain of Antipas. He lived among the excluded ones, seeking the reign of God and his justice.

Soon he invited the group of followers gathering around him to do the same. They would share the life of those poor. They would walk barefoot, like the poor who didn't have even a denarius to buy a pair of leather sandals. They would do without the second tunic that was used as a blanket, to shelter them from the cold night when they slept outdoors. They wouldn't carry even a pouch of food. They would live on God's care and the people's hospitality, just as the indigents did[7]. That was their place: among the dregs of the Empire. For Jesus, that was the best place to embrace and proclaim the reign of God.

He can't proclaim the reign of God and his justice without remembering the poor. He has to make room for them, to show everyone that they have a privileged place in the reign of God; he has to defend them so they will believe in a God who defends the last; he has to embrace, before anyone else, those who day by day confront the barriers raised by the families protected by Antipas and the rich landowners. He doesn't come to them as a fanatic or a complainer, nor by rejecting the rich. He only wants to be a clear sign that God does not abandon the last[8].

By identifying with them and suffering their needs at close hand[9], Jesus was becoming aware that for these men and women, the reign of God could only be «good news». Their situation was unjust and cruel. It did not respond to God's plan. The arrival of his reign would mean a total reversal: those vagabonds, deprived of even the necessities of life, would be the «first», and many of the pow-

---

7 Mark 6:8-11; Q Source (Luke 9:3-5; Matt 10:9-14); Luke 10:4-11; [apocryphal] *Gospel of Thomas* 13:4. The gist of these instructions to his followers came from Jesus.

8 Scholars have highlighted Jesus' attitude toward the last with graphic descriptions: «unheard-of concern for the lost» (Dodd), «a preference for the dehumanized» (Boff), «life in bad company» (Holl), «preference for the weak» (Fraijó), «downward inclination» (Bloch).

9 In Mark 2:23-28 Jesus' disciples, out of hunger, pluck heads of grain, crush them in their hands and begin to eat what they can. The episode is considered historically plausible (even by the Jesus Seminar [cf. Appendix 6, p. 493-498]). Certainly Jesus and his followers were hungry on more than one occasion.

erful who seemed to have everything would be the «last». Jesus expressed his condemnation very graphically in the parable of a rich man without compassion and a poor beggar named Lazarus. Everyone got the point. The beggars heard it with great joy. A new hope was awakening in their heart.

> There was a rich man who was dressed in purple and fine linen and who feasted sumptuously every day. And at his gate lay a poor man named Lazarus, covered with sores, who longed to satisfy his hunger with what fell from the rich man's table; even the dogs would come and lick his sores. The poor man died and was carried away by the angels to be with Abraham. The rich man also died and was buried.
>
> In Hades, where he was being tormented, he looked up and saw Abraham far away with Lazarus by his side. He called out, «Father Abraham, have mercy on me, and send Lazarus to dip the tip of his finger in water and cool my tongue, for I am in agony in these flames». But Abraham said, «Child, remember that during your lifetime you received your good things, and Lazarus in like manner evil things; but now he is comforted here, and you are in agony. Besides all this, between you and us a great chasm has been fixed, so that those who might want to pass from here to you cannot do so, and no one can cross from there to us».
>
> He said, «Then, father, I beg you to send him to my father's house — for I have five brothers — that he may warn them, so that they will not also come into this place of torment». Abraham replied, «They have Moses and the prophets; they should listen to them». He said, «No, father Abraham; but if someone goes to them from the dead, they will repent». He said to him, «If they do not listen to Moses and the prophets, neither will they be convinced even if someone rises from the dead»[10].

Jesus was talking about a powerful rich man. His tunic of fine linen from Egypt shows his life of luxury and ostentation. His purple clothes indicate that he belongs to royal circles. His life is a constant feast, because he holds splendid banquets every day, not only for special celebrations. Surely the poor who listen to Jesus have never seen such a person up close, but they know he belongs to the

10 Although this parable is found only in Luke 16:19-31, most scholars consider it a parable from Jesus (Jeremias, Scott, Herzog, Wright, Schweizer). The scandalous contrast between the rich man and the beggar, the absence of a judgment scene, and the reversal of the situation then prevailing in Galilee, are very much in Jesus' style. The dialogue in the afterlife is probably inspired by a popular Egyptian tale about the voyage of Si-Osiris to the world of the dead (Grossman). Many scholars believe that the second part of the dialogue between the rich man and Abraham (vv. 27-31) is Luke's creation (Bultmann, Crossan, Scott, Schotroff). Others attribute it to Jesus (Jeremias, Herzog).

highest level of the privileged sector living in Tiberias, Sepphoris, or Jerusalem. These are the people who possess wealth, wield power, and enjoy a lavish life beyond the wildest dreams of Jesus' followers.

Very close to this rich man, lying beside the beautiful gate of his mansion[11], there is a beggar. He has nothing except a name full of promises: «Lazarus», that is, «one helped by God»[12]. He is not covered in linen and purple, but with repugnant sores. He doesn't know about banquets; he can't even eat the crusts of bread that the guests drop under the table after using them to wipe their fingers. Only the stray dogs who wander through the city come near him. He seems exhausted, too weak even to ask for help. His repugnant skin makes him ritually impure, and he is further degraded by the contact with stray dogs. Isn't his situation of extreme misery the best sign that God has abandoned and condemned him? He is near his end. Perhaps some of Jesus' hearers shuddered: Lazarus could be any one of them. That was the future for those who lived in misery, the dregs of that society.

Jesus' penetrating gaze is unmasking the terrible injustice of that society. The most powerful classes and the oppressed underclass seem to belong to the same society, but they are separated by an almost invisible barrier, the one the rich man never crosses to come near Lazarus. The rich are celebrating splendid banquets in their palaces; the poor are outside, dying of hunger. Suddenly everything changes. Lazarus dies, and although nothing is said of his burial, he is carried off to the bosom of Abraham, who invites him to take part in his banquet. The rich man also dies and is buried with full honors; he ends up not in Abraham's bosom but in Hades[13].

This is a total reversal of the situation. While Lazarus is taken to the bosom of Abraham, the rich man stays in *sheol*, a place of affliction. Now he reacts for the first time. The man who had no compassion for the beggar, now cries out for compassion; the man who did not see Lazarus by his gate now sees him «far

---

11 The word *pylon* is not used for the door of an ordinary house, but the ornamental gate of a palace.

12 «Lazarus» is an abbreviated form of Eliezer («my God helps»). According to G. Vermes, it is a typical corruption of the Galilean dialect Jesus spoke. This is the only character in Jesus' parables who has a name.

13 The first-century Jews spoke of the afterlife in different ways. The Hades mentioned in the parable is not «hell», but *sheol*, a place of shadows and death where all the dead go. Apparently in Jesus' time it was considered a place of hope where both the righteous and sinners are taken, although separately, to wait for God's judgment. The *Book of Enoch* says: «When sinners die and are buried, if in their life they have not been subjected to judgment, their spirits are set apart in a place of great suffering until the day of judgment, punishment, and pardon arrives» (1:22).

away» and calls for him by name; the man who had not stepped through his gate to relieve the poor man's suffering now wants Lazarus to come and relieve his suffering. It is too late, Abraham tells him: that barrier, almost invisible on earth, has become an unbridgeable chasm.

The poor can hardly believe it. What is Jesus telling them? In Israelite tradition, prosperity is a sign of God's blessing; misery, in contrast, is a sign of condemnation[14]. How can that beggar, impure and miserable, go to the bosom of Abraham while the rich man, blessed by God, suffers in *sheol*? Aren't vagabonds and beggars under a curse? With his parable, Jesus is not naively describing life beyond death but unmasking what is happening in Galilee[15]. That state of things, in which some live in splendor while others die of hunger, is a painful injustice. Wealth built on the systematic oppression of the weak is not a sign of God's blessing. It is an intolerable injustice, which God will someday bring to an end. The arrival of God's reign will mean a total reversal of the situation.

Jesus is beginning to speak a new, surprising and provocative language. His voice echoes all over Galilee. In the villages he meets these downtrodden people who have no defense against the large landowners and cries out to them: «Blessed are you who are poor, for your king is God [NRSV: yours is the kingdom of God]». He sees with his own eyes the hunger of those malnourished women and children, and cannot hold back his feelings: «Blessed are you who are hungry now, for you will be filled». He sees the peasants weeping from anger and helplessness, after losing their land or watching the collectors carry away the best of their crops, and encourages them: «Blessed are you who weep now, for you will laugh»[16]. The reign of God is not «good news» for everyone, without distinction. Not everyone can hear it in the same way, the landowners feasting in Tiberias and the beggars dying of hunger in the villages. God wants justice among his sons and daughters. His heart cannot bear this cruel situation. The reign of God will bring change. His coming is good fortune for those who live under oppression, and a threat to those who live by oppressing.

---

14 The Psalms say repeatedly: «Those who seek the Lord lack no good thing» (34:10; 23:1), but Jesus' hearers lacked everything.

15 The parable is not a description of life after death, but carries a message about what is happening in Galilee between the rich and the poor (Hock, Bauckham, Wright, Herzog, Scott, Crossan).

16 No one doubts that these three beatitudes come from Jesus. Luke's version (6:20-21) is more authentic than Matthew's (5:3, 5-6). They probably were not part of a sermon, but cries raised by Jesus at different times to encourage the poor. They were collected later in the Christian community.

Is this a joke? Or cynicism perhaps? It might be, if Jesus were speaking in the palaces of Tiberias, the mansions of Sepphoris, or the villas of the high priests in Jerusalem. But Jesus is with these people. He is an indigent like them, talking to them with absolute faith and conviction[17]; the misery that dooms them to hunger and affliction does not come from God. On the contrary, it is a real scandal: God wants to see them filled, happy, and laughing. God is coming for their sake. That is what Jesus wants to write in their hearts: although no one else cares about them, God does; although they are expendable in human-made empires, they have a privileged place in his heart; although they have no patron to defend them, they have God as their Father.

Jesus is a realist. He has no political or religious power to transform that situation. He has no armies to rebel against the Roman legions or to overthrow Antipas. He is the prophet of God's mercy, himself one of the last. His word does

186 not mean an immediate end to the hunger and misery of these people, but it does mean unyielding dignity for all the victims of abuse and exploitation. Everyone needs to know that these people in particular are God's favorite children, which makes their dignity absolutely real. Their life is sacred. It is impossible, in Galilee or anywhere else, to build the life God wills except by freeing these men and women from hunger, misery, and humiliation. Neither the Jewish religion nor any other will be blessed by God unless it brings justice for them. The only way to accept God is to build a world whose first priority is the dignity of the last.

3

Foolishness or solidarity

In a society where some people live submerged in hunger or misery, there is only one choice: to live as fools, indifferent to the suffering of others, or to awaken hearts and move hands to help those in need. That is how Jesus sees it. The rich, oblivious to the suffering of the poor, exploiting the weak and enjoying their own selfish well-being, are fools. Their life is a failure. The idea that a rich person can «enter» the reign of God is not only impossible, but ridiculous: «It is easier for a camel to go through the eye of a needle than for someone who is rich to enter

---

17 Some authors, bearing in mind the Aramaic language patterns in which Jesus was speaking, believe that these beatitudes could be translated in the first person: «Blessed are we who have nothing… Blessed are we who are hungry now… Blessed are we who weep now».

the kingdom of God!»[18] In God's reign there cannot be rich people living at the expense of the poor. It is absurd to imagine that when God's will is finally achieved, the powerful will still oppress the weak.

The tragedy of the rich is that their well-being, together with the hungry, is incompatible with the reign of God who wants to see all his sons and daughters enjoying a full and just life. That is why Jesus exclaimed: «You cannot serve God and wealth»[19]. His words must have had an explosive impact. God and wealth are like two lords confronting one another. It is not possible to be a slave of wealth and spend one's life accumulating gold and silver coins to protect one's own well-being, and at the same time, expect to enter into the dynamic of the reign of God, who seeks a just and brotherly life for all. People have to choose. Jesus does not encourage the poor to thirst for vengeance against the rich[20]. He is only predicting the future of the rich: there is no place for them in God's reign. Unless they change, they are «fools». He made that clear in a parable, traditionally called «the rich fool»:

> The land of a rich man produced abundantly. And he thought to himself, «What should I do, for I have no place to store my crops?» Then he said, «I will do this: I will pull down my barns and build larger ones, and there I will store all my grain and my goods. And I will say to my soul, Soul, you have ample goods laid up for many years; relax, eat, drink, and be merry». But God said to him, «You fool! This very night your life is being demanded of you. And the things you have prepared, whose will they be?»[21].

---

18 Mark 10:24. The graphic and amusing picture of this dumb animal trying to go through the tiny hole in a needle is typical of Jesus' style. Everyone is inclined to believe that it reflects his sense of irony.

19 All the scholars consider this saying of Jesus, from the Q source (Luke 16:13; Matt 6:24), to be authentic: «No slave can serve two masters; for a slave will either hate the one and love the other, or be devoted to the one and despise the other. You cannot serve God and wealth».

20 In Luke we read three «curses» against the rich in contrast to the three «blessings» for the poor: «But woe to you who are rich, for you have received your consolation. Woe to you who are full now, for you will be hungry. Woe to you who are laughing now, for you will mourn and weep» (6:24-25). A majority of scholars think they did not come from Jesus (Dupont, Lambrecht, Klein, Crossan).

21 The parable is found in Luke 12:16-20 and in the [apocryphal] *Gospel of Thomas* 63:1. It certainly comes from Jesus. Although Crossan sees the version in the [apocryphal] *Gospel of Thomas* as closer to Jesus' original style, the majority of authors (Montefiore, Schürmann, Scott) see it as an abbreviated story that has lost the vitality it had in Luke. The ending (v. 21) was edited by the gospel writer, and does not convey the original meaning of the parable.

A rich landholder, owner of a great deal of land[22], is surprised by a harvest that exceeds all his expectations. His fields have produced so spectacularly that his granaries are too small to store the grain and other products. That is surprising, because ordinarily the large landowners had silos, granaries and warehouses well calculated to meet their storage needs[23]. «What shall I do?» he asks in view of this unexpected problem. Jesus' listeners are also wondering, what will he do? Such a bountiful harvest is a kind of miracle, a blessing from God. According to Israel's religious tradition Joseph, the Egyptian pharaoh's administrator, had stored grain so that the people would not die of hunger in a time of scarcity[24]. Would this landowner do something like that? Would he think about the laborers who work his land? Would he have compassion on the hungry?

The rich man makes the decision one expects of a powerful man: not to add one more granary to the ones he already has, but to destroy them all and build newer, larger ones. He isn't thinking about his workers or about the dispossessed and hungry. He alone will enjoy that unexpected harvest, a true blessing from God. From now on he will «relax, eat, drink, and feast [NRSV: be merry]»[25]. That is the smartest thing to do. The poor people listening to Jesus think differently. The man is inhuman and cruel: couldn't he give a thought to the hungry? Doesn't he know that by keeping the harvest for himself alone, he is depriving others of what they need to live? Don't they have a right to enjoy the harvest that God has bestowed on the land of Israel?[26]

God intervenes in an unexpected way. His words are harsh. That rich man will not enjoy his wealth. He will die in his sleep that night. His act is typical of the «fool» who ignores God and forgets other human beings. Jesus ends his parable with God's question, with which his hearers can identify: «Whose will they be?» The poor who have gathered around Jesus have no doubt about the answer. The crops with which God blesses the fields of Israel, do they not belong first to those who need bread in order to go on living?

22 The story uses the word *jora*, which does not mean just a piece of land but a region. It describes the large expanses of land accumulated by landowners who live in the city.

23 Underground chambers have been discovered in Sepphoris for the storage of wheat and other products from the fertile valley of Beth Netophah. They were undoubtedly used by landowners to assure their welfare and speculate on prices in times of scarcity (Freyne).

24 Gen 41:35-36.

25 The rich man's word has a typically epicurean tone. The hedonist philosophy of Epicurus was familiar to the urban elites.

26 The rich man does not realize that the goods of the earth are limited. If he keeps the harvest for himself, others will go hungry.

Jesus' parable is a challenge to the whole system. The rich man in the story is not a monster. He is acting like the other rich people in Sepphoris or Tiberias, who think only of themselves and their own welfare. It is always like that: the powerful accumulate goods, while the dispossessed sink deeper and deeper into misery. This state of things, Jesus is saying, is foolishness that destroys the weak and does not give security to the powerful. To enter the reign of God, the rich would have to look at those who suffer misery and hunger.

The gospel of Matthew has an impressive story that speaks of help for those in need as the criterion that will decide the final destiny of all people. The narrative combines a grandiose description of judgment on «all the nations», gathered before their king, with a simple pastoral scene that occurred every evening when the shepherds brought in their flocks[27].

When the Son of Man comes in his glory, and all the angels with him, then he will sit on the throne of his glory. All the nations will be gathered before him, and he will separate people one from another as a shepherd separates the sheep from the goats, and he will put the sheep at his right hand and the goats at the left.

189

Then the king will say to those at his right hand, «Come, you that are blessed by my Father, inherit the kingdom prepared for you from the foundation of the world; for I was hungry and you gave me food, I was thirsty and you gave me something to drink, I was a stranger and you welcomed me, I was naked and you gave me clothing, I was sick and you took care of me, I was in prison and you visited me». Then the righteous will answer him, «Lord, when was it that we saw you hungry and gave you food, or thirsty and gave you something to drink? And when was it that we saw you a stranger and welcomed you, or naked and gave you clothing? And when was it that we saw you sick or in prison and visited you» And the king will answer them, «Truly I tell you, just as you did it to one of the least of these who are members of my family, you did it to me».

Then he will say to those at his left hand, «You that are accursed, depart from me into the eternal fire prepared for the devil and his angels; for I was hungry and you gave me no food, I was thirsty and you gave me nothing to drink, I was a stranger and

27 This is traditionally called the parable of the «last judgment» or «the shepherd separating the sheep from the goats». The text is widely debated today: can Jesus' parable be understood apart from Matthew's editorial effort? What remains of Jesus' original message? Do «the least of these who are members of my family» represent Jesus' disciples, or all the poor and needy people in general? Is the story about judgment on all the nations of the world, or only about the behavior of «pagan nations» toward the Christian missionaries?

you did not welcome me, naked and you did not give me clothing, sick and in prison and you did not visit me».

Then they also will answer, «Lord, when was it that we saw you hungry or thirsty or a stranger or naked or sick or in prison, and did not take care of you?» Then he will answer them, «Truly I tell you, just as you did not do it to one of the least of these, you did not do it to me».

And these will go away into eternal punishment, but the righteous into eternal life[28].

It is a grandiose scene. The Son of Man arrives as a king with his cortege, «and all the angels with him», and sits on «the throne of his glory». The assembly of «all the nations» comes before him. This is the moment of truth. There are people from every race and nation, every culture and religion, every generation from all times. All the inhabitants of the earth, Israel, and the Gentile nations will hear the final verdict[29].

The king begins by separating them into two groups, as shepherds did with their flock: on one side the sheep, which are best left outdoors at night; on the other the goats, who must be sheltered against the cold of the night. The king and shepherd of all the nations holds a revealing dialogue with each group. He invites the first group: "Come, you that are blessed by my Father"; they are the men and women God has blessed to «inherit the kingdom prepared for you from the foundation of the world». To the second group he says, «You that are accursed, depart from me», without God's blessing and without God's reign[30]. Actually this is not a real judicial sentence. Each group goes to the place it has chosen. Those whose lives were oriented to love and mercy come to the love and mercy of God. Those who excluded people in need from their lives have excluded themselves from God's kingdom, where there is only acceptance and love.

The criterion separating the two groups is precise and clear: some have responded with compassion to those in need, while others have lived in indifference to their suffering. The king mentions six basic and fundamental situations of need. They are not hypothetical cases, but situations that everyone recognizes, which occur in all places and times. Everywhere there are hungry and thirsty

---

28 Matt 25:31-46. Many recent scholars consider this a composition by Matthew, formulated in the Christian community after the Resurrection (Funk, Crossan, Scott). I agree with the position of scholars like Jeremias, McBride, Wenham, France, and others, who seek to convey the basic content that may have come from Jesus.

29 This scene was probably composed by Matthew, based on the great vision of Dan 7:9-28.

30 However he does not say «accursed by my Father»; Jesus' Father never curses anyone.

people; there are immigrants and people without clothing; there are sick people and prisoners. The story does not use fancy words about justice and solidarity, but speaks of food, clothing, something to drink, protection from the elements. It doesn't recommend «love», but specific actions like «giving», «welcoming», «visiting», «taking care of». What matters is not a theoretical love, but compassion that helps the person in need.

The surprise comes when the king tells them: «just as you did it to one of the least of these who are members of my family, you did it to me». The first group is surprised because they never saw the king in these hungry, sick or imprisoned people; they were only thinking of those people's suffering. Their surprise is shared by the second group: it has never occurred to them that they were turning their backs on their king. But he insists that he was present in the suffering of «the least of these». What they did to them they were doing to him[31].

Those whom Jesus calls «blessed by my Father» were not acting out of religious motives, but out of compassion. It is not their religion or their explicit loyalty to Jesus that leads them into God's reign, but their help to people in need. The road that leads to God does not necessarily pass through religion, worship or a confession of faith, but through compassion toward «the least of these»[32]. The «last judgment» scene probably was not described this way by Jesus. It is not consistent with his style or his language. But no one can doubt that its message conveys the point of Jesus' whole message and activity. We can say with total confidence that «the great religious revolution» Jesus carried out was to open another way to God, different from the way of holiness: helping a brother in need. Religion does not have a monopoly on salvation; the surest way is to help the needy. Many men and women who do not know Jesus are taking that route.

31 Of course this way of describing Christ's presence in the suffering people was only possible when the Christian communities believed in Jesus, crucified by the Roman authorities and the temple representatives, but resurrected by God to a new life.

32 According to some scholars, Jesus was not talking about help to just anyone in need, but about «the least of these who are members of my family», that is, the disciples with whom he identified. That interpretation is supported especially by Matt 10:40-42. But it does not explain the people's surprise in this case: they could hardly have offered help to Jesus' disciples without knowing who they were. Also, Matt 10:40-42 specifically promises a reward for helping the disciples as such. Here they are rewarded simply for helping people in need.

Dignity for the undesirable

Jesus: An Historical Approximation

The lowest stratum of Galilean society, the indigents, not only lack everything; they are also condemned to living in shame, totally deprived of honor and dignity. They cannot take pride in belonging to a respectable family; they have been unable to defend their land; they cannot earn a living with a decent job. They are the undesirables, scorned by everyone. And they know it. Most Galilean beggars made their pleas from the ground, not even daring to raise their eyes; for the sake of survival, prostitutes gave up their sexual honor as women which was so highly valued in that society. Once they have lost their honor, these men and women can never get it back. Their fate is to live in degradation. They are nobodies. If they disappeared, no one would miss them[33].

The dishonor and indignity of these people was further aggravated by the prevailing system of ritual purity, which accentuated the existing discrimination within Jewish society. Ever since the invasion of the Hellenic culture, promoted by Alexander the Great, the Jews had been forced to defend their identity any way they could. Everyone understood that they could only survive by reaffirming unconditional loyalty to the law and the temple, and by observing a policy of separation from everything pagan. It was a matter of life and death.

This led to the development of a religious dynamic of «separation», in order to preserve the holiness that marked the people of God. The temple of Yahweh, the holiest of all places, must be protected from all contamination by excluding Gentiles and the ritually impure from its sacred spaces. Strict observation of the law was the best way to live in God's holy land, avoiding assimilation by foreign cultures. For this reason they emphasized keeping sabbath, the primary mark of Israel's identity in the midst of the peoples of the Empire; intermarriage was strictly forbidden; the payment of tithes and first-fruit offerings was given great importance. The «purity code» established in the law was enforced as a strategy of separation from whatever was impure, unholy, far from God[34].

---

33 Honor and shame were central categories in the Mediterranean societies of the first century (Malina, Rohrbaugh). Economic misery was experienced primarily as shame, indignity and dishonor.

34 The «purity code» is the collection of norms and prescriptions in the book of Lev 19-26. It was edited by the priestly circles of the temple, and insisted on separation from everything impure as a condition for access to the holy God.

In Jesus' time everyone accepted the central affirmation of this code of holiness, a command attributed to God: «You shall be holy, for I the Lord your God am holy»[35]. Everyone understood «holiness» to mean strict separation from everything impure. Some groups and sectors pursued it extremely rigorously. The Essenes of the Qumran community went so far as to leave the promised land in order to create a «holy community» in the middle of the desert. It was no longer possible, they said, to live a holy life in such a contaminated society. Only in the desert, dressed in white tunics and devoted to all kinds of purification, could they live as «men of holiness» and «sons of light», faithful to the holy God, separated both from the pagan Romans and from Jews who did not live in purity. The Pharisees generally did not go to such extremes, but the most radical groups tried to observe some purity laws that applied only to priests[36]. Apparently their goal was to turn the promised land into a kind of temple inhabited by the holy God, and to make the whole people a «priestly kingdom»[37]. Apparently they did not exclude from the Covenant everyone who did not meet their standard of purity, but they lived more or less «separate» from them, and certainly did not eat with them.

The system of ritual purity was intended to protect Jewish identity from the pagan culture, but it had another, perhaps unforeseen consequence: it hardened the differences and discrimination existing among the people themselves. Priests and Levites were born into a higher rank of holiness than other people; those who followed the holiness code enjoyed greater dignity than the impure. Among these were the people who lived in contact with pagans, or whose professions (for instance tax collectors and prostitutes) entailed regular transgressions of the code; lepers, eunuchs, the blind and crippled, who ranked lower than healthy people on the purity scale; and women, always at risk of impurity through menstruation or childbirth, naturally belonged to a lower level of dignity and holiness than men[38].

35 Lev 19:2.
36 We have little reliable information about the Pharisees before the year 70; apparently they were not all like the *haberim*, a radical minority group that sought to extend «priestly purity» to the whole people of Israel (Sanders).
37 Their goal was based on concepts similar to this from the book of Numbers: «You shall not defile the land in which you live, in which I also dwell; for I the Lord dwell among the Israelites» (35:34).
38 Borg has forcefully underlined the discriminatory nature of Jewish society, structured on the basis of purity. However, his affirmations should be modified by Sanders' recent observations: 1) most impurities did not stem from violations of the law; 2) falling into a state of ritual impurity did not automatically turn the person into a sinner; 3) contact with an impure person is not

One expects that in this type of society, where a person's degree of purity or impurity is a ritual matter, those who are socially disapproved of and devalued are broadly viewed as an «impure» sector, far away from the holy God of the temple. They are dirty, and many of them are sick, their skin covered with sores like Lazarus'. Among them are beggars, blind people, and prostitutes. Their life as vagabonds prevents most of them from meeting the requirements of purity and ritual purification. They have enough trouble getting something to eat. Their exclusion from the temple seems to show that God has rejected them. No one wants to be near dirty and disagreeable people; surely God doesn't, either.

That's not how Jesus sees it. In contrast to the command of the holiness code, «You shall be holy, for I the Lord your God am holy», he introduces a different requirement that radically transforms our way of understanding and living the «imitation» of God: «Be merciful, just as your Father is merciful»[39]. It is God's compassion, not his holiness, that we are to imitate. Jesus does not deny God's «holiness», but he defines holiness as compassionate love, not as separation from everything impure. God is great and holy, not because he is separated from impurity, but because he is compassionate toward all and «makes his sun rise on the evil and on the good, and sends rain on the righteous and on the unrighteous»[40]. Compassion is God's way of being, his first response to human beings, what comes from the «bowels» of the Father. God is compassion and «intestinal» love for all, including the impure, the dishonored, the people excluded from his temple[41]. For Jesus, compassion is the way to imitate God and to be holy as God is. To look on people with compassionate love is to be like God; to help the suffering is to act like God.

Thus Jesus is introducing a true revolution. The «holiness code» led to a discriminatory and exclusive society. Jesus is proposing a «compassion code» which would lead to a compassionate society, welcoming and inclusive even toward

a sin, although it should be avoided so the impurity will not spread further; 4) the purity laws regulate access to the temple, but not commensality (table hospitality); those who do not observe the holiness code or who never practice the rites of purification can be considered «sinners» for devaluing the law of Moses.

39 These words of Jesus appear in the Q Source (Luke 6:36; Matt 5:48). Matthew renders it as «Be perfect, therefore, as your heavenly Father is perfect». It is not clear which of the two evangelists more accurately reflects Jesus' original words. In any case they are not very different if we consider the context in Matthew, where Jesus was talking about loving one's enemy.

40 Matt 5:45.

41 The meaning of «compassion» is expressed in Aramaic as *rahamim*, which means «bowels». It is what a woman feels toward the child she carries in her womb. The word can also suggest «giving life», «nourishing», «caring for».

those dishonored, disreputable sectors. The God Jesus knows does not encourage separation and exclusion but welcome, embrace, and hospitality. In God's reign no one should be humiliated, excluded or separated from the community. The impure and the dishonored possess the sacred dignity of a child of God[42].

Compassionate love is behind all Jesus' activity, inspiring and shaping his whole life. For him compassion is not just another virtue, another attitude. His life is entwined with mercy: he aches with the people's suffering, makes it his, and turns it into the central principle of his activity. He is the first to live like the «father» in the parable who, «filled with compassion» (in his deepest bowels), embraces the son who comes back defeated by hunger and humiliation; or like the «Samaritan» who, «moved by pity», went to the aid of the man fallen by the wayside[43].

Jesus touches the lepers, allows the hemorrhagic woman to touch him and the prostitute to kiss him, and liberates those who were possessed by impure spirits. Nothing can keep him from coming close to those who suffer. His activity, inspired by compassion, is a direct challenge to the purity system. Perhaps he had a very specific vision: what is holy does not need to be protected from contamination by a strategy of separation; on the contrary, those who are truly holy can spread purity and transform the impure. When Jesus touches the leper, he does not become impure; the leper becomes pure.

5

Friend of sinners

Even more than his acceptance of the impure, it was his friendship with sinners that brought down scandal and hostility on Jesus. Nothing like this had ever happened in the history of Israel. Never had a prophet approached sinners with such respect, friendship and sympathy. What Jesus did was unheard of. People remembered the Baptist very differently. His main concern was to eradicate the sin that

---

42 In the Galilean cultural context, the language of the beatitudes is honorific language. Jesus attributes honor in God's eyes to those who cannot defend their dignity in human eyes (Malina/ Rohrbaugh). The first one could be translated: «How honorable you poor are, for you have God as your king!».

43 I use the words «mercy» and «compassion» interchangeably. Generally I prefer «compassion», perhaps because it suggests greater closeness, while «having mercy» can denote a relationship with someone at a lower level.

was contaminating the whole people and endangering the Covenant with God. It was the greatest evil and misfortune ever to fall on them. Their sin was upsetting God and provoking his «wrath»[44]. Could anything be more important than denouncing sinners, warning them of the punishment awaiting them, and offering a great rite of purification and penitence to bring them out of their sin?

The Baptist's approach didn't scandalize anyone. It was what they expected of a prophet, a defender of the people's Covenant with God. But Jesus' approach is surprising. He doesn't speak of sin as causing God's wrath. On the contrary, there is room in God's reign for sinners and prostitutes too. He doesn't address them in the name of a judge upset by such offenses, but shows them the Father's compassionate love. How can he associate with publicans and sinners without setting any conditions? How can a man of God accept them as friends? How dare he eat with them? This behavior is certainly Jesus' most provocative trait. Prophets don't act like that. Later on, the Christian communities would also have a hard time being so tolerant toward sinners[45].

Who were these sinners? In Jesus' time the word referred to a specific, recognizable group of people with clear sociological characteristics. They should not be confused with the ignorant masses who did not understand and therefore could not fully comply with the endless precepts of the law; nor with the many rural people who neglected to purify themselves properly after falling into a state of impurity. Nor should we arbitrarily count as sinners those included on the lists of occupations that were despised, especially by the most meticulous Pharisees[46]. Rather, «sinners» are people who have deliberately violated the Covenant, and who show no sign of repentance[47]. Not everyone deserves that description. «Sinners» are those who have rejected God's Covenant by radically disobeying the law: those who profane holy worship, who dishonor the great Day of Atonement, who collaborate with Rome in the oppression of the Jewish people, as well as usurers, swindlers, and prostitutes. They are seen as people who live outside the Covenant, who betray the God of Israel, and who are excluded from salvation. They are «the lost». They are the ones Jesus talks about in his parables[48].

---

44 Q Source (Luke 3:7; Matt 3:7).

45 1 Cor 5:1-13.

46 Studies carried out by Sanders have corrected the position of J. Jeremias, followed by many other experts, who identify as sinners the people who did not know the Law (*'am ha-'arets*), or who held dishonorable or stigmatized occupations. Only those whose behavior or occupation was seen as rejected by Israel's God were called «sinners».

47 Sanders believes the term «sinners» (in Hebrew, *resha'im*) should be translated as «evil ones».

48 For instance the parables of «the lost sheep», «the lost coin», «the prodigal son».

Along with sinners, the biblical sources constantly talk about another group: «publicans». Jesus is accused of eating with «sinners and tax collectors», and at least one tax collector belonged to his group of closest friends. Who are these «publicans» who are so closely associated with «sinners»? They should not be confused with the collectors of imperial tributes and direct taxes on land and farm products. That task was entrusted by Rome to prestigious, carefully selected families whose productivity was backed up by their fortune. Naturally these Roman fiscal bureaucrats carried out their task implacably, and at the same time sought to maximize their own profit.

The «publicans» in the gospels are the collectors of taxes on merchandise and transit rights through the major highways, bridges, or ports of some cities. There are also «chief tax collectors», who have gained control of these transit fees and customs duties in a given region[49], and work through their slaves and other subordinates who sit in the collection booths. As a group, these subordinate tax collectors have no better way to make a living. Their activity, like that of thieves and other dishonest people, is so shameful that it is sometimes assigned to slaves. It is these tax collectors that Jesus meets in his travels. They are a typical group of socially discredited sinners, much like «prostitutes» in female society[50].

Jesus also provoked scandal by associating with women of ill repute, from the lowest strata of the society. In the more important cities, the prostitutes worked in small brothels run by slaves; most prostitutes were also slaves, sometimes sold by their own fathers. The prostitutes who circulated in the villages were almost always repudiated wives or widows without a male protector, who looked for clients at parties and banquets. Apparently these were the prostitutes who came to meals organized in Jesus' circles.

What is scandalous is not that he associates with sinful and disreputable people, but that he sits with them at the dinner table. These meals with «sinners» are one of Jesus' most unique and surprising characteristics, perhaps the one that most distinguishes him from all his contemporaries and from the prophets and teachers of the past. Sinners are among his table companions; publicans and prostitutes are among his friends. Someone whom everyone considers a «man

---

49 The figure of the rich Zacchaeus has contributed to a widespread misperception of publicans. Luke carefully describes him as a «chief tax collector» (*arjitelonés*) in the region of Jericho, not as an ordinary tax collector seated in a collection booth.

50 It is significant that Matthew speaks of «the tax collectors and the prostitutes» together (21:31).

of God» would almost never do that[51]. It is certainly a provocative action, and an intentional one on Jesus' part. As a symbolic gesture it provoked an immediate reaction against him. The gospel writers faithfully report, first the surprise: «Why does he eat with tax collectors and sinners?»[52]. He doesn't keep a proper distance from them? How shameful! Then later the accusations, rejection and scorn: «Look, a glutton and a drunkard, a friend of tax collectors and sinners!»[53]. How dare he?

It is an explosive issue. To sit at table with someone is a sign of respect, trust, and friendship. One doesn't eat with just anyone; people eat with their own kind. Sharing the same table means belonging to the same group, and their differences with others are important. Gentiles eat with Gentiles, Jews with Jews, men with men, women with women, rich with rich, poor with poor[54]. One doesn't eat with just anyone, or just any way. This is especially important in view of the holiness of the true Israel. In the Qumran sect, meals were the center of community life; no one from outside the community could take part; the members themselves went through rigorous purification rites before sitting at the table; the meal followed a detailed ritual which established the place of each person in the hierarchical structure of the community. In radical Pharisaic groups the diners washed their hands before sitting down; the ritually impure were excluded, and the organizers had to ensure that the tithe had been paid on all the food to be served. Such table rules served to exclude outsiders, consolidate group identity, and demonstrate their vision of the true Israel.

Jesus surprises them all by sitting down to eat with just anyone. His table is open to everyone; no one feels left out. They don't have to be pure; they don't have to wash their hands[55]. Disreputable people can share his table, even sinners who forget the Covenant. Jesus doesn't exclude anyone. Everything will be different in God's reign: mercy takes the place of holiness. There's no need to gather at different tables. God's reign is an open table where even sinners can sit

---

51 Many authors consider this Jesus' most central and significant characteristic (Perrin, Fuchs, Jeremias, Vermes, Crossan, Aguirre, Borg).

52 Mark 2:16.

53 Q Source (Luke 7:34; Matt 11:9).

54 In almost every culture meals are a kind of «microcosm» that reveal what kind of society it is. What people eat, how, with whom, and where, all provide information about relationships, groups, traditions, and the nature of that society (Mary Douglas).

55 The practice of hand-washing is not a biblical law. It was probably gaining currency among the more fanatical groups in Jesus' time. It apparently was not very controversial in itself.

down and eat[56]. Jesus wants to show everyone what he experiences in his heart by sitting to eat with publicans, sinners, beggars, people recently cured of their illness, or people of doubtful morality. He tells them the parable of a man who held a great banquet and wouldn't stop until his house was filled with guests:

> Someone gave a great dinner and invited many. At the time for the dinner he sent his slave to say to those who had been invited, «Come, for everything is ready now». But they all alike began to make excuses. The first said to him, «I have bought a piece of land, and I must go out and see it; please accept my regrets». Another said, «I have bought five yoke of oxen, and I am going to try them out; please accept my regrets». Another said, «I have just been married, and therefore I cannot come».
>
> So the slave returned and reported this to his master. Then the owner of the house became angry and said to his slave, «Go out at once into the streets and lanes of the town and bring in the poor, the crippled, the blind, and the lame». And the slave said, «Sir, what you ordered has been done, and there is still room». Then the master said to the slave, «Go out into the roads and lanes, and compel people to come in, so that my house may be filled. For I tell you, none of those who were invited will taste my dinner»[57].

Jesus starts out talking about a «great dinner» that someone has organized. He is almost certainly a rich man. Naturally he doesn't invite just anyone. He invites his own kind, his rich and influential friends. The banquet will help strengthen their bonds of friendship and solidarity. Eating with such people will build up the host's honor, and they can also ensure his future success and patronage. Jesus' hearers know they will never be able to share in a banquet like that. The invitations are issued in advance. That way there will be time to prepare the dinner, and the guests can find out more about the party and the other people who will come. On the big day, the host again sends his servant to confirm the invitation: «Come, for everything is ready now». Rich people usually extend that kind of courtesy to one another.

---

56 Later the Christian community will follow Jesus' example by welcoming pagans into their midst.
57 This parable is found in Luke 14:16-24; Matt 22:2-13; and the [apocryphal] *Gospel of Thomas* 64:1-2. It comes from Jesus. Matthew, writing after the destruction of Jerusalem in 70 A.D., turned it into an allegory on the history of salvation. Although some see the version in the [apocryphal] *Gospel of Thomas* as an earlier version (Fitzmyer, Crossan), it is generally thought that the Lucan text brings us closer to Jesus' thinking. Probably v. 24 («For I tell you, none of those who were invited will taste my dinner») was added by the gospel writer.

Surprisingly, every one of them has an excuse. Their reasons vary. One says he has bought a field and wants to go see it, but who would buy a field in a region of such uneven quality, without first seeing how it looks and what it will produce? Another says he has bought ten oxen and wants to try them out, but who buys oxen without first seeing how strong they are and how well they work together? Another has just gotten married and naturally cannot attend, but didn't he know when he got the invitation that he would be getting married? The servant sees that no one is coming to the dinner. How can they leave their host alone and humiliated? Are their affairs and interests that important? Jesus' hearers must have been thinking the same thing: if they ever got an invitation like that, they'd be happy to go.

The lord in the parable has an unexpected reaction. One way or another, there will be a banquet. Suddenly he has a novel idea. He will invite people who are never invited to anything: «the poor, the crippled, the blind, and the lame», miserable people who have no honor to give him[58]. In order to call them, the servant will have to go into the «streets and lanes» of the poor neighborhoods in the city, far from the part of the city reserved for the elite. Jesus' hearers are surprised: What kind of dinner is that, where all the rules of honor and the purity codes are broken? They are even more surprised when the host gives another order: the servant must go out of the city, into «the roads and lanes» between the farms, and invite all the people who live as best they can outside the walls. Most of them are foreigners and disreputable people; they do not live in the city but are not peasants either. The servant is told to «compel people to come in» to the house, because otherwise they would not dare go into the elite neighborhood of the city.

What is Jesus saying? Who on earth would hold a banquet for everyone without guest lists, rules of honor and purity codes, where even strangers are invited in? Is God's reign like that? A table open to everyone without conditions: men and women, pure and impure, good and evil? A party where God is surrounded by poor people and undesirables, totally lacking in dignity and honor?

Jesus' message is incredibly seductive. But he speaks with total certainty: God is like that. He doesn't want to live forever in an «empty hall». A great celebration has been prepared for everyone, because God sees them all as his friends, wor-

58 The Qumran community excluded from its assembly precisely «those whose flesh is tainted, the crippled, blind, deaf, mute, or tainted in the flesh by a stain that the eye can see» (1Q Regla de la Congregación II:5-22 [English: *Rule of the Congregation*]).

thy to share his table. God's greatest joy is to share life with the poor and contemptible, the undesirables and sinners. Jesus is already doing that, by joyfully sharing meals with those who are scorned and marginalized by society. Those who have never been invited by anyone, will one day sit at God's table!

6

The forgiveness Jesus offers

Jesus sees and experiences these meals with sinners as a kind of healing. When he is admonished for his strange and provocative behavior, he replies with this saying: «Those who are well have no need of a physician, but those who are sick»[59]. These meals are therapeutic. Jesus offers his trust and friendship, frees the people from shame and humiliation, rescues them from their marginalization, accepts them as friends. Little by little they gain a sense of their own dignity: they do not deserve to be rejected by anyone. For the first time they feel accepted by a man of God. Their life may never be the same.

This is what makes these meals joyful and festive. They drink wine, and probably sing[60]. Deep in his heart, Jesus is rejoicing over the return of «the lost» to communion with the Father. They too are sons and daughters of Abraham. Jesus' happiness spreads to everyone. It is impossible to be sad in his company. That would be as absurd as fasting with the groom at his wedding[61]. Of course these are not Dionysian orgies, such as may have occurred in Sepphoris or Tiberias[62]. Jesus is not supporting libertinism. He does not justify sin, corruption, or prostitution. What he does is to break the vicious circle of discrimination, by opening up new space for a friendly encounter with God.

Jesus sits at the table with sinners, not as a severe judge but as a reassuring friend. Grace comes before judgment in God's reign. God is good news, not a threat. Sinners and prostitutes can rejoice, drink wine and sing with Jesus. These meals are a true «miracle» that is healing them from within. They begin to sense that

---

59 Researchers believe that this response is authentically Jesus' style (Mark 2:17a). However the words that follow may have been added later in the Christian community: «I have come to call not the righteous but sinners» (Mark 2:17b).

60 Wine was drunk at festive meals, and Jesus was called a «drinker of wine [NRSV: drunkard]» (Luke 7:33; Matt 11:19).

61 Mark 2:18-19.

62 Are Jesus' accusers perhaps trying to discredit his meals with sinners, by comparing them with Dionysian orgies? (S. Freyne).

God is not a sinister judge who waits for them in anger, but a friend who comes to them offering friendship. Jesus' acceptance gives these women and men the strength to recognize their own sinfulness. They have nothing to fear. Their social humiliation and exclusion had kept them from trusting God; Jesus' acceptance gives them back their lost dignity. They don't need to hide from anyone, not even from themselves. They can open themselves to God's life-changing forgiveness. Jesus makes it all possible.

The Christian sources give us two scenes in which Jesus solemnly offers forgiveness in God's name. In one moving scene at Capernaum, seeing a paralyzed man at his feet unable to walk, Jesus says with special tenderness: «Son, your sins are forgiven»[63]. In an equally moving scene with a prostitute who is anointing his feet amid tears, kisses and caresses, he speaks these words: «Your sins are forgiven»[64].

In the Jewish way of thinking, this behavior by Jesus was scandalous and blasphemous. We can certainly understand the scribes' accusation: «Who can forgive sins but God alone?»[65] Jesus answers firmly and clearly: «But so that you may know that the Son of Man has authority on earth to forgive sins» —he said to the paralytic— «I say to you, stand up, take your mat and go to your home»[66]. Jesus is not acting as a prophet or a priest, who declares in God's name that the sinner has been forgiven; rather he is acting as the «Son of Man» who has power on earth to forgive sins[67].

In speaking of Jesus' meals with sinners, the gospel sources never show Jesus offering God's forgiveness in a formula. We don't know whether he used one. Jesus acts as a close «friend» who accepts them at his table, offers them friendship, heals their lives of unworthiness, and turns them toward God. His behavior reflects the attitude of the same merciful God whom he describes in his parables as a father who puts on a festive banquet to welcome his lost son home, or as a shepherd who celebrates with his friends when he finds his lost sheep[68].

---

63 Mark 2:5.

64 Luke 7:48.

65 Mark 2:7.

66 Mark 2:11. Here Jesus is using language from Daniel 7:14, where God gives the Son of Man power (dominion, glory, kingship) to rule over the nations of the earth.

67 Although some scholars doubt that Jesus used this language to offer God's forgiveness, the similarity of the formulas used in both Judaism and the Christian communities does seem to support its authenticity (Broer, Schlosser).

68 Luke 15:4-31. J. Gnilka describes Jesus' behavior this way: «Forgiveness happens not so much through words as through the overt acceptance of the person being forgiven, through his or her effective rehabilitation, and through the new beginning that comes from restored communion».

It was probably especially at these meals that people learned to pray to God with the Lord's Prayer[69]. Calling on God as a Father, while they eat and drink together in Jesus' company, is a new experience that begins to heal them from the inside and helps them to return to God, whom they are beginning to sense as a Father. Little by little, with Jesus' encouragement, they begin to call him *Abba*, bless his holy name, and ask him to fulfill Jesus' great wish in them: «Your kingdom come». These men and women, scorned by almost everyone, are not thinking sublime thoughts. Jesus teaches them to be realistic. They ask for bread: that no one should go without a piece of bread every day, at least barley bread. They also ask for forgiveness, and are themselves willing to forgive and set aside the instincts of vengeance and resentment that rise up in their heart. They are not only thinking of God's reign as coming some day to free the world from evil. They ask for a chance to experience the arrival of God the Father right now, in order to live as God's sons and daughters: with a piece of bread to put in their mouths and with the strength to accept and forgive one another. Thus, eating and drinking with Jesus, these «lost» begin to experience God coming into their lives not with «great signs from heaven», as some wanted, but as compassionate strength that heals and transforms them. In Jesus' company they are entering a new world they have never dreamed of. He calls it «the reign of God».

7

Undeserved forgiveness

ℰℐℴ

Why did Jesus' way of offering sinners his acceptance and God's forgiveness provoke such scandal and indignation? What was so new about his way of acting? The Jewish people believed in the forgiveness of all sins, even homicide and apostasy. God can forgive anyone who repents. True, one had to follow a path. First, sinners must show repentance by making the appropriate sacrifices in the temple; they must abandon their life outside the Covenant and return to compliance with the law; finally they must make restitution or reparation for the harm

---

69 The Lord's Prayer is presented with no surrounding context in the Q source. Matthew later placed it with other sayings of Jesus in the Sermon on the Mount (Matt 6:9-13). Luke placed it in a scenario, probably of his own composition, in which Jesus «was praying in a certain place» when the disciples asked him to teach them to pray (Luke 11:1-4). Several scholars believe, based on the content of the prayer («give us bread», «forgive us»), that Jesus probably repeated it often at meals open to everyone (Breech).

and offense they have caused others. If Jesus had accepted sinners at his table in order to tell them to return to the Law, so that publicans and prostitutes would leave their sinful way of life, there would be no scandal. On the contrary, he would have been admired and applauded.

The surprise is that Jesus accepts sinners without first requiring repentance as it was traditionally understood, without even subjecting them to a penitential rite as the Baptist did. He offers his communion and friendship as a sign that God accepts them into his reign even before they return to the law and adhere to the Covenant. He accepts them as they are, sinners, trusting totally in God's mercy which is seeking them out. So Jesus was accused of being a friend of people who were still sinners. That was intolerable. How could he accept at his table people who were not reforming their lives as the Law requires, and assure them of their participation in God's reign?[70]

But Jesus' activity is very clear on this. He offers forgiveness without first requiring change. He brings them face to face, not with the tablets of the law but with God's love and tenderness. This is his personal therapy for the «lost» friends who have not found their way back to God through the law. He forgives them with no assurance that they will change their behavior in return[71]. He acts as a prophet of God's mercy. He is a friend of sinners before their conversion. That is God's way. God doesn't wait for his sons and daughters to change. He starts the process by offering them forgiveness.

The forgiveness Jesus offers is unconditional. His therapy doesn't follow the path of the law: establish blame, call to repentance, bring about change, and offer forgiveness on condition of further positive response. Jesus follows the paths of God's reign: he offers acceptance and friendship, gives the gift of God's forgiveness, and trusts in God's mercy, which is able to recover his lost sons and daughters. He comes near, accepts them, and starts them on a way to God that continues by God's infinite mercy alone. Never on earth has there been a more hope-filled, more gratuitous, or more absolute sign of God's forgiveness.

---

70 This seems to have been the main reason Jesus provoked such scandal and conflict (Sanders, Fredriksen). Apparently the Baptist stayed closer to the tradition, for his attitude toward sinners was not seen as scandalous.

71 There is a growing consensus that Luke was especially concerned with showing that Jesus brought about the repentance of sinners. Some examples are the scene with Zacchaeus (19:1-10), the scene with the sinful woman (7:36-50), and his additions to the parables of the shepherd with the lost sheep (15:7) and the woman with the lost coin (15:10).

Jesus brings everyone, unrighteous and righteous, to the bottomless well of God's forgiveness. There are no longer righteous people with special privileges, and sinners without privileges. Jesus has a different way. He offers everyone the reign of God; only those who do not accept God's mercy are excluded. He entrusts everything to the mystery of God's forgiveness. To his hearers, Jesus' message sounds like this: «When you are judged according to the law, know that you are understood by God; when you are rejected by society, know that God embraces you; when no one forgives your shame, feel God's inexhaustible forgiveness upon you. You don't deserve it. No one deserves it. But God is like that, love and forgiveness».

Jesus' main problem was whether or not morally righteous, legally correct people would understand his way of seeing things. The poor and the sick, the impure and sinners, the publicans and prostitutes understood him and accepted his message. For them, this God Jesus was talking about was the best kind of news. The Christian tradition gives us Jesus' response to those who resisted his message. Only he would have said it this way: «Truly I tell you, the tax collectors and the prostitutes are going into the kingdom of God ahead of you»[72].

72 Although these words are found only in Matthew 21:31, a majority of researchers see it as coming from Jesus. His friendship with publicans and prostitutes, the scandalous tone of the saying, and the strong contrast (like saying «the poor will enter the kingdom, but not the rich») are very like him. The text can be read two ways. One is strong and exclusive: the publicans and prostitutes will enter, but you will not. The other is gentle and not exclusive: they will enter first, you later (Jeremias).

A Friend of Women

Many of the poor people around Jesus were women. Those who lacked the protection of a man were certainly the most vulnerable, but in that patriarchal society all women were destined to a life of inferiority and subjection to men. Is this the will of the compassionate God of whom Jesus spoke? Couldn't women too achieve a life of dignity in God's reign? How does Jesus see and relate to women?

The first surprise is that there are so many women around Jesus. There are cherished friends like Mary, a woman from Magdala; two sisters from Bethany, Martha and Mary, whom he loved dearly; sick women like the one with a hemorrhage; pagans like the Syro-Phoenician woman; despised prostitutes; and faithful followers, like Salome and many others who went with him to Jerusalem and did not abandon him even at his execution. That had never been true of any Israelite prophet. What did these women see in Jesus? What was it that attracted them to him? How did they dare come to hear his message? Why did some of them leave their homes and follow him to Jerusalem, despite the scandal it would surely cause?[1].

1

The status of Jewish women

Jesus was born in a society whose collective consciousness had been shaped for centuries by stereotypes about women. As he grew up, Jesus saw those stereotypes in his own family, among his friends, and in daily life.

According to an ancient story, God had created woman only as a «helper» for the man. That was her destiny. But far from helping him, it was she who gave him the forbidden fruit to eat, thus provoking their expulsion from paradise[2]. Transmitted from generation to generation among the Jewish people, this story led to a negative view of women as a dangerous source of temptation and sin. It was always wise to treat them with great caution and keep them submissive[3]. That is what Jesus learned as a child.

1 To understand Jesus' relationship with women we must bear in mind three factors. First, all our sources of information are written by men, who naturally express a masculine experience and attitudes, which are different from what women felt and experienced in Jesus' presence. Second, the writers use generic, sexist language which «conceals» the women's presence: the «children» Jesus embraces included boys and girls, and there were men and women among his «disciples». Third, gospel commentators and scholars in the course of twenty centuries have imposed a traditional masculine reading on the text.

2 Gen 2:4-3:24. This story was written down around the ninth century B.C.

3 The Jewish wisdom literature repeatedly exhorts men to distrust women, and always to keep them under control (Ecclesiasticus [NRSV: Sirach] 25:13-26; 42:9-14; Prov 5:1-23; 9:13-18).

Another indisputable belief in that patriarchal society, dominated and controlled by men, was that women are the «property» of men. They belong first to their fathers; at marriage they belong to their husbands; if they become widows, they belong to their sons or return to their fathers and brothers. Autonomy is unthinkable in a woman. The holy Decalogue of Sinai classified women with the other properties of the man of the house: «You shall not covet your neighbor's house; you shall not covet your neighbor's wife; or male or female slave; or ox, or donkey, or anything that belongs to your neighbor»[4]. The social role of women was clearly defined: to bear children and faithfully serve the man.

Power over women was strongly enforced by the rules of sexual purity[5]. Women were ritually impure during menstruation and in the aftermath of childbirth. No one could come near an impure woman. Whoever and whatever they touched was contaminated. This is probably the main reason women were excluded from the priesthood, from full participation in worship, and from access to the most sacred areas of the temple. Women were a source of impurity. Jesus was surely warned about this as a child.

This negative view of women did not fade with the passage of the centuries. There are signs that it was even more negative and severe in Jesus' time[6]. Besides a temptation and occasion for sin, women were seen as frivolous, sensual, lazy, gossipy and disorderly. According to the Jewish writer Philo of Alexandria, a contemporary of Jesus, while men are guided by reason, women are carried away by sensuality. Flavius Josephus probably represents the generalized view in Jesus' time: «According to the Torah, the woman is inferior to the man in everything»[7].

On the other hand women were seen as vulnerable, needing male protection against sexual aggression by other men. Therefore they were kept at home, away from the sphere of public life. Men were responsible for the honor of the household and defended it publicly; women were responsible for their own reputation and for not shaming the family with dishonorable behavior. The safest way to guard their sexual honor was to keep them enclosed in the house. That way everyone in the villages could live in peace.

---

4 Exod 20:17
5 Lev 15:19-30.
6 The rabbinic literature is generally very negative toward women. However, since we are not sure when the rabbinic literature began, it does not take us back with any certainty to the time of Jesus.
7 Flavius Josephus, *Contra Apión* II, 201(English: *Against Apion*).

At her marriage a woman left her own family and was transferred, often without her consent, from the father's to the husband's authority. From then on her whole life was devoted to his service; he was called *ba'ali*, «my lord». Her duties were always the same: to grind wheat, bake bread, cook, spin, weave, and wash the man's face, hands and feet. Naturally her first duty was to satisfy him sexually and give him male children to ensure the survival of the family. However, women apparently had great influence within the family: many men respected and praised them as the mothers of their children. It was surely women who safeguarded the family and religious environment within the home[8].

Outside the home, women did not «exist». They could not leave the house without being accompanied by a man, and without hiding their faces behind a veil. They were not allowed to speak with men in public. They must be always withdrawn and silent. They did not have the rights men enjoyed. They could not take part in banquets. Except in clearly defined cases their testimony was not accepted as valid, or it carried less weight than a man's. In reality they had no place in social life. For a woman to leave the house alone, without a man's supervision, taking part in meals or activities reserved for men, was seen as wayward behavior typical of women who neglected their reputation and their sexual honor. Jesus knew that when he accepted them into his circle.

Religious life too, controlled as it was by men, placed women in an inferior status. They only had a role in family celebrations: lighting the candles, reciting certain prayers, and attending to some ritual details of the sabbath feast. In everything else their presence was secondary. Women were separated from men both in the temple and, probably, in the synagogue. The purity rules, rigidly interpreted, allowed them access only to the space set aside for pagans and women.

Men were the real «agents» in the Jewish religion; remember that circumcision was the rite that confirmed membership in the Covenant people. Women did not have the same dignity before the law that men had. Like men they were bound by all its prohibitions, but were not seen as active subjects of the people's religious life. They were not required to recite the *Shema*, Israel's official confession of faith, every day, or to make pilgrimages to Jerusalem for the feasts of Passover, Pentecost, or Booths. They weren't needed there. Only men were needed to maintain relations with God; everything was directed by the temple priests and the

---

8   We see great praise for women in the rabbinic literature after Jesus' time: «The world becomes more gloomy for the man who loses his wife» (Rabbi Alexandri); «The man without a wife does not know the good; he lives without help, without happiness, without blessing...» (Rabbi Jacob).

scribes of the law. For the same reason women did not need to be initiated in the Torah; they were not required to study the law, and the scribes did not accept them as disciples. There is a surprising harshness in some rabbinic sayings, which were written some time after Jesus but may still reflect the experience of his time: «Whoever teaches the Torah to his daughter teaches libertinism, because she will make bad use of what she learns»; «Better to burn the words of Torah than to entrust them to a woman»[9].

Thus without true autonomy, servants of their own husbands, kept inside their homes, always suspected of ritual impurity, religiously and juridically inferior, Jewish women were a profoundly marginalized sector of Jewish society[10]. Significantly, Rabbi Yehuda recommended the following prayer for daily recitation by men: «Blessed are you, Lord, for you have not created me a pagan, or made me a woman or an ignorant person». But was this God's will? What did the prophet think as he proclaimed God's compassionate love? What could women expect from the arrival of God's reign?

2

Friend of the last women

The women around Jesus generally belonged to the lowest sector of that society. Jesus had healed many of them, like Mary of Magdala[11]. Probably some of them had no male protector: defenseless widows, repudiated wives, and other single women without resources, without respect, and of ill repute. There were also some prostitutes, whom everyone saw as the worst sources of impurity and contamination. Jesus accepted them all[12].

---

9 However, some other sayings do encourage parents to teach Torah to their daughters.

10 There is reason to believe that customs in the small towns of Galilee were less strict than the rabbinic texts would indicate. Women left their houses more freely, worked in the fields with men and boys, and did not always cover their faces with a veil (Witherington III, Elisabeth Meier).

11 Luke 8:2.

12 Along with Mary Magdalene Luke mentions «Joanna, the wife of Herod's steward Chuza, and Susanna, and many others, who provided for them out of their resources» (8:3). It is hard to imagine rich matrons traveling around Galilee and supporting the group economically. Some scholars suspect that this information, which appears only in Luke, was probably offered by Luke to anticipate the conversion of those «distinguished women» referred to in the Acts of the Apostles 17:4-12 (Schüssler Fiorenza, Fitzmyer, Schweizer, Corley; Meier disagrees).

These women are among the sinners and undesirables who sit at Jesus' table. It is not the «holy table» at which the «holy men» of the Qumran community eat, where all women are excluded. Nor is it the «pure table» of the most radical sectors of Pharisees, who observe the same purity rites as priests when they eat[13]. For Jesus these meals are a symbol and foretaste of God's reign. With him they can already see that the «last» in the holy nation and the «last women» in that patriarchal society are the «first» to enter the reign of God[14].

The presence of these women at Jesus' meals was probably part of the scandal. Women who went out without husbands, in the company of men, were assumed to be at the disposal of any dinner guest[15]. The tax collectors were also notorious for their contact with the world of prostitution. Some of them ran small brothels or provided women for the banquets[16]. Jesus is not shocked, and does not condemn them. He accepts them with his Father's love and understanding. These women have never been so close to a prophet. They have never heard anyone talk about God that way. Some weep with gratitude. It's not hard for his adversaries to discredit him for ignoring the law, for being a «friend of sinful women». Once Jesus challenged them boldly: «the tax collectors and the prostitutes are going into the kingdom of God ahead of you»[17].

Even the «purity code» did not discourage Jesus from being close to women. The prescriptions of this code were apparently applied more strictly to women than to men[18]. During menstruation women are in a state of impurity for seven days; after childbirth, forty days if the baby is a boy and eighty if it is a girl. Indeed, «ritual impurity» is almost a permanent condition for women. It is hard to know how they experienced it, and what practical consequences it had in their daily life. Perhaps the worst effect was their sense of inferiority and of distance from the holy God who lives in the temple[19].

13 We do not know whether the Pharisees admitted women to special festive meals.

14 The gospel writers speak of «sinners», but the word clearly includes «sinful women» as well.

15 This explains the nervousness of Simon the Pharisee when a town prostitute approached Jesus at the height of the banquet, with gestures and attitudes that Simon saw as typical of a «sinful woman». Luke presents the story very carefully (7:36-50).

16 Kathleen E. Corley has shown in detail, both the suspicion of promiscuity that shadowed women who ate at public banquets and the links between tax collectors and prostitutes.

17 Matt 21:31. These words seem to confirm the close link that existed between «tax collectors» and «prostitutes». Jesus' acceptance of them must have caused a scandal.

18 This is Neusner's conclusion.

19 Sanders thinks, probably rightly, that scholars in general have exaggerated the repercussions of «ritual impurity».

Jesus does not go out of his way to criticize the «purity code». He never gets involved in issues of sex and ritual purity. That's not his problem. He simply starts acting with total freedom, out of his experience with God's reign. He doesn't look at women as a source of temptation or possible contamination. He approaches them without hesitancy and relates to them openly, without being affected by any prejudices. Women must have been attracted to his presence. For many it meant being free, at least for the moment, from the life of marginalization and work they led at home. Some even dared to follow him on the Galilean paths. These were probably single, unfortunate women who saw Jesus' travels as a way of living with greater dignity[20].

3
Breaking the mold

Certainly women see in him a different attitude. They never hear from him the disrespectful views that the rabbis would later express. He never exhorts them to be submissive to their husbands or to the patriarchal system. Jesus shows no animosity or carefulness toward them. Only respect, compassion, and unexpected sympathy.

Perhaps most surprising is his simple, natural way of defining the significance of woman, from his experience of God; he sets aside the prevailing stereotypes of that society. For example he does not accept the thoughtless view of women as a source of temptation and occasion of sin for men. Against the general tendency, he never warns men against the seductive arts of women but calls attention to their own lust: «everyone who looks at a woman with lust has already committed adultery with her in his heart»[21]. In a society that sees a man's lust as less serious than a woman's seductiveness, Jesus emphasizes the man's responsibility. They can't excuse themselves by blaming women for misbehaving.

Jesus also corrects the assumption that a woman's main task is to bear children. One exchange reported in the tradition has a strong Mediterranean flavor[22]. In that case a village woman expresses her admiration of Jesus by praising his mother

---

20 This is the opinion of scholars like Freyne, Corley, and Witherington III.
21 Matt 5:28.
22 Luke 11:27-28; [apocryphal] *Gospel of Thomas* 79:1-3. It is never easy to ascertain the historicity of this kind of episode. Certainly Jesus' reply reflects a conviction typical of him: those who fulfill God's will are his true family (Mark 3:35).

for the only female traits that mattered in that culture: a fertile womb and breasts to nurse her children. Jesus sees it differently; childbearing is not everything. As important as motherhood is to a woman, there is something even more important: «Blessed rather are those who hear the word of God and obey it!» A woman's dignity, like that of a man, stems from her ability to hear the message of God's reign and enter into it.

Another time, in the home of his friends Martha and Mary, we hear of Jesus correcting the generalized expectation that women should devote themselves exclusively to household tasks. Martha is determined to give Jesus a proper reception, while her sister Mary stays seated at his feet, listening to his words. When Martha asks for Mary's help, Jesus answers her: «Martha, Martha, you are worried and distracted by many things; there is need of only one thing. Mary has chosen the better part, which will not be taken away from her»[23]. Women should not be limited to household chores. They have the same right as men to the better part, which is hearing the Word of God.

In another captivating moment, Jesus reacts boldly to the moral double standard by which men and women are judged unequally[24]. They bring to Jesus a woman caught in a sexual act with a man. Nothing is said about the man. This usually happens in a society dominated by male supremacy. The woman is humiliated and condemned for dishonoring her family. Meanwhile no one mentions the man, although paradoxically, it is men who are exhorted by Torah not to possess or desire another man's wife[25]. The law is addressed to men as the ones responsible for society, but the punishment falls harshly on the women. Jesus does not accept this social hypocrisy created by men. The woman is not more to blame than the man: «Let anyone among you who is without sin be the first to throw a stone at her»[26]. The accusers withdraw one by one, beginning with the

23 Luke 10:38-42. Scholars generally believe that the scene was created by Luke. The speaking style is not typical of Jesus, but the content certainly reflects his attitude toward women.

24 John 8:1-8. This moving episode, incorporated in the gospel of John, is probably a fragment of a lost gospel or a story that circulated separately in the Christian community. The scene clearly has artificial aspects, but scholars (even those of the Jesus Seminar) believe that at some point Jesus did defend an adulterous woman in this way, so typical of his custom of accepting the most despised sinners and showing them God's compassion.

25 Exod 20:14-17 prohibits men from having sexual relations with another man's wife or fiancée. Adultery is equivalent to theft. The sin is not his unfaithfulness to his wife, but his possession of another man's wife. The true culprit is the adulterous man; the woman is only a victim, or at most an accomplice.

26 Apparently a stoning was usually initiated by the witnesses. Jesus' suggestion is a challenge to them.

oldest of them, shamed by Jesus' challenge. They know that they are the ones most responsible for the adultery committed in those towns.

The end of the story is heart-rending. The woman has not moved. She stands there, humiliated and ashamed. Jesus is alone with her. Now he can look at her tenderly, and express all his respect and affection: «Woman… Has no one condemned you?» The woman, who has just escaped death, responds fearfully: «No one, sir». Jesus' next words are unforgettable. The adulterous men who have gone home angry will not hear them, only the exhausted woman: «Neither do I condemn you. Go your way, and from now on do not sin again». That woman doesn't need any more condemnation. Jesus believes in her, wants the best for her, and encourages her not to sin. But she hears no condemnation from him.

4

A different way of seeing

Certainly Jesus sees women in a different way, and they can tell. He notices them right away among his hearers, covered by their veils, and he keeps them in mind as he tells his message. They too need to hear God's Good News and communicate it to other women who have not dared to leave their houses[27]. When he talks to people about God's care for his creatures, Jesus points out the birds which «neither sow nor reap, they have neither storehouse nor barn, and yet God feeds them». This gets the point across to the men who go out every day to work in the field. Then he also points out the field lilies, which «neither toil nor spin, yet I tell you, even Solomon in all his glory was not clothed like one of these»[28]. The women, who spend hours spinning and weaving their family's clothes in the patios of their houses, understand him perfectly.

With a sensitivity almost unknown in a patriarchal society, Jesus has a habit of talking specifically about women, making them «visible» and highlighting their activity. He tells the parable of the «persistent friend» who finally gets his neighbor's attention, but then he also tells about the «importuning widow» who tenaciously claims her rights until the judge agrees to do her justice[29]. Jesus does

Women probably passed on Jesus' message to other women who remained in the home environment (Witherington III).

28 Q Source (Luke 12:24-28; Matt 6:26-29); [apocryphal] *Gospel of Thomas* 36. No one doubts the authenticity of this saying. The language and images are typical of Jesus.

29 Luke 11:5-8 and 18:1-8.

not restrict himself to an androcentric language that considers everything from the man's viewpoint. He also puts himself in the women's place and makes them protagonists of his parables.

He tells the parable of the «sower» who goes out to plant seed, but also tells about the woman who mixes yeast into the bread dough[30]. The women appreciate that. At last someone has noticed what they do. Jesus does not only talk about planting, the most important job of those peasants. He is also thinking of the other indispensable work that the women do before daybreak, so that everyone can eat bread. That brings them close to Jesus, and helps them accept his message. God is mixing a transforming power into the world, just as women mix yeast into the bread.

One parable may have been especially surprising. Jesus wants everyone to share one of his most treasured convictions: God cares so much about those who are lost, that he doesn't stop until he finds them. He speaks of a compassionate father who runs down the road to embrace his lost son, and about a shepherd who doesn't stop until he finds his lost sheep; but he also talks about a woman in panic who carefully sweeps the whole house until she finds the small silver coin she has lost[31]. This language breaks all the traditional molds, in which God usually appears as a male figure. A father embracing his son and a shepherd looking for his sheep are worthy metaphors for God. But how does it occur to Jesus to talk about that poor woman? Of course women are like that: when they lose something they will tear the house apart until they find it. But for Jesus, that woman sweeping her house is a metaphor worthy of God's love for the lost.[32]

This is not only true of his parables. Jesus takes advantage of every opportunity to present women as a model of faith, generosity, and selfless commitment. A poor widow, a chronically ill woman, or a despairing pagan woman can be an example for everyone to follow. Mark tells a moving story[33]. A poor widow quietly goes up to one of the thirteen alms boxes in the temple near the women's patio. Many rich people are putting in large amounts of money. Almost ashamed, she

---

30 Mark 4:3-8 and Q Source (Luke 13:20; Matt 13:33).

31 Luke 15:4-6; 15:11-32; 15:8-9.

32 Some scholars believe it is Luke who has emphasized this special attention to women, because of his interest in the catechesis of the Christian community (Parrey, Corley, Elisabeth Meier). But there is no serious reason not to attribute this sensitivity to Jesus himself (Jeremias, Witherington III, Theissen/Merz).

33 Mark 12:41-44. Anecdotes in this style, showing that God appreciates the generosity of the poor, are also found in the rabbinic literature and in ancient Greek writings. There is no reason to doubt the historical roots of this one. Nothing in the episode is out of character with Jesus' style.

drops in two copper coins, the smallest in circulation in Jerusalem. No one has seen it. But Jesus has, standing near the alms boxes and watching everything. Moved by her gesture, he calls his disciples. He wants to show them what only the poor can teach: to give more than leftovers. «This poor widow has put in more than all those... she out of her poverty has put in everything she had, all she had to live on». For Jesus the quiet and complete devotion of this woman is the clearest example of generosity and the renunciation of worldly goods, which is the first thing he asks of anyone who wants to be his disciple[34].

In another story[35], a sick woman timidly approaches Jesus in hopes of being healed by touching his clothes. We don't know her name or anything about her life. She was probably always timid and withdrawn; the illness she suffers may have made her even more so. She has suffered a loss of blood for many years, and her state of ritual impurity requires her to stay away from others. She only wants to live in dignity. So great is her desire to be like other people, that she has spent everything she had on doctors. Now penniless, alone, and without a future, she touches Jesus' garment with faith and feels herself cured. Jesus wants to know who has touched him. He is not worried about being contaminated by an impure woman. What he wants is for her not to go away in shame; he wants her to live in dignity. What she has done is not inappropriate; it is proof of her faith. When she confesses «in fear and trembling», Jesus replies with great love and tenderness: «Daughter, your faith has made you well; go in peace, and be healed of your disease». This woman's action is an example of the faith that he sees as missing among his closest followers[36].

Perhaps even more surprising is the case of an unknown woman from the pagan region of Tyre[37]. Her daughter is not only sick and disoriented, but possessed by an unclean spirit. In her anguish the woman comes to Jesus, throws herself at his feet, and begs him over and over to free her daughter from the demon.

---

34 If those two coins, «worth a penny», are all the woman had to live on, we have to think she lived by begging. The text says literally, «she has given her life» (*bios*). She doesn't have anything else. Only her great heart and her total trust in God.

35 Mark 5:24-34. It is not possible to judge the historicity of this episode with certainty (Meier, Sanders). The healing of a woman who suffered hemorrhages is generally seen as its historical nucleus. The rest of the story may have come largely from the narrator's imagination.

36 The story does not explicitly mention the woman's state of ritual impurity, but it is surely in the background of the whole story.

37 Mark 7:24-30. The story may come from a layer of tradition earlier than Mark. Some scholars consider it an invention by the Christian community to justify preaching to the gentiles (Meier). Nevertheless its historicity is widely accepted. The early Christians probably would not have invented a story in which Jesus is shown using insulting language toward the pagans.

In her pleas we can easily sense the suffering and despair of her family. But Jesus' response is surprisingly cool. He feels called to the lost sheep of Israel; he can't be concerned with pagans just now. «Let the children be fed first, for it is not fair to take the children's food and throw it to the dogs». The dogs are not part of the family; they do not eat with the children of the household but lie under the table[38]. The woman does not take offense. What she's asking for is not unfair; she's not seeking anything for herself. All she wants is to see her daughter freed from her great torment. Picking up on the image Jesus used, she answers with wisdom and trust: «Sir, even the dogs under the table eat the children's crumbs». Her daughter will be satisfied with the crumbs and scraps dropped from the table. Suddenly Jesus understands: this woman's will is the same as God's, who doesn't want anyone to suffer. With compassion and admiration for her trust, he tells her: «Woman, great is your faith! Let it be done for you as you wish»[39]. This woman's great faith is an example for his disciples «of little faith». But the surprising part is that Jesus lets himself be taught and convinced by her. The woman is right: human suffering knows no borders, for it is present in every people and religion. Although his mission is to Israel, God's compassion will be felt by all God's sons and daughters. Against all expectation, in this story a pagan woman has helped Jesus understand his mission better[40].

5

A space not controlled by men

His experience of God as a Father and defender of the last, and his faith in the coming reign of God, lead Jesus to actions that critically challenge the customs, traditions and practices that oppress women[41]. Jesus cannot eliminate the overwhelmingly patriarchal character of that society. It would be simply impossible. But he introduces a new basis and attitude that can «depatriarchalize» the society. No one can use God's name to defend or justify the supremacy of men, or the subjection of women to their universal power. Jesus subverts all that by pro-

---

38 Jesus is following Jewish custom by speaking of the pagans as «dogs».

39 This is Jesus' reply in Matt 15:28.

40 This is the only time Jesus gives up his opinion and accepts that of his interlocutor (Patterson). He lets a pagan woman convince him!

41 Of course it would be anachronistic to present Jesus as a forerunner of modern feminism, committed to a struggle for equal rights between women and men.

moting relationships based on the fact that everyone, woman or man, is created and loved by God: God accepts them in his reign with equal dignity as his sons and daughters[42]. Jesus sees them all as persons, equally responsible before God. He never addresses anyone on the basis of their role as men or women. He is never seen exhorting men on the one hand and women on the other about their respective duties, as the Jewish rabbis did — and as the first Christian communities would do later, in establishing household rules for men and especially for women. Jesus calls them all, women and men, to live as sons and daughters of the Father; he does not establish a kind of «secondary morality» specifically and exclusively addressed to women and to men[43].

The hardest part for women probably is not living at the service of their husbands and children, but knowing that at any moment their husbands can repudiate them and leave them unprotected. This right for men is based on Jewish law itself:

> Suppose a man enters into marriage with a woman, but she does not please him because he finds something objectionable about her, and so he writes her a certificate of divorce, puts it in her hand, and sends her out of his house[44].

Experts in the law were heatedly debating the interpretation of these words even before Jesus was born. According to the followers of Shammai, the wife could only be repudiated in cases of adultery; for the school of Hillel, it was enough to find in her «something disagreeable», for instance if she had burned his meal. This was apparently the prevailing trend in Jesus' time. Later Rabbi Aqiba would go a step further: a man could even repudiate his wife if he preferred a different woman. While the male experts debated, women could not raise a voice to defend their rights.

At some point the issue comes before Jesus: «Can a husband repudiate his wife?» It is a totally sexist question, since a woman has no right to repudiate her husband. Jesus' answer surprises everyone; the women can't believe their ears.

---

42 This liberating attitude in Jesus coincides with a trend, both in Hellenistic circles and in Jewish society, toward the emancipation of women and a growing tension with the rigid patriarchal system (Schüssler Fiorenza).

43 It is unthinkable to find in Jesus' sayings anything like the *Nashim*, a part of the Mishna which regulates everything related to women; or like the exhortations on men's and women's household duties that appear in the first Christian communities (Col 3:18-4:1; Eph 5:22-6:9; 1 Pet 3:1-7).

44 Deut 24:1.

According to him, if the law permits repudiation it is because of the men's «hardness of heart» and their sexist attitude, but patriarchal marriage was not in God's original plan. God created the man and woman to be «one flesh», as persons called to share love, intimacy, and all of life in total communion. «Therefore what God has joined together, let no one separate»[45]. Here again Jesus is taking a position on the side of the victims, abolishing the male privilege of repudiating their wives at will, and claiming a more secure, dignified and stable life for the wives. God has no use for the structures of male superiority and female submission. There is no place for them in God's reign[46].

This is precisely what Jesus recommends for the «new family» he is forming with his followers in the service of God's reign. A non-patriarchal family where all are brothers and sisters. A community without male domination and without hierarchies established by men. A movement of his followers where there is no «Father» except the one in heaven.

The Christian sources have preserved another important episode in Jesus' life; we don't know where or when it happened. After breaking with his family, Jesus is surrounded by a group of followers seated in a circle, with whom he has formed a well defined group: women and men sitting together with no one in a position of superiority, no one with authority over the others, everyone listening to his word and seeking God's will together. Then someone tells Jesus that his mother and brothers have come to take him away, because they think he has gone crazy. They stay «outside», perhaps in order not to mix with that strange group around him. Looking around the circle, as may have been his custom, and contemplating the people he sees as his new family, Jesus responds: «Here are my mother and brothers! Whoever does the will of God is my brother and sister and mother»[47]. There are no fathers in this new family of his followers; only the one in heaven. No one can take his place. Patriarchal relationships do not exist in God's reign. Everyone sits in a circle around Jesus, renouncing power and dominion over others in order to live at the service of the weakest and most defenseless.

45 Jesus' declaration against a man's repudiation of his wife is reported in three independent sources: Mark 10:2-11; the Q Source (Luke 16:18; Matt 5:32); and Paul (1 Cor 7:10-11). Moreover the aphorism is typical of Jesus: «what God has joined together, let no one separate». All this supports the authenticity of the saying, which was later adapted for different contexts and situations.

46 Jesus does not speak specifically about divorce as it exists today, but about men's exclusive privilege of repudiating their wives.

47 Mark 3:20-21 and 31-35, and the [apocryphal] *Gospel of Thomas* 99:1-3. The episode has been reshaped in the Christian community, but it substantially retains its historical nucleus. After the Resurrection, no Christian would have «invented» a story in which Jesus' own mother thought of him as crazy.

Jesus says the same thing in a different situation. The disciples too have left their homes, their brothers and sisters, fathers, mothers and children; they have left the land, which was their source of survival, work and security. They are left with nothing and no one. What will they receive? That is Peter's question, to which Jesus replies: «There is no one… who will not receive a hundredfold now in this age: houses, brothers and sisters, mothers and children, and fields… and in the age to come, eternal life»[48]. Jesus' followers will find a new home and a new family. A hundred brothers and sisters, a hundred mothers! But they will not find «fathers». No one will hold dominating authority over them. There is no place for a «father» in the patriarchal sense: a dominant man, an owner imposed on them from above, a lord who holds women and children in submission. In Jesus' new family everyone shares brotherly life and love. Men lose their power, women gain their dignity. To accept the reign of the Father means making space for life together, without male domination.

Another Christian source also gives some words from Jesus, explaining this «absence of a father» in his movement. That is a strongly anti-hierarchical text in which he asks his followers not to become a group led by wise «rabbis», authoritarian «fathers», or «instructors» to be looked up to: «But you are not to be called rabbi, for you have one teacher, and you are all students. And call no one your father on earth, for you have one Father — the one in heaven. Nor are you to be called instructors, for you have one instructor, the Messiah»[49]. No one can be or be called «father» in the community of Jesus, except God. Jesus calls him «Father», not to legitimize earthly structures of patriarchal power, but precisely to prevent any of his people from trying to claim «paternal authority», which is reserved for God alone[50].

When patriarchal power disappears, children make their appearance. Along with women, children are the weakest and smallest members of the family, the least powerful and most in need of love. For Jesus they must be at the center of

---

48 Mark 10:28-30. Many scholars are reluctant to accept the authenticity of this passage, since it responds to the concerns of the early Christians. But the words can be attributed to Jesus if we take out some later additions («for my sake and for the sake of the good news», «with persecutions»).

49 Matt 23:8-11. In general this text was formulated by Matthew as a warning against the hierarchy that was emerging in the early Christian communities. But some scholars see it as an echo of something Jesus said, which is consistent with other authentic texts.

50 On the other hand, for Jesus the image of God as Father has intimate, motherly connotations. He speaks of a compassionate God who carries his daughters and sons in his womb, cares for the most fragile creatures, gives good things to his children, and effusively embraces and kisses his lost children when they come home alive (Luke 11:11-13, 12:29-32, 15:11-32).

God's reign. In Jewish society sons are a sign of God's blessing, but they are only important when they are of an age to fulfill the law and participate in the adult world. Daughters are never important until they bear children, preferably sons.

Jesus is suggesting a new and different world to his disciples. In a story from Mark[51], the male disciples are debating the distribution of powers and authority. Jesus does something to show them how he understands the community of his followers: the important thing is not who is first or most important, but to live as a servant: «Whoever wants to be first must be the last of all and the servant of all». Then he puts a little child in their midst as a sign of authority. He holds it in his arms as if to confer his own authority on the child. The disciples don't know what to make of this. He explains in a few words: «Whoever welcomes one such child in my name welcomes me, and whoever welcomes me welcomes not me but the one who sent me». In Jesus' movement it is the children, little as they are, who have authority. They are the most important and occupy the center, because they are most in need of care and love. All the others, the great and powerful, become important by putting themselves at the service of the small and weak.

Jesus' way of thinking is even clearer in another scene[52]. People bring children to him: if he is a man of God, he will infuse in them some of his power and his spirit[53]. The disciples, wanting to control things and impose their authority, try to stop them from going up to Jesus. His reaction is immediate. He angrily rejects his disciples' action: «Let the little children come to me; do not stop them; for it is to such as these that the kingdom of God belongs. Truly I tell you, whoever does not receive the kingdom of God as a little child will never enter it». Then he does something very characteristic of him. He embraces the children tenderly, infusing his life in them and receiving their tenderness and joy. Later he lays his hands on them so they will grow and live in health: he blesses them as the Creator blessed everything at the beginning of life. Jesus' movement, which is to prepare and anticipate the reign of God, must not be a group led by strong

---

51 Mark 9:33-37. Jesus' call to welcome children was apparently very important, for it led to a series of sayings that are retold in different ways in the Q Source and in John. They may well have begun with an act and a saying of Jesus, which are obscured by the editing in Mark and the later tradition.

52 Mark 10:13-16. Most biblical critics believe this story is based on a real incident in Jesus' life. It reflects his firm attitude toward those who are marginalized, excluded and defenseless. The affirmation that God's reign belongs to the children is in line with his conviction that God's reign belongs to the poor.

53 These may be children from the streets. It is not their mothers who bring them to Jesus.

men who impose on others from above. Rather it must be a community «of children» who do not impose on anyone, who enter God's reign simply because they need care and love. A community with women and men who, like Jesus, know how to embrace, bless and care for the weakest and smallest. In God's reign life does not come as an imposition by the great, but as a welcome of the small. Wherever the little ones are at the center of life, there the reign of God is coming. That was surely one of Jesus' great insights.

6

Women as Jesus' disciples

Women followed Jesus from Galilee to Jerusalem, and did not abandon him even at the moment of his execution. They heard his message, learned from him, and followed him close at hand, just as the male disciples did. This is an indisputable fact[54] but also a surprising one, since in the decade of the thirties and even later, women were not allowed to study the law with a *rabi*. Moreover, to follow a man around the countryside and sleep outdoors with a group of men was probably scandalous. Nothing like that ever happened in Galilee. The spectacle of a group of women, sometimes without their husbands, some of them former demoniacs, following a celibate man who accepts them into his circle along with his male disciples, could only inspire resentment. Who were those women? What were they doing among those men? Were they serving them in female roles, such as cooking, preparing the table, serving food, bringing water, washing their feet? Or were they disciples of Jesus at the same level and with the same rights as the male disciples?[55]

Women were part of the group following Jesus from the beginning. Some of them probably followed him along with their husbands[56]. Others were single

---

54 This is confirmed in all the Christian sources although some gospel writers, like Luke, attenuate their presence.

55 It was traditionally assumed that these women followed Jesus to carry out women's tasks. Since the study done by Winsome Munro (1982), most researchers have considered them true disciples (Schüssler Fiorenza, Witherington III, Moltmann-Wendel, Crossan, Meier, Kathleen E. Corley, Elisabeth Meier, and others).

56 The earliest gospel, that of Mark, never says that the disciples left their wives. They left their extended family, brothers, sisters, mother, father, children, but not wives (Mark 10:29). Only Luke, later and moved by his radical tendency, mentions leaving wives (Luke 14:26 and 18:19). The Q source (Luke 12:51-53; Matt 10:34-37) also does not mention confrontation with a wife.

women, unaccompanied by any man. The sources do not say that Jesus called them individually, as he apparently did with the Twelve but not with everyone. They probably came to him, attracted by his person, but they would not have dared stay with him if Jesus had not invited them. He never excludes or separates them for reasons of gender or impurity. They are «sisters» who belong to the new family Jesus is creating, and they are respected along with the «brothers»[57]. The prophet of God's reign only speaks of one discipleship, of equals.

We know a few of their names, though by no means all of them[58]. Mary of Magdala holds a pre-eminent place, as Peter does among the men. There is a group of three women, who are apparently the closest to Jesus: Mary of Magdala, Mary the mother of James the younger and of Joses, and Salome; just as among the men there are three who enjoy his special friendship: Peter, James and John. We also know the names of other women whom Jesus loved very much, such as Martha and Mary who welcomed him in their house at Bethany whenever he went up to Jerusalem, and who listened to him with great pleasure although they apparently did not accompany him in his travels[59].

The women who followed Jesus to Jerusalem had a very important presence in the last days of his life. There is no longer much doubt that they participated in the last supper. How could they be absent from that farewell dinner, since they did usually eat with Jesus? Who would have prepared and served the banquet without the women's help? Their exclusion would be even more absurd since it was a Passover meal, one of the feasts that women did attend. Where else would they have celebrated Passover, alone in the city of Jerusalem?[60] During those days the disciples always met in the same house where the dinner was held, even after Jesus' crucifixion; they included not only the Twelve, but also «certain women» including Mary the mother of Jesus, and his brothers[61].

The male and female disciples reacted differently to the execution of Jesus. While the men fled, the women remained faithful; although the Romans did not permit any interference with their criminal work, the women were «looking

---

57 Mark momentarily drops his sexist language and explicitly mentions women: «Whoever does the will of God is my brother and sister and mother» (3:35).
58 Mark says that in addition to the ones he names, there were «many other women who had come up with him to Jerusalem» (15:41).
59 Bethany was a small village near Jerusalem, about three kilometers from the temple.
60 John's gospel does not mention the Twelve. Jesus celebrated the last supper with «his own» (13:1). In the Christian community, women were accepted from the beginning at the «breaking of the bread» or Lord's supper (Acts 2:46).
61 Acts 1:14 and 2:1-4.

on from a distance» and later saw where he was buried[62]. But what is most important is the part they played in the origin of the resurrection faith. Women are identified with the first report of Jesus' resurrection[63]. Were they the first to experience the risen Jesus? We cannot easily say for certain. Mary of Magdala probably played an important role. Two traditions circulated in the Christian community; one attributes the first experience to Mary of Magdala, while the other gives primacy to Peter[64]. We cannot say anything more with certainty. If Mary was first in the group of women, and Peter among the men, it is probably because an important role was attributed to both in the origin of faith in the risen Jesus.

The women's presence in the group of disciples is not secondary or marginal. On the contrary. In many ways they are the model of true discipleship. The women do not debate who will be more powerful in God's reign, as the men did. They are used to always being the last. They are used to «serving»[65]. Indeed they were surely the ones primarily occupied with «serving the table» and other similar chores, but we should not see that service as their task in a logical distribution of work within the group. For Jesus, it was a model for the activity of every disciple: «For who is greater, the one who is at the table or the one who serves? Is it not the one at the table? But I am among you as one who serves»[66]. Perhaps at some point Jesus joined the women in serving, thus showing everyone the proper activity for their life as disciples. According to the sources, the women's activity was a model of discipleship for the men because of their commitment, their attitude of service, and their faithfulness to Jesus to the end, without betraying or abandoning him.

---

62 In the story of Jesus' execution the presence of the women seems to be a firmly historical fact (Mark 15:40-41). Luke, who sometimes tends to minimize the women's participation, says that «all his acquaintances» were there with the women (23:49). This last affirmation is not at all credible.

63 This is the most likely conclusion to be drawn from the gospel sources as a whole (Mark 16:1-8; Luke 24:10-11 and 23-24; John 20:11-18), although Paul only mentions men as witnesses to Jesus' resurrection (1 Cor 15:5-8). All the evidence suggests that Mark reflects an earlier tradition, which others were never able to set aside. In Acts 13:31, the risen Jesus «appeared to those who came up with him from Galilee to Jerusalem, and they are now his witnesses to the people».

64 John 20:19-29; Luke 24:34; 1 Cor 15:5.

65 In the Markan tradition, women «used to follow him and provided for him when he was in Galilee» (15:41).

66 Luke 22:27. According to scholars this saying, transmitted by Luke in the context of the last supper, is a better formulation of what Jesus said historically than the version in Mark 10:45, which is a Christian teleological view of Jesus' death as a means of salvation.

But these women are never called «disciples», simply because the word in Aramaic is always a masculine noun. For the same reason the gospels, written in Greek, do not speak of female disciples. The phenomenon of women integrated in the group of Jesus' disciples was so new that there were no adequate words to express it[67]. They are not called disciples, but Jesus sees and treats them as such.

But he could not send them to proclaim the reign of God throughout the Galilean countryside, to the places where he would be going. Their message would have been rejected. Women were not even permitted to read the Word of God, or to speak in public. How would men hear their message? If that wasn't possible, could he perhaps send them together with the men? If at some point he was sending out the disciples «two by two»[68], it is quite possible that there were married couples among them, or mixed pairs of men and women. Certainly in Galilee a woman could only travel safely in the company of a man. What we do know is that in the first years of the Christian mission most of the apostles, the brothers of the Lord, and Cephas in particular, took a «wife» or a «believing woman» with them in their travels[69]. On the other hand it is not surprising that no women are among the «Twelve» disciples chosen by Jesus to recall the restoration of Israel. That symbolic number represents the Jewish people, formed by twelve tribes descended, according to the tradition, from the twelve male sons of Jacob.

7

The woman closest to Jesus

Jesus treated all the women close to him with affection, like Salome or Mary, the mother of James and Joses. He had very dear women friends, like Martha and Mary, the sisters of Lazarus[70]. But his dearest friend was Mary, a woman from

---

67 The feminine form of «disciple» (*mathetria*) did not appear until the second century A.D., when it was applied to Mary Magdalene ([apocryphal] *Gospel of Peter* 12:50).

68 Researchers debate whether Jesus really sent the disciples out two by two during his period of public activity. I think he probably did.

69 Paul says specifically: «Do we not have the right to be accompanied by a believing wife, as do the other apostles and the brothers of the Lord and Cephas?» (1 Cor 9:5). Some scholars suggest that the «two disciples» on the road to Emmaus were a married couple. We know the man's name, Cleopas, but not his wife's since women's names were not usually given. It might have been the same «Mary the wife of Clopas» who appears near the cross in John 19:25. Some authors suggest that Jesus may have sent out pairs made up of a man and a woman. Crossan acknowledges, however, that we have no decisive evidence.

70 John's gospel tells us that «Jesus loved Martha and her sister and Lazarus» (11:5).

Magdala. She held a special place in his heart and in the group of disciples. Unlike the other women, her name is never linked to a man. She belongs to Jesus. She follows him faithfully to the end, leading the rest of the disciples. She is surely the first to meet the risen Jesus, although Paul doesn't even mention her in his list of witnesses to the resurrection.

Mary was born in Magdala, the ancient Tarichea, a city by the lake of Gennesaret, about five kilometers north of Tiberias, and famous for its fish-salting industry. Jesus went through Magdala on his way from Nazareth to Capernaum. We know nothing about Mary's life. However, one brief reference sheds considerable light on her relationship with Jesus. She was a woman «possessed by evil spirits», from whom Jesus had removed «seven demons»[71]. That was how it all started. Before meeting Jesus Mary was out of her mind, a broken woman, without her own identity, a defenseless victim of evil forces that were destroying her. She did not know what it was to live a healthy life.

For her, finding Jesus meant starting to live. Here for the first time was a man who loved her for herself, with God's own love and tenderness. She had found her center in him. From then on she could not live without him. He had everything she needed to be a healthy, living woman. It is said of the others that they left everything to follow Jesus. Mary had nothing to leave. Only Jesus could give her life. No man had ever approached her that way. No one had looked at her that way. She had lived for years in the dark, deprived of God's blessing. Now she felt closer to God than ever, thanks to the healing presence of Jesus.

According to one Christian tradition, Mary was the first to meet the risen Jesus and communicate her experience to the disciples, who didn't believe her. In this tradition, which combines and summarizes material from earlier sources, the risen Jesus appeared first to Mary Magdalene, from whom he had cast out seven demons. She went out and told those who had been with him, while they were mourning and weeping. But when they heard that he was alive and had been seen by her, they would not believe it[72].

John's gospel gives us a careful narrative of this encounter[73]. Jesus' execution had been especially traumatic for a woman whose life was so centered on him.

---

71 Luke 8:2. There is no reason to question the historicity of this information, although some scholars see in it an effort by Luke to downplay the importance of women, and specifically of Mary Magdalene (Elisabeth Meier).

72 Mark 16:9-11. This text is part of a later addition to Mark's original gospel.

73 John 20:11-18. The narrative may have come from the «Gospel of the Signs», a source which was probably used by the final editor of John's gospel. The scene is created by the narrator, who is

They had killed the one who was everything to her. She couldn't stop loving him; she clung to his person; she needed to hold on even to his dead body. Perhaps fear was growing within her: without Jesus she might again fall under the dark oppression of the powers of evil. She looked into the empty sepulcher, but the emptiness in her own heart was even greater. She had never been so terribly lonely. Blinded by her pain and tears, she did not recognize Jesus when he stood before her. He called to her with the same tenderness that was in his voice when they walked through Galilee: «*Miryam!*» Mary turned around quickly: «*Rabbouni! My Teacher!*» This woman who could not live without Jesus was the first to find him full of life[74]. Life was starting over for Mary. She could follow her beloved Teacher again, but it would not be the same as in Galilee. The risen one was sending her to his brothers: «Go to my brothers and say to them, "I am ascending to my Father and your Father, to my God and your God"». Mary would have to learn to embrace Jesus in her brothers and sisters, while she explained to them that there was no longer a chasm between God and human beings. United with Jesus, now they all had God as their Father[75].

Mary was not forgotten by the first Christians[76]. In second- and third-century Gnostic circles she is presented as a woman who «completely understood» and transmitted to the disciples the mystery of Jesus, although Peter and others could not accept «having to listen to a woman about secrets that they did not know». These writings narrate episodes and discourses that can only be correctly understood in the context of Gnostic doctrines. It is a mistake to attribute an historical character to them, although they do probably reflect the importance of Mary Magdalene in these circles as «an authorized interpreter of Jesus». We can also sense the rivalry that must have existed, not so much between Peter and Mary as among the groups that had chosen them as prototypes and representatives of their respective positions[77].

trying to show us the emotional intensity of the encounter. Scholars can affirm only that Mary was certainly one of the first witnesses to the resurrection event.

74 The narrator is trying to convey all the intensity and intimacy of the encounter by using Aramaic, the native language of Jesus and Mary.

75 According to the [apocryphal] *Gospel of Mary*, this is the woman who began to awaken faith in the disciples: «Mary stood up, kissed them all and said to her brothers: "Do not be afraid or doubtful, for his grace will go with you and protect you». Mary does not reserve her kisses and her tenderness for her Beloved alone. She gives everyone the love she carries in her heart.

76 The apocryphal books discovered at Nag Hammadi (Upper Egypt) in 1945 allow us to trace the profile of Mary Magdalene as she was remembered and discussed in Gnostic circles in the second century.

77 This is the general opinion of scholars studying the figure of the Magdalene in the Gnostic literature: *The Dialogue of the Savior*, the [apocryphal] *Gospel of Mary*, the [apocryphal] *Gospel of*

As we know, recent works of fiction have given a novelesque picture of Mary Magdalene as the «sexual companion» of Jesus. These works are built on two texts from the [apocryphal] *Gospel of Philip*[78]:

> There were three who always walked with the Lord: Mary his mother and her sister and Magdalene, the one who was called his companion. His sister and his mother and his companion were each a Mary.
>
> As for the Wisdom who is called «the barren», she is the mother of the angels and the companion of the Savior, Mary Magdalene. Christ loved her more than the rest of the disciples and used to kiss her often on her mouth[79].

It is unscientific and dishonest to read these texts in a «fundamentalist» way, without analyzing the Gnostic significance of the «holy kiss» as a sacrament of the reunification of men and women in Christ[80], and without studying their presentation of Mary Magdalene as the «personification» of Wisdom[81].

Especially after the fourth century, the image of Mary Magdalene underwent a rapid change. Gregory of Nyssa and Augustine of Hippo say that Mary was the first to receive the grace of the resurrection of Jesus, because a woman was the first to introduce sin into the world. Soon Mary was confused with the «woman who was a sinner» in Luke 7:36-50, and thus assumed to be a «prostitute». The degrading legend continued to grow. Male hierarchs, theologians and artists portrayed her as a lascivious, lustful woman, possessed by the «seven demons» or capital sins. Later, repentant and forgiven by Jesus, she had dedicated her whole life to doing penance. The Eastern Church was not influenced by this false and legendary image of the Magdalene as a prostitute and penitent. It has always venerated her as a faithful follower of Jesus and eminent witness to the risen Lord.

Philip,Pistis Sophia (Crossan, Jacobsen, Vouga, Karen Jo Torjesen, Margaret Y. MacDonald, Carmen Bernabé).

78 It was probably written in Syria, in the late second or early third century. Today we have a Coptic translation of the Greek original.

79 [Apocryphal] *Gospel of Philip* 59:6-11 and 63:1-2.

80 According to the Gnostic gospels, the primordial evil of humanity was that the original androgynous unity between men and women was broken with the separation of Eve and Adam. Reunification is achieved in Christ. The «holy kiss» is part of the sacramentalization of this saving event.

81 Mary is presented as the personification of «Wisdom». Wisdom is a «companion» (*koinonós*) to the Lord, as she was to the wise King Solomon, who decided to take her as a «companion» (*koinonós*) (Wis 8:9).

A Teacher of Life

Jesus went on sharing the experience he was living in his heart: «God is already here». God's saving presence was being felt quietly but in a real way. The sick, and those tormented by evil spirits, could feel in their own flesh the healing presence of God as a friend of life. The beggars and dispossessed, victims of all sorts of abuses, were sensing God as their defender and Father. Sinners, prostitutes, and undesirables felt accepted: as they ate with their friend Jesus, a new faith in God's forgiveness and friendship was awakening in their hearts. Even women began to enjoy a new, hitherto unknown dignity. With Jesus, everything was changing.

How should they respond to this new situation? How should they enter into the dynamic of the reign of God? How should they live in this new space, created by the saving irruption of God? Jesus can tell them how, from his own experience. He is the first to live by accepting God's reign. He can teach them. From the beginning people see him not only as God's prophet, healer, and defender of the last, but as a teacher of life who shows them a different way of living under the sign of God's reign.

1

An unconventional teacher

People call him *rabí,* because they see him as a teacher. It is not just a respectful term of address. His way of encouraging people to live differently fits the image of a teacher in his time. He is not only a prophet announcing the irruption, or in-breaking, of God's reign. He is a wise man, teaching them how to live in response to God[1].

But no one confuses him with the interpreters of the law, or with the scribes who work for the priestly hierarchy of the temple. Jesus is not an interpreter of the law[2]. He hardly ever cites the Holy Scriptures, and never quotes the teachers who came before him. He belongs to no school, and fits into no existing tradition. His authority surprises everyone. People have the impression of hearing from him about a radically different way of life[3].

1 It is true that the rabbinic writers only called educated people *rabí* after 70 A.D., but in Jesus' time there were teachers like Hillel, Shammai or Gamaliel (Theiessen/Merz, Marguerat).
2 Jesus never uses the traditional rabbinic terminology: «Thus says the Torah» (Borg, Chilton).
3 In Mark 1:22 we read that the people «were astounded at his teaching, for he taught them as one having authority, and not as the scribes». Although Mark's comment reflects later Christian thinking, it is still based on the real history of Jesus. This is how Jesus was remembered (Dunn).

As in all cultures, in the Jewish society of Jesus' time there was a conventional wisdom, shaped over the course of centuries and basically accepted by everyone. Its main source was the law of Moses and the traditions that had been passed down from generation to generation. This «religious culture», nurtured with weekly Scripture readings in the synagogues, refreshed in their great celebrations and temple feasts, conserved and updated by its official interpreters, was woven into the whole life of Israel. Internalized in the people's awareness, this religious tradition gave everyone their image of God and the framework of values that shaped their view of life: Israel as the chosen people, its covenant with Yahweh, the law, circumcision, and the sabbath rest. It nourished their identity as «children of Abraham»[4].

Although Jesus is rooted in the best of this tradition, his teaching has a subversive edge that challenges the conventional religion. One point is clear: the reign of God is coming. People can no longer live as if nothing were happening; they must move from a conventional religion to a life centered on God's reign. What is being taught in Israel no longer provides a basis for life as God wills it. They must learn a new way of responding to the new situation created by the irruption of God.

Jesus uses the language of popular wisdom to explain his purpose. He's not teaching them to go through the «wide door» that many people use, which leads to perdition. He wants to show them a new door; it is «narrow» and not many are going in through it, but it is the way that leads to life[5]. He doesn't want to be a blind guide for these people; there are already many «blind persons guiding blind persons», with the likelihood that they will all fall into a pit[6]. Nor does he want to patch an old garment with new cloth, since it only makes a worse tear; or put new wine in old wineskins, since both the wine and the wineskins will be lost[7]. The reign of God requires a new response, capable of transforming everything at its root. New wine goes in new wineskins!

4　According to Sanders, some authors distinguish between the «common Judaism» or «great tradition» that incorporates the essential content of Israel's religion, and more diverse «lesser traditions». Other writers consider this «common Judaism» an artificial construct of unproven value (Neusner, Hengel). Today's scholars increasingly recognize the pluralism of first century Judaism, within a basic religious framework (Perrot, Marguerat, Meier).

5　This image is reflected in the Q Source (Luke 13:24; Matt 7:13-14). It is often used in the Hebrew Scriptures, the apocryphal books of the Old Testament, and the writings of Qumran. Jesus clearly also liked using it. Luke's formulation is probably the most authentic.

6　Q Source (Luke 6:39; Matt 15:14) and the [apocryphal] *Gospel of Thomas* 34. Jesus is using a popular proverb in his own way.

7　Mark 2:21-22 (later used in Matt 9:16-17, Luke 5:36-38) and the [apocryphal] *Gospel of Thomas* 47:4-5. These are popular proverbs used by Jesus. The earliest version may be the one in the [apocryphal] *Gospel of Thomas*, since it has not been adapted to fit the Christian perspective.

This is why Jesus does not analyze the Scriptures and draw his teachings from them, as was done by the Pharisees or the Qumran community. He uses the Scriptures to show that God's plans are already being fulfilled with the irruption of God's reign. His experience as a son of God tells him that the message of the sacred texts is already being revealed, fully and decisively[8].

Jesus knew the biblical tradition, and the expressions and images it used, very well. It is hard to tell which texts he normally cited[9]. Probably his favorite book was that of the prophet Isaiah, and his most beloved texts were the ones that proclaimed a new world for the sick and the very poor. Of course he rejoiced to hear such texts as these read on the sabbath: «Be strong, do not fear! Here is your God... He will come and save you. Then the eyes of the blind shall be opened, and the ears of the deaf unstopped; then the lame shall leap like a deer, and the tongue of the speechless sing for joy». «On that day... the meek shall obtain fresh joy in the Lord, and the neediest people shall exult in the Holy One of Israel, for the tyrant shall be no more»[10].

Jesus apparently does not quote the Scriptures from the text of the Hebrew books that were kept in the synagogues. The people did not know Hebrew, and no one had books at home. Jesus quotes a more popular and less exact form of the Bible, following commentaries or translations (*targumim*) which were written in Aramaic so that people could understand the Word of God[11]. But he does more than repeat the text. He adapts the biblical language and images to his own experience of God. He reads and recreates everything from the viewpoint of his faith in the irruption of God's reign.

---

8 We do not know with certainty which texts Jesus knew and considered sacred.
9 Naturally the gospels, written in Greek, quoted the Old Testament from the Greek Septuagint version; it was completed in the second century B.C. and used among the Jews of the diaspora, who only spoke Greek. It is quite possible that some of the texts reportedly quoted by Jesus, which reflect the interests and preferences of the Christian communities, were introduced in the process of transmitting the tradition.
10 Isa 35:4-6; 29:18-20. Isa 61:1-2, quoted by Jesus in the Nazareth synagogue (Luke 4:18-19), reflects his experience but was probably introduced by Luke as a programmatic text: «The spirit of the Lord God is upon me, because the Lord has anointed me; he has sent me to bring good news to the oppressed, to bind up the broken-hearted, to proclaim liberty to the captives, and release to the prisoners, to proclaim the year of the Lord's favor».
11 This is the conclusion from Chilton's research, accepted by respected scholars (Evans, Theissen, Meier, Witherington III). Jesus was apparently familiar with a popular commentary on the book of Isaiah which later became the *Targum of Isaiah* (between 70 and 135 A.D.) The expression «reign of God», a central category of Jesus' message, often appears in that writing.

The people know that Jesus is not a teacher of the law. He has not studied with any famous teacher. He does not belong to any group dedicated to interpreting the Scriptures. Jesus moves among the people. He speaks in the plazas and fields, along the paths and by the lakeside. He has his own language and his own message. To convey his experience of God's reign, he tells parables that open up a new world to his hearers. To inspire the people to enter into the dynamic of that reign, he repeats brief sayings that reflect and condense his thinking. His direct and precise sayings urge everyone to live life in a different way.

His sayings were engraved in the memory of his hearers. Brief and concise, full of truth and wisdom, spoken forcefully, they obligate people to think about something they might otherwise miss. Jesus repeats them over and over, in different circumstances. Some of them help him to drive home in a few words what he has been saying at length. These sayings cannot be rattled off quickly, as a series[12]. People need time to think about each one.

Jesus has his own special teaching style. He knows how to touch people's hearts and minds. He often surprises them with paradoxical, disconcerting sayings: «For those who want to save their life will lose it, and those who lose their life for my sake... will find it»[13]. Is it really like that? A matter of life and death? A decision with everything at stake? Sometimes he provokes them with incredibly exaggerated sayings: «If your right eye causes you to sin, tear it out and throw it away... And if your right hand causes you to sin, cut it off and throw it away»[14]. Other times he speaks with irony and humor: «Why do you see the speck in your neighbor's eye, but do not notice the log in your own eye?»[15] People laugh heartily, but they will not forget the lesson. He uses funny word plays that amuse them greatly: «You blind guides! You strain out a gnat [in Aramaic, *galma*] but swallow a camel [in Aramaic, *gamla*]!»[16].

Jesus wants to reach even the most simple and ignorant. This is why he also uses sayings that everyone knows. People always love the anonymous proverbs that reflect the experience of generations. They are not original with Jesus, but he uses them in an original way to teach people how to enter the reign of God. «No one can serve two masters», we know from experience, but Jesus adds: «You

---

12 Many of Jesus' sayings in different circumstances have been gathered in the gospels as «collections» (for example Matthew 7). We should not be confused by their presentation as a package.

13 Mark 8:35.

14 Matt 5:29-30.

15 Matt 7:3.

16 Matt 23:24. People would laugh even harder because the camel was an impure animal.

cannot serve God and wealth»[17]. The people understand: you cannot follow the God who defends the last, and live by accumulating wealth. Another time he recalled a different saying: «Those who are well have no need of a physician, but those who are sick»[18]. Everyone knows doctors are there to attend to the sick. By the same token they should accept Jesus' way of relating to sinners and eating with them.

But more than popular proverbs, Jesus uses his own sayings, born of his way of understanding life in the perspective of God's reign[19]. These are brief and often very radical sayings. Jesus uses them authoritatively, not basing them on the Scriptures or other supporting arguments: «Love your enemies»; «Do not judge, so that you may not be judged». They are a kind of «counter-order» to live under the sign of the reign of God, against the way of life conventionally accepted by everyone[20].

2

Change your hearts!

∽

When Jesus proclaims the reign of God, he is trying to elicit a response. God is already acting. Israel cannot go on living in this new situation as if nothing is happening. They must enter into God's plan. This response is not needed in order to bring in God's reign, nor to earn it; God is offering compassionate love to all, without regard to merit. Jesus' concern is different: how should they respond to the Father, who is already acting? How should they live now, in the light of God's compassion? Jesus' life is already completely transformed by the reign of God, but these people need to hear a new summons that will touch their hearts.

---

17 Q Source (Luke 16:13; Matt 6:24).
18 Mark 2:17.
19 Crossan has analyzed 133 aphorisms. Aune has identified 167.
20 Different books of proverbs and wisdom sayings were known and appreciated in Jesus' time: the book of Proverbs, the final editing of which was completed around 480 B.C.; the book of Qohelet (or Ecclesiastes), written around 250 B.C.; the book of Jesus ben Sirach (or Ecclesiasticus), written around 132 B.C. and translated to Greek by a grandson of the author who lived in Alexandria. These books teach a common-sense, reasonable way of living: the search for wisdom; discernment of virtues and vices; work and family; relations with women; the traits of a sensible man, etc. Jesus never speaks about these life programs, but about a radical response to God's reign.

Jesus trusts entirely in God's saving power, but he sees the obstacles and resistance faced by his word. Not everyone is open to God. Will his project eventually fail? To explain how he sees things, Jesus tells the parable of a farmer sowing seed[21].

> Listen! A sower went out to sow. And as he sowed, some seed fell on the path, and the birds came and ate it up. Other seed fell on rocky ground, where it did not have much soil, and it sprang up quickly, since it had no depth of soil. And when the sun rose, it was scorched; and since it had no root, it withered away. Other seed fell among thorns, and the thorns grew up and choked it, and it yielded no grain. Other seed fell into good soil and brought forth grain, growing up and increasing and yielding thirty and sixty and a hundred fold[22].

Jesus is talking about something that happens regularly in Galilee. In fall the peasants go out to plant their fields; in June they bring in the harvest. His hearers know about planting, and they know what it means to live in expectation of the future harvest. What is he trying to tell them?

The story tells in great detail what happens in the planting. Part of the seed falls along the path beside the field. It is not good soil. The seed does not even germinate: the birds come and eat it right away. Here the sower's work has failed from the beginning. Another part falls in a rocky area, covered with a thin layer of soil. The seed springs up, but only for a while: when it fails to put down roots, the sun dries it up. Here too the sower's work has failed, although the seeds are not lost right away. Another part falls among thorns. It is apparently germinating and growing, but it does not bear fruit: the thorns grow stronger and strangle the seeds.

---

21 Although the story begins by talking about the sower, the focus of the parable is not on the sower but on what happens to the seed.

22 The parable appears in the synoptic gospels (Mark 4:3b-8; Matt 13:3b-8; Luke 8:5-8a) and in the [apocryphal] *Gospel of Thomas* 9. Mark's version is probably closest to the original story. To understand its message we must set aside the allegorical interpretation that appears in the synoptic gospels (Mark 4:14-20; Matt 13:18-23; Luke 8:11-15), which was the product of the Christian community. It is not in the [apocryphal] *Gospel of Thomas*. This allegorical interpretation uses the language of the Christian preachers, and responds to problems that were being experienced in the second and third generation. This has been a scholarly consensus since the publication of Jülicher's studies on the parables.

His followers listen in consternation. Is it worth it to go on planting? Can't the sower find a better field? Jesus continues the story. In spite of so much failure, most of the seed falls on good soil. The plants grow, develop, and bear fruit: thirty, sixty, even a hundredfold. In some areas the planting has been a failure; in others it has succeeded. But in spite of the failures, in the end the sower can enjoy a good harvest[23]. The people begin to «get it». Jesus is doing as the peasants do. They know when they set out to plant that part of the seed will be wasted, but that does not discourage them: the important thing is the final harvest. Something similar occurs with the reign of God. There is no lack of obstacles and resistance, but the power of God will bear fruit. Jesus is planting the seeds. Now is the time to respond.

What sort of response is he hoping for? Surprisingly, he never invites people to do penance with the ascetic rituals and actions that the prophets loved to call for. No one hears him talk about fasting, ashes, or mourning garments. That's not what the loving God is looking for as he holds out open arms to everyone. Jesus' call goes beyond such conventional penitence. Neither is he simply calling people to return to the law. He is not only calling sinners to renew their observance of the law, as the righteous do. He is calling the righteous too. Everyone must change in order to «enter» the reign of God, not in a penitential attitude, but moved by the joy and surprise of God's incredible love[24].

There is no time to wait. The reign of God is coming. They must «enter» into its dynamic right now. No one must be left out. Jesus is not calling all Israel to national penitence, as the Baptist did, but neither is he thinking of a select group. The Good News must come to everyone. Everyone is invited to believe. They will not find in God's reign a new code of laws to regulate their lives, but an impulse and a new horizon of life that transforms the world according to the true will of God.

23 The planting fails in three areas. In another three there is a good harvest, in varying degrees. In Mark's text, what has fallen in each of the first areas is only «a part» (singular), but the largest part, that is, the «other parts» plural has given a good harvest. [Editor's note: we must note that the NRSV does not support this singular/plural distinction].

24 Judaism around Jesus' time spoke of «returning to the God of the Law». For example, «abandon the way of corruption and return to the Law of Moses» (in the Qumran writings); «come away from impurity and observe the mandates of the supreme God» (book of *Jubilees*); «lead us to return to your law» (prayer of the *Eighteen blessings*). Jesus sets aside that language and talks about «entering the reign of God».

They can only enter God's reign with a «new heart», prepared to obey God at the deepest level. This radical transformation is decisive. God seeks to «reign» at the most intimate center of their hearts, that inner nucleus that determines their way of feeling, thinking, and behaving[25]. This is how Jesus sees it. A more humane world can never be born unless people's hearts are changed; life as God wills it cannot be built anywhere unless people are changed from within. «The good person out of the good treasure of the heart produces good, and the evil person out of evil treasure produces evil». Jesus illustrates the message with clear and penetrating images: «No good tree bears bad fruit, nor again does a bad tree bear good fruit… Figs are not gathered from thorns, nor are grapes picked from a bramble bush»[26]. Jesus wants to touch people's hearts. The reign of God must change everything from the roots[27]. Only men and women with new hearts can make a new world.

Jesus uses original language to describe the basic attitude needed to accept God. Some adults may take it as an insult. Jesus asks them to «become like children». Just what does he mean by that? «Children» are an archetype, used differently in different cultures. It is a universal metaphor for trust in one's parents, innocence, humility, sincerity, and many other things. Jesus never idealizes children. He knows very well those undernourished boys and girls who scamper around him and among his followers. Perhaps he knows of places in the Empire where newborn babies, especially baby girls, are abandoned by their parents; sometimes they are later rescued from the garbage dumps and brought up as slaves[28]. The Jews didn't do that, but for these poor Galilean families, a child was not only a blessing from God. It was also another mouth to feed.

---

25 In Semitic thinking, the «heart» is not only the center of love and affective life. Ir is the deepest level of the person, the source of perception, thinking, emotions, and behavior. People's whole lives are «determined» in their hearts.

26 This type of sayings is familiar in the proverbial wisdom of the time, but Jesus shapes it in his own way. The contrast between figs and thorns, and between grapes and brambles, is in Jesus' unmistakable style: Q Source (Luke 6:43-45; Matt 7:16-20) and the [apocryphal] *Gospel of Thomas* 45:1-4.

27 The Jewish people remembered a promise from God that Ezekiel had spoken among the exiles in Babylon, shortly after the destruction of Jerusalem (586 B.C.): «A new heart I will give you, and a new spirit I will put within you; and I will remove from your body the heart of stone and give you a heart of flesh» (Ezek 36:26).

28 In a papyrus discovered at Oxyrrhincus, near Cairo, an emigrant worker in Alexandria named Hilarion writes to his pregnant wife Alis, a letter dated June 18 in the year 1 B.C.: «I am staying in Alexandria. I beg you to take care of our child; I will send you my pay as soon as I receive it. *If the child you will bear is a son, let him live; but if it is a girl, expose her so she will die*» (cited by Crossan).

In Galilee in the decade of the thirties, a child was a nobody: a weak and needy creature, totally dependent on its parents. This is probably what Jesus is talking about. That is why he says: «Let the little children come to me; do not stop them; for it is to such as these that the kingdom of God belongs»[29]. The reign of God belongs to the children simply because they are the weakest and most needy, just as it belongs to the beggars, the hungry, and those who suffer. That is why Jesus, moved by that God, accepts, blesses and embraces them. Jesus lives and incarnates the reign of God by accepting the last.

Then Jesus goes a step further: «Truly I tell you, whoever does not receive the kingdom of God as a little child will never enter it»[30]. The way to enter the reign of God is to become like children. To let God embrace us, as children joyfully allowed Jesus to embrace them. Living before God means living differently from adults, who are almost always seeking power, greatness, honor or wealth. Jesus' language, asking adults to «become like little children», is about more than a change of behavior. He seems to be asking for a new beginning, the beginning of a new personality[31].

3

Beyond the law

The Jews talked proudly about the law. In their tradition, God himself had given the law to his people through Moses. It was the best thing they had received from their God. The scroll of the law was reverently protected in all the synagogues, in a chest kept in a special place. They did not see it as a heavy yoke or a bothersome burden. The law was their pride and joy, a precious and imperishable good for Israel, the promise and way of salvation. The will of the only true God was written in the law. There they could find everything they needed to live in faithfulness to the God of the Covenant[32].

---

29 Mark 10:14. These words are spoken in the same perspective as the beatitudes (Luke 6:20-21). God belongs to those who have no place in society (the dispossessed, the excluded). Now he adds the children, who are the last in society, the insignificant ones.

30 Mark 10:15. This saying probably circulated separately in the Christian community. It may have been reshaped in the context of early baptismal rites, but there is no reason to doubt its authenticity. It is typical of Jesus to invite people to a radically new life in the «kingdom of God».

31 The gospel of John makes explicit the idea of a «new birth»: «Very truly, I tell you, no one can see the kingdom of God without being born from above» (John 3:3).

32 The Hebrews spoke of *torá*, which literally means «teaching» or «instruction». At first, *torá* referred to a specific law. When the Pentateuch was put together around 500 B.C., all the laws and

But Jesus, totally seduced by the reign of God, does not focus on the Torah. He does not study it, or require his disciples to study it. He often talks about God without referring to the law, and without thinking about whether his teaching is in conflict with it. He is not concerned with scrupulous observance of the law, as the Qumran community was. For him the Torah is not the most important thing. He also does not intentionally get involved in debates over the correct interpretation of the legal norms. He is seeking God's will, based on a different kind of experience.

We really don't know what he thought about the law. He apparently never talked about it explicitly, either pro or con[33]. He does not offer a systematic doctrine of the Torah. Rather he takes positions in each situation, based on his own experience of God. Certainly he never promotes a campaign against the Israelite Torah. He sees a valid expression of God's will in many aspects of this law[34]. But the law no longer holds a central place. The reign of God is coming, and that changes everything. The law can rightly regulate many areas of life, but it is no longer the most decisive way to discover the true will of that loving God who is coming. It's not enough for the people to ask what it means to be faithful to the law. Now they need to ask what it means to be faithful to the God of compassion.

Jesus does not confront people with the laws that the scribes talk about, but with a compassionate God. It is not enough to be concerned with what the Torah says. They must seek the true will of God, which often takes us beyond what the laws say. What is important in the reign of God is not to have people who observe the laws, but sons and daughters who are like God and try to be good as God is. Those who do not kill are fulfilling the law, but if they do not root out aggression against their brother or sister from their hearts, they are not like God[35].

242

codes were incorporated into the history of God with his people. The whole collection was called Torah or Law. In Jesus' time, the Torah and the Temple were the two pillars of Judaism. Later with the destruction of the Temple, the Law became the only center. When we speak here of Law or Torah, we are talking about the collection of laws and prescriptions that the people must obey in order to live in faithfulness to the Covenant.

33 In Matthew Jesus says: «I have come neither to abolish nor to fulfill. For truly I tell you: until heaven and earth pass away, not one letter, not one stroke of a letter, will pass from the law until all is accomplished». There is a general consensus that this whole collection (Matt 5:17-19) is a Christian creation, reflecting later debates about the obligatory character of the Jewish law among Christians.

34 When someone asks him what he must do to inherit eternal life, Jesus reminds him of the requirements of the Law, and goes on to cite the second tablet which refers to social obligations: «You shall not murder; You shall not commit adultery; You shall not steal…» (Mark 10:17-22).

35 Matt 5:21-22. These words were shaped in the Christian community, but they reflect an echo of Jesus' teaching.

Those who do not commit adultery are fulfilling the law, but if they selfishly desire their brother's wife, they are not like God[36]. Those who love only their friends, but nourish an inner hatred against their enemies, do not have a compassionate heart as God does[37]. The law reigns in these people, but God does not; they are observant, but they are not like God.

Jesus seeks God's will with a surprising sense of freedom. He is not at all concerned with debating casuistic issues of morality; he goes straight to what is good for people. He criticizes, corrects and rectifies specific interpretations of the law when he finds them inconsistent with God's will, which above all is about compassion and justice for the weak and the people who need help[38].

His sense of freedom with respect to the norms and prescriptions of ritual purity probably surprised people greatly. Most of the «impurities» people might incur did not make them «sinners», morally culpable before God, but in the purity code they led to separation from the holy God, and prohibited the people from entering the temple and participating in worship. The observance of ritual purity was apparently quite rigorous in Jesus' time[39]. The Essenes of Qumran were surely the most rigorous. We know this from their obsessive purification of their bodies, over and over throughout the day. The Pharisaic groups did not go that far, although their way of observing the purity code was much stricter than that of other people[40].

In contrast, Jesus relates with total freedom to people who are considered impure, without caring about criticism from the most observant sectors. He eats with sinners and publicans, touches lepers, and mingles with undesirable people. Israel's true identity does not consist of excluding pagans, sinners, and the impure. The decisive factor in being the «people of God» is not «separating themselves», as most of the Pharisaic sectors did, or isolating themselves in the desert,

36 Matt 5:27-28.
37 Matt 5:43-45.
38 In Mark 7:8-13, Jesus criticizes a Pharisaic tradition by which if a son devotes something as Corban, that is, «an offering to God», he is excused from using those goods to assist his aging or needy parents. Jesus says that in doing so, «you no longer permit doing anything for a father or mother, thus making void the word of God through your tradition that you have handed on». This quote does not appear to be authentic, since Jesus did not intervene in matters as technical and subtle as a declaration of Corban. But scholars believe it reflects his attitude toward this type of issues.
39 Later in the Mishna, no fewer than twelve treatises were devoted to prescriptions related to purity.
40 We don't know the position of the Pharisaic groups with any certainty. The most respected scholars have widely divergent interpretations. Neusner affirms that even as lay people, the Pharisees were committed to observing the same purity laws as the temple priests. Sanders believes that only the most radical sectors followed that line.

as the Qumran Essenes did. In God's reign, their true identity consists of excluding no one but accepting everyone, especially the marginalized.

The Christian sources have preserved Jesus' words which express his thought well: «There is nothing outside a person that by going in can defile, but the things that come out are what defile»[41]. Some people were very concerned with observing the purity laws in order to remain unblemished. For Jesus, this type of impurity does not defile a person. Ritual impurity on the outside is less important, because it does not defile the heart. It is the «impurity» that comes from inside, which pollutes a person internally and is later expressed in evil words and actions. In accepting God, the important thing is not to avoid external contacts that can contaminate us, but to live with a clean, good heart[42].

Thus Jesus considers whether a specific law does good for people, and helps bring God's compassion into the world. We see this in his response to the law of sabbath, the weekly festival which everyone considered a gift of God. In the oldest traditions it was a blessed, holy day, instituted by God to give his creatures rest. Everyone should rest, including the animals that were used to work the fields. The sabbath was a day to take a deep breath and enjoy freedom. Even slaves were released from work on that day. There was tranquility and peace in the Galilean villages[43]. In Jesus' time, the sabbath was not only a law of faithfulness to the Covenant. It had become a sign and emblem of the Jewish people's identity vis-à-vis other nations[44]. The Romans, who did not interrupt their work rhythm with a weekly festival, admired, respected, and even «envied» this venerable custom. For the Jews it was a law so sacred and so rooted in their consciousness that in their struggles against Antiochus Epiphanes, many Jews died because they would not fight when they were attacked on the sabbath[45].

41 These words are cited in Mark 7:15 and in the [apocryphal] *Gospel of Thomas* 14:5. The saying reflects Jesus' authentic thinking, and probably circulated independently among the first Christians. Its context in Mark is the writer's own, rather complex construction.

42 Jesus apparently did not reject all the purity laws out of hand. As Sanders notes, if for example Jesus had affirmed that it was all right to eat pork, there would have been a violent negative reaction. Recall that in Maccabean times (175-134 B.C.), many Jews had died for their refusal to eat impure food. Even so, Jesus' words and behavior defied a purity system solidly established in the tradition.

43 The Jewish Scriptures interpreted the sabbath as a festival of «rest» in imitation of God, who had taken a day of rest after six days of creative labor (Exod 20:8-11). It was also seen as «liberation» from the workers' hard life, recalling their liberation from slavery in Egypt (Deut 5:12-15). The term «sabbath» comes from the Hebrew *sabbat*, which means «stop» or «rest».

44 The three best known customs distinguishing the Jewish people from others in the Roman Empire were the circumcision of men, the sabbath law, and abstaining from impure food.

45 A heart-rending episode is reported in 1 Macc 2:29-41. Later the sabbath law was interpreted less rigorously, permitting people to take up arms in defense of their own lives. Flavius Josephus

Because it was such an important sign of Israel's identity, there was real debate over the most perfect way to observe the weekly rest[46]. The Essenes of Qumran were certainly the most rigorous. We see this in some of their norms: «No one shall go to the fields to work on the sabbath… No one shall eat on the sabbath, anything that was not prepared the day before… No one shall assist livestock in giving birth on the sabbath, and if an animal falls into a well or a hole, it shall not be rescued on the sabbath… If a human being falls into a swamp or a pool of water, no one shall assist him with a ladder, a rope, or any other means»[47]. The Pharisees showed more understanding in their interpretation[48]. Specifically, they permitted breaking the sabbath in two situations: to defend one's own life against enemies, and to save a person or animal in danger of death. Healings on the sabbath were prohibited in principle, except where the sick person was in danger of death[49].

Jesus was never interested in suppressing the sabbath law. It was too great a gift for those people who needed to rest from their work and obligations. On the contrary, he restores its most genuine meaning: like everything that comes from God, the sabbath is always for the good, the rest, and the life of God's creatures. He does not share the perspective of either the Pharisees or the Essenes. He is not troubled by the scrupulous observation of a law that strengthens the people's identity. What he cannot tolerate, from his experience of God, is any law that keeps people from experiencing the Father's goodness.

That is why Jesus dares to cure people on the sabbath, even when they are not in imminent danger of death. His action apparently provoked a reaction from the most rigoristic sectors of his time, and Jesus used the occasion to explain the reason behind his action[50]. The sabbath is a gift of God. «The sabbath

says: «On the sabbath, the Jews only fight in self-defense» (*La guerra judía* I, 146. [English: *The Jewish War*]).

46 Opinions varied widely in Jesus' time. Apparently people did not force their opinions on others (Theissen, Sanders).

47 Flavius Josephus shows with various examples that the Essenes «avoid working on the seventh day of the week, with greater rigor than other Jews» (*La guerra judía* II, 147. [English: *The Jewish War*]).

48 The Essenes faulted the Pharisees for «easy interpretations» that «stray from the path».

49 The Pharisees also disagreed among themselves. The followers of Hillel were inclined toward more open and liberal interpretations, the partisans of Shammai toward more rigid and rigoristic positions.

50 The gospels report Jesus' transgressions of the sabbath law in detail (Mark 3:1-6; Luke 13:10-17; 14:1-6; John 5:1-18; 9:1-40). We cannot judge the authenticity of each episode, because they were recreated after 70 A.D. and largely reflect the Christian community's conflicts and polemics with orthodox Judaism (Gnilka, Meier, Schlosser, Sanders, Barbaglio). However, no one doubts that Jesus broke the sabbath to cure the sick.

was made for humankind, and not humankind for the sabbath»[51]. God did not create the sabbath to lay a burden on the people, or to shackle them to a set of norms. What God wants is the good of the people. That is the real intention of any law that comes from God. How can he not heal people on the sabbath? If the sabbath is for celebrating freedom from work and slavery, is it not the most appropriate day to free the sick from their suffering and help them experience the liberating love of God? God's reign is breaking into the world now; we can begin now to experience this weekly festival as an anticipation of the final rest and the enjoyment of life that God wills, especially for those who suffer most.

Jesus boldly defends his actions: «Is it lawful to do good or to do harm on the sabbath, to save life or to kill?»[52]. Is it permitted to «kill» an enemy in self-defense, but not to «heal»? Can we commit such an evil as homicide, and not do something so good for a sick person as to cure the sickness? Can we save a sheep that has fallen into a pit, and not heal a human being who is overcome by illness?[53] Jesus does not wait to heal the sick at the end of the sabbath. He cannot bear to see someone suffering, and not take immediate action. The next day he may be in another village, proclaiming the reign of God to other people. What is important is not the law, but the life that God wills for all who suffer.

The gospel writers also tell about another significant episode. Jesus is walking around Galilee as usual, with his disciples following him. It is a sabbath. In the villages, families gather on that day for the most important meal of the week, but Jesus and the disciples are out in the countryside and getting hungry. As they go through the fields, they see some ripe grain. The disciples don't hesitate for a moment. They pluck the grain, remove the husks by hand, and eat it. Apparently they are criticized, not for stealing what is not theirs, but because plucking and hulling the grain is work forbidden on the sabbath. Jesus defends them, recalling that when David and his followers were fleeing from Saul, they did not hesitate to satisfy their hunger by eating the «bread of the Presence» which only priests were allowed to eat. Jesus' attitude is always the same: no law that comes

---

51 Mark 2:27. Scholars consider this an authentic saying of Jesus which was probably circulated independently. We can read something similar, written years later by Rabbi Simeon ben Manasses (c. 180 A.D.): «The sabbath is given to you, and you are not the ones given to the sabbath».

52 Mark 3:4. We cannot affirm the authenticity of this saying with certainty.

53 Matt 12:11: «Suppose one of you has only one sheep and it falls into a pit on the sabbath; will you not lay hold of it and lift it out?» See also Luke 14:6 and 13:5. Such sayings echo the convictions of Jesus, but he probably was not accustomed to entering into this kind of casuistry.

from God can stop the sick or the hungry from satisfying their vital needs, precisely because God is the friend of life[54].

4

The important thing is love

The only appropriate response to the arrival of God's reign is love. Jesus is very certain about this. God's way of being and acting should be the program for everyone. A compassionate God is asking his sons and daughters to live a life inspired by compassion. Nothing would please God more. Love is an absolute imperative in order to build a life as God wills it.

Jesus often talks in his parables about compassion, forgiveness, accepting the lost, helping the needy. That is his language as a prophet of the reign of God. But sometimes he also speaks as a teacher of life, presenting love as the fundamental and decisive law. He draws an intimate, unbreakable connection between two great precepts that were deeply respected in the religious tradition of the Jewish people: love of God and love of the neighbor[55]. According to the Christian sources, when someone asks him which is the first of all the commandments, Jesus recalls first the one that Jews recite at the beginning and end of every day in the *Shema*: «The first is, "Hear, O Israel: the Lord our God, the Lord is one; you shall love the Lord your God with all your heart, and with all your soul, and with all your mind, and with all your strength"». Jesus himself has prayed those words that morning. They help him to live by loving God with all his heart and all his strength. That is the first one, but right away he adds another from the ancient book of Leviticus. «The second is this, "You shall love your neighbor as yourself." There is no other commandment greater than these»[56].

54 Mark 2:23-28; Matt 12:1-8; Luke 6:1-5. Researchers consider this episode historically plausible. The disciples were not carrying food as they followed Jesus through Galilee, and certainly they were often hungry before they reached a village. But although the words reflect Jesus' thinking, they have been recreated in the Christian community. It was not his style to argue from the Jewish Scriptures.

55 Jesus seldom uses the customary terminology for love. He speaks of *agape* (love) or *agapan* (to love) in the context of love for enemies. But in general he uses more concrete language: «have compassion» on those who suffer; «forgive» those who offend us; «give a cup of water», or «help the needy».

56 Mark 12:29-31. The episode was constructed by the editor of the book, but according to most researchers (not including Lüdemann), Jesus' reply is authentic. Its content reflects what Jesus really thinks. The two texts that Jesus brings together are Deut 6:4-5 and Lev 19:18.

The love of God and neighbor is the synthesis of the law, the supreme principle that sheds new light on the whole legal system. The commandment to love is not on the same level with the other precepts, mixed in with more and less important norms. Love makes everything else relative. If a precept is not derived from love or goes against love, it is meaningless; it is of no use in building a life according to God's will.

Jesus establishes a close connection between the love of God and the love of neighbor. They are inseparable. It is impossible to love God and forget about the neighbor. For those who seek God's will, the important thing is not to read laws written on stone tablets, but to discover the requirements of love in people's lives. There is no sacred place in which we can encounter God alone; we cannot worship God in the temple and neglect those who suffer; love of God becomes a lie when the neighbor is excluded. What goes against love, goes against God[57].

Jesus does not confuse love of God with love of neighbor, as if they were the same thing. The love of God cannot be reduced to love of neighbor; the love of neighbor is not, in itself, love of God. For Jesus the love of God holds absolute primacy, and nothing can replace it. It is the first commandment. It does not dissolve into human solidarity. Love of God comes first: seeking God's will, entering God's reign, trusting in God's forgiveness. We pray to God, not to our neighbor; we await the reign of God, not of our brothers and sisters.

On the other hand, the neighbor is not a means or an occasion for practicing our love of God. Jesus is not turning the love of neighbor into a kind of indirect love for God. He loves people and helps them because they suffer, because they need help. He is concrete and realistic. We must take a cup of water to the thirsty because they are thirsty; we must give food to the hungry so they will not die of hunger; we must give clothes to the naked to protect them from the cold. It would be rather strange to love people not for themselves, but for love of God. Certainly Jesus would have a hard time understanding it that way[58].

---

57 This synthesis between the love of God and the neighbor was already emerging in Judaism before Jesus' time. In the book of *Jubilees* (second century B.C.) we read: «Fear God and worship him, and at the same time each one shall love his brother with mercy and justice». The *Testament of the Twelve Patriarchs* (second century B.C.) says: «Love the Lord and your neighbor, have pity on the weak and the poor». According to Philo of Alexandria, a Jewish philosopher of Jesus' time, «the worship of God» and «philanthropy» are the two principal, twin virtues (*Virtutes* 51:95). What is most original in Jesus is that he cites the two precepts literally and places them above all the others, thus giving special emphasis to what was already being said.

58 Jesus cured people because their suffering was painful to him.

He thinks about it differently. Those who see themselves as God's sons and daughters love God with all their heart, all their soul, all their strength. Naturally this love requires humility, total availability and commitment to a Father who loves all his sons and daughters without limits or conditions. Therefore it is not possible to love God without desiring what he does, or without unconditionally loving those he loves as a Father. The love of God makes it impossible to shut ourselves off, indifferent to other people's suffering. It is precisely in our love of neighbor that we show the truth of our love for God.

So it is not surprising that Jesus gives special importance to love of the neighbor. He goes beyond repeating the famous command of Leviticus, «You shall love your neighbor as yourself», and makes it explicit by dictating what has become known as the golden rule: «Do to others as you would have them do to you»[59]. This rule was not new to Judaism. It appears as a negative in the book of Tobit, written in the second century B.C.: «And what you hate, do not do to anyone». Around the same time, a Hebrew book says: «Let no one do to his brother what he does not want done to him»[60]. There is a well known anecdote in a Jewish book, about two rabbis who lived shortly before Jesus. A Jewish man told Rabbi Shammai that he would become a proselyte, if the rabbi could teach him the Torah while standing on one foot. Shammai became angry and sent him away. Then he went to Rabbi Hillel, who answered him: «Don't do to others what you don't want done to you. That is all the Law. The rest is only commentary».

To love others «as yourself» simply means loving them as we want them to love us. It is impossible to describe love in precise formulas. Jesus never does that. Love requires imagination and creativity. That is the only way to understand Jesus' invitation: Do to others as you would have them do to you; your own experience can be the best viewpoint for imagining how to treat a specific person[61]. Put yourself in the other person's situation: what would you want if it were you? That way you can begin to see more clearly how to treat the other[62].

59 The golden rule is quoted in the Q Source (Luke 6:31; Matt 7:12) and in the [apocryphal] *Gospel of Thomas* 25:1-2.

60 Tob 4:5; *Testament of Nephtali* 1:6.

61 The different versions of the «golden rule» that circulated in Judaism formulated it in negative terms: «Do not do to others what you don't want them to do to you». In this formulation there is a risk of reducing love to «not doing harm» to the neighbor. Jesus' formulation is positive: «Do to others as you would have them do to you». Here love is not about not doing harm, but treating the other in the best possible way. Today's scholars do not place great importance on this change of formulation. It would be too subtle.

62 One author doubts that Jesus repeated this behavioral rule, so well known in Judaism. It does not seem to reflect his viewpoint, which was always so provocative, and which appears in sayings

Jesus could hardly have shown more incisively the unlimited nature of love. If what we ideally want for ourselves becomes a criterion and rule for our behavior toward others, we no longer have an excuse or a way out. We always want the best for ourselves. The «golden rule» forces us to seek the good of others, unconditionally. In the «new world» Jesus proclaims, this must be our basic attitude: availability, service and attention to a brother's or sister's need. There are no concrete norms. Loving our neighbors means doing everything we can for them in their specific situation[63]. Jesus is thinking about new relationships, governed not by self-interest or usefulness to others, but by concrete service to those who suffer most.

Jesus' call is clear and specific. Accepting the reign of God is not a metaphor. It simply means living the love of neighbor in every situation. That is the decisive point. We only live as sons or daughters of God by living with others as brothers or sisters. In God's reign, the neighbor takes the place of the law. We allow God to reign in our lives when we are totally open to God's call in the voice of any human being in need. In God's kingdom all human creatures, even the ones we find most contemptible, have a right to experience the love of others and to receive the help they need to live in dignity.

5

Love your enemies

The call to love is always appealing. Certainly many people accepted Jesus' message with pleasure. What they did not expect was to hear him talk about loving their enemies. For those with cruel experience of the Roman oppression and abuse from the powerful, this was a true scandal. Only a lunatic could say something so absurd with such conviction: «Love your enemies and pray for those who persecute you»; «forgive seventy-seven times», «if someone strikes you on

---

like these: «If anyone strikes you on the right cheek, turn the other also»; «invite those who cannot return the invitation». Perhaps this other rule would have better reflected Jesus' thinking: «Treat others as they want to be treated» (Lüdemann).

63 The parable of the good Samaritan describes, in surprising detail for the usually sober language of the gospels, the actions of someone who is moved by compassion, goes to the wounded man by the roadside, and does whatever he can for him: disinfects his wounds with wine, salves them with oil, bandages him, mounts him on his own horse, takes him to an inn, cares for him, and offers to pay for whatever else is needed (Luke 10:34-35).

the right cheek, turn the other also». What is Jesus talking about? Where is he leading them? Is this God's will? Living in meek submission to the oppressors?

The Jewish people had some very clear ideas about this. The God of Israel directs history by violently imposing his justice. The book of Exodus recalls the terrible experience that gave birth to the people of God. The Lord heard the cries of the Hebrews, and intervened powerfully to destroy the enemies of Israel and take vengeance for their unjust oppression. They worshiped him as the true God, precisely because his violence was more powerful than that of other gods. Again and again, God protected them by destroying their enemies. Only with God's violent help could they enter the promised land.

The crisis came when the people were again subjected to enemies more powerful than they. What could they think when the chosen people were exiled to Babylon? What could they do? Abandon Yahweh and worship the gods of Assyria and Babylonia? Learn to think of their God differently? They soon found the answer. God had not changed; it was they who had turned away from him by disobeying his commandments. Now Yahweh was directing his violent judgment against his disobedient people, somehow turning them into his «enemy». God is still great, because now he uses foreign empires to punish the people for their sin[64].

As the years went by, the people began to think it was excessive punishment. Their sin had been paid for, with interest. The hopes with which they returned from exile had been frustrated. The new invasion of Alexander the Great, and then oppression by the Roman Empire, were a cruel and undeserved injustice. Some visionaries began to talk about «apocalyptic violence». God would again intervene powerfully and violently, to liberate his people by destroying those who oppressed Israel and punishing those who rejected the Covenant. In Jesus' time, no one doubted God's violent power to impose his justice and take vengeance on the oppressors of his people. They only wondered when God would intervene, how he would do it, and what would happen when he came with his punishing power. Everyone was expecting a God of vengeance. They recited psalm after psalm, each one pleading for salvation and promising the destruction of

---

64 The author of Leviticus expounds in fearful terms this theology of a violent God who directs history by his destructive power. «If you follow my statutes... no sword will go through your land. You shall give chase to your enemies, and they shall fall before you by the sword... But if you will not obey me, and do not observe all these commandments... I will set my face against you, and you shall be struck down by your enemies; your foes shall rule over you» (Lev 26:3, 6-7, 14-17).

their enemies. This was their unanimous plea: «O Lord, you God of vengeance, you God of vengeance, shine forth! Rise up, O judge of the earth; give to the proud what they deserve!»[65].

In this climate, everything encouraged hatred toward the enemies of God and the people. It was a sign of their zeal for God's justice: «Do I not hate those who hate you, O Lord? And do I not loathe those who rise up against you? I hate them with perfect hatred; I count them my enemies»[66]. This hatred was nourished especially by the Essenes at Qumran. It was a fundamental principle for their members: «To love everything that God chooses and hate everything that he rejects». Members of the community were specifically required «to love all the sons of light, each one according to his place in God's plan, and to hate all the sons of darkness, each one according to his guilt in God's vengeance»[67]. The dark backdrop of hatred appears in various texts encouraging «eternal hatred against the men of corruption» or «anger against the men of evil». Fired up by this hatred, they prepared to take part in the final war of «the sons of light» against «the sons of darkness»[68].

Jesus starts using a new and surprising language. God is not violent but compassionate; he loves even his enemies; he does not seek anyone's destruction. His greatness does not consist of taking vengeance, punishing, and controlling history through destructive interventions. God is great, not because he has more power than anyone to destroy his enemies, but because of his unconditional compassion for all. «He makes his sun rise on the evil and on the good, and sends rain on the righteous and on the unrighteous»[69]. God does not jealously withhold his sun and his rain. He shares with his sons and daughters on earth, without distinguishing between the righteous and the guilty. He does not restrict his love to those who are faithful to him. He does good even to those who oppose him. He does not treat people according to their behavior. He does not respond to injustice with injustice, but with love[70].

---

65 Ps 94:1-2.

66 Ps 139:21-22.

67 1Q Rule of the Congregation 1:3-4, 9-11. According to Flavius Josephus, in forming their community the Essenes established a fearful oath «to hate… the unrighteous forever and struggle on the side of the righteous» (*La guerra judía* II, 139. [English: *The Jewish War*]).

68 The lame, blind, deaf, mute, mentally ill, etc. were probably excluded from the Qumran community because they could not participate in this final war. In contrast, Jesus accepts them because he is not preparing people for war and hatred, but for peace and love (Ranke-Heinemann, Nelson-Pallmeyer).

69 Q Source (Luke 6:35; Matt 5:45).

70 God's goodness in giving rain and crops to enemy peoples posed a problem for the rabbis, who tried to respond in different ways (Haninah, Eleazar). Jesus did not get involved in these debates.

God is accepting, compassionate and forgiving. Jesus knows this from experience. Therefore he is not in tune with messianic expectations of a bellicose God, or a Messenger of God who will destroy Israel's enemies. He also doesn't seem to believe in apocalyptic fantasies, proclaiming imminent catastrophic punishment for everyone who opposes God[71]. He doesn't want to nourish hatred against anyone, as the Qumran Essenes do. This God, who excludes no one from his love, will persuade us to act as he does. Jesus draws an irrefutable conclusion: Love your enemies, so that you will be worthy of your heavenly Father[72]. His message must have caused a stir, since the psalms encouraged hatred and the law, taken as a whole, taught people to fight against the «enemies of God»[73].

Jesus is not thinking only about the private enemies people might have in their own social groups or villages. He surely means all kinds of enemies: personal enemies, those who harm the family, group adversaries, and the oppressors of the people. God's love does not discriminate, but seeks the good of all. Those who are like God do the same; they seek the good of all. Jesus eliminates enmity from God's reign. His exhortation could be paraphrased as follows: «Don't be enemies to anyone, not even to your enemies. Be like God»[74].

Jesus does not turn the love of enemies into a universal law. From his experience as a child of God, he sees the love of enemies as the way to be like God, the way to destroy enmity among brothers and sisters. It is a process that takes work.

He simply contemplated the creation and saw that God is good to everyone. Around 260 A.D., a rabbi named Samuel affirmed something that Jesus would surely have agreed with: «The Lord is good to all and his mercy is for all, because this is his way of acting, since he is merciful» (*Beresit Rabbá* 33:3).

71 Jesus knew that God had not helped those who rebelled upon the death of Herod the Great (4 B.C.) He also saw that God had not intervened to save the Baptist from Herod Antipas. We don't really know if these events influenced his thinking, as some researchers suggest (Jewett, Nelson-Pallmeyer).

72 This is the gist of the message that we can attribute to Jesus from Matt 5:43-45; Luke 6:27-28, 35. The *Jesus Seminar* sees «Love your enemies» as one of the three sayings that most certainly came from Jesus.

73 There are fearful imprecations against enemies in the psalms (137:8-9; 58:11). In the Greek world, Plato's principle generally prevailed: «Do good to your friends and do evil to your enemies». However we see in Seneca an exhortation that is surprisingly close to Jesus' thinking: «If you want to imitate the gods, do good to the ungrateful, for the sun rises also on criminals and the seas are open to pirates».

74 It is misleading to introduce a distinction between personal enemies (*inimicus*) and public or political enemies (*hostis*) into Jesus' thinking. It is true that Jesus was almost always thinking primarily of the enemies his hearers might have in their own village context (Horsley), but he did not leave out the adversaries of the nation or the oppressors of the people (Schotroff, Theissen, Gnilka, Schrage). Probably in the transmission of the tradition, the focus shifted gradually toward the «persecutors» of the Christian communities (Matt 5:44).

Jesus is completely unsupported by his biblical tradition[75] —he is going against the psalms of vengeance which nourish his people's prayer life, opposing the general climate of hatred toward the enemies of Israel, rejecting the apocalyptic fantasies of a final war against the Roman oppressors— when he proclaims to all: «Love your enemies, do good to those who hate you»[76]. God's reign will be the beginning of the destruction of hatred and enmity among God's childrens. That is how Jesus sees it.

6

The nonviolent struggle for justice

All the people's hopes are focused on the powerful intervention of God, who will impose his justice by destroying the enemies of Israel. No one could think otherwise, hearing the promises of the prophets and the expectations of the apocalyptic writers. But Jesus' experience is different. God loves justice, but he is a healer, not a destroyer of life; he does not reject sinners but accepts and forgives them. Justice will come, but not because God imposes it violently and destroys those who oppose it.

Jesus' attitude goes directly against the general climate. He cannot believe in a Messenger of God charged with making war against the Romans; he expects nothing good to come from violent uprisings against the Empire; he does not listen to the apocalyptists who encourage people's hopes for imminent vengeance from God; he does not understand the Essenes living in the desert, preparing for the final war against «the sons of darkness». God's coming cannot be violent and destructive. On the contrary, it will mean the elimination of every kind of violence among individuals and peoples. As a result Jesus is constantly opposing different forms of violence, without ever resorting to the violence that destroys others. His mission is not to destroy but to heal, restore, bless, and forgive. That is how God's reign is breaking into the world[77].

75 The Q Source speaks of «praying» for enemies. Luke says, «Bless those who curse you, pray for those who abuse you» (6:28). Matthew writes, «Pray for those who persecute you». The *Oxyrrhincus* papyrus 1224 and the *Didache* transmit it literally: «Pray for your enemies».

76 Luke 6:27.

77 It is important to note that in describing Jesus' program or activity, the Christian sources draw on the prophet Isaiah — but cite only those texts that speak of healing, liberation, or restoration, ignoring those that speak of punishment, vengeance or destruction. In Luke 4:18-19 Jesus reads a text from Isaiah that says, «The Spirit of the Lord is upon me, because he has anointed me to

But if a warlike Messiah is not coming to defeat the Romans, and if God is not going to intervene violently to avenge the people and bring justice to the poor, what can they do? Submit meekly to the Roman oppressors? Accept the injustice of the large landowners? Hold their tongues in face of abuses by the temple priests? Give up forever their hopes for a just world? How can God's reign become reality in the face of such injustice? From his experience of a non-violent God, Jesus proposes a nonviolent practice of resistance to injustice. This means living in unity with a God whose heart is not violent but compassionate. God's sons and daughters are to be like God even when they are struggling against abuse and injustice.

Jesus' language is scandalous even today. He does not give norms or precepts. He simply suggests a way of acting that tests the limits of the possible. He does this by proposing specific situations that graphically show how to react against evil: «Do not [violently] resist an evildoer. But if anyone strikes you on the right cheek, turn the other also; and if anyone wants to sue you and take your coat, give your cloak as well; and if anyone forces you to go one mile, go also the second mile»[78].

This position is fully consistent with Jesus' way of acting, and seems to be a desperate attempt to eradicate injustice from the world without giving way to destructive violence. Jesus is not encouraging passivity. He is not leading them toward indifference, or toward a cowardly surrender to injustice. Rather he encourages them to take control of the situation by taking the initiative, throwing the adversary off balance with a positive act of friendship and grace.

He wants them to respond with dignity, creating a new situation which dramatizes the injustice and forces the violent ones to reflect, even perhaps to change their attitude. This does not mean playing the victim, but pursuing a friendly

bring good news to the poor. He has sent me to proclaim release to the captives and recovery of sight to the blind, to let the oppressed go free, to proclaim the year of the Lord's favor». The text stops there, without the rest of the sentence: «to proclaim the year of the Lord's favor, *and the day of vengeance of our God*». According to the Q Source (Luke 7:22; Matt 11:5), Jesus answers John's disciples: «The blind receive their sight, the lame walk, the lepers are cleansed, the deaf hear, the dead are raised, the people have good news brought to them». The reply is largely based on Isa 35:5-6, which says: «Then the eyes of the blind shall be opened, and the ears of the deaf unstopped; then the lame shall leap like a deer, and the tongue of the speechless sing for joy» — but it does not quote the preceding verse, which says: «He will come with vengeance, with terrible recompense».

78 Q Source (Luke 6:29; Matt 5:39-41). There is widespread scholarly agreement that these three examples come from Jesus. They reflect his paradoxical and provocative style. Some scholars doubt the authenticity of the third example, which does not appear in Luke.

strategy to forestall any possible escalation of violence. Perhaps Jesus is not so much thinking of the adversary's reaction, as of people's ability to overcome their own violent reaction and respond to aggression — not in the same way as the aggressor, but precisely the opposite way. For Jesus this is the action most worthy of people who are entering the reign of God[79].

A blow to the right cheek was apparently a common way to humiliate a subordinate in that culture. Masters struck their slaves, landowners their workers, husbands their wives, with impunity. How could the subordinate protest? It was normal to accept the humiliation and submit meekly to the abuse of the powerful. Jesus sees things differently; they can react in surprising ways. He is saying in effect, «When the aggressors strike you on the right cheek, don't let them take away your dignity. Look them in the eye, take away their power to humiliate you, offer the other cheek, let them see that their aggression has not intimidated you; you are as human as they are, or more so».

The same tactic works in different situations as well. If someone wants to take away the tunic you use to cover your body, take off the cloak you're wearing and hand it to him as well. Let everyone see you naked, but proud. The aggressors are ridiculed, their greed exposed for all to see[80]. Or imagine a different situation. If the Roman soldiers force you to carry a load for them one mile, why not offer to go another mile? This would cause them problems, because Roman law forbade them to force anyone to go more than one mile. It wouldn't be a great victory over Rome, but you would show your dignity and your rejection of unjust oppression[81].

The reign of God requires a world organized not around violence, but around love and compassion. Certainly Jesus is not thinking about a magic transformation of the unjust and cruel society that he knows so well. He would soon experience the brutal power of the violent ones in his own flesh. But he may have

---

[79] This is the most generalized interpretation, with different nuances (Schotroff, Theissen, Gnilka, Bruce, Nelson-Pallmeyer, Wink, Barbaglio). It has recently been opposed by Horsley. In his view Jesus is not talking about «nonviolent resistance to evil», but rather encouraging the Galilean villagers to «help one another, including even their enemies». In my judgment Horsley has contributed a better contextualization of Jesus' sayings, but that does not at all undermine their point about nonviolent resistance to those who mistreat us.

[80] The tunic (*khiton*) was an undergarment worn directly on the body. The cloak (*himation*) was the protective mantle worn over it. In the book of Exodus, it was forbidden to take a poor person's mantle, because it was his only protection against the nighttime cold (22:25-26).

[81] People were apparently obliged to carry a load for one mile if the military authorities requested it. Simon of Cyrene was forced to carry Jesus' cross in the passion narrative.

wanted to create radical, rebellious minority groups that instead of following the usual pattern, could free the people from the everyday violence that so easily takes control of everyone. Jesus is thinking of men and women who enter into the dynamic of God's reign with a nonviolent heart, confronting injustice responsibly and courageously, unmasking the inhumanity hidden in every society that is built on violence and indifference to the suffering of its victims. They are authentic witnesses to God's kingdom in the midst of an unjust and violent world. There will be few of them — only minorities, acting as sons and daughters of the God of compassion and peace. Jesus apparently is not thinking about large institutions. His followers will be «mustard seeds», or a small piece of «yeast». But their life, almost always on a cross, will be a light that proclaims God's new world in clear and credible ways.

Creator of a Renewal Movement

Jesus is surrounded by friends and supporters from the very beginning. The arrival of God's reign requires a change of course for the whole people, and it cannot be done by one preacher alone. He must start a movement of men and women from the people, who are one with him and can help others become aware of God's saving presence.

Jesus' intention is clear. His followers will accompany him in an itinerant life along the roads of Galilee and Judea; they will share his experience of God; they will learn from him to accept God's coming; with his guidance they will share the task of proclaiming the arrival of God's reign to everyone. He will educate and train them for this mission. How was this group of Jesus' closest disciples formed? Who helped him get the movement started? What was their life together like?

It was a brief but intense experience. There was no time for leisure activities. Apparently the group was energized by Jesus' charismatic power, rather than sustained by careful organization. Among them were his best and closest friends, who understood better than anyone his passion for God and for the last. They would not be a model of faithfulness at the moment of his execution, but later when they saw him full of life, they would become his strongest witnesses — the ones most capable of transmitting his message and passing on his spirit. It was they who would start the movement that gave rise to Christianity.

1

His power of attraction

Jesus has something that draws people to him. Most of them come out of curiosity and sympathy for the prophet of healing. But some are drawn by more than curiosity. They are convinced by his message. Some offer their full support; although they do not leave home to follow him, they provide help and hospitality when he comes to their village. There are other disciples who join his itinerant life and support him in different ways. Jesus chooses twelve of these to form his closest, most stable group[1].

---

1 A widespread scholarly consensus identifies four groups of Jesus' followers: the «crowds», who came mostly out of curiosity; the «initiates», who welcomed him in their homes; the «followers», who traveled with him; and his closest circle, the «Twelve» (Theissen, Sanders, Meier, Stegemann/Stegemann, Barbaglio).

Jesus had a real impact on the simple Galilean people. They were surprised and curious at first, then hopeful and enthusiastic. Many came to hear his parables. Quite a few brought their sick relatives, or asked him to go to their homes to cure a loved one. These people seemed to come and go. They probably accompanied him to neighboring villages, and then returned home. Clearly Jesus could mobilize people and spark their enthusiasm[2]. Flavius Josephus confirmed this at the end of the first century, saying that Jesus «attracted many Jews and many other people of Greek origin»[3]. This popularity never declined, but lasted to the end of his life[4].

It is not hard to come to Jesus, because he is almost always speaking outdoors. He is often on the shore of lake Galilee, near the small piers where people go for fish[5]. Sometimes he seeks out a quieter place on one of the hillsides facing that small sea, which the Galileans love so much. Sometimes he stops to rest at a bend in the road. Any place can be the right place to sit down and proclaim his message. He also speaks in the small village squares. Surely his favorite place is the synagogues, where villagers meet to celebrate the sabbath. The crowds can be overwhelming sometimes. The gospel writers may have occasionally exaggerated their numbers, but their descriptions give us an idea of Jesus' power of attraction. We know of one time when he had to talk to the people from a boat, while they sat on the shore. Sometimes the crowds «pressed in» on him until he could hardly walk. Once there were so many coming and going that Jesus asked his disciples to go with him to a deserted place where they could rest and eat[6].

---

2   The Christian sources affirm that Jesus attracted great crowds. They were described as «many», «a crowd», «all the people» in the region, etc. The most frequently used word is *ochlós*, which means «crowd», «multitude», a heterogeneous mass of people. Some of the descriptions were probably exaggerations, introduced by the Christian writers to emphasize the importance of a miracle or teaching (Meier), but the information is indisputable.

3   *Antigüedades de los judíos* 16, 3, 3 (English: *Jewish Antiquities*).

4   For a long time it was thought that after an early period of enthusiastic acceptance (the «Galilean spring»), people gradually pulled away from Jesus. More recent scholars argue persuasively that Jesus' popularity went on growing until his arrest in Jerusalem (R. Brown, Meier, Aguirre, Sobrino). An observation in the fourth gospel — «Because of this many of his disciples turned back and no longer went with him» (John 6:66) — probably reflects a conflict in the Johannine community around the end of the first century.

5   In addition to the ports of Capernaum and Bethsaida, the remnants of small piers have been found in protected estuaries (Aish, Kefar Aqavya, Ein Gofra, etc.) Some of them probably existed in Jesus' time (Duling).

6   Mark 3:9; 5:31; 6:31-32.

Most of the people who come to hear Jesus' parables and see his healings belong to the poorest and most despised social groups[7]. These are simple, ignorant people with no social status, fishers and peasants who live by their work; families who bring him their sick; women brave enough to go out to see the prophet; blind beggars who cry out for Jesus' attention; groups who have neglected the Covenant and are known as «sinners» for not observing the law; vagabonds and unemployed people who have nothing better to do. Jesus' heart is moved by them, for he sees them «harassed and helpless, like sheep without a shepherd»[8].

Their curiosity does not always translate into deep and lasting commitment. They listen with admiration, but they resist his message. The change of attitude he wants from them is too much. Apparently some towns like Chorazin, Bethsaida, and even the city of Capernaum rejected his message or remained indifferent[9]. Many others were attuned to him, however.

2

A widespread, warm welcome

Among these are individuals and whole families who welcome him warmly. This enthusiasm is not a passing fancy. Some follow him along the Galilean roads. Others cannot leave their homes, but are ready to support him in different ways. They are the ones who offer lodging, food, information and all kinds of help when he comes to their villages. The group of disciples who traveled with Jesus could hardly have moved around without them. Many of them are probably relatives of people Jesus has healed, or friends and neighbors who want to thank him as best they can for coming. These initiates, scattered around the towns of Galilee and Judea, form true «support groups» that collaborate closely with Jesus. He never calls them disciples, but they listen to him with the same faith and devotion as the people who accompany him in his itinerant life.

---

7 We also know of socially and economically prominent people who came to him: Zacchaeus, a rich tax collector from Jericho; Jairus, the head of the Capernaum synagogue; and a «centurion», also from Capernaum, who was a royal official in the service of Antipas.

8 Matt 9:36; Mark 6:34.

9 Jesus compares Chorazin and Bethsaida with Tyre and Sidon, the two rich, proud cities on the Phoenician coast. He warns Capernaum of a fate more tragic than Sodom's (Matt 11:21-24). Many scholars doubt that Jesus himself expressed this condemnation. They may reflect the frustration of the Christian prophets, whose itinerant mission in this region was a failure.

We don't know much about these home-based disciples. We know that when he goes to Jerusalem, Jesus doesn't stay in the holy city; he goes to Bethany, a small village three kilometers away, to stay at the home of an especially beloved family: Lazarus, Mary and Martha[10]. He may also have been invited to eat in Bethany with a leper whom he had previously cured. Someone in the village of Bethphage, very near Jerusalem, apparently loaned him a donkey to ride into the city. We also know of a friend in Jerusalem, who prepared a room to celebrate that memorable meal at which Jesus said farewell to those who had accompanied him from Galilee[11].

These are the people who make up Jesus' closest circle. It includes men and women who, attracted by his person, leave their families at least temporarily to follow him in his travels. For something over two years, from A.D. 28 to 30, they share his life, hear the message he repeats in each village, admire his faith in curing the sick, and are surprised again and again by his affection and freedom in welcoming fishermen and people of ill repute to his table.

Usually they walk a few meters behind Jesus. While they talk among themselves, Jesus is thinking over his parables in silence. Together they share moments of thirst and hunger[12]. On reaching a village they look for families of sympathizers who will give them shelter in their houses. They look for water and the other things they need to sit down and eat. The disciples are also concerned with helping the crowd listen to Jesus in peace. Sometimes they find him a boat, so people can see him better from the shore; sometimes they ask the multitude to sit around him where they can hear better. At the end of the day, they dismiss the people and prepare for the night's rest. Now they can converse more peacefully with Jesus. The disciples were his confidantes, the best friends he had during his life as an itinerant prophet[13].

We don't know exactly how many disciples there were, but there were more than just the «Twelve». Among them were men and women of different backgrounds. Some were fisherfolk, some peasants from Lower Galilee. But there

---

10 The gospel of John affirms that «Jesus loved Martha, her sister and Lazarus» (11:5).

11 It is hard to guarantee the authenticity of these details. The gospels sometimes reflect things that happened later, when itinerant Christian missionaries were supported by sympathetic families in the villages (Thiessen). But things like this probably did happen in Jesus' time (Horsley).

12 Mark 2:23-28. This story of Jesus' disciples plucking grain to satisfy their hunger is considered historically plausible (even by the *Jesus Seminar* group).

13 Most of the concrete details we have from the itinerant life of the disciples are from the gospel writers, but they reflect the type of activities we would expect.

was also a tax collector in Capernaum, named Levi, the son of Alphaeus. A few were with him from the beginning: Nathanael, a Galilean with a clean heart, and two men who were highly respected in the Christian community: Joseph Barsabbas, also known as Justus, and Matthias[14]. Bartimaeus, a blind man from Jericho whom Jesus had cured, also joined the group.[15]

The members of this heterogeneous group who shared Jesus' itinerant life are called «disciples». The term was not commonly used in that society[16]. Jesus or his followers may have begun using it among themselves, without giving it the technical meaning that would later be used to describe the disciples of the Jewish rabbis. Perhaps Jesus and some of the people around him were thinking of their experience as disciples of the Baptist[17]. Note also that in the region where Jesus traveled, there were still memories of two great prophets of the Northern Kingdom. Flavius Josephus writes that the younger of them, Elisha, «followed» the prophet Elijah and became his «disciple and servant»[18].

3

The Twelve

ᴄᴢᴏ

At some point Jesus chooses from these disciples following him, a special group of twelve to form his most intimate circle[19]. They are the core group of disciples, and the most stable. Most of them have no special status as individuals. The sources give more importance to the group as such, than to its individual members. The Twelve move in the shadow of Jesus. Their presence around him is a living sym-

---

14 According to a writing from around A.D. 80, which describes the beginning of Christianity, Joseph Barsabbas and Matthias were proposed as replacements for Judas Iscariot in the group of the Twelve (Acts 1:23).

15 See chapter 9 for information on the presence of women among Jesus' followers.

16 The Hebrew word «disciple» (*talmid*) almost never appears in the Jewish Bible, the writings of Qumran, or other books of the time. Neither was the Greek word «disciple» (*mathetés*) usually used for the first and second generation of Christians.

17 According to John 1:35-51 Andrew, Simon, Philip and Nathanael had been disciples of the Baptist.

18 *Antigüedades de los judíos* 8, 13, 7 (English: *Jewish Antiquities*).

19 Neither Jesus nor his other followers ever called them «apostles». Modern research has clarified much of the confusion surrounding the gospel writers' use of the different terms. All the men and women who followed Jesus' itinerant life are described as «disciples». The «Twelve» formed a special group within the wider circle of disciples. In contrast, the «apostles» or «messengers» were a specific group of Christian missionaries (there were more than twelve) who were sent out by the Christian communities to spread the faith in Jesus Christ (Rengstorf, Dupont, Rigaux, Meier).

bol of the hope Jesus carries in his heart: to accomplish the restoration of Israel as a seed of the reign of God[20].

Probably nearly all the members of the Twelve are Galileans[21]. Several of them are fishermen from the lake, the rest probably peasant farmers from nearby villages. The Twelve are simple men of little education, who live by their work[22]. There are no scribes or priests among them. But there are differences. The family of James and John belong to a socially prominent group. Their father, Zebedee, owned a boat and employed day workers. He probably had connections with families in the salt fish industry at Bethsaida and Tarichea (Magdala). In contrast, Peter and his brother came from a poor fishing family. They probably did not have a boat of their own, only a few nets for fishing in the shallow waters near the shore. Many lakeside villagers made their living that way. The two brothers worked together. They had come from Bethsaida, probably looking for better facilities for their modest work. Peter had married a woman from Capernaum, and their family was crowded into the household of his in-laws. They had nothing to leave but their nets when they followed Jesus[23].

It is quite a heterogeneous group. Some, like Peter, are married; others may be single. Most of them have left their whole families, but James and John come with their mother Salome; James the Younger and Joses also bring their mother, Mary. Most come from traditional Jewish families and have Hebrew names, but Simon, Andrew, and Philip, all born in Bethsaida, have apparently lived in a more hellenized environment and have Greek names[24]. Philip's father had named him after the tetrarch. Philip and Andrew probably spoke Greek, and may sometimes have served as intermediaries with visiting groups of pilgrims[25].

---

20 Jesus himself brought this group of Twelve together around him. We have this information from multiple sources, some of them in a pre-Pauline formulation (1 Cor 15:5). The names of the Twelve appear on different lists; it is said that Judas, the disciple who betrayed Jesus, was «one of the twelve». All this could hardly have been an invention of the Christian community (Dupont, Bornkamm, Roloff, Schürmann, Hengel, Sanders, Gnilka, Brown, Fitzmyer and Myer among others; Vielhauer, Braun, Conzelmann, and Crossan disagree).

21 Judas may be an exception, if we take Iscariot to mean «man from Kerioth», a small Judean village near Hebron, far away from Galilee.

22 The exception would be Levi, the tax collector from Capernaum, if he is correctly identified with Matthew (Matt 9:9; 10:3). That information cannot be confirmed.

23 Mark 1:18. Only Luke mentions «Peter's boat», but that seems to be an editorial gloss (5:3).

24 In the decade of the thirties, Philippus transformed the town of Bethsaida into a «city» (*polis*) and named it Julias, in honor of Augustus' wife.

25 John 12:20-22.

They may sometimes have had a hard time living together. Simon «the Cananean» —probably called that because of his zeal in fulfilling the Torah[26]—had to learn to accept Levi, the tax collector, in line with Jesus' insistence on accepting such undesirables as sinners, publicans and prostitutes. Likewise James and John, who were called *Boanerges* or «sons of thunder», were probably impetuous fellows[27] who created tension in the group with their ambition for an important position alongside Jesus[28].

Jesus apparently had a special relationship with Peter, and with the brothers James and John. The three fished in the same part of the lake, and knew each other before they met Jesus. He particularly enjoyed their company, and trusted them greatly. He gave them curious nicknames: he called Simon «the rock»[29], and the two brothers «sons of thunder». According to the Christian tradition, only those three were present at such special events as Jesus' «transfiguration» on a Galilean mountaintop, and his anguished prayer to the Father at Gethsemane on the night before his arrest[30].

Certainly Peter stands out among the Twelve. The sources show him as a spokesman and leader of the disciples in general, and the Twelve in particular. At some point Jesus names him *Kephas* (rock), which in its Greek version of *Petros* became his proper name; he always appears at the head of the Twelve with that name[31]. The Christian sources give an impression of Peter as a spontaneous, honest man, decisively and enthusiastically committed to Jesus, and at the same time capable of doubt, helplessness in crisis, and fear. The most solemn affirmation of faith in Jesus is attributed to him: «You are the Messiah, the Son of the Living God». So also is the most emphatic denial: «I do not know this man»[32]. His activity in the

26 The Aramaic word *qan'ana* means «zealous» or «enthusiastic». Its translation into Greek *(zelotés)* has led many people to think of him as a terrorist zealot. This is a misinterpretation; the revolutionary movement of the Zealots did not emerge until the winter of 67-68 A.D., in Jerusalem during the first Jewish War.

27 In a story that appears only in Luke 9:52-56, Jesus once had to admonish them severely. When a Samaritan village refused them hospitality, they asked him: «Lord, do you want us to command fire to come down from heaven and consume them?» Luke created the story to emphasize Jesus' peaceful attitude—so different from that of the prophet Elijah, who twice ordered fire to «come down from heaven and consume» the soldiers sent by the king to arrest him (2 Kgs 1:9-12).

28 Mark 10:35-40. There is debate over the historicity of this story. Meier considers the dialogue to be essentially historical.

29 *Kephas* (Peter) became Simon's proper name, and he was always called that in the Christian communities. Interestingly, though, when Jesus talked to him he regularly used his original name, Simon, and never called him Peter or Cephas.

30 Mark 9:2 and 14:33. This special treatment of the three men is not historically certain. We also see another special group formed by the two pairs of brothers, Peter and Andrew, James and John (Mark 1:26-20; 1:29; 13:2).

31 He always heads the list of the Twelve as transmitted by the Christian sources (Mark 3:16-19; Matt 10:2-4; Luke 6:14-16; Acts 1:1).

32 Matt 16:16 and Mark 14:71, respectively.

early Church had bright and dark spots: he was a zealous and committed leader of the Church in Jerusalem, but also capable of ambiguous and confusing actions, at least in Paul's eyes. All this made him especially appealing to Christians from the very beginning. After several periods of imprisonment in Jerusalem, he went to Antioch and later to Rome, where he died a martyr in the time of the emperor Nero between 64 and 68 A.D., possibly on Vatican Hill.

What was Jesus' goal in surrounding himself with this inseparable group of twelve men? Certainly everyone saw them as a symbol, somehow recalling the twelve tribes of Israel. But what was Jesus himself thinking of? To him the small group around him symbolized a new beginning for Israel. Once restored and rebuilt, that people so beloved of God would become the starting point for a new world, in which God's reign would reach the end of the earth. Brought into Jesus' mission of proclaiming God's arrival and healing the people, these Twelve would begin the true restoration of Israel in a modest but real way.

As they saw Jesus walk through the villages surrounded by the Twelve, a long-nourished dream was reawakening in many people: the reunification of all Jews in one kingdom like that of David (c. 1,000 B.C.) Israel saw itself as formed by twelve tribes, born of the twelve sons of Jacob, but that had changed in the eighth century B.C. The Assyrians destroyed the Northern Kingdom (Israel) in 721 B.C., and took its constituent tribes into exile. They never returned. In 587 B.C. the Babylonians invaded the Southern Kingdom (Judah), and deported the tribes of Judah and Benjamin to Babylon. The nation was never the same again. In 538 B.C. some of the exiles returned and began to rebuild the temple, but by then Israel was a broken people, its sons and daughters scattered all over the world. That was the situation in Jesus' time. Those Galilean villages were only a small part of the Jewish people; he wanted to reach all Israel, including those who lived strewn across the Empire. They were the children of the «diaspora». That is what they were called: the «Dispersion». Would they never be reunited by God?[33].

The prophets had always kept this hope alive in the hearts of the people: «He will… assemble the outcasts of Israel, and gather the dispersed of Judah from the four corners of the earth»[34]. In Jesus' time people were still waiting for that miracle. Jesus may have known of a writing that said the Messiah of David «will

[33] In Jesus' time there were over four million Jews of the diaspora, twice as many as lived in Palestine. They considered themselves members of the diverse tribes of Israel, although many had lost all memory of their ancestors. There were more than 150 Jewish colonies, including some very important ones in cities like Babylon, Antioch, Alexandria, Rome, Ephesus, Smyrna, and Damascus.

[34] Isa 11:12. The same hope is found in Mic 2:12; Jer 31:1; Ezek 20:27-44.

gather his holy people… and judge the tribes of a people sanctified by the Lord, their God»[35]. In Qumran there was frequent talk about the restoration of the «twelve tribes of Israel» in the last days; their symbol of that restoration was the presence of «twelve men» in the Council that presided over the community[36]. Jesus shared the same hope, not in terms of an ethnic and political restoration, but as a healing and liberating presence of God in his people, beginning with the sick, the excluded, and the sinners. That is why «he gave them power and authority over all demons and to cure diseases»[37]. Thus the restoration of Israel was beginning in an almost insignificant but real way. They should not expect the political triumph of Israel and the destruction of the pagans. Jesus worked for the restoration of Israel by showing them God's mercy in their own flesh. That is how he was making way for God's reign in the midst of the nations[38].

4

A radical summons

On returning from the Jordan desert, Jesus probably went first to Nazareth. His house and family were there. We don't know how long he stayed in his home town, but at some point his presence caused tension. This was not the Jesus they knew. They saw him transformed when he talked in the name of God. Moved by his Spirit, he was even trying to cure people and cast out demons. It was amazing and disconcerting to his neighbors. His childhood friends, who had played and grown up with him, had a hard time believing all that. They had seen him working as a craftsman; they knew his family. How dare he come to them now as a prophet? That was when Jesus left his town and traveled to the lake region[39]. It

---

35 *Psalms of Solomon* 17:26-32.

36 Especially in the *War Scroll*, the *Temple Scroll*, and the *Rule of the Community*.

37 Q Source (Luke 9:1-2; Matt 10:7-8).

38 The Twelve were important during Jesus' life and in the early days of the Church. But when Israel failed to respond to the call of Jesus, the group he intended to restore Israel lost its symbolic meaning for the gentiles, and soon disappeared from the scene. Only Peter, James and John remained in and around Jerusalem, until the year 43/44 when James was beheaded by Herod Agrippa, and Peter went first to Antioch, then to Rome. Paul, Barnabas, Apollo and the «apostles sent by the communities» are mentioned in letters to the early communities, but the Twelve are not.

39 Mark 6:1-6. It is impossible to reconstruct this sequence of events. Even Mark did not have it in exact order when he put together his gospel, but scholars generally agree that Jesus upset his neighbors and was not accepted by them. This may have been one of the reasons why he went away to the Galilean lake region.

was in and around Capernaum that he called his first disciples, to follow him on the plan that had been growing in his heart ever since he left the Baptist[40].

The other disciples come to Jesus in different ways. He calls some from their work. Others come after hearing from people who have met him[41]. Some may have come on their own initiative, and Jesus warns them about what following him can entail[42]. Women are probably attracted by his acceptance of them. Many people were surprised when Jesus accepted them into his group of followers. In any case the group is formed on Jesus' own initiative. His call is decisive. He does not stop to explain. He doesn't say what he is calling them to, or lay out a program for them. They will learn from him. Right now he is simply calling them to follow him[43].

The sources show him acting with surprising authority. He does not explain his goals or his logic. He does not accept conditions. They must follow him immediately. His summons requires total availability: absolute loyalty above all other loyalties, obedience even over religious duties that were considered sacred. He calls them with the passion for the reign of God that has been awakened in him. He wants to set in motion right now a movement to proclaim the Good News of God. The people have to feel his healing power now; the signs of mercy have to be planted among the nations.

Jesus' summons is radical. His followers have to drop whatever they are doing. Jesus is pointing their lives in a new direction. He pulls them out of security and launches them into an unpredictable experience. The reign of God is breaking in. They must not let anything distract them. From now on they will live in the service of God's reign, bound up intimately with Jesus' own life and prophetic task[44].

---

40 It is worth noting that none of Jesus' family members were followers. His mother and brothers did not join his disciples until after his death (Acts 1:14).

41 In John 1:35-51, Andrew brings his brother Simon to see Jesus. Philip does the same with his friend Nathanael. This story is very different from the version in Mark 1:16-18. We don't know anything with certainty. Some of Jesus' disciples had been disciples of the Baptist (as John says), but Jesus would have called them later on the shores of lake Galilee (as Mark says).

42 Q Source (Luke 9:57-62; Matt 8:18-22). Jesus probably held this type of conversation with would-be followers, even if the one related in the Q Source is not exact.

43 Jesus was not a stranger to the people he called. They already had some idea who he was (Hengel, Sanders, Gnilka).

44 It is undoubtedly an historical fact that Jesus called some people and set in motion a movement in the service of God's reign (Käsemann, Hengel, Meier). However the reports that describe his summons (Mark 1:16-20; Matt 4:18-22) are stylized narratives in the same line as the call from the prophet Elijah to Elisha (1 Kgs 19:19-21). This was the Christian writers' way of emphasizing the demands of discipleship and the exemplary responses of these people, in order to encourage the itinerant missionaries who continued Jesus' way of proclaiming the Gospel in the Syrian and Galilean regions; also in order to encourage the converts whose acceptance of the new faith in Jesus had forced them to leave their own Jewish family.

He invites them to leave their homes, their families, and their family lands[45]. This is not easy. The home is the basic institution in which everyone is rooted; it gives them a name and identity; it is where they find help and solidarity from the other family members. The home is everything: emotional shelter, place of work, symbol of social standing. To leave home is a grave offense to the family and a source of shame for all. But above all it means stepping out into total insecurity. Jesus knew that from his own experience, and he did not hide it from them: «Foxes have holes, and birds of the air have nests, but the Son of Man has nowhere to lay his head»[46]. Jesus has less security than animals do: he has no house, he eats what people give him, he sleeps wherever he can. He cannot give his followers honor or security. Those who follow him will live as he does, at the service of those who have nothing[47]. It is not surprising that vagabonds and homeless people would come to him, since he is living in the same unprotected and marginalized conditions[48].

Leaving home means neglecting their family, not protecting their honor, not working to support them or preserve their patrimony. How can Jesus tell them to «leave their lands», the peasants' most precious possession, their only means of subsistence, the only thing that gives their family social prestige? What he asks is just too much: an act of ingratitude and selfishness; a shame upon the whole family and a threat to their future. Jesus understands the conflict this can cause in those patriarchal families. Once he told them: «Do not think that I have come to bring peace to the earth; I have not come to bring peace, but a sword. For I have come to set a man against his father, and a daughter against her mother, and a daughter-in-law against her mother-in-law»[49]. The conflicts between fathers and sons were the most serious, because they undermined the father's authority. Relationships between mothers and daughters-in-law were not always easy, but they were very important in achieving the wife's integration into her hus-

45 Mark 10:28-30.
46 Q Source (Luke 9:58; Matt 8:20); [apocryphal] *Gospel of Thomas* 86:1-2. This saying had to come from Jesus: such lively images could only be his. Some authors see in these words a criticism of the two social groups that were expropriating the peasants' land and houses: the «birds» (pagans living in the Galilean cities) and the «foxes» (Herodian rulers). This has been pointed out by Manson, Bailey, and Oakman among others.
47 In Galilee during the decade of the thirties there were many beggars, vagabonds, and other people with no fixed address. It is quite possible that some of Jesus' followers were already homeless before they began following him (Thiessen, Guijarro).
48 It was said that itinerant missionaries in the early Christian communities lived «the way of life of the Lord» (*Didaché* 11:8).
49 Taken from the Q Source (Luke 12:51-53; Matt 10:34-36). The sayings probably come from Jesus.

band's household. A divided family would lose the stability it needed to protect its members and defend their honor. The family required total loyalty.

Jesus doesn't see it that way. For him the family doesn't come first; it is not above everything. There is something more important: service to the reign of God, which is already breaking in. The sources give us a disturbing saying from Jesus: «Whoever does not hate father and mother, son and daughter, cannot be my disciple»[50]. Jesus requires his disciples to be more faithful to him than to their own families. If that creates a conflict of loyalties, they must choose him. In that culture, «love» and «hate» do not refer only to personal sentiments; rather they pertain to group relationships. Jesus demands their unity and faithfulness (love), even if this entails disruption and opposition (hate) in the family.

According to one source, possibly a disciple, Jesus did not even let him take leave of his family. What that man wanted was not only to show courtesy toward his people. He wanted to be Jesus' disciple, but first he needed approval from his loved ones and the blessing of his father. How could he make such an important decision without them? Jesus answered sharply: «No one who puts a hand to the plow and looks back is fit for the kingdom of God»[51].

Why does he talk so much about the conflict his summons can cause in their families? Has he had problems with his own family? Probably so. Apparently Jesus' family members are not sympathetic to his activities around Galilee. They do not understand his behavior. At one point his mother and brothers come to take him home, because they think he has gone crazy. When told that they are there, he lets them wait outside the house where he is teaching, and says openly that the people around him, listening attentively to his word, are his true family[52]. Some of his followers probably had family conflicts like those Jesus experienced. The strange group Jesus led probably did not always have the sympathy of their families: weren't they all a little crazy?

---

50 Scholars generally agree on this proposed synthesis of the Q Source (Luke 14:26; Matt 10:37). These words come from Jesus. There is nothing like them in the Judaism of the time, and they go against the strongest pillar of that society. They were later softened by Matthew.

51 This reply probably did not come from Jesus. It was inserted later in the Christian community to contrast Jesus' radical demand with Elijah, who allowed his disciple Elisha to take leave of his family (1 Kgs 19:20). The demand of perseverance reflects a situation later than that of Jesus during those few months. Here an ancient agricultural proverb is adapted as a reference to the reign of God.

52 Mark 3:21, 31-35. Most scholars believe there really was a strong disagreement between Jesus and his family (Theissen, Meier). John agrees with Mark's interpretation when he says that «not even his brothers believed in him» (7:5).

Jesus knew those patriarchal families were controlled by the indisputable authority of the father. The father was the first defender of the family honor, the guardian of its patrimony, the coordinator of its labor. Everyone lived in submission to his authority. When Jesus asks his disciples to leave their fathers, he is requiring them to go against the first duty of any son, which is respect, obedience and total submission to the father's authority. To defy the father's supreme power, leaving him alone at home, is not only a sign of great ingratitude; it is also a public insult that no one can accept. So it must have caused a real scandal when Jesus told the man who wanted to «bury his father» before joining his followers: «Let the dead bury their dead; but as for you, go and proclaim the kingdom of God»[53]. Burying his father was a son's most important and sacred duty: the funeral honors, presided over by the son, were the sacred moment in which the father's authority and control over his family passed on to the heir. But what that man was asking Jesus probably was not to attend the burial of his recently deceased father, which would have taken only a few days. Rather he was asking to care for his father until the end. Wouldn't it be a violation of the continuity and honor of the family, to leave home without fulfilling that sacred obligation? Jesus answers with absolute clarity: God's plan comes first. Don't go on caring for the «world of your father», that patriarchal, authoritarian and exclusive family that is recreated at his death. You go and proclaim the reign of God, that new family which God is opening up to the weakest ones and the orphans. Leave your father and devote yourself to those who have no father to defend them.

Jesus' radical summons is not at all like the scrupulousness promoted by the teachers of the law. It is not inspired by the ideal of an ascetic life, superior to all others. Jesus is not trying to burden his followers with more demanding laws and norms. He is calling them to share his passion for God and his total availability for the service of God's reign. He wants to light a fire that will burn in their hearts. He would do anything for the reign of God, and he wants to see the same passion in his followers. Some of his sayings are especially telling: «For those who want to save their life will lose it, and those who lose their life for my sake, and for the sake of the gospel, will save it»[54]. With this paradoxical affirmation, which

53 Although these words appear only in Luke 9:59, there is no doubt about their authenticity. They are inconceivable in that culture (Schlätter, Hengel, Sanders). «Let the dead bury their dead» is a somewhat enigmatic word play. He probably means that the dead who must bury their dead are the people who have not yet entered into the life of God's reign. For Jesus they are «dead».

54 Mark 8:35. Few sayings are as well supported as this one; in addition to this text in Mark, it appears with minor differences in the Q Source (Luke 17:33; Matt 10:39) and in John 12:25. According to some scholars, «for my sake» and «for the sake of the gospel» may be later additions.

may reflect a popular wisdom saying, Jesus is asking his disciples to live as he does. By holding on blindly to their own life they may lose it; by generously, courageously risking their life they may save it. That's how it is. A disciple who grasps for the security, the goals and expectations that life offers, may lose the greatest of all its benefits: life according to God's plan. A disciple who risks everything and even loses the life he has been leading so far, will find life by entering into the reign of God.

The disciples may have heard something even more graphic and fearful from him. It would certainly have made them shudder: «If any want to become my followers, let them take up their cross and follow me»[55]. The disciples must forget about themselves, renounce their own interests, and center their lives on Jesus from now on. They no longer belong to themselves; their life belongs to Jesus; they will live by following him. Up to this point his summons was still appealing. What disturbed them was the metaphor he added. Everyone knew the fearful spectacle of a condemned man, lashed and bleeding, being forced to carry the horizontal beam of the cross on his own shoulders to the place of execution, where the vertical post was already standing. There were crosses scattered all over Palestine, before and after Jesus. Everyone knew how common it was to crucify slaves, thieves, rebels, and anyone who threatened the peace. They still remembered those awful days when general Varus had crucified two thousand Jews around Jerusalem. That was in 4 B.C., when Jesus was taking his first steps at home in Nazareth[56]. He could not have found more graphic language to impress on his disciples what he expected of them: their unlimited availability to follow him, taking the same risks, hostility, scorn, and possibly the same death he would suffer. Their destiny was to share the same fate as the wretched men and women who were «crucified» in so many ways in that society. They would all go together into God's reign.

---

55 Mark 8:34. This saying is attested by Mark, the Q Source (Luke 14:27; Matt 10:38), and the [apocryphal] *Gospel of Thomas* (55:2). Some scholars consider it a later Christian teaching, shaped in light of Jesus' crucifixion. But it asks followers to carry their own cross, not the cross of Jesus. The metaphor was not unknown in the first century. The Stoic philosopher Epictetus (c. 55-135 A.D.) tells his disciples: «If you want to be crucified, wait, and the cross will come». The scandalous character of the image and multiple citations point to Jesus as its source (Hengel, Meier, Gnilka).

56 Flavio Josephus, *La guerra judía* II, 72-75 (English: *The Jewish War*).

Living with Jesus

What were they thinking, this special group of people who traveled with Jesus in his life as an itinerant prophet? What had he called them to do? Would he teach them a new doctrine to be faithfully disseminated throughout Israel? If so, it was strange that he had not chosen people more educated than these ignorant fisherfolk and peasants. Why did he require of them such absolute, unconditional loyalty? Was he planning a «holy war» against Rome? This group was too insignificant to try something like that. Was he establishing a pure and holy community, like the one the Essenes had built in the Qumran desert? If so, what were women like Mary Magdalene and tax collectors like Levi doing in the group?

The image of Jesus surrounded by disciples might remind people of other teachers in that time. Flavius Josephus later described him as a «wise man» who was «a teacher of people who accepted the truth with pleasure, and attracted many Jews and gentiles»[57]. But his own people never confused him with a teacher of the law. They did call him *rabí*, but especially in the decade of the thirties, that title carried the generic meaning of «mister» and was used as a respectful term of address for anyone important. Only after A.D. 70 was it used for the «rabbis» who taught the Torah to their disciples. The rabbis would never have formed a group like this: it was not made up exclusively of men, but included women as well. And its members had not come to ask for admission to his school. Jesus had called them out of their homes to follow him and share in his service to God's reign.

The atmosphere around Jesus is very different from a rabbinical school. Jesus has not called them to study the law, or to memorize religious traditions. They are not devoted to the detailed study of innumerable precepts and norms. They are not there to become the teachers of Israel some day, experts dictating the ways of the law to the people. Their relationship with each other and with Jesus is not a scholarly one between students and their teacher. It is a personal bond with someone who is initiating them into God's plan. Jesus does not talk like a rabbi expounding the law, but as a prophet filled with God's spirit. Their goal is not some day to achieve the honorable status of a rabbi, but to share the uncertain and even dangerous fate of Jesus. These disciples are not there to learn the teacher's ideas, but to «follow» Jesus and live as he does, accepting the reign of God.

57 *Antigüedades de los judíos* 18, 3, 3 (English: *Jewish Antiquities*).

This strange group was also different from the great schools of Greece, where wise men like Pythagoras, Socrates, Plato and Aristotle taught their disciples wisdom. Following Jesus was not at all like the search for truth that the Greek philosophers cultivated[58]. Perhaps his itinerant life style, his way of dressing, and his argumentative life at the margin of society were like certain Cynical philosophers, who were apparently known in Gadara and other regions around Palestine in Jesus' time[59]. They were especially known for their dirty and unkempt appearance. Their only clothing was a threadbare mantle that showed naked arms, a knapsack and a walking stick. They walked barefoot like beggars, and slept on the hard ground. They could be seen in the public squares of the cities, or beside the thermal springs[60].

Their behavior was intentionally antisocial. The Cynics were a marginal, argumentative movement against the institutions and values of a society they considered rotten. They mocked authority, power, marriage, the family, and the ownership of property. They took pride in being happy with no help from anyone or anything. Freedom was their supreme good and highest aspiration. Free of all ties, they were not slaves to anyone; they were real kings. The words of Epictetus, a Cynic who lived shortly after Jesus (A.D. 50-130), are famous:

> Look at me; I have no city, no house, no goods, not even a slave. I sleep on the ground, I have no wife or children, no palace, only the sky and the earth and a threadbare mantle. And what do I lack? Do I not live without suffering? Do I not live without fear? Am I not free?... What is my attitude toward the people you fear or admire so much? Do I not treat them the same as slaves? Do those who see me not think they are seeing their king and lord?

58 However we do see characteristics in Socrates (469-399 B.C.) that resemble Jesus in some ways. He refused to be called a teacher and preferred to call his disciples «family members», followers, or «friends». His summons to Xenophon to follow him is well known. At the end of one dialogue he asked: «Where do perfect and good men come from?» When Xenophon remained silent Socrates said, «Follow me and learn». From then on Xenophon was one of his followers.

59 Some researchers (Downing, Mack, Crossan) have recently emphasized Jesus' similarity to the Cynics and even considered him one of them. Without denying the possibility of some influence, Horsley, Betz, Witherington III, Meier, Aguirre and others have challenged that approach, pointing out important underlying differences. Jesus was much more influenced by the Jewish wisdom tradition than by the ideas of the Cynics.

60 The Cynics had their golden age in the fourth and third centuries B.C.; after a time of eclipse, they flourished again in the first century A.D. The word «cynic» comes from the Greek *kynós*, which means «dog». Alexander the Great once presented himself as a «great king» to Diogenes, the founder of the Cynical movement; the latter replied, «I am Diogenes, the dog». The name came from their life in the streets, and their boldness in mocking the conventional society.

This total and absolute freedom led them to act in provocative and shameless ways. They felt bound only by the laws of nature, never those of society[61].

We don't know whether Jesus and his disciples ever met the Cynical philosophers. They probably never heard of them[62]. There are similarities, especially in their itinerant life, their argumentative message, and a way of dressing that graphically expresses their attitude toward society. But this group of rural Galileans has little in common with the urban phenomenon of the Cynics in the Hellenic cities. Their goals and underlying significance are completely different. The shoulder bag in which each Cynic carried his small provisions was a symbol of individualistic independence. In contrast Jesus wanted to build a family; that is why he asked his disciples to dispense with the bag and accept the hospitality of the villages. While the Cynics based their self-sufficiency on a simple life, Jesus taught his followers to trust God's solicitous love and each other's mutual acceptance. One would also never see in his group the contempt for others, the crude insults, or the indecent acts that were characteristic of the Cynics[63]. Jesus' actions are those of a prophet who wants to cure diseases, cast out evil, and tell everyone about the saving nearness of God. This is the radical difference: while the Cynics live according to nature in search of freedom, Jesus and his disciples live by accepting the reign of God and proclaiming God's love and justice.

What the people feel around Jesus is unheard of, something truly unique. His presence fills everything. He is the center. The difference is in his person, his whole life, the mystery of the prophet who spends his life healing, accepting, forgiving, liberating from evil, passionately loving people over any law, and telling everyone that the God who is already irrupting in their lives is like that: unfathomable love, and only love. They learn everything from Jesus. In him they can see what a life entirely dedicated to God's reign is like. They see how he trusts a good God, Father of all, Friend of life. From him they learn the Lord's Prayer,

---

61 The principal features of the Cynical groups are self-sufficiency (*autarchaeia*), freedom (*eleutheria*), imperturbability (*ataraxia*), and shamelessness (*anaidaeia*). The exchange between Diogenes and Alexander the Great is well known. When the emperor offered to grant him one wish, Diogenes replied: «Yes. Move your shadow; it's blocking out my sun».

62 The Cynical movement was apparently well rooted in Gadara, an Hellenic city a few kilometers from lake Galilee. In Gadara there were famous Cynics like Menippus, the inventor of satire (between the fourth and third centuries B.C.), Meleager (second century B.C.), and Theodore (first century A.D.) Witherington III considers it more likely that the Cynics had some influence in the tradition that passed on the memory of Jesus (especially the Q Source), than on Jesus himself.

63 They went so far as to practice sex in public.

and repeat it every day at the table along with people of all classes who join them along the way. They listen intently to the parables he tells in all the towns, to help everyone discover a new world. They see with amazement how he awakens the faith of the sick in order to cure their afflictions. They shudder to see his power to cast out demons and heal lives torn apart by evil. They see him filled with the Spirit of God.

From Jesus they learn a different way of understanding and living life. They see his tenderness toward the smallest and most helpless. They are moved by his compassion toward the misfortune and suffering of the sick; from him they learn to touch the lepers whom no one else will touch. They burn with his passion to defend each person's dignity, and his freedom to do good. They watch the growing tensions and conflict with the most rigorous sectors, but nothing and no one can stop their Teacher when he is defending the humiliated people. They are moved by his friendly acceptance of so many people victimized by sin; from him they learn to sit at the table with undesirables, women of ill repute, and sinners who neglect the Covenant. They admire his passion for the truth, his ability to go straight to the heart of the matter, beyond deceptive theories and legalisms. They struggle to understand the new language of their teacher, who insists on liberating the people from their fear so they can fully trust God. They hear him repeat, wherever he goes, something one doesn't hear from the teachers of the law: «Don't be afraid». He wishes the same thing to everyone: «Go in peace». Something new is awakening in the hearts of his disciples. That contagious peace, that purity of heart without a trace of envy or ambition, his ability to forgive, his acts of mercy in the face of weakness, humiliation or sin, his passionate struggle for justice on behalf of the weakest and most abused, his unbreakable trust in the Father… All this is awakening in them a new faith: God is in this man. Deep in his life they can sense the mysterious nearness of God as a friend and savior. Later they will begin to talk about the «Good News of God»[64].

---

64 The first generation of Christians used the Greek word *euaggelion* («good news») to describe what the disciples had learned from Jesus, and what they had experienced together with him (Mark 1:14; 1 Cor 15:1-3; Phil 1:27).

6

A new family

✍

There are people of different backgrounds in that group of followers, but Jesus sees them all as a family: the new family that God wants to see growing in the world. Around him they will learn to live together, not as in the patriarchal family they have left behind, but as a new family, united by their desire to do God's will. «Here are my mother and my brothers! Whoever does the will of God is my brother and sister and mother»[65].

They are not united by ties of blood or economic interests. They have not come together to defend their social status; for them, honor means doing the will of the Father of all. This family is not structured hierarchically; equality reigns among them. It is not a family closed in on itself, but open and accepting. These are the two characteristics that Jesus nourishes among his followers: the equality of all, and loving service to the last. This is the legacy he wants to leave: a movement of sisters and brothers in service to the smallest and most helpless. This service will be the symbol and seed of God's reign.

There are no teachers of the law in this family. The movement will not be led by educated people guiding the ignorant. They will all learn from Jesus. They will all be open to the experience of God's reign. Jesus rejoices especially to see God revealing himself to the little ones: «I thank you, Father, Lord of heaven and earth, because you have hidden these things from the wise and intelligent and have revealed them to infants; yes, Father, because this was your gracious will»[66]. In this new family there also are no fathers to impose their patriarchal authority on everyone else. No one in his group will hold dominant power. No one will even be called father. In Jesus' movement all patriarchal authority disappears, and God is seen as the Father close at hand who makes everyone brothers and sisters. No one is above the others. No one lords it over the others. There is no rank or class. There are no priests, Levites, and lay people. There is no place for intermediaries. Everyone has direct, immediate access to God, the Father of all.

---

65 Mark 3:35.

66 Q Source (Luke 10:21; Matt 11:25-26) and the [apocryphal] *Gospel of Thomas* 61:3. There is no doubt that these words came from Jesus, who emphasizes God's preference for the little ones in many ways, and says that the reign of God belongs to them (Mark 10:13-16).

The atmosphere around Jesus is very different from the hierarchical structure of Qumran. No one is admitted to that desert community without an examination «of their spirit and their works» and without perfecting their behavior[67]. In contrast, Jesus calls Levi straight from his tax booth to join the group, and accepts Mary of Magdala, who was once possessed by evil spirits, among his followers. In Qumran every community member is assigned his own place. «The small will obey the great», and they are all subject to the authority of the sons of Zadok, the priests who guard the Covenant»[68]. In contrast, in Jesus' family there are no lay people subject to the priests, nor small people obeying the great; the ideal is to become like a child, «for it is to such as these that the kingdom of God belongs»[69]. In meals and meetings at Qumran, all are seated according to their rank: «The priests are seated first, the elders second, and the rest of the people will be seated according to each one's rank»[70]. With Jesus it is different. His followers, men and women, sit in a circle around him; no one is seated above the others; they all listen to his word and seek God's will together. Nor is there any ceremonial or normative hierarchy at the meals; no seats of honor are reserved at Jesus' banquets[71].

Also within this equality there are no hierarchical differences between men and women. Women are not valued for their fertility, or disgraced by sterility. Jesus never talks about their purity or impurity. They are not in the group to take orders from the men. No one has special authority over them just because he is a man. Men and women, sons and daughters of God, live together with equal dignity in the service of God's reign.

That is why none of the gospel traditions show anyone carrying out hierarchical functions within the group of disciples. Jesus does not see the Twelve acting as «priests» for the others. He does not imagine his followers living according to the hierarchical system of the temple: a high priest, priests of different ancestral lines, and a group of Levites. The relationships he wants to promote among them are even less like the hierarchical model prevailing in the political struc-

---

67 *Regla de la Congregación* v, 24 (English: *Rule of the Congregation*).
68 *Regla de la Congregación* v, 1-2 and VI, 2-4 (English: *Rule of the Congregation*).
69 Mark 10:14b.
70 *Regla de la Congregación* VI, 8-9 (English: *Rule of the Congregation*).
71 In a parable retold only in Luke 14:8-10, Jesus suggests taking the lowest place at banquets. The parable probably is not from Jesus, but his concluding sentence is a saying that was circulated separately and expresses one of his favorite ideas: «For all who exalt themselves will be humbled, and those who humble themselves will be exalted».

tures of the Empire. The normal values of that society have been turned upside down among his followers. Greatness is not measured by one's degree of authority over others, but by the service one offers to others. Jesus gives the place of distinction to slaves, who hold the lowest status in the Empire: «You know that among the gentiles those whom they recognize as their rulers lord it over them, and their great ones are tyrants over them. But it is not so among you, but whoever wishes to become great among you must be your servant, and whoever wishes to be first among you must be slave of all»[72].

That is how Jesus imagines his family of followers: a group of brothers and sisters who follow his steps in order to accept and spread the reign of God. He is not thinking about brilliant doctors or astute rulers, but rather disciples who announce the saving nearness of God, and healers who transform the world with their attitude of service and love. Men and women who have learned to live as he does, serving the last. They will be his witnesses, the most effective symbol and sign of God's reign. Jesus' Church will begin with these witnesses, and with the same vocation and mission Jesus gave them.

7

In the service of God's plan

Clearly Jesus is not thinking about founding a rabbinical school. He has not called them to «serve him» in the style of the rabbis. He does not need a court of disciples, waiting to fulfill his wishes. Quite the contrary. He sees himself as a servant of all: «I am among you as one who serves»[73]. Neither does he want to create a ritually pure community of obedience to the law, like the most radical Pharisaic groups. He teaches them to share their table with people from outside the group; he wants them to go among the «lost sheep of Israel». He is not interested in a closed, exclusive group. He doesn't want to form a community of God's «elect» with them. He doesn't lead them into the desert, away from the contaminated people, to create a «new Qumran». Nor is he recruiting them for a «holy

---

72 Mark 10:42-44. These sayings grew out of the desire Jesus expressed to his disciples: «Whoever wants to be great, must become a servant». The idea of the slave as «number one» could only be his. Mark has shaped it in the context of the rivalries that were emerging in the early Christian community.

73 Luke 22:27. These words reflect Jesus' thinking. Luke's version seems to be more authentic than the one in Mark 10:45.

war» against Rome. His purpose is very different: he sends them out «like lambs into the midst of wolves»[74]. What the world needs is more peace, not more bloodshed.

Jesus calls them to share his experience of the irruption of God's reign, and to join him in the task of helping people to accept it. They leave their work, not to live in idleness and vagrancy, but out of wholehearted commitment to the reign of God. They leave their own fathers, to defend people who have no father and no protection. He wants to create a new family around the one Father of all. It is not an easy task. Following Jesus means becoming «displaced persons». He calls them away from the villages, families and employment that have always given them their identity, security and protection. But Jesus does not bring them into a new social system. He leads them toward a new space, full of possibilities, but with no specific place to develop a social identity. Following him is quite an

adventure. From now on their identity will be to live «on the way» toward the reign of God and its justice[75].

For Jesus, that small group is called to be a symbol of God's reign and its transforming power. There they will begin to live according to God's will. The group is modest and small, like a «mustard seed». It is hard to see the «yeast» transforming that society. But we can see something of God's plan in this group. A different kind of life is taking shape there, within the culture of the Empire: the life of God's reign. We can easily see some of its characteristics.

Jesus' disciples are no longer submissive to Caesar. They do not fear the tax collectors, since they have no land and no fishing business. They don't care about the emperor's decrees, but about «doing the will of God»[76]. God is their Father. That is what Jesus calls him; he never speaks of God as «King». He does not use imperial images, but metaphors taken from family life. He does not see his people as the seeds of a «new Empire», but of a «family» of brothers and sisters. The new social relationships that the reign of God needs cannot be understood by looking at the Empire, but at this humble family group conceived by Jesus.

---

74 Q Source (Luke 10:3; Matt 10:16). This suggestive image is common in the biblical and rabbinical literature. Jesus may very well have used it too.

75 Luke describes the Christian life as «belonging to the Way». The Christians «enter into the Way» (Acts 9:2; 18:25-26; 19:9-23; 22:4; 24:14-22).

76 Mark 3:35.

With them he opens a new space without masculine dominance. The men have left the privileged position they held at home as fathers, husbands or brothers. They have given up their leadership as men, and detached themselves from much of their identity as men in that patriarchal society. The new family that Jesus is creating does not mirror the patriarchal family. Even Jesus is not the «father» of the group, but a «brother». His followers can all see that there is no male dominance in God's reign[77].

By leaving the structures of the Empire and the family group, Jesus' followers are inevitably coming closer to people outside or at the margins of the system. This «family» is not like the Herodian families at the center of power. Rather it moves in the marginal spaces of the society. They do not have a house, land, or material goods. They do not hold a position of honor. They are among the smallest, least significant people in Galilee. By watching them we can see that God is accepted by the last.

Jesus' followers have to learn to live with insecurity. When they enter a town, they may be accepted or rejected. They can only find hospitality among their sympathizers. It wouldn't be surprising if they sometimes worried: What will they eat? What will they wear? All vagabonds worry about the same thing. Jesus conveys to them his trust in God: «Do not worry»[78]. The group must be at peace, filled with trust. How could God not care for them, as he cares for the birds of the air and the lilies of the field? He watches them knocking on doors in search of food and hospitality. They are not always well received, but Jesus reassures them: «Ask, and it will be given you; search, and you will find; knock, and the door will be opened for you. For everyone who asks receives, and everyone who searches finds, and for everyone who knocks, the door will be opened»[79]. He is very certain about this: the sympathizers who have joined his cause will accept them, and above all the Father will provide for their needs. Everyone will see that

77 According to some scholars (Sand, Blinzler, Braun, Meier, Moxnes, Freyne, and others), Jesus and his followers were vilified as «eunuchs» in some sectors (Matt 19:12). To that society they appeared to be «half men», neither men nor women, without the masculine honor that went with their sexual and patriarchal role. Jesus accepts their designation as «social eunuchs» who have abandoned the masculine place in patriarchal society in favor of God's reign. The expression, «who have made themselves eunuchs for the kingdom of heaven» could only have come from Jesus.

78 This insistent call comes from Jesus, and is at the heart of a collection of exhortations to trust God (Q Source: Luke 12:22-31; Matt 6:25-34). Apparently it was originally addressed to his disciples (or to the peasants, according to Horsley). Matthew later took it as an exhortation addressed to everyone who faces a situation of need.

79 Q Source (Luke 11:9-10; Matt 7:7-8).

for those who seek God's reign, life is sustained by mutual acceptance and the Father's care.

There was another trait that Jesus wanted to nourish in his group: joy. These men and women had left everything because they had found «the hidden treasure» or the «precious pearl». He could see in the eyes of some disciples the joy of those who have begun to discover the reign of God. They had no reason to fast or mourn. Living with him was a feast. It felt something like a village wedding feast. The meals were the best part. Jesus taught them to celebrate the recovery of so many lost people with joy. Sitting at the table with Jesus, the disciples felt like the «friends» of the shepherd in the parable, who rejoiced to see him come back with the lost sheep. The women disciples in turn rejoiced like the «neighbors» of the poor woman in another parable, who had found her lost coin. Everyone could see in the joy of Jesus' followers, that God is good news for the lost.

8

Sent out to proclaim God by healing

At some point Jesus sent his disciples out into the Galilean villages, to share in his task of preparing the way for God's reign[80]. All the signs are that it was a short mission, limited to the areas in which Jesus moved. Was this a well thought-out, practical strategy, or was it a trial run with a strongly symbolic purpose?[81] Perhaps Jesus wanted to show them how they could work with him on the plan for God's reign[82]. These messengers are not acting on their own initiative, but in Jesus' name. They do what he tells them, in the way he says to do it. They are his representatives[83].

80 Mark 6:7; Q Source (Luke 9:1; Matt 10:1). There is a significant scholarly consensus around the historical authenticity of this mission (Manson, Creed, Schweizer, Meier, Witherington III, Schlosser, Barbaglio). Crossan says it is impossible to imagine a group of men traveling through the Galilean villages in the decade of the thirties, but his arguments are not persuasive.

81 The disciples are never seen preaching, and it is hard to know how much they did so while Jesus was traveling in Galilee (Kaylor). They may only have been inviting people to come and hear Jesus.

82 It is hard to tell whether Jesus sent out only the Twelve (Pesch, Schneider, Meier), or an undetermined number of disciples (Karting). In addition to the mission of the Twelve to Israel, Luke has artificially created another mission of seventy-two (or seventy) disciples, emphasizing the universal character of the Christian mission (Luke 10:1).

83 The figure of the «messenger» or *shaliah* is well known in Judaism. The messenger acts in his lord's name and represents him: whoever accepts the messenger is accepting his lord, and whoever rejects him is rejecting his lord. In the Church, Jesus' «messengers» or *shalihim* would lead to the development of different missions or charismas whose bearers «represent» Jesus and receive his «ministerial authority» in the service of the prophetic proclamation of God's reign, leadership in the Christian community, teaching, or charitable service.

Jesus gives them specific power and authority, not to impose themselves on the people, but to cast out demons and cure sickness and affliction[84]. These are the two great tasks of his messengers: to tell the people how near God is, and to cure them of whatever causes evil and suffering in their lives. The two tasks are inseparable. They will do what they have seen him do: cure people by showing them how close God is to their suffering: «Cure the sick who are there, and say to them, "The kingdom of God has come near to you"»[85]. Thus Jesus is creating a network of «healers» to proclaim the irruption of God, just as the Baptist was planning a network of «the baptized» to warn about the imminent arrival of God's judgment. For Jesus, curing the sick and casting out demons is the first and most important task. It is the best sign he can find to proclaim God, the friend of life. In one story from the gospel sources, the disciples come to tell Jesus that they have seen someone from outside the group casting out demons in his name. They tried to stop him, but they want to warn Jesus about it. These disciples are not thinking about the joy that man has brought to the people he healed. They are concerned about their group: «He was not following us». Jesus tells them: «Do not stop him… Whoever is not against us is for us»[86]. How can Jesus stop the sick from being cured, if that is the best sign of God's saving power?

Jesus sees his disciples as «fishing for people». This is a surprising and evocative metaphor, typical of Jesus' creative and provocative language. It probably occurred to him along the Galilean shore, when he was calling some fishermen to leave their work and come with him. From now on they will fish for people instead of fish: «Follow me and I will make you fish for people»[87]. It was a rather enigmatic expression. Prophets like Jeremiah had used fishing and hunting as negative images for the capture of those who would be subjected to judgment and

---

84 Mark 6:7; Q Source (Luke 9:1; Matt 10:1).
85 Q Source (Luke 10:8-9; Matt 10:7-9). «Proclaiming the kingdom» and «curing the sick» are the two inseparable tasks that Jesus entrusted to his disciples. The commands to «teach» and «baptize», which appear in Matt 28:19-20, were formulated in the Christian community and reflect its thinking about the mission of the Church.
86 Mark 9:38-40, later summarized in Luke 9:49-50. It is hard to judge the historical authenticity of this episode. But Jesus' reply («Whoever is not against us is for us») is picked up in Mark, in the Q Source, and in the fragment of Mark preserved in the Oxyrrhincus papyrus 1224. Although it was a well known proverb, it was probably spoken by Jesus.
87 Mark 1:17. The expression «fishing for people» is a strange metaphor, invented by Jesus (Pesch, Meier, Witherington III, Guijarro). It had never before been used in the biblical tradition or the rabbinical literature, to describe a positive mission. The Old Testament sometimes spoke of gathering the «sheep», not of catching «fish».

condemnation; Qumran described the devil as a «fisher of men»[88]. Jesus isn't thinking of anything like that. Coming from him, the metaphor carries a salvific, liberating meaning. He is calling on his disciples to rescue people from the «abysmal waters» of evil, to free them from Satan's power, and in that way to bring them into the life of God's reign[89]. But it is still a strange image, and it was forgotten by the Christian missionaries; they never spoke of themselves as «fishing for people».

The disciples never forgot the instructions that Jesus gave them when he sent them on the mission[90]. He wanted to impress on them a prophetic and defiant life style. Everyone could see it in their way of dressing and equipping themselves, and in their activities in the Galilean villages. The surprising thing is that Jesus is not thinking about what they should take with them, but quite the contrary: he tells them what not to take, in order not to be separated from the last.

They should not take money or provisions of any kind. They should not even carry a shoulder bag, as the Cynical vagabonds did to keep the provisions and alms they collected. Going without a bag meant refusing to beg, trusting only in God's care and the acceptance of the people. They also should not carry a staff, as the Cynical philosophers and also the Essenes did, to defend themselves against wild dogs and attackers. They should present themselves to all as people of peace. They were to enter the villages peacefully, so as not to frighten the women and children even when the men were working in the fields.

They were to go barefoot, as slaves did. They would not wear sandals. Not even a spare tunic, like the one Diogenes the Cynic carried to protect himself from the cold when he slept outdoors. Everyone would see Jesus' followers identified with the most indigent people in Galilee. These instructions were typical of Jesus. He was the first to live like that: without money or provisions, without a beggar's bag, without a staff, barefoot, and without a spare tunic. The disciples were only following his example. This group — free of ties and possessions,

---

88 Thus we read in Jer 16:16: «I am now sending for many fishermen, says the Lord, and they shall catch them; and afterward I will send for many hunters, and they shall hunt them from every mountain and every hill, and out of the clefts of the rocks. For my eyes are on all their ways; they are not hidden from my presence, nor is their iniquity concealed from my sight». The prophet is referring to the Babylonian invasion.

89 In Semitic thinking the waters of the ocean readily evoke the abysmal waters, the chaos and horror of the world of evil, hostile to God. Jesus was probably referring to that image in this context (Manek, Witherington III).

90 They are preserved in Mark 6:8-11; the Q Source (Luke 9:3-5; Matt 10:9-14); Luke 10:4-11; and the [apocryphal] *Gospel of Thomas* 14:4. These instructions were later reshaped and combined to fit the varying practices of the Christian missionaries, but they could only have come from Jesus (Gnilka, Theissen, Crossan, Meier, Hengel, Witherington III, Schlosser, Barbaglio).

identified with the poorest people in Galilee, completely trusting God and the people's acceptance, and seeking peace for everyone — would bring Jesus' presence and the good news of God to the villages[91].

Jesus sends them out «two by two», so they can support each other. Also, for the Jews the testimony of two or more persons was considered more credible. As they come near a house, they are to wish its inhabitants peace. If they are offered hospitality, they are to stay there until they leave the village. If not, they are to «shake the dust off their feet» as they leave[92]. That was what Jews did when they left a pagan region that was considered impure. Perhaps we should not take this as a judgment of condemnation, but as a humorous gesture: «So much for you!».

In each village they do the same: proclaim the reign of God, sharing with the people their experience with Jesus, and at the same time cure the sick people of the village. They do it without charging a fee or asking for alms, but accepting in exchange a place at the table and in the house of the villagers. This is not a simple strategy for the sustenance of the mission. It is a way to build a new community in the villages, based on values radically different from honor and dishonor, patrons and clients. Here everyone shares what they have: some, their experience with God's reign and their ability to heal; others, their table and their house. The disciples' role is not only «giving», but «receiving» the hospitality they are offered[93].

The atmosphere they created in the towns was like that created by Jesus. The whole village was filled with joy by each report of a healing. It would be celebrated. The sick could now rejoin the community. The lepers and demon-possessed could again sit at the table with their loved ones. Seated at those meals with the two disciples, seeing relationships renewed and barriers removed, it was easier for the villagers to forgive one another the hurts they had caused. In a modest but real way they were sensing the arrival of God's reign in that village. Having no political or religious power of his own, in the midst of the immense Roman Empire Jesus had found the most effective way to initiate the new society that God willed: a more healthy and loving society, a society of self-respect and happiness.

91 Jesus' followers could not maintain his early, radical life style. An analysis of the tradition shows a clear evolution. According to the Q Source, the disciples were to take nothing at all; in the gospel of Mark they were allowed to wear «sandals» and carry a «stick»; in the *Didache* an apostle was allowed to «take enough bread to eat until you reach the place where you will stay» (Crossan).

92 Mark 6:11.

93 Not everyone accepts this view, proposed by Crossan. In any case Jesus' insistence is surprising: when they are accepted, they should «remain in the same house, eating and drinking whatever they provide» (Luke 10:7).

A Faithful Believer

His experience of God was central and decisive in Jesus' life. The itinerant prophet of God's reign, the healer of the sick and defender of the poor, the poet of mercy and teacher of love, the creator of a new movement in service to the reign of God, is not a dilettante attracted by different interests, but a person profoundly integrated by one core experience: God, the Father of all. It is God who inspires his message, integrates his intense activity, and polarizes his energies. God is at the center of this life. Jesus' message and activity can only be explained in terms of this radical, lived experience of God. To forget that is to lose the authenticity and deepest meaning of Jesus' life. Without it the figure of Jesus is distorted, his message devalued, his actions severed from the meaning he gave them[1].

But what is Jesus' experience of God? Who is God for him? How does he relate to God's mystery? How does he listen and trust in God's goodness? How does he live it? There are no easy answers to these questions. Jesus is very discreet about his inner life. But he speaks and acts in such a way that we can at least partly discern his experience from his words and actions[2].

One thing is evident right away. Jesus does not propose a doctrine of God. He never explains his idea of God. For Jesus, God is not a theory. God is an experience that transforms him, and shows him a fuller, more loving, happier life for everyone. He never tries to replace the traditional doctrine of God with a new one. His God is the God of Israel: the one Lord, creator of the heavens and the earth, savior of his beloved people, the nearby God of the Covenant in whom the Israelites believe. He has no debates with any Jewish group about God's goodness, his closeness to the people, or his liberating action. They all believe in the same God.

The difference is that the religious leaders identify God with their religious system, and not with the happiness and the life of the people. For them the first and most important thing is to worship God by observing the law, respecting the sabbath, and honoring the temple worship. In contrast, Jesus identifies God

---

1 Modern scholarship has unfortunately failed to explore Jesus' religious experience in depth. Seeking to avoid tangential discussions of his psychology, or confessional debates over his nature as Son of God, many scholars have neglected one indisputable historical fact: Jesus' activity was motivated by his experience of God, and he invited his hearers and followers to believe and accept God with the same trust he had. Jesus' relationship with God caused a deep impression in his followers.

2 Naturally, our historical approximation of Jesus cannot possibly prejudge what Church doctrine affirms and christology studies with regard to Jesus' filial and messianic consciousness, nor about the unique relationship of the incarnate Son of God with the Father in his unrepeatable singularity, nor about the legitimacy or illegitimacy of attributing faith to Jesus Christ, and the meaning of that faith. Such questions simply lie outside the field of historical research.

with life. For him the first and most important thing is for God's sons and daughters to benefit from a life of justice and dignity. The most religious sectors feel called by God to nurture the religion of the temple and the observance of the law. In contrast, Jesus feels sent to promote the justice and mercy of God.

What surprises them is not Jesus' new doctrines about God, but his different way of engaging in life. He does not criticize the idea of God that is taught in Israel, but he rebels against the dehumanizing effects of the way religion is organized. What they find most scandalous is that Jesus calmly invokes God in condemning or transgressing the religion that officially represents God, whenever that religion becomes an oppressive force rather than a principle of life. His experience of God compels him to liberate the people from the fears and enslavements that keep them from feeling and experiencing God as Jesus does, as a friend of life and of happiness for his sons and daughters.

1

Rooted in the faith of his people

Jesus was born into a nation of believers. Like all boys and girls in Nazareth, he learned his beliefs from his family and in sabbath meetings at the synagogue. Later, in Jerusalem, he would come to know the religious joy of this people, who throughout their history had felt accompanied by God as the friend they worshiped and praised at the great festivals. Can we get a sense of what Jesus was learning from the religious traditions that nourished the spirituality of Israel? What was most important to him in that learning process?[3].

God is Israel's friend. The Jewish *historical traditions* simply narrate, recall, and celebrate God's relationship with his people. God has been their ally from the beginning. When the Israelites were Pharaoh's slaves, God heard their cries, had compassion on the small nation oppressed by the powerful Egyptian Empire, liberated them from slavery and led them to the land he had chosen so that they might live in freedom. That is the central theme that Jesus learned from his people's faith. It is not a naïve faith. God acts in the history of Israel, but no one

---

3   We don't know with any certainty which biblical texts Jesus read or heard, which religious traditions were available to him, or which psalms he recited most often. But we do rightly try to understand the biblical background from which he was speaking and acting, so as to understand more clearly his «Jewish heritage» and the personal interpretations that influenced him (Haight).

confuses him with a human leader or king. God is transcendent. No one can see or experience God directly[4], but he acts at the deepest level of events. What happens in history has its own causes and protagonists. Everyone knows that, but God is acting in the midst of life, moved by his desire for the freedom and happiness of his people. The Israelites describe that action «suggestively» with a variety of symbols. God's action is like the «wind»; no one can see it, but they feel its effects[5]. It is also like the action of a «word»; no one sees it leave the person's mouth, but we see its power when the word is carried out[6].

From childhood Jesus carried with him the image of this saving God who cares about his people's happiness, a God close by, moved by tenderness toward those who suffer. His own name was a reminder: *Yeshua*, «Yahweh saves». This conviction fills his heart with joy: God wants the best for his sons and daughters. But Jesus is not so interested in what God has done in the past. He doesn't talk about the liberation from Egypt, or about the exodus of his people to the promised land; he barely mentions Israel's standing as the chosen people, or its covenant with Yahweh[7]. Jesus feels God acting now, in the present. God's creative action is not something from the past: as he walks the Galilean paths he can sense God encouraging life, feeding the birds of the sky and dressing the field lilies in bright colors. And God's saving action is not something that only the ancestors could contemplate: Jesus senses the presence of his Spirit when he heals the sick and liberates those who are possessed by «evil spirits». Moses and the great leaders of the people, in other times, were not the only ones to hear God's Word; Jesus rejoices that the most simple, ignorant people are now hearing the revelation of the Father[8].

Jesus was also coming to know the message of the *prophets of Israel*. Their word was listened to attentively in the synagogues, and then translated and commented on in Aramaic so that everyone could understand. The prophets were the sentinels who had always warned the people of their sin. The «people of God» was called to mirror God's justice and compassionate care for the op-

---

4 This is why Jews were strictly forbidden to use any images to represent God physically.

5 In Israel's religious tradition God is described as «Spirit» or *ruaj*, which literally means air, breath, or wind.

6 In the book of Genesis God creates the world with his word: «Then God said, "Let there be light"; and there was light» (1:3).

7 Jesus mentions the Covenant only in Mark 14:24, and his message does not clearly discuss God's election of Israel.

8 Jesus' emphasis on God's action in the present, and his lack of interest in the past, clearly distinguish him from his contemporaries (Schlosser).

pressed: Israel's treatment of the poor, orphans, widows, and foreigners should reflect what God had done for them when «you were a slave in Egypt[9]». The prophets were very clear on this: the people of God were destroying the Covenant by bringing injustice into their midst and committing abuses against the weakest people. God will not always remain indifferent. The prophets proclaimed judgment on Israel and its leaders in each case: «You who hate the good and love the evil, who tear the skin off my people, and the flesh from their bones... He will hide his face from them at that time, because they have acted wickedly»[10]. This judgment is not the reaction of an angry or vengeful God, but an expression of his love for the victims. His anger against the wicked is the other side of his compassion for the oppressed; the dramatic threats of the prophets only reveal more forcefully God's commitment to see his will carried out, in a world where God's justice reigns. That is all God asks of human beings: «to do justice, and to love kindness, and walk humbly with your God»[11].

That is how Jesus always understands it. God for him is the great defender of victims, the one who impels him to live with the poor and welcome the excluded. He invokes that God to fight against injustice, condemn the landowners, and even threaten the temple religion: a cult so devoid of justice and compassion deserves to be destroyed. God is love for the suffering, and for that very reason, he is judgment against everything that dehumanizes and makes them suffer. But Jesus is motivated more by God's saving love than by his judgment. He is fascinated by God's unfathomable forgiveness, totally undeserved by human beings.

He could hear this message from the prophets who comforted the people after their exile to Babylon in the year 587 B.C. The Israelites had been humiliated by their enemies, and needed to remember God's goodness. The prophet Jeremiah encouraged them to trust in his forgiveness. Here is the message he heard from God's heart: «I will forgive their iniquity, and remember their sin no more»[12]. Surely Jesus also heard that!. An anonymous prophet, a disciple of Isaiah, eloquently expressed God's unconditional love beyond all condemnation and punishment: «In overflowing wrath for a moment I hid my face from

9 Deut 24:17-22.
10 Mic 3:2,4. This prophet came from a peasant family as Jesus did, and railed against the social abuses and injustices that were being committed against the poor in Samaria and Jerusalem (738-693 B.C.)
11 Mic 6:8.
12 Jer 31:34. This prophet, born around 650 B.C. in the village of Anatoth near Jerusalem, proclaimed God's imminent punishment to his people; but after the disaster he encouraged them to trust God's forgiveness.

you, but with everlasting love I will have compassion on you… my steadfast love shall not depart from you, and my covenant of peace shall not be removed, says the Lord, who has compassion on you»[13]. We will never know exactly what impact words like these had in Jesus' heart; but his separation from the Baptist's threatening message, his lack of reference to God's anger, and his unconditional acceptance of sinners suggest that they helped to nourish his experience of God as a forgiving Father.

Jesus was also nourished by Israel's *wisdom tradition.* These «wise men» were not prophets, but they offered the people their reflection on life, humanity, sensible behavior and happiness. Their contribution was seen as enriching the Torah[14]. God is always on the horizon of this literature as the creator of human beings and the world; his Wisdom presides over all creation and is the source of wise behavior for human beings. This wisdom tradition was probably a greater influence on Jesus than is usually assumed[15]. Jesus sees the world as coming from God's Wisdom. It is God who cares for life, who feeds the birds of the sky and the lilies of the field. God is not only the Savior of Israel. He is present in all creation, blessing the children and making the crops grow. Jesus enjoys reflecting on the goodness of that God; everyone should emulate his activity and be good as he is good. We don't know if Jesus was familiar with the Book of Wisdom. He would have rejoiced to discover its beautiful vision of God as «a friend of life»[16].

Jesus probably nourished his experience of God, especially in praying the psalms. He knew some of them by heart, since the Jews repeated them every day on waking and going to bed, or blessing their meals; they recited others at sabbath prayers, or sang them on pilgrimage to Jerusalem and in celebrations at the temple. We don't know which were his favorite psalms, but we can imagine how deeply and intensely he prayed some of them. The poet of God's mercy must have found this psalm of thanksgiving especially meaningful:

---

13 Isa 54:8-10. This prophet is the author of what we now call the «Book of Consolation» (Isa 40-55), written in the last years of exile, shortly before Cyrus conquered Babylon in the year 539.

14 This wisdom literature developed especially after the return from exile, between 500 and 50 B.C. Some books, like the Proverbs, offer an optimistic view of life. Others, like Qohelet (Ecclesiastes), are marked by pessimism. The book of Job raises the problem of a just and good God in view of the suffering of the innocent.

15 Despite the important work of Ben Witherington III, Elisabeth Schüssler Fiorenza and others, scholars have not given much attention to this aspect.

16 Wis 11:26. This book was probably compiled in Alexandria between 100 and 50 B.C.

The Lord is gracious and merciful, slow to anger and abounding in steadfast love. The Lord is good to all, and has compassion over all that he has made. All your works shall give thanks to you, O Lord[17].

The prophet who unconditionally accepted sinners must have been encouraged by this psalm:

The Lord is merciful and gracious, slow to anger and abounding in steadfast love. He will not always accuse, nor will he keep his anger forever. He does not deal with us according to our sins… As a father has compassion for his children, so the Lord has compassion for those who fear him[18].

The defender of the poor and humiliated must have sung these words with special joy:

O Lord, who is like you? You deliver the weak from those too strong for them, the weak and needy from those who despoil them[19].

He must have identified passionately with this prayer for the poor:

Do not forget the life of your poor forever. Have regard for your covenant, for the dark places of the land are full of the haunts of violence. Do not let the downtrodden be put to shame; let the poor and needy praise your name[20].

And this psalm, which seems to anticipate Jesus' beatitudes, must have echoed in his soul:

Happy are those whose hope is in the Lord their God… who keeps faith forever; who executes justice for the oppressed, who gives food to the hungry[21].

It was in this deeply religious environment that Jesus nourished his experience of God.

17 Ps 145:8-10.
18 Ps 103:8-10, 13.
19 Ps 35:10.
20 Ps 74:19-21.
21 Ps 146:5-7.

2

A decisive experience

But Jesus does more than recall and relive the spiritual journey of Israel. He seeks God in his own existence, and like the prophets of other times, he opens his heart to hear God's voice for his people and himself in that particular moment. He goes into the desert and listens to the Baptist; he seeks solitude in secluded places; he spends long hours in silence. The God who speaks without human words becomes the center of his life, and the source of his whole being. The Christian sources all agree that Jesus' prophetic activity began with an intense and powerful experience of God. At the time of his baptism in the Jordan, Jesus goes through some kind of experience that decisively transforms his life. He does not stay long with the Baptist. Neither does he return to work as a craftsman in the village of Nazareth. Moved by an overpowering inner impulse, he begins to travel the Galilean paths, proclaiming to everyone the irruption of the reign of God.

We read in the earliest gospel: «And just as he was coming up out of the water, he saw the heavens torn apart and the Spirit descending like a dove on him. And a voice came from heaven, "You are my Son, the Beloved; with you I am well pleased"»[22]. This narrative was reworked in the Christian community, but there is no reason to doubt the historicity of Jesus' experience. The scene includes clearly mythic elements: the heavens are «torn apart», the Spirit of God descends gently on Jesus «like a dove», and immediately «a voice came from heaven». Writers use these elements to suggest a «theophany» or communication with God, beyond everyday experience. Thus the tradition has preserved the memory of Jesus' decisive experience that is hard to express, but key to our «understanding» of his activity and message[23].

The experience takes place at a very special moment. Jesus has gone to the Jordan to seek God, and has humbly joined others from his people in receiving John's baptism. Jesus comes before God. His attitude is one of total availability. That is when, according to the narrative, «he saw the heavens torn apart». The

---

22 We can read the story of this experience in Mark 1:10-11; Matt 3:16-17; Luke 3:21-22; John 1:32-34. It also appears in the [apocryphal] *Gospel of the Hebrews*, Justin, and Clement of Alexandria.

23 The historicity of this experience is supported by Scobie, Ernst, Jeremias, Hollenbach, Meier, Barret, and others. Even the *Jesus Seminar* group affirms that «Jesus probably went through some kind of very powerful religious experience» in the context of his baptism.

mysterious and unfathomable God is going to speak to him; the Father is entering into «dialogue» with Jesus. Coming out of the Jordan waters, this seeker of God is given a double experience. He discovers himself as a beloved Son: God is his Father! At the same time he feels filled with God's Spirit. These are really two aspects of a single experience that would mark Jesus forever[24].

Nothing expresses his experience better than these eloquent words: «You are my Son, the Beloved». It is very different from what happened to Moses thirteen centuries earlier on Mount Horeb, when he trembled to approach the burning bush, taking off his shoes so as not to defile the sacred ground[25]. God does not tell Jesus «I am Who I am», but «You are my Son». God does not reveal himself as ineffable Mystery, but as a Father close by who speaks to Jesus to reveal Jesus' mystery as a Son. God is saying, «You are mine, you are my son. Your whole being springs from me. I am your Father». The narrative shows the intimate, joyful nature of this revelation. This is how Jesus hears it: «You are my beloved son, I am pleased with you». I love you deeply. I rejoice to have you as my Son. I am happy[26]. Jesus responds with one word: *Abba*. From now on that is the name he will use when he communicates with God. That word says it all: his total trust in God and his unconditional availability. «We have good reason to affirm that Jesus perceived God as especially close and accessible, and that he related to him with a very special filial intimacy»[27].

Jesus' whole life exudes this trust[28]. He gives his life over completely to God. Everything he does is marked by this genuine, pure, spontaneous attitude of trust in his Father. He seeks God's will without reservation, calculation, or strategy. He does not rely on the temple religion or on the doctrine of the scribes; his power and his security do not come from the Scriptures and traditions of Israel. They come from the Father. His trust frees him from religious customs, traditions and models; his faithfulness to the Father leads him to act creatively, innovatively, and boldly. His is an absolute faith. That is why he grieves over the «little faith» of his followers, and rejoices over the great trust of a pagan woman[29].

---

24 It would be a mistake to try to analyze what happened to Jesus in his consciousness. All we can do is evoke what the narrative suggests, and follow the historical trajectory of this foundational experience.

25 Exod 3:1-14.

26 The text probably intends to convey God's joy over the goodness of his creatures (Gen 1:27-28), which reaches its full intensity with Jesus.

27 This is how J. Schlosser describes it.

28 Jewish writers see Jesus' trust as a sign of the *emuna* which marks the great believers of Israel (Flusser, Vermes).

29 Matthew contrasts the «little faith» of the disciples (16:8; 17:20) with the «great faith» of some pagans (8:10; 15:28).

This trust produces in Jesus an unconditional submissiveness to his Father. He seeks only to do God's will. That comes first for him. Nothing and no one can distract him from that path. As a good son he seeks to be the joy of his Father; as a faithful son he identifies with him and always emulates his way of acting. This is the inner motivation that inspires everything he does[30]. The Christian sources have preserved the memory that Jesus was tempted. This scene was developed later by the community; its intention is not to reproduce an event from a specific place and time in his life, but to evoke the climate of testing and difficulty in which Jesus lived out his faithfulness to the Father[31]. These are not just moral temptations. They go deeper than that; the crisis tests Jesus' fundamental attitude toward God. How will he live out his task, by seeking his own interest or faithfully listening to God's Word? How will he act, by dominating others or serving them? Will he seek glory for himself, or do God's will?[32] The memory preserved by his followers leaves no room for doubt: Jesus lives situations of inner darkness, conflict and struggle throughout his life, but he remains faithful to his beloved Father.

At the Jordan Jesus lives more than his experience of being God's beloved Son. At the same time he feels filled by God's Spirit. He has seen «the Spirit descending on him» from that open heaven. God's Spirit which creates and sustains life, which cures and nourishes every living creature, has come to fill him with its life-giving power. Jesus experiences it as the Spirit of grace and life. It comes down on him murmuring gently, «like a dove»[33]. It fills him with its power, not to judge, condemn, or destroy, but to cure, liberate from «evil spirits», and give life.

Jesus feels the Spirit moving in him so forcefully that his awareness of its life-giving power leads him to cure sick people of their affliction; all he asks of them is faith in the power of God acting in him and through him. Filled with the good

---

30 The words «obedience» and «obey» never appear in Jesus' sayings (Schlosser). His attitude toward the Father is not one of fulfilling his «laws», but identifying with him and seeking what will please him: abundant life for his sons and daughters.

31 We can read the temptation narrative in Mark 2:12-13 and in the Q Source (Luke 14:1-13; Matt 4:1-11). Most scholars interpret it as a theological reflection on the internal struggles Jesus experienced throughout his life. According to the Q Source, Jesus is tempted in the desert after forty days of fasting, thus reliving the temptations of idolatry that Israel faced as a result of hunger in the desert. This way of reading the past into the present was a literary genre well known to the Jews, which they called *haggadah*.

32 These three quotations from Deuteronomy (8:3; 6:13; 6:16), with which Jesus answers the tempter, are a way of expressing God's will.

33 Comparing the Spirit with a dove was unknown in ancient Judaism. Scholars have not explained it very satisfactorily. The author probably does not mean that the Spirit was shaped like a dove, but that it came down and rested gently on Jesus, as a dove would do (Jeremias).

Spirit of his Father, he is not at all afraid to confront the evil spirits in order to bring God's mercy to the people who are most defenseless and enslaved by evil. He sees the «finger of God» or as Matthew says, the «Spirit of God», in these healings. When he casts out demons it is the liberating Spirit of God acting in him and through him; his victory over Satan is the best sign that God seeks health and liberation for his children[34]. Luke probably composed the description of Jesus in the Nazareth synagogue, as «anointed» by God's Spirit to bring good news to the poor and to liberate the captives and oppressed; however it expresses very well what all the sources tell us[35].

3

Withdrawing to pray

Jesus never forgot his experience by the Jordan. Through all his intense activity as an itinerant prophet, he always nurtured his communication with God in silence and solitude. The Christian sources have preserved the memory of a custom that deeply impressed his followers: withdrawing for prayer[36]. He was not satisfied with praying at the times prescribed for all pious Jews, but personally sought out intimate, silent encounters with his Father. This experience, often repeated and always new, is not an obligation added on to his daily work. It is what the heart of the Son longs for, the well he needs to drink from to nourish his being.

Jesus was born into a people who knew how to pray. Israel was not going through a religious crisis like that of other peoples in the Empire. No one laughed at the people who prayed to God; no one parodied their prayers[37]. The pagans pray to their gods, but they don't know whom to trust; just to be sure, they build altars to them all, even «unknown gods»; they try to use different divinities by pronouncing

---

34 Q Source (Luke 11:20; Matt 12:28).

35 Luke 4:16-22. In citing a text from Isaiah, Luke intentionally uses the words which speak of the Spirit of grace and blessing for the poor and oppressed, omitting those which speak of the «day of vengeance» (compare Isa 61:1-2 with Luke 4:18-19). There is no doubt in Luke's mind: Jesus has brought the «year of the Lord's favor», not the «day of vengeance». He is the bearer of God's salvation, not God's wrath.

36 Modern scholars view this custom of Jesus as an historical fact.

37 Such laughter and parodies of prayer are famous in the comedies of Aristophanes (446-385 B.C.), or in Seneca's criticism to discourage faith in the gods.

magic names; they try to «wear out» the gods with prayer in order to win favors from them; if that doesn't work, they try threatening or scorning them[38].

The environment around Jesus in Israel is very different. All pious Jews begin and end the day by confessing their God and blessing his name. According to the historian Flavius Josephus, «Twice a day, early in the morning and as the time for sleep approaches, they recall thankfully before God all the things God has done from the time they left Egypt»[39]. This custom of morning and evening prayer was already well established in Jesus' time, both in Palestine and in the Jewish diaspora[40]. All the men were obliged to practice it from age thirteen on. Jesus probably never went a day in his life without praying in the morning at sunrise and in the evening before he went to sleep[41].

Both morning and evening prayer began with a recitation of the *Shema*, which is not exactly a prayer but a confession of faith. Curiously, the person praying does not speak to God but listens: «Hear, O Israel, the Lord is our God, the Lord is one. You shall love the Lord your God with all your heart, and with all your soul, and with all your might. And these words that I command you today shall be in your heart…»[42]. How did Jesus understand this insistent call every morning and evening, to love God with all his heart and soul and might? Apparently it was deeply engraved within him, for he remembered it during the day and on one occasion quoted it explicitly[43].

The *Shema* is followed by a prayer made up of eighteen blessings (*Shemone Esre*)[44]. Jesus repeated it twice every day. Some of the blessings surely echoed deep in his heart. The prophet who ate with sinners and undesirables during the day, must have been moved by this blessing: «Forgive us, our Father, for we have sinned against you. Erase and remove our sin from before your eyes, for your mercy is great. Blessed are you, O Lord, abounding in forgiveness». The one who

---

38 The Latin expression, *fatigare deos*, is well known. The gods had to be «worn out» with prayer in order to gain their help.

39 *Antigüedades de los judíos* 4, 212 (English: *Jewish Antiquities*).

40 The Essenes at Qumran and the Therapeutae of Alexandria also prayed at sunrise and sunset.

41 There was also a prayer to be recited at three in the afternoon, when the «vesper sacrifice» was offered in the Jerusalem temple. Apparently this prayer too was well established in the first century, perhaps through the influence of Pharisaic groups. Jesus probably also practiced it. In the Acts of the Apostles we read that «Peter and John were going up to the temple at the hour of prayer, at three o'clock in the afternoon» (3:1).

42 The *Shema* is composed of three texts: Deut 6:4-9; Deut 11:13-21; and Num 15:37-41.

43 Mark 12:29.

44 This was also called *Amida*, because it was spoken standing up; or simply *Tefila*, the quintessential prayer.

healed wounds and cured the sick must have spoken this one with great trust and joy: «Cure us, O Lord our God, of all the wounds of our heart. Remove sadness and tears from us. Come quickly to cure our wounds. Blessed are you, who cure the sick of your people». These words twice a day must have warmed his heart: «You alone reign over us. Blessed are you, O Lord, who love justice». And these words, invoking God's name: «Hear, O Lord, our God, the voice of our prayer. Show us your mercy, for you are a good and merciful God. Blessed are you, O Lord, who hear our prayer»[45].

For Jesus it is not enough to follow this practice routinely. Sometimes he gets up early in the morning and goes to pray in a solitary place before sunrise; other times, he leaves everyone at the end of the day and continues the afternoon prayer late into the night[46]. Jesus' prayers do not consist of a verbal repetition of the prescribed prayers. He prays without words, in a contemplative way; the important thing is his intimate encounter with God. That is what Jesus seeks in this environment of silence and solitude[47].

We know very little about Jesus' physical posture for prayer. He almost always prayed standing up, as all pious Jews did, in a serene and trusting attitude toward God. But the sources say that the night he spent at Gethsemane, on the eve of his execution, «he threw himself on the ground» in a gesture of defeat, but also of total submission to the Father[48]. Jesus expresses himself to God with total sincerity and transparency, including his bodily position. He was apparently accustomed to «looking up to heaven» when he prayed[49], which was unusual in his time, since Jews ordinarily looked toward the temple in Jerusalem; according to Israel's faith that was where the Shekinah, the earthly Presence of God, resided[50]. In raising his gaze toward heaven Jesus was turning his heart, not toward the God of the temple, but toward the good Father of all. Curiously,

---

45 From blessings # 6, 8, 11 and 15 respectively.

46 Mark 1:35; 6:46; 14:32-42; Luke 6:12. The gospel writers (especially Luke) have probably independently inserted some of the texts that speak of Jesus' prayers, but the fact related in the tradition is authentic: Jesus sought solitude and silence in order to pray.

47 Different texts of the Mishnah and some *targumim* emphasize the importance of prolonged silence to center the heart on God. It is said that «in other times, the first *hasidim* waited in silence for an hour before beginning to pray, so as to direct their hearts toward God» (Mishnah *Berakot* 5,1). Jesus may have done something similar.

48 Mark 14:35. A Christian writing dated around 65 to 67 A.D., traditionally called the letter to the Hebrews, says that at Gethsemane Jesus prayed «with loud cries and tears» (5:7).

49 Mark 7:34; John 11:41; 17:1.

50 This custom is reflected in writings as early as 1 Kgs 8:48-49 and Dan 6:11. According to the Mishnah, «those who pray must turn toward the Holy of Holies» (*Berakot* 4:5). Apparently both the Essenes and the Therapeutae turned their faces toward the sun when they prayed.

the Mishnah says that looking toward heaven goes with acceptance of the reign of God: those who raise their eyes to heaven must turn their hearts to accept the demands of God's reign[51].

Jesus nourishes his daily life with this contemplative prayer, going out early in the morning to a secluded place or spending a good part of the night alone with his Father[52]. But the sources also suggest that he stayed in communion with God during his daytime activities as well. Once, seeing that the wise and educated were closed to the message of God's reign while the small and ignorant accepted it with simple faith, a joyful blessing to God sprang from the depths of his being. Jesus was rejoicing over God's goodness to the little ones. There's no need to wait until evening to bless God. Right there, in the midst of the people, he praises God out loud: «I thank you, Father, Lord of heaven and earth, because you have hidden these things from the wise and the intelligent and have revealed them to infants; yes, Father, for such was your gracious will»[53]. Jesus can bless God at any time of day. He spontaneously bursts out with such typical Jewish prayers of «blessing», which is not exactly an act of thanksgiving for a favor received, but a heartfelt exclamation to the one who is the source of everything good. In «blessing», the Jewish believer turns everything toward God and yields everything to its original goodness[54].

Jesus also prays when he cures the sick. We see it in his act of laying hands on them, to bless them in God's name and envelop them in his mercy. While his hands are blessing those who feel condemned, and convey power and encouragement to those who suffer, by raising his heart to God he conveys to the sick the life he himself is receiving from the Father[55]. He does the same thing with

---

51 Some texts of the Mishnah (period of the tannahs) speak of *qawana*, an attitude of prayer which includes looking toward heaven and heartfelt submission to the demands of the reign of God (Manns).

52 The rabbinic literature says that charismatics like Honi or Hanninah ben Dosa withdrew to pray alone on the roof of their house, or in the upper room (Vermes).

53 Q Source (Luke 10:21; Matt 11:25-26); [apocryphal] *Gospel of Thomas* 61:3. Both style and content are typical of Jesus, especially God's preference for the little ones. There is no serious reason to doubt its authenticity.

54 The blessing or *berakah* usually begins with an introduction, «Blessed are you, O Lord...», followed by the reason for the blessing and a brief summary. Jesus probably often recited this blessing as part of the prayer after meals: «Blessed are you, O Lord our God, king of the universe; you feed the world with your goodness, your love and your mercy; you give bread to all flesh. His love for us is eternal, and we have not lacked his great goodness. We will lack nothing good in his great Name, for he feeds and supplies us all. Blessed are you, O Lord, who give food to us all».

55 Mark 8:23; Luke 4:40; 13:13. According to the Markan tradition, when the disciples ask why they were unable to cast out the evil spirit of an epileptic, Jesus replies: «This kind can come out only through prayer» (9:29). Jesus is able to cast out evil with God's power because unlike his disciples, he lives in prayer.

the children. Sometimes «he took them up in his arms, laid his hands on them, and blessed them». The little ones above all must feel God's tenderness. While he blesses them, he asks the Father to give them everything good[56].

Jesus' prayer has unmistakable characteristics. It is simple prayer, «in secret». He prays without great gestures or solemn words, not for the sake of appearance, not to nourish narcissism or self-deception. He stands before God, not anyone else. We should not pray in the public square where others will see us: «Whenever you pray, go into your room and shut the door and pray to your Father who is in secret»[57]. And it is spontaneous, natural prayer; it comes out without effort or special techniques; it comes from the depth of his being; it is not an afterthought or an artifice, but a humble, sincere expression of his life. Neither is it a mechanical prayer or a quasi-magical repetition of words. We should not pile up formulas, as the pagans do to «wear out» the gods so that they will listen. It is enough to present ourselves to God as sons and daughters in need: «for your Father knows what you need before you ask him»[58]. Jesus' prayer is absolute trust in God.

Jesus' prayer can only be understood in the context of the reign of God. Beyond the customary prayers prescribed by Jewish piety, he seeks out God to accept God's reign and make it a human reality. His prayer at Gethsemane is surely the most dramatic example of his search for God's will, even at the moment of a total crisis of meaning. His trust in the Father is firm in the midst of his anguish. His desire is clear: for God's reign to come without the need for so much suffering. His position of filial obedience is also clear and definitive: «*Abba*, Father, for you all things are possible; remove this cup from me; yet not what I want, but what you want»[59].

---

56 Mark 10:16. Although we can see traces of Christian baptismal rites in this text, the story may reflect a real incident in Jesus' life; it shows his attitude toward the small and defenseless.

57 Matt 6:5-6. Since none of the village houses had private rooms, Jesus withdrew to a hill or a secluded place.

58 Matt 6:7-8.

59 Mark 14:36. The scene at Gethsemane was carefully constructed by the Christian community, but its core is considered historical by most scholars.

4
God as the Father

Jesus' whole life is based on his experience of God as Father. That is what he feels during his nights of prayer, and what he lives throughout the day. God takes care of even his most fragile creatures, makes the sun rise on good and evil, reveals himself to the little ones, defends the poor, heals the sick, seeks out the lost. This Father is the center of his life.

In ancient times the Jews gave God the name «Yahweh», to distinguish him from the gods of other people[60]. However, after the exile this name was used less often. Other names were introduced to evoke God without directly naming him. The holy «name» of Yahweh was reserved for the official temple cult[61]. In everyday conversation people used expressions like «the Heavens», «the Power», «the Place», «the One who lives in the Temple», «the Lord»[62]. Jesus used this language as everyone else did, but it was not characteristic of him. What comes from his heart is to call God «Father».

This is not completely new with Jesus. Israel's Scriptures also speak metaphorically of God as a «father» in order to emphasize his authority, which demands respect and obedience, but especially his goodness, care, and love, which invite trust. This image of God as «father» is not central. It is one more image, along with God as «husband», «shepherd», or «liberator». Jesus knows that the biblical tradition sees God's relationship with Israel as one of a father and his sons. There are moving prayers in the book of Isaiah: «Yet, O Lord, you are our Father; we are the clay, and you are our potter; we are all the work of your hand»[63]. «You, O Lord, are our father; our Redeemer from of old is your name. Why, O Lord, do you make us stray from your ways, and harden our heart, so that we do not fear you?»[64].

The Jews always kept this vision of God as «father». At the time Jesus was traveling around Galilee, a wise Jew from Alexandria named Philo spoke of God

---

60 In the words of Micah, a Jewish prophet between 738 and 693 B.C.: «For all the peoples walk, each in the name of its god, but we will walk in the name of the Lord our God forever and ever» (4:5).
61 We know the high priest pronounced the name on the day of Atonement (*Yom Kippur*), when he entered the holiest area of the temple.
62 «Lord» (*Kyrios*) was a divine title deeply rooted in hellenistic Judaism in the first century, but Jesus seldom used it. He apparently chose not to emphasize God's lordship (Schlosser).
63 Isa 64:8.
64 Isa 63:16b-17a.

as «father and author of the universe» to emphasize his nature as creator of the universe, the source and beginning of everything. A writing called the book of Wisdom, also compiled in Alexandria around the end of the first century B.C., repeatedly affirms that the righteous have God as their «father». He wasn't called that in Qumran, but this moving text has been discovered: «You will care for me until my old age, for my father did not recognize me and my mother abandoned me to you, because you are a father to all your children»[65]. Jesus the Galilean peasant could hardly have known all that, but we do know he recited the *Eighteen Blessings* every day, in which God is repeatedly invoked as «our father and our king»[66].

Jesus likes to call God «Father». It springs from within him, especially when he wants to emphasize God's goodness and compassion[67]. But it is especially typical of Jesus to call on God with the seldom-used expression, *Abba*. He experiences God as someone so close, so good and so intimate, that this one word comes spontaneously to his lips when he is talking to God: «*Abba*, my dear Father»[68]. This is the most characteristic feature of his prayer. He has no deeper expression for God than this: *Abba*. It had such an impact that years later, in the Greek-speaking Christian communities, they left the Aramaic word *Abba* untranslated as an echo of Jesus' personal experience[69]. This is not a conventional way of addressing God. This consciousness of filial intimacy with God, his Father, is different from the consciousness that other sons and daughters of God might have. Jesus speaks out of his awareness that he is the Son sent by God: «whoever welcomes me welcomes not me but the one who sent me»[70]; «and

---

65 1Q Hymns IX, 34-35.

66 The rabbinical literature describes God as a father, but never uses the term as an invocation of God (Schlosser).

67 After carefully studying all the sources, Schlosser concludes that Jesus' custom of calling God «Father» is firmly attested in the Markan tradition (11:25; 14:36) and in the Q Source (Luke 6:36; 10:21; 11:13; 12:30; Matt 5:45). In the exclusively Lucan and Matthean material all the texts appear to be secondary, except Luke 12:32 and possibly Luke 23:34.

68 The view of Jeremias, widely known and accepted for many years, has been reshaped and corrected by modern scholarship: 1) It is not certain that Jesus always used the term *Abba* in speaking of God (Schlosser, Marchel); 2) he may not have been the only one to address God that way (Dunn, Vermes); 3) *Abba* comes from the language of children, but it was also used as a solemn, mature form of address (Barr, Vermes, Schlosser).

69 We see this in two letters from Paul of Tarsus. The first was written in 55 A.D. to the communities in Galatia: «And because you are children, God has sent the Spirit of his Son into our hearts, crying, "Abba! Father!"» (Gal 4:6). The second was written in 58 A.D. to the Christians in Rome: «You have received a spirit of adoption. When we cry, "Abba! Father" it is that very Spirit bearing witness...» (Rom 8:15-16).

70 Mark 9:37.

whoever rejects me rejects the one who sent me»[71]. By speaking this way, Jesus is expressing his awareness of his mission and his unique relationship to God, his Father. We should also recall the very meaningful way in which Jesus uses the definitive term, «the Son», which expresses the singular, unique relationship between Jesus, the Son, and God, the Father: «All things have been handed over to me by my Father; and no one knows the Son except the Father, and no one knows the Father except the Son and anyone to whom the Son chooses to reveal him»[72]. Many scholars consider this saying, with its very Johannine tone, as the earliest evidence in the synoptic tradition of Jesus' clear awareness of his filial relationship with God[73]. It comes from his most intimate experience, and is very different from the solemn tone his contemporaries generally used to speak to God, emphasizing distance and reverential awe[74].

The first words a Galilean toddler learned were *imam* (mama) and *abba* (papa). Jesus used those names for Mary and Joseph too. So for him *abba* evoked a small child's affection, intimacy and trust for his father. But we should not exaggerate. Adults apparently also used the word to express their respect and obedience to the father in a patriarchal family. To call God *Abba* conveyed affection, intimacy and closeness, but also respect and submission[75]. Jesus had learned the importance of the father in his own home. Joseph was the center of the family. Everything turned on him. The father cares for and protects his own. If he's not there, the family is at risk of disintegration and disappearance. The father sustains and assures everyone's future. There are two characteristics of a good father. The first is solicitude for his children: it is he who must provide their sustenance, protect and help them in everything. At the same time, the father is the author-

71 Luke 10:16.
72 Matthew 11:27.
73 Jesus' well-documented custom of calling on God with the Aramaic word *abbá*, which connotes a singular closeness and immediacy (Mark 14:36); his awareness that he had the authority to forgive sins on earth (Mark 2:10); his claim to act as «Lord of the sabbath» (Mark 2:28); his two basic attitudes of absolute trust and unconditional submission to God, his Father, even in death (Mark 14:36); the Jordan River experience in which God does not appear to him as an ineffable Mystery, but as a Father who dialogues with him to reveal his mystery as the Son (Mark 1:10-11): these constitute the historical basis from which his disciples came to their faith in Jesus Christ as the Son of God in the light of paschal faith.
74 Neither the rabbinical literature nor the official prayers of later Judaism use *Abba* directly in addressing God. Many authors emphasize the novelty of Jesus' custom in this context (Jeremias, Marchel, Van Iersel, Schillebeeckx, Fitzmyer, Schlosser, Guijarro). Jewish authors like Flusser and Vermes disagree.
75 The affection implicit in Jesus' use of *abba* is not the opposite of respect, but of distance. It suggests closeness and immediacy, but does not exclude respect and obedience (Schlosser, Schillebeecks, Guijarro, Dunn).

ity of the family: he gives the orders to organize their work and assures the good of all. He instructs his children, teaches them a trade, and corrects them when necessary. The children in turn are called to be the joy of their father. Above all they must trust him: to be a child is to belong to the father and joyfully accept what he gives them. At the same time they must respect his paternal authority, listen to him and obey his orders. They owe their father affection and submission. He is the ideal for all his children. This family experience helped Jesus to deepen his experience of God as his Father.

5

Jesus' good Father

❧

308   But Jesus never confused God with those Galilean fathers, concerned as they were for maintaining their patriarchal authority, their honor and their power[76]. Although he sometimes speaks of God as a Father who demands obedience and respect, this is not God's most characteristic feature. Jesus is entranced by his goodness. God is good. Jesus grasps his unfathomable mystery as a mystery of goodness. He does not base that on any text from the sacred Scriptures. For him it is a primordial, unarguable, self-evident fact. God is a good Presence which blesses all life. The Father's loving care, almost always mysterious and hidden, is present and all-encompassing in the life of every creature.

What defines God is not his power, like that of the pagan divinities of the Empire; nor his wisdom, as in some currents of Greek philosophy. Jesus understands the ultimate reality of God, the mystery we cannot think through or imagine, as his goodness and salvation. God is good to him, and to all God's sons and daughters. People are the most important thing for God, much more important than sacrifices or the sabbath. God only wants what is good for them. Nothing should be used against people, especially not religion.

This good Father is a God close by. His goodness is already breaking into the world, in the form of compassion. Jesus lives this loving closeness of God with amazing simplicity and spontaneity. It is like a grain of wheat sowed in the ground, which we do not see now, but it will soon become a splendid head of grain. God's goodness is like that: now it is hidden in the complex reality of life, but one day it

---

76 The Father God of whom Jesus spoke, far from being a sexist symbol, actually implied a radical critique of the «patriarchal ideology» and what today we call sexism (Hamerton-Kelly, Haight).

will triumph over evil. This is not a theory for Jesus. God is close and accessible to everyone. Anyone can have a direct and immediate relationship with him in the secrecy of their hearts. He speaks to everyone without human words. Even the smallest ones can discover his mystery[77]. We can meet him without ritual mediations or sophisticated liturgies, like those of the temple. Jesus invites us to live by trusting the ineffable Mystery of a nearby, good God: «When you pray, say, Father!»[78]. This nearby God seeks out people wherever they are, even those who are lost, far from the Covenant of God.

This God is good to everyone. «He makes his sun rise on the evil and on the good, and sends rain on the righteous and on the unrighteous»[79]. The sun and rain are for everyone. No one has an exclusive claim to them. No one owns them. God offers them as a gift to all, breaking with the moralistic tendency to discriminate against bad people. God does not belong to good people; his love is also open to the wicked. Jesus' faith in the universal goodness of God surprises everyone. For centuries they have heard something very different. They often talk about God's love and tenderness, but that love has to be earned. Said a well known psalm: «As a father has compassion for his children, so the Lord has compassion» — but only for «those who fear him»[80]. As late as 190 B.C., a Jewish writer from Jerusalem named Jesus ben Sira affirmed that «the Most High hates sinners»[81].

Jesus often speaks of God as a good Father, but never as masterfully as in his parable about a father welcoming home his lost son[82]. God the good Father is not like an authoritarian patriarch, concerned only for his honor, implacably controlling his family. He is like an ever-present father who is not concerned with his legacy, respects his children's decisions, and allows them freedom to follow their own path. One can always return to this God without fear. When the father in the parable sees his son arriving, hungry and humiliated, he runs to meet him, embraces and kisses him as effusively as a mother would, and shouts his joy for everyone to hear. He interrupts the son's confession to avoid humiliating him further; he doesn't need that to accept him as he is. He doesn't mete

---

77 Q Source (Luke 10:21; Matt 11:25).

78 Luke 11:2. In Matt 6:6 we see this recommendation: «Whenever you pray, go into your room and shut the door and pray to your Father who is in secret». Some scholars doubt that Jesus would have given such specific details on prayer, but the underlying attitude is typical of him.

79 Q Source (Luke 6:35; Matt 5:45). The Lucan and Matthean versions are somewhat different, but the idea that God does not restrict his love exclusively to good people comes from Jesus.

80 Ps 103:13. See also Psalms 5:6; 11:5-6; and others.

81 Ecclesiasticus (Sirach) 12:6.

82 Luke 15:11-32.

out punishment; he doesn't set conditions on the son's return to the house; he doesn't require a ritual of purification. He doesn't seem to feel a need to forgive him; he has always loved him and only seeks his happiness. He gives him back his dignity as a son: the household ring and the best robe. He holds a feast with banquet, music and dancing. He wants to teach his son to enjoy the good feast of life, instead of the false distraction he has been living among the pagan prostitutes.

This is not God the guardian of the law, watching the sins of his children, who gives everyone their just deserts and only forgives those who have scrupulously met his conditions. This is the God of forgiveness and life; we can come into his presence without humiliation or self-degradation. He demands nothing of the son. All he asks of him is to trust his father. When we understand God as the absolute power who rules and imposes himself by the force of his law, we have a religion based on harshness, merits and punishment. When we experience God as goodness and mercy, we have a religion based on trust. God does not terrify us with his power and majesty; he seduces us with goodness and closeness. We can trust him. Jesus said this in a thousand ways to the sick, suffering, undesirables and sinners: God is for those who need him to be good.

6

The God of life

༄

Jesus cannot think about God without thinking about his plan to transform the world. He never distinguishes between God and his reign. He does not contemplate God enclosed in his own world, isolated from the people's problems; he is committed to humanizing life. The priests in Jerusalem think of God in terms of the cultic system of the temple; the Pharisaic sectors see him as the foundation and guarantor of the law that governs Israel; the Essenes in Qumran experience him as the inspiration of their pure life in the desert. Jesus senses him as the presence of a good Father who is stepping in to the world to humanize life[83]. Thus for Jesus the best place to understand God is not at worship, but wherever he is making his reign of justice a reality among human beings. Jesus understands God in the midst of life, as an accepting presence for the excluded ones, as a

---

83 Jesus doesn't really talk about God, but about the reign of God. Underlying his religious experience is a decisive change of emphasis: God is for humanity, and not humanity for God (Schillebeeckx, Sobrino). That is why no sabbath or cultic practice pleases God unless it is for the good of human beings.

healing power for the sick, as gratuitous forgiveness for the guilty, as hope for those who have been defeated by life.

This God is a God of change. His reign is a powerful force of transformation. His presence among human beings is inflammatory, provocative, challenging: it pulls them toward conversion. God is not a conservative force, but a call for change: «The kingdom of God has come near; repent [change your way of thinking and acting], and believe in the good news»[84]. It is not a time to be passive. God has a great plan. We must begin building a new earth, the way he wants it. Everything must be turned toward a more human life, beginning with those whose life is no life. God wants those who weep to laugh, those who are hungry to eat; he wants everyone to live.

What human beings want is to live, and live well. And what God wants is to turn that wish into reality. The better people live, the better reality is made of God's reign. For Jesus, God's will is not at all mysterious: it is abundant life for everyone. We will never find a better «ally» for our happiness than God. The idea of a God who cares about receiving honor and glory, forgetting about the good and the happiness of his sons and daughters, is not from Jesus. God cares about his children's well-being, health, community, peace, family, enjoyment of life, real and eternal fulfillment.

That is why God is always on the side of human beings and against evil, suffering, oppression and death. Jesus accepts God as a power that seeks only the good, stands against whatever is evil and painful for human beings, and thereby seeks to liberate human life from evil. This is how he experiences and communicates God through his whole message and activity. Jesus struggles constantly against the idols that oppose this God of life, and become divinities of death. Idols like Wealth or Power, which dehumanize everyone who worships them, and which demand victims for their own sustenance. His faith in God impels him to go straight to the root of the problem: defending life and helping the victims. This is his whole life story[85].

His healing activity is inspired by the God who stands against whatever diminishes or destroys human wholeness. God cares about the health of his sons and daughters. Suffering, disease and misfortune are not God's will; they are not

84 This is Mark's summary of Jesus' message (1:15).
85 Jesus' position toward Caesar or toward Wealth (*mammon*) is important: they are quintessentially idols that offer salvation but produce misery, starvation and death: «You cannot serve God and wealth» (Luke 16:13; Matt 6:24). «Give to the emperor the things that are the emperor's, and to God the things that are God's» (Luke 20:25; Matt 22:21).

punishments, tests, or purifications that God sends upon his children. It is impossible to imagine Jesus talking about them that way. He does not come to the sick to offer them a pious vision of their unhappy state, but to empower their life. The blind, deaf, lame, lepers, and demon-possessed belong to the world of those whose life is «no life». Jesus gives them something as basic and elemental as walking, seeing, feeling, speaking, regaining ownership of their own mind and heart. There is a message for everyone in their healed bodies: God wants his sons and daughters to be filled with life.

His defense of the last reveals the same thing. Jesus turns his back on the rich and powerful, those who create hunger and misery, and moves in solidarity toward the dispossessed. The rich are creating a barrier between themselves and the poor: they are the great obstacle against a more just life together. Their wealth is not a sign of God's blessing, for it is accumulating at the cost of suffering and death for the weakest. Jesus is very clear about this: misery is against God's plans. The Father does not want more death among his children. Only abundant life for everyone will satisfy his plan.

Therefore Jesus also takes the side of the excluded ones. He cannot do otherwise. The God he knows is a Father whose heart's desire is a world of wholeness. There must be no people of status, contemptuous of the undesirables; no holy people condemning sinners; no strong people abusing the weak; no men forcing women into submission. God does not bless abuse and discrimination, but equality and solidarity; he does not exclude or excommunicate, but embraces and accepts. Instead of John's «baptism», the symbolic act of a community awaiting God in an attitude of penitence and purification, Jesus offers his «open table» to sinners, undesirables, and excluded ones as the symbol of a community accepting the reign of the Father.

His filial experience of God also impels Jesus to unmask the machinery of a religion that is not at the service of life. We cannot justify in God's name the fact that some people go hungry when they could be filled[86]; we cannot turn away from someone in need of healing, in the name of some cultic observance. Is not the sabbath the best day, in the eyes of the God of life, to restore them to health and liberate them from suffering?[87] A religion that works against life is a false religion; no divine law is unchangeable if it harms people who are already so vulnerable. When a religious law harms people and plunges them into despair,

---

86 Mark 2:23-27.
87 Mark 3:1-6; Luke 13:10-16.

it loses its authority; it does not come from the God of life. Jesus' view is forever enshrined in that unforgettable aphorism: «The sabbath was made for humankind, and not humankind for the sabbath»[88].

Impelled by this God of life, Jesus comes to those whom religion has forgotten. The Father cannot be monopolized by a pious elite, or by a priestly class controlling the religion. God doesn't give anyone special status over others; he doesn't give anyone religious power over the people, but rather the power and authority to do good. Jesus always acts that way: not by authoritarian imposition, but by healing power. He does not instill fear in people but frees them from the fears instilled by religion; he nurtures freedom, not enslavement; he calls people to God's mercy, not to the law; he inspires love, not resentment.

7
The prayer of Jesus

Jesus left his followers the legacy of a prayer that distills in a few words his most intimate experience of God, his faith in God's reign, and his concern for the world. In that prayer we see the great desires of his heart, and the cries he raised to his Father in those long hours of silence and prayer. It is a brief, concise and direct prayer, which must have come as a surprise to people who were used to praying in more solemn, rhetorical language[89].

The earliest Christians considered this prayer, sometimes called the «Our Father» or «Lord's Prayer», to be the only one Jesus taught to nourish the life of his followers. A group's way of praying expresses its relationship with God; it is the experience that unites its members in one faith. Thus the first Christians saw the «Our Father» as the best sign of their identity as followers of Jesus. The Baptist's disciples had their own way of praying. We don't know what it was, but to reflect his message their prayer would probably have modeled a penitential attitude toward the imminent judgment, begging God to free them from his «wrath to come». In contrast, Jesus' prayer is filled with trust in the beloved Fa-

---

88 Mark 2:27.

89 The first two desires in Jesus' prayer are brief and concise: «Hallowed be your name. Your kingdom come». Scholars generally agree that these two petitions come from the *qaddish*, the conclusion to prayer in the synagogue, which Jesus surely knew. However the tone and atmosphere of that Jewish prayer is different: «Exalted and sanctified is his great name, in the world which he has created according to his will. And may he establish his kingdom… in your lifetime and in your days, and in the lifetimes of all the House of Israel, speedily and soon».

ther. It combines his two great desires, centered on God, with three cries of petition centered on the urgent, basic needs of humanity. Jesus tells the Father the two desires in his heart: «Hallowed be your name. Your kingdom come». Then the three cries of petition: «Give us bread», «forgive our debts», and «do not bring us to the time of trial»[90].

We have the Lord's Prayer in two slightly different versions. A rigorous analysis of the texts enables us to detect later additions and modifications, and identify a brief, simple prayer with an Aramaic flavor which is probably very close to the one Jesus taught. That is: «Father, blessed be your name; may your kingdom come; give us today our daily bread; forgive us our debts as we forgive our debtors, and do not put us to the test»[91]. Can we come closer to the «secret» of this prayer?

Father! That is always Jesus' first word when he speaks to God. It is not just an introductory invocation. It opens up the atmosphere of trust and intimacy that shapes all the petitions that follow. His desire is to teach people to pray as he does, aware of themselves as beloved sons and daughters of the Father, brothers and sisters in solidarity with everyone[92]. God is the «Father in heaven». He is not tied to the temple in Jerusalem or any other holy place. He is the Father of all, with no discrimination or exclusion. He does not belong to a privileged people. He is not owned by any religion. Everyone can call on him as Father[93].

Hallowed [blessed, sanctified] be your name. This is not just another petition. It is the first desire of Jesus' heart, his most burning aspiration. He is saying in effect: «May your name of Father be recognized and venerated. Let everyone know the goodness and saving power contained in your holy name. Let no one

---

90 Luke describes the specific circumstances in which Jesus taught the prayer to his disciples: «He was praying in a certain place, and after he had finished, his disciples said to him, "Lord, teach us to pray, as John taught his disciples"» (11:1). The episode was developed by the gospel writer, but it helps us see how the early Christians understood Jesus' prayer.

91 Q Source (Luke 11:2-4; Matt 6:9-13). The Matthean text is more extensive; several additions were made to give it the more solemn, filled-out tone characteristic of Jewish piety. Luke has made some less important changes. The prayer comes from Jesus. Some scholars believe it includes «unrelated petitions» that the disciples heard him make, which were later compiled into a single prayer. There is no strong evidence for this hypothesis.

92 Jesus does not see it as his exclusive right to call God «Father»; he invites everyone to do so. That is why Christian liturgy has always surrounded the Our Father with great respect and veneration: «Faithful to the Savior, and following his divine teaching, we are bold to say: Our Father» (Roman liturgy). «Condescend, O Lord, to allow us joyfully and fearlessly to dare invoke you as the Father» (Oriental rite).

93 Matthew adds «in heaven» to Jesus' invocation of the Father, following the style of some Jewish prayers. But it is close to the spirit of Jesus, who «raised his eyes to heaven» when praying to the Father who «makes his sun rise on the evil and on the good, and sends rain on the righteous and on the unrighteous» (Matt 5:45).

ignore or disrespect it. Let no one profane it by abusing your sons and daughters. Make your saving power and your holy goodness fully manifest now. Let the names of other gods, and of the idols who kill your poor ones, be exiled from the land. May everyone bless your name of good Father»[94].

Your kingdom [reign] come. This is the passion of Jesus' life, his ultimate goal. He's saying: «Let the path of your reign be opened among us. Let the "seed" of your saving power continue growing, let the "yeast" of your reign ferment everything. Let your Good News come now to the poor and abused. May the suffering feel your healing action. Fill the world with your justice and truth, with your compassion and forgiveness. If you reign, the rich will no longer reign over the poor; the powerful will no longer abuse the weak; men will no longer dominate women. If you reign, no Caesar will be given what is yours; no one will serve Wealth along with you»[95].

Your will be done on earth as it is in heaven. This petition, probably added by Matthew, simply repeats and reinforces the previous two; it commits us even more to God's plan of salvation. He's saying: «Let your will, not ours, be done. May your desires be fulfilled, for you seek only what is good for us. Let your will be done in all creation, and not the will of the powerful in this world. Let the will of your heart as a Father become reality among us»[96].

Give us today our daily bread. Now Jesus focuses on specific human needs[97]. «Give us each the food we need to live. Let no one go without bread today. We do not ask for abundant wealth and well-being, we do not want riches to accumulate, only bread for everyone[98]. Let those who are hungry eat; let your poor

---

94 In Semitic cultures, a «name» is not only a term designating a person; it represents the being or the nature of that person. The «name» of God is his reality as a good and saving God. Thus a psalm says: «I will proclaim [or wait for] your name, for it is good» (52:9).

95 In the Lord's prayer Jesus is calling for God's «definitive reign» to become a «present reality» among us; the bread of the eternal banquet and bread for today; the ultimate forgiveness and the forgiveness we need now; the final victory over evil and liberation in the trials of today.

96 A general scholarly consensus views Matt 6:10 as a later addition. The petition can be understood in two different ways. If we understand «heaven and earth» as the totality of everything that exists, we are asking for God's will to fill the whole creation. If we understand «heaven» as the place where God lives and «earth» as the space inhabited by human beings, we are asking for God's present reality to be made real among human beings as well. I have tried here to reflect both interpretations.

97 The first two petitions, on God's «name» and God's «kingdom» are probably inspired by the *qaddish*. The subsequent ones on bread, forgiveness, and liberation from evil make up the new element Jesus is adding. He cannot ask God to sanctify his name and make his kingdom come, without immediately thinking about the specific needs of the people as well.

98 Here Matthew surely reflects the petition authentically, exactly as it springs from Jesus' life as an itinerant vagabond. Trusting in the Father's providence, he only asks for today's bread: «Give us

people stop weeping and begin to laugh; let us see them living with dignity. Give us all a foretaste of the bread that one day we will all eat together, seated at your table. We want to see it now»[99].

Forgive us our debts as we, in the act of saying this, forgive our debtors. We are in debt to God. This is our great sin: not responding to the Father's love, not entering into his reign. Thus Jesus is praying: «Forgive us our debts, not only our offenses against your law, but the enormous emptiness of our failure to respond to your love[100]. We need your forgiveness and your mercy. Our prayer is sincere. In asking this we are forgiving those who are indebted to us. We do not want to nurture resentment or feelings of revenge against anyone. We want your forgiveness to transform our hearts and make us live in mutual forgiveness»[101].

Do not let us fall into temptation. We are weak, exposed to all kinds of dangers and risks that can ruin our life and remove us permanently from God's reign. We are threatened by the mystery of evil. That is why Jesus teaches us to pray: «Do not let us be tempted to reject your reign and your justice definitively. Give us your power. Don't let us be defeated in the final trial. In the midst of temptation and evil, let us depend on your powerful help»[102].

Rescue us from the evil one. Matthew adds this final petition to reinforce and complete Jesus' previous petition. Thus while Jewish prayers almost always end with praise to God, the Our Father ends with a cry for help that still echoes in our life: Father, rescue us from evil!

---

today our daily bread» (*semeron* = today). In contrast, Luke is writing from the perspective of the early Christians, who pray for each day's bread as it is needed: «Give us each day our daily bread» (*kath'emeron*—from day to day).

99 The Greek word *epiousios* is usually understood as «daily» or «everyday» bread, but it can also be translated as bread «for tomorrow», the bread of the future ([apocalyptic] *Gospel of the Nazarenes*). In that interpretation the petition would be: «Give us today our bread for tomorrow».

100 Matthew's version is probably the most original. Jesus knows firsthand the anguish of the peasants, who are deeply in debt and losing their lands. His plea for forgiveness is shaped by this concern: «Forgive us our debts as we forgive our debtors». On the other hand, Luke forgets the economic situation and substitutes «sins» for «debts», although in the next line he returns to the word «indebted»: «forgive us our sins, for we ourselves forgive everyone indebted to us». Subsequent liturgical translations completely leave out the reference to debts: «Forgive us our trespasses [offenses], as we forgive those who trespass against us».

101 God's forgiveness is totally gratuitous. He does not condition his forgiveness of us on our forgiveness of others, but we need to forgive others if our prayer is to be sincere. We cannot adopt a double standard: one in asking the Father for forgiveness, the other in refusing forgiveness to our brothers and sisters. This is why I have used the interpretation of J. Jeremias: «Forgive us our debts as we, in the act of saying this, forgive our debtors».

102 The text [as translated by the NRSV] says literally: «Do not bring us to the time of trial». However the plea is not to be free from temptation or testing, but for help to avoid falling into the trap.

Combative and Dangerous

Jesus did not enjoy a peaceful old age. He died violently in the summer of his life. He was not defeated by illness. He wasn't an accident victim. He was executed outside Jerusalem, beside an old rock quarry, by soldiers under the orders of Pilate, the highest authority of the Roman Empire in Judea. It was probably the 7th of April, in 30 A.D. The prefect had sentenced him to death as the instigator of an insurrection against the Empire. Thus his passionate life as a prophet of God's reign ended on a cross-shaped gallows.

What brought him to this tragic end? Was it all an incredible mistake? What had the prophet of God's compassion done to deserve such torture, which was only applied to criminal slaves or to rebels who threatened the order imposed by Rome? What crime had the healer of the sick committed, to deserve being tortured on a cross? Who was afraid of this preacher of the love of enemies? Who felt threatened by his activity and his message? What did they kill him for?

His tragic end did not come as a surprise. It had been developing day by day, ever since he began his passionate proclamation of the divine plan he was carrying in his heart. While the common people almost always accepted him enthusiastically, alarms were being raised in other sectors. The freedom of this God-filled man was disturbing and dangerous. His strange, nonconformist behavior was troubling. Jesus was an obstacle and a threat. His insistence on changing the situation, and his specific plan for accepting the reign of God, were a threat to the system. Probably everyone found his activity disconcerting and reacted in different ways, but this rejection did not come from the people; it came from those who saw him as a threat to their religious, political or economic power. What made him such a dangerous prophet in just a few months?

1

Conflict with the Pharisaic sectors

According to the gospels, Jesus came into conflict with the Pharisees early on. They were apparently very well known among the people. The «monks» of Qumran lived in their secluded «monastery» beside the Dead Sea; we know very little about the other Essenes. The Sadducees were an aristocratic minority centered around the temple, not particularly concerned with gaining a following in the villages. It was probably the Pharisees who worked hardest to influence the life of the people. Naturally Jesus would come into collision with them[1].

The Pharisees were educated men, very knowledgeable in the traditions and customs of Israel. Many of them had administrative or bureaucratic roles, especially in Jerusalem; they probably earned their living as scribes, teachers, judges, or officials serving the ruling classes. We know almost nothing of their organizational structure. The people identified them in terms of their shared set of beliefs and practices. But they were not a homogeneous bloc. There were disagreements and different viewpoints among them. Teachers like Hillel, Shammai, and Judas, «the founder of the fourth philosophy» according to Flavius Josephus, each had an enthusiastic following[2].

The first concern of the Pharisaic movement was to ensure Israel's faithful response to the holy God, who had given them the law that distinguished them from the other peoples of the earth. This explains their extensive study of Torah and their zeal for strict compliance with all its prescriptions, especially the ones that strengthened the identity of God's holy people: the sabbath, the payment of tithes for the temple, and ritual purity. Along with the written law of Moses they made an obligation of the so-called «traditions of the fathers», which favored more rigorous compliance with the Torah. Out of concern for the holiness of Israel, the most radical sectors urged the people to fulfill purity laws that only applied to priests carrying out their cultic tasks in the temple.

It is hard to reconstruct Jesus' relationship with the Pharisaic sectors. The gospels suggest that he was always in conflict with them. They are his quintessential adversaries: the ones who challenge him, ask him devious questions, and try to discredit him in the eyes of the people. For his part Jesus peppers them with threats and condemnations: they do not want to enter God's reign, but

---

1 The Pharisees evolved as a group in the early Hasmonean period, around 150 B.C. They represented a reaction against the hellenizing influence of Antiochus Epiphanes. They were very powerful in the time of Salome Alexandra. They were marginalized under Herod the Great, but never gave up their political influence among the people. After the destruction of Jerusalem in 70 A.D. the Pharisees, along with other sectors of scribes and pious men, gave rise to the rabbinical movement which became the basis of modern Judaism.

2 It is hard to reconstruct the Pharisaic movement without direct sources. Recent studies suggest that they were not a «religious group» devoted to the study of Torah (which was the traditional understanding); neither were they an academic «school» (Rivkin), although their members were well educated; they had some of the traits of a «sect» centered around meals (Neusner identifies them as a table fellowship); but at the same time they sought to influence the Jewish society (Saldarini). The important studies by Neusner, Sanders and Saldarini are contributing to a better understanding of the Pharisees in the social-religious context of the decade of the thirties.

they lock out those who want to enter; they are «full of hypocrisy and lawlessness»; they are «blind guides», concerned only with details and neglecting «justice and mercy and faith»; they are like whitewashed tombs, «which on the outside look beautiful, but inside they are full of the bones of the dead and of all kinds of filth»[3]. However, this level of hostile confrontation needs to be reviewed and corrected.

In the decade of the thirties, Pharisaism as a group phenomenon was more an urban than a rural movement. It was apparently concentrated in and around Jerusalem. We have no reason to think they were particularly active in Galilee during the time of Jesus. In any case they did not possess a high level of political or religious power. They were a minor social force in Jesus' time, seeking to increase their influence among the people. In Galilee they probably represented the interests of the temple, and some of them may have been bureaucrats or scribes in the service of Antipas. Jesus may have met some of them in the larger Galilean villages, but his contacts with them would have been mostly in and around Jerusalem. So why do they appear in the Christian tradition as his great adversaries?[4]. There is one likely reason. The gospels were compiled after 70 A.D., when there was great hostility between Jesus' followers and the Pharisaic scribes, the only group that had survived the destruction of Jerusalem, and which was struggling to unify its forces and restore Judaism. The gospel writers' descriptions reflect those later confrontations more than the real conflicts between Jesus and the Pharisees in Galilee in the decade of the thirties. However they are so strongly present in all the sources, that we can hardly dismiss the possibility of such confrontations. It would not be surprising, since Jesus and the Pharisees were competing for popular support for their own movements[5].

Chapter 12

321

---

3   This mutual hostility solidifies and deepens with the development of later traditions about Jesus. By the time of Matthew's gospel it has reached the point of extreme virulence. Jesus' «woes» against the «scribes and Pharisees» are well known (Matt 23:2-36).
4   The gospels often speak of the «scribes and Pharisees». We should not confuse the two groups. The «scribes» are not an autonomous organization. They are individuals who copied and edited legal documents, wrote letters, kept accounts, educated the youth of the urban elites, guaranteed the written transmission of religious traditions, and so on. They lived and worked in the service of the ruling classes. In Jesus' time they lived in the service of the temple or the circle of Antipas and the Herodian families; in the villages they may have carried out administrative tasks for the landowners. Some may have achieved a certain level of power as advisors. Some scribes probably belonged to the Pharisaic groups (Saldarini).
5   Some scholars deny, or significantly downplay, Jesus' confrontations with the Pharisees (Mack, Sanders, Fredriksen). The majority practice a critical analysis of the gospel witness, in order to identify the historical core of the confrontation between the prophet of God's reign and the Pharisaic position of his time (Meier, Borg, Schürmann, Schlosser, Léon-Dufour, Rivkin, Gourgues).

The Pharisees cannot ignore a man who so passionately seeks God's will. They are surely pleased to hear his ardent call to all the people to seek God's justice. They like his radical approach. They share his hope in the final resurrection. But they are disconcerted by his proclamation of the reign of God. Jesus does not understand and live by the law as they do. His heart is focused on God's imminent irruption. The more they hear, the more they have to disagree with him.

What bothers them most is his pretentious way of speaking directly in God's name, on his own authority, rather than referring to what other teachers say. This uncommon freedom contrasts with the behavior of their teachers, who always refer to the «traditions of the fathers» or the teachings of their own school[6]. While the Pharisees are struggling to interpret, explain, and apply the will of God as expressed in the law and traditions, Jesus insists on communicating his own experience of a Father God who is establishing his reign in Israel. What matters to Jesus is not observance of the law, but hearing God's call to «enter» his reign. The absolute criterion is no longer the Torah, but the irruption of God in favor of a more human way of life.

The Pharisees probably don't know what to think of Jesus. They are attracted by his healings as everyone else is; they see in him a healing prophet like Elijah, who was so popular among the people. Perhaps the forcefulness of his words reminds them of Isaiah, Jeremiah, or one of the great prophets, but they find his behavior disconcerting. They don't see how he dares to eliminate a Mosaic tradition like the man's right to repudiate his wife[7]. They are irritated by his freedom to transgress something as sacred as the sabbath. They are annoyed that he does not feel obliged to practice the norms of ritual purity in the way they teach them[8].

There is one thing about Jesus that the Pharisees find especially perplexing. On the one hand they are captivated by this prophet who feels the suffering of the sick, the humiliation of the poor, and the loneliness of the excluded as if it

---

6 Mark says that the people were astounded by Jesus' teaching, «for he taught them as one having authority, and not as the scribes» (1:22). Scholars generally agree that this was the impression Jesus left on the people.

7 Most scholars believe Jesus' attitude toward repudiation was scandalous. However, Sanders believes that in the customary practice of rabbinical disputes, it was not a violation of the law to interpret a provision of the Torah by referring to another text of the Torah, as Jesus did in the case of repudiation.

8 However Sanders affirms in a detailed study that «there was no significant conflict between Jesus and the Pharisees over issues of the sabbath, meals, and the purity laws». This position has become quite influential in current scholarship.

were his own: it is truly moving to see him come to them with God's compassion. What they can't understand is his acceptance of sinners. Prophets of God don't act that way. He sees himself as a friend of the «lost». His table is open to all, even those who live outside the Covenant and show no signs of repentance. They find it offensive that he treats sinners as friends in God's name, without demanding the penitence and sacrifices required of all who have separated themselves from the law[9].

So there was confrontation between Jesus and the Pharisaic sectors, but it was not as violent and fanatical as the gospels describe it. The Pharisees were not the instigators of his execution. They may have been annoyed by his activity; they surely argued with him and tried to discredit him; perhaps they exchanged harsh words with him, but they did not seek his death. This was not the way the Pharisees, and probably other groups, did things. They argued among themselves, defended their own positions passionately, but there is no reason to think that they sought Jesus' death because he did not share their vision[10]. Jesus' death is not a result of these confrontations with the Pharisees. Indeed in the passion narratives they are never seen as a group participating in his conviction or execution. The real threat to Jesus comes from other sectors: from the priestly and lay aristocracy of Jerusalem, and from the Roman authorities[11].

2

Opposition to the religious authorities

The Jerusalem aristocracy comprised a rich and important minority of the citizenry, many of them priests. Some members of these ruling classes, but not all, were Sadducees[12]. Many of them were very wealthy. Their elegant mansions in

9 We must not forget that the Pharisees were fundamentally a «table fellowship sect» (Neusner). According to Sanders it was primarily Jesus' behavior toward sinners that provoked the indignation of the Pharisees and other pious sectors.
10 Rivkin has noted the coexistence of different groups and tendencies in Jesus' time, based on an attitude of «live and let live». The reports of Mark and John, that the Pharisees sought Jesus' death, are not historically plausible.
11 This is the most widely accepted position today (Meier, Schlosser, Sanders, Rivkin, Crossan, and others). Some of Caiaphas' scribes or advisors, of a Pharisaic tendency, may have acted individually against Jesus. Others surely defended him (Meier).
12 During the Hasmonean dynasty, the Sadducees enjoyed power until the arrival of Salome Alexandra (76-67 B.C.), who relied on the Pharisaic sectors and contributed to their decadence. When Herod the Great ascended the throne, he named chief priests from the Jewish families in Babylon

the upper city of Jerusalem, and the properties they acquired by different strategies and pressure tactics, were well known. The people apparently considered them a powerful, corrupt sector that lived on the tithes, fees and donations that came to the temple from all over the Jewish diaspora[13]. In fact they did not have supporters or sympathizers in the villages and rural towns.

In Jesus' time the high priest held ruling power both in Jerusalem and in Judea. On the one hand he enjoyed full autonomy in the affairs of the temple: regulation of the sacrificial system, fees, tithes, administration of the treasury; for this purpose he had different services and a police force responsible for maintaining order in the temple area and in Jerusalem. On the other he intervened in the everyday litigation and affairs of the inhabitants of Judea, applying the laws and traditions of Israel. A variety of members of the priestly and lay aristocracy assisted in his tasks as a ruler. When the gospels speak of the «chief priests» they are referring to a group that includes the current high priest, others who have held that role in the past, and the priests responsible for important services, such as the temple commander and the chief treasurer. This aristocracy based in the temple acted as a «branch of power» on which the Roman prefect relied in governing Judea[14].

We don't know whether Jesus ever met the Sadducees directly[15]. Most of the time he spoke to ordinary Jews in the towns of Galilee and Judea, not to the small

and Egypt. Thus they marginalized the priestly aristocracy of Jerusalem, who according to tradition were descendants of Zadok, the priest who served the kings David and Solomon in Jerusalem. When Judea came under the direct rule of a Roman prefect (6 A.D.), the Sadducees recovered some of the power they had held in the time of Hyrcanus I and his Hasmonean successors (134-76 B.C.)

13 Flavius Josephus describes abuses committed by the chief priests around 50-60 A.D.; they even sent servants to extort tithes from the lower-ranking priests, beating up those who resisted (*Antigüedades de los judíos* 20, 179-181, 206 [English: *Jewish Antiquities*]). When the people rebelled against Rome in 66 A.D., they set fire to the house of the high priest Ananias and burned the public archives to prevent him from collecting their back debts (*La guerra judía* II, 426-427 [English: *The Jewish War*]).

14 It is an error to consider the chief priests as an exclusively religious authority whose role was limited to the temple environment. They exercised political power in close collaboration with the Roman prefect, who appointed them and could remove them. Defending the frontiers, protecting the *pax romana* against any kind of sedition, collecting tributes on time, and handing down death sentences, were tasks reserved to Rome.

15 Because the Sadducees disappeared with the destruction of the temple (70 A.D.), and the rabbinical literature gives only a negative and distorted view of them, it is practically impossible to reconstruct the Sadducees as a group. We can only say with certainty that they were a well established minority group; they included some lay and priestly members of the Jerusalem aristocracy; they had their own traditions, different from those of the Pharisees and Essenes; as a power group they collaborated with the Roman authorities to maintain the *status quo* that favored their power and prosperity; they were not interested in «the next life», and rejected the doctrine of resurrection.

group of wealthy aristocrats from Jerusalem. But Jesus was not unknown to them when he went up to Jerusalem to celebrate the Passover in 30 A.D. They had heard about him, and some may have heard him speak[16]. It was not the first time Jesus had come to the city to proclaim his message during a Jewish feast. And naturally he taught in the temple area, where the people gathered and where Sadducean groups were also to be found[17].

The religious leaders in Jerusalem had to be alarmed and suspicious about what Jesus was saying. They knew he came from the circle of John the Baptist, the wilderness prophet who offered forgiveness in the Jordan river, bypassing the process of purification from sins which was controlled by the temple. They never approved of baptism by that rural priest who had suddenly left them and abandoned his duties[18]. Now with the Baptist gone, they must have been really bothered by Jesus' charismatic activity along the same prophetic line, outside the sacrificial system of the temple. Perhaps more so, because Jesus didn't require a penitential rite as John did; he was friendly with sinners, and offered them God's gratuitous forgiveness. In his scandalous practice, even tax collectors and prostitutes had a place in the reign of God, without first going through the official process of atonement! How could they tolerate such disrespect for the temple?

They may also have disapproved of the healings and exorcisms that made Jesus so popular, which seemed to undermine their power as the exclusive intermediaries of God's forgiveness and salvation for Israel. When Jesus cured people or freed them from evil spirits, he was not only curing them but pulling them out of sin (which was believed to be the source of all illness) and re-incorporating them into the people of God. Apparently no Jew had the right to exercise that mediation of God's blessing, except those who belonged to a priestly lineage. Jesus' activity was a challenge to the temple as the exclusive source of salvation for the people[19].

16 The gospels mention only one confrontation between Jesus and the Sadducees (Mark 12:18-27). That scene, set in the temple, is a debate over the resurrection of the dead. The story may reflect a basically historical episode.

17 We know from the gospel of John that Jesus visited Jerusalem several times: three times for the Passover (2:13; 6:4; 11:55); during the feast of Booths (7:2); the feast of Dedication (10:22); and once for an unidentified feast (5:1). In Mark he goes up only once, for the Passover feast when he is executed. But in Mark's description, once Jesus arrives he acts as if he had been there before; he has friends and acquaintances who help him prepare the last supper.

18 In an episode at the temple, reported in Mark 11:27-33, Jesus asks the chief priests, scribes, and elders: «Did John's baptism come from heaven, or was it of human origin? Answer me». His adversaries avoid answering, because they have never believed in baptism in the Jordan. Not all scholars accept the historicity of this story.

19 The theory that Jesus' healings were seen as a subversion of the temple, which is emphasized by Crossan, Herzog, Kaylor and other authors, is not unanimously accepted by scholars.

It raised a decisive question: could the religious leaders in Jerusalem still exercise God's authority over the people of Israel, or was Jesus opening up a new way outside the religious control of the temple? The Christian tradition has preserved a parable, which Mark describes as addressed to the temple authorities[20]. We can no longer reconstruct Jesus' original story, traditionally known as the parable of the murderous tenants, but it probably conveyed a strong criticism to the religious authorities in Jerusalem: they had failed to care for the people entrusted to them. They thought only of their own interests and considered themselves the owners of Israel, when they were only its managers. Worse yet: they had not accepted the messengers of God, but rejected them one by one. The time was coming when the owner «will give the vineyard to others». The priestly aristocracy would be stripped of God's power to serve the people of Israel[21]. If this was really the message of the parable, Jesus' life was in serious danger. The chief priests could not tolerate such defiance.

There are other echoes of Jesus' criticism toward the religious leaders of the temple. At some unknown time he proclaimed what was probably a prophetic lament over Jerusalem, in the style of Amos and other prophets. He was not thinking of the whole city, but especially of its religious leaders. We can still discern in the text the sad rhythm of the lament and Jesus' deep sorrow:

Jerusalem, Jerusalem,

the city that kills the prophets

and stones those who are sent to it!

How often I have desired to gather your children together

as a hen gathers her brood under her wings,

and you were not willing!

See, your house is left to you.

---

20 The parable of the murderous vineyard tenants is found in Mark 12:1-8 and parallels (Luke 20:9-15 and Matthew 21:33-39), and in the [apocryphal] *Gospel of Thomas* 65. The text of the synoptic gospels has been shaped into an allegorical vision of the history of salvation (especially by Matthew): the owner of the vineyard is God, the tenant workers are the priests in Jerusalem, the servants sent to them are the prophets, the son they kill is Jesus, and the others who replace them are the disciples who are to form the Church. The more restrained version in the [apocryphal] *Gospel of Thomas*, without the allegorical interpretation, appears to be closer to the original.

21 This criticism of the ruling aristocracy in Jerusalem was probably shaped by the later Christian community into an allegory which identified the Church as the successor to Israel.

And I tell you, you will not see me until the time comes when you say, «Blessed is the one who comes in the name of the Lord»[22].

Here again Jesus is talking about the defiant attitude of the religious rulers, who kill the prophets God has sent them. He too has tried to restore the true Israel, but they were not willing. Anticipating the imminent judgment of God, he already sees the ill-fated city as destroyed: the temple will be abandoned without God's presence[23].

3
The defensiveness of the Roman powers

This confrontation with the ruling powers of the temple was much more threatening than Jesus' disputes with the scribes and Pharisees over practical issues of behavior. But along with the temple authorities, the greatest threat to Jesus came from the highest power of all. His proclamation of the imminent establishment of God's reign, his critical view of the existing situation, his program of solidarity with the excluded, and his freedom, represented a radical and dangerous alternative to the system imposed by Rome. Jesus was becoming a disturbing prophet: a source of concern at first, and later, as the impact of his activity became more widely known, a dangerous threat of subversion. He could be executed in any territory controlled by Rome, whether in Galilee under the emperor's faithful vassal Antipas, or in Judea where the Roman prefect ruled directly.

Although Jesus is active mainly in Galilee, it is not Antipas who executes him. Certainly Antipas knows about Jesus. He knows about his potentially dangerous relationship with the Baptist. He may occasionally have Jesus followed, but he never arrests him[24]. He is probably held back by the popular resentment that followed his arbitrary execution of the Baptist. He doesn't want to stir up any

---

22 Q Source (Luke 13:34-35; Matt 23:37-39). The prophetic tone and the image of the hen are typical of Jesus' language. The episode apparently occurred before the last entry of Jesus into Jerusalem. The text implies that Jesus has visited the city several times before.

23 «Your house is left to you» literally means, «is left desolate». It probably refers to the temple, known then as «the house of God». Horsley suggests that Jesus is thinking of «the ruling house». That would be the Sadducean family of Annas, a powerful manipulator; even after being deposed as chief priest in 15 A.D., he was able to keep his five sons and his son in-law Caiaphas in that post for another 35 years. They were the most powerful Jewish family in Jesus' time.

24 In Luke 13:31 some Pharisees warn Jesus: «Get away from here, for Herod wants to kill you». He may in fact have received such a warning.

more trouble[25]. Jesus in turn shows only contempt for the tetrarch who executed the prophet whom he so admired and loved. He calls Antipas «that fox», knowing that he wants to entrap him as he did the Baptist[26], and he derides the emblem stamped on Antipas' coins as a mere «reed shaken by the wind», no matter how elegantly he dresses and how splendidly he lives in his palace at Tiberias[27].

Probably in Pilate's palace at Caesarea by the Sea, and in the garrison where soldiers kept watch at the Antonia tower in Jerusalem, everyone is worried by the puzzling reports from Galilee; but they are not overly concerned. It is only when they see the great attraction Jesus holds for the people, and especially when they see him freely performing his provocative acts in the capital city itself, in the explosive atmosphere of the Passover feast, that they become aware of his dangerous potential.

One thing may have worried them from the beginning. Jesus uses a political term as a key symbol of his message. He wants everyone to know that «God's empire» is imminent. In the decade of the thirties the word *basileia*, which the Christian sources consistently use to translate «kingdom» or reign of God, was only used to describe the Roman «empire». It is the Roman Caesar and his legions who establish the *pax romana* and impose their justice on the whole world. Caesar gives well-being and security to the peoples, and in exchange for that protection he exacts an implacable tribute. What does Jesus mean by inviting people to «enter into the empire of God», which unlike Tiberius' empire does not seek power, wealth and honor, but justice and compassion for those who have been most excluded from and humiliated by the Roman Empire?

When Jesus speaks of an «empire», even if he calls it God's empire, the rulers have to be worried. His talk about building a different «empire», on the basis of God's will, implies a radical criticism of Tiberius, the Caesar who dictates his own will uniformly to all the peoples[28]. But they are more worried by his social

---

25 Flavius Josephus reports that later, when Antipas' army was destroyed by Aretas, the king of Nabatea and father of the Galilean tetrarch's repudiated wife, some people interpreted the defeat as «just vengeance» for what he had done to the Baptist (*Antigüedades de los judíos* 18, 114-116. [English: *Jewish Antiquities*]).

26 Luke 13:32. The epithet may have come from Jesus, although the statement that follows has been reshaped by the Christian community.

27 «What did you go out into the wilderness to look at? A reed shaken by the wind?... Someone dressed in soft robes? Look, those who put on fine clothing and live in luxury are in royal palaces. What then did you go out to see? A prophet? Yes, I tell you, and more than a prophet» (Q Source: Luke 7:24-27; Matt 11:7-9). Antipas' coins were stamped with the rustic image of a «reed», like those that grew abundantly on the shores of the sea of Tiberias (Theissen).

28 Beginning in 27 A.D., Tiberius was living in his refuge on the island of Capri; the powerful Sejanus ruled in his name. His hostility toward the Jewish people was well known.

location than by his language. Again and again the Galilean prophet says that the people most excluded and marginalized by the Empire have priority in God's plan. This man is telling everyone that God's will goes against Caesar's will. His message is clear to anyone who listens: the whole society must be made over on a different basis, restoring the true will of God. To «enter» into the empire of God, they must «leave» the empire of Rome.

Jesus certainly is not planning a suicidal uprising against Rome, but his activity is dangerous. Wherever he goes, he arouses the hope of the dispossessed with an unheard-of passion: «Blessed are you who are poor, for the empire of God is yours». When he sees hungry people in one of the villages, he infects them with his faith: «Blessed are you who are hungry now, for you will be filled». When he sees peasants overwhelmed by helplessness, he proclaims his conviction to them: «Blessed are you who weep now, for you will laugh». These are inflammatory words. What does he mean by proposing to turn the situation upside down? He has one particularly blunt and provocative saying: «Many who are first will be last, and the last will be first»[29]. Is this only the dream of a naïve prophet? Jesus knows that nothing will be changed by struggling against the Roman legions. But he directs all his energy to the God of Israel, and with incredible faith encourages his followers to keep praying: «Father, let your empire come». Where will it all end?[30].

The Roman authorities are also hearing about his healings, and his extraordinary power to liberate people from demonic powers. Apparently Jesus is committed to a struggle between God and the evil powers that control the people. It is hard for us to imagine the political-religious tragedy that Israel was experiencing. They are God's chosen people, but they live in subjection to the evil power of Rome. The Jews cannot conceive of such cruel oppression without seeing it as the intervention of superhuman powers against Israel. There has to be something demonic in all that. Demon-possession, apparently so common in that period, can only be a tragic expression of the people's real situation. The Romans are the evil powers that have taken control of the people and are strip-

---

29 Jesus probably used this aphorism on different occasions. We find it in Mark 10:31, in the Q Source (Luke 13:30; Matt 20:16), and in the [apocryphal] *Gospel of Thomas* 4:2-3. It circulated in the Christian communities as one of Jesus' sayings; the gospel writers set it in different contexts with different meanings.

30 Fierce criticism of the empire was common, and the Roman authorities must have been listening carefully. Among the most famous were the words attributed by Tacitus to a British rebel leader: «To ravage, slaughter, usurp, they call this "empire"; they make a desert, and call it "peace"» (*Vida de Agricola*, 30. [English: *Life of Agricola*]).

ping them of their identity[31]. One question is eating at them: is the God of Israel still in charge of history? Why then are they subjected to the gods of Rome? Where is their God? This is what makes Jesus' exorcisms unexpectedly powerful. If God is overcoming Satan, as he says, then the days of Rome are numbered. He is signaling the defeat of Rome by casting out the demonic forces. God is already taking action. His empire is beginning to make itself felt. Jesus said so: «If it is by the finger of God that I cast out the demons, then the kingdom of God has come to you»[32]. The simple people of Galilee may have sensed the approaching defeat of the Romans behind this religious interpretation of Jesus' exorcisms, but it is unlikely that the Romans saw this strange behavior as a threat to the Empire[33].

What may have worried them more, if they knew about it, was Jesus' ambiguous position on the tribute exacted by Rome. This was a smoldering issue. It had exploded with special virulence a few years earlier, in 6 A.D. when Jesus was ten or twelve years old. Archelaus had been deposed as tetrarch of Judea, and Rome had taken over direct rule in the region. From then on the tribute would be paid directly to the Roman prefect, and not to a Jewish authority subordinate to Rome. The new situation provoked a fierce reaction, promoted by a Galilean named Judas and a Pharisee named Zadok. Their challenge was direct and to the point: God was «the only lord and owner of Israel»; paying tribute to Caesar meant denying the lordship of the God of the Covenant over Israel. In reality everyone felt this way, but Judas and Zadok put it in radical terms: the Jews must accept Yahweh's exclusive empire in the land of Israel and refuse to pay the tribute to Caesar[34].

Rome had put an end to that movement, but the debate did not end there. At some point Jesus was asked directly: «Is it lawful to pay taxes to the emperor? Should we pay them, or should we not?»[35] They could not have asked him a

---

31 In Mark 5:1-20 the man from Gerasa is possessed by many demons that are called «legion», like the armed divisions controlling the Empire. When they are cast out they enter a herd of «pigs», the most impure of all animals, used to describe the Romans. The wild boar was the symbol of Legion X Fretense, which controlled the Palestinian area from Syria (Warren Carter).

32 Q Source (Luke 11:20; Matt 12:28). Most scholars believe this affirmation comes from Jesus. Luke's version is closest to his language.

33 A growing number of scholars emphasize a possible political dimension in Jesus' exorcisms (Hollenbach, Horsley, Crossan, Sanders, Evans, Herzog II, Guijarro).

34 Flavius Josephus calls this movement the «fourth philosophy», after the Pharisees, Sadducees, and Essenes. They should not be confused with the «zealots», an armed group that only appeared in the decade of the seventies in Jerusalem, during the first uprising against Rome.

35 The episode appears in Mark 12:13-17 and parallels, in the [apocryphal] *Gospel of Thomas* 100:1-4, and in the *Egerton Papyrus* 3:1-6. Its historicity is well attested.

more difficult question. If he responds in the negative he can be accused of rebellion against Rome. If he accepts the tax he will be discredited in the eyes of the people, who are squeezed dry by the taxes, and whom he has always loved and defended. Jesus asks them to show him the coin in question. He doesn't have one, because he lives as an itinerant vagabond without land or fixed employment; he hasn't had a problem with the tax collectors in a long time. Then he asks whose image is on that silver denarius. It is Tiberius' image, and the legend says: *Tiberius Caesar, Divi Augusti Filius Augustus*; on the back it says, *Pontifex Maximus.* That says it all. His adversaries are slaves to the system; by using those coins engraved with political and religious symbols, they are recognizing the emperor's sovereignty. He does not; his life is poor but free, devoted to the poor and excluded subjects of the Empire. Jesus is not a subject of Caesar's empire; he has entered into God's reign.

Out of that freedom he proclaims his position: «Give [return] to the emperor the things that are the emperor's, and to God the things that are God's»[36]. Does he mean they should pay the tribute to avoid a massacre like the last one? Does he mean they should not recognize any Caesar above God? Is he supporting the position of Judas and Zadok?[37]. Jesus' aphorism seems to show a conflict of loyalties between God and Caesar. But for Jesus, how could there be anything that doesn't belong to God? What could still be Caesar's? Only his money. Is Jesus talking to the people who use those silver denarii? Maybe his message is very simple: «If you are benefiting from the system and collaborating with Rome, then fulfill your obligations to the tax collectors and "return" to Caesar what you got from him. But don't leave in Caesar's hands what belongs to God». Jesus has often told them that the poor belong to God; the little ones are his favorite children. The reign of God belongs to them. No one must abuse them, not even Caesar.

Jesus' answer was surely a clever way out of the trap they had set for him, but his resistance to the Roman oppressors and his absolute loyalty to the God of the poor were clear. Luke says later that Jesus was accused before Pilate of «perverting the nation, forbidding us to pay taxes to the emperor»[38]. We don't know

36 Mark 12:17. There is general consensus in affirming the authenticity of this saying. It probably circulated independently among the early Christians.

37 There is no scholarly consensus on what Jesus meant by this saying. Some historians say he was suggesting collaboration with Rome through the tribute (Bruce, Jeremias, and Stauffer in part). Others say he was supporting a radical criticism by reminding his questioners of God's absolute primacy (Belo, Tannenhill, Evans). My reading follows suggestions from recent studies (Kennard, Horsley, Herzog II).

38 Luke 23:2. This verse was probably created by Luke.

if he did that. But the prophet of God's reign was a disturbing element for everyone who depended on the Roman Empire: the temple aristocracy, the Herodian families, and Caesar's circle of representatives.

4
Single-minded to the end

Jesus knew the odds of a violent end. He was not naïve. He knew the danger he was in if he continued his activity and kept insisting on the irruption of God's reign. Sooner or later it could lead to his death. There was danger on several fronts. As he went from village to village he may not have thought much about an intervention by Pilate, who finally did execute him; his palace in Caesarea by the Sea was a long way from the peasant environment in which Jesus moved. At the beginning he also may not have seen the danger coming from the Sadducean temple aristocracy. Only when he went up to Jerusalem would he see their power and hostility up close[39].

It was dangerous to seek a just and dignified life for the last. He could not promote God's reign as a project of justice and compassion for the excluded and rejected, without provoking persecution from those who did not want to see any change in the Empire or in the temple. It was impossible to live in solidarity with the last, as he did, without suffering the reaction of the powerful. Jesus knew that both Herod and Pilate had the power to kill him. Perhaps the threat from the Roman prefect seemed remote; more likely, what happened to the Baptist could happen to him at any moment. Everyone knew he had come from John's circle; Antipas saw him as a prophet who was lengthening the shadow of the Baptist. Jesus was well aware of that. One source tells us that on hearing about the execution of the Baptist, he withdrew to a deserted place. We don't know anything for sure[40]. What happened to the Baptist was no accident. It was the tragic fate that prophets could expect. Jesus knew the same thing could happen to him. He too was a prophet. Most first-century Jews believed that the fate in

---

39 We cannot test the authenticity of the three predictions of his death that are attributed to Jesus in Mark 8:30; 9:31; and 10:33-34. Most scholars consider them, at least in part, a composition developed after the fact from the theological perspective of the later Christian community.

40 Matthew says: «Now when Jesus heard this, he withdrew from there in a boat to a deserted place by himself». This was probably an editorial gloss by Matthew.

store for a prophet was incomprehension, rejection and persecution[41]. Would the same fate befall him?

Jesus probably understood early on that a fatal outcome was possible. First it was only a possibility; later it seemed quite probable; then it was a certainty. People cannot live from day to day with a violent end always on the horizon. Can we learn anything from Jesus' behavior? He certainly was not suicidal. He did not seek martyrdom. That was not the purpose of his life[42]. He did not seek out suffering, for himself or others. Suffering is evil. His whole life was devoted to combating it in illness, injustice, marginalization, sin, and hopelessness. If he accepted persecution and martyrdom, it was out of faithfulness to the plan of the Father, who does not want to see his sons and daughters suffer. So Jesus was not chasing death, but he also did not pull back from it. He did not flee from the threats; neither did he change his message by adapting or softening it. He could easily have avoided death. He needed only to stop insisting on things that might prove annoying in the temple or in the palace of the Roman prefect. He didn't do that. He kept going. He would rather die than betray the mission for which he knew he had been chosen. He would be a faithful Son to his beloved Father. That faithfulness meant more than accepting a violent end. It meant living from day to day in a climate of insecurity and confrontation; not being able to proclaim God's reign in tranquility and serenity; being continually exposed to scorn and rejection.

Many questions must have troubled his conscience: How could God call him to proclaim the decisive arrival of his reign, and then let the mission end in failure? Was God contradicting himself? How could his death be reconciled with his mission?[43]. It took a lot of trust for Jesus to let God act, and put himself in God's hands in spite of everything. That's what he did. There was nothing resigned or submissive about his attitude[44]. He was not passively carried along by

---

41 The martyrdom of the prophets is not reported anywhere in Israel's sacred Scriptures, except for the death of a few relatively unimportant ones. But those isolated events developed into the idea that martyrdom was the fate of the prophets. A first century writing called the *Ascension of Isaiah* gives a detailed description of Isaiah's death, cut in half with a wood saw. Another, titled *The Life of the Prophets*, tells of the death of Isaiah, Micah, Joel, Zechariah and others. Apparently Jesus was also familiar with the memorials built to the prophets around Jerusalem (Jeremias).

42 Modern scholars no longer believe that when Jesus went up to Jerusalem at Passover in 30 A.D., he was seeking his own death in order to bring about the irruption of God's reign.

43 The story of his temptations in Mark 1:12-13, the Q Source (Luke 4:1-13; Matt 4:1-11), and the prayer at Gethsemane (Mark 14:36; Matt 26:39; Luke 22:42) allow us to discern, albeit from a distance, the darkness and the struggles Jesus experienced.

44 It may be misleading to imagine Jesus as a lamb that «did not open its mouth» (Isa 53:7). Jesus did not submit in silence. He was executed because he «opened his mouth» to defend the claims of God's reign.

events to an inexorable death. He reaffirmed his mission, insistently repeated his message. He did it courageously, not only in the remote Galilean villages but in the dangerous environment of the temple. Nothing could stop him.

He would die faithful to the God he had always trusted. He would go on accepting sinners and «the excluded», no matter who didn't like it; if they rejected him to the end he would die as an «excluded one», but his death would confirm what he had always lived: total trust in a God who rejects no one and excludes no one from his forgiveness. He would go on proclaiming «God's reign» to the least and the last, identifying with the poorest and most despised people in the Empire, no matter how much it bothered the people around the Roman ruler. If they eventually tortured him to death on the cross, like a slave with no rights, he would die as the poorest and most despised of all; but his death would seal his message of a God who defends all the poor, oppressed and persecuted by the powerful. He would go on loving God with his whole heart, refusing to give any «caesar» or any «chief priest» what belongs only to God; he would go on defending the poor to the very end. He would accept God's will, even now when God's will seemed to be his martyrdom.

Jesus apparently never developed a theory about his death, never theologized about his crucifixion. He saw it as the logical consequence of his unconditional commitment to God's plan. In spite of his pain and fear as he died in agony on the cross, he saw no contradiction between the definitive establishment of God's reign and his failure as its definitive messenger and bearer. The reign of God would achieve its fullness beyond his death. Jesus did not interpret his death from a sacrificial perspective. He did not understand it as a sacrificial atonement offered to the Father. He didn't use that kind of language. He never connected God's reign with the cultic practices of the temple, never understood his service to God's plan as a ritual sacrifice. It would be strange if at the end of his life, to give meaning to his death, he had resorted to concepts from the world of atonement. He never imagined his Father as a God whose honor, rightly offended by sin, needed to be restored by his death and destruction so that he would forgive human beings in the future. We never see Jesus offering his life as an immolation to the Father, in exchange for clemency for the world. The Father doesn't need to preserve his honor with anyone's destruction. His love for his sons and daughters is gratuitous, his forgiveness unconditional[45].

45 None of Jesus' authentic sayings interpret his death as a sacrifice of atonement. Most scholars (Schillebeeckx, Leon-Dufour, Schürmann, Sobrino) believe that the saying attributed to him

Jesus understands his death as he has always understood his life: as a service to God's reign for the benefit of all. Day by day he has poured out his life for others; now if necessary he will die for them. The attitude of service that inspired his life will now inspire his death. Apparently that was how Jesus wanted people to understand everything he did: «I am among you as one who serves»[46]. That is also how he will be on the cross: as «one who serves». It is the characteristic feature that defines him from the beginning to the end, that inspires and gives ultimate meaning to his life and his death. This was probably his basic attitude toward his death. We can say little more than that: total trust in the Father and a will to serve to the end[47].

What salvific value did Jesus see in his death? Could he foresee what his violent, painful death would contribute to the reign of God? All his life he had offered «salvation» to those who suffered evil and sickness, given «acceptance» to those who were excluded from the society and the religion, and held out God's gratuitous «forgiveness» to sinners and lost people, who could not find their way back to his friendship. He did more than talk about God's life and salvation. He gave it to them, impelled by his trust in God's incredible love for all. He lived his service by curing, accepting, blessing, offering God's gratuitous forgiveness and salvation. All the evidence suggests that he died as he had lived. His death was the ultimate, supreme service to God's plan, his supreme contribution to the salvation of all[48].

The gospel attributes to Jesus these words which clearly reflect his commitment to a life of redemptive value: «For the Son of Man came not to be served but to serve, and to give his life a ransom for many»[49]. This allows us to say, although

in Mark 10:45 («For the Son of Man came not to be served but to serve, and to give his life a ransom for many») is a creation of the gospel writer. A comparison with Luke 22:27 shows that Mark has converted this saying on service into a theological affirmation on redemptive death. Moreover, the term «ransom» (*lytron*) is not used in the Greek Bible to refer to a «vicarious atonement» offered to God for sin. It means payment to a master for the liberation of a slave.

46 This saying in Luke 22:27 is viewed as a more authentic approximation to Jesus' thinking than the equivalent in Mark 10:45.

47 The Christian communities would very soon come to interpret Jesus' death in the light of the «Servant of Yahweh» celebrated in the book of Isaiah (1 Pet 2:21-24; 1 Tim 2:6; Mark 10:45b).

48 Although Jesus probably did not see himself as the «Servant of Yahweh». and did not formulate any theology on the redemptive nature of his death, he did experience it as a service and offering of God's salvation. H. Schürmann has coined the term «proexistence» (later accepted by Leon-Dufour, Grelot and others) to suggest Jesus' consciousness and existential attitude in his life and death, prior to the theologies that were later, with all legitimacy, formulated in the Christian communities (Paul, Hebrews, and other writings), based precisely on this attitude of Jesus as remembered by his disciples.

49 Mark 10:45.

we have no certain evidence that Jesus described himself as the «Servant of Yahweh»[50], that he lived his death with that attitude, understanding it as redemptive service and a source of salvation for all. Some authors use the term «proexistence» to evoke Jesus' awareness and existential attitude in his life and in his death[51]. In this sense Jesus' existence, not for himself but for others, should not be understood as a merely philanthropic attitude; it constitutes the very being of Jesus and his redemptive mission[52].

5

A dangerous pilgrimage to Jerusalem

It was the month of *nisan*[53] in the year 30 A.D. The winter rains were gently tapering off. Spring was beginning to warm the Galilean hills; the fig trees were budding. Every spring reminded Jesus of the nearness of God's reign, filling the earth with new life. The weather was pleasant. People were preparing to go up as pilgrims to Jerusalem, to celebrate the great Passover feast. It would be a three- or four-day walk from Galilee; they could comfortably sleep outdoors on the way. And the moon was getting brighter; Passover Day would be a full moon. Jesus told his disciples of his decision: he wanted to make the pilgrimage with them.

What impelled him to make the trip? Did he simply want to join his people once more in the Passover celebration, as one pilgrim among others? Was he going to the holy city to await the glorious manifestation of God's reign? Was he planning to challenge the religious leaders of Israel, in order to provoke a response that would lead everyone to accept the irruption of God in their midst? Did he plan to confront the whole people and press for the restoration of Israel?

---

50 Isaiah 53 describes the figure of a «Servant of Yahweh» who accepts all kinds of humiliation and suffering, giving his life as «an offering for sin» (v. 10). The poem develops this theme in different ways: «he has borne our infirmities and carried our diseases» (v. 4); «he was wounded for our transgressions, crushed for our iniquities» (v. 5); «upon him was the punishment that made us whole» (v. 5); «he was cut off from the land of the living, stricken for the transgression of my people» (v. 8); «the righteous one, my servant, shall make many righteous, and he shall bear their iniquities» (v. 11).

51 The term «proexistence» originated with H. Schürmann and was later accepted by X. Léon-Dufour, P. Grelot, and many other scholars, especially Catholics.

52 J. Ratzinger-Benedict XVI considers that Jesus' «proexistence» should be understood «not only as one dimension among others of his existence, but as that which constitutes his most intimate and integral aspect». *Jesús de Nazaret. Desde la entrada en Jerusalén hasta la resurrección.* Madrid, Encuentro, 2011, p. 160 (English: Jesus of Nazareth: Vol II).

53 The month of *nisan* corresponds to March-April in our calendar.

We don't know for sure[54]. Until now Jesus had been proclaiming the reign of God in the villages of Galilee, but his call was addressed to all Israel. It wouldn't be surprising if at some point he extended it to Jerusalem as well.

It would be an opportune place and time. The holy city was the center of the chosen people; Jews all over the world turned their eyes and their hearts to Jerusalem. And the time was right; thousands of pilgrims from Palestine and all over the Empire were gathering to renew their yearning for liberation at the Passover feast. Apparently the disciples found it an alarming prospect. Jesus too was aware of the risks he would run in Jerusalem. His message would upset the temple leaders and the Roman authorities. But Jesus went up to the holy city anyway. And he would not be coming back.

They probably take the easternmost road for their pilgrimage to the holy city. The group leaves Capernaum, walks the length of the Jordan river, passes through Jericho, and then takes the highway that climbs up through the *wadi* Kelt to the Mount of Olives. This is the best place to contemplate the holy city in all its splendor and beauty. When they see it, the pilgrims fall silent and cry for joy. This probably isn't Jesus' first visit to Jerusalem, but everything is different this time. His heart is full of joy and sorrow, fear and hope[55]. We have no way of knowing what he is thinking. It will be only a few days until his execution.

From the Mount of Olives they can see the whole city. In the distance, on the highest hill, stands the old palace of Herod with its sumptuous halls and gardens, now an occasional base of operations for the Roman prefect; perhaps Pilate was there, to monitor the Passover festivities. Not far away is the residence of Antipas, the tetrarch of Galilee, who usually would not miss the chance to be seen by the multitudes at such an event. His palace brings tragic memories to the pilgrims; that was once the residence of the pagan king Antiochus IV, who brought down such suffering on Jews who remained faithful to their God. Near these two palaces are the luxurious villas of the upper city; Annas and most of the temple aristocracy live there. To the south they see the Roman theatre and circus, built by Herod so that Jerusalem would be like the other important cities of the Empire. Jesus probably never walked the streets in that part of the city,

---

54 The sources say nothing about Jesus' reasons for going up to Jerusalem. We have no clear grounds on which to build a hypothesis.

55 John is the only gospel writer who tells us that Jesus went to Jerusalem several times for the Passover, the feast of Booths, and another unspecified occasion. The Q Source suggests that Jesus had failed on earlier attempts to preach in Jerusalem (Luke 13:34-35; Matt 23:37-39). In any case he was not very well known in the holy city.

where the priestly class and the richest, most powerful families lived[56]. In the other direction they see the poor and popular neighborhoods, covering the lower part of the city. From the Mount of Olives they cannot see the bustle and confusion that prevail there. The narrow streets are lined with workshops, bazaars and all sorts of businesses. The merchants hawk their wares: cloth, sandals, tunics, perfumes, costume jewelry, souvenirs of the holy city. Stands selling grain, fruit, and other farm products are concentrated around the gates of the city. It is not easy to move among so many people, all eagerly gathering provisions for the coming feast days.

But the pilgrims' eyes were drawn especially to the great esplanade[57] where the holy temple rose in splendor, dominating a complex of buildings, galleries and halls for different activities. This was the house of God! According to the historian Flavius Josephus, «it was almost entirely covered with sheets of solid gold; at sunrise it shone with such brilliance that no one could look at it directly. Travelers approaching Jerusalem might think they were seeing a snow-covered mountain»[58]. The pilgrims would go there in a few days to offer their ritual sacrifices, sing hymns of thanksgiving, and slaughter the lambs for the Passover meal. Now the festivities would begin in a few hours, and they must first undertake the rite of purification. The conditions of purity were strict. Pagans must stay outside in the large «Court of the Gentiles», along with the lepers, blind, and lame. Women were restricted to the «Court of the Women», and men went on to the «Court of the Israelites» where they would participate in different rituals. No pilgrim could enter the area reserved for priests, where the altar of sacrifice stood. Only the high priest, the one mediator between Israel and its God, could come into God's presence in the _sancta sanctorum_.

They may have wondered about the imposing building with four towers that rose at one end of the esplanade, dominating the entire holy area. It was a fortress built by Herod and popularly known as the «Antonia tower». According to Flavius Josephus, «the temple was the fortress dominating the city, and the Antonia

---

56 Systematic excavations by Nahman Avigad, beginning in 1969, have revealed the luxury and wealth enjoyed by the priestly aristocracy that mobilized against Jesus: villas with beautiful gardens and patios; multi-level pools adorned in stucco for private use; mosaics and frescos of great artistic quality; ceramics and fine tableware, splendid jars and basins imported from the West; Ephesian lamps, perfume flasks made of Phoenician glass, etc.

57 It covered 144,000 meters² and was five times as large as the Acropolis in Athens. Artificial terraces were under construction in Jesus' time, to expand it over the Cedron river valley.

58 Flavius Josephus, _La guerra judía_ v, 222-223 (English: _The Jewish War_).

tower dominated the temple»[59]. The garrison of Roman soldiers was there to keep watch for any possible disruption of order. A few unfortunates were probably locked in its jail cells, awaiting their hour of execution.

Jesus and his disciples had to come closer, to sense the mood of excitement in Jerusalem. Groups of pilgrims were coming in from every direction. The Cedron, Hinnon and Tyropoeon valleys around Jerusalem were full to overflowing with crowds walking toward the several gates of the city. People were setting up camp wherever there was space: beside the walls, on the surrounding hills, and on the Mount of Olives. More than a hundred thousand pilgrims would take part in the festivities[60]. After their incorporation into the Roman Empire, the communities of the Jewish diaspora no longer faced border problems on the way to Jerusalem. Herod's impressive reconstruction of the temple had also given new impetus to the pilgrimages. Every year there were more pilgrims from Egypt, Phoenicia or Syria; from Macedonia, Thessalonica or Corinth; from Pamphylia, Cilicia, Bithynia and the shores of the Black Sea; even from Rome, the capital of the Empire. Jerusalem at Passover had become a world city, the «religious capital» of the Jewish world at the heart of the Roman Empire[61].

Such a large multitude in the holy city, so full of memories, meant potential danger. The gathering of so many kinfolk from all over the world increased their sense of belonging: they were all God's privileged, chosen people. The Passover celebration inspired their hearts even more. The feast recalls that memorable night when the people were liberated from slavery under Pharaoh. They celebrate it with a mixture of nostalgia and hope. Rome has taken the place of Egypt. The promised land of Yahweh is no longer a land of freedom; now they are slaves in their own land. Those days of prayer become an outcry: God will surely hear the cry of his oppressed people, and will come again to liberate them from slavery. Rome is very aware of the danger. That is why Pilate has come to Jerusalem for the duration, and reinforced the garrison in the Antonia tower: any subversive moves must be cut off at the root before they can spread to the throngs of pilgrims[62].

59 *La guerra judía* v, 243-245 (English: *The Jewish War*).

60 There is a wide range of scholarly estimates. According to J. Jeremias there may have been around 125,000 pilgrims at Passover during Jesus' time; Shamuel Safrai speaks of 100,000; the most recent study, by Ph. Abadie, puts it as high as 200,000. The city population at the time was between 25,000 and 55,000 inhabitants.

61 The number of diaspora Jews in the first century has been estimated at six to eight million.

62 Flavius Josephus tells about serious incidents that occurred during Passover feasts. The first was in 4 B.C. when Archelaus, fearful of the crowd gathered in the temple and pressuring him with their demands, with other pilgrims still arriving, ordered his infantry and cavalry forces to attack

As they enter Jerusalem, Jesus' group and many other pilgrims are singing with joy at the end of their long walk. Now they are near the gates of the city. Jesus has planned to make this last part of the trip on a donkey, as a humble pilgrim who enters the city, wishing everyone peace. Just then, enlivened by the festive mood of the Passover — and by the imminence of God's reign, which Jesus has talked about so much — they begin to cheer him on[63]. Some of them cut whatever branches or foliage they find along the road; others lay out their tunics as he passes. They are expressing their faith in God's reign, and their gratitude to Jesus. It is not a solemn reception organized to welcome an illustrious, powerful celebrity. It is a spontaneous act of homage by the disciples and followers who have come with him. In Mark's words, he is acclaimed by «those who went ahead and those who followed». Their cry was probably «*Hosanna!* Blessed is the one who comes in the name of the Lord!»[64].

Jesus' prophetic act was surely intentional. His entry into Jerusalem on the back of a donkey said more than many words could. Jesus is seeking a reign of peace and justice for all, not an empire built through violence and oppression. Mounted on a small donkey, he appears to the pilgrims as a prophet, the bearer of a new and different order, in contrast to the one imposed by the Roman generals on their war horses. His humble entry into Jerusalem becomes a satire and mockery of the triumphal processions organized by the Romans to take possession of conquered cities. Many people see it as an amusing criticism of the Roman prefect who has just ridden into the city on his powerful horse, adorned

---

them; around three thousand people were killed (*La guerra judía* II, 10-13 [English: *The Jewish War*] = *Antigüedades de los judíos* 7, 204-205 [English: *Jewish Antiquities*]). The second was between 48 and 52 A.D. when a crowd angrily protested an indecent, mocking gesture by a soldier. Cumanus, the Roman prefect, sent his men to invade the temple porticos; Josephus speaks of thirty thousand fatalities! (*La guerra judía* II, 224-227 [English: *The Jewish War*] = *Antigüedades de los judíos* [English: *Jewish Antiquities*] 20, 106-112).

63 This narrative is in Mark 11:1-11 and parallels, and in John 2:13-22. Most scholars believe Jesus did enter Jerusalem riding a donkey, carrying out a symbolic act to proclaim God's reign of peace and justice, in contrast to the Roman Empire which was built on violence and injustice. That event was later developed theologically, to become the triumphal entry of the Messiah into Jerusalem (Gnilka, Roloff, Schlosser, Crossan).

64 The later transformation of Jesus' prophetic act into an affirmation of his messianic mission included two important editorial additions: the legend of the disciples finding «a colt that has never been ridden» (Mark 11:1-6); and a second cry of acclamation, «Blessed is the coming kingdom of our ancestor David!» Matthew and John then independently added a quotation from the prophet Zechariah, taken from the Greek Bible, to illustrate the meaning of the event: «Lo, your king comes to you... humble and riding on a donkey, on a colt, the foal of a donkey» (9:9).

with all the symbols of his imperial power[65]. The Romans probably aren't at all amused. We don't know how widely this symbolic act was reported in the midst of all the crowds. In any case that «anti-triumphal» entry, cheered on by his followers, is a mockery that could easily ignite the people's spirits. As a public act proclaiming a nonviolent anti-kingdom, it would have been enough to lead to a decree of execution[66].

6

A very dangerous act

Something much more dangerous happens a few days later. Jesus has apparently been staying in the nearby town of Bethany with his friends Lazarus, Mary and Martha[67]; on returning to the city he carries out the most dangerous public act of his life. Indeed his intervention in the temple probably led to his arrest and rapid execution[68]. No one doubts that Jesus took this bold and provocative action. He strides firmly into the great Court of the Gentiles, in the midst of a variety of cultic activities. The different currencies of the Empire are being exchanged for the *shekel* of Tyre, the only coin accepted in the temple, probably because it was the strongest and most stable currency in that time. Then the pilgrims buy pigeons, turtledoves, and other animals for the sacrifices and fulfillment of vows; they prefer to buy them in Jerusalem rather than bringing them from home, since any injury on the way would make them unacceptable as sacrifices.

According to the earliest source[69], Jesus «began to drive out those who were selling and those who were buying in the temple»; he also «overturned the tables of the money changers and the seats of those who sold doves»; finally, «he

Chapter 12

341

---

65 We know of the imperial visit that Adrian made through the eastern provinces in A.D. 129-130. He entered cities like Philadelphia, Petra, Gerasa, [Aeschitopolis] or Caesarea, on a ritual white horse with ceremonial armor, and was received with hymns and speeches by local dignitaries. That was customary for an emperor going into his cities.

66 This is the opinion of Crossan and several other authors.

67 Bethany was about 3 kilometers from Jerusalem, away from the road followed by the pilgrims.

68 Most scholars agree on this point (Roloff, Brown, Sanders, Horsley, Borg, Fitzmyer, Schlosser, Crossan, and Evans among them).

69 The episode appears in two probably independent versions: Mark 11:15-19 and John 2:13-22. It is certainly authentic. It happened at the end of Jesus' life and not at the beginning, as John implies. Quotations from Isa 56:7 and Jer 7:11 were later attributed to Jesus as a way of explaining its meaning. John adds a new dimension to the original story: in his version, Jesus makes «a whip of cords» and drives out the sellers of sheep and cattle, as well as doves.

would not allow anyone to carry anything through the temple». It was probably a mild intervention, which only temporarily interrupted the day's routine. The Court of the Gentiles is huge, taking up most of the temple esplanade; thousands of pilgrims would have been there in those days; there were dozens of exchange tables and stands selling sacrificial animals. The temple security guard and hundreds of priests make sure everything runs smoothly; Pilate's soldiers keep watch from the Antonia Tower. Perhaps Jesus knocked down a group of buyers and sellers, overturned a few tables and bird-sellers' stands, and tried to interrupt their activities for a few minutes. He could hardly have done much more. It would take many people to obstruct the functioning of the temple. His gesture was small and limited, but it was full of prophetic power and unpredictable consequences.

But an attack on the temple was an attack on the heart of the Jewish people, the symbol around which everything else revolved, the center of their religious, social and political life. The God of the Covenant lived in that holy place, the sign of Israel's election: his presence guaranteed their protection and security. The temple made visible the unity of heaven and earth, the communion between Israel and its God. Only there could they offer God a pleasing sacrifice, and receive his forgiveness. And that holy place, protected from all impurity and contamination, was where one day the final victory of Israel's God would be made manifest. Any aggression against the temple was a dangerous, intolerable offense, not only for the religious leaders but for the whole people. What would become of Israel without God's presence in their midst? How could they survive without the temple?

It was certainly a gesture of hostility and protest, but what specific meaning did this prophetic act hold for Jesus?[70] To grasp its full dimensions, we have to understand the ambivalent feelings that surrounded the temple and the high dignitaries who controlled it during that time. The people's concern dated back to the beginning of the temple reconstruction. No one questioned the beauty

---

70 There are many different interpretations of what the action meant to Jesus. They are not all mutually exclusive. They are also not equally plausible. Here are some of the most important: purifying the Jewish cult from profanation by commercial activities (Edersheim, Fitzmyer); a protest against priestly injustice and abuse (Evans, Taylor); a protest against the exclusion of Gentiles (Borg, Freyne); a signal for a messianic uprising to take the temple by force (Brandon); God's judgment against a corrupt temple (Derret); a symbolic act of destruction prior to the restoration of a new temple (Sanders); a prophetic call for the end of an unjust system and preparation for the reign of God (Roloff, Crossan, Horsley, Herzog II, Wright, and others, each with variations of tone and content).

and splendor of the new temple, but what was Herod's real motivation? Was he trying to build a house for the God of Israel, or to magnify his image in the Empire? What was the purpose of the enormous Court of the Gentiles, which took up three-fourths of the esplanade? Was it to gather pilgrims faithful to the Covenant, or to draw pagan travelers to admire his power? What was the temple now, the house of God or a sign of collaboration with Rome? A temple of prayer, or a warehouse for the peasants' tithes and first fruit offerings? A sanctuary of forgiveness, or a symbol of injustice? Was the temple there to serve the Covenant, or to benefit the interests of the priestly aristocracy?

This place of worship had given rise to an enormous organization, maintained by an oversized bureaucracy of officials, scribes, administrators, accountants, security guards, and servants of the large priestly families[71]. They all made their living from the temple, and represented an additional burden on the peasant population. The popular criticism focused mainly on the powerful priestly families. Although they were based on lineage, the dynasty of Zadok had been broken long ago; Herod had imported priestly families of dubious legitimacy from Babylon and Egypt; now the Roman authorities named and removed high priests at will. So it is not surprising that the chief priests were more concerned with staying in power than serving the people; they handed out the most lucrative positions to their relatives, kept close control over debts, and according to Josephus, even sent their slaves to extort tithes from the poorest priests[72].

The people were probably most upset by the priests' life of luxury at the cost of the rural people. When the promised land was divided up, the tribe of Levi did not receive a territory. Its inheritance would be God: the Levites would live from sacrifices, tithes and tributes[73]. Nevertheless, some priests owned land soon after their return from Babylonian exile; by the time of Jesus, many had bought large farms and properties. Naturally they continued to claim their share of the sacrificed animals, pressured the people for their first fruits and tithes on farm products, and demanded the annual payment of a half *shekel* in tribute. This income alone would not have enabled them to live in opulence, but the develop-

71 According to Flavius Josephus, the priests and other temple service personnel added up to some 20,000 people.
72 The Babylonian Talmud has preserved a poem that severely denounces the house of Boeto, Annas, Katros and Ishmael, priestly families in the first century: «Woe to me... because they are the high priests, and their sons are the treasurers, and their sons in-law the administrators, and their servants beat the people with sticks!» (*Pesahim* 57a).
73 Deut 18:1-5.

ment of currency facilitated the accumulation of wealth in the temple treasury, and astute money-lending did the rest. The temple became a source of power and wealth for an aristocratic minority that lived at the cost of the weakest people[74]. Was this the temple that the God of the Covenant wanted?

Jesus' act is a symbolic gesture[75]. His apparently brief intervention in the large temple esplanade is not very important in itself, but he uses it to draw attention to something very important to him. He has carefully chosen the time and place: he is surrounded by pilgrims from all over the world, the temple police are on the lookout for any disruption, and the Roman soldiers are watching from the Antonia Tower. It is a good place to give his message the appropriate resonance. Jesus is not trying to «purify» the temple. He doesn't go to the place of sacrifice, to denounce abusive practices. His act is deeper and more radical than that. He is interrupting and obstructing everyday activities, necessary for the function-

ing of the temple, such as the exchange of currency or the sale of pigeons. His act is not aimed at a liturgical reform, but at the elimination of the institution itself. Without money no one can buy unblemished animals; without animals there can be no sacrifices; without sacrifices there is no atonement for sin, and no absolution[76]. His intervention also does not appear to be a protest against the exclusion of pagans from worship. Jesus expects that Gentiles will be accepted in the definitive reign of God, but he does nothing to enable them to participate now in the temple sacrifices. Nor is it specifically intended to denounce the corrupt life of the priestly aristocracy, although their abusive activities are clearly in the background of his action.

Jesus' gesture is more radical and total. He proclaims God's judgment not on the temple building, but against an economic, political and religious system that cannot be pleasing to God. The temple has become a symbol of everything that oppresses the people. Wealth is being accumulated in «the house of God», while poverty and indebtedness are growing in the villages of God's children. The

---

74 Flavius Josephus gives clues to the high level of wealth accumulated in the temple: In 40 B.C. the prefect Sabinus took over the temple treasury, used it to reward his soldiers handsomely, and kept 400 talents for himself. During his rule, Pilate provoked a serious incident by taking money from the temple to build an aqueduct, bringing water to Jerusalem.

75 Jesus performed other symbolic acts: his meals with sinners, choosing the Twelve, the entry into Jerusalem, the last supper. In this he followed the example of the great prophets, like Isaiah and Jeremiah.

76 Jesus' intervention has been mistakenly described as a «purification» of the temple. Recent scholarship speaks of a symbolic act of «destruction» of the temple (Sanders, Crossan, Horsley, Wright, Theissen, Herzog II, Schlosser).

temple is not serving the Covenant. No one there is defending the poor, or protecting the goods and the honor of the most vulnerable. What Jeremiah denounced in his time, is occurring here too: the temple has become a «den of robbers». The den is not the place where the crimes are committed, but where the thieves and criminals take refuge afterwards. That is what is happening in Jerusalem. The crimes are not committed in the temple but outside it; the temple is where the thieves take refuge and store up their booty[77]. Sooner or later there will be a head-on collision between the reign of God and that system. Jesus' gesture is a symbolic and prophetic «destruction», not a real and effective one, but it proclaims the end of that state of things[78]. The God of the poor and excluded does not and will not reign from that temple: he will never legitimize that system. With the coming of God's reign, the temple loses its reason for being.

Jesus' action has gone too far. The temple security guards and the soldiers at the Antonia fortress know what they have to do. They must wait until the city quiets down, and the pilgrims are less agitated. The matter is not only of concern to the temple priests; the Roman authorities are also upset. The temple is always a place of conflict; that is why they watch it so closely. Any incident in that holy place gets their guard up: whoever threatens the power of the high priest, Rome's faithful servant, is a threat to peace. One thing is certain: unless he changes his attitude and stops his subversive activity, this man will be eliminated. It is not advisable to arrest him in public, while he is surrounded by followers and sympathizers. They will find a way to capture him discreetly.

7

A memorable farewell

∽

Jesus too knows his hours are numbered. But he is not planning to hide or flee. Instead he arranges a special farewell dinner with the men and women closest to him. It is a solemn and intimate moment for him and his disciples; he wants

77 Most scholars believe it was not Jesus who justified his action by saying the temple had become a «den of robbers», but Mark who attributed the quote from Jeremiah to him in order to show the meaning of his action. However S. Freyne leaves open the possibility that Jesus was searching the Scriptures as other Jews did, to discern God's will on the most decisive issues. In any case it is a telling expression: Jeremiah condemns those who «oppress the alien, the orphan, and the widow», and then seek safety from God's punishment in the temple (7:6, 10-11).

78 Mark says literally that Jesus «overturned» the money changers' and dove-sellers' tables. The word in Greek, *katastrefo*, also readily evokes the catastrophic «destruction» of the temple.

to experience it in all its depth. This is a well thought-out decision. Aware of his imminent death, he needs to convey to them his total trust in the Father, even in this hour. He wants to prepare them for the crushing blow that awaits them; his execution must not plunge them into sadness or hopelessness. They need to share the questions that they are all pondering: what will become of God's reign without Jesus? What should they do? Where will they turn now, to nourish their hope for the coming reign of God?

Apparently it is not a Passover meal. Some sources say Jesus intended to share with his disciples a Passover meal, or *seder*, in which Jews recall their liberation from slavery in Egypt. But the description of the banquet never once alludes to the Passover liturgy; it says nothing of the paschal lamb or the bitter herbs that Jews eat that night; it does not ritually recall the departure from Egypt, as the liturgy prescribes. Moreover it would be unthinkable, on that evening when families are celebrating the most important meal in the Jewish calendar, for the chief priests and their assistants to drop everything to arrest Jesus and arrange a late-night meeting to decide on the specific charges against him. Another source reports more plausibly that Jesus held the dinner before the Passover feast; it says he was executed on the 14th of *nisan*, on the eve of Passover. In short, we cannot clearly identify the last supper with a Passover meal[79]. Probably Jesus did make the Jerusalem pilgrimage to celebrate Passover with his disciples, but he could not fulfill his wish, because he was arrested and tried before then. He did have time to celebrate a farewell dinner, however.

In any case it was not an ordinary meal but a solemn dinner, the last of so many that they had celebrated in the villages of Galilee. They drank wine, as they did on special occasions; they reclined at the table for peaceful conversation, rather than sitting as they normally did. It is probably not a Passover meal, but the excitement of the paschal festivities is all around them. All the pilgrims are making their final preparations: obtaining unleavened bread, buying the paschal lamb, seeking out a place in the local inns or on household patios and terraces. Jesus' group is also

---

79 Mark, Matthew and Luke give sufficient information to identify the meal with the Jewish Passover (Mark 14:1, 12, 16-17, 18 and parallels). Luke even says that this was Jesus' wish: «I have eagerly desired to eat this Passover with you before I suffer» (22:15). Jeremias, Gnilka and others believe Jesus did celebrate the Passover meal. But according to John he was crucified on the day before Passover (18:28); Paul also says nothing about a Passover meal (1 Cor 11:23-26). Most authors today doubt that it was a paschal celebration, or leave the question open (Schürmann, Leon-Dufour, Theissen, Schlosser, Roloff, and others).

looking for a peaceful place[80]. Jesus does not spend that night at Bethany as usual. He stays in Jerusalem. His farewell dinner must be held in the holy city. The narratives say he celebrated the meal with the Twelve, but we cannot exclude the presence of other men and women disciples who have come with him on the pilgrimage. Given his custom of sharing his table with all kinds of people, even sinners, it would be surprising if he suddenly adopted such a selective, exclusive attitude. Do we have any way of knowing what really happened at that meal?[81].

For Jesus the meals and dinners in Galilee were a symbol and anticipation of the final banquet in God's reign. Everyone remembers those meals, enlivened by Jesus' faith in the definitive reign of the Father. It is one of the most distinctive features of his life in the villages[82]. On this evening too, the meal reminds him of the final banquet in the reign of God. Jesus is weighed down by two feelings. First, the certainty of his imminent death, which he cannot avoid. This is the last cup of wine that he will share with them, and everyone knows it; there must be no illusions. At the same time, his unbreakable trust in God's reign, to which he has devoted his whole life. He speaks very clearly: «Truly I tell you, I will never again drink of the fruit of the vine until that day when I drink it new in the kingdom of God»[83]. His death is near. Jerusalem does not want to answer his call. His activity as a prophet and bearer of God's reign is going to be violently cut off, but his execution will not stop the coming of the reign of God which he has been proclaiming to all. Jesus' faith in God's saving intervention never wavers. He is certain of the truth of his message. His death must not destroy anyone's hope. God will not be held back. One day Jesus will sit at the table, with a cup in his hands, to celebrate God's eternal banquet with his sons and daughters. They will drink the

---

80 Mark 14:13-15 and parallels, on the preparation of the paschal meal, show some marks of legend and do not support any historical conclusion.

81 The last supper is related in Mark 14:22-26; Matt 26:26-30; Luke 22:14-20; and 1 Cor 11:23-26. No one doubts the historicity of the event. But these are highly condensed, opaque texts that do not attempt to describe in detail what happened; rather they proclaim Jesus' action which gave rise to a liturgical practice that the Christian communities have followed. The stories are different because each writer tells about the meal in the context of his own community's cultic practice. We can readily see that they are liturgical texts which specify the essence of the ritual: gestures to make, words to pronounce. Through these clues we can approximate what people experienced in the meal with Jesus.

82 Jesus compares the reign of God to a meal in which «the poor, the crippled, the blind, and the lame» take part (Q Source = Luke 14:15-24; Matt 22:2-10). Even Gentiles will take part in that banquet (Q Source = Luke 13:28-29; Matt 8:11-12).

83 Mark 14:25 and parallels. In general, scholars see the echo of a genuine saying of Jesus in these words. There are no theological traces of the Christian community in the saying. Jesus is engaged in «commensality» at the table of God's reign, without a christological title.

wine «new», and share together the final feast of the Father. Tonight's meal is a symbol.

Impelled by that conviction, Jesus sets out to enliven the meal by sharing his hope with his disciples. He begins the meal according to the Jewish custom: he stands up, takes the bread in his hands, and blesses God in the name of them all; they all reply, «Amen». Then he breaks the bread and distributes a piece to each person. They all know that gesture. They have probably seen him do it more than once. They know the meaning of that ritual by their host: in giving them that piece of bread, he is giving them God's blessing. How moving it was to see him give it to sinners, tax collectors and prostitutes! Receiving the bread, they all felt united with one another and with God[84]. But this time Jesus adds words that give new and unexpected meaning to his gesture. As he distributes the bread he tells each one: «*This is my body*. I am this bread. See me in these pieces of bread, *giving myself* to the end, to bring you the blessing of God's reign»[85]. What must these men and women have felt, hearing these words for the first time?

What he does at the end of the meal surprises them even more. They all know the accustomed ritual. Near the end of the meal their host, still seated, takes a cup of wine in his right hand, holds it a palm's width above the table, and pronounces over it a prayer of thanks for the meal, to which everyone responds, «amen». Then he drinks from the cup, the signal for everyone else to do the same. But that evening Jesus changes the ritual and invites his disciples to drink from a single cup: his! They all share the «cup of salvation» that Jesus has blessed[86]. Passing the cup around and offering it to everyone, Jesus sees in it something «new» and special that he wants to explain: «*This cup is the new Covenant in my blood*. My blood will open up a new future for you and for everyone»[87]. Jesus is not only thinking of his closest disciples. At this decisive and crucial moment,

---

84 For Jews the «breaking of the bread» was an important act at the beginning of a meal. Already in Jesus' time it was apparently done in a fixed and ritualized way. It created «table communion» among the people before God (Jeremias, Schürmann, Leon-Dufour).

85 We cannot reconstruct Jesus' exact words on the basis of the different versions. Great scholars like Jeremias, Schürmann, and Leon-Dufour have renounced the challenge. The most widespread view is that Mark (= Matthew) gives us the earliest layer: «This [is] my body»; Paul adds, «for you»; Luke brings them together: «This is my body, which is given for you» (Schlosser, Roloff, Theobald). The Aramaic word for «body» is equivalent to «a specific person», «I myself».

86 Jesus may have been following a custom that consisted of sending a «blessed cup» to someone he wanted to share in the blessing, even though the person was not at the table (Dalman, Billerbeck, Schürmann). This was called the «cup of salvation» (Ps 116:13), and it apparently had a meaning like our custom of toasting a person: «To your health!»

87 All the sources speak of the «covenant», but in different ways. Paul and Luke say: «This cup is the new covenant in my blood»; Mark and Matthew, in contrast, say «this is my blood of the

the horizon he has in view becomes universal: the new Covenant, the definitive reign of God will be for many, «for all»[88].

With these gestures of distributing the bread and wine to be shared by all, Jesus transforms that farewell meal into a great sacramental action, the most important one in his life, the one that best sums up his service to the reign of God. Moreover, his double gesture of passing a piece of bread to each one, and inviting them all to drink the wine from his cup, constitutes the definitive gift of his body and blood. Whenever they eat that bread and drink that wine, they will be nourished by his body and by his blood. Jesus wants them to stay connected with him, and to let him nourish their hope. He wants them to remember him always, as one committed to serving them. He will always be the «one who serves», the one who has offered his life and his death for them, the servant of all. That is who he is now, in their midst, and that is how he wants them always to remember him[89]. More than anything else, the bread and the cup of wine will remind them of the final feast in God's reign; the distribution of the bread to each person and their drinking from the same cup will remind them of Jesus' total commitment[90]. The words «for you» sum up very well his life in service to the poor, the sick, the sinners, the despised, the oppressed, everyone in need. These words also express the meaning of his approaching death: he has given his whole life over to bring acceptance, healing, hope and forgiveness to all in God's name. Now he will give up his life to death, offering the Father's salvation to all[91].

covenant». Scholars are hesitant to choose one text over another. Some prefer the version of Paul and Luke, because the parallelism of Mark and Matthew — «this is my body», «this is my blood» — seems more appropriate to a liturgical act than to words spoken at a meal (Theissen). Others question the historicity of the words about blood, because Jesus was not known to use the word «covenant» anywhere else, although he might have said it on this occasion.

88 In Mark 14:24 he says that the blood is «poured out for many». The Greek word *hyper pollon* literally means «for many», but in the Aramaic language Jesus is speaking it does not have an exclusive meaning; it suggests the idea of totality. The best translation is «for all».

89 The commands, «Do this in remembrance of me» (1 Cor 11:24; Luke 22:21) and «Do this, as often as you drink it, in remembrance of me» (1 Cor 11:25), do not come from the earliest tradition. They probably come from the later Christian liturgy, but this was unquestionably Jesus' wish in celebrating the solemn farewell.

90 The broken bread is not a metaphor for the dead and broken body of Jesus, nor the wine for his blood (its red color is never mentioned). Rather they are an image of the banquet and feast of God's reign. It is Jesus' gesture, handing a piece of bread to each one and having them all drink from his cup, that signifies his commitment unto death.

91 Mark goes deeper into the theme of Jesus' commitment unto death, saying that Jesus' blood is «poured out for many» (14:24); Matthew adds, «for the forgiveness of sins» (26:28); Paul and the letter to the Hebrews present it theologically as «a sacrifice of atonement» for the sin of humanity.

This was Jesus' farewell, as it was engraved forever in the memory of the Christian communities. His followers will not be left as orphans; their communion with him is not broken by his death; it will remain until the day they all drink «new wine» together in the reign of God. They will not feel the emptiness of his absence: in repeating this meal they will be nourished by his memory and his presence. He will be with his people, upholding their hope; they will prolong and reproduce his service to God's reign until they meet at the end. Thus Jesus has built into this farewell the broad outlines of his plan for his movement of followers: a community fed by him and totally devoted to opening the way for God's reign, in an attitude of humble and all-inclusive service, with their hope placed in the feast that will bring them together at last[92].

Is Jesus also giving a new sign, inviting his followers to a shared life of service? John's gospel says that at some point during the supper, Jesus got up from the table and «began to wash the disciples' feet». In this narrative, he did it to set an example and to show his followers that they should live in mutual service: «You also ought to wash one another's feet». The scene is probably a creation of the gospel writer, but it reflects Jesus' thinking wonderfully[93]. It is an unusual gesture. In a society where individual and group roles are so clearly defined, it is unthinkable that anyone at a festive meal — especially not the host — should undertake this humble task of slaves or servants. In the story Jesus leaves his seat and begins washing his disciples' feet like a slave. It would be hard to find a more expressive image for his life, and for the message he wants to impress forever on his followers. Jesus has said it many times: «whoever wishes to be first among you must be slave of all»[94]. Here he says it graphically: by washing his disciples' feet he is acting as a servant and slave of all. Within a few hours he will die on the cross, a punishment reserved especially for slaves.

---

92 Some recent scholars have seen the «last supper» as an act that «complements» Jesus' earlier prophetic gesture against the temple. In this hypothesis, Jesus understood the meal as a new and radical alternative to the temple system. Their service to the reign of God and his justice would not be connected to the religious-political-economic system of the Jewish temple, but to their shared experience of a meal where Jesus' followers would be nourished by that spirit of service to God's plan, and by their trust in the final feast with the Father (Theissen, Neusner, Chilton, and Wright, each with variations).

93 This story appears only in John 13:1-16. Although some scholars defend its authenticity (Dodd, Robinson, Bauckham), a majority are inclined to see it as a later composition. The introduction (13:1-3), which reflects the characteristic language and theology of John's gospel, does not ensure a connection between this episode and the historical context of the last supper.

94 Mark 10:43-44; see also Mark 9:35.

Martyr of the Reign of God

Jesus had only a few hours of freedom left after his farewell dinner. Toward midnight he was arrested by the temple police in a garden in the Cedron valley, at the foot of the Mount of Olives, where he had gone to pray. A man who publicly denounced the temple system, and who talked to Jews from all over the world about an «empire» that wasn't the Roman empire, could not be allowed to continue moving freely in the explosive atmosphere of the Passover festival.

What can we learn about the events of Jesus' last days? One thing is certain: he was «condemned to death during the reign of Tiberius, by the governor Pontius Pilate». We have that information from Tacitus, the famous Roman historian[1]. Flavius Josephus says the same thing, and adds some interesting details: Jesus «attracted many Jews and many people of Greek origin. And when Pilate, because of an accusation lodged by some of our leaders, condemned him to the cross, those who had loved him did not stop loving him»[2]. These details coincide with what we know from the Christian sources. We can summarize them as follows: Jesus was executed on a cross; the sentence was handed down by the Roman governor; he had been accused earlier by the Jewish authorities; Jesus alone was crucified, with no attempt to eliminate his followers. This means that Jesus was considered dangerous because he denounced the roots of the prevailing system, but neither the Jewish nor the Roman authorities saw him as the leader of an insurrectionist group; otherwise they would have taken action against the whole group[3]. In this case it was enough to eliminate the leader, but at the same time they needed to terrorize his followers and sympathizers. Nothing could do that more effectively than a public crucifixion, witnessed by the crowds that filled the city.

The gospels offer a detailed narrative of the passion of Jesus[4]. But in order to use this information correctly, we need to bear several things in mind. First, we

353

---

1 *Anales* 15, 44,3 (English: *The Annals*).
2 *Antigüedades de los judíos* 18, 3,3 (English: *Jewish Antiquities*. Translation by J.P. Meier).
3 That is what happened in 45 A.D. when the governor Fadus sent a cavalry squadron against Theudas and his followers, killing many people (*Antigüedades de los judíos* 20, 90 [English: *Jewish Antiquities*]). Between 53 and 55, Felix sent his soldiers against a popular prophet called the Egyptian, killing 400 of his followers (*Antigüedades de los judíos* 18, 85-89 [English: *Jewish Antiquities*]).
4 Mark 14-15; Matt 26-27; Luke 22-23; John 18-19; the [apocryphal] *Gospel of Peter* (a fragment of a lost gospel which preserves the passion narrative beginning with the intervention of Herod). No one has yet developed a convincing theory about the relationship between these documents. There is general agreement on the importance of Mark as a source for Matthew and Luke. Matthew in particular follows Mark closely, adding a few details. Luke is noticeably more independent, so some scholars believe that the author of Luke drew on some other tradition in addition to Mark. There is still some debate over whether John used another source besides Mark. J.D. Crossan

don't know who may have witnessed the events directly. The disciples fled to Galilee; the women may have watched from a distance and witnessed the public events, but who could have heard Jesus' conversations with the high priest or his encounter with Pilate? The early Christians probably had reports on the general course of events (his interrogation by the Jewish authorities, his betrayal to Pilate, the crucifixion), but not the details[5]. Furthermore, the passion narrative is different from the other gospel stories, which were composed of short scenes and episodes transmitted by the tradition. This narrative is a long composition describing a sequence of interrelated events[6]. All the evidence suggests that it was composed by «scribes» who were searching the sacred Scriptures for the deeper meaning of the events. What we see in the background is not so much the transmission of traditions as the careful work of scribes, who could identify texts from the Old Testament that would help to explain the underlying meaning of what happened. The problem is to figure out whether the stories describe real events on which a biblical text can shed light, or whether the biblical texts have led the scribe to «invent» a particular episode or a part of it[7].

We must also keep in mind the latent tendencies in these stories, which modern research is identifying with increasing scholarly precision. We can easily summarize these tendencies. In response to those who could not make sense of the passion events, these writings are an effort to show, sometimes very artfully, that they were a providential fulfillment of God's designs[8]. The tradition also moves gradually toward exempting the Romans from blame by emphasizing the innocence of Pilate, while insisting with increasing forcefulness on the cul-

has recently reconstructed, on the basis of the [apocryphal] *Gospel of Peter*, a brief text which he calls *The Gospel of the Cross*, which he proposes as the single source of all the passion narratives we know of. His theory is supported only by some members of the *Jesus Seminar*.

5 This is the current opinion of many authors (Sanders, Harvey, Reumann, Roloff, Schlosser and others).

6 In keeping with the Roman time frame, Mark notes what happened «as soon as it was morning» (15:1), at the sixth hour [«when it was noon»] (15:33), and at the ninth hour [«three o'clock»] (15:34).

7 The two most recent, authorized monographs on the passion reflect different approaches within modern research. R.E. Brown generally considers the stories as «history remembered» in the Christian communities, subsequently interpreted in the light of the scribes' biblical references. In contrast, J.D. Crossan believes that most of the stories are «historicized prophecy», that is, compositions by the scribes which are not derived from specific events but developed on the basis of biblical texts.

8 Matthew in particular uses explicit references or implicit allusions to the Old Testament when he speaks of the flight of the disciples, Jesus' reply to the high priest, the thirty pieces of silver Judas received for his betrayal, the cries of the crowd demanding Jesus' execution, the division of his clothes, his execution between two criminals, his cry of lament to God, and other details.

pability of the whole Jewish people in the crucifixion of the Messiah, Son of God[9]. At the same time we also see their desire to present Jesus as an innocent martyr, unjustly executed by wicked men but rehabilitated by God, following a pattern well known in Jewish tradition. In this way the crucified one becomes a model for Christians under persecution. There is also a tendency to develop legendary episodes, which are always popular in folk narratives[10].

1

Handed over by the temple authorities

The action against Jesus was clearly precipitated by the incident in the temple. He wasn't arrested immediately, because the operation had to be carried out without causing a major riot; but the high priest did not forget Jesus[11]. He surely issued the order of arrest, since he was the one empowered to take measures against anyone who disrupted the sacred grounds. It was the temple police, not Roman soldiers from the Antonia tower, who came into the Garden of Gethsemane[12]. They were appropriately armed; their orders were to take Jesus to the high priest, Caiaphas. Apparently the temple guards asked for help in identifying Jesus, and especially in finding him and capturing him discreetly. The sources tell us that Judas, one of the Twelve, offered to help them. This report appears to be histori-

9 This interpretation, which led to so much persecution of the Jews, is due to the fact that the Christians, who were gaining a following among the Gentiles, did not want to evoke the hostility of Rome by identifying with someone who had been condemned by the Roman authorities as a threat to the Empire. They also wanted to distinguish themselves clearly from the other Jews, who were being persecuted by Rome after the fall of Jerusalem. Although historically it was Pilate who pronounced the death sentence, Luke shows him declaring Jesus innocent three times (23:4, 14, and 22). In Matthew, Pilate declares himself innocent and washes his hands (27:24). John shows him handing Jesus over to the Jews so that they will be the ones to crucify him (19:16). On the other side, while the earlier Mark 14:1 speaks only of a conspiracy by the chief priests and scribes, Matthew 27:25 insists that the whole people demanded Jesus' crucifixion («His blood be on us and on our children»). In John it is «the Jews» who ask for his death (18:31, 38). Thus «the trial of Jesus» sometimes becomes «the trial of the Jews» (A. Marchadour).

10 Some examples are the amputation of Malchus' ear (John 18:10), the dream of Pilate's wife (Matt 27:19), and the «Field of Blood» (Matt 27:3-10).

11 Mark 14:12 tells about a conspiracy among the chief priests and scribes, two days before Passover; they sought to arrest Jesus without causing a riot. This report may be correct.

12 John 18:3 and 12 mention the presence of a «detachment» or cohort, a military unit comprised of 600 soldiers. That is most unlikely, not only because of the exaggerated number, but because Roman soldiers would have taken Jesus to the prefect, not the high priest. The scene described in 18:1-9 was composed by John to emphasize the lordship of Jesus; when he says «I am he», they all fall to the ground.

cal, although the act of kissing him publicly was probably created to dramatize the infamy of Judas' act[13]. Once Jesus is arrested, his disciples flee to Galilee in terror. Only a few women remain in Jerusalem, perhaps because they are in less danger than the men. The flight of the disciples seems to be an instinctive reaction by people who fear for their lives; there is no reason to interpret it as a sudden loss of faith in Jesus[14].

Jesus is taken to the house of Caiaphas, the strongman of Jerusalem in the decade of the thirties[15]. The high priest not only ruled the temple and the holy city, but he was the highest authority over the Jewish people in dispersion throughout the empire. He presided over the Sanhedrin and represented the people of Israel before the Roman authorities. He was clearly a very astute man. He was related to the most powerful priestly family in Jerusalem, through his marriage to a daughter of Annas. His father in-law arranged for him to be named high priest by Valerius Gratus in 18 A.D. Eight years later, when Gratus was replaced by Pontius Pilate, Caiaphas succeeded in being confirmed by Pilate; he continued in the post until 36 A.D. when they were both removed by Vitelius, the governor of the Roman province of Syria. Caiaphas had been in power 18 years. No other high priest held the post that long under Rome's control[16].

Behind Caiaphas was a powerful clan that dominated the religious and political scene in Jerusalem during Jesus' time: Annas' descendants, also known as the *Ben Hanan* family. Annas, the founder, had been high priest for many years. Named by Quirinius in 6 A.D., early in the Roman occupation, he left the post in 15 A.D. but did not lose his influence and power. As a personal friend of Valerius Gratus and Pontius Pilate, he was able to get five of his sons, a grandson,

---

13 There seems to be no doubt that Judas played a part. The Christian community would not have invented such a tradition featuring one of the Twelve (R.E. Brown). There is no convincing basis for the theory that Judas' figure and action were invented by Mark to symbolize the Jewish people as traitors (Judas = Yehuda = Judah). Even J.D. Crossan considers Judas a real person, a «follower» of Jesus whom he betrayed (although a majority of the *Jesus Seminar* disagree).

14 Mark 14:50. The flight of the disciples is generally seen as an historical fact. The details of the young man who ran off naked, and the disciple (Peter?) cutting off the ear of the high priest's slave and Jesus restoring it, probably belong to the world of legend. However, Brown sees cutting off his ear as a disconcerting and scandalous detail that was conserved in the earliest tradition.

15 Flavius Josephus gives his full name as Joseph Caiaphas. In fact *Caiaphas* was probably a humorous nickname. Some authors believe it comes from *qof* (monkey), and reflects the popular view of him as a pet monkey who went along with the Romans. Others think it comes from *kuf* (to force), and means a «big stick» or a «tyrant».

16 Both Herod the Great and the Roman prefects tended to change high priests regularly, sometimes every year. That kept the priests from entrenching their power, and ensured their submissiveness.

and especially his son in-law Caiaphas, named in his place. Jewish tradition remembers the priestly clan of Annas as a rapacious family, which used all kinds of intrigues, pressures and machinations to turn the most influential and profitable positions into a family monopoly[17]. The *Ben Hanan* family was the most powerful and opulent in the priestly aristocracy; its principal members lived in the residential neighborhood of the priests, in the upper city, near the palace where Pilate stayed when he was in Jerusalem[18].

There is increasing scholarly certainty about the good relations and close collaboration that existed between Caiaphas and Pilate. It is worth noting that the prefects did not select high priests for their religious piety, but for their willingness to collaborate with Rome; the high priests in turn generally maintained a «prudent» collaboration that would ensure their longevity in power. Caiaphas is a case in point. He never supported the people in their angry protests against Pilate, first for bringing imperial banners into the holy city, and later for raiding the temple treasury to build an aqueduct. Caiaphas cleverly succeeded in navigating the conflicts and keeping his post at Pilate's side. Not until Vitelius, the Roman governor of Syria, ordered Pilate to return to Rome and explain his actions to the emperor, was Caiaphas removed from his post as the high priest[19].

What did happen that last night of Jesus' life on earth, in custody of the temple security guards? It is not easy to reconstruct the events, because the sources give very different versions[20]. One gets an impression from the gospel sources

17 In 30 A.D. Jonathan, a son of Annas and brother in-law of Caiaphas, was the «chief of the clergy» who monitored worship and controlled the temple police. There is reason to suspect that the sale of animals for sacrifice was a profitable business controlled by the family of Annas (J. Jeremias). Several members of the clan owned shops and businesses in Jerusalem.

18 Excavations by the Israeli archeologist Nahman Avigad between 1969 and 1980 have uncovered a palace which may have belonged to the family of Annas. It was a sumptuous building, adorned with Roman-style frescos and mosaics, whose façade faced the temple and the Mount of Gethsemane. It had a large audience hall, four pools for ritual baths, and three small dining rooms (*cubiculi*). Both Valerius Gratus and Pontius Pilate, friends of the family, were probably invited to dine in one of them (J. Genot-Bismuth).

19 In 1990 on the south side of the old city of Jerusalem, a splendid first-century family ossuary was discovered with the inscription: «Yehosef bar Caifa». Archeologists believe it is the ossuary of the high priest who participated in Jesus' execution (Greenhut, Reed).

20 According to Mark, Jesus is taken from Gethsemane to the high priest. «All the chief priests, the elders, and the scribes were assembled»; that is, the groups that made up the Sanhedrin, which would indicate that he was facing a death sentence (14:53-64). The next morning they meet again, but only to «bind» Jesus and «hand him over to Pilate» (15:1). In Luke's version there is no night-time meeting; the Sanhedrin only meets the next morning, but the scene ends without any judicial proceedings (22:66-71); he is then taken to Pilate (23:1). According to John he is taken to Annas, the father in-law of Caiaphas (18:13), who questions him «about his disciples and about his teaching»; then he is bound over to Caiaphas, where nothing happens (18:24). Finally he is

that it was a confusing night. It is also possible that the gospel writers didn't know much in detail about the relationships prevailing among the chief priests, the elders, the scribes, and the Sanhedrin[21]. What we can deduce is that there was a confrontation between Jesus and the Jewish authorities who had ordered his arrest, and that the high priest Caiaphas and the chief priests played an important part in it. Recent scholars have been moving closer to a basic reconstruction of the events[22].

In Mark's narrative, the Sanhedrin meets at night and solemnly condemns Jesus for having proclaimed himself Messiah and Son of God, and for claiming that one day he would come in the clouds and be seated at the right hand of God. His attitude elicits an indignant cry from the high priest. The poor man who stands bound before him is not the Messiah or the Son of God: he is a blasphemer! The Sanhedrin hands down a unanimous decision: execution. In reality there are many signs that Jesus' trial before the Sanhedrin never happened. This dramatic scene was probably a later Christian composition, constructed to show that Jesus was crucified because of the titles «Messiah» and «Son of God», which the Christians ascribed to him and which so scandalized the Jews[23].

The Sanhedrin of Jesus' time was probably similar to the one described by the Jewish Mishnah years later; it certainly did not have the power to hand down, or at least to carry out, a death sentence. Today we know that Rome never left this power (*ius gladii*) in the hands of local officials[24]. Moreover the «trial» before the Sanhedrin, as the gospels describe it, contradicts what we know from the Mishnah. In describing the functions of the Sanhedrin, it says that such meetings were prohibited during feast days and the preparation leading up to them; could not be held at night; and must take place in the temple atrium, not in the palace of the high priest.

taken to Pilate's headquarters (18:28); the Sanhedrin is totally absent in this scene, and there is nothing to suggest a trial by the Jewish authorities.

21 This is the opinion of Sanders and others.

22 My interpretation closely follows the research of such respected scholars as Brown, Theissen, Gnilka, Schlosser, Legasse, Lemonon, Rivkin, and others. I exclude the radical position of J.D. Crossan, who believes that the trial before the Jewish authorities is not an historical event but was entirely invented by the early Christians. In any case, Crossan says, a reconstruction is no longer possible; a man like Jesus could have been arrested and executed without such a formal trial before either Caiaphas or Pilate.

23 The gospel of John also reflects this sensitive distinction: «It is not for a good work that we are going to stone you, but for blasphemy, because you, though only a human being, are making yourself God» (10:33).

24 For many years scholars have disagreed on whether or not the Sanhedrin possessed *ius gladii*. There is general agreement today that it did not have that power in the time of Jesus. The decisive arguments were presented by A.N. Shervin-White, an expert on Roman history.

Thus there could not have been an official session of the Sanhedrin that night, let alone a fully legal trial by the Jewish authorities; rather it was an informal meeting by a private council of Caiaphas to carry out the necessary inquiries and clearly establish the terms in which the matter would be presented to Pilate[25]. Once Jesus was arrested, they were mainly concerned with clarifying the accusation they would bring to the Roman prefect the next morning; they needed to show that it justified a death sentence[26]. We have no way of knowing who was present that night, interrogating Jesus. It was probably a small group led by Caiaphas, the current high priest; his father in-law Annas, the former high priest and head of the clan; and other members of their family[27].

The decision to eliminate Jesus was apparently made from the beginning, but what were the real reasons that motivated this group of Jewish leaders to condemn him? His attitude toward the Torah, his criticism of the «traditions of the elders», his acceptance of sinners, and his healings on the sabbath, are never mentioned. These issues had caused conflict and debate between Jesus and some Pharisaic sectors, but it was not customary for Jewish groups to take punitive action against members of other groups because of their differing positions[28]. The Pharisees as a group did not take part in this council of Caiaphas; besides, the council was mainly concerned with the political repercussions that Jesus' activity might cause.

In the narrative Jesus is condemned as a blasphemer for proclaiming himself «Messiah», «Son of God», and «Son of Man». Since this combination of three great christological titles was the core of faith in Jesus, as expressed by Christians in the decade of the sixties, it seems unlikely that the scene is historically accurate. Blasphemy is not the reason for Jesus' condemnation. In the monotheistic culture of the Jewish people, «Son of God» is a messianic title which does not

---

25 Brown thinks there was a formal session of the Sanhedrin at which Jesus' death was decreed, but it was held long before his arrest (John 11:47-53; see also Mark 11:18). Brown also thinks that on that last night, it would make more sense to interrogate Jesus prior to handing him over to the Romans, than to hold a nighttime trial before the Sanhedrin.

26 Rivkin has argued persuasively that Jesus was not taken before the great Sanhedrin (*bet din hamigdol*), but to a «private council» of Caiaphas whose role was to advise the Sanhedrin, not on religious matters, but on issues of governance with serious political repercussions.

27 Researchers like Brown and Lemonon emphasize the importance of astute participation by Annas. John's report is quite credible: that Jesus was taken first to the palace of Annas, who «questioned Jesus about his disciples and his teaching» — two key questions for determining just how dangerous he was (John 18:12, 19).

28 «Live and let live» was apparently the ruling principle in relations among Jewish groups like the Sadducees, Pharisees, and Essenes (Rivkin).

yet explicitly express the meaning it would take on later, when Christians began to confess Jesus as divine. Nor is he condemned for claiming to be the promised «Messiah». Some of his followers may have seen him as the Messiah and passed the word to other people, but Jesus apparently never openly said it of himself. His answer to the messianic question was usually ambiguous; he neither affirmed nor denied it. This is partly because he had his own idea of what he should do as a prophet of God's reign; partly because he left the manifestation of that reign, and of his own person, in the hands of the Father. In any case we know that since the return from exile, several people had claimed to be God's «Messiah» without provoking persecution from the Jewish authorities. We know of no messianic claimant who was judged under the law or accused of blaspheming against God. Quite the contrary. In 132 A.D. when Simon bar Kosiba presented himself as the Messiah to lead an uprising against Rome, he was solemnly recognized as such by Aqiba, the most respected rabbi at the time. Such a messianic claimant might be accepted or rejected, but he would not be condemned as a blasphemer.

Of course none of the participants in this interrogation believe that Jesus is the Messiah. They're not really concerned with establishing his identity. They see him as a false prophet, who is becoming a danger to them all. Claiming to be the Messiah is not «blasphemy», but it is a politically explosive charge that they can use to accuse him before Rome, especially when his attitude in the capital is beginning to threaten the stability of the system. The attack in the temple is certainly the main reason for the Jewish authorities' hostility against Jesus, and the decisive reason for handing him over to Pilate. The Christian narrative cannot conceal this[29]. The temple scene is also Jesus' last public action. They don't let him do anything after that. His intervention in the sacred area is a grave act against the «heart» of the system. The temple is untouchable. Ever since the time of Jeremiah, the authorities have reacted violently against anyone who dared to attack it[30].

An episode that occurred in Jerusalem thirty years after Jesus' execution sheds considerable light on what may have happened to him. The report comes from

---

29 The attack in the temple as the cause of hostility against Jesus never disappears from the horizon in the Christian sources. Mark recalls it in the scene before the high priest (14:57-58); it appears again in the mocking scene at the cross (Mark 15:29-30; Matt 27:39-40); and it is recalled in the accusation against Stephen (Acts 6:13-14).

30 Around 610 B.C., the prophet Jeremiah entered the court of the temple and delivered the curse that God had ordered him to pronounce against that holy place. Immediately the priests, prophets, and all the people captured him, saying that he «deserves the sentence of death». Jeremiah barely escaped with his life (Jer 26:1-19).

Flavius Josephus. Just before the first great uprising against Rome, a strange and solitary man named Jesus, son of Ananias, began to walk the streets of the holy city night and day, crying: «Voice of the East! Voice of the West! Voice of the Four Winds! A voice against Jerusalem and the temple! A voice against husbands and wives! A voice against the whole people!» Some Jewish leaders arrested and beat him, but when they could not silence his cries they «handed him over» to the Roman governor Albinus, who ordered him to be cruelly whipped but could not get him to answer any questions. Finally he was released as a crazy man[31]. Jesus the son of Ananias had no followers, and did not proclaim any plan. He was a relatively harmless eccentric, yet the leaders in Jerusalem did not hesitate to arrest him and hand him over to the Roman authorities. The case of Jesus of Nazareth, who had a group of followers and invited people to «enter the reign of God», is much more serious. His action against the temple is so threatening to the public order that he is handed over to the Roman prefect. The Romans are not indifferent to problems at the temple, as if they were only an internal religious problem for the Jews. The prefect knows very well how dangerous any disruption of order in Jerusalem can be, especially at Passover when the city is full of Jews from all over the Empire. The council of Caiaphas decides to hand him over to Pilate. The Roman prefect will almost certainly execute him as an undesirable subversive.

2

Condemned to death by Rome

Pontius Pilate arrived in Caesarea by the Sea in 26 A.D. Tiberius had named him prefect of Judea[32], and he was coming to take over that position. He belonged to the lower nobility of the equestrian order, not to the more aristocratic senatorial class; in the eyes of those above him, he was a man who had to «make a career». Pilate usually lived in his palace at Caesarea, about a hundred kilometers from Jerusalem, but for the most important Jewish feasts he led his auxiliary troops to monitor the situation in the holy city. In Jerusalem he stayed at the fortress-

---

31 *La guerra judía* VI, 300-309 (English: *The Jewish War*).

32 He may have been named directly by Sejanus, who was charged with handling the ordinary affairs of the Empire when Tiberius withdrew to his villa on the island of Capri. If so, Pilate's position was probably greatly weakened when Sejanus lost favor with Tiberius and was executed in October of the year 31 A.D.

palace built by Herod the Great on the highest hill in the city. It stood out over the other buildings with its enormous towers, built to defend the upper city of Jerusalem. Flavius Josephus says it was a palace of indescribable luxury and extravagance. That is where, one April morning in 30 A.D., a fettered, defenseless prisoner named Jesus of Nazareth meets the representative of the most powerful imperial system ever known to history[33].

It is hard to get a clear idea of Pilate's personality. According to Philo of Alexandria, a contemporary of Jesus, Pilate is known for his «bribery, insults, robbery, abuse, unjustified harm, frequent executions without trial, and endless, horrible cruelty»[34]. According to other sources, Pilate probably was neither more nor less cruel than other Roman governors. They all used and abused their power, to execute with impunity anyone they considered dangerous to the public order. Flavius Josephus reports some incidents provoked by Pilate which show his lack of diplomacy, his ignorance of the religious sensitivity of the Jewish people, and his ability to control the masses by brutal means. Nevertheless his attitude is not always consistent.

The first serious episode occurred at the beginning of his rule as prefect: a great crowd, angry because he had brought military banners with the emperor's image into Jerusalem at night, surrounded his residence at Caesarea and stayed there for five days and five nights, demanding that he withdraw the banners. Pilate summoned them to the great stadium, surrounded them with his soldiers by surprise, and threatened to behead them all if they did not cease their protest. When the soldiers unsheathed their swords the Jews bared their necks, prepared to lose their lives rather than permit this transgression of the law. Pilate was disconcerted, disarmed by that peaceful, rational and disciplined behavior. He considered it more prudent to give in to their demands and withdraw the banners[35]. This prefect does not seem to be a heartless despot. He knows how to pull back. He can even weaken under pressure. Does this tell us anything about the action of Pilate who, according to the gospels, gave in to the coercion of the Jewish authorities and the crowd when they demanded that he condemn Jesus?

---

[33] Although some scholars still identify the Antonia fortress as the praetorium where Jesus was sentenced, a growing number believe it happened in this palace.

[34] *Ad Gaium* 28, 302. Most authors consider this negative picture of Pilate to be tendentious and rhetorical.

[35] *La guerra judía* II, 169-174 (English: *The Jewish War*); *Antigüedades de los judíos* 18, 55-59 (English: *Jewish Antiquities*).

Yet Pilate acted differently a few years later. He had decided to build an aqueduct fifty kilometers long, to bring water from the Bethlehem area to Jerusalem. Since it was a public work in everyone's interest, he took it as his right to draw on the temple treasury; that money was considered *korban*, consecrated to God. On one of his visits to Jerusalem, a crowd surrounded his palace and began to shout at him. This time Pilate did not pull back. He infiltrated the crowd with soldiers in civilian dress, ordered not to use their swords but to beat the demonstrators with sticks. Flavius Josephus reports that many people died: some from the beatings, others trampled in the panic[36]. In 36 A.D. his action was even more brutal. A Samaritan prophet called all the people to Mount Gerazin to see the place where Moses had buried the sacred urns. Nervous about his fanaticism, Pilate sent out cavalry and infantry troops to stop him. Some Samaritans died in the confrontation, many were taken prisoner, and the leaders were executed[37]. That was his last official act. Vitelius, the legate of Syria, heard the Samaritans' complaints and ordered the prefect back to Rome to give an account of his action to the emperor. Pilate spent his last days in the Gauls (Vienna). He probably was not as bloodthirsty and evil as Philo of Alexandria describes him, but as governor he did not hesitate to resolve conflicts brutally and expeditiously.

On his arrival in Judea, Pilate found Caiaphas installed as high priest by the previous prefect, Valerius Gratus. Pilate kept him in that post until they were both removed in 36/37 A.D. Apparently he found Caiaphas to be a reliable collaborator who would support him, or at least not take any position against him, at the critical moments when his action provoked popular protests[38]. Scholars are increasingly convinced that there was mutual understanding and even «complicity» between Caiaphas and Pilate about Jesus, who posed a problem for them both.

What really happened? The gospels give only a few legal details of Jesus' trial before Pilate. That isn't the purpose of their narrative. Besides, they don't seem to know exactly what happened in the prefect's palace[39]. They do agree with what

---

36 *La guerra judía* II, 175-177 (English: *The Jewish War*); *Antigüedades de los judíos* 18, 60-62 (English: *Jewish Antiquities*).

37 *Antigüedades de los judíos* 18, 85-89 (English: *Jewish Antiquities*).

38 In the matter of the temple, Caiaphas probably did not support the popular protest because he had given prior approval for the use of the temple money (McLaren). Caiaphas himself may have encouraged the massacre of the Samaritans, so that Mount Gerazin would not compete with the temple on Mount Zion in Jerusalem (Brown).

39 Mark (15:1-15) says that Jesus is taken to Pilate, who asks him if he is «the King of the Jews». The chief priests accuse him generically of «many things», and Jesus does not answer them (vv. 1-5). Then comes Pilate's attempt to resolve the impasse by releasing Jesus and condemning Barrabas; when the people insist on crucifying Jesus, Pilate gives in and sends him to the cross (6-15).

we have from non-Christian sources, however. It was Pilate who sentenced Jesus to death and ordered him crucified; he did so mostly at the instigation of the temple authorities and the powerful families of the Jewish capital. This is the clearest historical information we have: Jesus was executed by soldiers under orders from Pilate, but behind the execution was the high priest Caiaphas, assisted by members of the priestly aristocracy in Jerusalem[40].

But was there really a trial before the Roman prefect? Pilate could easily have executed the Galilean pilgrim without worrying about such formalities. His way of doing things was not exactly marked by a humanitarian streak. For some people the naïve style of the narrative, the vagueness of the accusations, and the legendary episode of Barabbas suggest that this trial is a Christian composition rather than an historical report[41]. Such radical skepticism is unjustified. As flawed as it may have been, there was a trial in which the Roman prefect condemned Jesus to die on a cross, for claiming to be the «king of the Jews». There is sufficient evidence of that in the sources, and it is confirmed by the tablet of condemnation placed on the cross[42].

The trial is probably held in the palace where Pilate stays on his visits to Jerusalem. It is early morning. In the custom of the Roman magistrates, the prefect begins to impart justice soon after sunrise. Pilate takes his seat in the court

---

Matthew (27:11-26) is based on Mark, but adds two historically unsubstantiated episodes: the dream of Pilate's wife (v. 19), and his theatrical gesture of washing his hands, which elicited a terrible self-condemnation from the Jewish people: «His blood be on us and on our children!» (24-25). Luke (23:1-5) is quite different from Mark. He shows the chief priests raising several specific charges against Jesus (vv. 2 and 5), and tells us of an appearance before Herod (6-12). John in turn offers a long and elaborate story (18:28-19:16). This is an artificial construction in which Pilate moves back and forth between the «inside» of the palace, where he is talking with Jesus, and the «outside» where he talks to «the Jews». Although John includes details of interest to historians, his composition is a «lesson on christology» that Pilate receives from Jesus.

40 The Jewish historian Flavius Josephus, in *Antigüedades de los judíos* (English: *Jewish Antiquities*), which was written in 93 A.D., says this about Jesus: «When Pilate, because of an accusation brought by the leading men among us, condemned him to the cross, those who had loved him before did not stop loving him» (18,3). Around 116/117 A.D. the Roman historian P. Cornelius Tacitus, explaining the origin of the Christians whom Nero had accused of having burned Rome, explains that «this name comes from Christ, who was executed under Tiberius by the governor Pontius Pilate». *Anales* 15, 44. (English: *Annals*).

41 This is the position of J.D. Crossan and most members of the *Jesus Seminar*, who consider the story to be a Christian creation based on Psalm 2.

42 This is the opinion of most recent scholars, who affirm the historicity of the Roman trial against Jesus, based on the gospel sources and on available information about judicial practices in the Empire (Brown, Theissen, Rivkin, Gnilka, Lemonon, Bovon, Legasse, Schlosser, Roloff, and others). My reconstruction of the events is mainly based on these studies.

where he will hand down his sentences[43]. Several criminals are waiting for the verdict of Caesar's representative this morning. Jesus is brought in with his hands bound. He is just another criminal. The temple authorities have brought him here. When his time comes, Pilate does more than ratify whatever trial or investigation Caiaphas may have carried out. He does not simply dictate an *exequatur*, «let it be done». He wants to present the case in his own way. Although Jesus was brought to him as guilty by the Jewish authorities, the prefect wants to see for himself whether the man deserves to be executed. It is he who will impose the justice of the Empire.

Pilate does not act arbitrarily. He can choose one of two judicial procedures in force at the time, to judge a case like this in a province like Judea. He apparently does not follow the practice of *coertio*, which gives him absolute power to take whatever measures he considers necessary to maintain the public order, including immediate execution; that would be a legal judgment. Instead, from what we know, he uses the *cognitio extra ordinem*, which is ordinarily practiced by Roman governors in Judea: an expedited way of administering justice which does not follow all the steps required in ordinary trials[44]. It is sufficient to attend to the essentials: hearing the accusation, questioning the defendant, assessing guilt and handing down a sentence. Pilate apparently takes considerable liberties and applies his own style in developing the *cognitio* procedure. He listens to the accusers, allows the defendant to speak, and without further proof or investigation, focuses on what particularly interests him: the potential threat of agitation or insurrection that this man poses. This is the question cited by all the sources: «Are you the King of the Jews?» Is it true that Jesus is trying to establish himself as king of this Roman province? This is a new question, not previously asked of the temple authorities from a political perspective. From the viewpoint of the Empire it is the key question.

For Pilate, Jesus' intervention in the temple and any possible debate over his stature as a true or false prophet are, in principle, an internal issue of the Jews. As prefect of the Empire, he is more concerned with the political repercussions of the case. This kind of prophet, who raises strange expectations among the people, can be dangerous in the long run. Attacks on the temple are also a serious

43 Only John 19:13 mentions the seat or «judge's bench» (*bema*) on which Pilate sits. This information is very plausible. It probably stood at the front of the small courtyard in front of the palace, a very appropriate place for a public trial.

44 For example, there is no intervention by the defense in Jesus' case.

matter. Anyone who threatens the temple system is trying to impose some kind of new power. Jesus' earlier words against the temple and his recent threatening act might undermine the power of the priests, who are currently faithful to Rome and play a key role in the maintenance of public order.

Thus the prefect's question puts the accusation in a new light. If the verdict is confirmed, Jesus is lost. «King of the Jews» is a dangerous title[45]. The Hasmonean priests were the first to claim that title, in proclaiming the independence of the Jewish people after the Maccabean rebellion (143-63 B.C.) Later Herod the Great (37-4 B.C.) was called «king of the Jews», by the authority of the Roman senate. Does anyone really think that Jesus is trying to establish a monarchy like that of the Hasmoneans or Herod the Great? He is not armed. He is not leading an insurrectionist movement or preaching a direct uprising against Rome. But his fantasies of an «empire of God», his criticism of the powerful, his firm defense of the most oppressed and humiliated sectors in the Empire, and his insistence on a radical change in the situation, all amount to a powerful challenge to the Roman emperor, the prefect, and the high priest named by the prefect: he is saying that God does not bless this state of affairs. Jesus is not harmless. A rebel against Rome is a rebel, even if he is preaching about God[46].

What always worries rulers is the unpredictable reaction of the crowds. That was also Pilate's concern. It was true that Jesus' followers were unarmed, but there were a lot of them. Cases like that had to be cut off at the roots, before they could spread. The religious motivations of these visionaries weren't the problem[47]. Nothing good could come of what was happening during those days in Jerusalem, full of Jewish pilgrims from all over the empire in the explosive atmosphere of the Passover feast: Jesus was publicly defying the temple system, and some of the pilgrims were apparently acclaiming him in the streets of the city. The public order, the *pax romana*, was in danger[48].

---

45 Its real meaning is «king of Judea» (G. Soslayan).

46 Luke gives the most plausible account of the trial, with the following accusations against Jesus: «We found this man perverting our nation, forbidding us to pay taxes to the emperor, and saying that he himself is the Messiah, a king» (23:2). «He stirs up the people by teaching throughout all Judea, from Galilee where he began even to this place» (23:5).

47 Pilate's decision in the case of Jesus is like that of Herod Antipas in the case of John the Baptist. Both were fearful of the unpredictable reactions of the people, and both killed the leaders but left their followers alone.

48 Luke says that Jesus also appeared before Antipas (23:8-12). It is hard to determine the historicity of this information. Although he was from Galilee, and was thus a subject of Antipas, Jesus could be tried in Judea by the Roman prefect at any time. The episode is probably a Christian composition, based on Psalm 2, to re-emphasize Jesus' innocence: «The kings of the earth set themselves, and the rulers take counsel together, against the Lord and his anointed» (2:2).

Pilate considers Jesus so dangerous that he has to be eliminated. It is enough to execute him. His followers are not an insurrectionist movement[49], but his execution must serve as a deterrent for anyone who dreams of challenging the Empire. Publicly crucifying Jesus, in full view of the crowds who have come from all over, is a perfect way of terrorizing those who might be tempted to rebel against Rome. Scholars debate whether the sentence was based on the crime of *perduellio* (sedition, or a grave attack against Rome) or on *crimen laesae majestatis populi romani* (harm to the Roman nation and its rulers). It doesn't matter which; Jesus is executed as a dangerous man[50].

So Jesus' crucifixion is not a terrible mistake, or the result of an unfortunate combination of circumstances. The prophet of God's reign is executed by the representative of the Roman Empire, at the instigation and on the initiative of the local temple aristocracy. Some of them see Jesus as dangerous. Their actions are not especially monstrous. Powerful people often respond that way to what they see as a threat to their interests. Tiberius has appointed his prefects to defend his control of all the provinces in the Roman empire. Pilate's job is to uproot any disruption that might endanger the public order in Judea. Caiaphas and his council have to defend the temple and guard it against unruly «fanatics». The soldiers are following orders. Probably some of the people of Jerusalem, who don't know much about Jesus and whose livelihood is largely dependent on the temple and the regular arrival of pilgrims, accept their leaders' view and take a position against Jesus[51]. Meanwhile his sympathizers are intimidated into silence. His closest followers take flight. The prophet of God's reign is left alone.

49 It is surprising that no one went after Jesus' followers. Quite the contrary: after his death they were allowed to form a community in Jerusalem itself. Rome clearly never saw Jesus as the organizer of an uprising against the Empire (*contra* Brandon and Carmichael).

50 Although the gospels all proclaim Pilate's innocence in different ways, it is not credible. Recent studies suggest that the exculpatory evidence they cite to justify the Roman prefect is not historical truth, but «Christian propaganda». Behind it is the early Christians' concern not to be seen in the Empire as successors of a man condemned as a threat against Rome. However, Brown considers it an exaggeration to say that the gospels have justified Pilate by creating a totally fictitious image of him.

51 It is hard to determine the historicity of the Barabbas episode. No one has yet found documentary evidence for the custom of releasing a prisoner at Passover (Brown, Crossan, Theissen, Gnilka, Schlosser, Bovon). Therefore some think the episode was created by Mark to dramatize the injustice against Jesus (Crossan, *Jesus Seminar*). Others think there really was a man named Barabbas, imprisoned for an uprising and later released by Pilate. After Jesus' conviction the Christians pointed to the irony of what happened in Jerusalem: the «criminal» who had participated in an uprising was released, while the «innocent man» who had never harmed anyone was executed (Brown). It is plausible that some group, hostile to Jesus, was present at the trial along with the temple leaders (Brown, Theissen, Bovon, Legasse, Gnilka, Schlosser). It may not have been an

The underlying situation is clear. The reign of God defended by Jesus is a simultaneous challenge to the whole Roman structure and to the temple system. The Jewish authorities, faithful to the God of the temple, feel obliged to react: Jesus is getting in the way. He is invoking God to defend the life of the least and the last. Caiaphas and his people are invoking the same God to defend the interests of the temple. They condemn Jesus in the name of their God, but in so doing they are condemning the God of the reign, the one living God in whom Jesus believes. The same thing is true of the Roman Empire. In Jesus' view, the system defended by Pilate is not a world organized in line with God's heart. Jesus is defending the most neglected people in the Empire; Pilate is protecting the interests of Rome. The God of Jesus is concerned with the last; the gods of the Empire are protecting the *pax romana*. No one can be a friend of Jesus and of Caesar at the same time[52]; no one can serve both the God of the reign and the

state gods of Rome. The Jewish authorities and the Roman prefect take action to protect order and security. But it is not just a matter of pragmatic politics. Underneath it all, Jesus is crucified because his activity and his message have shaken the roots of the system, which is organized to serve the interests of the most powerful people in the Roman empire and in the temple religion. It is Pilate who pronounces the verdict: «You will go to the cross». But that death sentence is signed by all those who, for different reasons, have refused Jesus' call to «enter the kingdom of God»[53].

«acclamation» (*acclamatio*) against him, as if they had voice and vote in the trial, but a more general popular pressure. The repeated and terrible outcry, «crucify him!» is a deplorable dramatization fostered by the Christian communities against the Jews of the synagogue. In those first days of Christianity it was a relatively innocent invention by Christians who felt threatened and were trying to defend themselves against the power of the Jewish religious authorities. But later when the Roman Empire embraced Christianity, these fantastic and unreal stories fed the terrible accusation of deicide against the Jewish people; it became a lethal weapon inspiring anti-Jewish feeling, provoking anti-Semitic persecution and genocide.

52 John's gospel attributes these words to the Jews: «If you release this man, you are no friend of the emperor» (19:12).

53 Jesus probably heard the sentence of the Roman prefect in Latin: «*Ibis ad crucem*». This was the usual formula. Pilate spoke Latin and Greek. Jesus spoke Aramaic, and perhaps some Greek. There was probably some translation during the trial.

The horror of the crucifixion

ᚖ

Jesus hears the verdict in terror. He knows what crucifixion is. He has heard about that terrible punishment ever since he was a child. He also knows there is no appeal. Pilate is the supreme authority. Jesus is a subject of a province occupied by Rome, with none of the rights of a Roman citizen. Everything has been decided. The bitterest hours of his life are ahead of him[54].

In those days crucifixion was the most fearful, terrible form of execution. Flavius Josephus calls it «the most miserable of all deaths», and Cicero describes it as «the cruelest, most terrible punishment»[55]. The three most ignominious forms of execution among the Romans were a slow death on the cross (*crux*), being devoured by wild animals (*dammatio ad bestias*), and being burned alive on a bonfire (*crematio*). Crucifixion was not a simple execution, but a slow torture. The victim's vital organs were not directly damaged, so death could last many hours or even days. Furthermore, it was customary to combine the basic punishment of crucifixion with other types of humiliation and torment. The historical details are chilling[56]. It was not unusual to mutilate the victim, put out his eyes, burn, lash, or otherwise torture him before hanging him on the cross. The methods used were left entirely to the sadism of the torturers. Seneca tells of men crucified head-down, or obscenely impaled on the post of the cross. In describing the fall of Jerusalem, Flavius Josephus says that the vanquished «were

---

54 The four gospels tell what happened in detail. The earliest narrative is in Mark 15:15-39. Matt 27:27-54 comes soon after; he develops in more detail the supernatural events that attended Jesus' death (vv. 51-54). Luke 23:24-28 has some unique features. He omits the flogging; mentions some women who wept for Jesus on the way to Calvary; and attributes to him words of forgiveness for those who were crucifying him (34), of salvation for the good thief (39-43), and of trusting prayer to the Father on giving up his spirit (46). John 19:17-29 also bears the writer's own seal. He omits the episode of Simon of Cyrene; gives great importance to the inscription on the cross (19-22); tells of Jesus' brief dialogue on the cross with his mother and the beloved disciple (25-27); and quotes two other brief words from the cross (28-30). The [apocryphal] *Gospel of Peter* gives a very condensed narrative of the crucifixion (10-20), with some interesting details to which we shall return.

55 *Crudelissimum teterrimumque supplicium* (*Against Verres* 2, 5,165). Crucifixion was practiced in many ancient nations. Persians, Assyrians, Celts, Germans, and Carthaginians used it in different forms. Rome learned it from Carthage, and made it the punishment of choice in the worst criminal cases.

56 An impressive study by M. Hengel gives abundant details of testimonies and reports on crucifixion in the ancient world.

whipped and subjected to all types of torture, before being crucified beside the walls... Out of anger and hatred, to mock them, the Roman soldiers hung the people they caught in different ways, and there were so many victims that there was not enough room to put the crosses, nor enough crosses to hang the bodies»[57]. Jesus' crucifixion apparently was not an act of unusual barbarity on the part of the torturers. The Christian sources mention only the flogging and crucifixion, along with different kinds of mocking and humiliation.

The cruelty of crucifixion was intended to terrorize the population and serve as a general deterrent. It was always a public act. The victims were left totally naked, dying in agony on the cross, in a visible place: a well-traveled crossroads, a small hill not far from the doors of a theatre, or the place where the crucified person had committed the crime. The spectacle of those men writhing in pain, moaning and cursing, was unforgettable. In Rome there was a special place for crucifying slaves. It was called the *Campus Esquilinus*. This killing field, full of crosses and instruments of torture, usually surrounded by vultures and wild dogs, was the most powerful deterrent. The little hill of Golgotha (place of the Skull), not far from the city walls, near a well-traveled road to the Ephraim gate, may have been the «killing field» for the city of Jerusalem.

Roman citizens were not subject to crucifixion, except in extraordinary cases or to enforce military discipline. It was too brutal and shameful, the typical punishment for slaves. It was called *servile supplicium*. The Roman writer Plautus (c. 250-184 B.C.) describes how easy it was to crucify slaves in order to terrorize others, cutting off any attempt at rebellion, escape, or robbery[58]. It was also the most efficient punishment for anyone who dared to rebel against the Empire. For many years it was the most common instrument for «pacifying» rebellious provinces. The Jewish people experienced it repeatedly. The historian Flavius Josephus reports four massive crucifixions in one period of seventy years, around the time of Jesus' death. In 4 B.C. Quintilius Varus crucified two thousand rebels in Jerusalem; between 48 and 52 A.D. Quadratus, the legate of Syria, crucified all the people captured by Cumanus in a confrontation between Jews and Samaritans; an uncounted number of Jews were flogged and crucified under the pre-

---

57 *La guerra judía* v, 449-451 (English: *The Jewish War*). Beginning with the emperor Constantine, crucifixion was gradually replaced by hanging, a quicker and more humane form of punishment.

58 450 slaves were crucified in the first slave revolt in Sicily (139-132 B.C.) After the defeat of Spartacus, Crassus ordered 6,000 slaves crucified along the Appian Way, between Capua and Rome.

fecture of the cruel Florus in 66 A.D.; at the fall of Jerusalem in September 70, many defenders of the holy city were brutally crucified by the Romans[59].

Those who pass by Golgotha on this April 7, 30 A.D., do not see an uplifting scene. Once more, at the height of the Passover festivities, they are forced to witness the cruel execution of a group of convicts. They won't be able to put it out of their minds at tonight's paschal meal. They know how that human sacrifice ends. The ritual of crucifixion requires the bodies to be left naked on the cross as food for the vultures and wild dogs; what is left will be buried in a common grave. Thus their name and identity are erased forever. Maybe it will be different this time; it is only a few hours until the beginning of Passover, Israel's most solemn feast day, and among the Jews it is customary to bury the victims of execution before nightfall. In the Jewish tradition, «anyone hung on a tree is under God's curse»[60].

4

The final hours

ᑯ

What is Jesus going through in his last hours?[61]. The violence, beatings and humiliation begin on the night he is arrested. In the passion narratives there are two parallel scenes of mistreatment. They come immediately after Jesus' condemnation by the high priest and by the Roman prefect, and they are closely related to the themes discussed in each place. In the palace of Caiaphas people «spit on» Jesus and «strike» him; they blindfold him and mock him, saying, «Prophesy to us, you Messiah! Who is it that struck you?» Here the mocking focuses on Jesus as a «false prophet», which was the accusation behind the Jews' condemnation. In Pilate's praetorium he is again beaten and spat upon, and

59 *La guerra judía* II, 75; II, 241; II, 305-308; V, 449-451 (English: *The Jewish War*). The Jews practiced stoning, not crucifixion. However, Alexander Janeus crucified 800 Pharisees. Herod the Great ended that practice when he ascended to the throne.

60 Thus Deut 21:22-23: «When someone is convicted of a crime punishable by death and is executed, and you hang him on a tree, his corpse must not remain all night on the tree; you shall bury him that same day, for anyone hung on a tree is under God's curse».

61 The passion narratives do not give us an objective report of events; the Christians began by searching the sacred Scriptures, especially the psalms of innocent suffering (22 and 69), to make sense of this horrible outcome of Jesus' life. This scriptural interpretation has deeply influenced the way they present the passion, but that does not mean that it was all invented on the basis of biblical texts. To judge the historicity of each detail we must discern carefully between what may be historical reminiscences and what is interpretation based on the biblical texts.

made the object of a masquerade: they put a purple cloak on him, press a crown of thorns on his head, put a reed in his right hand like a scepter, and kneel before him, saying «Hail, King of the Jews!» Here the mocking focuses on Jesus as «king of the Jews», which was the concern of the Roman prefect[62].

Probably neither of the two scenes is fully historical, in exactly the way they are described. The first is derived in part from the figure of the «suffering servant of Yahweh», who offers his back to those who strike him and does not hide his face from «insult and spitting»[63]. The soldiers' masquerade is probably inspired by the royal investment ritual, with its well known symbols of a purple riding mantle, a crown of wild leaves, and the gesture of prostration — in which, according to Mark, «the whole cohort» (600 soldiers!) took part. The two scenes have clearly been profoundly reshaped into rituals through which — indirectly and with a strong sense of irony — the Christians portray Jesus' adversaries confessing him as the prophet of God and king, which is how the Christians see him.

This does not at all mean the scenes are entirely fictional. Behind the first scene, at Caiaphas' palace, there apparently is an underlying memory of one or more of the high priest's guards striking Jesus on the night of his arrest[64]. Such humiliating treatment of prisoners was a routine practice. Thirty years later, in the decade of the sixties, Jesus son of Ananias was arrested by the Jewish authorities for prophesying against the temple; he was repeatedly struck before being handed over to the Romans[65]. Pilate's soldiers probably did the same thing. This incident does not come from a Hebrew text and is entirely plausible. Pilate's soldiers were not disciplined Roman legionnaires, but auxiliary troops recruited from the Samaritan, Syrian or Nabatean population — all strongly anti-Jewish peoples. It is entirely likely that they would be tempted to mock this Jew, disgraced and condemned by their prefect. We don't know exactly what they did to Jesus. The specific description that appears in the gospels was apparently inspired by incidents like one reported by the Jewish writer Philo of Alexandria, in which king Herod Agrippa was ridiculed on a visit to Alexandria around 38 A.D.: A mob «enthroned» a madman named Carabas in the city gymnasium, putting a pa-

---

62 The Jews' mocking of Jesus is described in Mark 14:65, Matt 26:67-68, and Luke 22:63-65. The mocking by Pilate's soldiers is in Mark 15:16-20, Matt 27:27-31, and John 19:2-3. Luke tells about the mocking in Herod's palace (23:11).

63 The suffering servant, whom the earliest Christians saw as the figure of Jesus, says «I gave my back to those who struck me... I did not hide my face from insult and spitting» (Isa 50:6).

64 John mentions a guard striking Jesus on the face during the interrogation (18:22-23).

65 Flavius Josephus, *La guerra judía* VI, 302 (English: *The Jewish War*).

pyrus-leaf crown on his head, a rug on his shoulders for a mantle, and a papyrus stalk in his hand for a scepter. Then two youths stood beside him like bodyguards, while others paid him homage[66].

Pilate's soldiers take a more official role when Pilate orders them to flog Jesus[67]. This is not an independent abuse or another game of the soldiers. It is part of the ritual of execution, which usually begins with flogging and ends with the actual crucifixion[68]. After the sentence is read, the soldiers probably lead Jesus to the palace courtyard, called the «tiled court», to begin the flogging. It is a public act. We don't know if any of his accusers are present at the sad spectacle. Jesus' most terrible hours are beginning. The soldiers remove all his clothes and tie him to a column or other post. There is a special instrument for flogging called a *flagrum*; it has a short handle and is made of leather thongs to which lead balls, sheep bones, or sharp metal pieces are attached. We don't know exactly what Jesus' torturers used, but the result is always the same. His skin is shredded; he is too weak to stand. That is also what happened to Jesus the son of Ananias, when Albinus had him flogged in 62 A.D. Flavius Josephus describes him as «skinned to the bones by the lashing»[69]. The whipping is so brutal that some victims die on the spot. That didn't happen with Jesus, although the sources tell us he had little strength left. He apparently had to have help carrying the cross, because he couldn't do it alone, and in fact his agony didn't last as long as some: he died sooner than the two prisoners who were crucified with him.

After the flogging comes the crucifixion. They can't afford to delay it. It takes time to crucify three people; in a few hours the sun will set, and the Passover feast will begin. The pilgrims and the people of Jerusalem are hurrying to finish their last preparations. Some are going up to the temple to buy a sheep and ritually slaughter it; others are on their way home to prepare the meal. The very air they breathe is festive. Meanwhile a somber procession is setting out from the prefect's palace to Golgotha. It is a relatively short walk, perhaps less than 500 meters. They probably follow the narrow street that runs from Pilate's fortress-palace to the city walls; just outside the Ephraim gate is the place of execution[70].

66 Philo, *In Flaccum* 6, 36-40.
67 Almost all scholars (including J.D. Crossan and the *Jesus Seminar* group) affirm the historicity of the flogging.
68 The Romans distinguished between *fustigatio*, a less brutal pre-emptive action, and *flagellatio* [NRSV: «flogging»], a terrible prelude to crucifixion. Scholars believe that what Jesus suffered was the flogging that precedes execution.
69 *La guerra judía* [English: *The Jewish War*] VI, 304.
70 There is scholarly debate over the exact route Jesus walked on his way to the cross.

The three doomed men are escorted by a small squad of four soldiers. Pilate apparently figures that is enough to ensure security and order. Jesus' closest followers have fled; there won't be any great resistance to the execution of these three prisoners. The procession also includes the torturers who will carry out the execution. There are three prisoners, so it will require some skill. They are carrying their tools: nails, ropes, hammers and other objects. Jesus walks in silence. Like the other two, he carries the *patibulum* or horizontal crossbar on which he will be nailed; when they get there it will be affixed to one of the vertical poles (*stipes*) that stand permanently at Golgotha for use in executions. Around his neck is a small tablet (*tabella*) on which the charge against him is written. Each prisoner carries one. It is important to show everyone what can happen to anyone who imitates them: the crucifixion must be a general deterrent. According to some sources, Jesus was unable to drag the cross all the way. At some point the soldiers, afraid that he might die before they got there, stop a man on his way from the country to celebrate Passover and make him carry Jesus' cross to Calvary. His name is Simon; he comes from Cyrene (now a part of Libya) and has two sons, Alexander and Rufus[71].

The walk to Golgotha doesn't take long. Although it is less famous than Rome's *Campus Esquilinus*, the field is probably known in Jerusalem as a place of public executions. Its sinister name is a clue: «place of the skull». «Calvary» comes from the Latin, *Calvariae Locus*[72]. It is a small, rocky hill, ten or twelve meters above the surrounding area. It was once a quarry for stones used in city buildings; in Jesus' time the rock cavities may have served as burial places. At the top of the hill stand the vertical poles, firmly planted in the rock bed. A heavily traveled road goes past, toward the nearby Ephraim gate. It is an ideal place for making a public example of the punishment.

The execution begins immediately. Jesus' crucifixion is probably the same as many others that have been described in greater detail. He is stripped naked, in order to strip him of all dignity; he is thrown to the ground, his arms stretched out to the two ends of the crossbar; he is nailed to the bar by his wrists, which are

---

71 Mark 15:21 (Matt 27:32, Luke 23:26). This episode is not mentioned in John. Some scholars consider Simon a fictitious character, invented to represent a faithful follower of the crucified one. Simon Peter did not carry Jesus' cross, but ran away; in contrast, Simon of Cyrene takes up Jesus' cross and follows him (Reinach, *Jesus Seminar*, Crossan). However as Brown points out, Simon's act is not voluntary but forced. Thus it does not work as an example of following Jesus, but may rather be an historical fact (Taylor, Gnilka, Brown).

72 The name «Golgotha» comes from the Aramaic *gulgultá* which also means «Place of the Skull».

easily penetrated by the long, heavy nails and will sustain the weight of his body. Then the crossbar and his body are raised and attached to the vertical pole, and his feet nailed together to the pole[73]. Ordinarily the cross was not much higher than two meters, so his feet would be only thirty to fifty centimeters above the ground. This way he would be within easy reach of his torturers throughout the long process of asphyxiation, and the wild dogs could get at him as soon as he was dead[74].

As always in these cases, the soldiers attach to the top of the cross a small white tablet, with clearly visible black or red letters, identifying the crime for which he is being executed[75]. Jesus' tablet is apparently written in Hebrew, the sacred language most commonly used in the temple; in Latin, the official language of the Roman Empire; and in Greek, the common language of the eastern nations and the one most used by the Jews of the diaspora[76]. His crime must be made very clear: «king of the Jews». These words are not just a christological title invented later by the Christians[77]. Neither is it an official announcement summarizing the findings of the trial before Pilate. It is rather a warning to the people who are to be deterred by Jesus' execution. It tells them, simply and with a touch of mockery, what will happen to them if they follow the example of this man on the cross.

Jesus is executed with other convicts. Group executions like this were apparently quite common. The Christian sources mention two other men; there may have been more. We don't know whether they were «bandits» captured in some

73 We do not have any more details. Apparently Jesus' arms were not tied to the cross, but nailed at the wrists. We don't know whether his two feet were nailed to the pole separately, or together with one long nail. Apparently they did not use either a *sedile*, a small wooden seat attached to the vertical pole to hold some of his body weight, or a *suppedaneum* to hold up his feet; they were not interested in prolonging his agony.

74 In June 1968, archeologists discovered a tomb dug into the rock at Giv'at ha-Mitvar, northeast of Jerusalem. In one of the ossuaries were the bones of a man about twenty or thirty years old, named Yehojanan, who had been crucified. His arms had not been nailed but tied to the crossbar. His feet were separated and nailed on the two sides, not at the front of the vertical pole. Each foot was attached by a long nail which ran first through an olive-wood board (so he could not pull out his feet), then the heel, and finally into the wooden pole. One of the nails had bent as it went into the knotty pole, and could not be extracted from the foot of the cadaver; the nail, the heel, and the olive-wood board were still together in the ossuary. The cadaver of Yehojanan, whom archaeologists call the «crucified one of Giv'at ha-Mitvar», sheds a sinister light on the agony that Jesus suffered.

75 For most historians, this inscription or *titulus* identifying the crime is one of the most certain details in Jesus' passion narrative (Legasse, Fitzmyer, Brown, Bovon, Gnilka and others); Bultmann and Linnemann are skeptical.

76 Only John 19:20 mentions the three languages on the *titulus* affixed to the cross.

77 The first Christians never called Jesus «king of the Jews». They would have put other titles on the cross, for example «Messiah», «Savior of the world,» or «Lord».

skirmish with the Roman authorities, or «common criminals» convicted of a capital offense[78]. Some scholars are doubtful about this detail; they think it may have been invented on the basis of texts like Isa 53:12 or Ps 22:17 to dramatize the atrocity committed against Jesus, an innocent man executed like any criminal[79]. That may be why the gospels report this detail, but it does not seem to be fictitious. Jesus was very probably executed with other criminals, as was often done. However, placing him at the center, between two bandits, may have been a matter of «Christian esthetics»[80].

After the crucifixion, the soldiers do not leave. Their job is to make sure no one comes to take down the bodies, and to wait until the dying men heave their last gasp. Meanwhile, according to the gospels, they cast lots to see who gets to keep Jesus' garments[81]. That probably did happen. In Roman custom the victim's possessions could be taken as spoil (*spolia*). The victims must know they no longer belong to the world of the living[82].

The gospels have also preserved the memory that at some point, the soldiers offered Jesus something to drink. It is hard to know exactly what happened. In Matthew and Mark, when they reach Golgotha before the crucifixion, the soldiers offer him «wine mixed with gall», an aromatic drink which dulled the senses and helped the victim to withstand the pain; they tell us that «he would not drink it»[83]. Something very different happens at the end, just before he dies. On hearing Jesus cry out loudly to God, one of the soldiers runs to bring him vinegary «sour wine», called *posca* in Latin, a strong drink popular among the soldiers, who used it to recover their strength and revive their spirits. This time it is not an act of compassion to relieve the victim's suffering, but a final mockery suggesting that he hold on a little longer in case Elijah comes to help him (!). It doesn't say whether Jesus drank it. He probably didn't have enough strength. This offer of vinegar in his last moments is so rooted in all the sources that it proba-

---

78 According to Mark and Matthew, they are two «bandits» (the plural of *lestes*). Luke calls them «criminals» (the plural of *kakourgos*). Perhaps Luke avoids the word «bandit» because of its anti-Roman implications for some readers.

79 Isa 53:12 says of the Servant of Yahweh, a figure of Christ for the early Christians: «The righteous one... poured out himself unto death, and was numbered with the transgressors». In Ps 22:16 an innocent man cries out: «a company of evildoers encircles me». Crossan sees these texts as the basis of the scene described in the gospels.

80 This is the view of R.E. Brown.

81 Mark 15:24.

82 John 19:23-24 expands this detail and mentions a «seamless tunic», probably an allusion to the tunic worn by the high priest. John explains it theologically by quoting Ps 22:18: «They divided my clothes among themselves, and for my clothing they cast lots».

83 Mark 15:23; Matt 27:34.

bly is historical: one more mockery, this time at the height of his agony[84]. But it is surely mentioned in the tradition because it takes on special meaning in light of a psalm of lament which says: «They gave me poison for food, and for my thirst they gave me vinegar to drink»[85].

Now there is nothing to do but wait. Jesus has been nailed to the cross from nine in the morning until noon[86]. His agony will not last much longer. For Jesus these are the hardest moments. While his body is being deformed by its own weight, the anguish of his progressive asphyxiation is growing. Little by little he is losing blood and strength. His eyes can barely see. Nothing reaches him from outside himself except for an occasional taunt, and the cries of despair and anger from the men who are dying beside him. Soon the convulsions will begin; then, the final gasp for air[87].

5
In the hands of the Father

How does Jesus experience this tragic martyrdom? What does he feel as he sees the failure of his plan for the reign of God, the abandonment of his closest followers, and the hostility surrounding him? How does he react to a death so ignominious and cruel? It would be a mistake to try getting inside Jesus' inner world through a psychological inquiry. The gospel sources do not give us a psychological description of his passion, but they do invite us to understand his basic attitude in light of the «suffering of the righteous innocent», as described in psalms well known to the Jewish people.

---

84 All the gospel writers mention this detail in different ways: Mark 15:36, Matt 27:48-49, Luke 23:36 and John 19:28-30. In the [apocryphal] *Gospel of Peter* (15-16), they give Jesus this «mixture» to poison him so that he will die before sundown (!).

85 Ps 69:21.

86 Mark has apparently organized the narrative chronologically in three-hour periods. The cock crows at three in the morning (14:72); Jesus is taken before Pilate at six o'clock (15:1, «as soon as it was morning»); at nine he is crucified (15:25); at noon darkness comes over the land (15:33); he dies at three in the afternoon (15:34); at six («when evening had come») he is buried. Though clearly artificial, this chronology is fundamentally in line with the reality: Jesus was crucified between nine a.m. and noon, and died around three p.m.

87 The gospel writers do not seek to incite anger by describing the horror of Jesus' final agony. We have deduced the details from available information on the Roman practice of crucifixion (Hengel, Sloyan, Legasse and others). Various medical theories about the physiological cause of Jesus' death (LeBec, Barbet, Behaut, Gilly, Edwards and others) are based in part on details from the gospels which are more theological than historical.

There is a memory among the early Christians that near the end of his life, Jesus experienced an anguished inner struggle. He even asked God to liberate him from such a painful death[88]. Probably the early Christians don't know exactly what words he used. To come closer to his experience they study Psalm 42; its anguish seems to echo what Jesus must have felt[89]. They also associate his prayer at that terrible moment with forms of prayer that they recite, which came from Jesus: he was surely the first to feel them deep in his heart[90]. Perhaps at first they do not know when and where Jesus went through this crisis, but they soon come to associate it with the «garden of Gethsemane», and with the dramatic moment before his arrest[91].

It is a wrenching scene. Jesus enters the «olive orchard» amid the dark shadows of the night. He becomes more and more «distressed and agitated». Then he walks away from his disciples, as was his custom, seeking silence and peace. He «throws himself on the ground» prostrate, with his face touching the earth[92]. The texts portray his distress with a variety of terms and expressions. Mark speaks of «sadness»: Jesus is deeply, mortally sad; nothing can put joy in his soul. A lament escapes him: «I am deeply grieved, even to death». He also speaks of «anguish»: he is alone and overwhelmed; one thought has overpowered him; he is going to die. John sees him as «perturbed»; Jesus is disconcerted, internally broken. Luke emphasizes his «anguish»; what Jesus is feeling is not fearfulness or worry, but horror at what is coming. The letter to the Hebrews says that he prayed «with loud cries and tears»[93].

88 This is recalled in different testimonies: Mark 14:32-42 (Matt 26:36-46); Luke 22:39-45; John 12:23, 27, 28 and 29; letter to the Heb 5:7-10.

89 The speaker says: «Why are you cast down, O my soul, and why are you disquieted within me? Hope in God, for I shall again praise him, my help and my God. My soul is cast down within me; therefore I remember you» (Ps 42:5-6).

90 «*Abba*, Father» (Mark); «Your will be done» (Matthew); «Father, glorify your Name» (John); «Pray that you may not come into the time of trial» (Mark).

91 Scholars differ among themselves on the historicity of the scene at Gethsemane. Some consider it entirely an invention of the Christian community, not a fact transmitted by witnesses (Lüdemann, Crossan, *Jesus Seminar*). Many accept it as a certain fact; no one would have invented a scene so unfavorable to Jesus (Lietzmann, Schnackenburg, Gnilka and others). Others see it as «substantially historical», but heavily reworked by the Christian tradition, since no one knew Jesus' exact words (Leon-Dufour, Grelot, Brown). I follow this more nuanced position.

92 In Luke he «knelt down», in a posture that can serve as an model of Christian prayer (22:41). John doesn't show him «falling to the ground», but he does say in John that the grain only bears fruit when it «falls into the earth and dies» (12:24).

93 Heb 5:7. This image of Jesus perturbed and anguished, falling on the ground to plead with God to save him from his fate, contrasts strongly with Plato's description of the death of Socrates. Forced to take poison, Socrates accepts his death without tears or pathetic pleas, with the certainty that he is going to a world of perfect truth, beauty, and kindness.

There on the ground, Jesus begins to pray. The earliest source quotes him as saying, «*Abba*, Father, for you all things are possible; remove this cup from me; yet, not what I want, but what you want»[94]. In this moment of anguish and total defeat, Jesus comes back to his original experience of God: *Abba*. With this prayer in his heart he plunges trustingly into the unfathomable mystery of God, who is offering him such a bitter cup of suffering and death. He doesn't need many words to communicate with God, saying in effect: «You can do everything. I don't want to die. But I will do whatever you want». God can do anything; Jesus doesn't doubt that. God could bring his reign into reality some other way, without this terrible punishment of crucifixion. So Jesus cries out his desire: «Take this cup far away from me. Don't show it to me again. I want to live». There must be another way to fulfill God's plans. A few hours ago, as he bid his friends farewell with a cup in his hands, Jesus himself was talking about his total commitment in service to the reign of God. Now in anguish he is asking God to take the cup away. But he is available for anything, even death, if that is the Father's will. «Your will be done». Jesus gives himself up completely to the Father's will, at a moment when his will seems absurd and incomprehensible[95].

What is behind this prayer? What is the source of Jesus' anguish, and his plea to the Father?[96] Surely the source of his affliction is having to die so soon, and so violently. Life is God's greatest gift. For Jesus, as for any Jew, death is the greatest misfortune; it destroys everything good that life offers, and leads only to a dark existence in *sheol*[97]. Perhaps his soul recoils even more from the thought of a death as ignominious as crucifixion, which many see as a sign of abandonment and even the curse of God. But for Jesus there is something even more tragic. He

94 Mark 14:36.

95 It is important to understand this very well. The gospels never say that God wills the «destruction» of Jesus. The crucifixion is a «crime» and an «injustice». How could the Father want Jesus tortured? What God wills is that Jesus remain unambiguously faithful in service to God's reign, that he not renounce his message of salvation in this hour of decisive confrontation, that he not pull back from his defense and solidarity with the last, that he continue to show everyone God's mercy and forgiveness.

96 Different theological currents have attributed the anguish of Gethsemane to a variety of causes. Jesus is becoming aware that his sacrifice is a failure, that many people will be «condemned» in spite of him; or he is feeling in his own person the «condemnation of sin», the «punishment that awaits sinners», the «wrath of God». This is reading too much into the texts, which do not speak of «sin» or of «punishment». The cup is not a symbol of «God's wrath» against the wicked, but of the painful and imminent fate of crucifixion that awaits him.

97 *Sheol* is the land of the dead. In Jewish faith it is in the depths of the earth. There is no light there, only darkness and deep shadows. There is no life, no song, no praise to God. All the dead go down to *sheol*, whether good or evil, and no one ever returns to this life. In Jesus' time many people thought of it as the place of waiting for resurrection.

is going to die without seeing his plan fulfilled. He has lived his commitment so passionately, he is so identified with God's purpose, that now he is even more horribly lost. What will become of the reign of God? Who will defend the poor? Who will think about the suffering? Where will sinners find God's acceptance and forgiveness?

The insensitivity and abandonment of his disciples plunge him deeper into loneliness and sorrow. Their behavior shows him how utterly he has failed. He has gathered a small group of disciples around him; with them he has begun to form a «new family» of service to God's reign; he has chosen «the Twelve» as a symbolic number for the restoration of Israel; he has brought them together at a special meal to share with them his trust in God. Now they are about to flee, leaving him alone. Everything is falling apart. The scattering of his disciples is the clearest sign of his failure. Who will bring them together now? Who will live in service to God's reign?

Jesus is totally alone. No one hears his suffering and his cries; God is not answering, and the disciples are «sleeping». When he is taken by the temple security forces, there is no longer any doubt: the Father has not heard his wish to go on living; his disciples are running for their own safety. He is alone! The narratives show us his aloneness throughout his passion. The small group of convicts being executed outside the city are not with him, as the people of Jerusalem and the pilgrims in the streets were. The temple is full of activity; at this very moment thousands of sheep are being slaughtered in the sacred court. People are feverishly completing their preparations for the paschal meal. The only people who notice him are the ones who see the convicts on the road or who happen to be passing by Golgotha. In ancient societies people are used to the spectacle of a public execution. They react in different ways: with curiosity, shouts, laughter, scorn, here and there a word of pity. From the cross, Jesus probably only sees rejection and hostility[98].

---

[98] We cannot fully evaluate the historicity of the different reactions at the foot of Jesus' cross. The Christian sources emphasize the scorn and insults, based on Ps 22:7-9. Different versions mention the mockery from «passers-by», «the chief priests», «the soldiers», and even those who were «crucified with him». Only Luke (and the [apocryphal] *Gospel of Peter*) speak of expressions of sympathy from a few people.

Only Luke tells about a more friendly, compassionate attitude among some women in the crowd watching the procession, who come near Jesus and weep for him[99]. And a group of women disciples are present in the Golgotha scene, «watching at a distance» because the soldiers do not let anyone come near the crucified men at the top of the hill[100]. We have the names of these courageous women who stayed to the end. All the gospels agree on the presence of Mary of Magdala, the woman who loved him so deeply. Mark and Matthew mention another two women: Mary the wife of Alphaeus, mother of James the younger and Joses; and Salome, the mother of James and John. Only the fourth gospel mentions «the mother of Jesus», her sister (Jesus' aunt), and «Mary the wife of Clopas». Although it is often said that Jesus must have been comforted by their presence, that is unlikely. Surrounded as he was by Pilate's soldiers and the executioners, it is hard to believe that in his agony he could have seen them there, forced to stand at a distance, lost among the other onlookers.

The first generations of Christians probably didn't know exactly what words Jesus might have murmured on the cross. No one was close enough to hear them[101]. The Christians knew that he had died praying to God, and also that he had cried out strongly near the end[102]. Not much more than that. Almost all the specific words that the gospel writers attribute to Jesus are probably derived from the reflections of the Christian community, who tried to fathom Jesus' death from different perspectives, each emphasizing different aspects of his prayer: desolation, trust, or self-abandonment into the Father's hands. Since the writers could not draw on specific memories preserved in the tradition, they turned to psalms that were well known in the Christian community, and which invoked God in the midst of suffering[103].

---

99 Luke 23:27-31. Might Luke have had a special source, unknown to the other gospel writers (Fitzmyer, Taylor)? Certainly the hand and spirit of Luke are visible in almost every line (Brown).

100 This detail is generally accepted as historical, although it was probably recorded under the influence of Ps 38:11: «and my neighbors stand far off».

101 The «seven words» of Jesus on the cross are only weakly rooted in the tradition. Only one cry is attested by more than one writer (Mark and Matthew): «My God, my God, why have you forsaken me?» Each of the other words appears only once, some in Luke and some in John.

102 This seems to be historical, according to most authors. Perhaps it was remembered because it was unusual for a victim on the cross, dying of asphyxiation, to cry out.

103 Although readers may find this way of understanding the «seven words» disconcerting, it is the position of most scholars, including very balanced ones like Brown, Leon-Dufour, Grelot, and Dunn.

Must we then be resigned to knowing nothing with any certainty? It seems quite clear that the «dialogue» between Jesus, his «mother», and the «beloved disciple» is a scene constructed in the gospel of John[104]. The same can be said of the «dialogue» between the two criminals and Jesus, which was almost certainly composed by Luke[105]. It is also discouraging to learn that the most beautiful prayer in the whole passion narrative is textually doubtful. According to Luke, on being nailed to the cross Jesus said, «Father, forgive them; for they do not know what they are doing». That is, and always was, his inner attitude. He asked his followers to «love your enemies» and «pray for those who persecute you»; he insisted on forgiving as many as «seventy-seven times». Those who knew him were sure he died forgiving, but he probably did so in silence, or at least outside the hearing of witnesses. It was Luke, or perhaps a second-century copyist, who expressed what the whole Christian community was thinking as words from his own mouth[106].

Jesus' silence in the final hours is heart-rending. As he died, however, he «cried out with a loud voice». This last, inarticulate cry is the most historically certain memory in the tradition[107]. The Christians never forgot it. Three gospel

104 In John 19:26-27: «When Jesus saw his mother and the disciple whom he loved standing beside her, he said to his mother, "Woman, here is your son." Then he said to the disciple, "Behold your mother"». It is hard to accept the historicity of this episode. No other source mentions the presence of Jesus' mother at the cross, and the figure of the «beloved disciple» appears only in the gospel of John. The scene was probably composed in the Johannine community.

105 In Luke 23:39-43, while one of the criminals is insulting Jesus, the other rebukes his companion and defends Jesus' innocence. Then he says, «Jesus, remember me when you come into your kingdom». Jesus replies: «Truly I tell you, today you will be with me in Paradise». This dialogue between the two criminals hanging beside Jesus, which is mentioned only in Luke, is artificial. The first criminal's insults are drawn from the taunts of the bypassers in Mark 15:30. Furthermore, Jesus' language is uncharacteristic: he talked only about the «reign of God», not about «Paradise». According to the [apocryphal] *Gospel of Peter* (13-14), one of the criminals rebuked the soldiers for mistreating Jesus; by way of revenge, «they ordered that there be no leg-breaking, so that he might die tormented». Apparently there was no clear memory of the two criminals' behavior on the cross. Luke's intention was probably to present Jesus as the righteous man insulted by the wicked, and to proclaim forgiveness to anyone who repents.

106 Jesus' beautiful prayer of forgiveness for his torturers does not appear in some of the earliest and most important codices, such as the Vaticanus, Beza, or the Syriac and Coptic versions of the Codex Sinaiticus. The prayer is probably inspired by the Lord's prayer. Could it have been spoken by Jesus and preserved only by Luke? Was it perhaps a saying that circulated independently and was later inserted by a copyist in the gospel of Luke, but was unknown to the other writers? Might it have been put in by Luke because it reflected Jesus' attitude, but later suppressed by a copyist who disapproved of forgiving the Jews? We don't know for sure.

107 All three synoptic gospels and the [apocryphal] *Gospel of Peter* attest to it. The letter to the Hebrews also speaks of the «loud cries» that Jesus addressed «to the one who was able to save him from death» (5:7).

writers quote the dying Jesus as saying three different things, derived from three psalms. In Mark (=Matthew) he cries out, «My God, my God, why have you forsaken me?» Luke omits these words but quotes him as saying, «Father, into your hands I commit my spirit». In John, shortly before he dies Jesus says, «I am thirsty»; after taking the vinegar they offered him, he exclaims, «It is finished». What do we know about these words? Were they spoken by Jesus? Are they Christian words, inviting us to penetrate the mystery of Jesus' silence which was broken only by his heart-rending cry at the end?

It is not hard to understand the description given us by John, the last of the gospel writers. In his theological vision, for Jesus being «raised up on the cross» means «returning to the Father» and entering his glory. Thus John's passion narrative is Jesus' serene and solemn walk toward death. There is no anguish or terror. There is no resistance to drinking the bitter cup of the cross: «Am I not to drink the cup that the Father has given me?»[108] His death is simply the culmination of his deepest desire. Thus he says, «I am thirsty»; I want to finish my work; I feel a thirst for God, I want to enter into his glory now[109]. And after drinking the vinegar he exclaims, «It is finished». He has been faithful to the end. His death is not a descent into *sheol,* but a passage from this world to the Father. Everyone in the Christian communities is certain of that.

We can also understand Luke's response. Jesus' anguished cry of protest over God's abandonment seems harsh to Luke. Mark had no problem attributing it to Jesus, but people might misunderstand. So Luke takes the liberty of replacing it with other words, more appropriate from his viewpoint: «Father, into your hands I commit my spirit»[110]. He needs to make clear that Jesus' anguish never altered his attitude of trust and total commitment to the Father. Nothing and no one could ever separate him from God. At the end of his life Jesus trustingly gave himself up to the Father who had been the source of all his activity. Luke wants to make that clear.

108 John 18:11.

109 John is certainly drawing on Ps 69:22: «and for my thirst they gave me vinegar to drink». But Jesus' exclamation also echoes other psalms: «My soul thirsts for God, for the living God. When shall I come and behold the face of God?» (42:2); «O God, you are my God, I seek you, my soul thirsts for you» (63:1).

110 Luke replaces Jesus' anguished cry, taken from Psalm 22:1, with a prayer of trust taken from Ps 31:5. He also emphasizes Jesus' trust by adding the term «Father» (Leon-Dufour, Grelot, Brown and others).

But in spite of these concerns, the cry quoted by Mark — «Eloi, Eloi, lema sabachthani?», that is, «My God, my God, why have you forsaken me?» — is the oldest in the Christian tradition and may well have come from Jesus. There is amazing sincerity in these words, spoken in Aramaic, Jesus' mother tongue, in the midst of his loneliness and total abandonment. If he hadn't spoken them, would anyone in the Christian community have dared put them in his mouth? Jesus is totally alone at his death. He has been condemned by the temple authorities. The people have not come to his defense. His followers have fled. Around him he can only hear mockery and scorn. In spite of his cries to the Father in Gethsemane, God has not come to help him. His beloved Father has left him alone to face an ignominious death. Why? Jesus is not calling God by his usual name *Abba*, Father. He calls him *Eloi*, «my God», as any human being would[111]. Yet his prayer is still an expression of trust: *My God!* God is still his God in spite of everything. Jesus does not doubt God's existence or his power to save him. His complaint is about God's silence: Where is he? Why doesn't he say something? Why has God forsaken him just when he needs him most? Jesus dies in the dark of night. He doesn't enter his death enlightened by a sublime vision. He dies with «why?» on his lips. Now it is all in the hands of the Father[112].

---

111 In the [apocryphal] *Gospel of Peter*, Jesus cries out: «My power, my power, thou hast forsaken me!» (19).

112 Some authors (Sahlin, Boman, Leon-Dufour, Brown and others) hold open the possibility that Jesus cried out only these words at his death: *'Eli 'atta*, «you are my God». This expression is also found in the same psalms that inspired the gospel writers to attribute three different prayers to Jesus. Ps 22, which Mark draws on, begins with «My God, my God, why have you forsaken me?» but continues in verse 11: «since my mother bore me you have been my God». Ps 31, which gives Luke the words «Into your hand I commit my spirit», says in verse 14: «But I trust in you, O Lord; I say, "You are my God"». Ps 63, which may have inspired John's quote «I am thirsty», begins as follows: «O God, you are my God, I seek you, my soul thirsts for you».

Raised by God

«Why?» we want to know, and so do Jesus' followers. «Why did God abandon that innocent man, executed unjustly for defending God's cause?» They have just seen him go to his death in an act of total obedience and faithfulness. How could God turn away from him? The memory of the last supper is still engraved in their hearts. In his farewell words and gestures they can feel the immensity of his kindness and his love. How can a man like that end up in *sheol?*[1].

Will God leave this man in the «land of the dead», this Spirit-filled man who has filled so many sick and handicapped people with health and life? Will he lie forever in the dust like a «shadow» in the land of «darkness», this man who has raised so many hopes in his followers? Can he no longer live in communion with God, this man who so completely trusted his Father's goodness? When and how will he ever fulfill his desire to «drink new wine» with them in the final banquet of God's reign? Was it all a naïve illusion on Jesus' part?

Certainly they are mourning the death of a man whose goodness and great-heartedness they came to know so well, but sooner or later death comes to everyone. What scandalizes them more is his brutal, unjust execution. Where is God? Won't he react to what they did to Jesus? Isn't he the defender of innocent victims? Was Jesus wrong in proclaiming his justice on behalf of the crucified ones?

1

God has raised him!

We can never fully measure the impact of Jesus' execution on his followers. We know only that his disciples fled to Galilee. Why? Did their loyalty to Jesus collapse? Did their faith die with Jesus on the cross? Or did they return to Galilee simply to save their own lives? We don't know for sure. Only that the rapid execution of Jesus has plunged them, if not into total despair, at least into a radical crisis. Probably rather than losing their faith, they have become desolate followers escaping danger, disconcerted by what has happened[2].

1 In the most ancient biblical understanding, people who die go down to a place under the earth called *sheol*, filled with total silence, darkness, and dust. It is the «place of darkness». There are no signs of life there. The dead are like «shadows» (*rephaim*) who sleep in the dust, unable to praise God. No one comes back from *sheol*. They are left there, forgotten even by God (Ps 115:17; 88:6-13; Job 17:13-14; 38:17).

2 Most scholars accept the flight of the disciples as an historical fact. Some consider it a sign of their «loss of faith» in Jesus (Vögtle, Kessler). Others think it can be more fairly and accurately described as a «radical crisis» (Pesch, Schillebeeckx, Müller, Torres Queiruga).

But then something happens which is hard to explain. Those men come back to Jerusalem and gather in Jesus' name, proclaiming to everyone that the prophet who was sentenced to death a few days earlier by the temple authorities and the imperial representatives is alive. What makes them leave the safety of Galilee and return to Jerusalem, a truly dangerous place where they will soon be arrested and persecuted by the religious leaders? Who has pulled them out of their cowardice and confusion? Where have they suddenly gotten all this audacity and conviction? Why do they come back to gather in the name of the one they abandoned when they saw him being condemned to death? They give only one answer: «Jesus is alive. God has raised him». Their conviction is unanimous and unassailable. We know that, because it appears in all the traditions and writings that have been passed down to us. What do they tell us?

They all say the same thing, in different ways and different words: «Death has not overcome Jesus; the crucified one is alive. God has raised him». Jesus' followers know they are talking about something beyond human existence. No one knows from experience just what happens in death, let alone what can happen to someone who is resurrected by God after death. But they are soon able to express the essence of their faith in simple formulas. These short, very stable formulas began to circulate among the first generation of Christians between 35 and 40 A.D. The Christians used them to transmit their faith to new believers, to proclaim their joy in celebrations, and perhaps to reaffirm their loyalty to Christ in times of persecution. This is the heart of their confession: «God has raised Jesus from among the dead»[3]. He was not a passive observer of Jesus' execution. He has stepped in to rescue Jesus from the power of death. They express the idea of resurrection with two words: «awakening» and «raising»[4]. These two metaphors suggest something impressive and extravagant. God has gone down even to *sheol*, has entered the land of death where everything is darkness, silence and solitude. The dead are lying there, covered by dust, sleeping the sleep of death. God has «awakened» the crucified Jesus from among them, has stood him on his feet and «raised» him to life.

---

3 Researchers say this was the earliest way of expressing faith in Jesus' resurrection. There is a typical example in Paul's letter to the Romans: «if you confess with your lips that Jesus is Lord and believe in your heart that God has raised him from the dead, you will be saved» (10:9).
4 The first Christians used two Greek terms: *egeirein*, «waking up» the dead person from his sleep, and *anistanai*, «raising» or «standing up» the dead person lying in the dust of *sheol*.

Then came other formulas, confessing that «Jesus died and has risen». This is no longer about God's intervention. Their attention has shifted to Jesus. It is he who awoke and rose from death, but in reality it was all God's doing. Jesus is awake because God wakened him; he is standing up because God raised him; he is full of life because God filled him with God's life. The loving act of God, his Father, is always there in the background[5].

In all these formulas, the Christians speak of the «resurrection» of Jesus. But in the same period we also find liturgical songs and hymns acclaiming God for having exalted and glorified Jesus as Lord after his death. They do not speak of «resurrection». In these hymns, born of the early enthusiasm of the Christian communities, the believers are expressing themselves in another mental framework and a different language: God «has exalted» Jesus, he has «taken him up in glory», he has «seated him at the right hand of his throne» and has «established him as Lord»[6].

This language is as old as the one that speaks of «resurrection». For the first Christians, the exaltation of Jesus to the glory of the Father is not something that happens after his resurrection, but a different way of affirming what God has done with the crucified one. To be «raised» is already to be exalted, that is, to be introduced into God's own life. To be «exalted» is to rise, to be pulled away from the power of death. The two languages enrich and complement each other, to suggest the action of God on the dead Jesus[7].

We find the most important and meaningful confession of faith in a letter that Paul of Tarsus wrote around 55/56 A.D. to the Christian community of Corinth, a cosmopolitan city where different hellenist and oriental religions live together in a strange mix with temples erected to Isis, Serapis, Zeus, Aphrodite, Aesclepios, or Cybele. Paul encourages them to remain faithful to the gospel that he taught them on his visit around 51 A.D., the «good news… through which also you are being saved». This «news» is not Paul's invention. It is a teaching he has received, and is now transmitting faithfully along with other preachers of great stature who live and proclaim the same faith:

5   A typical example of these confessions of faith is found in the earliest letter we have from Paul: «For since we believe that Jesus died and rose again, even so, through Jesus, God will bring with him those who have died» (1 Thess 4:14).
6   Typical examples are the pre-Pauline hymn found in Phil 2:6-11, and the one in 1 Tim 3:16. We can also detect this language in hymnic fragments like Eph 4:7-10 or Rom 10:5-8.
7   According to Luke the first preachers used these two languages interchangeably: «The God of our ancestors raised up Jesus, whom you had killed by hanging him on a tree. God exalted him at his right hand as Leader and Savior» (Acts 5:30-31).

For I handed on to you as of first importance what I in turn had received: that Christ died for our sins in accordance with the scriptures, and that he was buried, and that he was raised on the third day in accordance with the scriptures, and that he appeared to Cephas, then to the Twelve…[8].

One thing in this confession may surprise us. Why does it say that Jesus «was raised on the third day in accordance with the scriptures»? Did anyone witness that crucial moment? Why do the gospel writers speak of appearances on the «first day of the week», before the «third day»? In reality, in biblical language the «third day» means the «decisive day». After days of suffering and tribulation, the «third day» brings salvation. God always saves and liberates on the «third day». God has the last word; the «third day» belongs to him. Thus we read in the prophet Hosea: «Come, let us return to the Lord; for it is he who has torn, and he who will heal us; he has struck down, and he will bind us up. After two days he will revive us; on the third day he will raise us up, that we may live before him»[9]. Different rabbinical commentaries interpret this «third day» announced by Hosea as «the day of the resurrection of the dead», «the day of consolation on which God will revive the dead and will raise us up»[10]. The first Christians believe that this definitive «third day» has come for Jesus. He has entered into full salvation. We are still going through days of trial and suffering, but the «third day» has dawned with Jesus' resurrection[11].

This language might have been understood in the Jewish culture, but the missionaries who traveled through the cities of the Empire felt that people in the Greek culture were resistant to the idea of «resurrection». Paul could see that, when he started talking about the risen Jesus at the Areopagus in Athens. «When they heard of the resurrection of the dead, some scoffed, but others said, "We will hear you again about this"»[12]. So some sectors found a different language

8 1 Cor 15:3-5. Linguistic analysis suggests that this confession of faith is of Jewish origin and has been adapted to the Greek world. The tradition probably came from the Church in Jerusalem and was embraced by the leaders of the Church in Antioch around 35 or 40 A.D. Paul surely came to know it during his stay in that great city around 40 or 42 A.D.

9 Hos 6:1-2.

10 These are midrashic writings, like the *Midrash Rabbah* or the targums that translate and comment on the Hosea text.

11 This is the most commonly accepted interpretation today (Vögtle, Leon-Dufour, Grelot, Schillebeeckx). Some scholars recall, however, that in the Jewish way of thinking a dead person is really dead «after three days». The expression in the Christian confession would then mean that God raised Jesus, not from apparent death after one or two days, but from real death after three days (Kegel, Goguel, Schmitt).

12 Acts 17:32.

which, without distorting faith in the risen one, was more appropriate and easily accepted by people of a Greek mentality. Luke in particular may have helped to introduce a new language presenting the risen one as «he who lives», «the living one». Thus in his gospel the women at the tomb are asked, «Why do you look for the living among the dead?»[13]. Years later the book of Revelation has the risen one making strong statements, very different from the first formulas of faith: «I am the first and the last, and the living one. I was dead, and see, I am alive forever and ever, and I have the keys of Death and of Hades»[14].

2

What happened in Jesus' resurrection?

⸎

What do these first generation Christians mean by «the risen Christ»? What do they mean by «the resurrection of Jesus»? How do they think of it?

Resurrection is something that has happened to Jesus. Something that took place in the crucified one, not in the imagination of his followers. Everyone is convinced of this. It is not just a way of saying that their faith in Jesus has been reawakened. Certainly a new faith in Jesus has been awakened in the disciples' hearts, but his resurrection came before that; it preceded everything that they have experienced since then. It is in fact the event that pulled them out of their confusion and frustration, transforming their relationship with Jesus at its roots.

This resurrection is not a return to his earlier life on earth. Jesus does not return to biological life as we know it, to die irreversibly some other day. The sources never suggest that. This resurrection is not the reanimation of a cadaver. It is much more than that. The first Christians never confuse Jesus' resurrection with what might have happened in the gospel stories about Lazarus, Jairus' daughter, or the young boy at Nain. Jesus does not return to this life; he enters definitively into «the Life of God»[15]. A liberated life, where death has no power over him. Paul makes this very clear: «We know that Christ, being raised from the dead, will never die again; death

---

13 Luke 24:5. See also Luke 24:23; Acts 1:3; 25:19.
14 Rev 1:17-18 and 2:8. This book, the last of the writings in the New Testament, was composed around 95 A.D. at the end of the reign of Domitian, in Asia Minor.
15 John's gospel does not confuse the raising of Lazarus, who came out of the tomb with «his hands and feet bound with strips of cloth, and his face wrapped in a cloth», with the resurrection of Jesus, who left the «linen wrappings» and the cloth behind in the tomb. Lazarus returns to this life full of enslavements and darkness. In contrast, Jesus enters into the land of freedom and light.

no longer has dominion over him. The death he died, he died to sin, once and for all; but the life he lives, he lives to God»[16]. However, the gospel narratives about the «appearances» of the risen Jesus may leave us somewhat confused[17]. According to the gospel writers Jesus can be seen and touched, he can eat, he can go up into heaven until he is hidden by a cloud. If we understand these narrative details in a material way, it seems as if Jesus has come back to this earth to go on living with his disciples as they were before. But the gospel writers themselves tell us that's not what happened. It is the same Jesus, but not the Jesus they knew before; he comes to them full of life, but they do not recognize him right away; he is in their midst, but they cannot hold on to him; he is someone real and concrete, but they cannot live with him as they did in Galilee. It is certainly Jesus, but in a new existence.

Jesus' followers also do not understand his resurrection as a kind of mysterious survival of his immortal soul, which is how the Greek culture would think of it[18]. The risen one is not someone who survives death, stripped of his corporality. They are Hebrews, and in their way of thinking, the «body» is not simply the physical or material side of a person, something that can be separated from a different, spiritual side. The «body» is the whole person, who experiences his or her own rootedness in the world and in life with others. When they speak of the «body» they are thinking of a person in his or her whole world of relationships and shared experiences, a whole history of conflicts and hurts, joys and suffering. They cannot imagine Jesus risen without a body; he would be something else, but not a human being[19]. But naturally they are not thinking of a physical, flesh and blood body, subject to the power of death; rather it is a «glorious body» that expresses and gives fullness to the real life he lived in this world. When God raises Jesus he raises up his earthly life, marked by his commitment to God's reign, his acts of kindness to the little ones, his youth so violently cut short, his struggles and conflicts, his obedience unto death. Jesus is raised with a «body» that expresses and gives fullness to his whole earthly life[20].

16 Rom 6:9-10.

17 Later we shall discuss these narratives, composed between 70 and 90 A.D. They are not biographical narratives. They do not try to give us information on which to reconstruct the events as they happened, beginning on the third day after the crucifixion. They are wonderful «catechetical resources» which evoke the first experiences, in order to explore more deeply our faith in the risen Christ and draw out its meaning for believers.

18 In speaking of the risen one they used the language of «resurrection», of «exaltation» to the glory of God, or of «life», but they were never thinking of the «immortality of the soul» of Jesus.

19 This reflects studies on the «corporality of the risen one» by authors like Kessler, Boismard, Deneken, Bouttier, Sesboüé, Martelot and others.

20 Phil 3:21.

For the first Christians, more than any other representation or mental frame of reference, Jesus' resurrection is an act of God, whose creative power rescues him from death and brings him fully into God's own life[21]. This is what the early Christian confessions and the first preachers say again and again. In one way of saying it, God embraces Jesus at the very center of death, filling him with all God's creative power. Jesus dies crying out, «My God, why have you abandoned me?»; in dying he meets his Father, who embraces him with immense love and prevents his life from being extinguished. At the very moment when Jesus feels that his whole being is being lost forever, as is the sad fate of all human beings, God intervenes to give him God's own life. Where everything is ending for Jesus, God is beginning something radically new. When everything seems irremediably lost in the absurdity of death, God is beginning a new creation.

This creative action by God, accepting Jesus into his unfathomable mystery, is an event that overflows all the structures of life as we know it. It transcends any experience we might have in this world. We have no way of describing it. That is why no gospel writer has tried to describe Jesus' resurrection. No one can be a witness to that transcendent act of God[22]. The resurrection no longer belongs to the visible, tangible world. Thus we say that it is not properly speaking an «historical event», like others which happen in the world and which we can observe and verify, but it is a «real event» that really happened. Therefore, «the resurrection of Jesus goes beyond history, but it has left its mark in history». For the same reason, «it opens history beyond itself, and creates something definitive»[23]. For believers in Jesus it is the most real, important and decisive event that has ever occurred in human history, because it is the foundation and the true hope of history[24].

21 Although the resurrection is ordinarily described as an act carried out by God (transitive verb), we also say that «Jesus rose» from the dead (intransitive verb). This linguistic fact suggests that in a more fully developed, global understanding of the early Christian faith, the life-giving force always comes from God; at the same time it also pertains to the Son, who is one with the Father.

22 Only the [apocryphal] *Gospel of Peter*, probably composed around 150 A.D. in Syria, dares to report that the Roman soldiers saw «three men come forth from the tomb, and two of them supporting one, and a cross following them: and the heads of the two reached up to heaven, but the head of the one they led was higher than the heavens».

23 J. Ratzinger-Benedict xvi, *Jesús de Nazaret. Desde la entrada en Jerusalén hasta la resurrección.* Madrid, Encuentro, 2011, p. 160 (English: Jesus of Nazareth: Vo. II).

24 In everyday conversation we tend to think of «historical events» as «real events», things that have happened. In the technical language used by theology, the only «historical events» are those that can be empirically verified. Thus some theologians affirm the resurrection of Jesus as a «real» event, but consider it inappropriate to call it an «historical event» without further explanation, since its full reality cannot be empirically analyzed.

How do the first generation Christians speak of this creative act of God, which we cannot observe? Paul's language is helpful. In his words, Jesus has been raised by the «power» of God, who gives Jesus his new, risen life; because he is filled with this divine power he can be called «Lord», the same name that the Greek-speaking Jews used for Yahweh. Paul also says that he was raised by the «glory» of God, that is, by that creative, saving force that reveals God's greatness. That is why the risen Jesus possesses a «glorious body», by which Paul does not mean radiant or resplendent, but rather overflowing with God's own glorious power. Finally, Paul says that he has been raised by the «spirit» of God, by his creative force. That is why his risen body is a «spiritual body», that is, fully enlivened by the vital and creative force of God[25].

The first Christians believe that this intervention by God is the beginning of the final resurrection, the fullness of salvation. Jesus is only the «firstborn from the dead»[26], the first one born into the definitive life of God. He has gone before us into the enjoyment of a fullness that will also be there for us. His resurrection is not something private, only for him; it is the foundation and guarantee of resurrection for all humanity and all creation. Jesus is the «first fruits» of a universal harvest to come[27]. «And God raised the Lord and will also raise us by his power»[28]. In raising Jesus, God begins the «new creation». He comes out of his hiddenness and reveals his ultimate plan, the purpose for which he first created the world: to share his infinite happiness with humanity.

3

On the way to new faith in the risen Christ

What happened, to make Jesus' disciples believe something so amazing about him? What caused such radical turnaround in these disciples, who had given him up as a lost cause just a few days earlier? What is happening to them now, since his death? Can we come closer to the early experience that sparked their enthusiasm for the risen Christ?

---

25 Jesus is raised by the «power» (*dynamis*) of God (2 Cor 13:4; Eph 1:19-20); by the «glory» (*doxa*) of God (Rom 6:4; Phil 3:21); and by the «spirit» (*pneuma*) of God (Rom 8:11; 1 Cor 15:35-49).
26 Col 1:18.
27 1 Cor 15:20.
28 1 Cor 6:14.

The stories that have come down to us do not provide a clear basis for understanding just what happened after Jesus' death. We cannot penetrate the meaning of their experience by using historical methods. It is clear, however, that the faith of his followers did not come out of nowhere. Something happened to them. Indeed the apostolic preaching, with all its enthusiasm and audacity, would be unthinkable unless the witnesses were in real contact with the totally new and unexpected event that had happened to them, that is, the manifestation of the risen Christ and the fact that he had spoken with them[29]. All the sources tell us that what they went through not only revived their faith in Jesus, but opened them to a new and surprising experience of his presence in their midst.

It was a rich and complex process, caused by more than one factor. Jesus' followers have been reflecting on what happened, pondering their faith in God's faithfulness and his power over death, and thinking about the life they shared with Jesus so intensely. This process is made up of questions, reflections, unexpected events, and amazing experiences of faith. Together these things have awakened in them a new faith in Jesus; their growing sense of his presence with them after his death does not only come from reflection on the past. They think it comes from God. Something so great and unexpected could only be a revelation of God. Without God's action they would be lost in their questions and doubts, unable to reach any joyful certainty about what happened to Jesus[30]. What can we learn about this process?

Jesus' disciples, like almost all the Jews of his time, expected the «resurrection of the righteous» at the end of time. Without that expectation they could hardly have imagined such a thing as resurrection. It was not an ancient Jewish belief but a relatively new faith, still being formulated in different ways. The problem arose most sharply in 168-164 B.C., when an uncounted number of Jews were martyred by Antiochus Epiphanes for remaining faithful to the Law: would God abandon to death those who had loved him enough to die for him? Wouldn't he give back life to those who have sacrificed their lives out of faithfulness to him?

29 J. Ratzinger-Benedict xvi, Jesús de Nazaret, p. 320 (English: Jesus of Nazareth: Vo. II).

30 Recent scholarship has moved away from the traditional tendency to explain the birth of faith in the risen Christ as a result of concrete experiences, and now focuses more on an overall process (Müller, Kessler, Torres Queiruga), including such factors as Jewish expectations about life after death (Berger), faith in the final resurrection of the dead (Pannenberg, Wilckens), the interpretive models that were available to the disciples (Marxsen, Boismard), the cognitive process (Schillebeeckx), or their memories of the message and activity of Jesus (Pesch). Dunn and others also point out that we don't know how long the process lasted; Luke was applying a conventional formula in fitting the appearances of the risen Christ into a 40-day period.

Jesus' followers were probably asking themselves the same thing in view of his death. The response of the prophet Daniel was to proclaim a new faith: at the end of time, those who have remained faithful to God will be saved. «Many of those who sleep in the dust of the earth shall awake, some to everlasting life, and some to shame and everlasting contempt. Those who are wise shall shine like the brightness of the sky, and those who lead many to righteousness, like the stars forever and ever»[31]. The martyrs who are faithful to God, and the wise who lead many on the right path, will awake from the sleep of death. Now they are dust, but God will make them shine like the stars.

Certainly Jesus' disciples shared this faith. It was widely accepted in their time, especially by apocalyptic writers[32], although it was the Pharisees who most actively promoted it among the people; only the Sadducees rejected it as a «novelty» not supported by the earliest traditions. Like most pious Jews, the disciples

probably also recited this blessing every day at sunrise and sunset: «Blessed are you, Lord, who make the dead live»[33]. This hope surely helped them understand what they were going through. If they were experiencing Jesus as alive, didn't it mean the final resurrection of the righteous was here? Wasn't Jesus living God's full salvation?

But the early resurrection of one person, before the end of time, was something new. The disciples were expecting the «resurrection of the righteous» in general, and in the plural. They had surely heard about the martyrdom of seven brothers, tortured along with their mother by Antiochus Epiphanes. It was a very popular story, with an impressive scene in which the brothers challenge the king, confessing their faith in their own resurrection[34]. We don't know for sure, but the idea of specific martyrs being raised by God may have helped the disciples overcome the scandal of the cross. Jesus, unjustly assassinated for his faithfulness to God, cannot be annihilated by death; God's vindication for the martyr has been completely fulfilled in him.

---

31 Dan 12:2-3.

32 Books like 1 Enoch 92-105 and the *Testament of the Twelve Patriarchs* clearly affirm it: «Those who die in pain will rise up in joy… and those who die in the name of the Lord will awaken to life».

33 This is in the second blessing of the *Shemone esre*: «You are powerful and bring low the proud, you are strong and judge oppressors, you live forever and raise the dead, you command the wind and make the dew fall, you give food to the living and give life to the dead. In one moment you make our salvation spring up. Blessed are you, Lord, who make the dead live» (from a brief Palestinian text of the Cairo *genizah*).

34 The brothers say among other things: «You accursed wretch, you dismiss us from this present life, but the King of the universe will raise us up to an everlasting renewal of life, because we have died for his laws». Meanwhile their mother encourages them: «The Creator of the world… will-

But this vision is not quite enough. The resurrection of these specific martyrs only affects each one individually; it has nothing to do with salvation for the rest of humanity[35]. This is different: Jesus' followers eventually start talking about his resurrection as a source of salvation for all humanity, the «first fruit» of a universal resurrection, the beginning of the last times. The disciples have been deeply «marked» by Jesus. The crucifixion cannot erase all that they have experienced with him. In Jesus they have experienced God irrupting in the world, in a new and definitive way. His healing power has destroyed Satan's power and rescued the sick and demon-possessed from evil, showing them a new world of abundant life. His acceptance of the last as the first in God's reign has awakened the hope of the poor in a God who is beginning to show his liberating power in the face of so much injustice and abuse. His meals with sinners and undesirables have shown them the final banquet and the joy that will come in the last times. With Jesus they have felt the irruption of God's saving power and love. Could it be that in his resurrection, they were experiencing God's liberating irruption to establish the definitive reign of life here and now?

4

The decisive experience

God is in the very heart of this process: inspiring their search, throwing light on their questions, clearing away their doubts, and opening up their incipient faith to new horizons. The disciples are convinced of this: God is making the risen Jesus present in their hearts. At some point they realize that it is God who is revealing the crucified one to them, full of life. That wasn't clear to them at first, but now they are really «seeing» him in all his risen «glory». Without that experience, perhaps they would have revered his memory for a while; then it would have begun to fade[36].

How do the disciples understand what is happening to them? A very early formula, repeated always in the same way, is their first way of expressing it: Jesus

---

in his mercy give life and breath back to you again, since you now forget yourselves for the sake of his laws» (2 Macc 7:9, 23).

35 The same can be said of Enoch or the prophet Elijah who were mysteriously taken up into heaven, in events unconnected to the final salvation in the last times (Sirach 44:16; 48:9,12).

36 Something similar may have happened with John the Baptist; rumors began circulating about him as a prophet «returned to life» (Mark 6:16; 8:28).

«let himself be seen»[37]. They had lost him in the mystery of death, but now he shows himself to them, full of life. The term comes from the Greek Bible, which uses it to speak of God's «appearances» to Abraham, Jacob, and others. In reality God does not appear in these scenes in a visible way, but comes out of his unfathomable mystery to establish real communication with human beings: Abraham and Jacob experience his presence. Thus their words alone do not tell us how the disciples perceive the presence of the risen Jesus. What the words suggest is not so much that the risen one has appeared as a visible figure, but rather that he is acting within the disciples, creating conditions in which they can perceive his presence[38].

It is even more enriching to read what Paul says from his own experience, since he is the only witness who speaks directly of what happened to him[39]. He never describes or explains it in psychological terms. What has happened is a «grace». It is a gift, which he attributes to God's initiative or to the intervention of the risen one. He can only say that he has been «reached» by Christ Jesus; the risen one has taken control of him, has made him his own. In that experience he has «discovered the power of his resurrection». Paul is aware that the mystery of Jesus is being revealed to him. What he is experiencing is «the revelation of Jesus Christ». All the veils are being removed; Jesus becomes diaphanous and luminous to him. It is not an illusion. It is an amazing reality: «God has revealed his Son in me». The impact is so powerful that it causes a total reorientation of his life. His encounter with the risen one makes him «understand» the mystery of God and the reality of life in a radically new way. Paul is not the same person he was. He who persecuted the followers of the crucified Jesus is now proclaiming to everyone the Good News that he was trying to destroy before. A total revolution of values is being produced in his life. Paul feels himself as a «new person». His own transformation is the best testimony to what he has experienced. From his own experience he can proclaim to all: «it is no longer I who live, but it is Christ who lives in me»[40].

---

37 1 Cor 15:5-8. The Greek word *ofthe* is usually translated «he appeared». According to all the scholars, a better translation would be «he made himself visible» or «he let himself be seen».

38 This is the most commonly accepted scholarly interpretation (Michielis, Pelletier, Leon-Dufour, Kessler, Lorenzen, Deneken and others).

39 Paul speaks of his experience in 1 Cor 15:8-11; 1 Cor 9:1; Gal 1:13-23; Phil 3:5-14. My description is drawn from these texts, except where otherwise noted.

40 Gal 2:20.

Somewhat later, when Christians have already been living their faith in the risen Christ for forty or fifty years, we find stories filled with the delight that came from the disciples' first «encounters» with the risen Christ. These stories build on earlier traditions, reworked by each writer according to his own theological vision as a conclusion to his gospel about Jesus[41]. We see right away that they are not trying to give us detailed information about what happened forty or fifty years earlier. Indeed it is impossible to reconstruct the events on the basis of what they tell us[42]. Rather they are «catechetical resources» composed to help people explore different aspects of the resurrection of Christ, with important consequences for his followers. They did not spring up out of nothing, with no basis in reality, but represent a collection of experiences that the Christians could still remember: experiences of Jesus' unexpected presence after his death, their doubts and uncertainties in the first moments, their processes of conversion, reflections on the Scriptures that helped them understand what was happening. However the gospel writers are not trying to add more information to what they have already said about Jesus. Their purpose is to make everyone understand that his life and his death must be understood in a new dimension. The Jesus that their readers have been able to follow through their narrative, proclaiming and dying for the reign of God, is not dead. He has been raised by God and is still full of life, accompanying his followers.

41 These stories are found in all the gospels except Mark, and they form the conclusion to each writer's work (Matt 28; Luke 24; John 20-21). Some time later, someone added a brief summary of a few appearances to Mark's gospel (16:9-20). These descriptions have decisively shaped the ideas held by many Christians about the «appearances» of the risen Jesus.

42 It is practically impossible to harmonize the «information» they offer, because they do not agree on who witnessed the appearances, in what order, where, when, and under what circumstances. We can say nothing for certain about those questions. Nevertheless, those who have tried to trace the historical steps agree along some general lines, which can be summarized as follows: 1) It was an experience shared by different followers, and repeated in different circumstances. 2) The first experiences of the men probably took place in Galilee. 3) It is not clear whether the first appearance was to Peter or Mary Magdalene; a growing number of scholars contend that Mary's came first, but was later suppressed in the tradition (Hengel, Benoit, Schüssler Fiorenza, Theissen/Merz, Lorenzen, and others). 4) Some experiences may have occurred in the context of meals or dinners, where the memory of Jesus was more intense (Leon-Dufour). 5) The psycho-historical hypothesis of Lüdemann, which explains these experiences as a way of overcoming repressed guilt, especially by Peter (who denied Jesus) and Paul (who persecuted him), is highly debatable and not well supported by the texts. The same is true of J.D. Crossan's suggestion that these stories grew out of «feminine eulogies» or ritual mourning by a group of women: this position is based on a combination of hypotheses that cannot be easily justified.

What do these stories tell us about the experience that transformed Jesus' followers?[43] The core of the stories is a personal encounter with Jesus, full of life. That is the key: Jesus lives and is with them again; everything else comes later. The disciples have met the one who called them to serve the reign of God, the one they abandoned at the critical moment of his crucifixion. While they were still behind closed doors, filled with fear of the Jewish authorities, «Jesus came and stood among them»[44]; nothing and no one can stop the risen Jesus from returning to be with his followers. The women have met the one who defended their dignity and accepted them in his company: «Jesus met them and said, "Greetings!" And they came to him, took hold of his feet, and worshiped him»[45]; once more they can feel his intimate presence. Mary Magdalene has met the Teacher who cured her and whom she loves forever; once more, with tears in her eyes, she hears Jesus call her by name in his own voice; no one else has ever spoken to her that way[46]. No. That's probably not exactly how it happened, but it is the most expressive way possible to communicate what happens to those men and women when they experience Jesus again in their lives[47].

This encounter with the risen Jesus is a gift. The stories say repeatedly that the disciples don't take the initiative; Jesus does. It is he who comes to them full of life, pulling them out of their confusion and incredulity. The disciples are taken by surprise when Jesus lets himself be seen in the midst of that group of fearful men. Mary Magdalene is looking for a cadaver when Jesus calls to her. No one is expecting the risen Jesus. It is he who becomes present in their lives, beyond all their expectation. That is a «grace» of God, as Paul puts it.

The stories show it as a peacemaking experience, reconciling them to Jesus. The disciples know they have abandoned him. The sorrow in their hearts is not only sadness over Jesus' death; it is the sadness that comes from guilt. But the stories never show a sign of reproach or condemnation. Their encounter with Jesus is an experience of forgiveness. A meaningful greeting is repeatedly attrib-

---

43 The right way to read these texts is to see in their graphic images, not specific descriptions of what happened, but narrative processes that try somehow to evoke the experience of the risen Christ.

44 John 20:19.

45 Matt 28:9.

46 John 20:16.

47 Many scholars, following H. Kessler, consider the idea of «meeting» the most appropriate way to describe the central and irreducible experience that the disciples were feeling. We should make clear that it is not the disciples who meet Jesus. It is he who «goes out to meet them» and takes them by surprise.

uted to him: «Peace be with you»[48]. The risen one gives them the gift of God's peace and blessing; the disciples feel forgiven and accepted again into communion with him[49]. He is still the same Jesus. He is giving them the same peace that he gave to the sick and to sinners when he walked with them in Galilee. That is also the great gift that God offers to all his sons and daughters through the dead and risen Christ: forgiveness, peace, and resurrection.

According to the stories, their encounter with the risen Christ transforms his disciples at their very roots. Once more Jesus offers them his trust: their disloyalty has been cured by forgiveness, and they can begin a new life. All things are possible with Jesus. Their joy is so great that they cannot believe it. Jesus fills them with his spirit and liberates them from sadness, cowardice, and the fears that paralyze them[50]. The Emmaus story is an unequalled description of the way the disciples are transformed by accepting the risen Jesus into their life. They were walking sadly, but when they heard his words «their hearts were burning within them». They were crushed by Jesus' death, but when they experienced him full of life, they discovered that their hopes were not exaggerated but too small and limited. They had left the group of disciples, frustrated by all that had happened, but now they return to Jerusalem to tell the others «what had happened on the road»[51]. A new life is beginning for them.

This encounter with the risen one has to be communicated and shared with others. To meet him is to feel called to proclaim the Good News of Jesus. Above all the stories emphasize the experience of the Eleven. They are the beginning of the proclamation of Jesus Christ to all nations. There are as many as three versions of this «official» encounter. They were composed later on, in response to the needs of different communities[52]. In John, he tells them: «Peace be with you. As the Father has sent me, so I send you[53]». The Eleven must feel «sent» by Jesus. He doesn't say to what or to whom he is sending them; they are to do what they have seen him doing. Their mission is the same as the one he received from the

---

48 John 20:19, 21, 26; Luke 24:36.
49 According to Schillebeeckx, this forgiveness is «the experience which, in the light of their memory of Jesus' earthly life, becomes the matrix in which faith in Jesus as the risen one is born».
50 John 20:19-22.
51 This extraordinary story is in Luke 24:13-35. It deserves to be read and enjoyed slowly.
52 Of course the words attributed to the risen Jesus by each gospel writer are not the words he spoke in a particular appearance. Each editor uses his own language to emphasize different aspects of the mission that began to unfold after the paschal experience. John focuses on the «sending»; Luke characteristically focuses on their «witness»; Matthew on «teaching» and «baptizing».
53 John 20:21.

Father; their job is simply to extend his work into the future. In Luke, the Eleven are called to testify to this experience of the risen one: «You are witnesses of these things»[54]. These witnesses will be the core of a new movement to proclaim, in the name of the risen Jesus, «repentance and forgiveness of sins» to all nations[55]. Matthew in turn presents Jesus as the universal Lord of heaven and earth, who sends the Eleven «to make disciples of all nations, baptizing them»[56]. It is not just about proclaiming a doctrine, but raising up disciples who will learn to live with Jesus as their focal point, and who commit themselves to follow him faithfully through the act of baptism[57].

This evangelizing mission is not given only to the Eleven. All those who meet the risen Christ feel his call to share their own experience with others. He tells Mary Magdalene: «Go to my brothers and say to them…»; with amazing docility she stops holding on to him, goes to where the disciples are, and tells them: «I have seen the Lord»[58]. The disciples at Emmaus do the same, when their eyes are opened and they recognize the risen one: they return to Jerusalem with burning hearts and tell the others «what had happened to them on the road, and how he had been made known to them in the breaking of the bread»[59]. The second and third generation of Christians recall that it was the encounter with the living Jesus after his death that had sparked the contagious proclamation of the Good News of Jesus[60].

---

54 Luke 24:48.

55 Luke 24:47.

56 Matt 28:19-20. This very specific language reflects a missionary practice and liturgical customs that were established later by the Christian community.

57 At the end of Mark, Jesus tells them: «Go into all the world and proclaim the good news to the whole creation» (16:15).

58 John 20:17-18.

59 Luke 24:35.

60 Luke is the only gospel writer who tells of Jesus' «ascension» into heaven. In Matthew Jesus does not leave his disciples or say goodbye. The risen one is always with them: «I am with you always, to the end of the age» (28:20). John also does not speak of the «ascension». The risen one is with his disciples, filling them with inspiration: «Receive the Holy Spirit» (20:22). The «ascension» is a literary device imagined by Luke with a clear theological purpose. He offers two different versions. At the end of his gospel he presents it as a solemn culmination of Jesus' time on earth (Luke 24:50-53): the risen one is carried up into heaven (to the unfathomable world of God) while he is blessing the disciples. The disciples worship him for the last time, return to Jerusalem overflowing with joy, and stay there blessing God in the temple. Later the same Luke describes the «ascension» as the point of departure for the time of the Church and its evangelizing mission (Acts 1:6-11): Jesus «was lifted up and a cloud took him out of their sight», and they are told that he «will come in the same way as you saw him go into heaven». Here too they return to Jerusalem, not to the temple but to the «room upstairs», where they receive the Spirit that impels them into the evangelizing mission (Conzelmann, Lohfink, Leon-Dufour and others).

Was Jesus' tomb empty?

$\mathcal{S}$

All the gospel writers say that early in the morning after the crucifixion, some women went to the sepulchre where Jesus' body had been taken, and found it open and empty[61]. Naturally they recoiled in amazement. According to the story, an «angel» of God reassured them with the words: «Do not be alarmed. You are looking for Jesus of Nazareth, who was crucified. He has been raised; he is not here. Look, there is the place where they laid him. But go, tell his disciples and Peter that he is going ahead of you to Galilee; there you will see him»[62]. This story developed later. The earliest confessions and liturgical hymns that speak of Jesus' resurrection, or of his exaltation to the life of God, do not mention the empty tomb. Paul of Tarsus also does not speak of it in his letters. The empty tomb is not mentioned until the decade of the sixties. By all the evidence, it did not play a significant role in the birth of faith in the risen Jesus. It only gained importance when the report of it was integrated into other traditions that spoke of «appearances» by the risen Jesus.

It is hard to know whether things happened just as the gospels describe them. To begin with, it is hard to know for sure how and where Jesus was buried. The Romans usually left crucified bodies on the cross, available to the wild dogs and vultures, and later threw their remains into a common grave or dumping place without ritual or funerary honors. This final humiliation for the convict was part of the rite of crucifixion. Did Jesus end up there, in a common grave with many other convicts, expelled from life with no honor at all? Historically that seems unlikely. According to one tradition Jesus was buried by Jewish authorities who «asked Pilate to have him killed», and later «took him down from the tree and laid him in a tomb»[63]. This information is plausible. The authorities in Jerusalem

---

61 Mark 16:1-8; Matt 28:1-8; Luke 24:1-12; John 20:1-18. All the narratives probably draw on Mark, although John's version, which speaks of the appearance to Mary Magdalene, may be somewhat independent.

62 Mark 16:6-7. The bearer of this message from God is described differently in the different versions: «a young man, dressed in a white robe» (Mark); «an angel of the Lord» (Matthew); «two men in dazzling clothes» (Luke); «two angels in white» (John).

63 Acts 13:28-29. John's gospel says: «The Jews did not want the bodies left on the cross during the sabbath, especially because that sabbath was a day of great solemnity. So they asked Pilate to have the legs of the crucified men broken and the bodies removed» (John 19:31).

are concerned: the Passover festivities are beginning; those bodies, hanging on the cross, stain the earth and contaminate the whole city. Jesus and his two companions have to be buried in haste, without any ceremony, before the beginning of that solemn Passover sabbath.

But the gospels tell a different story. They recognize honestly that it was not the disciples who buried Jesus: they had all fled to Galilee. And the women could not have done it; they followed the burial «at a distance». But a good man named Joseph of Arimathea, unknown to the sources before this point, asks Pilate for authorization and buries him «in a tomb that had been hewn out of the rock». The identity and action of Joseph of Arimathea are not at all clear[64], but it might well have happened that way. We know that occasionally the authorities did authorize a more dignified and respectable burial by friends or relatives for a crucified body[65]. It is hard to know what happened. Certainly Jesus was not buried

with funeral honors. His followers were not there; the men were in hiding, and the women could only look on from a distance. It all happened very quickly, because it had to be done by nightfall. We don't know for sure who had possession of the body, the Roman soldiers or servants of the temple authorities. We don't know if he ended up in a common grave like so many others, or if Joseph of Arimathea was able to bury him in a tomb nearby[66].

---

64 The story appears in Mark 15:42-47; Matt 27:57-61; Luke 23:56-56; and John 19:38-42. According to Mark, Joseph of Arimathea was «a respected member» of the Sanhedrin; he does not appear as a follower of Jesus, but he also was «waiting expectantly for the kingdom of God». Luke describes him as «a good and righteous man» who did not agree with the other Sanhedrin members in condemning Jesus. Matthew goes an important step further, and tells us that he «was also a disciple of Jesus» (!), despite being «a rich man». John describes him as «a disciple of Jesus, though a secret one because of his fear of the Jews». We can also see a gradual development in the tradition about Jesus' burial. In Mark, Joseph of Arimathea did the best he could: «he wrapped the body in a linen cloth, and laid it in a tomb that had been hewn out of the rock». Luke specifies a tomb «where no one had ever been laid»; Matthew adds that it was «a new tomb» that Joseph himself «had hewn in the rock». In John the hasty burial has become dignified and even solemn: Nicodemus comes to help Joseph with «a mixture of myrrh and aloes, weighing about a hundred pounds» (!) Together they «took the body of Jesus and wrapped it with the spices in linen cloth, according to the burial custom of the Jews»; then they lay it in «a new tomb in which no one had ever been laid», which by some miracle is there «in a garden».

65 Philo mentions crucified bodies that «were brought down and handed over to their relatives so that they might receive burial honors» (*In Flaccum*, 83). Flavius Josephus persuaded Titus to hand over to him three crucified men, relatives of his, before they were dead; one of them even survived (*Autobiography*, 420-421). In addition, in 1968 at Giv'at ha-Mitvar north of Jerusalem, archeologists discovered the body of a man crucified in Jesus' time, named Yehojanan; the body was in a family ossuary, indicating that he was buried by family members.

66 Each of the possibilities is defended by some modern scholars. The one thing they agree on is that Jesus did not receive the care that usually goes with a burial (Benoit, Leon-Dufour, Vögtle, Parrot, Pannenberg and others).

For many researchers it is also unclear whether the women found Jesus' tomb empty. They ask, does this narrative reflect the memory of what happened, or is it a literary composition that tries to describe graphically what everyone believes: that if Jesus has risen, they should not look for him in the world of the dead? Certainly the event is plausible, and there are ample reasons to affirm it. If the story had been invented as realistic support for the resurrection of Jesus, it is hard to imagine choosing a group of women, whose testimony carried so little weight in Jewish society, as the protagonists; wouldn't that lead people to believe that something as fundamental as the resurrection was «a woman thing»? Besides, how could Christians proclaim the resurrection in the city of Jerusalem, where people could see if Jesus' body was still there in the tomb?[67].

A close reading of the narrative enables us to see it from a more than purely historical perspective. Indeed the key to the narrative is not the empty tomb, but the «revelation» by the messenger of God to the women. That scene apparently is not intended to present Jesus' empty tomb as a proof of his resurrection. In fact it does not inspire the women to faith, but to fear and trembling. What we need to hear is the voice of the angel, which naturally calls for faith. Only those who believe the explanation given by God's messenger, can discover the true meaning of the empty tomb[68].

So it is hard to establish an historically irrefutable conclusion. What we can say is that the story simply lays out in narrative terms what the first and second generations of Christians were already confessing: «Jesus of Nazareth, who was crucified, has been raised by God». The specific words attributed to the angel are a simple, almost literal repetition of the preaching of the first disciples[69]. This is another way of proclaiming God's victory over death, a graphic way of saying that God has opened the gates of *sheol* so that the crucified Jesus could escape

67 This argument was widely accepted after the study of H. von Campenhausen, but it does not carry too much weight because we do not know when the Christians began proclaiming the resurrection of Jesus in Jerusalem, or whether the tomb was accessible then. It is also interesting to note that people had been talking about the resurrection of the Baptist without feeling a need to show that his tomb was empty (Mark 6:14-16).

68 Finding Jesus' tomb empty would not be an irrefutable proof of his resurrection, because it could be explained in different ways. The body might have been stolen (as the soldiers were bribed to say in Matt 28:13); it could have been taken to another place (as Mary Magdalene first thought, according to John 20:15); the women might have gone to the wrong tomb; or the body could have been «revived» without entering into God's life (Lazarus' tomb was also left empty).

69 See the Acts 3:15; 4:10; 5:30 and others, especially 2:23-24: «You crucified [Jesus]... But God raised him up, having freed him from death, because it was impossible for him to be held in its power».

from the power of death. More than historical information, what we find in these stories is the preaching of the first Christians on the resurrection of Jesus. Everything leads to the conclusion that their faith in the risen Christ was inspired, not by the empty tomb but by the «encounter» with him, full of life after his death, that his followers experienced.

Then why was the story written? Some believe it was intended to explain the origins of a Christian celebration that took place beside Jesus' tomb at least once a year, going up in pilgrimage to that sacred place at sunrise on the day of Passover. The culmination of that celebration was a reading of this narrative. It proclaimed the Good News to the pilgrims at the tomb: «You are looking for Jesus of Nazareth, who was crucified. He has been raised; he is not here. Look, there is the place where they laid him». This is a suggestive hypothesis that cannot be dismissed, but it is very hard to prove[70]. A simpler explanation is that the story developed in popular circles, where the bodily resurrection of Jesus was understood in a material and physical way, as the continuation of his earthly body. The story held great fascination for these believers. What better place to grasp the victory of God over death than in an empty tomb?

In any case there is general agreement that the exegetical details do not resolve the issues raised by the narratives. The narratives certainly take as given the disappearance of the cadaver; without it the resurrection would be unimaginable in the biblical mentality[71]. The story of the empty tomb, as it is given at the end of each gospel, carries a message of great importance. It would be a mistake to look for the crucified Jesus in a tomb; he is not there; he does not belong to the world of the dead. It would be a mistake to worship and acknowledge him for what he did in the past. He has risen. He is more full of life than ever. He is still enlivening and guiding his followers. We must «go back to Galilee» and follow his steps: curing those who suffer, accepting those who are excluded, forgiving sinners, defending women and blessing children. We must offer meals open to everyone, and go into people's houses proclaiming peace; we must tell parables about the goodness of God, and denounce all religion that works against people's happiness; we must go on proclaiming the nearness of God's reign. A

---

70 This hypothesis is strongly defended by L. Schenke and Van Iersel. It is not widely accepted by other scholars.

71 It is not surprising that in our time some theologians, who confess their faith in the «fact» of Jesus' resurrection, still disagree on «how» it happened. Of course that debate is beyond the purpose and limits of the present book.

different, more friendly, abundant and just life is possible with Jesus. There is hope for everyone: «Go back to Galilee. He is going ahead of you; there you will see him»[72].

6

God has vindicated Jesus and done him justice

Jesus' execution raised doubts about his whole message and activity. The tragic end of his story raised serious questions for even his most faithful followers: who was right, Jesus or his executioners? Whose side was God on? It was not only Jesus who died on the cross. They had also killed his message, his plan for God's reign, and his aspirations for a new world. Only God could say whether or not he was right.

Even today, in the texts that have come down to us, we can see the joy of the first disciples on discovering that God has not abandoned Jesus. He has stepped forward to defend him. He has identified with him, forever dispelling any ambiguity. For Jesus' followers, the resurrection is not only a victory over death; it is God's own response, confirming his beloved Jesus and denying those who condemned him. This is the first thing the early preachers say, over and over, in the vicinity of the temple and the streets of Jerusalem: «You crucified and killed [Jesus] by the hands of those outside the law. But God raised him up…»; «Jesus Christ of Nazareth, whom you crucified, whom God raised up from the dead»; «The God of our ancestors raised up Jesus, whom you had killed by hanging him on a tree»[73]. By raising him, God has confirmed Jesus' life and message, his plan for God's reign, and everything he has done. What Jesus proclaimed in Galilee about the Father's tenderness and mercy is true: God is exactly as Jesus described him in the parables. Jesus' way of being and acting are true to the Father's will. His solidarity with those who suffer, his defense of the poor, his forgiveness for sinners, are exactly what God wanted. Jesus was right to seek a happier,

---

72 Scholars have interpreted the invitation to return to Galilee in different ways. A growing number understand Galilee in a symbolic sense: as the place of evangelically following Jesus (Beasley-Murray); as the point of departure for the Church's mission to all nations (Evans); as a symbol of the Christian life lived from day to day (Leon-Dufour); as the place of the *parousia* (Lohmeyer, Lichfoot, Marxsen in part).

73 This formula of «contrast», between their action and God's reaction, is a central element in the early preaching (Acts 2:23-24; 4:10; 5:30 and other passages).

more dignified life for all. That is the greatest desire God holds in his heart. It is the way of life that pleases the Father. It is the pathway to life.

God has not only vindicated Jesus, he has also done him justice. God was not passively, silently watching what they were doing to Jesus; he has returned in all its fullness the life that was so unjustly taken from him. In the resurrection Jesus' followers can see God's wonderful response to the abuses that were committed against him. Evil has a great deal of power, but only to the point of death; the Jewish authorities and powerful Romans have killed Jesus, but they could not annihilate him. Beyond death, there is no power besides the unfathomable love of God. The torturers cannot triumph over their victims.

But why did Jesus have to die? If God loves him so, why has he let him die this way? Why so much humiliation and suffering? What good can ever come from the crime that was committed against him? It took the Christians a long time to find some explanation for something so scandalous and unjust. Around 40 or 42 A.D. they developed a strange formula: «Christ died for our sins in accordance with the Scriptures»[74]. But what does the death of one man have to do with all the sinful people of all times? Death is the end of life; how can others be saved by one man's death?

The resurrection forces the early believers to explore Jesus' death in a new light. They have just discovered that on his death, Jesus entered into God's «glory». He died trusting in the Father, and the Father has accepted him into his unfathomable life. What happened to Jesus was a «death-resurrection». He didn't die into emptiness and nothingness, but into full communion with God. The Father has not saved him *from* death, but *in* his death. We might say that in raising him, God has begotten him as his most beloved son. The early Christians found it perfectly natural to interpret Jesus' resurrection in light of a well known psalm: «by raising Jesus, as also it is written in the second psalm, "You are my Son; today I have begotten you"»[75]. In rising, Jesus is begotten by God into life.

This God who embraces Jesus in the midst of death has never really been away from him. Now in the resurrection we see that while Jesus was dying in agony God was with him, upholding him with faithful love, suffering with him and for him, totally identified with him. The Father does not want to see Jesus suffer. That was never his will. How could he will the unjust destruction of an innocent person? How could he will such a tragic end for his most beloved son?

74 1 Cor 15:3.
75 Acts 13:33.

The Father's will is that Jesus remain faithful to the end, that he continue to identify with all the world's unfortunate people, that he seek God's reign and its justice for everyone. The Father does not will an ignominious death for Jesus, and Jesus does not offer his blood expecting it to please him. The early Christians never thought anything like that. Father and Son are united in the crucifixion, not for the sake of blood and destruction, but in confronting the ultimate consequences of evil. The suffering is evil; the crucifixion is a crime. No one wants it but the Jewish authorities and the representatives of the Empire, who are closed to the reign of God. Jesus does not want them to kill him; he resists drinking that absurd, unjust «cup» of suffering. But he will go to his death if need be, to be faithful to God's reign; everyone will see the depth of his trust in the Father and his love for humanity. For his part, the Father does not want them to kill his beloved Son: nothing they do could hurt him more. But he will let him be sacrificed if need be. He will not intervene to destroy the people who are crucifying Jesus; he will go on loving the world, and he will reveal to everyone the unfathomable depth of his «foolish love» for humanity.

The first Christians said this in amazement: «God so loved the world that he gave his Son»[76]. On the cross, no one is making an offering to God so that he will show a more benevolent face to humankind. It is God who is offering what he loves most: his own Son. His love comes first. Paul is clear about this: «God proves his love for us in that while we still were sinners Christ died for us»[77]. There can be no more unequivocal way for God to reveal his love. He doesn't stay his hand, even from what he loves most. «He who did not withhold his own Son, but gave him up for all of us, will he not with him also give us everything else?»[78]. This love of God is unheard of. He doesn't do or say anything while Jesus is dying. He doesn't intervene. He respects what they are doing to his Son. He doesn't grant Jesus' anguished plea in Gethsemane. He simply suffers the death of his beloved Son out of his love for human beings, who would otherwise be lost forever. This «crucifixion-resurrection» is the supreme revelation of God's love. No one could have imagined it. In the «crucified-risen» Jesus God is *with* us, thinking only *about* us, suffering *like* us, dying *for* us[79].

---

76 John 3:16.
77 Rom 5:8.
78 Rom 8:32.
79 In different ways, with different nuances, today's theologians generally explore the mystery of the cross from this perspective of the sorrow it means for God (Pannenberg, Moltmann, Rahner, Kitamori, Sobrino, Durrwell).

God's silence at the cross never meant he was abandoning the crucified one, or in complicity with the crucifiers. God was with Jesus. That is why, at his death, Jesus was raised in God's arms. The resurrection shows that God was with him in a real way, not intervening against his torturers but assuring his final triumph. That is the most amazing thing about God's love: it has the power to annihilate evil without destroying the evil people. He does justice for Jesus without destroying the men who crucified him. Paul says it wonderfully: «In Christ God was reconciling the world to himself, not counting their trespasses against them»[80]. All this seems incredible. The message of the cross is «foolishness». Paul knows that, for it has brought him constant rejection.

> For Jews demand signs and Greeks desire wisdom, but we preach Christ crucified, a stumbling block to Jews and foolishness to Gentiles, but to those who are the called, both Jews and Greeks, Christ the power of God and the wisdom of God. For God's foolishness is wiser than human wisdom, and God's weakness is stronger than human strength[81].

In that cross which seems like «foolishness» to us, we see the supreme «wisdom» of God finding a way to save the world. In that crucified Christ who seems like «weakness» and impotence, we see the saving «power» of God. That is why the Christians say Christ died for our sins «in accordance with the Scriptures». God's plan has been fulfilled on the cross. «It was necessary» for Christ to suffer. With God it has to be that way, for in his incredible foolishness he loves his children to the end.

The early Christians draw on different models to explain the «foolishness» of the crucifixion in some way. They describe it as a «sacrifice of atonement», a «new covenant» between God and humankind, sealed with the blood of Jesus; they like to compare his death with that of the «suffering servant» in the book of Isaiah, a righteous and innocent man who carries the guilt and sin of others and thus becomes their salvation[82]. We need to understand this language well, because it never denies or distorts the gratuitous love of God which Jesus proclaimed so forcefully.

---

80 2 Cor 5:19.
81 1 Cor 1:22-25.
82 Especially Isa 53:1-12.

God does not appear as one who requires Jesus' suffering and destruction in order to satisfy his honor and justice, or to enable him to «forgive» human beings. Jesus does not appear as using his suffering to influence God, to get him to look on the world more benevolently. It never occurs to the early Christian communities to put it that way. If God required the blood of an innocent person to save humanity, the image of the Father that Jesus portrayed would have been totally false. He would be a «vengeful» God who does not forgive gratuitously, an implacable creditor who cannot save anyone until the debt owed to him is paid. If God were like that, who could love him with all their heart and soul and strength? The best response to such a rigorous and threatening God would be to act cautiously and defensively, making sure to keep him satisfied with all kinds of rituals and sacrifices.

God also does not appear as taking out his wrath on Jesus. The Father never holds him responsible for sins he has not committed; he never thinks of his Son as a «substitute» for sinners. How could a just God impute sins to Jesus that he has not committed?[83]. Jesus is innocent; sin has not entered into his heart. He is not suffering any punishment from God on the cross. He is suffering the rejection of those who oppose God's reign. He is not a victim of the Father, but of Caiaphas and Pilate. Jesus bears the suffering unjustly inflicted on him by human beings, and the Father bears the suffering of his beloved Son. That is what we read in a writing attributed to Peter: «He committed no sin... When he was abused, he did not return abuse; when he suffered, he did not threaten; but he entrusted himself to the one who judges justly. He himself bore our sins in his body on the cross»[84].

It is love, not suffering, that gives redemptive value to the punishment of the cross. What saves humanity is not some «mysterious» saving power in blood spilled before God. Suffering in itself is evil; it has no redemptive power. It does not please God to see Jesus suffer. The only salvific thing about Calvary is the unfathomable love of God, incarnate in the suffering and death of his Son. There is no saving power outside of that love.

---

83 It is hard to interpret one short line from Paul: «For our sake he made him to be sin who knew no sin, so that in him we might become the righteousness of God» (2 Cor 5:21). He probably intends to emphasize Jesus' solidarity with sinners. Of course we should not take this sentence too literally, because it starts out by affirming Jesus' absolute innocence.

84 1 Pet 2:22-24. Sins are something that cannot be carried on one's body. The writer is using an image to express the great weight that falls upon Jesus in his solidarity with those who reject him and God's reign.

Suffering is still evil, but precisely for that reason, it becomes the most solid and real way to live and express love within human experience. That is why the first Christians saw the crucified Jesus as the most realistic and extreme expression of God's unconditional love for humanity, the mysterious and unfathomable sign of his forgiveness, compassion, and redemptive tenderness. Only the incredible love of God can explain what happened on the cross. Only in the luminous shadow of the cross could the Christians make this transcendent and miraculous affirmation: «God is love»[85]. This is Paul's great insight when he writes so passionately about «the Son of God, who loved me and gave himself for me»[86].

[85] 1 John 4:8, 16.
[86] Gal 2:20.

Exploring the Identity of Jesus

It is hard to imagine the impact that Jesus' resurrection had on his closest follow-ers. His execution on the cross had plunged them into confusion. Who was right? The beloved Prophet whose presence, words and actions had made the reign of God real to them? Or the people who had delivered him up to death in God's name, and to save their own honor? The resurrection confirms the belief that Jesus himself had instilled in their hearts as they walked around Galilee: God is with him. Everyone has turned away from him at the moment of his cru-cifixion. Everyone but God. The God whom Jesus trusted so deeply has con-firmed that he was right; God has taken his side.

Who is this Jesus, through whom the disciples have so powerfully experienced the saving nearness of God, and whose death and resurrection showed his total identification with God? In the early stages of faith in Jesus Christ, the disciples were especially concerned with answering one question: who is it that they were living with in Galilee? Who is this Jesus whose life brought so much hope to their hearts, and whose death, ending in resurrection, now offers them hope for eter-nal life in God? What mystery is hidden in this man, whom death could not overcome? What is the real identity of the crucified one, whom God has raised by filling him with his own life? What should they call him? How should they proclaim him?

It is hard to know all the questions, hopes and expectations that Jesus inspired among those who came to him and followed him most closely in Galilee. There is more here than curiosity and momentary enthusiasm. It is warm, heartfelt loyalty. They don't fully understand their Teacher's message or his actions, and he often criticizes their «little faith». But for them Jesus is not John the Baptist come back to life; he is not Elijah or Jeremiah or any other prophet, as some peo-ple apparently thought[1]. Who is he, really? How can he talk with such intimate trust about God as his «Father», suggesting that he has a unique, incomparable relationship with God? What is it about his acts of healing that shows the saving nearness of God so powerfully? What mysterious power enables this prophet to cast out the Evil One by the Spirit of God? Where does he get his certainty that God belongs to the poor, the hungry, the last, the helpless? How does he dare, not only to proclaim God as a Father merciful and compassionate to all, but even to grant forgiveness in God's name? What enables him to teach the true will of God, without deferring to the law of Moses as the central, absolute and indis-

1 Mark 8:27-30; Matt 16:13-20; Luke 9:18-21.

putable authority for the Jewish people? How can he hold God up to everyone so directly, presenting himself as a prophet and bringer of God's ultimate salvation?

Out of their experience of Jesus' resurrection, his followers begin looking back over his whole life[2]. That surprising, fascinating life which they knew up close and now treasure in their hearts, is suddenly opening up to them in greater depth. The resurrection has shed a new light on what they knew of Jesus through everyday contact, and given it new and unexpected meaning. The personal characteristics they remember so vividly are coming clear in all their authentic truth, as Christian communities gather around the first witnesses; now they are seeing things that they could not understand before, in the light of their paschal experience.

According to the earliest gospel, the young man «dressed in white» who tells the women that Jesus has risen also confers this task on them: «Go, tell his disciples and Peter that he is going ahead of you to Galilee; there you will see him, just as he told you»[3]. These words seem to invite readers to go back to Galilee in order to «see» the Risen One. To go back to the beginning and reflect, from the perspective of the resurrection, on all that they remember of Jesus, his activity and his message. It is the resurrection experience that can reveal the real identity of Jesus and the profound content of his message and activity[4].

Indeed that is the goal of the gospel writers: to read the story of Jesus with new eyes. To re-live what they experienced in his presence, this time in the light of his resurrection. Impelled by faith in the risen Jesus they begin recalling his words, not as the legacy of a dead teacher who now belongs forever to the past, but as the words of one who «lives» among them and still talks to them with the power of his Spirit. Their writings are not a collection of sayings spoken by a famous rabbi in another time, but the message of one raised by God, who is here and now conveying his spirit and his life to the communities of believers that follow him[5]. The sayings collected here must be heard as words that represent

---

2 In revisiting Jesus' life from the perspective of his resurrection, the disciples are thinking about the Jesus they knew in Galilee — not the «historical Jesus» whom modern scholars attempt, with varying degrees of success, to recover or «reconstruct». The memory of those who knew him as «Good News» during his life, now interpreted in the light of the resurrection that followed his death, becomes the starting point of christological faith.

3 Mark 16:7.

4 This is the view of important scholars who study the origin and narrative development of the gospels (Rhoads, Dewey, Michie, Kingsbury, Aletti and others).

5 The community of believers is so convinced that Jesus is alive, that they feel entirely free to attribute to him words that express his spirit even though they are not the exact words he spoke in Galilee.

«spirit and life», «words of eternal life»[6], conveying the happiness and peace of the Risen One.

The gospels recall more than Jesus' words. They also tell about his actions and his life. They are not just the biography of a great man from the past, nor a historical or psychological portrait of him. That's not their purpose[7]. The purpose of the gospels is to reveal the saving presence of God, who raised Jesus but who was acting in his life even before that. When Jesus healed the sick, he was conveying to them the power, the health, and the life of the same God who has now revealed all his saving power by raising Jesus from death. When he defended the poor, victims of so much injustice, he was demanding the justice of the same God who defended him by raising him from among the dead. When he accepted «sinners and tax collectors» at his table, he was offering them the same forgiveness and peace of God that the disciples are now enjoying in the presence of the Risen One.

This new view of Jesus, inspired by faith in a God who so completely identifies with him that he raised him from among the dead, opens an unexpected perspective for his Galilean followers. They can see God breaking in through the story of Jesus[8]. The story they tell is a story of God, living in the flesh of his Son. A story full of conflicts and challenges, but especially of promises and hopes. The gospel writers are telling the story of Jesus as «the central event of the history of the world». From now on, the past and the future are tied to this fragment of history in which we can clearly see the face of God incarnate in Jesus[9].

417

6 John 6:63.68.
7 Indeed they pay little attention to such typically biographical factors as education and physical characteristics. Except for some notes in Luke's gospel, they also are not much concerned with placing Jesus' activity in the specific socio-political context of his time.
8 According to D. Marguerat, «in some ways we can read the whole gospel as one long narrative about an appearance of the Risen One».
9 From the Christian perspective, this process of re-reading Jesus in the light of his resurrection is not only a literary act; it is part of the process by which God reveals himself in human words. As believers we recognize the action of the Spirit of the Risen One in this process, guiding the disciples step by step toward a fuller understanding of Jesus.

The Gospel of Mark

Mark isn't writing a «life of Jesus» in the same way Tacitus or Suetonius wrote histories of the emperors. As he says in the title of his short gospel, what Mark wants is to proclaim «the good news of Jesus Christ, the Son of God»[10]. Jesus' activity brings in an element of «suspense» from the very beginning. His behavior raises questions: «What is this?» «Who then is this?»[11]. His disciples don't understand him. His adversaries ask him for a «sign from heaven», not realizing that Jesus himself is the sign. The demons know his secret, but Jesus tells them to be still; they don't know enough to worship his mystery and his saving action. Mark shows the path that leads to faith in Jesus as the true Messiah and Son of God.

The mystery of Jesus *as Messiah or Christ* is first revealed in the region of Caesarea Philippi. There are different rumors about him: some say he is John the Baptist returned to life, some think Elijah, or maybe one of the prophets. When Jesus asks his disciples, «But who do you say that I am?» Peter replies for them all: «You are the Messiah»[12]. Peter is thinking of a Messiah who will lead the liberation of Israel, destroying all its adversaries. Jesus then patiently begins teaching them that his destiny is to suffer an ignominious death and then rise again. He is not the powerful and glorious Messiah they are expecting. This Messiah will follow the way of the cross; he will become the last and the servant of all, «for the Son of Man came not to be served but to serve, and to give his life a ransom for many»[13]. His disciples will understand his true messianic identity when they take up the cross, learn to be the last, the servants of all, and follow him to crucifixion. His mystery will be revealed to them on the cross[14].

The mystery of Jesus *as Son of God* is revealed to readers from the beginning. God himself introduces Jesus as his Son. Jesus has just come out of the Jordan river where he was baptized, when he sees the heavens torn apart and hears a

---

10 Mark 1:1.
11 Mark 1:27; 4:41; 6:3.
12 Mark 8:29.
13 Mark 10:45.
14 Jesus' teaching about the way through suffering and humiliation to death-resurrection, and the disciples' failure to understand, are found in three sections: 8:31-34; 9:30-35; and 10:32-44.

voice: «You are my Son, the Beloved; with you I am well pleased»[15]. Apparently no one else is present. God's decisive action will have to come before he can be confessed as Son of God, but Jesus is already acting as such «in secret». Later the voice from heaven is heard again, on a mountaintop where Jesus is «transfigured». This time his closest disciples are there. They also hear the voice: «This is my Son, the Beloved; listen to him!»[16]. God himself invites them to see Jesus as his Son, and to hear what he is teaching them about the way of the cross and resurrection. But when they come down from the mountain, Jesus tells them «to tell no one about what they had seen, until after the Son of Man had risen from the dead»[17]. Then they would be able to understand and confess his mystery. Only at the end can a pagan centurion, watching Jesus die abandoned by everyone, confess: «Truly this man was God's Son!»[18]. It is precisely in the abandonment of the crucifixion that one can confess Jesus, not as the powerful Son of an omnipotent God, but as a crucified Son, given by his Father out of love for humanity.

It is not easy, and Mark knows that. As the crucifixion approaches, the disciples who have followed Jesus to Jerusalem all «deserted him and fled»[19]. The women now take the place of the men. They follow Jesus to the cross. But after his death, when they are told that the crucified one «has risen», the women run away from the tomb; «for terror and amazement had seized them, and they said nothing to anyone, for they were afraid»[20]. It is a fearful thing to explore the mystery of Jesus' death and resurrection. It is easy to leave him and flee. But to help us believe in him as the true Messiah and Son of God, Mark invites his readers to stand before «the crucified Jesus» and before his «empty tomb». That is where God reveals his Son to us.

This life of Jesus the Messiah, Son of God, who ends up crucified by his adversaries but raised by God, is a proclamation of «God's Good News». Mark summarizes his message by saying that Jesus proclaimed: «The time is fulfilled, and the kingdom of God has come near; repent, and believe in the good news»[21]. In Mark's narrative it is Jesus' actions, more than his words, that bring God's reign close to the people: «hearing all that he was doing, they came to him in great

419

15 Mark 1:11.
16 Mark 9:7.
17 Mark 9:9-10.
18 Mark 15:39.
19 Mark 14:50.
20 Mark 16:8.
21 Mark 1:14-15.

numbers»[22]. Filled with the Spirit of God, his life becomes a source of life and healing. As he walks through Galilee, the evil spirits come out of people and run away[23]. By his authority as God's Son he offers God's free forgiveness: «Son, your sins are forgiven»[24]. His saving power cleanses lepers, gives sight to the blind, and gives life back to Jairus' daughter[25]. Jesus is the Son of God who brings God's salvation — in contrast to the Roman emperor, who is called the «son of God» (*divi filius*) although he cannot save. Jesus, the Messiah and Beloved Son, is God's Good News because he brings salvation.

2

The Gospel of Matthew

420   After the fall of Jerusalem in 70 A.D., after the destruction of the temple by the Romans, the Pharisaic rabbis are doing their best to restore Judaism with the law of Moses at its center. Meanwhile Jesus' followers are establishing Christian communities among the Jews of the diaspora. This often leads to tensions and conflicts. It is at this crucial moment that Matthew wants to confess what Jesus' followers are discovering in him by the light of the resurrection. Matthew is convinced that the Jesus whom the disciples remember, and the risen Jesus present in the Christian communities, are one and the same. Thus he proclaims that Jesus is not a false prophet executed on the cross, but the true «Messiah» in whom the history of Israel is fulfilled; not a failed rabbi, but the «new Moses» bringing a new Law of life. Jesus is giving birth to the «new Israel», the Church brought together by the Risen One; in place of the destroyed temple, Jesus, the beloved Son of God, is the new presence of God in the world. Let us look at some of the most important features of Matthew's gospel.

Jesus is the *Messiah* (the Christ) in whom the history of Israel is fulfilled. His resurrection makes that clear. There's no need to wait for anyone else. By raising Jesus, God has identified with his life and teaching, dispelling the doubts that might arise among the Jews who accept Jesus or those who reject him. Jesus is the fullness, the fulfillment, the realization of Israel's hopes. He alone deserves

22 Mark 3:8.
23 Mark 1:27; 5:13.
24 Mark 2:1-12.
25 Mark 5:37-43.

to be called by the messianic titles of the Jewish tradition: Son of David, Messiah, Son of Man. Matthew's purpose is to describe the messianic identity of Jesus in terms that his Jewish readers can understand. Jesus belongs to the family of David[26]; he was born in Bethlehem, where the Messiah would be born according to the Jewish scriptures[27]; and his life fulfills the prophecies remembered by Israel[28].

Just when the Pharisees are working to restore Judaism on the basis of Mosaic law after the destruction of the temple, Matthew is describing Jesus as the only «Teacher»[29] — not only an interpreter of the law of Moses, but the «new Moses», bringing a new and definitive Law of God[30]. This is why Matthew organizes the essential message of Jesus in five great discourses, which serve as the five structural pillars of his gospel[31]. Together they make up the «new Law», ratified by the God who has raised Jesus; this is the message that the risen Lord tells his disciples to teach people to obey, because he has commanded it[32]. Matthew recommends this Law of Jesus Christ not only to the communities addressed in his gospel, but to all nations. It can be summarized in three formulations:

The so-called golden rule: «In everything do to others as you would have them do to you; for this is the law and the prophets»[33].

The double commandment of love: «"You shall love the Lord your God with all your heart, and with all your soul, and with all your mind". This is the greatest and first commandment. And a second is like it: "you shall love your neighbor as yourself"»[34].

«The weightier matters of the law: justice and mercy and faith»[35].

---

26 Matthew's gospel begins with «the genealogy of Jesus the Messiah, the Son of David, the Son of Abraham», in whom the history of the chosen people is fulfilled (1:1-17).

27 Matt 2:1-12.

28 In telling the story of Jesus, Matthew repeatedly points out that it is all happening to fulfill the Scriptures. There are more than seventy citations from the Old Testament in his gospel.

29 Matt 23:8.

30 In the gospel of the infancy, Matthew attributes some apparently Mosaic features to Jesus: he was saved from a massacre of children (2:13-14), came out of Egypt (2:14-15), and «will save his people» (1:21).

31 The five are the *discourse on the mountain* (5-7), which hands down the law and the spirit that guide those who are entering into the reign of God; the *discourse on mission* (10), to guide those who are sent to proclaim God's reign; the *discourse of parables* (13), on diverse aspects of God's reign; the *discourse on the Church* (18) and on life in the community of disciples; and the *eschatological discourse* (24-25) on hope, vigilance, and the final judgment.

32 Matt 28:20a.

33 Matt 7:12.

34 Matt 22:37-40.

35 Matt 23:23.

Matthew describes Jesus as the Messiah, Son of God, who *convokes* or calls together the «new Israel». His story emphasizes the failure of the Messiah's own people to understand and accept him. When Jesus was born in Bethlehem, Herod «was frightened, and all Jerusalem with him»[36]. When he goes up to Jerusalem at the end of his life, the temple leaders condemn him and the people of the city demand his crucifixion[37]. Matthew's gospel also speaks explicitly about the «Church»[38], whose root meaning is «convocation», «congregation», «assembly». It is the community formed by those who hear Jesus' call to follow him; it is not a new rabbinical school, not the religion of one specific people or race like Israel. It is a community open to a universal mission[39]. This Church belongs to Christ. He is building it on Peter, its «rock» or foundation. In this Church everyone is a «disciple», because Christ is the one Teacher from whom all must learn. Everyone is a «brother or sister», because they are sons and daughters of the one Father in heaven[40]. In this Church everyone must care especially for the «little ones», because they need it most[41]. The Church as a community must practice loving correction and unconditional forgiveness[42].

For Matthew, Jesus is not only a prophet or messenger of God. He is God's Son. Matthew explains this in a typically Jewish way. Jesus is more than David, more than Solomon, more than the prophets and popular sages: «Something greater than Jonah is here!»[43]. «Something greater than Solomon is here!»[44]. Jesus is «the Son» who knows the Father as no one else can, and reveals him to whomever he wants[45]. But perhaps an even more characteristic feature of Matthew is his description of Jesus as the «new presence of God» in the world. In the biblical tradition, God is with his chosen people and lives in their midst. His presence in the temple is the center of Israel's religious experience. After the destruction of the temple Matthew proclaims that Jesus, the one raised by God, has taken its

---

36 Here Matthew's perspective (2:3) contrasts sharply with that of Luke, who shows Jesus being joyfully accepted in the temple (2:22-32).

37 Matt 27:25.

38 Matt 16:18; 18:17.

39 Matt 28:19.

40 Matt 23:8-12.

41 Matt 18:10-14.

42 Matt 18:19-20; 21-22.

43 Matt 12:41.

44 Matt 12:42.

45 This saying has a surprisingly Johannine flavor: «All things have been handed over to me by my Father; and no one knows the Son except the Father; and no one knows the Father except the Son and anyone to whom the Son chooses to reveal him» (Matt 11:27).

place. Jesus is the new presence of God in the world. In fulfillment of Isaiah's prophecy, Mary's son will be called «*Emmanuel,* which means "God is with us"»[46]. In the resurrection, God is so identified with Jesus that only he can be called *Emmanuel,* «God with us». In reading his gospel, Matthew wants us to see the presence of God among us in Jesus and in all his actions: we hear the Word of God in his words, we feel God's saving Love in his actions. That is why Matthew quotes a promise from Jesus that is becoming reality in the community of his followers: «For where two or three are gathered in my name, I am there among them»[47]. His gospel also ends with an unforgettable promise of the Risen One: «And remember, I am with you always, to the end of the age»[48]. A new age is beginning; Jesus is the saving presence of God in the world forever.

3

The Gospel of Luke

The protagonist in Luke's narrative is also the «Messiah» and «Lord» confessed by the followers of Jesus, but Luke describes him above all as «Savior». That is how the angel of the Lord announces his birth: «To you is born this day in the city of David a Savior, who is the Messiah, the Lord»[49]. When Simeon takes the baby in his arms, he sings gratefully to God: «Master, now you are dismissing your servant in peace, according to your word; for my eyes have seen your salvation»[50]. Jesus is the salvation of God. In him we can see, touch, grasp the salvation that God offers[51]. Before he is born, Jesus' presence makes John «leap for joy» in his mother's womb[52]. At his birth the angel brings «good news of great joy for all the people»[53]. The life of Jesus the Savior spreads joy wherever he goes. His

---

46 Matt 1:23.
47 Matt 18:20. These words may be a reference to a Jewish text that said: «Where two or three are gathered to study Torah, there is the *Shekina* [Presence] of God». Now Jesus makes God present wherever the new law is being studied and lived.
48 Matt 28:20.
49 Luke 2:11.
50 Luke 2:30.
51 Earlier, Zechariah blesses God for the birth of his son John, who «will go before the Lord to prepare his ways, to give knowledge of salvation to his people by the forgiveness of their sins» (Luke 1:77).
52 Luke 1:44.
53 Luke 2:11. When Matthew writes, the «joy» and «peace» of which the angels sing have already been felt by the disciples at their encounter with the risen Lord (24:36-43).

healings inspire great praise: «God has looked favorably on his people!»[54]. When he arrives in Jerusalem for the last time, «the whole multitude of the disciples began to praise God joyfully with a loud voice for all the deeds of power that they had seen»[55]. Luke also emphasizes another characteristic aspect of his theology: Jesus is the «today» of salvation. God always offers salvation in Jesus today, now. «To you is born *this day*… a Savior»[56]. «*Today* this scripture has been fulfilled» which promised a liberating Messiah; Jesus' saving presence brings Good News to the poor, release to the captives, sight to the blind, freedom to the oppressed, and the year of the Lord's favor[57]. This is also why Jesus could say, visiting Zacchaeus, «*Today* salvation has come to this house»[58], and he could promise the good thief on the cross, «t*oday* you will be with me in Paradise»[59]. We are always being offered salvation in Jesus, who was raised by God.

This salvation is the fruit of God's mercy. Luke describes Jesus as the «incarnation» of God's mercy. In Zechariah's blessing we are promised that «By the tender mercy of our God, the dawn from on high will break upon us, to give light to those who sit in darkness and in the shadow of death, to guide our feet into the way of peace»[60]. This mercy of God, enfleshed in Jesus, can be seen in different ways. We see it first in the *forgiveness* he offers sinners: «The Son of Man came to seek out and to save the lost»[61]. Jesus is like the father in the parable who accepts his lost children and celebrates festive meals with them; like the shepherd who seeks the lost sheep, and celebrates with his friends when he finds them; like the poor village woman who seeks and joyfully finds her lost penny[62]. He offers friendship and forgiveness to sinners and tax collectors[63], and asks God to forgive those who are nailing him to the cross: «Father, forgive them, for they do not know what they are doing»[64]. Jesus also shows God's mercy in his «healings», which are signs both of God's saving power and his compassion. He is like the good Samaritan who is «moved with pity», «comes near», and merci-

---

54 Luke 7:16; 13:17; 18:43.
55 Luke 19:37-38.
56 Luke 2:11.
57 Luke 4:21.
58 Luke 19:9.
59 Luke 23:43.
60 Luke 1:78-79.
61 Luke 19:10.
62 Luke 15:1-32.
63 The scenes of acceptance toward the sinful woman (7:36-50), and Zacchaeus, the chief tax collector (19:1-10), are unforgettable.
64 Luke 23:34.

fully cures the wounds of the man fallen by the roadside[65]. More than the other writers, Luke emphasizes Jesus' compassion for women: he liberates Mary Magdalene and others from their demons[66]; has compassion on the widow at Nain[67]; and consoles the women who mourn for him on his way to the cross[68].

The people did not fully understand him in Galilee, but now that Jesus has been raised by God's Spirit, Luke encourages everyone to see that the same Spirit was always giving him life. Jesus is the «Bearer of the Spirit of God». The Holy Spirit, giver of life, is made present in the world through him. John the Baptist is «filled with the Holy Spirit» even before his birth[69]. Jesus is conceived by the Holy Spirit in the Virgin Mary, as the angel tells her: «The Holy Spirit will come upon you, and the shadow of the Most High will overshadow you; therefore the child to be born will be holy; he will be called Son of God»[70]. The Savior of the world does not come into human history as the fruit of the love between husband and wife, but as the fruit of God's love for humanity. The Messiah, Son of God, is not born as an expression and confirmation of the human love between Mary and Joseph, but as an expression and confirmation of God's love for us[71]. It is this same Spirit, which gave rise to Jesus' presence in the world, that «descended on him in bodily form» while he prayed after his baptism[72]. This Spirit leads him into the desert and guides him with its «power» as he walks through Galilee[73]. Anointed by this Spirit, he spends his life proclaiming the Good News of liberation to the poor, oppressed, and humiliated[74]. Later, in the light of the resurrection, Luke is able to formulate more deeply the memory Jesus has left to his followers: «how God anointed Jesus of Nazareth with the Holy Spirit and with power, how he went about doing good and healing all who were oppressed by the devil, for God was with him»[75].

Chapter 15

425

---

65 Luke 10:33-37.
66 Luke 8:2.
67 Luke 7:13.
68 Luke 23:27-31.
69 Luke 1:15.
70 Luke 1:35.
71 In announcing the birth of the Savior, the Messiah, the Lord, the angel tells the shepherds: «to you is born this day»... The child is not born to Mary and Joseph as the fruit of conjugal love. He is born to us all.
72 Luke 3:22.
73 Luke 4:1,14.
74 Luke 4:7-20.
75 These are Luke's words, not in his gospel but in the Acts of the Apostles 10:38.

The Gospel of John

John's gospel portrays the life of Jesus in a different way from the earlier gospels. This, the author explains, is because in his narrative the disciples are «remembering» Jesus' words and actions in the light of his resurrection. An example is Jesus' prophetic intervention in the temple: «After he was raised from the dead, his disciples remembered that he had said this, and they believed the scripture and the word that Jesus had spoken»[76]. The same thing occurs in the solemn welcome Jesus receives on entering Jerusalem: «His disciples did not understand these things at first; but when Jesus was glorified, then they remembered that these things had been written of him and had been done to him»[77]. This «remembering» is not the result of their effort alone. The Holy Spirit is working in them. John calls the Holy Spirit the «Paraclete», the «Advocate». The Father sends it to the disciples «to remind you of all that I have said to you»[78]. It is the «Spirit of truth» who will faithfully «testify on my behalf»[79]. This Spirit «will guide you into all the truth»[80]. Thus the writer wants us to read his story as the result of his disciples looking back on Jesus in the light of the resurrection. That looking is guided by the Spirit of the Risen One, and enables them to grasp the «whole truth» enclosed in Jesus.

Jesus is the *Word of God made flesh*. The prologue tells us that this is the framework in which we are to read the narrative. The story that will be told in the gospel is not about just another prophet acting and speaking in God's name. It is the story of the Word of God made flesh in Jesus. This Word has always existed together with God. This Word is God. This Word, hidden in God, contains the origin of all things. The whole of reality was created by it. The wonderful thing is that this «Word became flesh and lived among us, and we have seen his glory»[81]. God has become enfleshed in Jesus. We are meeting God in his words, his actions, his life and his death. In this specific story of Jesus we will hear God

---

76 John 2:22.
77 John 12:16.
78 John 14:26.
79 John 15:26.
80 Cf. John 16:13-15.
81 John 1:14.

talking to us through the fragile, vulnerable life of a human being[82]. Within this ambitious framework the gospel of John will introduce us to Jesus as the Son of God, the *messenger* sent by the Father to save the world; as the authentic *revealer* who can show us the mystery of this God whom no one has ever seen; and as the *savior* who fulfills and goes beyond all the hopes of human beings.

Jesus is the *Messenger* sent by the Father. He is the Son who has always existed in the Father's bosom, whom God sends to the world as an act of love[83]. As the messenger of the Father, Jesus makes him present in the world; he «represents» him. The words he speaks are not his, but the words he hears from the Father[84]; the works he performs are not his, but those of his Father[85]; he does not follow his own will, but that of the Father[86]. Jesus is only the «voice» and the «hand» of the Father. The Father speaks to us in Jesus' words; he holds out his hand to us in Jesus' actions. The gift God gives the world by sending his Son is motivated by love alone: «For God so loved the world that he gave his only Son, so that everyone who believes in him may not perish but may have eternal life. Indeed, God did not send the Son into the world to condemn the world, but in order that the world might be saved through him»[87]. In short, Jesus «came from God»[88]. The Father is so present in him that Jesus tells Philip: «Whoever has seen me has seen the Father»[89].

This Jesus, who comes directly from the heart of the Father, is the only one who can reveal him. He is God's great *Revealer*. «No one has ever seen God. It is God the only Son, who is close to the Father's heart, who has made him known»[90]. In God's becoming flesh «we have seen his glory, the glory as of a father's only son, full of grace and truth»[91]. The «glory» that Jesus receives as a Son from the Father is seen in the miracles he performs. John calls them «signs», and they have been written down «so that you may come to believe that Jesus is the Messiah, the Son of God, and that believing you may have life in his name»[92]. These «signs»

---

82 We shall say more about the Word of God incarnate in Jesus, on p. 436.
83 In John's gospel, Jesus most frequently speaks of God as «the Father, who has sent me».
84 John 14:10; 17:8,14.
85 John 14:10; 5:15,36; 8:28; 14:10.
86 John 4:34; 5:30; 6:38.
87 John 3:16-17.
88 John 7:28; 8:42; 16:27-28.
89 John 14:8.
90 John 1:18.
91 John 1:14.
92 John 20:30.

reveal the power of Jesus as Son of God, and show his compassion; Jesus performs them in order to inspire faith[93]. Perhaps from John's viewpoint, Jesus is revealing the whole content of his message from the Father when he reveals the commandment of love. At that point he says explicitly that Jesus has told his disciples «everything»:

> This is my commandment, that you love one another as I have loved you. No one has greater love than this, to lay down one's life for one's friends. You are my friends if you do what I command you. I do not call you servants any longer, because the servant does not know what the master is doing; but I have called you friends, because I have made known to you everything that I have heard from my Father[94].

This commandment of love really does say everything that Jesus has to convey from his intimacy with the Father. Jesus has brought the commandment of love to earth from the Father. It supercedes all previous revelation, because «the law indeed was given through Moses; grace and truth came through Jesus Christ»[95]. Up until this point, the disciples were «servants» of God and Jesus. Now they have become «friends».

Besides the Revealer, John's gospel presents Jesus as the *Savior* who at once fulfills and surpasses the human hope of salvation. From the beginning of this gospel, the disciples say they have met the «Messiah», and Nathanael confesses Jesus as the «Son of God»[96]. But that is only the beginning. Jesus tells Nathanael, «You will see greater things than these»[97]. Jesus is not yet fully known, when his identity is described only with traditional titles. It is more important to hear how he reveals himself when he says, «I am». The images attributed to him give us a sense of all the saving power of Jesus Christ, the messenger from the Father who responds completely to the most fundamental needs of human existence[98].

---

93 The stories of the «signs» appear in different episodes: the wedding at Cana (2:1-12), the healing of the royal official's son at Cana (4:46-54), the healing of the sick man at Bethsaida (5:1-18), the multiplication of the loaves (6:1-15), the healing of the man blind from birth (9:1-40), and the raising of Lazarus (11:1-43). These signs are the still-discreet manifestation of his glory, waiting for the full manifestation which will come at the time of his death-resurrection, leading to his definitive «elevation» and «glorification».

94 John 15:12-15.

95 John 1:17.

96 John 1:41-49.

97 John 1:50.

98 In John's gospel, the «christology of titles» is less important than the «christology of images».

The gospel seems to follow an intentional order in presenting these images. When Jesus speaks of himself as the «bread of life», he invites us to *go* to him: «I am the bread of life. Whoever comes to me will never be hungry»[99]. Human beings seek different kinds of bread to feed their deep hunger; only in Jesus will they find the bread of life that feeds it completely. As the «light of the world», he invites us to *follow* him: «I am the light of the world. Whoever follows me will never walk in darkness but will have the light of life»[100]. Human beings need light in order to stay on the right path; only in Jesus will they find the light that leads to life. Those who follow him will enter into a new world, so Jesus presents himself as «the gate»: «I am the gate. Whoever enters by me will be saved»[101]. Many gates and many paths are open to human beings; only by going through Jesus will they find salvation. That brings them into a new realm of existence where they are protected and nourished by Jesus, who offers himself as the «good shepherd»: «I came that [my sheep] may have life, and have it abundantly. I am the good shepherd»[102]. Human beings are fragile, helpless, victimized by bad shepherds; only in Jesus will they find a «good shepherd» to give them the life they long for. With Jesus as their shepherd, human beings find *resurrection* and life in him: «I am the resurrection and the life. Those who believe in me, even though they die, will live, and everyone who lives and believes in me will never die»[103]. Those who believe in Jesus have life, not only in the future, but as a present reality. Later in his farewell discourses, Jesus summarizes and deepens his self-revelation in two more sayings about the Father. «I am *the way, the truth, and the life.* No one comes to the Father except through me»[104]. In offering us his life and his truth, Jesus opens the way to the Father for us. Then after his death and resurrection, the most important thing is to «stay» on that way, in that truth and that life. So he tells his disciples, «I am the *true vine,* and my Father is the vinegrower»[105]. The disciples must never forget: they must stay in Jesus like the branches on the vine. «Abide in me… abide in my love… If you keep my commandments, you will abide in my love, just as I have kept my Father's commandments and abide in his love… This is my commandment: that you love one another as I have loved you»[106].

99   John 6:35.
100   John 8:12.
101   John 10:9.
102   John 10:10-11:15.
103   John 11:25-26.
104   John 14:6.
105   John 15:1.
106   John 15:4.9.10.12.

Finding the right name for Jesus

Even before the gospel stories are written down, providing us with a rich re-reading of Jesus in the light of the paschal experience, another important development is occurring among his followers. The impact of his resurrection moves them to look for «names» and «titles» that can express the «mystery» they sense in the prophet they have been following around Galilee. What is his real identity? What should they call him? By what name should they proclaim him? In Semitic thinking, one's «name» is very important. You don't put just any name on people. Their names describe their being, their mission, their destiny[107].

The mystery his followers sense in Jesus cannot be expressed by that name alone. Matthew finds deep meaning in «Jesus»: his father was inspired by an «angel of the Lord» to call him that, «for he will save his people from their sins»[108]. But that is not enough to express all that is being revealed in the Risen One. Soon new titles and names begin to circulate in the Christian communities, taken from the Jewish cultural world or from more hellenized circles[109]. In spite of their diversity, there seems to be no separation or confusion among them. All the names refer to Jesus, the wonderful Prophet they knew in Galilee, and they all reflect his person and activity: Jesus is the «Lord», but a Lord who «serves» rather than dominates; he is the «Messiah», but a crucified Messiah, not a victorious king who destroys his adversaries.

5.1. MESSIAH

The Christians call Jesus «Messiah» or «Christ» from the beginning[110]. It is a key title, the one everyone uses most. The first preachers enthusiastically describe him that way: «God has made him both Lord and Messiah, this Jesus whom you crucified»[111]. The Messiah whom some people have waited so long to see, has

---

107 This is why God changed Abram's name to *Abraham* (father of many); from then on he would be «the ancestor of a multitude of nations» (Gen 17:5). Jesus did the same when he called Simon *Peter* (*kefa* = rock), saying that he would build his Church on this rock.

108 Matt 1:21. The Hebrew name Yehoshua means «Yahweh saves».

109 More than thirty names, titles, and forms of address have been identified (Sabourin).

110 The word «messiah» comes from the Hebrew *mashiah*, meaning «anointed». The Greek equivalent is «Christ».

111 Acts 2:36; 5:42; 9:22 and others.

been crucified. It's hard to believe, but it's true. There's no need to wait for another; Jesus is the Messiah. So his followers spontaneously begin to call themselves «Christians» or «Messianists». They first took on the name in Antioch[112]. It must have come from the impact of the resurrection on them, for the disciples remembered that Jesus was reluctant to be called «Messiah» or «Christ». Indeed the biblical figure of the Messiah had become vague, and sometimes ambiguous. Most people saw the Messiah as a descendant of the royal family of David. Some thought in terms of a priestly role. Either way, most people imagined him as a warlike liberator: he would put an end to Roman domination, cleanse Israel of the pagan presence, restore the chosen people and establish peace. Jesus probably raised some expectations that reminded people of the Messiah: could this be the liberator they were waiting for? Jesus apparently resisted that idea[113]. He didn't want to be thought of as a nationalistic Messiah; his plan for the reign of God was much more than that.

The crucifixion puts an end to all such confusion. It is no longer possible to think of Jesus as a nationalistic warrior like Judas the son of Ezekias, Simon of Perea, or Atronges. Paul says clearly: «For I decided to know nothing among you except Jesus Christ, and him crucified»[114]. Jesus is the true Messiah who brings salvation, not by destroying the Romans, but seeking the reign of God and his justice for everyone. He is not a victorious Messiah, but one crucified for liberating people from oppression and injustice. That is how everyone knows him. Little by little, under Paul's influence, the term «Christ» becomes a personal name for Jesus. The Christians no longer distinguish among the names «Jesus», «Christ», and «Jesus Christ». Unfortunately, the name «Christ» began to lose its original power in everyday usage. People would soon forget its real meaning[115].

---

112 Acts 11:26.
113 This is the view of most biblical scholars. Gospel texts like Matt 16:13-20, which show Jesus accepting being called Messiah, reflect the faith of the early Christians rather than Jesus' own behavior.
114 1 Cor 2:2.
115 Many people today probably believe in Christ without knowing that «Christ» means a liberator from injustice and oppression, a fighter for a more just and human life, a seeker of the reign of God and his justice. And they call themselves «Christians» without realizing that the word means «Messianists», seekers after a new world according to God's will, fighters for peace and justice, bringers of hope to all victims.

Apparently Jesus never called himself «Messiah» or «Christ». When speaking of himself and his mission, he often used a strange, typically Semitic expression: «Son of man»[116]. This expression was unintelligible and puzzling to Greek ears, but even to Aramaic speakers there was something mysterious about referring to himself that way[117]. «Son of man» is not a specific title attributed to Jesus by others. No one in the Christian community confesses him, or invokes him, by that name. The gospel writers describe it as a way in which he spoke of himself, mainly to emphasize his human nature: Jesus is a vulnerable human being, a «son of man» who has nowhere to lay his head; who has not come to be served but to serve, and to give his life as a ransom; who always seeks out the excluded ones and sinners, in order to save the lost; and finally, who will be crucified and raised on the third day.

432

But Jesus also talks about the «Son of Man seated at the right hand of the Power, and coming with the clouds of heaven»[118]. Did he say this during his life, or did the Christian community, in the light of the resurrection, imagine him as the Son of man who appears in the powerful vision of the book of Daniel?[119]. Many scholars believe the first Christians, probably based on Jesus' habit of calling himself «son of man», saw in him the «Son of man» now exalted and glorified at the right hand of God, who will come as the ultimate Judge of the world. In any case they see Jesus as a truly human being who has struggled to the death for abundant life for all, and whom God has made the ultimate Judge who will one day come to bring justice to the world. This will not be arbitrary judgment; Jesus knows what it is to be human. He will judge humanity from within. Every-

---

116 The gospels use the Greek expression *huios tou anthropou*, a literal translation of the Aramaic *bar enasha*. It is a characteristically Semitic way of saying «human being».

117 There has been endless, sometimes confused debate over the term «Son of man» (Vielhauer, Cullmann, Bultmann, Stuhlmacher, Perrin, Vermes, Merklein, Vögtle, González Faus and others). Scholars disagree over whether Jesus used the expression himself, whether it was meant to create mystery about his identity, whether he expected the glorious coming of a Son of man different from himself, whether it was the Christian community that developed this way of speaking out of the figure of the «Son of man» who appears in the book of Daniel. There is no consensus as yet. In this section I am following the most widely accepted interpretations.

118 Mark 14:62; 13:26.

119 In Daniel's vision, after the four beasts from the sea who represent the powerful kingdoms that have oppressed the chosen people, «I saw one like a human being [or son of man] coming with the clouds of heaven. And he came to the Ancient One and was presented before him. To him was given dominion and glory and kingship, that all peoples, nations, and languages should serve him. His dominion is an everlasting dominion that shall now pass away, and his kingship is one that shall never be destroyed» (7:13-14).

thing will confront the truth of God, enfleshed in the humanity of Jesus. Then what is authentically human will be made clear. At last people will see what is true and what is false, who has acted justly and who has been wicked and inhuman.

Early in 58 A.D., Paul of Tarsus writes a letter from Greece to the Christian community in Rome. He too sees Jesus as the Man in whom true humanity is manifest. But his theological reflection moves in a new and different direction. Paul thinks of Jesus as the «new Adam», a new Man inaugurating a new humanity[120]. In his religious vision, the first Adam's «disobedience» gave rise to a history of sin which leads inevitably to destruction and death. But Jesus, the «new Adam», with his faithful and loyal «obedience» to God, has inaugurated a new era of justice leading to salvation. Injustice, suffering and death came into human history with the first Adam. With Jesus, grace and salvation are within everyone's reach. Paul cannot conceal his joy and excitement. Sin and evil have abounded since Adam, but since Jesus, «where sin increased, grace abounded all the more»[121].

5.3. **HIGH PRIEST**

As rich as it was, the title «Son of man» soon fell into disuse. It had little meaning for new Christians in the Empire. Something similar happened with another name, introduced in a writing that calls Jesus the «High priest»[122]. It didn't go very far. Still, this startling and even scandalous title sheds a special light on the mediating role played by Jesus between God and humanity. The high priests had fallen into disrepute in Jesus' time. The high priest was still the great «mediator» between God and his people, but in the view of many people, he was serving his own interests and those of the Empire rather than defending God's poor people. How could anyone give Jesus that title? What did he have in common with Annas or Caiaphas?

The writer of the letter to the Hebrews was expressing a bold and fascinating insight. Calling Jesus the «High priest» was the best way to demystify the religion

---

120 Rom 5:12-21.

121 Rom 5:20. It might be closer to Paul's thinking to say that human beings are born, not into «original sin» but into «original redemption». The saving power of Jesus cannot be compared to the wickedness of Adam.

122 This is the term used in the letter to the Hebrews, an exhortation addressed to a community of Jews converted to following Jesus, probably in Alexandria. We know it was written before the destruction of the temple, since at the time of writing (64 A.D.?), ritual sacrifices were still being performed.

of the temple, and an impressive way to identify Jesus to the Jewish world. What better way could there be to get the attention of Jews who were still making pilgrimages to Jerusalem to offer sacrifices to the God of the Covenant? Priests are still holy men, separated from the impure so they can make acceptable offerings to God for people's sins[123]. In contrast, Jesus has accepted sinners and prostitutes, and touched lepers and other people banned from the temple because of their infirmity. He does not get close to God by separating himself from others; he moves among the people and is close to everyone, in order to make his beloved Father present in the midst of the most forgotten and humiliated people. Moreover, the high priests' sacrifices cannot bring forgiveness of sins: «For it is impossible for the blood of bulls and goats to take away sins»[124]. Jesus does not offer any ritual sacrifice, for that is not what pleases God; he has come to do God's will, and his offering is his own life[125].

434

Hebrews has a wonderful description of Jesus as the true «mediator» between God and human beings. On one hand he is «the reflection of God's glory and the exact imprint of God's very being»[126], the first-born Son, seated at God's right hand, not like the angels who sit at his feet or around him[127]. On the other hand, this same Jesus who shares the life of God is fully human. He is in total solidarity with human beings, and is «not ashamed to call them brothers and sisters»[128]. Unlike the high priests whom the people see far off, solemnly entering the holiest and most inaccessible places of the temple, and unlike the family of Annas who lost credibility by exploiting the people mercilessly for years, Jesus «had to become like his brothers and sisters in every respect, so that he might be a merciful and faithful high priest»[129]. Even more, Jesus identifies with everyone who suffers; «Because he himself was tested by what he suffered, he is able to help those who are being tested»[130]. The author cannot find words to describe this incredible solidarity: «For we do not have a high priest who is unable to sympathize with our weaknesses, but we have one who in every respect has been

---

[123] «Every high priest chosen from among mortals is put in charge of things pertaining to God on their behalf, to offer gifts and sacrifices for sins» (Heb 5:1).
[124] Heb 10:4.
[125] Heb 10:5-10.
[126] Heb 1:3.
[127] Heb 1:5-14.
[128] Heb 2:11.
[129] Heb 2:17.
[130] Heb 2:18.

tested as we are, yet without sin»[131]. He is like us: «Although he was a Son, he learned obedience through what he suffered»[132]. He too has to live by faith; therefore we must walk «looking to Jesus the pioneer and perfecter of our faith»[133].

5.4. LORD

Jesus was called «Lord» from the beginning. This is not only an honorific title. This title carries a deeper meaning. According to the first preachers, God himself « has made him both Lord and Messiah, this Jesus whom you crucified»[134]. For the Christians there is no doubt about this. From the moment of resurrection, «Jesus is Lord». For Paul this confession synthesizes the whole Christian faith: «if you confess with your lips that Jesus is Lord and believe in your heart that God has raised him from the dead, you will be saved»[135]. This confession is so important that «no one can say "Jesus is Lord" except by the Holy Spirit»[136]. Why is it so important? What makes the title of «Lord» such a central affirmation for Jesus' followers[137]? The Christians know that gods are called *Kyrios* («Lord») in Syria, Greece, Asia Minor or Egypt. They have also seen the cult of the emperor developing in the Roman Empire. Perhaps the title did not have such strong connotations of divinity in late 54 A.D. when Claudius began to be called *Kyrios*, but a little later Caligula, Nero, and especially Domitian (81-96) would require people to worship them as «divine Lords». Domitian in particular was invoked as «Lord and God» (*Kyrios kai Theos*). Jesus' followers reacted negatively. Paul had already written years earlier: there are many so-called «gods» and «lords», but «for us there is one God, the Father, from whom are all things... and one Lord, Jesus Christ»[138]. Luke attributes to Peter an affirmation of faith that would be vital to the early generations of Christians facing the imperial theology, which saw the emperors as «lords» who bring peace. They are not. It is God who sent a message «to the people of Israel, preaching peace by Jesus Christ — he is Lord of all»[139]. A moving scene in John's gospel challenges Domitian's

131 Heb 4:15.
132 Heb 5:8.
133 Heb 12:2.
134 Acts 2:36.
135 Rom 10:9.
136 1 Cor 12:3.
137 The Greek word *kyrios* simply meant «lord», «master», «owner of the house». Its Aramaic equivalent, *mar*, referred to the father, judge, or king. Both words acquired a much deeper meaning when used for God or Jesus.
138 1 Cor 8:5, 6.
139 Acts 10:36.

pretensions in an especially graphic and bold way when Thomas, kneeling before the risen Christ, makes precisely the confession that the emperor was claiming for himself: «My Lord and my God!»[140]. Only Jesus is Lord. Not because he arrogantly claimed that title, as Caligula and Domitian did, but because in the words of an early Christian hymn:

> Christ Jesus,
>
> though he was in the form of God… emptied himself, taking the form of a slave… and became obedient to the point of death — even death on a cross. Therefore God also highly exalted him, and gave him the name that is above every name, so that… every tongue should confess that Jesus Christ is Lord, to the glory of God the Father[141].

The lordship of Jesus is not an apotheosis of power. Jesus is not Lord in order to dominate, oppress, rule, or control. All his life he has been serving and giving life to the poorest and neediest people. His lordship is not despotic, authoritarian, or imposed from above. It is power that enlivens, energy that gives life. The Roman emperors «lord it over» the people, and the powerful become tyrants. But it is not so with Jesus, and must not be so among his followers[142]. This Jesus, exalted by God, is the only Lord of the community. The life of his followers must be shaped by him. «If we live, we live to the Lord, and if we die, we die to the Lord; so then, whether we live or whether we die, we are the Lord's. For to this end Christ died and lived again, so that he might be Lord of both the dead and the living»[143]. This is how the first generations of Christians lived: hearing the «Word of the Lord», celebrating the «Lord's Supper», waiting for the «Day of the Lord». And it is how they called upon him in those communities: *Marana tha*, «Come, Lord Jesus»[144].

5.5. INCARNATE WORD OF GOD

This is how Jesus is described in a kind of «prologue» at the beginning of John's gospel. Then the expression disappears, even in the same gospel. The first generations never speak of him that way again. Later, however, the expression would

---

140 John 20:28.
141 Phil 2:6-11. This is probably a very early Christian hymn, which Paul is quoting verbatim.
142 Mark 10:42-45.
143 Rom 14:8-9.
144 1 Cor 16:22; Rev 22:20; *Didache* 10:6. Jesus taught his disciples to cry out: «Your kingdom come». Now, convinced that the kingdom has fully come, his followers cry out to him: «Come, Lord Jesus».

help to deepen the very core of the mystery of Jesus as seen from the viewpoint of faith[145].

The language of this prologue echoes with the Greek concept of *Logos*, with Jewish faith in the «Word» of God, and with ancient meditation on «Wisdom». As we have said, Greek culture perceives reality as interwoven with rationality and meaning. Reality is not something chaotic and incoherent, but contains a *Logos*; everything has an internal «logic». Meanwhile in Jewish faith, God has no visible image that can be painted or sculpted, but he has a voice; God creates the universe and saves his people through the power of his «Word». Thus in Israel's wisdom tradition the world and human history are not an absurd reality; everything is sustained and directed by the «Wisdom» of God.

The prologue is a beautiful Johannine hymn, reflecting the Jewish faith in particular. The Word is «in the beginning» of everything. We are not to understand this Word as something created. It is God speaking, communicating, revealing himself in creation and in the dramatic history of humanity. Everything is created and directed by that Word. We can sense its movement everywhere. In that Word is «life», and the «true light» that shines on everyone who comes into this world. There is also darkness in the world, but «the light shines in the darkness».

Jews believe this, and it can also be accepted by many people in the hellenic culture. Then comes the bold and startling proclamation: «And the Word became flesh and lived among us»[146]. Now we can see the Word of God enfleshed in Jesus, this Galilean prophet. It is not easy. Indeed he did come into the world, and the world did not know him; even his own people did not accept him. But in Jesus Christ we are being offered «grace and truth». No one else can talk to us as he does. God has become flesh in him. We are meeting God in his words, his acts, and his whole life. This is how God is, Jesus tells us. God looks at people as Jesus does; he accepts, heals, defends, loves, forgives as Jesus does. God is like Jesus. More than that: Jesus is God, speaking to us in the fragility and vulnerability of this one human being.

5.6. SON OF GOD

This is another title that helped the Christians to think out the relationship between Jesus and God. It did not emerge separately in a particular writing; Jesus was called «Son of God» very early on, in almost all the communities. It must

145 John 1:1-18. The prologue is a kind of triumphal «hymn» that precedes the gospel narrative.
146 John 1:14.

surely have come from their memory of Jesus, from his lifelong attitude of obedience, faithfulness, and intimate trust in the God he called *Abba*. At the same time the title suggested the ineffable mystery of God, which enabled them to connect Jesus with the Father who had raised him by infusing his own life in him.

There was a real danger of idolatry. Many people were attracted to the oriental world of gods and goddesses. They liked the protective nearness of Artemis, Cybele, Dionysius, and other gods who offered «salvation» to their worshipers. And the cult of emperor worship was becoming increasingly popular: in 40 A.D. Caligula had tried to bring a statue of Zeus, looking just like Caligula, into the temple at Jerusalem. Under the impact of God's action in raising Jesus, the Christians were looking for an emphatic way to affirm their relationship with him, but how could they do it without falling into idolatry? How could they express their union with God, without turning Jesus into another god like all the others?

The title «son of God» was very meaningful to the Jews. In the biblical tradition the people of Israel, whom God so loved and cared for, was called that; the king, as representative of the people, was also seen as a «son of God»; even some righteous individuals, for their outstanding faithfulness to God, were called his sons. How could they not say it of Jesus? Then too, they remembered his unique way of relating to God. He experienced God as a beloved Father, and called him *Abba*; he trusted him totally, and gave him absolute obedience and faithfulness. Jesus is not just another «son» of God. He is «*the* Son». The one God loved most. The Father himself «sent his Son» Jesus into the world[147]. Jesus comes from God. His relationship with God is not like ours. God is Jesus' Father in a different way. The early Christians always make note of that difference. They never attribute the words «Our Father» to Jesus; he talks about «my Father» and «your Father»[148].

It probably was not so unusual in the first century to describe a man as a «son of God». What was absurd and horrendous was to say it of an unknown man, executed on a cross by the Roman authorities. The Christians know that. Yet Mark boldly has a Roman centurion say of Jesus on the cross, those words which could only be spoken of the emperor: «Truly this man was God's Son!»[149]. For the Christians, Jesus is not a «Greek god». Calling him «Son of God» is not an *apotheosis*, like the one that was cultivated around the emperor. It means discerning and confessing the mystery of God, incarnate in this man who gave

147 Gal 4:4.
148 John 20:17.
149 Mark 15:39.

himself up to death for the sake of love[150]. Jesus is *truly man*, and has made visible what it really means to be human: to show solidarity, to have compassion, to liberate, to serve the last, to seek the reign of God and his justice. And he is *truly God*, making present the God of the victims and crucified ones, the God who is Love, the Father who seeks only life and abundant happiness for his sons and daughters, beginning with the crucified ones[151].

6

Encounter with the living Jesus Christ

After Jesus' execution, his followers went through a process that led them to «believe» in the risen Jesus, overcoming their doubts, uncertainty, questions, and confusion. They began to explore the mystery of Jesus in the light of this faith, often with difficulty, until they could confess him in different ways as the incarnation of the mystery of God in the fragility of a human being. What paths can men and women take today, to go through a similar process? Christians in the second and third generation were asking the same thing. They were thinking of people in the future who would believe without having directly witnessed the events they had lived with Jesus[152]. They even suggested ways to come to faith in Jesus Christ. What experiences do we have that can bring us closer to the faith of Jesus' first disciples?

150 In any case, to avoid misunderstanding the early Christians do not talk about a «son» begotten by a «father god» as Greek gods were. Only Luke suggests, discreetly, that Mary's son originally came from God, by saying he was conceived by the «Holy Spirit» and is therefore called «Son of God» (1:30-35).

151 As they came into contact with other ways of thinking, and with views they considered incomplete or distorted, the early Christians were forced to look for new formulas that would express their faith in Jesus Christ as clearly as possible. The Councils of Nicaea (325), Constantinople (381), Ephesus (431), and Chalcedon (451) were milestones in that search. Chalcedon served as the conclusion of the efforts carried out in the earlier councils, and the starting point for later Christian reflection. In the cultural language of its time, which like all human language can be made more perfect, Chalcedon confesses Jesus Christ as «truly God and truly man» (*Deum vere et hominem vere*), «consubstantial with the Father in his divinity, and consubstantial with us in our humanity» (*consubstantialem Patri secundum deitatem et consubstantialem nobis secundum humanitatem*); «like us in everything except in sin» (*per omnia nobis similem absque peccato*). This abstract confession takes on life and warmth when we see it through a living reading of the gospel narratives, and when we make the effort to see Jesus' life in a more concrete, contextualized way. Then perhaps believers and non-believers, people of weak faith and no faith, can more clearly hear the invitation to come with a livelier faith to the mystery of God incarnate in the fragility of Jesus.

152 In John 20:29, the risen Jesus tells Thomas: «Blessed are those who have not seen and yet have come to believe».

This story suggests some very important ideas[153]. Two disciples have left the group meeting in Jerusalem. They are «looking sad»; after Jesus' execution their spirits have been engulfed by sadness, desolation and despair. Their faith in Jesus has been extinguished. They no longer expect anything of him. They apparently have everything they need to bring them to faith in Jesus Christ. They know the Scriptures of Israel; they have lived with Jesus, heard his message, seen him act as a «mighty prophet», heard the women's news «that he was alive», and the other disciples' report of the empty tomb. None of that helps. Their faith is still dead. They don't have what they most need: recognizing the presence of the Risen One in their lives, meeting the living Christ in person.

Although they walk in sadness and discouragement, these disciples are re-membering Jesus and «talking and discussing» about him. As they walk, Jesus himself «comes near», enters into their conversation and begins walking with them. He invites them to tell him what they were discussing. The disciples re-live for the stranger their memories of «Jesus of Nazareth»: he was «a prophet mighty in deed and word before God and all the people», but was crucified by the religious leaders; he had inspired them to hope «that he was the one to re-deem Israel», but his execution had put an end to that hope; not even the news that he was alive could revive their faith in him. That is when Jesus begins to ex-plain to them, in the light of the Scriptures, the true meaning of the events and the need for the Messiah to suffer and be raised again.

What Luke is telling us is very important. Wherever a group of people are walking through life, trying to understand the meaning of the words and deeds of the prophet Jesus of Nazareth, wherever his passion is remembered and the news of his resurrection is heard, there the Risen One is made present. It is the real presence of one who walks with us on the road, a presence not easily grasped because our eyes may be unable to recognize him; a presence that invites us to see that we are «slow of heart to believe». But this presence is what awakens their hope. Later they confess that while Jesus was talking to them on the road, their hearts were «burning» within them. One way to meet the risen Christ and feel our hearts light up with his presence is to meet each other in his name, read the

---

153 Luke 24:13-35. It is a unique story. It avoids the traditional language of «appearances», and in-stead emphasizes the recognition of a presence. It is the only story in which the Risen One spends hours with the disciples, living with them: he accompanies them along the road, enters into their discussion, and stays to eat with them.

gospels in an effort to discover the deepest meaning of his words and deeds, remember his crucifixion and listen from within, with trusting hearts, to the news of his resurrection.

But that is not enough. We also need to experience the eucharistic meal in order to recognize the presence of the risen Lord, not only as one whose Word shines a light on our life, but as one who feeds us at his Table. That is what Luke's story tells us. The disciples ask the unknown traveler not to leave them, and Jesus «stays with them». The three of them sit together at the table, to eat together as friends and brothers/sisters. When Jesus takes the bread, blesses it, breaks it and gives it to them, «their eyes are opened and they recognize him». It is enough to recognize his presence, even for just a few moments. The experience of being fed by him transforms their life. Now they know that the hope they had in Jesus was not too great, but too small and restricted. They recover the meaning of their life. They return to tell the community of disciples «what had happened to them on the road, and how he had been made known to them in the breaking of the bread»[154].

Our faith in the risen Christ does not come only from the sign of the empty tomb, or from the testimony of those who lived the experience of meeting him. We also need to recognize the presence of the living Christ in our own life. Luke's story conveys two privileged experiences of the Christian community: personally hearing the Word interpreted by Christ and in Christ, and experiencing the shared eucharistic meal.

6.2.   MARY'S ENCOUNTER WITH THE RISEN ONE

This story also suggests something important about coming to faith in Jesus Christ[155]. Mary Magdalene is sad and desolate. Her heart is weeping. Above all the story describes her as a woman who is looking for Jesus. She cannot resign herself to living without him. Her life would have no meaning. One after another she tells people why she is crying: «They have taken the Lord out of the tomb, and we do not know where they have laid him». The answers she receives reflect an intentional progression. Simon Peter and the disciple whom Jesus loved reply with silence: they don't know where he is either. The «two angels» beside the tomb invite her to search within herself when they ask: «Woman, why

---

154 «The breaking of the bread» is the technical term used by the Christian community to describe the eucharist (Acts 2:42).
155 John 20:11-18.

are you weeping?» Then Mary goes to someone she thinks is the «gardener». In fact it is Jesus. He is standing there, but she «did not know that it was Jesus». He asks her the full question: «Woman, why are you weeping? Whom are you looking for?» John's story suggests that not just any questions will bring us to an encounter with the risen Christ. We have to undertake an inner search, asking the key questions about our existence.

This inner search may not be enough. Mary only recognizes Jesus when she hears him call her by name: «Jesus said to her, "Mary!" She turned and said to him in Hebrew, "*Rabbouni!*" (which means Teacher)». To meet the risen Jesus Christ, we need to hear our own name on his lips. We need to feel called by him in person. Then our life changes from the bottom up. Mary still needs to discover that Jesus is more than the Teacher she has known. He is the Son of God who is going to his Father and our Father. She has to learn to live with the risen Lord, without being able to enjoy his physical presence as she did in Galilee. She will be able to embrace him in her brothers and sisters. The risen Jesus sends her to convey the Good News to them: we are all brothers and sisters. We all share one God and Father with Jesus. Jesus is the only Son, our older brother. Together we all make up the family of God. Jesus Christ is our hope. With him and through him, we will come one day into the bosom of the Father.

Epilogue

According to one gospel story, as Jesus and the disciples were walking through the region of Caesarea Philippi, Jesus asked them what people were saying about him. After they told him about the rumors and expectations that were circulating in the villages, he asked them directly: «But who do you say that I am?»

Twenty centuries later, anyone who earnestly and honestly comes near to Jesus is faced with the same question: «Who is he?» The answer will necessarily be very personal. I have to speak for myself. The question is, who do I say Jesus is? He's not asking for christological dogmas formulated by ecumenical Councils, the explanations of theologians, or the results of modern scholarly research on Jesus.

Throughout this study, I too have asked myself who Jesus really is for me. My purpose is not to confess my own faith in Jesus Christ in these pages. Like all Christians, I have to do that in my daily life. What I do want is to share with you who think of yourselves as Christians, some of the convictions that have been growing forcefully within me as I moved forward in this effort to come closer to the person of Jesus.

I do not want to impose these convictions on people who think differently. They are only an expression of my faith in Jesus Christ. I want to share them with you who love Jesus, who believe in his plan for the reign of God, and who carry the same concern for the future of humankind deep in your hearts.

1

Coming back to Jesus

This is the first and most decisive part: putting Jesus at the center of Christianity. Everything else comes later. What could be more urgent and necessary for Christians, than awakening our passion for faithfulness to Jesus? He is the best the Church has to give, the best we can offer and communicate to today's world.

The essential thing is for Christians to confess Jesus Christ as «Son of God», «Savior of the world», or «Redeemer of humankind», without reducing him to a «sublime abstraction». I do not want to believe in a disembodied Christ. I cannot nourish my faith on doctrine alone. I don't think we Christians can live today with a set of truths about Christ as our only motivation. We need a living connection to him; we need to know Jesus better, and become vitally attuned to him. I have no other way to deepen and enrich my faith in Jesus Christ, the Son of God, who became human for our salvation.

We are all in danger of turning Christ into a mere «object of worship»: an icon to venerate, with an attractive and majestic face to be sure, but a more or less washed-out version of the fiery Prophet who walked around Galilee in the decade of the thirties. What we Christians need is to see him alive and up close, understand his message, grasp his deepest insights, and feel the heat of his passion for God and humanity.

We have very different images of Jesus. Not all of them look like the beloved Teacher remembered by the first men and women who knew him and followed him. Each of us has developed a personal image of Jesus. Internalized over the years, those images «mediate» the presence of Christ in our life. Those images affect the way we read the gospel, or hear it preached to us; they affect the way we nourish our faith, celebrate the sacraments, and shape our own Christian life. If we have a poor and partial image of Jesus, our faith will be poor and partial; if it is a distorted image, our way of living the Christian experience will be distorted. Even the good Christians among us, who sincerely believe in Jesus and love him, may sometimes need to «change» and purify their image of Jesus in order to joyfully discover the grandeur of the faith we carry in our hearts.

2

Believing in the God of life

In these times of deep religious crisis, it is not enough to believe in just any God; we need to discern the true God. It is not enough to say that Jesus is God; we need to know what kind of God is embodied and revealed in Jesus. Within the Church and in today's society, it seems very important to me to reaffirm the authentic God of Jesus — not a «god» we have created out of our own fears, ambitions, and illusions, but the very different God that Jesus experienced and communicated. I believe the time has come to put our hearts into the challenge of learning, through Jesus, about God: who God is, how he cares for us, how he seeks us out, what he wants for us as human beings.

What joy it would bring to people, to be able to discern the features of the true God in Jesus! How brightly their faith would burn, if they could see with new eyes the face of God incarnate in Jesus! If there is a God, he is like Jesus. Jesus' way of being, his words, his actions and reactions are details of the revelation of God. Studying what Jesus was like, I have often been surprised by the thought: that's exactly the way God cares for people. That's how God sees their suffering, searches for the lost, accepts them, understands them, forgives them, loves them.

I cannot imagine a better way to approach the mystery that we call God. Jesus' way of living God has become a part of me. It is immediately clear that for Jesus God is not a concept, but a friendly, intimate presence that leads him to live and love life in a different way. Jesus lives God as the best friend of humanity: the «Friend of life». He is not a stranger who controls the world and orders our poor lives around from far away; he is the Friend within us who shares our existence, whose bright light and trustworthy power enable us to face the hardships of life and the mystery of death.

What God cares about is not religion, but a more human and friendly world. What he seeks is a more abundant, healthy and happy life for all, beginning with the «last». Jesus said that in many different ways: if our religion goes against life, either it is a false religion or we have misunderstood it. What makes God happy is to see us happy, now and forever. That is the Good News revealed to us in Jesus Christ: God gives himself to us just as he is, as Love.

3
Living for the reign of God

ᐤᐤ

As we seek to become attuned to Jesus, we need to ask first of all: What is the most important thing for him, the center of his life, the cause he always pursued, his absolute priority? There can be only one answer: Jesus lives for the reign of God. That is his true passion. It is the cause for which he struggles and pours out his life, for which he is persecuted and finally executed. For Jesus, «only the kingdom is absolute and it makes everything else relative»[1].

What is central in Jesus' life is not just God, but God with his plan for human history. He does not speak only of God, but of God and his reign of peace, compassion, and justice. He does not call people to do penitence before God, but to «enter into» God's reign. He does not invite us only to seek God, but to «seek the kingdom of God and his justice». When he launches a movement of his followers to prolong his mission, he does not send them to organize a new religion, but to proclaim and promote the reign of God.

1 PAUL VI, *Evangelii nuntiandi*, 8.

What would life be like if we all acted a little more like God? That is Jesus' great desire: to build a life in line with God's will. That would mean doing many things, but Jesus gave special emphasis to some of them. He emphasized bringing God's compassion into the world; focusing people's concern on the «last» of humanity; building a more just world, beginning with the most neglected; sowing acts of kindness to relieve suffering; trusting in God the Father, who wants a life of happiness for his sons and daughters.

Unfortunately, the reign of God is not a priority for many Christians. Many have not even heard of God's plan; they do not see that it is the only task of the Church and its people. They do not realize that to look at life through the eyes of Jesus means seeing it from the perspective of God's reign; to follow Jesus means living out his passion for the reign of God.

What could be more important for followers of Jesus in our time, than committing ourselves to a true conversion of Christianity to the reign of God? That is God's plan, and our first objective. In that perspective the ultimate truth of the Christian faith is revealed to us: to love God means hungering and thirsting for justice as God does; to follow Jesus means living for the reign of God as Jesus does; to belong to the Church means committing ourselves to a more just world.

4

Following Jesus

Jesus did not establish a «school», as the Greek philosophers did, to continue exploring the ultimate truth of reality. Neither was he thinking about an institution designed to establish the true religion in the world. Jesus launched a movement of «followers» to proclaim and promote his plan for the «reign of God». That is how the Church of Jesus began. For this reason, nothing is more important for us than to reactivate a faithful following of Jesus in the Church, again and again. Following Jesus is the only thing that makes us Christians.

Although we sometimes forget it, that is the first choice that a Christian must make: to follow Jesus. That decision changes everything. It is like starting all over again to live faith, life, and everyday reality in a different way. It means finding — at last — the center, the truth, the reason, the way to life. It gives real meaning to faith in Jesus: believing in what he believed, living what he lived, giving importance to what was important to him, caring about what mattered to him, treating people as he treated them, seeing life as he saw it, praying as he prayed, sharing hope with others as he shared it.

I know there are many ways to follow Jesus. The path of Francis of Assisi is not the one taken by Francis Xavier or Teresa de Jesús. Jesus showed us many aspects and nuances of service to the reign of God. But some basic features are essential in truly following Jesus. Here are a few of them.

Following Jesus means focusing our attention and our heart on *the poor*. Seeing through the eyes of those who suffer. Making their suffering and their aspirations our own. Taking sides with them. Following Jesus means living with *compassion*. Shaking off our indifference. Not living by theoretical abstractions and principles, but coming near to people in their concrete situation. Following Jesus requires us to develop *acceptance*. To renounce sectarian ways of thinking. Not to exclude or excommunicate anyone. To emulate Jesus' inclusive, integrating way of doing things. To break down walls and build bridges. To eliminate discrimination.

Following Jesus means accepting *crucifixion* for God's reign. Not refusing to take sides out of fear that it might get us into trouble. Carrying the weight of the «anti-kingdom», and taking up the cross of daily life in communion with Jesus and the crucified people. Following Jesus means *trusting* the Father of all, calling on his holy name, praying for the coming of his reign, and sowing Jesus' hope against hope.

5

Building the Church of Jesus

It is important to talk about Jesus and the Church, but to do so can be difficult and sometimes conflictive. We Christians do not all have the same vision of ecclesial reality; our perspective and our approach, our way of perceiving and living the mystery of the Church, may be not only different but contradictory. Jesus did not exclude any believers from his Church, or turn the Church against them. That at least has been my experience. I have found Jesus in the Church more than anywhere else; in Christian communities I hear his message and feel his Spirit moving.

But something is changing inside me. I love the Church just as it is, with all its virtues and sinfulness, but now more and more I love it because I love Jesus' plan for the world: the reign of God. That is why I hope to see it converted to

Appendices

Brief historical profile of Jesus

A brief, basic historical outline of Jesus' life may be useful here. I include only those facts which are considered highly reliable by a majority of scholars. Many more things can be affirmed about Jesus, but these provide a point of departure from which to approximate his life and message more closely.

1
His birth

Jesus was born during the reign of the Roman Emperor Augustus, certainly before the death of Herod the Great in the spring of 4 B.C. It is not possible to establish a more exact date. Most historians agree that he was born between 6 and 4 B.C.[1]. He was probably born in Nazareth, although Matthew and Luke set his birth in Bethlehem for theological reasons. In any case, Nazareth was his true homeland. His parents' names were Mary and Joseph.

2
His native language

Jesus' mother tongue was Aramaic. He spoke it in a dialect commonly used in Galilee. It is not clear whether he knew how to read and write. He certainly knew Hebrew, the literary language used at the time for liturgy in the temple and synagogues; the sacred Scriptures were read aloud in Hebrew and then translated into Aramaic. A growing number of scholars believe that Jesus may also have spoken some Greek. He did not know Latin.

3
His life in Nazareth

Jesus spent his childhood, youth, and early adulthood in Nazareth, a small town on a hillside in the Galilean mountain region, far from the important commer-

---

1 The calendar we use was devised by the monk Dionysius Exiguus in the late fifth century. By miscalculating Jesus' date of birth, he set the starting point of the Common or Christian Era (A.D.) about five years late.

cial roads. His mentality was more rural than urban. By studying his socio-cultural and religious context, we can plausibly establish some aspects of his vocation as an artisan, and his upbringing in a Jewish family setting. It is not certain whether or not he worked in the restoration of Sepphoris, which was being re-built by Herod Antipas during those years.

4
Meeting the Baptist

At some point Jesus heard about John the Baptist, who was developing a move-ment of conversion in a desert area near the Jordan river. He left his town of Nazareth, heard John's message and accepted his baptism. Jesus had a very im-portant religious experience at the Jordan; he never returned to live with his family in Nazareth, but neither did he stay very long with the Baptist. At first he too may have developed a practice of baptism, but he soon left the desert and started a new and unique type of activity, different from John's.

5
Breaking with his family

Jesus did not enjoy his family's support. His immediate family did not approve of his activity as an itinerant prophet. They came to think that he had lost his mind, and was bringing shame to the whole family. Jesus developed new relationships, forming a group of followers around him. Seeing family ties as an obstacle to his mission, he left his home at Nazareth for good and went to Capernaum. Some members of his family apparently joined his movement later on.

6
His itinerant ministry

Around 27 or 28 A.D., Jesus changed to an itinerant life style which led him from Galilee to Jerusalem, where he was probably executed on April 7 in the year 30 A.D. Thus it was a brief but intensive ministry, lasting less than three years. We cannot identify the places he stayed and the routes he traveled with any precision. Certainly he traveled around the lake of Galilee. He went from one village to another, but seems never to have visited the most important Galilean cities of Sepphoris and Tiberias. For some time his base of operation was Capernaum, on the lakeshore. Jesus moved from place to place, accompanied by male and female disciples. He had two main activities: curing the sick of diverse afflictions, and proclaiming his message about the «reign of God». His fame increased rapidly, and people traveled to meet him. Jesus had a habit of going out to pray at night in remote places.

7
Prophet of the reign of God

Jesus used a characteristic, suggestive way of speaking. The brief, trenchant sayings, aphorisms, and especially the beautiful parables he told were unmistakably his. He seldom talked about himself. His preaching focused on what he called the «reign of God». Jesus' message was rooted in the Jewish tradition, but it did not grow directly out of apocalyptic literature or the official teaching of the scribes. It came from his deep experience of God, which Jesus tried to communicate in a symbolic, poetic language derived from everyday life. At the center of his preaching was an experience of God as a Father who «makes his sun rise on the evil and the good», and who seeks out and embraces his lost sons and daughters. What was essential was his exhortation to «enter» the reign of God, and to be «compassionate» like the Father in heaven. This exhortation culminated in his call to forgive one's enemies.

8
Healing activity

Although it is hard to establish the historicity of all the healings reported in the gospels, it is clear that Jesus cured a wide variety of sick people, and that these healings were seen as miracles by his contemporaries. He also practiced exorcism on people whom the culture viewed as possessed by evil spirits, freeing them from the evil. In the society of his time Jesus drew many people to him as a popular exorcist and healer. He described these healings and exorcisms as signs that the reign of God had come to the most suffering, alienated sectors of society. But he always refused to produce the spectacular signs that some critics apparently demanded.

9
Deviant behavior

Jesus behaved in strange and provocative ways. He constantly flouted the prevailing codes of conduct in that society. He did not observe the accepted norms of ritual purity. He did not care about the rite of hand-washing before meals. He did not engage in fasting. He sometimes violated the prescribed norms of sabbath practice. He surrounded himself with undesirable people, like tax collectors and prostitutes. He was seen in the company of beggars, hungry people, and the socially marginalized. More specifically, he fraternized and ate with «sinners and tax collectors». He socialized with women in ways inappropriate to that culture, and accepted them among his disciples; Mary Magdalene had an especially important role in Jesus' movement. He apparently had an unusually welcoming attitude toward children. There was nothing haphazard about the way Jesus did these things. He was intentionally, graphically showing people that God's reign is open to everyone, with no one excluded or marginalized.

10
The disciples around him

It was never Jesus' intention to break with Judaism or to establish a separate institution over against Israel. He constantly called on people to enter the reign of God. But a small group of followers did form around him, including a certain number of women. Beyond that small group there was a wider circle of supporters who stayed at home, but who identified with his message and welcomed Jesus and his group into their villages. Jesus also formed a closer group of «Twelve», symbolizing his wish to achieve the restoration of Israel.

11
Reactions against Jesus

∽

Beyond the small group of disciples and the wider circle of supporters, Jesus attained considerable popularity in Galilee and the nearby regions. This popular resonance apparently did not diminish during his brief time of itinerant activity. Indeed Jesus mobilized a fairly significant mass of followers, and this was what made him dangerous from the viewpoint of the ruling authorities. He also provoked rejection from some sectors, which tried to stigmatize and discredit him in order to limit his influence. He drew the disapproval of local leaders, and the opposition of religious leaders in both Galilee and Jerusalem. He was criticized for eating with sinners, and accused of being possessed by the devil. He firmly defended himself against both accusations.

(

12
His execution

∽

In the spring of 30 A.D., Jesus went up to Jerusalem in the territory of Judea, which unlike Galilee was ruled by a Roman prefect. At the time the city of Jerusalem was directly controlled by a high priest named Caiaphas. Jesus carried out a hostile act against the temple, which led to his arrest. He apparently was not formally brought to trial before the Jewish authorities. Instead, because of what had happened in the temple, the priestly aristocracy identified him as a threat and conspired to eliminate him. He died by crucifixion, probably on April 7 in the year 30 A.D., under a death warrant issued by the Roman prefect Pontius Pilate. Apparently expecting his violent death, Jesus celebrated a farewell dinner with his disciples, at which he performed a symbolic gesture with bread and wine. His closest followers abandoned him at the time of his arrest.

Faith in the risen Jesus

We can historically verify that between 35 and 40 A.D., the first generation of Christians were using a variety of formulas to confess the belief they all shared, which spread rapidly across the Roman Empire: «God has raised Jesus from among the dead».

General criteria of interpretation

Catholic exegesis does not practice its own exclusive method of interpretation. Rather it uses all the currently accepted methods, based on an historical-critical approach to the original sources. The principal criteria of interpretation were established in 1993 by the Pontifical Biblical Commission[1]. The most important of them are mentioned here.

1
Rejection of a fundamentalist interpretation

A fundamentalist reading assumes that the Bible must be read and interpreted literally, in every detail. No scientific method is required for this task. This way of reading the gospels does not make allowance for the human language of the writers; it is usually linked to a specific translation, and often gives pious but false interpretations. Fundamentalism amounts to a kind of «intellectual suicide».

2
Historical-critical method as an indispensable tool

In order to understand the meaning expressed by the writers as clearly as possible, this historical-critical method considers textual criticism, linguistic and semantic analysis, the study of literary genres, and the redaction process. It is «the indispensable method» for the scientific study of ancient texts. A right understanding of the gospel texts «requires the use of this method». Therefore, «exegetes have to make use of the historical-critical method. They cannot, however, accord to it a sole validity».

1 Pontifical Biblical Commission, *La interpretación de la Biblia en la Iglesia* (English: *The Interpretation of the Bible in the Church*). Madrid, PPC, 2007 (originally published April 15, 1993). All the texts quoted here are from this important document.

3
The importance of an approach from cultural anthropology

Cultural anthropology endeavors to define the anthropological characteristics of the society of origin of the biblical texts (recognized values, ways of exercising social control, concepts of the family, the condition of women, social structure, etc.) This approach to the texts is of paramount importance. «In the texts which report the teaching of Jesus, for example the parables, many details can be explained thanks to this approach. This is also the case with regard to fundamental ideas, such as that of the reign of God». However we need to remember that this approach alone cannot account for the deep meaning that believers find in Jesus' message.

4
The contribution of liberation theology

The theology of liberation has promoted a liberationist approach to the Bible which contributes «elements of undoubted value»: greater attention to the «God of the poor, [who] cannot tolerate injustice and oppression»; insistence on the communitarian dimension of the faith; the urgency of a liberating praxis rooted in justice and love. This committed reading of the Bible entails risks. «It is true that exegesis cannot be neutral, but it must also take care not to become one-sided».

5
The contribution of the feminist approach

Many positive contributions have come out of feminist exegesis. Women «have succeeded, often better than men, in detecting the presence, the significance and the role of women in the Bible, in Christian origins and in the church». A growing feminine sensitivity «helps to unmask and correct certain commonly accepted interpretations which were tendentious and sought to justify the male domination of women». However we must avoid the risk of «arguments *ex silentio*» or «fleeting indications in the text».

6
The importance of affinity with the content of the text

ℭℐℴ

It is important to remember that a «lived affinity between the interpreter and the object» is a requirement for the understanding of a biblical text. Therefore all interpreters must ask: «Which hermeneutical theory best enables a proper grasp of the profound reality of which Scripture speaks and its meaningful expression for people today?» There can be no doubt that being attuned to the message of Jesus, positively accepting his call, and following him faithfully, all improve the exegete's ability to understand that profound reality.

7
The contemporary meaning of the biblical message

ℭℐℴ

The expression of faith must be continually renewed, in order to confront new situations. Thus «the interpretation of the Bible should likewise involve an aspect of creativity; it ought also to confront new questions so as to respond to them out of the Bible». It is true that exegetes «arrive at the true goal of their work only when they have explained the meaning of the biblical text as God's word for today». To attain that goal, «they must take into consideration the various hermeneutical perspectives which help toward grasping the contemporary meaning of the biblical message and which make it responsive to the needs of those who read Scripture today». This is why it is important to adapt our interpretation to the mentality and language of our own time.

Literary sources

Here is some general information and observations on the different literary sources, and their importance to current research on Jesus.

1
The importance of the gospel of Mark

There is widespread consensus that Mark's gospel is the earliest one that has come down to us. It was probably written in Rome at the height of the Jewish war against Rome (perhaps around 66-67 A.D.), shortly before the destruction of Jerusalem in August of the year 70. The author has compiled oral and written traditions that go back to the decade of the 50s or earlier[1]. Thus the existence of this gospel is important, for it includes the recent memories that were circulating among Jesus' followers, and places them in the framework of a great foundational narrative that was developing during the transition from the first to the second generation of Christians. This writing would later become the model for gospel writing, and a source used by Matthew and Luke. The chronological and geographical outline of the document is somewhat artificially constructed, but the materials it uses are tremendously helpful in understanding how Jesus, his activity and his message were remembered from the beginning.

2
The decisive importance of the Q Source

There was also another gospel, written before 70 A.D. It has not come down to us as a separate writing, but Matthew and Luke used it as an important source in their respective gospels. Scholars have deduced its existence from the discovery that Matthew and Luke, writing independently of each other, incorporated many of the same moments, sometimes with identical wording. That can only be explained by both authors copying from an earlier source. This writing by an unknown author has been called the «Gospel of the Sayings», or the «Q Source» from the German word *Quelle*, meaning «source». It was written in Greek,

---

1 The only available written sources on the Buddha, who died around 480 B.C., are legends compiled at least half a millennium after his death. On Confucius, his contemporary in China, we have two sources of doubtful credibility; they were written 400 and 700 years after that Teacher's lifetime.

almost certainly in Palestine before the destruction of Jerusalem. It is made up entirely of sayings and parables. It does not include any kind of acts by Jesus, nor any narrative of the Passion or appearances of the risen one. These sayings were probably collected by the earliest itinerant missionaries, who imitated Jesus' way of living and preaching, and who were very interested in learning about his teachings. The Q Source is of special interest to many authors, and has become one of the most exciting objects of modern research on Jesus. Scholars are still learning about the different stages of its composition, about the itinerant prophets who composed it, and about the countercultural life style it advocates. Although we still cannot speak of consensus on many points, today the Q Source is considered the most important basis on which to reconstruct Jesus' teachings.

3
The gospel of Matthew

This gospel was written in the decade of the eighties, after the destruction of Jerusalem. It probably appeared in Syrian territory, perhaps in the Damascus region. It is written in the context of strong polemics between the Christian sectors and Jewish leaders. Its sources include the gospel of Mark, the Q Source, different traditions of sayings and parables gathered by Matthew, and some legendary material which he uses to compose his narrative of Jesus' infancy. Matthew generally follows Mark's themes, but organizes much of the material along his own plan. Sometimes he is clearly adapting Jesus' words to fit the conflictive situation in which he is living, but maintains their essential content.

4
The gospel of Luke

Like Matthew, this gospel was written in the decade of the eighties, probably somewhere in western Palestine. It is presented as the first part of a large, two-part work: the gospel of Jesus and the Acts of the Apostles. In addition to Mark and the Q Source, it draws on abundant material that Luke himself collected, which makes up almost half the gospel. This allows him to compose beautiful scenes and tell some very moving stories. He also uses his own traditions to create his gospel of Jesus' infancy. He generally follows Mark's themes, with a few changes and some important omissions. Luke shapes the figure of Jesus from his own perspective, but his aim is to highlight an image that already existed in the traditions on which he draws.

5
The historic contribution of John's gospel

This gospel is structurally similar to Mark, Matthew and Luke, but it is very different. It probably appeared in the region of Syria, around the end of the first century. The narrative scheme is different from that of the synoptics; unlike them, John speaks of Jesus traveling three times to the Passover feast in Jerusalem, which suggests that his activity lasted longer than two years. The language and content of his message are also different. In the synoptics, Jesus talks in beautiful parables or short sayings; in John he develops long discourses, very different from that unmistakable style. In the synoptics, Jesus' preaching is centered on God's reign; in John he talks about his own person and his mission. Also, in the synoptics Jesus is constantly defending the cause of the poor and oppressed; in John he says almost nothing about them. Scholars believe that the synoptic gospels offer us better information on the memory of Jesus that was passed on by the traditions, although John sometimes gives information of great historical value. He tells us that Jesus' first disciples came from the Baptist's circle; that there was not a Jewish trial against Jesus, but an interrogation prior to referring the accusation to Pilate; that Jesus was executed on the eve of Passover (the 14th of Nisan), and not on the feast day.

6
The debate over the [apocryphal] Gospel of Thomas

Scholars today view the Gospel of Thomas as the most interesting of all the apocryphal gospels. The text does not contain any narrative material. It does not tell about Jesus' healings, or his death and resurrection. It does not attribute any christological title to him. It is simply a collection of 114 sayings (*logia*) of Jesus: wisdom or prophetic sayings, parables, or brief dialogues. The title of the document says: «These are the secret sayings that the living Jesus spoke and Didymos Judas Thomas recorded». At present there is lively debate over its date and its relation to the synoptic gospels. One group of authors (almost all members of the Jesus Seminar) give it equal standing with the Q Source, date it as early as 50-70 A.D., and consider it independent of the synoptic tradition; if so, the Gospel of Thomas would be one of the most important sources for research on Jesus. However most authors believe it was composed in Syria after 70 A.D., probably before the end of the first century, and that its content is not independent of the synoptic gospels. Everyone agrees that the document is tinged by Gnosticism to one degree or another. The Gospel of Thomas may be useful in measuring the depth and impact of the memory of Jesus in different environments, and in studying the changes that the tradition may have undergone in the process of transmission.

474

7

The critical study of historian Flavius Josephus

Modern scholars have analyzed the writings of Flavius Josephus more critically than in the past. His most relevant works are *La guerra judía* (English: *The Jewish War*) and *Antigüedades de los judíos* (English: *Jewish Antiquities*), both written in Rome in the decade of the 90s. Both give very important information on the political, social and cultural context of Palestine in the time of Jesus. Josephus knows Galilee very well, for he was the supreme commander of the Jewish forces from that region in the war against Rome (66-67). He mentions Jesus on two occasions. Speaking of the stoning of James in Jerusalem in 62 A.D., he describes him as «the brother of Jesus, called Christ». The most important citation, if we remove the glosses added by medieval Christian transcribers, says the following:

> Now there was about this time Jesus, a wise man. He was a doer of wonderful works, a teacher of those who receive the truth with pleasure. He attracted to him many Jews and many people of Greek origin. And when Pilate, because of an accusation by the principal men amongst us, had condemned him to the cross, those who loved him at the first did not forsake him. And the tribe of Christians, named after him, have not disappeared (*Jewish Antiquities* 18, 3, 3).

The neutral witness of Roman writers

℘

The historian Tacitus (50-120 A.D.), the writer Suetonius (around 120), and Pliny the Younger (61-120), legate of the emperor Trajan in Bithynia, offer brief information about Jesus. Their references have an important documentary value, since they are neutral observers or even hostile to the Christian movement. They never cast doubt on the existence of Jesus. They give only a schematic image of him: Jesus came from Judea, was executed under Tiberius by the governor Pontius Pilate, and at the time of writing, he was being worshiped by his followers «like a god». Their information fits completely with what the Christian sources say.

9

The Qumran manuscripts

℘

Today's researchers have an almost complete translation of the non-biblical manuscripts that were recovered from the caves around Qumran (north of the Dead Sea), after 1947 when an Arab herdsman found in one of them seven handwritten scrolls of exceptional importance. Three of the writings in particular shed light on the richness and diversity of the Jewish world in the time of Jesus: the *Rule of the Congregation* at Khirbet Qumran (100-75 B.C.); the *War Scroll* (37-4 B.C.), preparation for the war of the end times between the «sons of light and the sons of darkness»; and the *Hymns,* some thirty psalms infused with a spirituality of great tenderness toward God. The Qumran manuscripts also shed great light on the first Christian communities: the images they use, the idea of the «new covenant», the use of wine in sacred banquets. There is no serious reason to believe that Jesus was an «Essene» from Qumran. On the contrary, scholars believe that his activity and his message would have been immediately rejected in Qumran.

The hostility of the rabbinical literature

Jesus is mentioned in about a dozen passages of the Talmud. There he is called *Yeshu,* or contemptuously referred to as *Ben Pandira* or *Ben Pantera,* implying that he is the illegitimate son of a Roman soldier who raped Mary. Their image of Jesus can be summarized as follows: He «practiced witchcraft» (performed miracles); he mocked the words of the «wise men» (teachers of the law); he expounded Scripture as the Pharisees did; he had five disciples; he «led Israel astray»; he was «hung» (crucified) as a false prophet and deceiver on the eve of a Passover feast. Still, this hostile image fits substantially with the information given in the gospels.

11

Interest in the apocryphal gospels

In 1945, the discovery of the codices of Nag Hammadi (Upper Egypt) stimulated new interest in the «apocryphal gospels», which have since become a source of all kinds of biographies and works of fiction about Jesus. Some people naively believe that these writings reflect a pure version of the life and message of Jesus, before it came under dogmatic control by the Church. These gospels come from various places in the Mediterranean basin. Some of them may date back to the middle of the second century; most were composed much later, and after a long process, Christian communities selected the gospels that were considered authentic by them.

There are important differences among the apocryphal gospels. Some were written to satisfy popular curiosity, by filling «gaps» in the gospels about Jesus' infancy and childhood (e.g. *Protoevangel of James, Gospel of Pseudo-Matthew, The Birth of Mary, The Story of Joseph the Carpenter*) or about his passion and resurrection (*The Gospel of Peter,* and the *Gospel of Nicodemus* or *Acts of Pilate*). A quick glance at these fantasy-filled tales will show that they do not offer reliable information (except for the *Gospel of Peter,* which is similar to the passion narrative in the synoptics).

We also have fragments of apocryphal gospels from Jewish-Christian circles (e.g. *The Gospel of the Nazarenes, Gospel of the Ebionites, Gospel of the Hebrews*). These are the oldest of the apocryphal gospels. They provide some helpful elements for comparison with the traditions in the synoptic gospels, but they do not offer new information.

Some of the apocryphal gospels were written by marginal groups, to present their own beliefs as coming from Jesus. Thus they speak of Jesus' «secret teachings» to Mark, Peter, Thomas, or Mary Magdalene. Most of these writings come from gnostic circles (e.g. *Dialogue of the Savior, Gospel of Mary, Gospel of Philip, Pistis Sophia*).

Researchers today are re-evaluating these non-canonical sources. In order to get closer to the historical figure of Jesus, in principle we need to use all the available sources, not only the officially accepted gospels, and rigorously analyze the possible historicity of each one. But the results have been disappointing. Except for J.D. Crossan and some authors in the orbit of the *Jesus Seminar*, most scholars agree with the pessimistic judgment of J.P. Meier: «I do not think that the rabbinical material, the *agrapha*, the apocryphal gospels and the Nag Hammadi codices (particularly the *Gospel of Thomas*) offer new and reliable information, or authentic sayings apart from those in the New Testament».

Criteria of historicity

Here is a brief summary of the principal criteria used by today's researchers to evaluate the historicity of the material contained in the literary sources.

1
The criterion of difficulty

Facts about Jesus, and acts or sayings by him, are considered highly credible if they would have caused problems for the early Christians, and thus are unlikely to have been invented by them. We can sometimes see that this «embarrassing» material has been softened and even removed in the process of transmission. For example there is scholarly unanimity based on this criterion, regarding the historicity of Jesus' baptism by John the Baptist.

2
The criterion of discontinuity

We can confidently attribute to Jesus those deeds and words which cannot be derived from the Judaism of his day, or from the early Church. Some examples are his meals with «tax collectors and sinners»; his call to «enter the reign of God»; his calling on God as *Abba*. This criterion is helpful in understanding the unique and irreducible content of his message and activity, but it does not explain everything. Used as an absolute and exclusive criterion, it would leave us with an «unreal» Jesus — reduced to a minimum, artificially isolated from his people, and disconnected from the movement of followers that he established. Therefore some scholars (Theissen, Sanders, Meier and others) use it together with the principle of «plausibility», which allows for Jesus' relationship with the Jewish people on the one hand (Jesus is a Jew), and on the other his impact on the Christian movement (Jesus is the origin of Christianity).

3
The criterion of multiple witnesses

Jesus' deeds and words are more historically credible when they appear independently in more than one literary source (for example in Mark, the Q Source, John, and Paul) and in more than one literary form (sayings, parables, healing stories). This criterion supports the credibility, for example, of Jesus' healing activity, his menacing intervention in the temple, his preaching on the reign of God. A tradition may be authentic, however, even if it appears in only one source (for instance the Aramaic word *Abba* is mentioned only in Mark 14:36).

4
The criterion of consistency

Once we have gathered a set of materials in accordance with the criteria mentioned above, other deeds and words of Jesus can be accepted as probably historical if they are consistent with the «data base» thus established (e.g. sayings on the coming of God's reign, disputes with his adversaries). However, some sentences that are very consistent with Jesus' message may not have originated with him, but with Christian missionaries who knew his preaching well.

5
Rejection and crucifixion

Since there is no doubt that Jesus was crucified under orders from Pilate, it makes sense for researchers to look for explanations of this execution in his message and actions. It would be hard to believe in a Jesus whose teaching and activity bore no relation to his death on the cross.

6

Other less important criteria

∽

There are also some secondary criteria of historicity, not as strong as the ones listed above. They include vestiges of Aramaic or Semitic expressions (which might also come from Jewish Christians); Palestinian «local color» (which might also reflect the context of a Palestinian Christian group); and stories told with specific, vivid details (which is not by itself a sufficient proof of historicity).

C

Basic Archeological Information

Here is a brief list of the most interesting discoveries in recent research on Jesus:

1

The Qumran manuscripts

In 1947, an Arab herdsman found some clay jars in a cave on the northeast side of the Dead Sea, containing seven scrolls of exceptional importance. Ten other caves were explored in subsequent years, and a great «monastic» center was excavated on a site near the Dead Sea called Khirbet Qumran. The manuscripts found there date from approximately 200 B.C. to 70 A.D. None of them mention Jesus, because almost all were written before his birth. Nevertheless, the publication of this complete «library» from Qumran has given scholars a close look at a religious community and some documents from the same time, and in the same geographical area, as the life of Jesus. Today the Qumran manuscripts are considered indispensable for studying an assortment of viewpoints and concerns from the society in which Jesus lived.

2

The Nag Hammadi codices

In 1945 a worker near the Egyptian city of Nag Hammadi, 600 kilometers south of Cairo, happened upon a collection of papyri made up of 45 Christian texts. They were transcriptions in the Coptic language dating to the sixth century A.D., of materials written several centuries earlier. These apocryphal gospels («apocryphal» means «secret») were of different types, but they almost all present Jesus from the perspective of a sectarian movement called «Gnosticism». They were written after the gospels of Mark, Matthew and Luke, and offer no reliable information beyond what is in the officially accepted gospels. Some are fantastic recreations of the figure of Jesus, allegedly «hidden away» by the Church; they do not stand up to even minimal critical analysis, and have not been authenticated by any specialists in research on Jesus. The only apocryphal gospel that merits careful attention is the one called *The Gospel of Thomas* (see Appendix 3).

3

The inscription of Pilate

In 1962 some Italian archeologists were pulling weeds from the ruins of the theatre at Caesarea by the Sea, headquarters of the Roman government during the time of Jesus, when they found an inscription with the name of the prefect Pontius Pilate. The inscription is in Latin and commemorates Pilate's dedication of a public building erected in honor of the emperor Tiberius. It is the first physical evidence of the existence of Pilate, the prefect who sentenced Jesus to death.

4

The ossuary of the high priest Caiaphas

In November 1990, some builders working on the south side of the ancient city of Jerusalem, opposite Mount Zion, accidentally discovered an elaborately decorated ossuary like those used to bury members of upper-class families in first-century Jerusalem. On one compartment of the ossuary, roughly carved in Aramaic, is the name *Yehosef bar Caiafa*. That is the name by which Flavius Josephus calls the high priest Caiaphas. This compartment contains the bones of six people: two newborn infants, another between two and five years old, an adolescent, an adult woman, and a man about sixty years old. Archeologists believe it is the tomb of the family of Caiaphas, who was the high priest between 18 and 36 A.D. and played an important role in delivering Jesus to the Roman authorities.

5

Yehonanan, crucified in Jerusalem

In June 1968, archaeologist Vassilio Tzaferis discovered a first-century tomb dug into the rock at Giv'at ha-Mitvar, northeast of Jerusalem. One of the ossuaries contained the bones of a man between twenty and thirty years old, named *Yehonanan*, who had been crucified. His arms had been tied, not nailed, to the crossbar. His feet were separated and nailed, not to the front but on the sides of the vertical post. Each foot was held by a long nail that went first through a piece of olive wood (so he could not free the foot), then through the heel, and into the wooden post. One of the nails had been twisted on its way into the knotty wood, and could not be pulled out of the dead man's foot. The heel, the nail, and the piece of olive wood were still together in the ossuary. The body of *Yehonanan*, whom the archeologists call «the crucified one at Giv'at ha-Mitvar», sheds a sinister light on what Jesus must have suffered.

6

The location of the praetorium and Golgotha

Recent excavations at Jerusalem have helped to locate some biblical sites more exactly. Archeologists today believe that the «praetorium», Pilate's official residence in Jerusalem, was not in the Antonia tower but in the upper part of the city, in the former palace of Herod the Great. Jesus probably heard his death sentence in a small plaza facing the palace, which was paved with large stone tiles (*lithostroton*). Also, a study of the ancient walls of Jerusalem has confirmed with a high degree of probability that Jesus was crucified on the small rock which can now be seen in the Church of the Holy Sepulchre. It has been shown that in Jesus' time, this rock (Golgotha) was outside the city walls. Jesus may have been buried nearby.

7

Excavations at Sepphoris and Tiberias

In recent decades four teams of archeologists, in limited excavations at Tiberias and more extensively at Sepphoris, have shown the importance of both these cities in Jesus' time; however the Roman theatre, the underground aqueduct and the villa of Dionysius discovered at Sepphoris are of later origin. Today's scholars attribute great importance to the building of the two cities, in the short period of twenty years during Jesus' life. This urbanization led to a new socio-economic situation in Galilee, provoking crisis and impoverishment for many families. It was in this context that Jesus proclaimed his message of the reign of God in the Galilean villages, without setting foot in Sepphoris or Tiberias.

8

The villages of Jotapata and Gamla

Jotapata (or Yodfat) in Lower Galilee, and Gamla on the Golan Heights, were destroyed by the Roman legions in 67 A.D.; they remained buried and intact until a recent series of excavations. This archeological work has brought to light a lot of evidence about the life of a Jewish village in the time of Jesus, which enables us to see more clearly how Jesus might have lived in Nazareth.

9

Excavations in Galilee

Excavations in different parts of Galilee have confirmed many details about the Jewish way of life among the people who lived there. Stone vessels, pools for ritual purification, burial sites with ossuaries, and a pork-free diet are evidence of Jewish ethnicity and religion in Jesus' time. These signs also appear in Sepphoris and Tiberias, which suggests that although these cities were more hellenized than the peasant villages, a majority of their population was Jewish.

10

Vestiges of ancient Nazareth

Systematic excavations are hard to carry out in the modern city of Nazareth, but for some years there have been explorations to the east of the first-century Nazareth. The findings include some well-built terraces for vineyards on a hillside, a round tower that was also associated with a vineyard, and a wine press dug into the rock. We cannot dismiss the possibility that Joseph and Jesus were engaged in this type of construction.

A Galilean fishing boat

In 1986, when a severe drought reduced lake Galilee to a very low level, two members of the Ginnosaur kibbutz discovered the profile of a boat emerging from the coastal mud. Inside it were bowls and lanterns which have been dated to the first century A.D. through the use of carbon-14 methods. The boat was made of cedar, measuring 8.12 meters in length and 2.35 meters at the beam. It must have had a mast for a square sail, but it also carried oars. There was room for thirteen people. It was the kind of boat used in Jesus' time for fishing or crossing the lake. It may have sunk in a storm in the early first century.

Appendix 5

491

Current methods of research on Jesus

Here are some directions that scholars are currently following in their study of Jesus[1].

• The skepticism sown by R. Bultmann has been overcome. Scholars now move in a climate of relative optimism and confidence. There is less inclination to see historical research on Jesus as irrelevant to the Christian faith, and to believe that we cannot really know much about him. Except for Flavius Josephus, and perhaps Paul of Tarsus, «Jesus is the best-known Jewish personality of his time» (D. Flusser).

• There is widespread consensus that it is not possible to write a biography of Jesus, in the modern sense of that word. It is understood that the gospels, the principal source of the history of Jesus, reflect the impact he had on his followers and conserve memories that date back to him, although they were composed by believers who interpreted Jesus' life from the standpoint of their faith in the risen Christ. Their work does not constitute a «biography», but proclaims the Good News of Jesus: Messiah, Lord, and Son of God.

• Scholars in general, with some noteworthy exceptions (J.P. Meier), do not restrict their work to the critical study of literary sources; rather they use many methods to learn about Jesus through archeology, sociology, cultural anthropology, the economics of pre-industrial agrarian societies, etc.

• There is also a consensus that research on the figure of Jesus should draw on all the available sources, although the synoptic gospels are the most important and decisive source. There has been progress in understanding the apocryphal gospels, the works of Flavius Josephus, the rabbinical literature, the *targumim*, and the intertestamental apocryphal or pseudepigraphal writings. The works of Flavius Josephus are studied with particular critical rigor, bearing in mind the pro-Roman bias in his presentation of the facts (Freyne, Horsley). Critical analysis of the rabbinical literature has also been important, in order not to draw false conclusions about Judaism prior to 70 A.D. (Neusner, Sanders).

• We have also seen growing attention to archeological data on Roman Palestine before 70 A.D. Researchers are not expecting sensational discoveries, but they are gathering and evaluating the results of their ongoing work: for instance on the Jewish life style of the Galilean people, everyday life in the Galilean vil-

[1]   There is debate about whether this period, since the 1980s, should be called a «Third Quest». The period from Reimarus (1694-1768) to Schweitzer (1875-1965) was called the first «Quest for the Historical Jesus»; from E. Käsemann (1953) to E. Schillebeeckx (1979) has been called the «Second» or «New Quest».

lages, their degree of hellenization, and the impact of construction in Sepphoris and Tiberias (Reed, González Echegaray, Charlesworth).

• Today's scholars are making an important effort to locate Jesus within the Judaism of his time, which was much more complex and pluralistic than was understood until recently. We must remember that Jesus was the founder of a «Jewish renewal movement» (Theissen). The tendency which prevailed until a few years ago, to emphasize only the originality and uniqueness of Jesus, has been corrected by using the «criterion of discontinuity» less exclusively and more flexibly. It is true that models of Jesus apart from Judaism have been offered (for example the «itinerant cynic» presented by Downing, Mack, and in part, Crossan), but they have been widely subjected to sharp criticism.

• In recent years the study of Galilee has become important as a more specific way to understand the context in which Jesus moved, since most of his activity and the preaching of his message occurred in the Galilean villages and around the lake (Freyne, Horsley, Reed, Charlesworth). Special attention is focused, for example, on the degree of possible hellenization of the region, socio-economic influences from the urban centers of Sepphoris and Tiberias, the burden of tributes and taxes on the peasant classes, and the presence in Galilee of Pharisees and teachers of the law.

• In these same years there have been notable developments in the application of the social sciences and cultural anthropology to the study of Jesus (Malina, Rohrbaugh, E.W. Stegemann and W. Stegemann, Moxnes, Aguirre, Guijarro, and members of the *Context Group*). There has also been progress toward understanding the economic situation (Hanson, Oakman). These scholars are working from a double conviction: that in the society in which Jesus lived it was not possible to separate religion from sociopolitical concerns; and that Jesus was not a social revolutionary, but through his activity and his message he did directly challenge the social order (Horsley).

• There is deepening understanding of Jesus' specific activity from the viewpoint of the social sciences and anthropology. His healings have been the focus of socio-cultural research on ancient medicine, magic, and miracles (Kee, Pilch, Avalos, Guijarro, Stevan). The same is true of his exorcisms (Twelftree, Strecher, Chilton, Guijarro); his custom of eating with «tax collectors and sinners» has also been studied from the viewpoint of the anthropology of meals and the purity system (Douglas, Malina, Neusner, Aguirre, Crossan).

- The state of current research has been described as «chaotic creativity», because of its variety of models: Jesus as a «marginal Jew» (Meier); as a «social reformer» (Horsley, Theissen, Kaylor); as an «itinerant cynic» (Downing, Mack, Crossan); as a «wisdom teacher» (Ben Witherington III, Schüssler Fiorenza); as a «pious Jew» or *hasid,* filled with the Spirit (Vermes, Borg); and as an «eschatological prophet» or Messiah (Meier, Wright, Dunn, Stuhlmacher, Bocmuehl). Certainly there is a risk of focusing the research on a single aspect, to the neglect of others that were gathered in the Jesus tradition. Thus we need to attend to the most solid, well-reasoned contribution of each model. The same Jesus who acts as an «eschatological prophet» also promotes the «social change» required by the coming of God's reign, because he is moved by the Spirit of God, which also impels him to cure illness and offer forgiveness; he is not only proclaiming the definitive reign of God, but its real presence in the search for God's justice. We can probably come closer to Jesus if we avoid the risk of compartmentalizing models and bring in compatible aspects of different approaches.

- James D.G. Dunn has recently reminded us of two questions that have been neglected in modern research on the historical Jesus. First, we tend to forget that our research will not bring us to a «pure Jesus» by eliminating from the tradition everything that was subsequently added or modified, but should be aimed at the clearest possible understanding of the «impact» that he had on his followers. Second, accustomed as we are to a culture of writing, modern researchers sometimes forget the importance of oral transmission in the Jesus tradition; we do not understand its characteristic features and how it works. Dunn's critique is now apparently being taken seriously.

- Three features mark the work of today's scholars. The research is moving away from Europe toward the Anglo-Saxon world, where the number of studies and publications is increasing; there is an increasing development of interdisciplinary research; and teamwork has played a growing role. One thinks, for example, of the creation of the Historical Jesus Section within the Society of Biblical Literature in 1983; the foundation of the controversial Jesus Seminar in 1985, with about a hundred members; the Context Group, which meets regularly to study the cultural context of the Bible, or the International Q Project.

- Research on Jesus today is carried out by an impressive army of exegetes, linguists, historians, anthropologists and archeologists, working intensively on this exciting task of coming to know Jesus better. In the *United States* they include D.C. Allison (Pennsylvania), B.L. Blackburn (Georgia), C.L. Blomberg (Colorado),

M.J. Borg (Oregon), the late R.E. Brown (New York), J.H. Charlesworth (New Jersey), B. Chilton (New York), J.D. Crossan (Chicago), W. Farmer (Texas), P. Fredriksen (Massachusetts), R. Funk (California), W.R. Herzog (New York), R.A. Horsley (Massachusetts), D. Kaylor (North Carolina), H.C. Kee (Pennsylvania), H. Koester (Massachusetts), B. Malina (Nebraska), J.P. Meier (New York), J.H. Neyrey (Indiana), D.E. Oakman (Washington), S.J. Patterson (Missouri), J.L. Reed (California), A.J. Saldarini (Massachusetts), E.P. Sanders (North Carolina), B.B. Scott (Oklahoma), and E. Schüssler Fiorenza (New York).

In the *United Kingdom*: R.J. Bauckham (Scotland), J.D.G. Dunn (England), J.H. McDonald (Scotland), M.B. O'Donell (England), and N.T. Wright (England). In *Ireland*: S. Freyne. In *Canada*: C.A. Evans, J.S. Kloppenborg, B.F. Meyer, and R.L. Webb. In *Australia*: G.H. Twelftree.

On the European continent: In *France*: S. Légasse, J.-P. Lémonon, A. Paul, Ch. Perrot, and J. Schlosser. In *Germany*: J. Gnilka, M. Hengel, M. Karrer, H. Merklein, R. Pesch, J. Roloff, L. Schotroff, H. Schürmann, P. Stuhlmacher, Gerd Theissen. In *Holland*: E. Schillebeeckx. In *Italy*: the late G. Barbaglio and R. Fabris. In *Scandinavia*: P. Borgen, T. Holmen, H. Moxnes, and H. Rieselfed. In *Spain*: R. Aguirre, S. Guijarro, J. González Echegaray, X. Pikaza, A. Puig, and S. Vidal. In *Switzerland*:, F. Bovon, P. Buhler D. Marguerat, and E. Norelli.

In *Latin America*: J.L. Segundo (Uruguay) and J. Sobrino (El Salvador).

Jewish scholars: D. Flusser, D. Mendels, J. Neusner, E. Rivkin, and G. Vermes.

Jesus in science fiction

While scientific research on the Bible continues apace, a large number of books, articles, and science-fiction novels are promoting images of Jesus that are quite at odds with the information authenticated by biblical scholars and exegetes.

Some of these works are derived from the esoteric and gnostic trends that have become fashionable as part of the «New Age» movement. Their images of Jesus can be traced to esoteric traditions; to gnostic religiosity; to the «secret» Jesus of the Templars; to the Theosophical Society; to the anthroposophy of Rudolf Steiner; to the Rosicrucian Order (AMORC) and *The Mystical Life of Jesus* by H.S. Lewis; to the movement of the Holy Grail; to the Universal White Brotherhood; to stories of contact with extraterrestrials, and so on. The response of biblical scholars to this sort of literature is unanimous: its image of Jesus has nothing to do with the Jesus who lived in Galilee in the early first century[1].

There are also hastily prepared books by writers in other fields besides historical research on Jesus, such as journalism, fantasy literature, and occultism. These books on Jesus are offered together with others on UFOs, the secrets of the Egyptian pyramids, inexplicable historical events, and so on. They have titles like *Jesus lived and died in Kashmir; The secret history of Jesus; Jesus the man without gospels; Jesus and Mary Magdalene;* or *Jesus the great unknown.* Without analyzing each of these in detail, we can make the following general observations:

• They are written without consulting modern research: their superficial portraits of Jesus are not at all based on historical information, but generally contradict it. Their stories are sometimes supported by frivolous references to «recent research» or «the latest scientific data», without naming any credible experts on the subject.

• Uninitiated readers may never suspect the arbitrary use they make of sources, without any effort to evaluate their historicity. For example Dan Brown, in his novel *The DaVinci Code*, bases his theory that Mary Magdalene was married to Jesus on the [apocryphal] *Gospel of Philip*, claiming that it was earlier, more original and more authentic than the canonical gospels. The uninitiated will not know that in a study of that gospel, the highly respected German author Hans-Josef Klauck has concluded that «no one has dated it earlier than the second century».

• These books make provocative claims in opposition to what first-hand researchers have found. One claims that Jesus was an Essene; scholars have con-

---

1 For full information see Jean VERNETTE, *Jésus dans la nouvelle religiosité. Ésoterismes, gnoses et sects d'aujourd'hui.* Desclée, Paris, 1987. Also by the same author, *Jésus au peril des sects.* Desclée, Paris, 1994.

cluded that Jesus' activity and teachings were roundly rejected in Qumran. Another calls Jesus' marriage to Mary Magdalene «the most important and best-kept secret of all time»; no competent researchers had found evidence of it before Dan Brown came along. According to Michel Benoit, «Judas was assassinated by Peter»; scholars would never have guessed that.

• Writers in this genre use selected episodes of decidedly secondary importance, for purely sensationalistic purposes: Jesus' love for Mary Magdalene, the betrayal by Judas, the «secret teachings» of Jesus, etc. At the same time they pay no attention to the historical core of Jesus' teaching and activity: his message about God, his defense of the poor, his criticism of the powerful, his call to conversion, or his plan for a more just world for everyone.

Chronology

YEARS	JESUS	EVENTS
6-4 B.C. 5 B.C.	*His birth*	Judas and Matthias, teachers of the law, and 42 young disciples are burned alive by Herod, accused of destroying the «imperial eagle» placed in the temple.
		At the end of March, 4 B.C., Herod the Great dies at his palace in Jericho. On April 11 (Passover), his son Archelaus takes his body to the Herodion fortress.
4 B.C.	*Jesus takes his first steps*	Soon afterward, the suppressed rage of the people explodes. In Galilee, Judas occupies Sepphoris and takes control of a weapons arsenal. The slave Simon and his men sack and burn the Jericho palace.
c. 3 B.C.	*Jesus is 3-5 years old*	The soldiers of Varus, governor of Syria, destroy Sepphoris (only 6 km. from Nazareth) and raze the surrounding villages, beheading their inhabitants or taking them away as slaves.
		Varus crucifies about 2,000 Jews in the area around Jerusalem.
		Augustus names Archelaus ethnarch of Judea and Samaria. Antipas is named tetrarch of Galilee, Perea and Iturea.
6 A.D.A	*youth of 10-12 years*	Archelaus is deposed by the emperor Augustus, who sends him into exile at Vienne (the Gauls).
		Quirinius is named governor of Syria.
		Judas and Zadok rebel against the payment of tributes to Rome.
6-9 A.D.	*Between 10-12 and 13-15 years*	Coponius rules as prefect of Judea from 6-9 A.D.
		Annas is named high priest by the newly arrived Roman prefect, Coponius.
		Under the rule of Coponius, with Annas as high priest, a group of Samaritans defile the temple by scattering human bones on the eve of the Passover. In reprisal, Samaritans are forbidden from then on to enter the holy area.

10 A.D.A	*youth of 14-16 years*	The reconstruction of the Jerusalem temple, begun by Herod the Great 30 years earlier, is completed.
14 A.D.	*18-20 years of age*	On August 9, the emperor Augustus dies in Rome at age 77. He is succeeded by Tiberius, age 56.
15 A.D.	*19-21 years of age*	The prefect Valerius Gratus deposes Annas as high priest, although his family continues to exercise great power in Jerusalem.
18 A.D.	*22-24 years of age*	Valerius Gratus names Joseph Caiaphas, married to a daughter of Annas, as high priest. It is he who will deliver Jesus to the Roman authorities 12 years later.
c. 19 A.D.	*23-25 years of age*	Antipas completes the construction of Tiberias, on the shore of lake Galilee, and takes up residence there. Jesus apparently never entered that city.
26 A.D.	*30-32 years of age*	The new prefect Pontius Pilate lands at Caesarea by the Sea. Four years later he will order Jesus' execution.
26-27 A.D.	*30-33 years of age*	Pilate begins his rule by bringing military banners with images of the emperor and imperial eagles into Jerusalem, provoking a strong negative reaction.
27-28 A.D.	*31-34 years of age*	Activity of John the Baptist at the Jordan river. Jesus hears his call and is baptized by John.
28 A.D.	*32-34 years of age*	The Baptist is imprisoned by Antipas at the Machaerus fortress, later beheaded.
		Jesus' prophetic activity in Galilee.
30 A.D.	*34-36 years of age*	Jesus is crucified on the outskirts of Jerusalem, near an old rock quarry, on April 7 (the eve of Passover).

Bibliography by Chapters

Chapter 1

1. STUDIES OF GALILEE

FREYNE Sean, *Galilee and Gospel*, Brill, Boston - Leiden 2002.

———, *Jesus, a Jewish Galilean. A New reading of the Jesus-story*, Clark International, London - New York 2005.

———, «The Geography, Politics and Economics of Galilee and the Quest for the Historical Jesus» *in* CHILTON Bruce - EVANS Craig A., *Studying the Historical Jesus. Evaluations of the State of Current Research*, Brill, Leiden-Boston-Cologne 1998, 75-121.

HORSLEY Richard A., *Galilee. History, Politics, People*, Trinity Press International, Valley Forge, PA 1995.

———, *Archaeology, History and Society in Galilee*, Trinity Press International, Harrisburg, PA 1996.

———, *Sociology and the Jesus Movement*, Continuum, New York 1994, 67-101.

HANSON K. C. - OAKMAN Douglas E., *Palestine in the time of Jesus. Social Structures and Social Conflicts*, Fortress Press, Minneapolis 1998.

THEISSEN Gerd - MERZ Annette, *El Jesús histórico*, Sígueme, Salamanca 1999, 151-176; 189-206.

COUSIN Hugues (ed.), *Le monde où vivait Jésus*, Cerf, París 1998, 11-128.

DEBERGÉ Pierre, «Le monde où vivait Jésus» *in* MARCHADOUR Alain (ed.), *Que sait-on de Jésus de Nazareth?*, Bayard, París 2000, 71-106.

SANDERS Ed Parish, «Jesús en Galilea» *in* DONNELLY Doris (ed.), *Jesús. Un coloquio en Tierra Santa*, Verbo Divino, Estella 2004, 11-38.

———, *La figura histórica de Jesús*, Verbo Divino, Estella 2000, 33-53.

VERMES Geza, *Jesús el judío*, Muchnik, Barcelona 1977, 47-62.

SAULNIER Christianne - ROLLAND Bernard, *Palestina en tiempos de Jesús*, Verbo Divino, Estela 1998[12].

AGUIRRE Rafael, *Del movimiento de Jesús a la Iglesia cristiana. Ensayo de exégesis sociológica del cristianismo primitivo*, Verbo Divino, Estella 2001[2], 23-32.

EHRMAN Bart D., *Jesús, el profeta apocalíptico*, Paidós, Barcelona 2001, 135-159.

FABRIS Rinaldo, *Jesús de Nazaret. Historia e interpretación*, Sígueme, Salamanca 1985, 59-70.

GNILKA Joachim, *Jesús de Nazaret. Mensaje e historia*, Herder, Barcelona 1993, 45-63; 83-93.

2. THE CONTRIBUTION OF ARCHAEOLOGY
CHARLESWORTH James H. (ed.), *Jesus and Archaeology*, Eerdmans, Grand Rapids — Cambridge 2006 (especially the articles by CHARLESWORTH, «Jesus, Research and Archaeology: A New Perspective», 11-63, and S. FREYNE, «Archaeology and the Historical Jesus», 64-83).

GONZÁLEZ ECHEGARAY Joaquín, *Arqueología y evangelios*, Verbo Divino, Estella 1999.

_____, *Jesús en Galilea. Aproximación desde la arqueología*, Verbo Divino, Estella 2000.

REED Jonathan L., *El Jesús de Galilea. Aportaciones desde la arqueología*, Sígueme, Salamanca 2006.

CROSSAN John Dominic - REED Jonathan L., *Jesús desenterrado*, Crítica, Barcelona 2003, especially 33-172.

3. SOCIOLOGICAL AND ANTHROPOLOGICAL APPROACHES
MALINA Bruce J., *El mundo social de Jesús y los evangelios*, Sal Terrae, Santander 2002.

_____, *El mundo del Nuevo Testamento. Perspectivas desde la antropología cultural*, Verbo Divino, Estella 1995.

_____, *The Social Gospel of Jesus. The Kingdom of God in Mediterranean Perspective*, Fortress Press, Minneapolis 2000.

MALINA Bruce J. - ROHRBAUGH Richard L., *Los evangelios sinópticos y la cultura mediterránea del siglo I. Comentario desde las ciencias sociales*, Verbo Divino, Estella 1996.

STEGEMANN E. W. - STEGEMANN W., *Historia social del cristianismo primitivo. Los inicios en el judaísmo y las comunidades cristianas en el mundo mediterráneo*, Verbo Divino, Estella 2001, especially 19-258.

4. THE ROMAN EMPIRE AND JEWISH RESISTANCE
SCHÜRER Emil, *La historia del pueblo judío en tiempos de Jesús*. I. *Fuentes y marco histórico*, Cristiandad, Madrid 1985.

LEIPOLDT, J. - GRUNDMANN, W., *El mundo del Nuevo Testamento*, Cristiandad, Madrid 1973, especially 19-188.

PAUL André, *El mundo judío en tiempos de Jesús. Historia política*, Cristiandad, Madrid 1982.

HORSLEY Richard A., *Jesus, and the Spiral of Violence. Popular Jewish Resistance in Roman Palestine*, Fortress Press, Minneapolis 1993.

_____, *Jesús y el Imperio. El Reino de Dios y el nuevo desorden mundial,* Verbo Divino, Estella 2003, 27-74.

HORSLEY Richard A. - HANSON John S., *Bandits, Prophets and Messiahs. Popular Movement at the time of Jesus,* Harper, San Francisco 1988.

5. SOME SPECIFIC ISSUES
PORTER Stanley E., «Jesus and the Use of Greek in Galilee» *in* CHILTON Bruce - EVANS Craig A., *Studying the Historical Jesus. Evaluations of the State of Current Research,* Brill, Leiden-Boston-Cologne 1988, 123-154.

OAKMAN Douglas E., «Money in the Moral Universe of the New Testament» *in* STEGEMANN W. - MALINA Bruce - THEISSEN Gerd, *The Social Setting of Jesus and the Gospels,* Fortress Press, Minneapolis 2002, 335-348.

6. OTHER WORKS OF INTEREST
WITHERINGTON III Ben, *The Jesus Quest. The Third Search for the Jew of Nazareth,* Inter-Varsity Press, Downers Grove, IL 1997, 14-41.

SICRE José Luis, *El cuadrante.* II. *La apuesta. El mundo de Jesús,* Verbo Divino, Estella 2002, 29-109.

GUEVARA Hernando, *Ambiente político del pueblo judío en tiempos de Jesús,* Cristiandad, Madrid 1985.

Chapter 2

1. FOR GENERAL STUDY
MEIER John Paul, *Un judío marginal. Nueva visión del Jesús histórico.* I. *Las raíces del problema y de la persona,* Verbo Divino, Estella 2001, 219-377 (English: *A Marginal Jew*).

BARBAGLIO Giuseppe, *Jesús, hebreo de Galilea. Investigación histórica,* Secretariado Trinitario, Salamanca 2003, 113-136.

SANDERS Ed Parish, *La figura histórica de Jesús,* Verbo Divino, Estella 2000, 55-61.

FABRIS Rinaldo, *Jesús de Nazaret. Historia e interpretación,* Sígueme, Salamanca 1985, 68-86.

COUSIN Hugues (ed.), *Le monde où vivait Jésus,* Cerf, París 1998, 199-219.

THEISSEN Gerd - MERZ, Annette, *El Jesús histórico,* Sígueme, Salamanca 1999, 191-193.

GNILKA Joachim, *Jesús de Nazaret. Mensaje e historia,* Herder, Barcelona 1993, 95-99.

CHILTON Bruce, *Rabbi Jesus. An Intimate Biography.* Doubleday, New York 2002, 3-22.

2. THE CONTRIBUTION OF ARCHEOLOGY
CHARLESWORTH James (ed.), *Jesus and Archaeology,* Eerdmans, Grand Rapids— Cambridge 2006, especially 206-222 and 236-282.

GONZÁLEZ ECHEGARAY Joaquín, *Jesús en Galilea. Aproximación desde la arqueología,* Verbo Divino, Estella 2000, especially 121-152.

REED Jonathan L., *El Jesús de Galilea. Aportaciones desde la arqueología,* Sígueme, Salamanca 2006, especially 133-177.

CROSSAN John Dominic - REED Jonathan L., *Jesús desenterrado,* Crítica, Barcelona 2003, especially 37-58.

3. SOCIOLOGICAL AND ANTHROPOLOGICAL APPROACHES
MALINA Bruce J., *El mundo social de Jesús y los evangelios,* Sal Terrae, Santander 2002.

_____ , *El mundo del Nuevo Testamento. Perspectivas desde la antropología cultural,* Verbo Divino, Estella 1995, especially 45-83 and 145-180.

MALINA Bruce J. - ROHRBAUGH Richard L., *Los evangelios sinópticos y la cultura mediterránea del siglo I. Comentario de las ciencias sociales,* Verbo Divino, Estella 1996.

4. THE RELIGIOUS CONTEXT
COUSIN Hugues (ed.), *Le monde où vivait Jesús,* Cerf, París 2002, especially 287-373.

MAIER J., *Entre los dos Testamentos. Historia y religión en la época del segundo templo,* Sígueme, Salamanca 1996.

SICRE DÍAZ José Luis, *El cuadrante.* II. *La apuesta. El mundo de Jesús,* Verbo Divino, Estella 2002, especially 115-170.

MANNS Frédéric, *La prière d'Israël à l'heure de Jésus,* Franciscan Printing Press, Jerusalem 1986.

ARON R., *Los años oscuros de Jesús.* Taurus, Madrid 1963.

Chapter 3

1. GENERAL DISCUSSION OF THE RELATIONSHIP BETWEEN JOHN THE BAPTIST AND JESUS
MEIER John Paul, *Un judío marginal. Nueva visión del Jesús histórico* II/1. *Juan y Jesús. El reino de Dios,* Verbo Divino, Estella 2001, 47-290.

THEISSEN Gerd - MERZ Annette, *El Jesús histórico,* Sígueme, Salamanca 1999, 226-244.

TATUM W. Barnes, *John the Baptist and Jesus. A report of the Jesus Seminar*, Polebridge Press, Sonoma, CA 1994.

BARBAGLIO Giuseppe, *Gesù, ebreo di Galilea. Indagine storica*, Ed. Dehoniane, Bologna 2003, 183-213.

FABRIS Rinaldo, *Jesús de Nazaret. Historia e interpretación*, Sígueme, Salamanca 1985, 89-101.

GNILKA Joachim, *Jesús de Nazaret. Mensaje e historia*, Herder, Barcelona 1993, 100-108.

BEAUDE Pierre-Marie, *Jesús de Nazaret*, Verbo Divino, Estella 1988, 98-104.

2. RECENT RESEARCH ON JOHN THE BAPTIST AND JESUS
WEBB Robert L., «John the Baptist and his Relationship to Jesus» *in* CHILTON Bruce - EVANS Craig A. (eds.), *Studying the Historical Jesus. Evaluations of the State Current Research*, Brill, Leiden 1998, 179-229.

3. JOHN THE BAPTIST AND JESUS IN THE CONTEXT OF BAPTIST MOVEMENTS AND QUMRAN
PERROT Charles, *Jesús y la historia*, Cristiandad, Madrid 1982, 80-110.

STEGEMANN Hartmut, *Los esenios, Qumrán, Juan Bautista y Jesús*, Trotta, Madrid 1996.

4. COMPARISON OF JOHN THE BAPTIST'S AND JESUS' MISSIONS
VIDAL Senén, *Los tres proyectos de Jesús y el cristianismo naciente*, Sígueme, Salamanca 2003, 61-124.

Chapter 4

1. GENERAL DISCUSSION OF THE REIGN OF GOD
BARBAGLIO Giuseppe, *Jesús, hebreo de Galilea. Investigación histórica*, Secretariado Trinitario, Salamanca 2003.

BEASLEY-MURRAY, G. R., *Jesus and the Kingdom of God*, Eerdmans, Grand Rapids 1986.

CHILTON Bruce, *Pure Kingdom. Jesus' Vision of God*, Eerdmans, Grand Rapids 1996.

————, (ed.), *The Kingdom of God in the Teaching of Jesus*, Fortress Press, Philadelphia 1984.

FUELLENBACH John, *The Kingdom of God. The Message of Jesus Today*, Orbis Books, New York 1995.

GNILKA Joachim, *Jesús de Nazaret. Mensaje e historia*, Herder, Barcelona 1993.

MEIER John Paul, *Un judío marginal. Nueva visión del Jesús histórico.* II/1. *Juan y Jesús. El reino de Dios,* Verbo Divino, Estella 2001.

MERKLEIN Helmut, *La signoria di Dio nell'annuncio di Gesù,* Paideia, Brescia 1994.

PERRIN Norman, *The Kingdom of God in the Teaching of Jesus* SCM Press, London 1975[3].

_____, *Jesus and the Language of the Kingdom,* Fortress Press, Philadelphia 1976.

SANDERS Ed Parish, *La figura histórica de Jesús,* Verbo Divino, Estella 2000.

_____, *Jesús y el judaísmo,* Trotta, Madrid 2004.

THEISSEN Gerd - MERZ Annete, *El Jesús histórico,* Sígueme, Salamanca 1999.

VIDAL Senén, *Los tres proyectos de Jesús y el cristianismo naciente,* Sígueme, Salamanca 2003.

2. RECENT RESEARCH ON DIFFERING INTERPRETATIONS OF THE REIGN OF GOD
BORG Marcus J., *Jesus in contemporary Scholarship,* Trinity Press International, Valley Forge 1994, especially pp. 47-126.
CHILTON Bruce, «The Kingdom of God in recent Discussion» *in* CHILTON Bruce - EVANS Craig A. (eds.), *Studying the Historical Jesus. Evaluations of the State Current Research,* Brill, Leiden 1998.

SAUCY Mark, *The Kingdom of God in the Teaching of Jesus in 20th Century Theology,* Word Publishing, Dallas 1997.

WITHERINGTON III Ben, *The Jesus Quest. The Third Search for the Jew of Nazareth,* Inter-Varsity Press, Downers Grove, IL 1997[2], especially pp. 116-136 y 137-160.

3. EXPECTATIONS OF THE REIGN OF GOD
GRELOT Pierre, *L'espérance juive à l'heure de Jésus,* Desclée, Paris 1978.

4. ON THE POLITICAL AND SOCIAL DIMENSION OF THE REIGN OF GOD
HORSLEY Richard A., *Jesus and the Spiral of Violence. Popular Jewish Resistance in Roman Palestine,* Fortress Press, Minneapolis 1993, especially pp. 167-326.

_____, *Jesús y el Imperio. El reino de Dios y el nuevo desorden mundial,* Verbo Divino, Estella 2003, especially pp. 105-163.

KAYLOR R. David, *Jesus the Prophet. His vision of the Kingdom on Earth,* Westminster-John Knox Press, Louisville 1994, especially pp. 70-120.

5. ON THE REIGN OF GOD AS A KINGDOM OF LIFE, JUSTICE AND LIBERATION

CASTILLO José María, *El reino de Dios. Por la vida y dignidad de los seres humanos,* Desclée de Brouwer, Bilbao 1999.

LOIS Julio, *Jesús de Nazaret, el Cristo liberador,* HOAC, Madrid 1995.

SOBRINO Jon, *Jesucristo liberador. Lectura histórico-teológica de Jesús de Nazaret,* Trotta, Madrid 1991.

Chapter 5

1. RECENT RESEARCH ON THE PARABLES

BLOMBERG Craig L., «The Parables of Jesus: Current Trends and Needs in Research» *in* CHILTON Bruce - EVANS Craig A. (eds.), *Studying the Historical Jesus. Evaluations of the State of Current Research,* Brill, Leiden-Boston-Cologne 1998², pp. 231-254.

GOWLER David B., *What are they saying about Parables?* Paulist Press, New York 2000.

PARKER Andrew, *Painfully Clear. The Parables of Jesus,* Academic Press, Sheffield 1996, pp. 10-121.

SNODGRASS Klyne R., «From Allegorizing to Allegorizing: A History of the Interpretation of the Parables of Jesus» *in* LONGENECKER Richard N. (ed.), *The Challenge of Jesus' Parables,* Eerdmans, Cambridge 2000, pp. 3-29.

WEDER Hans, *Metafore del Regno. Le parabole di Gesù: ricostruzione e interpretazione,* Paideia, Brescia 1991.

2. GENERAL OVERVIEW OF JESUS' POETIC AND PARABOLIC LANGUAGE

ESPINEL José Luis, *La poesía de Jesús,* San Esteban, Salamanca 1986.

SCOTT Brandon Bernard, *Jesus, Symbol-Maker for the Kingdom,* Fortress Press, Philadelphia 1981.

3. LITERARY ANALYSIS OF THE PARABLES

BOUCHER Madeleine, *The Mysterious Parable. A Literary Study,* Catholic Biblical Association, Washington 1977.

CROSSAN John Dominic, *In Parables. The Challenge of the Historical Jesus,* Polebridge Press, Sonoma 1992.

DUPONT Jacques, *Il metodo parabolico di Gesù*, Paideia, Brescia 1978.

FUSCO V., *Oltre la parabola. Introduzione alle parabole di Gesù*. Borla, Roma 1983.

HARNISCH Wolfgang, *Las parábolas de Jesús. Una introducción hermenéutica*, Sígueme, Salamanca 1989.

4. IMPORTANT STUDIES OF JESUS' PARABLES

DODD Charles Harold, *Las parábolas del Reino*, Cristiandad, Madrid 1974.

JEREMIAS Joachim, *Las parábolas de Jesús*, Verbo Divino, Estella 1971.

LINNEMANN Eta, *Jesus of the Parables. Introduction and Exposition*, Harper and Row, New York—Evanston (First edition published in German 1961).

VIA Dan Otto, *The Parables. Their Literary and Existencial Dimension*, Fortress Press, Philadelphia 1977.

5. COMMENTARIES ON JESUS' PARABLES

BATAGLIA Oscar, *Le parabole del Regno. Ricerca exegetica e pastorale*, Cittadella, Asís 1999².

BEASLEY-MURRAY G. R, *Jesus and the Kingdom of God*, Eerdmans, Grand Rapids 1986, pp. 108-143 and 194-218.

CAPON Robert Farrar, *The Parables of Grace*, Eerdmans, Grand Rapids 1988.

CERFAUX Lucien, *Mensaje de las parabolas*, Fax, Madrid 1969.

DONAHUE John R, *The Gospel in Parable*, Fortress Press, Minneapolis 1990.

ETCHELLS Ruth, *A reading of the Parables of Jesus*, Darton, Longman and Todd, London 1998.

HARRINGTON W., *Il parlait en paraboles*, Cerf, Paris 1967.

LONGENECKER Richard N. (ed.), *The Challenge of Jesus' Parables*, Eerdmans, Cambridge 2000.

MCBRIDE Denis, *Les paraboles de Jésus*, Eds. de l'Atelier, Paris 2001.

SCOTT Brandon Bernard, *Hear Then the Parable. A Commentary on the Parables of Jesus*, Fortress Press, Minneapolis 1990.

SHILLINGTON V. George (ed.), *Jesus and his Parables. Interpreting the Parables of Jesus Today*, T. & T. Clark, Edinburgh 1997.

6. READING THE PARABLES FROM SOME SPECIFIC VIEWPOINTS

BAILEY Kenneth E., *Poet and Peasant. Through Peasant Eyes. A Literary-Cultural Approach to the Parables in Luke*, Eerdmans, Grand Rapids 1983.

HEDRICK Charles W., *Parables as Poetic Fictions. The Creative Voice of Jesus*, Hendrikson, Massachusetts 1994.

HERZOG II William R., *Parables as Subversive Speech. Jesus as Pedagogue of the Oppressed*, Westminster-John Knox Press, Louisville 1994.

7. OTHER WORKS OF INTEREST

FORD Richard Q., *The Parables of Jesus. Recovering the Art of Listening*, Fortress Press, Minneapolis 1997.

FUNK Robert W. - SCOTT Bernard Brandon - BUTTS James R., *The Parables of Jesus. Red Letter Edition*, Polebridge Press, Sonoma 1988.

SCHWEIZER Eduard, *Jesús, parábola de Dios*, Sígueme, Salamanca 2001, pp. 37-55.

STEIN Robert H., *The Method and Message of Jesus' Teachings*, Westminster-John Knox Press, Louisville 1994, pp. 7-59.

Chapter 6

1. RECENT RESEARCH ON JESUS' MIRACLES

BARTOLOMÉ Juan José, «Reseña de la investigación crítica sobre los milagros de Jesús» *in* GUIRRE Rafael (ed.), *Los milagros de Jesús*, Verbo Divino, Estella 2002, pp. 15-52.

BLACKBURN Barry L., «The Miracle of Jesus» *in* CHILTON Bruce - EVANS Craig A. (eds.), *Studying the Historical Jesus. Evaluations of the State of Current Research*, Brill, Leiden-Boston-Cologne 1998, pp. 353-394.

2. SOCIO-CULTURAL RESEARCH ON MEDICINE, MAGIC, AND MIRACLES IN NEW TESTAMENT TIMES

AVALOS Hector, *Health, Care and the Rise of Christianity*, Hendrickson, Peabody, MA 1999.

EVANS Craig A., *Jesus and His Contemporaries*. Brill, Boston-Leiden 2001, pp. 213-243.

GEORGE Augustin, «Milagros en el mundo helénico» *in* LÉON-DUFOUR Xavier (ed.), *Los milagros de Jesús*, Cristiandad, Madrid 1979, pp. 95-108.

GUIJARRO Santiago, «Relatos de sanación y antropología médica. Una lectura de Mc 10,46-52» *in* AGUIRRE Rafael (ed.), *Los milagros de Jesús*, Verbo Divino, Estella 2002, pp. 247-267.

KEE Howard Clark, *Medicina, milagro y magia en tiempos del Nuevo Testamento*, El Almendro, Córdoba 1992.

PILCH John J., *Healing in the New Testament. Insights from Medical and Mediterranean Anthropology*, Fortress Press, Minneapolis 2000.

PIÑERO Antonio (ed.), *En la frontera de lo imposible. Magos, médicos y taumaturgos en el Mediterráneo antiguo en tiempos del Nuevo Testamento*, El Almendro, Córdoba 2001.

YAMAUCHI Edwin, «Magic or Miracle? Diseases, Demons and Exorcism» *in* WENHAM David - BLOMBERG Craig, *Gospel Perspectives. The Miracle of Jesus* VI, Wipf and Stock, Eugene, OR 1986, pp. 89-183.

3. MONOGRAPHIC STUDIES ON THE MIRACLES OF JESUS

GONZÁLEZ FAUS José Ignacio, *Clamor del Reino. Estudio sobre los milagros de Jesús*, Sígueme, Salamanca 1982.

LATOURELLE René, *Milagros de Jesús y teología del milagro*, Sígueme, Salamanca 1997².

LÉON-DUFOUR Xavier (ed.), *Los milagros de Jesús*, Cristiandad, Madrid 1979.

MEIER John Paul, *Un judío marginal. Nueva visión del Jesús histórico.* II/2. *Los Milagros*, Verbo Divino, Estella 2002.

PENNDU Theophile, *Jésus nous fait signe. Les miracles de Jésus*, Anne Sigier, Sillery (Quebec) 1997.

PERROT Charles - SOULETIE Jean-Louis - THÉVENOT Xavier, *Les miracles*, Eds. de l'Atelier, Paris 1995.

RICHARDSON Alan, *Las narraciones evangélicas sobre Milagros*, Fax, Madrid 1974.

SMITH Morton, *Jesús el Mago*, Martínez Roca, Barcelona 1988.

THEISSEN Gerd, *The Miracle Stories of the Early Christian Tradition*, Fortress Press, Philadelphia 1982.

TWELFTREE Graham H., *Jesus, the Miracle Worker*, Inter-Varsity Press, Downers Grove, IL 1999.

WENHAM David - BLOMBERG Craig (eds.), *Gospel Perspectives. The Miracle of Jesus* VI, Wipf and Stock, Eugene, OR 1986.

4. STUDIES ON THE MIRACLES IN MORE GENERAL WORKS ON JESUS

BARBAGLIO Giuseppe, *Gesù, ebreo di Galilea. Indagine storica*, Ed. Dehoniane, Bologna 2003, pp. 215-253.

CROSSAN John Dominic, *Jesús: Vida de un campesino judío,* Crítica, Barcelona 1994, pp. 177-208 and 352-408.

_____, *El nacimiento del cristianismo,* Sal Terrae, Santander 2002, pp. 291-304.

GNILKA Joachim, *Jesús de Nazaret. Mensaje e historia,* Herder, Barcelona 1993, pp. 145-171.

SANDERS Ed Parish, *Jesus and Judaism,* SCM Press, London 1999, pp. 157-173.

_____, *La figura histórica de Jesús,* Verbo Divino, Estella 2000, pp. 155-190.

5. SPECIFIC STUDIES ON EXORCISM

CHAPA Juan, «Exorcistas y exorcismos en tiempos de Jesús» *in* GUIRRE Rafael (ed.), *Los milagros de Jesús.* Verbo Divino, Estella 2002, pp. 121-146.

CHILTON Bruce, «An Exorcism of History: Mark 1,21-28» *in* HILTON Bruce - VANS Craig A. (eds.), *Authenticating the Activities of Jesus,* Brill, Boston-Leiden 2002, pp. 215-245.

GONZÁLEZ FAUS José Ignacio, «Jesús y los demonios» in *Fe y justicia,* Sígueme, Salamanca 1981.

GUIJARRO Santiago, «La dimensión política de los exorcismos de Jesús. La controversia de Belzebú desde la perspectiva de las circunstancias sociales» in *Estudios Bíblicos* 58 (2000), pp. 51-77.

_____, «The Politics of Exorcism» in STEGEMANN W. - MALINA Bruce J. - THEISSEN Gerd (eds.), *The Social Setting of Jesus and the Gospels,* Fortress Press, Minneapolis 2002, pp. 159-174.

MARCUS Joel, «The Beelzebul Controversy and the Eschatologies of Jesus» *in* CHILTON Bruce - EVANS Craig A. (eds.), *Authenticating the Activities of Jesus,* Brill, Boston-Leiden 2002, pp. 247-277.

STRECKER Christian, «Jesus and the Demoniacs» *in* STEGEMANN W. - MALINA Bruce J. - THEISSEN Gerd (eds.), *The Social Setting of Jesus and the Gospels,* Fortress Press, Minneapolis 2002, pp. 117-133.

TWELFTREE Graham H., *Jesus, the Exorcist. A Contribution to Study of the Historical Jesus,* Hendrickson, Peabody, MA 1993.

6. OTHER STUDIES OF INTEREST

DAVIES Stevan L., *Jesus the Healer,* SCM Press, London 1995.

HOOKER Morna D., *The Signs of a Prophet. The Prophetic Actions of Jesus,* Trinity Press International, Harrisburg, PA 1997.

Chapter 7

1. FOR A STUDY OF THE SOCIAL DIMENSION OF THE REIGN OF GOD

MALINA Bruce J., *The Social Gospel of Jesus. The Kingdom of God in Mediterranean Perspective*, Fortress Press, Minneapolis 2000.

HORSLEY Richard A., *Sociology and the Jesus Movement*, Continuum, New York 1994.

FREYNE Sean, *Galilee and Gospel*, Brill, Boston-Leiden 2002.

HANSON K. C. - OAKMAN Douglas E., *Palestine in the Time of Jesus*, Fortress Press, Minneapolis 1998.

STEGEMANN E. W. - STEGEMANN W., *Historia social del cristianismo primitivo. Los inicios en el judaísmo y las comunidades cristianas en el mundo mediterráneo*, Verbo Divino, Estella 2001, pp. 81-138 and147-178.

2. JESUS' INTERACTION WITH THE POOR

SCHOTROFF Louise - STEGEMANN Wolfang, *Jesús de Nazaret, esperanza de los pobres*, Sígueme, Salamanca 1981.

JEREMIAS Joachim, *Teología del Nuevo Testamento* I, Sígueme, Salamanca 1973, 133-148.

MOLTMANN Jürgen, *El camino de Jesucristo*, Sígueme, Salamanca 1973, 141-151.

SOBRINO Jon, *Jesucristo. Lectura histo-rico-teológica de Jesús de Nazaret*, Trotta, Madrid 1991, 110-122.

LOIS Julio, *Jesús de Nazaret, el Cristo liberador*, HOAC, Madrid 1995, 83-99.

FRAIJÓ Manuel, *Jesús y los marginados*, Cristiandad, Madrid 1985.

ESCUDERO FREIRE Carlos, *Jesús y el poder religioso. El Evangelio y la liberación de los oprimidos*, Nueva Utopía, Madrid 2003.

3. JESUS' INTERACTION WITH THE IMPURE AND UNDESIRABLES

SANDERS Ed Parish, *Jesús y el judaísmo*, Trotta, Madrid 2004, 269-277.

BORG Marcus J., *Conflict, Holiness and Politics in the Teaching of Jesus*, Trinity Press International, Harrisburg, PA 1998.

_____, *Jesus. A New Vision*, Harper, San Francisco 1998.

_____, *Meeting Jesus Again for the First Time*, Harper, San Francisco 1991, 46-68.

FREDRIKSEN Paula, *Jesus of Nazareth, King of the Jews*, Vintage Books, New York 2000, 51-73.

PATTERSON Stephen J., *The God of Jesus. The Historical Jesus and the Search for Meaning*, Trinity Press International, Harrisburg, PA 1998, 56-87.

4. JESUS' INTERACTION WITH SINNERS
SANDERS Ed Parish, *Jesús y el judaísmo*, Trotta, Madrid 2004, 257-310.

SCHLOSSER Jacques, *Jesús, el profeta de Galilea*, Sígueme, Salamanca 2005, 139-148.

SOBRINO Jon, *El principio-misericordia*. Sal Terrae, Santander 1992, pp. 31-45 and 133-158.

PIKAZA Xabier, *El Evangelio. Vida y pascua de Jesús*, Sígueme, Salamanca 1990, 67-80.
CASTILLO José María, *Víctimas del pecado*, Trotta, Madrid 2004, 61-81.

5. JESUS' TABLE OPEN TO ALL
AGUIRRE Rafael, *La mesa compartida. Estudios del Nuevo Testamento desde las ciencias sociales*, Sal Terrae, Santander 1994, 26-133.

CROSSAN John Dominic, *Jesús: Vida de un campesino judío*, Crítica, Barcelona 1994, 383-408.

———, *Jesus. A Revolutionary Biography*, Harper, San Francisco 1995, 66-70.

Chapter 8

1. FOR GENERAL STUDY OF JESUS AND WOMEN
WITHERINGTON III Ben, *Women in the Ministry of Jesus*, University Press, Cambridge 2001.

SCHÜSSLER FIORENZA Elisabeth, *En memoria de ella. Una reconstrucción teológico-feminista de los orígenes del cristianismo*, Desclée de Brower, Bilbao 1989.

BAUTISTA Esperanza, *La mujer en la Iglesia primitiva*, Verbo Divino, Estella 1993, 21-61.

MOLTMANN-WENDEL Elizabeth, *The Women Around Jesus*, Crossroad, New York 1982.

CONRAD WAHLBERG Rachel, *Jesus according to a Woman*, Paulist Press — Paramus, New York - Toronto 1975.

2. FOR GENERAL STUDY OF THE STATUS OF WOMEN IN FIRST-CENTURY PALESTINE
JEREMIAS Joachim, *Jerusalén en tiempos de Jesús*, Cristiandad, Madrid, 1977, 371-387.

STEGEMANN E. W. - STEGEMANN W., *Historia social del cristianismo primitivo*, Verbo Divino, Estella 2001.

FREYNE Sean, *Galilee and Gospel*, Brill, Boston-Leiden 2002, 271-286.

HANSON K. C. - OAKMAN Douglas E., *Palestine in Time of Jesus. Social Structures and Social Conflicts*, Fortress Press, Minneapolis 1998, 23-26.

3. WOMEN AS DISCIPLES
TUNC Suzanne, *También las mujeres seguían a Jesús*, Sal Terrae, Santander 1999.

MEIER Elisabeth, *Women and Ministry in the New Testament: called to serve*, University Press Lanham, New York — London 1980.

MEIER John Paul, *Un judío marginal. Nueva visión de Jesús histórico. III. Compañeros y competidores*, Verbo Divino, Estella 2003, 98-105.

CORLEY Kathleen E., *Private Women, Public Meals: Social Conflict in the Synoptic Tradition*, Hendrickson, Peabody, MA 1993.

THEISSEN Gerd - MERZ Annette, *El Jesús histórico*, Sígueme, Salamanca 1999, 250-256.

PIKAZA Xabier, *Sistema, libertad, Iglesia. Instituciones del Nuevo Testamento*, Trotta, Madrid 2001, 135-158.

4. OTHER WORKS OF INTEREST ON VARIOUS ASPECTS
MACDONALD, Margaret Y., *Las mujeres en el cristianismo primitivo y la opinión pagana. El poder de la mujer histérica*, Verbo Divino, Estella 2004.

VOUGA François, *Los primeros pasos del cristianismo. Escritos, protagonistas, debates*, Verbo Divino, Estella 2001, 196-198.

PIKAZA Xabier, *Hombre y mujer en las religions*, Verbo Divino, Estella 1996, 275-300.

BERNABÉ Carmen, *María Magdalena. Tradiciones en el cristianismo primitivo*, Verbo Divino, Estella 1994.

HORT Weiss, *¿Vino nuevo en odres viejos? Consecuencias sociopolíticas del evangelio*, Studium, Madrid 1973, 99-119.

LEVINE Amy-Jill (ed.), *Una compañera para Mateo*, Desclée de Brouwer, Bilbao 2003.

Chapter 9

1. FOR THE STUDY OF JESUS AS A TEACHER OF WISDOM

BARBAGLIO Giuseppe, *Jesús, hebreo de Galilea. Investigación histórica*, Secretariado Trinitario, Salamanca 2003, 391-449.

BRUCE F. F., *Hard Sayings of Jesus.* Inter-Varsity Press, Downers Grove, IL 1983.

CHILTON Bruce - EVANS Craig A., «Jesus and Israel's Scriptures» *in* CHILTON Bruce - EVANS Craig A. (eds.), *Studying the Historical Jesus*, Harper and Row, San Francisco 1983.

CROSSAN John Dominic, *In Fragments. The Aphorisms of Jesus*, Harper and Row, San Francisco 1983.

GRENIER Brian, *Jesús, el Maestro*, San Pablo, Madrid 1996, 15-63.

MARGUERAT Daniel, «Jésus le sage et Jésus le prophète» *in* MARGUERAT Daniel - NORELLI Enrico - POFFET Jean-Michel (eds.), *Jésus de Nazareth. Nouvelles approches d'une énigme*, Labor et Fides, Genève 1998, 293-317.

PERKINS Pheme, *Jesús como Maestro. La enseñanza de Jesús en el contexto de su época*, El Almendro, Córdoba 2001.

STEIN Robert H., *The Method and Message of Jesus' Teachings*, John Knox Press, Louisville, KY 1994, 1-32.

WINTON Alan P., *The Proverbs of Jesus. Issues of History and Rhetoric*, Academic Press, Sheffield 1990.

WITHERINGTON III Ben, *Jesus the Sage. The Pilgrimage of Wisdom*, Fortress Press, Minneapolis 2000.

2. FOR THE STUDY OF JESUS' POSITION ON THE LAW

BARBAGLIO Giuseppe, *Jesús, hebreo de Galilea. Investigación histórica*, Secretariado Trinitario, Salamanca 2003, 443-449.

GNILKA Joachim, *Jesús de Nazaret. Mensaje e historia*, Herder, Barcelona 1993, 249-303.

LOADER William, *Jesus' Attitude towards the Law. A Study of The Gospels*, Grand Rapids, MI — Eerdmans, Cambridge 2002.

SANDERS Ed Parish, *Jesús y el judaísmo*, Trotta, Madrid 2004, 353-386.

———, *La figura histórica de Jesús*, Verbo Divino, Estella 2000, 219-227.

SCHLOSSER Jacques, *Jesús, el profeta de Galilea*, Sígueme, Salamanca 2005, 159-181.

THEISSEN Gerd - MERZ Annette, *El Jesús histórico*, Sígueme, Salamanca 1999, 389-448.

WRIGHT N. Thomas, *Jesus and the Victory of God*, Fortress Press, Minneapolis 1996, especially 369-442.

3. FOR THE STUDY OF THE ETHICAL DIMENSION OF JESUS' MESSAGE
CHILTON Bruce - MCDONALD J. I. H., *Jesus and the Ethics of the Kingdom*, Eerdmans, Grand Rapids, MI 1987.

HARRINGTON Daniel / KEENAN, James, *Jesus and Virtue Ethics*, Sheed and Ward, Lanham, MD — Chicago, IL 2002.

SCHRAGE Wolfgang, *Ética del Nuevo Testamento*, Sígueme, Salamanca 1987, 27-146.

SPOHN William C., *Go and do Likewise. Jesus and Ethics*, Continuum, New York 2000.

WIEBE Ben, *Messianic Ethics. Jesus' Proclamation of the Kingdom of God and the Church in Response*, Herald Press, Waterloo, Ontario 1992.

4. ON JESUS' NON-CONVENTIONAL CHARACTER
BORG Marcus J., *Spirit, Culture and Life of Discipleship*, Harper, San Francisco 1991, 79-124.

SANDERS Ed Parish, «La rupture de Jésus avec le judaïsme» *in* MARGUERAT Daniel - NORELLI Enrico - POFFET Jean-Michel (eds.), *Jésus de Nazareth. Nouvelles approches d'une énigme*, Labor et Fides, Genève 1998, 209-222.

WRIGHT N. Thomas, *El desafío de Jesús*, Desclée de Brouwer, Bilbao 2003, 71-96.

5. ON NON-VIOLENT RESISTANCE TO INJUSTICE
HORSLEY Richard A., *Jesus and the Spiral of Violence. Popular Jewish Resistance in Roman Palestine*, Fortress Press, Minneapolis 1993, 255-284.

NELSON-PALLMEYER Jack, *Jesus against Christianity. Reclaiming the missing Jesus*, Trinity Press International, Harrisburg, PA 2001.

SWARTLEY Willard M (ed.), *The Love of Enemy and Nonretaliation in the New Testament*, Louisville, KY, Westminster - John Knox Press 1992 (especially the articles by D. J. WEAVER, «Transforming Nonresistance: From *Lex Talionis* to "Do not Resist the Evil One"» [pp. 32-71]; Richard A. HORSLEY, «Ethics and Exegesis: "Love your Enemies" and the Doctrine of Nonviolence» [pp. 72-101]; W. WINK, «Neither Passivity nor Violence: Jesus' Third Way [Matt. 5:38-42 par.]» [pp. 102-125]).

WINK Walter, *Engaging the Powers: Discernment and Resistance in a World of Domination*, Fortress Press, Minneapolis 1992.

6. OTHER STUDIES OF INTEREST

HERZOG II William R., *Jesus, Justice, and Reign of God. A Ministry of Liberation*, John Knox Press, Louisville, KY 2000, especially pp. 144-167.

TOMSON Peter, *L'affaire Jésus et les Juifs*, Cerf, Paris 2003.

Chapter 10

1. FOR GENERAL STUDY

BARBAGLIO Giuseppe, *Jesús, hebreo de Galilea. Investigación histórica*, Secretariado Trinitario, Salamanca 2003, 337-386.

GNILKA Joachim, *Jesús de Nazaret. Mensaje e historia*, Herder, Barcelona 1993, 203-236.

MATEOS Juan, *Los «Doce» y otros seguidores de Jesús en el evangelio de Marcos*, Cristiandad, Madrid 1982.

MEIER John Paul, *Un judío marginal. Nueva visión del Jesús histórico*. III. *Compañeros y competidores*, Verbo Divino, Estella 2003, 43-300.

PUIG I TARRECH Armand, *Jesús. Un perfil biográfico*, Proa, Barcelona 2004, 237-286.

SANDERS Ed Parish, *La figura histórica de Jesús*, Verbo Divino, Estella 2000, 140-153.

SCHLOSSER Jacques, *Jesús, el profeta de Galilea*, Sígueme, Salamanca 2005, 95-112.

THEISSEN Gerd - MERZ Annette, *El Jesús histórico*, Sígueme, Salamanca 1999, 244-250.

2. FOR A SOCIOLOGICAL STUDY OF JESUS' MOVEMENT

DRAPER Jonathan A, «Wandering Charismatics and Scholarly Circularities» *in* HORSLEY Richard A.- DRAPER Jonathan A., *Whoever Hears You Hears Me*, Trinity Press International, Harrisburg, PA 1999, 29-45.

STEGEMANN E. W. - STEGEMANN W., *Historia social del cristianismo primitivo*, Verbo Divino, Estella 2001, 259-302.

THEISSEN Gerd, *El movimiento de Jesús. Historia social de una revolución de los valores*, Sígueme, Salamanca 2005, especially pp. 35-130.

_____, *Sociología del movimiento de Jesús. El nacimiento del cristianismo primitivo*, Sal Terrae, Santander 1979.

_____, *Estudios de sociología del cristianismo primitivo*, Sígueme, Salamanca 1979.

3. FOR A STUDY OF JESUS' FOLLOWERS

BEST Ernest, *Disciples and Discipleship. Studies in the Gospel according to Mark*, T. & T. Clark, Edinburgh 1986.

CASTILLO José María, *El seguimiento de Jesús*, Sígueme, Salamanca 1986.

DUNN James D. G., *La llamada de Jesús al seguimiento*, Sal Terrae, Santander 2000.

GUIJARRO Santiago, *Fidelidades en conflicto. La ruptura con la familia por causa del discipulado y de la misión en la tradición sinóptica*, Universidad Pontificia, Salamanca 1998.

_____, *Jesús y el comienzo de los evangelios*, Verbo Divino, Estella 2006, 87-101.

HENGEL Martin, *Seguimiento y carisma. La radicalidad de la llamada de Jesús*, Sal Terrae, Santander 1981.

MOXNES Halvor, *Poner a Jesús en su lugar. Una visión radical del grupo familiar y el Reino de Dios*, Verbo Divino, Estella 2005.

4. FOR A COMPARISON OF JESUS WITH THE CYNICAL PHILOSOPHERS

AGUIRRE Rafael, «La teoría de Jesús como un predicador cínico» *in* PIÑERO Antonio (ed.), *Biblia y helenismo. El pensamiento griego y la formación del cristianismo*, El Almendro, Córdoba 2006, 209-260.

CROSSAN John Dominic, *Jesús: vida de un campesino judío*, Grijalbo-Mondadori, Barcelona 1994, 110-126; 383-408.

_____, *Jesus. A Revolutionary Biography*, Harper, San Francisco 1994, 102-122.

KLOPPENBORG John S., *Q. El evangelio desconocido*, Sígueme, Salamanca 2005, 236-251.

WITHERINGTON III Ben, *Jesus the Sage. The Pilgrimage of Wisdom*, Fortress Press, Minneapolis 2000, 118-145.

5. ON THE RELATIONSHIP BETWEEN ITINERANT AND HOME-BASED FOLLOWERS

CROSSAN John Dominic, *Jesús: vida de un campesino judío*, Grijalbo-Mondadori, Barcelona 1994, especially pp. 383-408.

KAYLOR, R. David, *Jesus the Prophet. His Vision of the Kingdom on Earth*, John Knox Press, Louisville, KY 1994, 174-191.

KOENIG John, *New Testament Hospitality*, Wipf and Stock, Eugene, OR 1985, 26-38.

THEISSEN Gerd, *El movimiento de Jesús. Historia social de una revolución de los valores*, Sígueme, Salamanca 2005, 35-100.

6. OTHER WORKS OF INTEREST

GESTEIRA Manuel, «La llamada y el seguimiento de Jesucristo» *in* GARCÍA TOMAS Juan Manuel - GARCÍA-MURGA José Ramón (eds.), *El seguimiento de Cristo.* PPC, Madrid 1997, 33-72.

LOIS Julio, «Universalidad del llamamiento y radicalidad del seguimiento» *in ¿Quién decís que soy yo? Dimensiones del seguimiento de Jesús.* Verbo Divino, Estella 2000, 105-150.

MATURA Thaddée, *Le radicalisme évangélique. Aux sources de la vie chrétienne*, Cerf, Paris 1978.

PIKAZA Xabier, *Sistema, libertad, Iglesia. Instituciones del Nuevo Testamento*, Trotta, Madrid 2001, 141-164.

VIDAL Senén, «El seguimiento de Jesús en el Nuevo Testamento. Visión general» *in* GARCÍA LOMAS Juan Manuel - GARCÍA-MURGA José Ramón (eds.), *El seguimiento de Cristo*, PPC, Madrid 1997, 13-31.

WITHERINGTON III Ben, *The Christology of Jesus*, Fortress Press, Minneapolis 1990, 118-143.

Chapter 11

1. FOR GENERAL STUDY OF THE EXPERIENCE OF GOD THAT JESUS LIVED AND COMMUNICATED

AGUIRRE Rafael, *El Dios de Jesús*, Fundación Santa María, Madrid 1985.

DUNN James D. G., *Jesús y el Espíritu*, Secretariado Trinitario, Salamanca 1981, 31-160.

DUQUOC Christian, *Dios diferente*, Sígueme, Salamanca 1978.

GUIJARRO Santiago, *Jesús y el comienzo de los evangelios*, Verbo Divino, Estella 2006, 37-69.

HAIGHT Roger, *Jesus, Symbol of God*, Orbis Books, Maryknoll, NY 1999, 88-118.

PIKAZA Xabier, *Dios judío. Dios cristiano*, Verbo Divino, Estella 1996.

SCHILLEBEECKX Edward, *Jesús. La historia de un Viviente*, Cristiandad, Madrid 1981, 209-246.

SCHLOSSER Jacques, *El Dios de Jesús. Estudio exegético*, Sígueme, Salamanca 1995.

SOBRINO Jon, *Jesucristo liberador. Lectura histórico-teológica de Jesús de Nazaret*, Trotta, Madrid 1991, 179-250.

VERMES Geza, *La religione di Gesù l'ebreo*, Cittadella, Assisi 2002.

2. ON JESUS' EXPERIENCE OF GOD AS FATHER

GUIJARRO Santiago, «Dios Padre en la actuación de Jesús» in *Estudios Trinitarios* 34/1 (january-april 2000), 33-69.

JEREMIAS Joachim, *Teología del Nuevo Testamento* I, Sígueme, Salamanca 1974, 80-87; 210-238.

_____, *Abba. El mensaje central del Nuevo Testamento*, Sígueme, Salamanca 1981, 19-89.

SCHNEIDER Gerhard, «El Padre de Jesús. Visión bíblica» in *Estudios Trinitarios* 24/3 (september-december 1990), 401-441.

TORRES QUEIRUGA Andrés, *Creo en Dios Padre. El Dios de Jesús como afirmación del hombre*, Sal Terrae, Santander 1986, 73-97.

3. ON OTHER ASPECTS OF JESUS' GOD

AGUIRRE Rafael, «El Dios de Jesús y la realidad social de su pueblo» in ID., *Del movimiento de Jesús a la Iglesia cristiana. Ensayo de exégesis sociológica del cristianismo primitivo*, Verbo Divino, Estella 2001, 53-77.

BORG Marcus J., *Jesus, a New Vision. Spirit, Culture and the Life of Discipleship*, Harper, San Francisco 1991, 23-56.

JOHNSON Elizabeth A., *She Who Is. The Mystery of God in Feminist Theological Discourse*, Crossroad, New York 1992.

ROSSÉ G., «Dieu Amour dans le Nouveau Testament» in *Dieu Amour dans la tradition chrétienne et la pensée contemporaine*, Nouvelle Cité, Paris 1993, 51-84.

SCHÜSSLER FIORENZA Elisabeth, *Cristología feminista crítica. Jesús, hijo de Miriam, Profeta de la Sabiduría*, Trotta, Madrid 2000.

4. ON JESUS' PRAYER LIFE AND THE LORD'S PRAYER

BOFF Leonardo, *El padrenuestro. La oración de la liberación integral*, Ed. Paulinas, Madrid 1982.

DI SANTE Carmine, *El Padrenuestro. La experiencia de Dios en la tradición judeo-cristiana*, Secretariado Trinitario, Salamanca 1998.

HELEWA Juan, *Orar. Enseñanzas del evangelio*, Monte Carmelo, Burgos 1994.

MANNS Frédéric, *La prière d'Israël à l'heure de Jésus*, Franciscan Printing Press, Jerusalem 1986.

PAGOLA José Antonio, *Padrenuestro. Orar con el espíritu de Jesús*, PPC, Madrid 2002.

SCHÜRMANN Heinz, *El Padrenuestro*, Secretariado Trinitario, Salamanca 1982.

SOBRINO Jon, «La oración de Jesús y del cristiano» *in* SOBRINO Jon - GALILEA Segundo - CASTILLO José María (eds.), *Oración cristiana y liberación*, Desclée de Brouwer, Bilbao 1980, 55-94.

5. OTHER WORKS OF INTEREST
GIROUX Gertrude, *La spiritualité de Jésus perdue et retrouvée*, Carte Blanche, Outremont, Quebec 2002.

PIKAZA Xabier, *Para descubrir el camino del Padre. Nuevos itinerarios para el encuentro con Dios*, Verbo Divino, Estella 1999, 71-119.

SEGUNDO Juan Luis, *La historia perdida y recuperada de Jesús de Nazaret. De los sinópticos a Pablo*, Sal Terrae, Santander 1991, 149-232.

VIVES Juan, «*Si oyerais su voz*». *Exploración cristiana del misterio de Dios*, Sal Terrae, Santander 1998.

Chapter 12

1. THE COMBATIVE NATURE OF JESUS' ACTIVITY
BORG Marcus J., *Conflict Holiness and Politics in the Teaching of Jesus*, Trinity Press International, Harrisburg, PA 1998, 88-173.

BRAVO Carlos, *Jesús, hombre conflictivo*, Sal Terrae, Santander 1986.

EVANS Craig A., «From Public Ministry to the Passion: can a link be found between the (Galilean) Life and the (Judean) Death of Jesus?» in *Jesus in his Contemporaries*, Brill, Boston-Leiden 2001, 301-318.

HORSLEY Richard A., *Jesus and the Spiral of Violence. Popular Jewish Resistance in Roman Palestine*, Fortress Press, Minneapolis 1993, 147-284.

———, *Jesús y el Imperio. El Reino de Dios y el nuevo desorden mundial*, Verbo Divino, Estella 2003, 105-163.

LÉMONON Jean-Pierre, «Les causes de la mort de Jésus» *in* MARGUERAT Daniel - NORELLI Enrico - POFFET Jean-Michel (eds.), *Jésus de Nazaret. Nouvelles approches d'un énigme*, Labor et Fides, Genève 1998, 349-369.

MEIER John Paul, *Un judío marginal. Nueva visión del Jesús histórico*. III. *Compañeros y competidores*, Verbo Divino, Estella 2003, 301-653.

RIVKIN Ellis, *What crucified Jesus?*, UAHC Press, New York 1997, 1-77.

SALDARINI Anthony J., *Pharisees, Scribes and Sadducees in Palestinian Society*, Eerdmans, Grand Rapids, MI — Cambridge 2001.

SANDERS Ed Parish, *Jesús y el judaísmo*, Trotta, Madrid 2004, 387-420.

SOBRINO Jon, *Jesucristo liberador. Lectura histórico-teológica de Jesús de Nazaret*, Trotta, Madrid 1991, 253-272.

THEISSEN Gerd - MERZ Annette, *El Jesús histórico*, Sígueme, Salamanca 1999, 256-271.

WRIGHT N. Thomas, *El desafío de Jesús*, Desclée de Brouwer, Bilbao 2003.

2. JESUS' PROPHETIC ACT IN THE TEMPLE
BORG Marcus J., *Conflict Holiness and Politics in the Teaching of Jesus*, Trinity Press International Harrisburg, PA 1998, 174-212.

CROSSAN John Dominic, *Who killed Jesus?*, Harper, San Francisco 1996, 50-65.

CROSSAN John Dominic - REED Jonathan L., *Jesús desenterrado*, Crítica, Barcelona 2003, 226-273.

EVANS Craig A., «Jesus' Action in the Temple and Evidence of Corruption in the First Century Temple» in *Jesus in his Contemporaries*, Brill, Boston-Leiden 2001, 319-344.

_____, «Jesus and the "Cave of Robbers": Towards a Jewish Context for the Temple Action» in *Jesus in his Contemporaries*, Brill, Boston-Leiden 2001, 345-365.

_____, «Jesus and Predictions of the Destruction of the Herodian Temple» in *Jesus in his Contemporaries*, Brill, Boston-Leiden 2001, 367-380.

GNILKA Joachim, *Jesús de Nazaret. Mensaje e historia*, Herder, Barcelona 1993, 337-341.

HERZOG II William R., *Jesus, Justice, and Reign of God. A Ministry of Liberation*, Westminster-John Knox Press, Louisville, KY 1999, 111-143.

SANDERS Ed Parish, *Jesús y el judaísmo*, Trotta, Madrid 2004, 99-142.

SCHLOSSER Jacques, *Jesús, el profeta de Galilea*, Sígueme, Salamanca 2005, 225-239.

3. THE LAST SUPPER
BAUCKHAM R. J., «Did Jesus Wash His Disciples' Feet» *in* HILTON Bruce - VANS Craig A. (eds.), *Authenticating the Activities of Jesus*, Brill, Boston-Leiden 2002, 411-429.

GNILKA Joachim, *Jesús de Nazaret. Mensaje e historia*, Herder, Barcelona 1993, 342-353.

JEREMIAS Joachim, *La última cena*, Cristiandad, Madrid 2003.

LÉON-DUFOUR Xavier, *La fracción del pan. Culto y existencia en el Nuevo Testamento*, Cristiandad, Madrid 1983, 72-232.

_____, *Jesús y Pablo ante la muerte*, Cristiandad, Madrid 1982, 100-111.

SCHILLEBEECKX Edward, *Jesús, la historia de un Viviente*, Cristiandad, Madrid 1981, 279-285.

SCHLOSSER Jacques, *Jesús, el profeta de Galilea*, Sígueme, Salamanca 2005, 241-258.

SCHÜRMANN Heinz, *El destino de Jesús: su vida y su muerte*, Sígueme, Salamanca 2003, 211-240.

THEISSEN Gerd - MERZ Annette, *El Jesús histórico*, Sígueme, Salamanca 1999, 450-485.

Chapter 13

1. GENERAL STUDY ON THE DEATH OF JESUS

BARBAGLIO Giuseppe, *Jesús, hebreo de Galilea. Investigación histórica*, Secretariado Trinitario, Salamanca 2003, 451-511.

BORG Marcus J. - CROSSAN John Dominic, *La última semana de Jesús. El relato día a día de la semana final de Jesús en Jerusalén*, PPC, Madrid 2007.

BORG Marcus J. - WRIGHT N. Thomas, *The Meaning of Jesus. Two Visions*, Harper, San Francisco, 1998, 79-107.

BOVON François, *Los últimos días de Jesús. Textos y acontecimientos*, Sal Terrae, Santander 2007.

BROWN Raymond E., *La muerte del Mesías. Desde Getsemaní hasta el sepulcro* (2 vols), Verbo Divino, Estella 2005-2006.

CARROLL John T. - GREEN Joel B., *The Death of Jesus in Early Christianity*, Hendrickson, Peabody, MA 1995.

CROSSAN John Dominic, *Who killed Jesus?*, Harper, San Francisco 1995.

GNILKA Joachim, *Jesús de Nazaret. Mensaje e historia*, Herder, Barcelona 1993, 355-388.

HORSLEY Richard A., «The Death of Jesus» *in* CHILTON Bruce - EVANS Craig A. (eds.), *Studying the Historical Jesus. Evaluations of the State of Current Research*, Brill, Leiden-Boston-Cologne 1998, 395-422.

LOHSE Eduard, *La storia della passione e morte di Gesù Cristo*, Paideia, Brescia 1975.

NEITZEL R. - WAYMENT Th. A. (eds.), *From the Last Supper through the Resurrection. The Savior's Final Hours*, Deseret, Salt Lake City 2003.

PUIG I TARRECH Armand, *Jesús. Una biografía*, Destino, Barcelona 2004, 455-594.

ROLOFF Jürgen, *Jesús*, Acento, Madrid 2002, 152-170.

SANDERS Ed Parish, *Jesús y el judaísmo*, Trotta, Madrid 2004, 421-456.

SCHILLEBEECKX Edward, *Jesús: la historia de un Viviente*, Cristiandad, Madrid 1981, 248-302.

SCHLOSSER Jacques, *Jesús, el profeta de Galilea*, Sígueme, Salamanca 2005, 259-276.

SOBRINO Jon, *Jesucristo liberador. Lectura histórico-teológica de Jesús de Nazaret*, Trotta, Madrid 1991, 253-272.

THEISSEN Gerd - MERZ Annette, *El Jesús histórico*, Sígueme, Salamanca 1999, 487-521.

VERMES Geza, *La pasión. La verdad sobre el acontecimiento que cambió la historia de la humanidad*, Crítica, Barcelona 2007.

WRIGHT N. Thomas, *Jesus and the Victory of God*, Fortress Press, Minneapolis 1996, 540-611.

2. THE TRIAL OF JESUS

BAMMEL Ernst (ed.), *The Trial of Jesus*, SCM Press, London 1971.

BLINZLER Josef, *El proceso de Jesús*, Herder, Barcelona 1960.

JOSSA Giorgio, *Il processo di Gesù*, Paideia, Brescia 2002.

LÉGASSE Simon, *El proceso de Jesús*. I. *La historia*, Desclée de Brouwer, Bilbao 1994.

_____, *El proceso de Jesús*. II. *La pasión en los cuatro evangelios*, Desclée de Brouwer, Bilbao 1996.

LÉGASSE Simon - TOMSON Peter, *Qui a tué Jésus?*, Cerf, Paris 2004.

LÉMONON Jean-Pierre, «Les causes de la mort de Jésus» *in* MARGUERAT Daniel / NORELLI Enrico / POFFET Jean-Michel (eds.), *Jésus de Nazareth. Nouvelles approches d'une énigme*, Labor et Fides, Genève 1998, 349-369.

RIVKIN Ellis, *What crucified Jesus?*, UAHC Press, Nueva York 1997, 3-77.

WINTER Paul, *El proceso de Jesús*, Muchnik, Barcelona 1983.

3. THE CRUCIFIXION
HENGEL Martin, *Crucifixion in the ancient world and the folly of the message of the cross*, Fortress Press, Philadelphia 1997.

SLOYAN Gerard S., *The Crucifixion of Jesus. History, Myth, Faith.* Fortress Press, Minneapolis 1995, 9-44.

4. JESUS' ATTITUDE TOWARD HIS DEATH
BASTIN M., *Jésus devant sa passion*, Cerf, Paris 1976.

CHORDAT J. L., *Jésus devant sa mort dans l'évangile de Marc*, Cerf, Paris 1970.

GOURGUES Michel, *Jesús ante su pasión y su muerte*, Verbo Divino, Estella 1995.

LÉON-DUFOUR Xavier, *Jesús y Pablo ante la muerte*, Cristiandad, Madrid 1982, 73-165.

SCHÜRMANN Heinz, *¿Cómo entendió y vivió Jesús su muerte?*, Sígueme, Salamanca 1982.

_____, *El destino de Jesús: su vida y su muerte*, Sígueme, Salamanca 2003.

5. OTHER BOOKS OF INTEREST
FREDRIKSEN Paula - REINHARTZ Adele (eds.), *Jesus, Judaism, and Christian Anti-Judaism. Reading the New Testament after the Holocaust*, John Knox Press, Louisville, KY — London 2002.

LOUPAN Victor - NOËL Alain, *Enquête sur la mort de Jésus*, Presses de la Renaissance, Paris 2005.

VARONE François, *El Dios «sádico». ¿Ama Dios el sufrimiento?*, Sal Terrae, Santander 1988.

Chapter 14

1. GENERAL STUDIES ON THE RESURRECTION OF JESUS
ALVES Manuel Isidro, *Ressurreiçao e fe pascal*, Didaskalia, Lisbon 1997.

BONY Paul, *La résurrection de Jésus*, Eds. de l'Atelier, París 2000.

BRAMBILLA Franco Giulio, *El crucificado resucitado*, Sígueme, Salamanca 2003.

DENEKEN Michel, *La foi pascale. Rendre compte de la résurrection de Jéus aujourd'hui*, Cerf, Paris 1997.

EVANS C. F., *Resurrection and the New Testament*, SCM Press, London 1970.

KESSLER Hans, *La resurrección de Jesús. Aspecto bíblico, teológico y sistemático*, Sígueme, Salamanca 1989.

LÉON-DUFOUR Xavier, *Resurrección de Jesús y mensaje pascual*, Sígueme, Salamanca 1992⁵.

LORENZEN Thorwald, *Resurrección y discipulado. Modelos interpretativos, reflexiones bíblicas y consecuencias teológicas*, Sal Terrae, Santander 1999.

534

MOINGT Joseph, *El hombre que venía de Dios* II, Desclée de Brouwer, Bilbao 1995, 49-88.

PERKINS Pheme, *Resurrection. New Testament Witness and Contemporary Reflection*, Geoffrey Chapman, London 1984.

RIGAUX Beda, *Dieu l'a ressuscité. Exégèse et théologie biblique*, Duculot, Gembloux 1973.

RUCKSTUHL Eugen - PFAMMATER Josef, *La resurrección de Jesucristo. Hecho histórico-salvífico y foco de la fe*, Fax, Madrid 1973.

SCHMITT J., *Jésus ressuscité dans la prédication apostolique. Étude de théologie biblique*, Gabalda, Paris 1968.

THEISSEN Gerd - MERZ Annette, *El Jesús histórico*, Sígueme, Salamanca 1999, 523-560.

WILCKENS Ulrich, *La resurrección de Jesús. Estudio histórico-crítico del testimonio bíblico*, Sígueme, Salamanca 1981.

WRIGHT N. T., *The Resurrection of the Son of God*, Fortress Press, Minneapolis 2003.

2. ON NEW APPROACHES TO JESUS' RESURRECTION, THE TOMB, THE APPEARANCES, AND THE ORIGINS OF PASCHAL FAITH

ALEGRE Xavier, «Perspectiva de la exégesis actual ante la resurrección de Jesús y el nacimiento de la fe pascual» *in* FRAIJÓ Manuel - ALEGRE Xavier - TORNOS Andrés, *La fe cristiana en la resurrección*, Sal Terrae, Santander 1998, 33-62.

BOISMARD Marie-Émile, *¿Es necesario aún hablar de «resurrección»? Los datos bíblicos*, Desclée de Brouwer, Bilbao 1996.

BORG Marcus J. - WRIGHT N. T., *The Meaning of Jesus. Two Visions*, Harper, San Francisco 1998, 111-142.

CROSSAN John Dominic, *El nacimiento del cristianismo. Qué sucedió en los años posteriores a la ejecución de Jesús*, Sal Terrae, Santander 2002, 481-573.

D'ACOSTA Gavin (ed.), *Resurrection reconsidered*, Oneword, Oxford 1996.

DAVIES S. - KENDALL D. - O'COLLINS G., *The Resurrection. An Interdisciplinary Symposium on the Resurrection of Jesus*, University Press, Oxford 1998.

DELORME Jean, «La résurrection dans le langage du Nouveau Testament» in *Le langage de la foi dans l'Écriture*, Cerf, Paris 1972, 101-182.

DE SURGY E. - GRELOT Pierre - CARREZ Maurice - GEORGE Augustin - DELORME Jean - LÉON-DUFOUR Xavier, *La résurrection du Christ et l'exégèse moderne*, Cerf, Paris 1969.

HAIGHT Roger, *Jesus, symbol of God*, Orbis Books, Maryknoll, NY 2002, 119-151.

KREMER J. - SCHMITT J. - KESSLER H., *Dibattito sulla risurrezione di Gesù*, Queriniana, Brescia 1969.

LÜDEMANN Gerd - ÖZEN Alf, *La resurrección de Jesús. Historia. Experiencia. Teología*, Trotta, Madrid 2001.

MARXSEN Willy, *La resurrección de Jesús de Nazaret*, Herder, Barcelona 1974.

MÜLLER Ulrich B., *El origen de la fe en la resurrección de Jesús*, Verbo Divino, Estella 2003.

SCHENKE L., *Le tombeau vide et l'annonce de la Résurrection (Mc 16,1-8)*, Cerf, Paris 1970.

SCHILLEBEECKX Edward, *Jesús: la historia de un viviente*, Cristiandad, Madrid 1981, 482-509.

_____, *En torno al problema de Jesús. Claves de una cristología*, Cristiandad, Madrid 1983, 103-128.

TORRES QUEIRUGA Andrés, *Repensar la resurrección*, Trotta, Madrid 2003.

WEDDERBURN A. J. M., *Beyond Resurrection*, Hendrickson, Peabody, MA 1999.

3. FOR GENERAL STUDY ON THE MEANING OF JESUS' RESURRECTION

BEASLEY-MURRAY Paul, *The Message of the Resurrection*, Inter-Varsity Press, Downers Grove, IL 2000.

COUNE M. - DELORME Jean - GAIDE G. - GAMBIER J. M. - MARTINI Carlo Maria - MOLLAT Daniel - RIDOUARD A. - SEINAVE J. - TRILLING Wolfgang, *La Bonne Nouvelle de la Résurrection*, Cerf, Paris 1981.

KANNENGIESSER Charles. *Foi en la Résurrection. Résurrection de la foi*, Beauchesne, Paris 1974.

LECLERC Éloï, *Pâques en Galilée ou la rencontre de Christ pascal*, Desclée de Brouwer, Paris 2003.

MICHIELS Robrecht, *Jésus-Christ, hier, aujord'hui, demain*, Casterman, Tournai 1971, 95-135.

MOULE C. F. D., *The significance of the Message of the Resurrection for Faith in Jesus Christ*, SCM Press, London 1968.

PIKAZA Xabier, *El evangelio. Vida y Pascua de Jesús*, Sígueme, Salamanca 1990, 245-428.

VIDAL Senén, *La resurreción de Jesús en las cartas de Pablo. Análisis de las tradiciones*, Sígueme, Salamanca 1982.

WAGNER Guy, *La résurrection, signe du monde nouveau*, Cerf, Paris 1970.

4. ON THE SALVIFIC CONTENT OF THE DEATH-RESURRECTION OF JESUS

DUQUOC Christian, «Actualidad teológica de la cruz» in *Teología de la cruz*. Sígueme, Salamanca 1979, 19-25.

DURRWELL François-Xavier. *La mort du Fils. Le mystère de Jésus et de l'homme*, Cerf, Paris 2006.

KARRER Martin, *Jesucristo en el Nuevo Testamento*, Sígueme, Salamanca 2002, 25-96.

LÉON-DUFOUR Xavier - VERGOTE Antoine - BUREAU R. - MOINGT Joseph, *Mort pour nos péchés*, Facultés Universitaires Saint Louis, Brussels 1976.

REY Bernard, *Nous prêchons un Messie crucifié*, Cerf, Paris 1989.

SABOURIN Léopold, *Redención sacrificial. Encuesta exegética*, Desclée de Brouwer, Bilbao 1969.

SESBOÜÉ Bernard, *Jesucristo, el único Mediador. Ensayo sobre la redención y la salvación* I-II, Secretariado Trinitario, Salamanca 1990.

_____, «Redención y salvación en Jesucristo» in GONZÁLEZ DE CARDEDAL Olegario - GONZÁLEZ FAUS José Ignacio - RATZINGER Joseph (eds.), *Salvador del mundo*, Secretariado Trinitario, Salamanca 1997, 113-132.

SOBRINO Jon, *Jesucristo liberador. Lectura histórico-teológica de Jesús de Nazaret*, Trotta, Madrid 1991, 281-320.

VARONE François, *El Dios «sádico». ¿Ama Dios el sufrimiento?*, Sal Terrae, Santander 1988.

5. OTHER WORKS OF INTEREST

BERTEN I. - BOISMARD Marie-Émile - BOUTIER M. / CARREZ Maurice - DUQUOC Christian - GEFFRÉ Claude - MOINGT Joseph, «La Résurrection» *in* Monographic issue of *Lumière et Vie* XXI, n. 107 (March-May) 1972.

BONNET G., *Jésus est ressuscité*, Desclée, Paris 1969.

BULTMANN Rudolf - RAD Gerhard von - BERTRAN G. - OEPKE A., «Vie, mort, résurrection» *in* KITTEL Gerhard (ed.), *Dictionnaire biblique*, Labor et Fides, Genève 1972.

BUSTO José Ramón, «El resucitado» *in* TAMAYO ACOSTA Juan José (dir.), *10 palabras clave sobre Jesús de Nazaret*, Verbo Divino, Estella 1999, 357-399.

CHARPENTIER Étienne, *¿Cristo ha resucitado?*, Verbo Divino, Estella 1981.

DUNN James D. G., *Jesús y el Espíritu*, Secretariado Trinitario, Salamanca 1981, 163-255.

GUILBERT Pierre, *Il ressuscita le troisième jour*, Nouvelle Cité, Paris 1988.

MARTIN-ACHARD Robert, *De la muerte y la resurrección según el Antiguo Testamento*, Marova, Madrid 1969.

MUSSNER Franz, *La resurrección de Jesús*, Sal Terrae, Santander 1971.

PUECH Émil, «Mesianismo, escatología y resurrección en los manuscritos del mar Muerto» *in* TREBOLLE BARRERA Julio (coord.), *Paganos, judíos y cristianos en los textos de Qumrán*, Trotta, Madrid 1999, 245-286.

RAMSEY A. Michael, *La resurrección de Cristo*, Mensajero, Bilbao 1971.

SCHLIER Heinrich, *De la resurrección de Jesucristo*, Desclée de Brouwer, Bilbao 1970.

SEIDENSTICKER Philip, *La resurrezione di Gesù nel messagio degli evangelisti*, Paideia, Brescia 1972.

SPONG John Shelby, *Resurrection. Myth or Reality*, Harper, San Francisco 1994.

Chapter 15

1. RE-READING THE STORY OF JESUS IN THE LIGHT OF THE PASCHAL EXPERIENCE

GUIJARRO Santiago, *Jesús y el origen de los evangelios*, Verbo Divino, Estella 2007.

MARGUERAT Daniel, *Le Dieu des premiers chrétiens*, Labor et Fides, Genève 1997, especially pp. 147-163.

_____, (ed.), *Introducción al Nuevo Testamento. Su historia, su escritura, su teología*, Desclée de Brouwer, Bilbao 2008.

THEISSEN Gerd, *El Nuevo Testamento. Historia, literatura, religión*, Sal Terrae, Santander 2003, especially pp. 137-176.

GNILKA Joachim, *El evangelio segun san Marcos*, Sígueme, Salamanca 1986.

LÉGASSE Simon, *L'évangile de Marc*, Cerf, Paris 1997.

MICHIE Donald, *Marcos como relato. Introducción a la narrativa de un evangelio*, Sígueme, Salamanca 2002.

BONNARD Pierre, *El evangelio según san Mateo*, Cristiandad, Madrid 1976.

LUZ Ulrich, *El evangelio según Mateo*, Sígueme, Salamanca 1993-2003.

STIEWE Martin / VOUGA François, *Le Sermon sur la Montagne. Un abrégé de l'Évangile dans le miroitement de ses interprétations*, Labor et Fides, Genève 2002.

TRILLING Wolfgang, *El verdadero Israel. La teología de Mateo*, Fax, Madrid 1972.

ALETTI Jean-Noël, *El arte de contar a Jesucristo*, Sígueme, Salamanca 1992.

BOVON François, *L'Évangile selon saint Luc*, 3 vols. Labor et Fides, Genève 1991-2001.

CONZELMANN Hans, *El centro del tiempo. La teología de Lucas*, Fax, Madrid 1974.

FITZMYER Joseph A., *Luke the Theologian. Aspects of his Teaching*, Paulist Press, New York 1989.

BROWN Raymond E., *El Evangelio según Juan*, Cristiandad, Madrid 1999².

_____, *La comunidad del discípulo amado. Estudio de la eclesiología joánica*, Salamanca, Sígueme 1987².

LÉON-DUFOUR Xavier, *Lectura del evangelio de Juan*, Sígueme, Salamanca 1989-1998.

MATEOS Juan / BARRETO Juan, *El Evangelio de Juan*, Cristiandad, Madrid 1979.

MOLONEY Francis J., *El Evangelio de Juan*, Verbo Divino, Estella 2005.

2. ON THE NAMES AND TITLES ATTRIBUTED TO JESUS

CULLMANN Oscar, *Cristología del Nuevo Testamento*, Sígueme, Salamanca 1998.

DUNN James D. G., *Christology in the Making. A New Testament Inquiry into the Origins of the Doctrine of the Incarnation*, Michael Glazier, London 1980.

DUQUOC Christian, *Mesianismo de Jesús y discreción de Dios. Ensayo sobre los límites de la cristología*, Cristiandad, Madrid 1985, 117-193.

FREDRIKSEN Paula, *From Jesus to Christ*, Yale University Press, 2000.

HAIGHT Roger, *Jesus, Symbol of God*, Orbis Books, Maryknoll, NY 2002, 152-184.

HENGEL Martin, *El Hijo de Dios. El origen de la cristología y la historia de la religión judeohelenista*, Sígueme, Salamanca 1977.

MARTÍNEZ Felicísimo, *Creer en Jesucristo. Vivir en cristiano. Cristología y seguimiento*, Verbo Divino, Estella 2005, 195-273.

PERROT Charles, *Jésus, Christ et Seigneur des premiers chrétiens. Une christologie exégétique*, Desclée, Paris 1997.

PIKAZA Xabier, *El evangelio. Vida y pascua de Jesús*, Sígueme, Salamanca 1990, 287-428.

POKORN Petr, *The Genesis of Christology. Foundations for a Theology of the New Testament*, T. & T. Clark, Edinburgh 1987.

QUESNEL Michel, *Jésus, l'homme et le Fils de Dieu*, Flammarion, Paris 2004, 125-193.

SABOURIN Leopold, *Los nombres y títulos de Cristo*, San Esteban, Salamanca 1966.

SCHIERSE Franz Joseph, *Cristologia*, Queriniana, Brescia 1990, 59-114.

SOBRINO Jon, *La fe en Jesucristo. Ensayo desde las víctimas*, Trotta, Madrid 1999, 169-313.

General Bibliography

We mainly refer to recent Studies.
For Books on the Resurrection of Jesus,
please see Chapter 15.

AGUIRRE R., *Del movimiento de Jesús a la Iglesia cristiana. Ensayo de exégesis sociológica del cristianismo primitivo*, Verbo Divino, Estella 2001.

_____, *Ensayo sobre los orígenes del cristianismo. De la religión política de Jesús a la religión doméstica de Pablo*, Verbo Divino, Estella 2001.

_____, *La mesa compartida. Estudios del Nuevo Testamento desde las ciencias sociales*, Sal Terrae, Santander 1994.

_____, (ed.), *Los milagros de Jesús. Perspectivas metodológicas plurales*, Verbo Divino, Estella 2002.

ALLISON D.C., *Jesus of Nazareth, millenarian prophet*, Fortress Press, Minneapolis 1998.

ÁVALOS H., *Health care and the rise of christianit*, Hendrickson, Peabody, MA 1999.

BARBAGLIO G., *Jesús, hebreo de Galilea. Investigación histórica*, Secretariado Trinitario, Salamanca 2003.

BARTOLOMÉ J.J., *El evangelio y Jesús de Nazaret*, CCS, Madrid 1995.

BAUCKHAM R. (ed.), *The Gospels for all christians. Rethinking the Gospel audiences*, Eerdmans, Grand Rapids, MI 1998.

BAYLEY K.E., *Poet and peasant. Through peasant eyes. A literary-cultural approach to the parables in Luke*, Eerdmans, Grand Rapids, MI 1983.

BEASLEY-MURRAY G.R., *Jesus and the Kingdom of God*, Eerdmans, Grand Rapids, MI 1986.

BEAUDE P.-M., *Jesús de Nazaret*, Verbo Divino, Estella 1988.

BERNABÉ C., *María Magdalena. Tradiciones en el cristianismo primitivo*, Verbo Divino, Estella 2003.

BEST E., *Disciples and discipleship. Studies in the Gospel according to Mark*, T. & T. Clark, Edinburgh 1986.

BLOMBERG C.L., *Interpreting the parables*, Inter-Varsity Press, Downers Grove, IL 1990.

_____, *Preaching the parables. From responsible interpretation to powerful proclamation*, Baker Academic, Grand Rapids, MI 2004.

BOCHMUEHL M. (ed.), *Jesus*, University Press, Cambridge 2001.

BOFF L., *Jesucristo y la liberación del hombre*, Cristiandad, Madrid 1981.

BOISMARD M.-É., *À l'aube du christianisme. Avant la naissance des dogmes*, Cerf, Paris 1998.

_____, *Jésus, un homme de Nazareth raconté par Marc l'évangeliste*, Cerf, Paris 1996.

BORG M.J., *Conflict, holiness and politics in the teaching of Jesus*, Trinity Press International, Harrisburg, PA 1998.

_____, *Jesus. A new vision. Spirit, culture and the life of discipleship*, Harper, San Francisco 1987.

_____, *Meeting Jesus again for the first time. The historical Jesus and the heart of contemporay faith*, Harper, San Francisco 1994.

BORG M.J. – CROSSAN J.D., *La última semana de Jesús. El relato día a día de la semana final de Jesús en Jerusalén*, PPC, Madrid 2007. (English: *The Last Week*, Harper, San Francisco 2006).

BORG M.J. – WRIGHT N.T., *The meaning of Jesus. Two visions*, Harper, San Francisco 1998.

BORNKAMM G., *Jesús de Nazaret*, Sígueme, Salamanca 1975. (English: *Jesus of Nazareth*, Harper & Row, New York 1960).

BOUCHER M., *The mysterious Parable. A literary study*, Catholic Biblical Association, Washington 1977.

BOVON F., *Los últimos días de Jesús. Textos y acontecimientos*, Sal Terrae, Santander 2007.

BREECH J., *The silence of Jesus. The authentic voice of the historical man*, Fortress Press, Philadelphia 1987.

BROWN R.E., *La muerte del Mesías. Desde Getsemaní hasta el sepulcro*, 2 vols., Verbo Divino, Estella 2005-2006. (English: *The Death of the Messiah*, Vols. 1-2, Doubleday, New York 1994).

_____, *El nacimiento del Mesías. Comentario a los relatos de la infancia*, Cristiandad, Madrid 1982. (English: *The Birth of the Messiah*, Doubleday, New York 1977).

BRUCE F.F., *Testimonianze extrabibliche su Gesù. Da Giuseppe Flavio al Corano*, Claudiana, Torino 2003.

CARREIRA DAS NEVES, J., *Jesus de Nazaré, quem és tu?* Franciscana, Braga 1991.

CARROLL J.T. – GREEN J.B., *The death of Jesus in early christianity*, Hendrickson, Peabody, MA 1995.

CASTILLO J.M., *El Reino de Dios. Por la vida y la dignidad de los seres humanos*, Desclée de Brouwer, Bilbao 1999.

CARLESWORTH J.H. (ed.), *The Messiah. Developments in earliest Judaism and Christianity*, Fortress Press, Minneapolis 1992.

_____, *Jesus and archaeology*, Eerdmans, Grand Rapids, MI-Cambridge 2006.

_____, *Gesù nel giudaismo del suo tempo alla luce delle piu recenti scoperte*, Claudiana, Torino 1998. (English: *Jesus within Judaism*, Doubleday, New York 1988).

——, *L'ebraicità di Gesù*, Claudiana, Torino 2002. (English: *Jesus Jewishness*, Crossroad, New York 2005).

CHILTON B. (ed.), *The Kingdom of God in the teaching of Jesus*, Fortress Press, Philadelphia 1984.

——, *Jesus' baptism and Jesus' healing. His personal practice of spirituality*, Trinity Press International, Harrisburg, PA 1998.

——, *Pure Kingdom. Jesus vision of God*, SPCK, Michigan 1996.

——, *Rabbi Jesus. An intimate biography*, Doubleday, New York 2002.

CHILTON B. – EVANS C.A. (eds.), *Authenticating the activities of Jesus*, Brill, Boston-Leiden 2002.

——, *Authenticating the words of Jesus*, Brill, Boston-Leiden 2002.

——, *Studying the historical Jesus. Evaluations of the state of current research*, Brill, Boston-Leiden-Colonia 1998.

CHILTON B. – MCDONALD J.I.H., *Jesus and the ethics of the Kingdom*, Eerdmans, Grand Rapids, MI 1988.

COLERIDGE M., *Nueva lectura de la infancia de Jesús. La narrativa como cristología en Lucas 1-2*, El Almendro, Córdoba 2000.

CORLEY K.E., *Private women, public meals: social conflict in the Synoptic Tradition*, Hendrickson, Peabody, MA 1993.

COUSIN H. (ed.), *Le monde où vivait Jésus*, Cerf, Paris 1998.

CROSSAN J.D., *In fragments. The aphorisms of Jesus*, Harper and Row, San Francisco 1983.

——, *Jesús. Biografía revolucionaria*, Grijalbo-Mondadori, Barcelona 1896. (English: *Jesus. A Revolutionary Biography*, Harper, San Francisco 1995).

——, *In parables. The challenge of the historical Jesus*, Polebridge Press, Sonoma, CA 1992.

——, *Jesús: vida de un campesino judío*, Crítica, Barcelona 1994. (English: *The Historical Jesus*, Harper, San Francisco 1992).

——, *Who is Jesus?*, Harper, New York 1996.

——, *Who killed Jesus?*, Harper, San Francisco 1996.

——, *El nacimiento del cristianismo. Qué sucedió en los años inmediatamente posteriores a la ejecución de Jesús*, Sal Terrae, Santander 2002. (English: *The Birth of Christianity*, Harper, San Francisco 1999).

CROSSAN J.D. – REED J.L., *Jesús desenterrado*, Crítica, Barcelona 2003. (English: *Excavating Jesus*, Harper, San Francisco 2003).

DAVIES S.L., *Jesus the Healer*, SCM Press, London 1995.

DE HAVEN-SMITH L., *The hidden teachings of Jesus. The political meanings of the Kingdom of God,* Phanes Press, Grand Rapids, MI 1999.

DE JONGE M., *God's final envoy. Early cristology and Jesus' own view of his mission,* Eerdmans, Grand Rapids, MI 1998.

DODD Ch.H., *Las parábolas del Reino,* Cristiandad, Madrid 1974. (English: *The Parables of the Kingdom,* Nisbet, London 1935).

DONAHUE J.R., *The Gospel in Parable,* Fortress Press, Filadelfia 1990.

DUNN J.D.G., *Jesús y el Espíritu. Un estudio de la experiencia religiosa y carismática de Jesús y de los primeros cristianos, tal como aparece en el Nuevo Testamento,* Secretariado Trinitario, Salamanca 1981. (English: *Jesus and the Spirit,* Eerdmans, Grand Rapids MI 1997).

_____, *Jesus remembered,* Eerdmans, Grand Rapids, MI-Cambridge 2003.

_____, *Redescubrir a Jesús de Nazaret. Lo que la investigación sobre el Jesús histórico ha olvidado,* Sígueme, Salamanca 2006. (English: *A New Perspective on Jesus,* Baker, Grand Rapids MI 2005).

DUPONT J., *Les béatitudes,* I, *Le problème littéraire,* II, *La bonne nouvelle,* III, *Les évangelistes,* Gabalda, Paris 1969-1973.

EDELMANN E., *Jesus parlait araméen. À la recherche de l'enseignement originel,* Les Éditions du Relié, Gordes 2000.

EHRMAN B.D., *Jesús, el profeta judío apocalíptico,* Paidós, Barcelona 2001. (English: *Jesus. Apocalyptic Prophet of the New Millenium,* Oxford University Press, Oxford 1999).

ESCUDERO FREIRE C., *Jesús y el poder religioso. El evangelio y la liberación de los oprimidos,* Nueva Utopía, Madrid 2003.

ESPINEL J.L., *La poesía de Jesús,* San Esteban, Salamanca 1986.

ETCHELLS R., *A reading of the Parables of Jesus,* Darton, Longman and Todd, London 1998.

EVANS C.A., *Jesus and his contemporaries,* Brill, Boston-Leiden 2001.

FABRIS R., *Jesús de Nazaret. Historia e interpretación,* Sígueme, Salamanca 1985.

FERNÁNDEZ RAMOS F. (ed.), *Diccionario de Jesús de Nazaret,* Monte Carmelo, Burgos 2001.

FLUSSER D., *Jesús en sus palabras y en su tiempo,* Cristiandad, Madrid 1975. (English: *Jesus,* Herder and Herder, New York 1969).

_____, *La secte de la mer Morte. L'histoire spirituelle et les manuscrits,* Desclée de Brouwer, Paris 2000.

FORTE B., *Jesús de Nazaret. Historia de Dios. Dios de la historia,* Ediciones Paulinas, Madrid 1989.

FRAIJÓ M., *Jesús y los marginados. Utopía y esperanza cristiana,* Cristiandad, Madrid 1985.

_____, *El cristianismo. Una aproximación,* Trotta, Madrid 1997.

FREDRIKSEN P., *Jesus of Nazareth, King of the Jews,* Vintage Books, New York 1999.

_____, *From Jesus to Christ,* Yale University Press, New Haven-London 2000.

FREDRIKSEN P. – REINHARTZ A. (eds.), *Jesus, Judaism and Christian anti-judaism,* John Knox Press, Louisville, KY-London, Westminster 2002.

FREYNE S., *Galilee and Gospel,* Brill, Boston-Leiden 2002.

_____, *Jesus, a jewish galilean,* Clark International, London-New York 2005.

FUELLENBACH J., *The Kingdom of God. The message of Jesus today,* Orbis Books, Maryknoll, NY 2002.

FUNK R.W., *Honest to Jesus. Jesus for a New Millenium,* Harper, San Francisco 1996.

FUNK R.W. – HOOVER R.W., *The five Gospels. What did Jesus really say?,* Harper, San Francisco 1993.

FUNK R.W. – JESUS SEMINAR, *The acts of Jesus. What did Jesus really do?,* Harper, San Francisco 1998.

FUNK R.W. – SCOTT B.B. – BUTTS J.R., *The Parables of Jesus. Red letter edition,* Polebridge Press, Sonoma, CA 1988.

FUSCO V., *Oltre la parabola. Introduzione alle parabole di Gesù,* Borla, Roma 1983.

GIBERT P. – THEOBALD Ch., *Le cas Jésus Christ. Exégètes, historiens et théologiens en confrontation,* Bayard, Paris 2002.

GNILKA J., *Jesús de Nazaret, Mensaje e historia,* Herder, Barcelona 1993. (English: *Jesus of Nazareth,* Hendrickson Publishers, Peabody MA 1997).

GONZÁLEZ ECHEGARAY J., *Arqueología y evangelios,* Verbo Divino, Estella 1999.

_____, *Jesús de Galilea. Aproximación desde la arqueología,* Verbo Divino, Estella 2000.

_____, *Pisando tus umbrales, Jerusalén. Historia antigua de la ciudad,* Verbo Divino, Estella 2005.

GONZÁLEZ FAUS J.I., *Acceso a Jesús,* Sígueme, Salamanca 1979.

_____, *Clamor del Reino. Estudio sobre los milagros de Jesús,* Sígueme, Salamanca 1982.

GORDON T., *The life and inevitable crucifixion of Jesus,* Lion Publishing, Oxford 1997.

GOWLER D.B., *What are they saying about Parables?* Paulist Press, New York 2000.

GRAPPE Ch., *Le Royaume de Dieu. Avant, avec et après Jésus*, Labor et Fides, Genève 2001.

GREEN J.B. – MC KNIGHT S. – MARSHALL I.H. (eds.), *Dictionary of Jesus and the Gospels*, Inter-Varsity Press, Downers Grove, IL 1992.

GREEN J.B. – TURNER M. (eds.), *Jesus of Nazareth: Lord and Christ. Essays on the Historical Jesus and New Testament Christology*, Eerdmans, Grand Rapids, MI 1994.

GRELOT P., *L'espérance juive à l'heure de Jésus*, Desclée de Brouwer, Paris 1978.

GUEVARA H., *Ambiente político del pueblo judío en tiempos de Jesús*, Cristiandad, Madrid 1977.

GUIJARRO S., *Fidelidades en conflicto. La ruptura con la familia por causa del discipulado y de la misión en la tradición sinóptica*, Universidad Pontificia, Salamanca 1998.

_____, *Dichos primitivos de Jesús. Una introducción al «Proto-evangelio de dichos Q»*, Sígueme, Salamanca 2004.

_____, *Jesús y el origen de los evangelios*, Verbo Divino, Estella 2006.

_____, *Jesús y sus primeros discípulos*, Verbo Divino, Estella 2007.

HANSON K.C. – OAKMAN D.E., *Palestine in the time of Jesus. Social structures and social conflicts*, Fortress Press, Minneapolis 1998.

HARRINGTON D. – KEENAN J., *Jesus and virtue ethics*, Sheed and Ward, Lanham 2002.

HARVEY A.E., *Strenuous commands. The ethic of Jesus*, SCM Press, London 1990.

HEDRICK Ch.W., *Parables as poetic fictions. The creative voice of Jesus*, Hendrikson, Peabody, MA 1994.

HELLER A., *La resurrección del Jesús judío*, Herder, Barcelona 2007.

HENGEL M., *Crucifixion*, Fortress Press, Philadelphia 1977.

_____, *Seguimiento y carisma. La radicalidad de la llamada de Jesús*, Sal Terrae, Santander 1981 (English: *The charismatic leader and his followers*, Crossroad, New York 1991).

HERZOG II W.R., *Parables as subversive Speech. Jesus as Pedagogue of the oppressed*, John Knox Press, Louisville, KY, Westminster 1994.

_____, *Jesus, justice, and the Reign of God. A ministry of liberation*, John Knox Press, Louisville, KY, Westminster 2000.

HILL B.R., *Jesus the Christ. Contemporary perspectives*, Twenty-Third Publications, Mystic, CT 2004.

HOOKER M.D., *The signs of a Prophet. The prophetic actions of Jesus*, Trinity Press International, Harrisburg, PA 1997.

HORSLEY R.A., *Jesus and the spiral of violence. Popular Jewish resistance in Roman Palestine*, Fortress Press, Minneapolis 1993.

_____, *Sociology and the Jesus movement*, Continuum, New York 1994.

_____, *Galilee history, politics, people*, Trinity Press Internacional, Harrisburg, PA 1995.

_____, *Archeology, history and society in Galilee. The social context of Jesus and the Rabbis*, Trinity Press International, Harrisburg, PA 1996.

_____, *Jesús y el imperio. El Reino de Dios y el nuevo desorden mundial*, Verbo Divino, Estella 2003. (English: *Jesus and Empire*, Augsburg Fortress, MN 2003).

HORSLEY R.A. – DRAPER J.A., *Whoever hears you, hears me. Prophets, performance and tradition in Q*, Trinity Press, Harrisburg, PA 1999.

HORSLEY R.A. – SILBERMAN N.A., *La revolución del Reino. Cómo Jesús y Pablo transformaron el mundo antiguo*, Sal Terrae, Santander 2005. (English: *The Message and the Kingdom*, Augsburg Fortress, MN 2002).

HOUZIAUX A. (ed.), *Jésus. De Qumrâm à l'Évangile de Thomas. Les judaïsmes et la genèse du christianisme*, Bayard, Paris 1999.

_____, *Jésus-Christ, de quoi est-on sûr?*, Ed. de l'Atelier, Paris 2006.

JEREMIAS J., *Las parábolas de Jesús*, Verbo Divino, Estella 1971.

_____, *Teología del Nuevo Testamento*, Sígueme, Salamanca 1974.

_____, *Jerusalén en tiempos de Jesús*, Cristiandad, Madrid 1977.

_____, *La última cena. Palabras de Jesús*, Cristiandad, Madrid 1980.

_____, *Abba. El mensaje central del Nuevo Testamento*, Sígueme, Salamanca 1981.

JOSSA, G., *I gruppi giudaici ai tempi di Gesù*, Paideia, Brescia 2001.

_____, *Il processo di Gesù* Paideia, Brescia 2002.

KARRER M., *Jesucristo en el Nuevo Testamento*, Sígueme, Salamanca 2002.

KAYLOR R.D., *Jesus, the prophet. His vision of Kingdom on Earth*, John Knox Press, Louisville, KY, Westminster 1994.

KINGSBURY J.D., *Conflicto en Marcos. Jesús, autoridades, discípulos*, El Almendro, Córdoba 1991.

KISTEMAKER S.J., *The Parables. Understanding the stories Jesus told*, Baker Books, Grand Rapids, MI 2005.

KLAUCK H.-J., *Los evangelios apócrifos. Una introducción*, Sal Terrae, Santander 2006.

KLAUSNER J., *Jesús de Nazaret. Su vida, su época, sus enseñanzas*, Paidós, Barcelona 1991. (English: *Jesus of Nazareth*, Menorah Pub, New York 1925).

KLOPPENBORG J.S., *Q. El Evangelio desconocido*, Sígueme, Salamanca 2005.

KNIGHT J., *Jesus. An Historical and Theological investigation*, Clark International, New York 2004.

KNOHL I., *El mesías antes de Jesús. El siervo sufriente de los manuscritos del mar Muerto*, Trotta, Madrid 2004.

LAPIDE P., *Predicava nelle loro sinagoghe. Esegesi ebraica dei Vangeli*, Paideia, Brescia 2001.

LEIPOLDT J. – GRUNDMANN W., *El mundo del Nuevo Testamento*, Cristiandad, Madrid 1973.

LEIVESTAD R., *Jesus in his own Perspective. An examination of his Sayings, Actions and Eschatological Titles*, Augsburg, Minneapolis 1987.

LÉON-DUFOUR X., *Jesús y Pablo ante la muerte*, Cristiandad, Madrid 1982.

_____, *Agir selon l'Évangile*, Seuil, Paris 2002.

_____, (ed.), *Los milagros de Jesús*, Cristiandad, Madrid 1979.

LEVINE A.-J. (ed.), *Una compañera para Mateo*, Desclée de Brouwer, Bilbao 2003.

LINNEMANN E., *Jesus of the Parables. Introduction and exposition*, Harper and Row, New York 1976.

LOADER W., *Jesus' attitude towards the Law. A study of the Gospels*, Eerdmans, Grand Rapids, MI 2002.

LOIS J., *Jesús de Nazaret, el Cristo liberador*, HOAC, Madrid 1995.

LONGENECKER R.N. (ed.), *The challenge of Jesus' parables*, Eerdmans, Grand Rapids, MI-Cambridge, 2000.

LÜDEMANN G., *Jesus after two thousand years. What he really said and did*, Prometheus Books, Amherst, NY 2001.

LUNY W.J., *The Jesus option*, Paulist Press, New York 1994.

MAGNANI G., *Origini del cristianesimo. Gesù costruttore e maestro. L'ambiente: nuove prospettive,* Citadella, Assisi 1996.

MAIER J., *Entre los dos Testamentos. Historia y religión en la época del segundo Templo,* Sígueme, Salamanca 1996.

MALINA B.J., *El mundo del Nuevo Testamento. Perspectivas desde la antropología cultural,* Verbo Divino, Estella 1995. (English: *The New Testament World,* J. Know, Westminster 2001).

_____, *The Social Gospel of Jesus. The Kingdom of God in mediterranean Perspective,* Fortress Press, Minneapolis 2000.

_____, *El mundo social de Jesús y los evangelios,* Sal Terrae, Santander 2002. (English: *The Social World of Jesus and the Gospels,* Routledge, London-NY 1996).

MAILINA B.J. – ROHRBAUGH R., *Los evangelios sinópticos y la cultura mediterránea del siglo I,* Verbo Divino, Estella 1996. (English: *Social-Science Commentary on the Synoptic Gospels,* Fortress, MI 1992).

MANNS F., *La prière d'Israël à l'heure de Jésus,* Franciscan Printing Press, Jerusalem 1986.

MANSON T.W., *The Teaching of Jesus. Studies in its form and content,* University Press, Cambridge 1963.

MARGUERAT D. – NORELLI E. – POFFET J.-M. (eds.), *Jésus de Nazareth. Nouvelles approches d'une énigme,* Labor et Fides, Genève 1998.

MARSHALL I.H., *I believe in the Historical Jesus,* Eerdmans, Grand Rapids, MI 1977.

MARXSEN W., *Jesus and the Church. The beginnings of Christianity,* Trinity Press International, Philadelphia 1992.

MATEOS J., *Los «Doce» y otros seguidores de Jesús en el evangelio de Mateo,* Cristiandad, Madrid 1982.

MCBRIDE D., *Les paraboles de Jésus,* Eds. De l'Atelier, Paris 2001.

MCKNIGHTS S., *A new vision for Israel. The teachings of Jesus in national contex,* Eerdmans, Grand Rapids, MI 1999.

MEADORS E.P., *Jesus, the Messianic Herald of Salvation,* Hendrickson, Peabody, MA 1997.

MEIER E., *Women and Ministry in the New Testament: called to Serve,* University Press, Lanham-New York-London 1980.

MEIER J.P., *Un judío marginal. Nueva visión del Jesús histórico,* I, *Las raíces del problema y de la persona,* II/1, *Juan y Jesús. El Reino de Dios,* II/2, *Los milagros.* III, *Compañeros y competidores,* Verbo Divino, Estella 2001-2003. (English: *A marginal Jew. Rethinking the Historical Jesus,* Vol. I 1991; Vol. II 1994, Vol. III 2001, Vol. IV 2009).

MERKLEIN H., *La signoria di Dio nell an-nuncio di Gesù*, Paideia, Brescia 1994.

MEYER B.F., *The aims of Jesus*, Pickwic, Eugene, OR 2002.

MOLTMANN J., *El camino de Jesucristo*, Sígueme, Salamanca 1993. (English: *The Way of Jesus Christ*, Harper, NY 1990).

MOLTMANN J. – WENDEL E., *The women around Jesus*, Crossroad, New York 1982.

MORRICE W., *Dichos desconocidos de Jesús. Palabras atribuidas a Jesús fuera de los cuatro evangelios*, Sal Terrae, Santander 2002.

MOXNES H., *Poner a Jesús en su lugar. Una visión radical del grupo familiar y el Reino de Dios*, Verbo Divino, Estella 2005. (English: *Putting Jesus in His Place*, Westminster, Louisville 2003).

NEITZEL R. – WAYMENT T.A. (eds.), *From the last Supper through the Resurrection, the savior's final hours*, Desert Books, Salt Lake City, UT 2003.

NELSON-PALLMEYER J., *Jesus against Christianity. Reclaiming the missing Jesus*, Trinity Press International, Harrisburg, PA 2001.

NEYREY J.H., *Honor y vergüenza. Lectura cultural del evangelio de Mateo*, Sígueme, Salamanca 2005

NODET É., *Histoire de Jésus? Nécessité et limites d'une enquête*, Cerf, Paris 2003.

PAGOLA J.A., *Jesús de Nazaret. El hombre y su mensaje*, Idatz, San Sebastián 1981.

PARKER A., *Painfully clear. Parables of Jesus*, Academic Press, Sheffield 1996.

PATTERSON S.J., *Beyond the passion. Re-thinking the death and life of Jesus*, Fortress Press, Minneapolis 2004.

_____, *The God of Jesus. The historical Jesus and the search for meaning*, Trinity Press International, Harrisburg, PA 1998.

PAUL A., *El mundo judío en tiempos de Jesús. Historia política*, Cristiandad, Madrid 1982.

_____, *Jésus Christ, la rupture. Essai sur la naissance du christianisme*, Bayard, Paris 2001.

PERRIN N., *Rediscovering the teaching of Jesus*, SCM Press, London 1967.

_____, *The Kingdom of God in the teaching of Jesus*, SCM Press, London 1975.

PERROT Ch., *Jesús y la historia*, Cristiandad, Madrid 1982.

PIKAZA X., *El evangelio. Vida y pascua de Jesús*, Sígueme, Salamanca 1990.

_____, *La figura de Jesús. Profeta, taumaturgo, rabino, mesías*, Verbo Divino, Estella 1992.

_____, *Sistema, libertad, Iglesia. Instituciones del Nuevo Testamento*, Trotta, Madrid 2001.

_____, *La nueva figura de Jesús. Guía evangélica*, Sígueme, Salamanca 2003.

PILCH J.J., *Healing in the New Testament insights from medical and mediterranean Anthropology*, Fortress Press, Minneapolis 2000.

_____, *Cultural tools for interpreting the Good News*, The Liturgical Press, Collegeville, MN 2002.

PIÑERO A., *Fuentes del cristianismo. Tradiciones primitivas sobre Jesús*, El Almendro, Córdoba 1993.

_____, *El otro Jesús. Vida de Jesús según los evangelios apócrifos*, El Almendro, Córdoba 1996.

_____, *En la frontera de lo imposible. Magos, médicos y taumaturgos en el Mediterráneo antiguo en tiempos del Nuevo Testamento*, El Almendro, Córdoba 2001.

_____, *Textos gnósticos. Biblioteca de Nag Hammadi*, II, *Evangelios, Hechos, cartas*, Trotta, Madrid 2004.

_____, (ed.), *Biblia y helenismo. El pensamiento griego y la formación del cristianismo*, El Almendro, Córdoba 2006.

POWELL M.A., *Jesus as a Figure in History. How modern historians view the man from Galilee*, John Knox Press, Louisville, KY-London, Westminster 1998.

PUIG A., *Jesús. Una biografía*, Destino, Barcelona 2005.

RAUSCH T., *¿Quién es Jesús? Introducción a la cristología*, Mensajero, Bilbao 2006.

REED J.L., *El Jesús de Galilea. Aportaciones de la arqueología*, Sígueme, Salamanca 2006. (English: *Archaeology and the Galilean Jesus*, Trinity Press, Harrisburg 2000).

RICHARDSON A., *Las narraciones evangélicas sobre milagros*, Fax, Madrid 1974.

RILEY G.J., *Un Jésus, plusieurs Christs. Essai sur les origines plurielles de la foi chrétienne*, Labor et Fides, Genève 2002.

RIVKIN E., *What crucified Jesus? Messianism, Pharisaism, and the development of Christianity*, UAHC Press, New York 1997.

ROBINSON J.M. – HOFFMANN P. – KLOPPENBORG J.S. (eds.), *El documento Q en griego y en español*, Sígueme, Salamanca 2002.

ROLOFF J., *Jesús*, Acento, Madrid 2003.

ROVIRA BELLOSO J.M., *Jesús, el Mesías de Dios*, Sígueme, Salamanca 2005.

SALDARINI A.J., *Pharisees, Scribes and Saducees in Palestinian Society*, Eerdmans, Grand Rapids, MI-Cambridge 2001.

SANDERS E.P., *La figura histórica de Jesús,* Verbo Divino, Estella 2000. (English: *The Historical Figure of Jesus,* Allen Penguin NY 1993).

_____, *Jesús y el judaísmo,* Trotta, Madrid 2004. (English: *Jesus and Judaism,* SCM, London 1987).

SANFORD J.A., *The Kingdom within. The inner meaning of Jesus sayings,* Harper, San Francisco 1987.

SAUCY M., *The Kingdom of God in teaching of Jesus in 20th Century Theology,* Word Publishing, Dallas-London-Vancouver-Melbourne 1997.

SCHILLEBEECKX E., *Jesús. La historia de un viviente,* Cristiandad, Madrid 1981.

_____, *En torno al problema de Jesús. Claves de una cristología,* Cristiandad, Madrid 1983.

SCHLOSSER J., *El Dios de Jesús,* Sígueme, Salamanca 1995.

_____, *Jesús, el profeta de Galilea,* Sígueme, Salamanca 2005.

SCHNACKENBURG R., *Reino y reinado de Dios,* Fax, Madrid 1967.

SCHOTTROFF L. – STEGEMANN W., *Jesús de Nazaret, esperanza de los pobres,* Sígueme, Salamanca 1981.

SCHRAGE W., *Ética del Nuevo Testamento,* Sígueme, Salamanca 1987.

SCHÜRER E., *Historia del pueblo judío en tiempos de Jesús,* 2 vols., Cristiandad, Madrid 1985.

SCHÜRMANN H., *La prière du Seigneur. À la lumière de la prédication de Jésus,* Eds. de l'Orante, Paris 1965.

_____, *¿Cómo entendió y vivió Jesús su muerte?* Sígueme, Salamanca 1982.

_____, *El destino de Jesús: su vida y su muerte,* Sígueme, Salamanca 2003.

SCHÜSSLER FIORENZA E., *En memoria de ella. Una reconstrucción teológico-feminista de los orígenes del cristianismo,* Desclée de Brouwer, Bilbao 1989. (English: *In Memory of Her,* Crossroad, San Francisco 1984).

_____, *Cristología feminista crítica. Jesús, el hijo de Miriam, profeta de la sabiduría,* Trotta, Madrid 2000. (English: *Jesus. Miriam's Child,* Continuum, New York 1994).

SCHWEIZER E., *Jesús, parábola de Dios,* Sígueme, Salamanca 2001.

SCOTT B.B., *Jesus. Symbol Maker for the Kingdom,* Fortress Press, Philadelphia 1981.

_____, *Hear then the Parable. A Commentary on the Parables of Jesus,* Fortress Press, Minneapolis 1990.

SCOTT F., *What did Jesus do? Gospel profiles of Jesus' personal conduct*, Trinity Press International, Harrisburg, PA-London-New York 2003.

SEGUNDO J.L., *El hombre de hoy ante Jesús de Nazaret*, 3 vols., Cristiandad, Madrid 1982.

SHANKS H., *The search for Jesus. Modern scholarship. Looks at the Gospels*, Biblical Archaeology Society, Washington 1994.

SHILLINGTON V.G. (ed.), *Jesus and his parables. Interpreting the parables of Jesus today*, T. & T. Clark, Edinburg 1997.

SLOYAN G.S., *The Crucifixion of Jesus. History, Myth, Faith*, Fortress Press, Minneapolis 1995.

SNYDER H.A., *Models of the Kingdom*, Wipf and Stock, Eugene, OR 1991.

SOBRINO J., *Jesucristo liberador. Lectura histórico-teológica de Jesús de Nazaret*, Trotta, Madrid 1991.

———, *La fe en Jesucristo. Ensayo desde las víctimas*, Trotta, Madrid 1999.

———, *Jesús en América Latina. Su significado para la fe y la cristología*, Sal Terrae, Santander 1982.

SÖLLE D. – SCHOTTROFF L., *Jesus of Nazareth*, John Knox Press, Louisville, KY-London, Westminster 2002.

SPOHN W.C., *Go and do likewise. Jesus and Ethics*, Continuum, New York 1999.

STEGEMANN E.W. – STEGEMANN W., *Historia social del cristianismo primitivo. Los inicios en el judaísmo y las comunidades cristianas en el mundo mediterráneo*, Verbo Divino, Estella 2001.

STEGEMANN H., *Los esenios, Qumrán, Juan Bautista y Jesús*, Trotta, Madrid 1996.

STEGEMANN W. – MALINA B.J. – THEISSEN G., *The Social Setting of Jesus and the Gospels*, Fortress Press, Minneapolis 2002.

SYEIN R.H., *The Method and Message of Jesus' Teachings*, John Knox Press, Louisville, KY, Westminster 1994.

STIEWE M. – VOUGA F., *Le sermon sur la montagne. Un abrégé de l'Évangile dans le miroitement de ses interprétations*. Labor et Fides, Genève 2002.

STUHLMACHER P., *Jesús de Nazaret. Cristo de la fe*, Sígueme, Salamanca 1996.

SWARTLEY W.M. (ed.), *The Love of the Enemy and Non-retaliation in the New Testament*, John Knox Press, Louisville, KY, Westminster 1992.

TATUM W.B., *John the Baptist and Jesus. A report of the Jesus Seminar*, Polebridge Press, Sonoma, CA 1994.

TAUSSIG H., *Jesus before God. The Prayer Life of the Historical Jesus*, Polebridge Press, Santa Rosa, CA 1999.

THEISSEN G., *Sociología del movimiento de Jesús. El nacimiento del cristianismo primitivo*, Sal Terrae, Santander 1979.

―――, *The Miracle Stories of the early Christian Tradition*, Fortress Press, Philadelphia 1983.

―――, *Colorido local y contexto histórico en los evangelios. Una contribución a la historia de la tradición sinóptica*, Sígueme, Salamanca 1997.

―――, *La religión de los primeros cristianos*, Sígueme, Salamanca 2002.

―――, *El Nuevo Testamento. Historia, literatura, religión*, Sal Terrae, Santander 2003.

―――, *El movimiento de Jesús. Historia social de una revolución de los valores*, Sígueme, Salamanca 2005.

THEISSEN G. – MERZ A., *El Jesús histórico*, Sígueme, Salamanca 1999.

TOMSON P., *L'affaire Jésus et les juifs*, Cerf, Paris 2003.

TRAGÁN P.-R., *La preistoria dei Vangeli. Tradizione cristiana primitiva*, Servitium, Fontanella di Sotto il Monte 1999.

TREBOLLE J. (coord.), *Paganos, judíos y cristianos en los textos de Qumrán*, Trotta, Madrid 1999.

TREVIJANO R., *Orígenes del cristianismo. El trasfondo judío del cristianismo primitivo*, Universidad Pontificia, Salamanca 1996.

TRILLING W., *Jesús y los problemas de su historicidad*, Herder, Barcelona 1970.

TUNC S., *También las mujeres seguían a Jesús*, Sal Terrae, Santander 1999.

TWELFTREE G.H., *Jesus the Exorcist. A contribution to the Study of the Historical Jesus*, Hendrickson, Peabody, MA 1993.

―――, *Jesus. The Miracle Worker*, Inter-Vasity Press, Downers Grove, IL 1999.

VERMES G., *Jesús el judío*, Muchnik, Barcelona 1977. (English: *Jesus the Jew*, Collins, London 1973).

―――, *Jesus and the World of Judaism*, SCM Press, London 1983.

―――, *La religione di Gesù l'ebreo. Una grande sfida al cristianesimo*, Citadella, Assisi 2002.

―――, *Enquête sur l'identité de Jésus. Nouvelles interprétations*, Bayard, Paris 2003.

―――, *La pasión. La verdad sobre el acontecimiento que cambió la historia de la humanidad*, Crítica, Barcelona 2007.

VIA D.O., *The Parables. Their Literary and Existential Dimension*, Fortress Press, Philadelphia 1977.

VIDAL S., *Los tres proyectos de Jesús y el cristianismo naciente*, Sígueme, Salamanca 2003.

———, *Jesús el Galileo*, Sal Terrae, Santander 2006.

VOUGA F., *Los primeros pasos del cristianismo. Escritos, protagonistas, debates*, Verbo Divino, Estella 2000.

WEDER H., *Metafore del Regno: le parabole di Gesù: ricostruzione e interpretazione*, Paideia, Brescia 1991.

WENHAM D. – BLOMBERG C. (eds.), *Gospel Perspectives. The Miracles of Jesus*, VI, Wipf and Stock, Eugene, OR 1986.

WHITE L.M., *De Jesús al cristianismo*, Verbo Divino, Estella 2007. (English: *From Jesus to Christianity*, Harper, San Francisco 2004).

WILLIS W. (ed.), *The Kingdom of God in 20th Century Interpretation*, Hendrickson, Peabody, MA 1987.

WINTON A.P., *The Proverbs of Jesus. Issues of History and Rhetoric*, Academic Press, Sheffield 1990.

WITHERINGTON III B., *Jesus the Sage. The Pilgrimage of Wisdom*, Fortress Press, Minneapolis 1994.

———, *The Jesus Quest. The Third Search for the Jew of Nazareth*, Inter-Varsity Press, Downers Grove, IL 1997.

WRIGHT N.T., *Following Jesus. Biblical reflections on Discipleship*, Eerdmans, Grand Rapids, MI 1994.

———, *Jesus and the Victory of God*, Fortress Press, Minneapolis 1996.

———, *The Resurrection of the Son of God*, Fortress Press, Minneapolis 2003.

YODER J.H., *The Politics of Jesus*, Eerdmans, Grand Rapids, MI 2002.

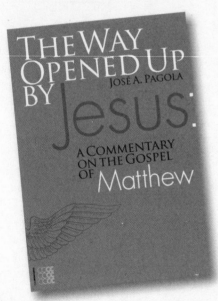

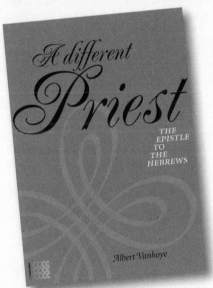

Is Life in Society Possible without Morality?

Sergio Bastianel answers the question by addressing the responsibility of Christians to confront issues of justice within society in ways that promote the common good. The author, who views one's relationship with the «other» as foundational to the moral experience, places a priority on human relationships based on sharing and solidarity. He emphasizes the interconnections between personal morals and social justice and raises fundamental questions about such issues as political life and economics, about hunger and development, and about the true meaning of «charity», all of which are relevant issues in our contemporary societies.

Sergio Bastianel s.j. is currently professor of moral theology at the Pontifical Gregorian University in Rome and also serves as its academic vice-rector. He spent his early years teaching and lecturing at the Pontifical Theological Faculty of San Luigi in Naples, Italy, and in later years he served as dean of the theological faculty of the Pontifical Gregorian University.

Morality in Social Life
Sergio Bastianel
ISBN: 978-1-934996-14-0
360 Pages
Series Episteme

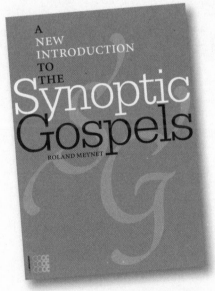

A new reading of freedom and liberation through Israel's History

Rediscovering freedom in the Bible

Meynet posits that the concept of freedom in the Hebrew Bible is the guiding core of all the socio-political distinctions within Israel's religious experience and history. This original study leads us through the experience of the people of Israel in the Exodus. It guides us into a new reading of the Law in the two narrative sections of the Decalogue, seeing it as an expression of the search for the authentic meaning of human freedom. He also introduces Israel's Psalms as hymns of freedom.

Roland Meynet S.J. is presently professor of Biblical theology at the Pontifical Gregorian University in Rome and was the former director of its Department of Biblical Theology. He is a founding member and currently the secretary of the International Society for the Studies of Biblical and Semitic Rhetoric.

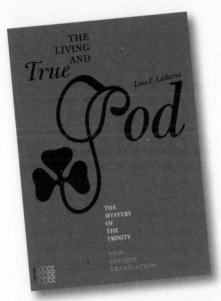

A Beautiful and Simple Proposal to Construct Our Spiritual Life through Discernment and Prayer of the Heart

One of the greatest experts in the spirituality of Eastern Christianity, Cardinal Špidlík, deals in this book with prayer and spiritual life, with the experience of grace and goodness, through discernment of evil and human passions in everyday experience. It is a beautiful and simple proposal to construct our spiritual life through discernment and prayer of the heart.

Tomáš Špidlík was born in Boskovice, now in the Czech Republic, in 1919. In 1951, Špidlík began broadcasting programs from Vatican Radio calling for freedom behind the Iron Curtain. He met with Alexander Dubcek, former First Secretary of the Central Committee of the Communist Party of Czechoslovakia, and Václav Havel, who became President of Czechoslovakia. Špidlík is Professor of Eastern Spiritual Theology, and Cardinal, and is known as one of the greatest experts in Eastern Christianity today. He has been chosen «Man of the Year, 1990» and «the most admired person of the decade» by the American Bibliographical Institute of Raleigh in North Carolina.

Jesus: An Historical Approximation

This book was printed on *thin opaque smooth white Bible paper*, using the *Minion* and *Type Embellishments One* font families.
This edition was printed in Panamericana Formas e Impresos, S.A., in Bogotá, Colombia, during the last weeks of the ninth month of year two thousand and thirteen.

Ad publicam lucem datus mense septembre in nativitate Sancte Marie